HUMAN DEVELOPMENT REPORT 2000

Published
for the United Nations
Development Programme
(UNDP)

New York   Oxford
Oxford University Press
2000

Oxford University Press

Oxford   New York

Athens   Auckland   Bangkok   Bombay
Calcutta   Cape Town   Dar es Salaam   Delhi
Florence   Hong Kong   Istanbul   Karachi
Kuala Lumpur   Madras   Madrid   Melbourne
Mexico City   Nairobi   Paris   Singapore
Taipei   Tokyo   Toronto

and associated companies in
Berlin   Ibadan

Published by Oxford University Press, Inc.
198 Madison Avenue, New York, New York, 10016

Oxford is a registered trademark of Oxford University Press

ISBN 0-19-521679-2 (cloth)
ISBN 0-19-521678-4 (paper)

9 8 7 6 5 4 3 2 1
Printed in the United States of America on acid-free, recycled paper, using soy-based ink.

Cover, design and photos: Gerald Quinn, Quinn Information Design, Cabin John, Maryland

Editing, desktop composition and production management: Communications Development Incorporated,
Washington, DC

Foreword

Support for human rights has always been integral to the mission of the United Nations, embodied in both the UN Charter and the Universal Declaration of Human Rights. But throughout the cold war serious discussion of the concept as it relates to development was too often distorted by political rhetoric. Civil and political rights on the one hand and economic and social rights on the other were regarded not as two sides of the same coin but as competing visions for the world's future.

We have now moved beyond that confrontational discussion to a wider recognition that both sets of rights are inextricably linked. As Mary Robinson, United Nations High Commissioner for Human Rights, often reminds us, the goal is to achieve all human rights—civil, cultural, economic, political and social—for all people. Access to basic education, health care, shelter and employment is as critical to human freedom as political and civil rights are. That is why the time is right for a report aimed at drawing out the complex relationship between human development and human rights.

As always, the result is a *Human Development Report* that is unapologetically independent and provocative. But it clearly underlines the fact that human rights are not, as has sometimes been argued, a reward of development. Rather, they are critical to achieving it. Only with political freedoms—the right for all men and women to participate equally in society—can people genuinely take advantage of economic freedoms. And the most important step towards generating the kind of economic growth needed to do that is the establishment of transparent, accountable and effective systems of institutions and laws.

Only when people feel they have a stake and a voice will they throw themselves wholeheartedly into development. Rights make human beings better economic actors.

And it is clearly not enough for countries simply to grant economic and social rights in theory alone. You cannot legislate good health and jobs. You need an economy strong enough to provide them—and for that you need people economically engaged. People will work because they enjoy the fruits of their labour: fair pay, education and health care for their families and so forth. They will build the wealth that allows them to be compensated. But if the rewards of their labour are denied them again, they will lose their motivation. So economic and social rights are both the incentive for, and the reward of, a strong economy.

That is why a broad vision of human rights must be entrenched to achieve sustainable human development. When adhered to in practice as well as in principle, the two concepts make up a self-reinforcing virtuous circle. Many countries have made enormous strides in human rights in recent years. Most have now ratified the core covenants and conventions on political, economic, social and cultural rights, and are struggling to implement them.

Yet the legal advance does not tell the whole truth: to be poor is still to be powerless and vulnerable. Life remains a torment for children in the teeming barrio of a developing country city, for refugees caught up in a conflict, for women in a society that still denies them equality and freedom—every day bringing physical and psychological threats. And still too many of the 1.2 billion people living on less than a dollar a day lack even the most basic human security. So while the progress on human rights allowed by the end of the cold war marks a great breakthrough, for these people it is still just the thin end of the wedge. It has not yet affected the quality of their lives.

While the Report cites and examines many examples of egregious human rights violations across the world, it is not aimed at producing legalistic rankings of the worst offenders.

Instead, it is intended primarily to help promote practical action that puts a human rights–based approach to human development and poverty eradication firmly on the global agenda. I believe it has done so admirably, and I warmly congratulate its authors, particularly Richard Jolly, who has completed his last *Human Development Report.*

Mark Malloch Brown

The analysis and policy recommendations of the Report do not necessarily reflect the views of the United Nations Development Programme, its Executive Board or its Member States. The Report is an independent publication commissioned by UNDP. It is the fruit of a collaborative effort by a team of eminent consultants and advisers and the Human Development Report team. Richard Jolly, Special Adviser to the Administrator, together with Sakiko Fukuda-Parr, Director of the Human Development Report Office, led the effort.

Team for the preparation of
Human Development Report 2000

Principal Coordinator
Richard Jolly

Director
Sakiko Fukuda-Parr

UNDP team
Deputy Director: Selim Jahan
Members: Christian Barry, Sarah Burd-Sharps, Haishan Fu, Petra Mezzetti, Laura Mourino-Casas, Omar Noman, Andreas Pfeil, Kate Raworth and David Stewart, with Håkan Björkman, Marixie Mercado, Nadia Rasheed and Gül Tanghe-Güllüova

Editor: Bruce Ross-Larson
Designer: Gerald Quinn

Panel of consultants
Philip Alston, Sudhir Anand, Abdullahi A. An-Na'im, Radhika Coomaraswamy, Meghnad Desai, Ayesha Dias, Cees Flinterman, Jayati Ghosh, Leo Goldstone, Savitri Goonesekere, Maria Green, Julia Häusermann, Nadia Hijab, Scott Leckie, Juan E. Mendez, Vitit Muntarbhorn, Makau Mutua, Kassie Neou, Roger Normand, Joseph Oloka-Onyango, Siddiq R. Osmani, Paulo Sergio Pinheiro, Pablo Rodas-Martini, Amartya Sen, A. K. Shiva Kumar and Darko Šilovic

Acknowledgements

The preparation of the Report would not have been possible without the support and valuable contributions of a large number of individuals and organizations.

The team is particularly grateful for the close collaboration with the United Nations High Commissioner for Human Rights, Mary Robinson, and the Deputy High Commissioner, Bertrand Ramcharan, and their staff, especially Stefanie Grant and Sylvie Saddier. The team also expresses its gratitude to Professor Amartya Sen, who, as the author of chapter 1, provided the conceptual framework for the Report.

ADVISORY PANEL

The Report benefited greatly from intellectual advice and guidance provided by the external Advisory Panel of eminent experts, which included Shin-ichi Ago, Medea Benjamin, Charlotte Bunch, Antonio Cancado-Trindade, Clarence Dias, Mohammed Fayek, Thomas Hammarberg, Ann Christine Hubbard, Stephen Marks, Simon Maxwell, Malini Mehra, Solita Monsod, Aryeh Neier, Barney Pityana, Gita Sen, Arjun Sengupta, Paul Streeten, Laila Takla, Katarina Tomasevski and Danilo Türk. An advisory panel on statistics included Jean-Louis Bodin, Paulo Garonna, Denise Lievesley, Angela Me, Darryl Rhoades, Alain Tranap and Willem de Vries.

CONTRIBUTORS

Many background studies were prepared on thematic issues in human rights and human development as well as analyses of experiences in countries and regions. These were contributed by M. M. Akash, Philip Alston, Sudhir Anand, Abdullahi A. An-Na'im, Radhika Coomaraswamy, Jorge Correa Sutil, Meghnad Desai, Ayesha Dias, Bahey El-Din Hassan, Cees Flinterman, Jayati Ghosh, Leo Goldstone, Felipe González Morales, Savitri Goonesekere, Maria Green, Julia Häusermann, Nadia Hijab, Asma Khader, Scott Leckie, Sandra Liebenberg, Juan E. Mendez, Vitit Muntarbhorn, Makau Mutua, Irina Nemirovsky, Kassie Neou, Roger Normand, Martha Brill Olcott, Joseph Oloka-Onyango, Siddiq R. Osmani, Andrés E. Pérez, Paulo Sergio Pinheiro, Pablo Rodas-Martini, Rocio Rosero Garcés, Jean Rubaduka, Akmal Saidov, Johan Saravanamuttu, Amartya Sen, A. K. Shiva Kumar, Darko Šilovic, Noël Twagiramungu and Polly Vizard.

Many organizations generously shared their data series and other research materials: the Carbon Dioxide Information Analysis Center, Centre for Research on the Epidemiology of Disasters, Co-operative Programme for Monitoring and Evaluation of the Long-Range Transmission of Air Pollutants in Europe, Food and Agriculture Organization, Inter-Parliamentary Union, International Fund for Agricultural Development, International Institute for Democracy and Electoral Assistance, International Institute for Strategic Studies, International Labour Organization, International Monetary Fund, International Organization for Migration, International Telecommunication Union, Joint United Nations Programme on HIV/AIDS, Luxembourg Income Study, Office of the United Nations High Commissioner for Refugees, Organisation for Economic Co-operation and Development, Stockholm International Peace Research Institute, United Nations Centre for Social Development and Humanitarian Affairs, United Nations Children's Fund, United Nations Conference on Trade and Development, United Nations Department of

Economic and Social Affairs, United Nations Division for the Advancement of Women, United Nations Economic and Social Commission for Asia and the Pacific, United Nations Economic and Social Commission for Western Asia, United Nations Economic Commission for Africa, United Nations Economic Commission for Europe, United Nations Economic Commission for Latin America and the Caribbean, United Nations Educational, Scientific and Cultural Organization, United Nations Population Division, United Nations Research Institute for Social Development, United Nations Statistics Division, World Bank, World Health Organization, World Trade Organization and World Resources Institute.

UNDP READERS AND ADVISORY PANEL

Colleagues in UNDP provided extremely useful comments, suggestions and input during the drafting of the Report. In particular, the authors would like to express their gratitude to Adel Abdellatif, Dominique Aitouyahia-McAdams, Omar Bakhet, Jamal Benomar, Stephen Browne, Nilufer Cagatay, Edmund Cain, Nikhil Chandavarkar, Shabbir Cheema, Bertrand Coppens, Djibril Diallo, Hans d'Orville, Elizabeth Fong, Walter Franco, Marit Gjelten, John Hendra, Noeleen Heyzer, Nay Htun, Abdoulie Janneh, Macharia Kamau, Inge Kaul, Normand Lauzon, Thierry Lemaresquier, José Carlos Libanio, Carlos Lopes, Kamal Malhotra, Abdoulaye Mar Dieye, Elena Martinez, Jan Mattsson, Saraswathi Menon, Hamed Mobarek, Jana Ricasio, Rebeca Rios-Kohn, Jordan Ryan, Mia Seppo, Nessim Shallon, Rosine Sori-Coulibaly, R. Sudarshan, Antonio Vigilante, Eimi Watanabe, David Whaley, Caitlin Wiesen-Antin, Kanni Wignaraja, Oscar Yujnovsky and Agostinho Zacarias.

CONSULTATIONS

Many individuals took part in special meetings. In consultations with UN organizations: Gonzalo Abad, Francoise Belmont, Peter Crowley, Virginia Leary, Lars Ludvigsen, Themba N. Masuku, Steven Oates, Steven Olejas, Reinaldo Figueredo Planchart, Norman Scott, Lee Swepston, Andrew Whitley and Daniel Wikler. In consultations on human rights indicators: Ignacio Aymerich, David Cieslikowski, Gerhard Haensel, Ellen Hagerman, Stephen Hansen, Aart Kraay, Richard Leete, Patrick Molutsi, Goro Onojima, Ali Piano, Massimo Tommasoli and Joann Vanek. On developing a collaborative study for progress in human development: Halis Akder, Robert Greener, Ricardo Henriques, Jong-Wha Lee, Osman M. Osman, Gustav Ranis and Frances Stewart. On corporations and human rights: Ron Berenbeim, Rainer Braun, Johanna Breman, Jonathan Cohen, Amy Davidsen, Arvind Gamesan, Lauren Goldblatt, Scott Greathead, Elizabeth Howard, Kiku Loomis, David Lowry, Wendy Rhein, Bob Turner, Larry Walsh and Joanna Weschler.

Many individuals consulted during the preparation of the Report provided invaluable advice, information and materials. Lack of space precludes naming all of them here, but we would like to especially recognize the contributions of Yasmin Ahmad, Özer Babakol, Shaida Badiee, Maria Baquero, Hazel Bennett, Douglas Bettcher, Yonas Biru, Tom Boden, Adam Bouloukos, Brigitte Brandt, Ewa Brantley, Mathieu Brossard, Claude Cahn, Rolf Carriere, Vittoria Cavicchioni-Molcard, Shaohua Chen, Noam Chomsky, S. K. Chu, Alice Clague, Adam Cohen, Patrick Cornu, Carlos Correa, David Donat-Cattin, Marie-Therese Dupre, Graham Dutfield, Julian Fleet, Julio Frank, Lisa Frederiksson, Judy Gearhart, Patricia Georget, Dorota Gierycz, Peter Gleick, Erlinda Go, Emmanuel Guindone, Kul Guntham, Björn Hagelin, Katherine Hagen, Brigitte Ham, Abrar Hasan, Michael Henriques, Bela Hovy, Kareen Jabre, Phil James, Bruce Jones, Gareth Jones, Urban Johnnson, Alex Julca, Georg Kell, Alison Kennedy, Shulamith Koenig, Miloon Kothari, John Langmore, Todd Larson, Paul Gordon Lauren, Elisa Levy, Myriam Linster, Nyein Nyein Lwin, Serguei Malanitchev, Carolyn McAskie, Caroline Michellier, Zafir Mirza, Roeland Monasch, Srdan Mrkic, Aimée Nichols,

David Nyheim, Rosario Pardo, David Patterson, Rachel Pedersen, Tatjana Peric, Thomas Pogge, Kiernan Prendergast, Will Prince, Agnès Puymoyen, Sonya Rabeneck, Sadig Rasheed, Socarro Reyes, Wolfgang Rhomberg, Santiago Romero, Kenneth Roth, Karl Sauvant, Bernhard Schwartländer, Simon Scott, Hy Shellow, Henry Shue, Elizabeth Sköns, Timothy Smeeding, Herbert Spirer, Louise Spirer, Petter Stålenheim, Elissavet Stamatopoulou-Robbins, Romila Sudhir, Eric Swanson, Kari Tapiola, Gordon Telesford, Jessica Vivian, Michael Ward, Tessa Wardlaw, Aurelie von Wartensleben, Kevin Watkins, Patrick Werguin, Siemon Wezeman, Robin White, Robert Wintemute, Mania Yannarakis and Ann Zammit.

ADMINISTRATIVE AND LOGISTICAL SUPPORT

Secretarial and administrative support for the Report's preparation was provided by Oscar Bernal, Wendy Chen, Renuka Corea-Lloyd, Rekha Kalekar, Chato Ledonio-O'Buckley, Aida Liza-Mayor, Stephanie Meade, Maria Regina Milo and Emily White.

The United Nations Office for Project Services provided the team with critical administrative support. Particular thanks go to Oscar Hernandez, Liliana Izquierdo, Maarten Poolman and Ingolf Schuetz-Mueller.

The Report also benefited from the dedicated work of interns. Thanks are due to Ana Budin, Ali Buzurukov, Hyun Go, Vivian Herrera, Claes Johansson, Hoster Lifalaza Bebi, Christopher Pinc and Danny Sriskandarajah.

EDITING, PRODUCTION AND TRANSLATION

As in previous years, the Report benefited from the editing and pre-press production of Communications Development Incorporated's Bruce Ross-Larson, Fiona Blackshaw, Carole-Sue Castronuovo, Garrett Cruce, Terrence Fischer, Wendy Guyette, Walter Hemmens, Megan Klose, Daphne Levitas, Molly Lohman, Alison Strong and Elfranko Wessels. The Report also benefited from the translation, design and distribution work of Elizabeth Scott Andrews, Maureen Lynch and Hilda Paqui.

• • •

The team expresses sincere appreciation to Philip Alston, Anne Bayefsky, Radhika Coomaraswamy, Meghnad Desai, Stefanie Grant, Paul Hunt, Bruce Jenks, Barney Pityana, Rebeca Rios-Kohn, Jordan Ryan and Joanna Weschler for their advice to the Administrator and for acting as readers of the final draft of the Report.

Last but not least, the authors are especially grateful to Mark Malloch Brown, UNDP Administrator, who has given the Report his full support and strong intellectual leadership.

Thankful for all the support that they have received, the authors assume full responsibility for the opinions expressed in the Report.

AIDS	Acquired immunodeficiency syndrome
CAT	Convention Against Torture and Other Cruel, Inhuman or Degrading Treatment or Punishment
CEDAW	Convention on the Elimination of All Forms of Discrimination Against Women
CIS	Commonwealth of Independent States
CRC	Convention on the Rights of the Child
ECOSOC	Economic and Social Council (of the United Nations)
EU	European Union
GATT	General Agreement on Tariffs and Trade
GDI	Gender-related development index
GDP	Gross domestic product
GEM	Gender empowerment measure
GNP	Gross national product
HDI	Human development index
HIPCs	Heavily indebted poor countries
HIV	Human immunodeficiency virus
HPI	Human poverty index
ICCPR	International Covenant on Civil and Political Rights
ICERD	International Convention on the Elimination of All Forms of Racial Discrimination
ICESCR	International Covenant on Economic, Social and Cultural Rights
ILO	International Labour Organization
IMF	International Monetary Fund
NGO	Non-governmental organization
ODA	Official development assistance
OECD	Organisation for Economic Co-operation and Development
PPP	Purchasing power parity
TRIPS	Trade-Related Aspects of Intellectual Property Rights
UNCTAD	United Nations Conference on Trade and Development
UNDP	United Nations Development Programme
UNESCO	United Nations Educational, Scientific and Cultural Organization
UNICEF	United Nations Children's Fund
UNIFEM	United Nations Development Fund for Women
WHO	World Health Organization
WTO	World Trade Organization

Contents

HUMAN DEVELOPMENT INDICATORS

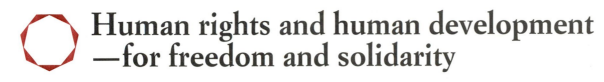 Human rights and human development —for freedom and solidarity

Human rights and human development share a common vision and a common purpose—to secure the freedom, well-being and dignity of all people everywhere. To secure:

• Freedom from discrimination—by gender, race, ethnicity, national origin or religion.

• Freedom from want—to enjoy a decent standard of living.

• Freedom to develop and realize one's human potential.

• Freedom from fear—of threats to personal security, from torture, arbitrary arrest and other violent acts.

• Freedom from injustice and violations of the rule of law.

• Freedom of thought and speech and to participate in decision-making and form associations.

• Freedom for decent work—without exploitation.

One of the 20th century's hallmark achievements was its progress in human rights. In 1900 more than half the world's people lived under colonial rule, and no country gave all its citizens the right to vote. Today some three-quarters of the world lives under democratic regimes. There has also been great progress in eliminating discrimination by race, religion and gender—and in advancing the right to schooling and basic health care.

In 1948 the Universal Declaration of Human Rights was adopted, for the first time in history acknowledging human rights as a global responsibility. Today all but one of the six core covenants and conventions on civil, political, economic, social and cultural rights have each been ratified by 140 or more countries. All but one of the seven core labour rights conventions have been ratified by 125

or more countries. There is still far to go—but the progress has been spectacular.

The 21st century's growing global interdependence signals a new era. Complex political and economic interactions, coupled with the rise of powerful new actors, open new opportunities. They also call for a more visionary commitment to building the institutions, laws and enabling economic environment to secure fundamental freedoms for all: all human rights, for all people in all countries.

Individuals, governments, non-governmental organizations (NGOs), corporations, policymakers, multilateral organizations—all have a role in transforming the potential of global resources and the promise of technology, know-how and networking into social arrangements that truly promote fundamental freedoms everywhere, rather than just pay lip service to them.

Many countries—poor and rich—are already demonstrating a new dynamism in taking initiatives for human rights and human development. South Africa, since ending apartheid, has put human rights at the core of its development strategy, with the government establishing one of the world's most forward-looking structures of rights. In India, the world's largest democracy, the supreme court has insisted on the rights of all citizens to free education and basic health care. Europe is making human rights a key priority—as with the pioneering approaches of the Council of Europe and the European Court of Human Rights.

The mark of all civilizations is the respect they accord to human dignity and freedom. All religions and cultural traditions celebrate these ideals. Yet throughout history they have been violated. Every society has known racism, sexism, authoritarianism, xenophobia—depriving

The mark of all civilizations is the respect they accord to human dignity and freedom

men and women of their dignity and freedom. And in all regions and cultures the struggle against oppression, injustice and discrimination has been common. That struggle continues today in all countries, rich and poor.

Human freedom is the common purpose and common motivation of human rights and human development. The movements for human rights and for human development have had distinct traditions and strategies. United in a broader alliance, each can bring new energy and strength to the other.

Human rights and human development are both about securing basic freedoms. Human rights express the bold idea that all people have claims to social arrangements that protect them from the worst abuses and deprivations—and that secure the freedom for a life of dignity.

Human development, in turn, is a process of enhancing human capabilities—to expand choices and opportunities so that each person can lead a life of respect and value. When human development and human rights advance together, they reinforce one another—expanding people's capabilities and protecting their rights and fundamental freedoms.

Until the last decade human development and human rights followed parallel paths in both concept and action—the one largely dominated by economists, social scientists and policy-makers, the other by political activists, lawyers and philosophers. They promoted divergent strategies of analysis and action—economic and social progress on the one hand, political pressure, legal reform and ethical questioning on the other. But today, as the two converge in both concept and action, the divide between the human development agenda and the human rights agenda is narrowing. There is growing political support for each of them—and there are new opportunities for partnerships and alliances.

Human rights can add value to the agenda of development. They draw attention to the accountability to respect, protect and fulfil the human rights of all people. The tradition of human rights brings legal tools and institutions—laws, the judiciary and the process of litigation—as means to secure freedoms and human development.

Rights also lend moral legitimacy and the principle of social justice to the objectives of human development. The rights perspective helps shift the priority to the most deprived and excluded, especially to deprivations because of discrimination. It also directs attention to the need for information and political voice for all people as a development issue—and to civil and political rights as integral parts of the development process.

Human development, in turn, brings a dynamic long-term perspective to the fulfilment of rights. It directs attention to the socio-economic context in which rights can be realized—or threatened. The concepts and tools of human development provide a systematic assessment of economic and institutional constraints to the realization of rights—as well as of the resources and policies available to overcome them. Human development thus contributes to building a long-run strategy for the realization of rights.

In short, human development is essential for realizing human rights, and human rights are essential for full human development.

The 20th century's advances in human rights and human development were unprecedented—but there is a long unfinished agenda.

The major advances in human rights and human development came after the horrors of the Second World War. The 1945 Charter of the United Nations, followed by the Universal Declaration of Human Rights in 1948, ushered in a new era of international commitment to human freedoms:
• Emphasizing the universality of rights, centred on the equality of all people.
• Recognizing the realization of human rights as a collective goal of humanity.
• Identifying a comprehensive range of all rights—civil, political, economic, social and cultural—for all people.

In short, human development is essential for realizing human rights, and human rights are essential for full human development

- Creating an international system for promoting the realization of human rights with institutions to set standards, establish international laws and monitor performance (but without powers of enforcement).
- Establishing the state's accountability for its human rights obligations and commitments under international law.

Work on international human rights legislation also continued. But polarized by the cold war, the rhetoric of human rights was reduced to a weapon in the propaganda for geopolitical interests. The West emphasized civil and political rights, pointing the finger at socialist countries for denying these rights. The socialist (and many developing) countries emphasized economic and social rights, criticizing the richest Western countries for their failure to secure these rights for all citizens. In the 1960s this led to two separate covenants—one for civil and political rights, and the other for economic, social and cultural rights.

The 1980s brought a strong renewal of international interest and action, propelled by the women's movement, the children's movement and a surge of activity by civil society. The Convention on the Elimination of All Forms of Discrimination Against Women (CEDAW) was agreed to in 1979, the Convention on the Rights of the Child 10 years later.

In 1986 the Declaration on the Right to Development was adopted. And further strong commitments were made at the World Conference on Human Rights in Vienna in 1993. This was followed by the creation of the position of United Nations High Commissioner for Human Rights and the growing advocacy for rights internationally and nationally.

The late 1990s brought other developments:
- The 1998 Rome statute to establish the International Criminal Court. By April 2000 it had been signed by nearly 100 countries.
- Establishment of international tribunals for Rwanda and the former Yugoslavia—for the first time since the Nuremberg and Tokyo trials, enforcing individual accountability for war crimes.
- The optional protocol to CEDAW, opening the way for individuals to appeal to an international body.

In 1990, 10% of the world's countries had ratified all six major human rights instruments, but by February 2000—in 10 years—this increased spectacularly to nearly half of all countries.

Freedom from discrimination—for equality. The 20th century's progress towards equality—regardless of gender, race, religion, ethnicity or age—was propelled by social movements. One of the most significant has been the movement for women's rights, with roots back over the centuries. The struggle against discrimination has also led to civil rights and anti-racism movements the world over.
- More than three-quarters of the world's countries have ratified CEDAW and the International Convention on the Elimination of All Forms of Racial Discrimination (ICERD)—165 for CEDAW and 155 for ICERD.
- National institutions and legal standards for affirmative action have emerged in Australia, Canada, India, New Zealand and the United States, where ethnic minorities and indigenous and tribal peoples form a significant part of the population.

But discrimination by gender, ethnic group, race and age continues all over the world.
- In Canada in 1991, the life expectancy of an Inuit male, at 58 years, was 17 years less than the life expectancy of 75 years for all Canadian males.
- In the Republic of Korea the female wage rate is only three-fifths the male, a disparity typical of many countries.
- Police reports record hundreds of violent hate crimes and discrimination against immigrants and ethnic minorities in Germany, Sweden and elsewhere in Europe.

Freedom from want—for a decent standard of living. The world has made much progress in achieving freedom from want and in improving the standard of living of millions.
- Between 1980 and 1999 malnutrition was reduced: the proportion of underweight chil-

Polarized by the cold war, the rhetoric of human rights was reduced to a weapon in the propaganda for geopolitical interests

dren fell in developing countries from 37% to 27% and that of stunted children from 47% to 33%.

• Between 1970 and 1999 in rural areas of the developing world, the percentage of people with access to safe water increased more than fourfold—from 13% to 71%.

• Some countries made spectacular progress in reducing income poverty—China from 33% in 1978 to 7% in 1994.

Yet many deprivations remain:

• Worldwide, 1.2 billion people are income poor, living on less than $1 a day (1993 PPP US$).

• More than a billion people in developing countries lack access to safe water, and more than 2.4 billion people lack adequate sanitation.

Freedom to develop and realize one's human potential. The achievement of human potential reached unprecedented heights in the 20th century.

• Worldwide, 46 countries, with more than a billion people, have achieved high human development.

• In developing countries during the past three decades, life expectancy increased by 10 years—from 55 years in 1970 to 65 in 1998. The adult literacy rate increased by half—from 48% in 1970 to 72% in 1998. And the infant mortality rate declined by more than two-fifths—from 110 per 1,000 live births in 1970 to 64 in 1998.

• The combined net primary and secondary enrolment ratio increased from 50% in 1970 to 72% in 1998.

Yet such progress has been uneven across regions and among groups of people within countries.

• Some 90 million children are out of school at the primary level.

• By the end of 1999 nearly 34 million people were infected with HIV, 23 million in Sub-Saharan Africa. Life expectancy, after huge gains in the 1970s, is slipping.

Freedom from fear—with no threats to personal security. No other aspect of human security is so vital as security from physical violence. But in poor nations and rich, peo-

ple's lives are threatened by violence. For years civil society movements have mobilized public opinion to eliminate such threats, as have international groups. The right of habeas corpus, vital as a tool against arbitrary detention, now prevails in many more countries. Laws for rape are stricter. Significant advances are evident in the respect for human rights.

• The incidence of torture is lower in many countries. In Honduras the number of torture cases reported to the Committee for the Defence of Human Rights, a major NGO, fell from 156 in 1991 to 7 in 1996.

• Worldwide, the number of major armed conflicts—almost all internal—declined from 55 in 1992 to 36 in 1998.

• The appointment of a Special Rapporteur on Violence against Women did much to raise public awareness and change public policy on the issue.

Yet the security of people all over the world is still under threat—from conflicts, political oppression and increasing crime and violence.

• Around the world on average, about one in every three women has experienced violence in an intimate relationship.

• Worldwide, about 1.2 million women and girls under 18 are trafficked for prostitution each year.

• About 100 million children are estimated to be living or working on the street.

• About 300,000 children were soldiers in the 1990s, and 6 million were injured in armed conflicts.

Freedom from injustice. Without the rule of law and fair administration of justice, human rights laws are no more than paper. But there has been much progress on the institutional front.

• The Universal Declaration of Human Rights inspired many constitutions in the newly independent countries of Asia and Africa during the 1950s and 1960s. And in recent times Cambodia, South Africa, Thailand and most countries in Eastern Europe and the Commonwealth of Independent States (CIS) have incorporated its articles in their new constitutions. Egypt recently became the second of the Arab States, after Tunisia, to grant equal divorce rights to

Without the rule of law and fair administration of justice, human rights laws are no more than paper

women. Some 66 countries have abolished the death penalty for all crimes.

• To improve the protection of women's rights, many domestic laws have been changed. In 1995 an amendment to the Citizenship Act in Botswana, citing the commitment of the government to CEDAW, granted the children of women married to foreigners the right to assume their mother's citizenship.

• Public interest litigation cases—in education and environment in such countries as India—have been important in securing people's economic and social rights.

• Human rights ombudsmen are working in more than a dozen countries.

Still, there is a long way to go. In many countries the fair administration of justice remains elusive because of inadequate institutional capacity.

• Of 45 countries having data, more than half have fewer than 10 judges per 100,000 people.

• The average custody while awaiting trial in 1994 was 60 weeks in Mexico, 40 weeks in Hungary and 30 weeks in the Czech Republic.

Freedom of participation, speech and association. The 20th century's brutal militaries, fascist regimes and totalitarian one-party states committed some of the worst abuses of human rights. But thanks to impressive struggles, most of these ugly regimes have given way to democracies.

• By 1975, 33 countries had ratified the International Covenant on Civil and Political Rights—by 2000, 144 had.

• One person in five is estimated to participate in some form of civil society organization. People are participating in national poverty hearings, peasants associations, indigenous peoples associations and truth and reconciliation commissions in post-conflict situations—and at the local level, in tenants associations, school boards, water users associations and community policing.

• People are also demanding more transparency and accountability, and in many cases the legal framework is helping. Thailand's new constitution allows people to demand accountability from public officials for corruption and misdeeds, with 50,000 signatures against any parliamentarian triggering a review. In Brazil the Federal Audit Tribunal, linked to the legislative branch, holds a mandate to audit all expenditures of the central government.

• In 1900 no country had universal adult suffrage. Today nearly all countries do.

• Between 1974 and 1999 multiparty electoral systems were introduced in 113 countries.

All these are impressive testimony to the advance of freedom, but many setbacks and dangers need to be addressed.

• About 40 countries do not have a multiparty electoral system. And democracies remain fragile. In the 1990s several countries reverted to non-electoral regimes.

• Women hold about 14% of parliamentary seats worldwide.

• In 1999, 87 journalists and media people were killed while doing their job.

Freedom for decent work—without exploitation. Productive and satisfying livelihoods give people the means to buy goods and services. They empower people socially by enhancing their dignity and self-esteem. And they can empower people politically by enabling them to influence decision-making in the workplace and beyond.

• Employment in the formal labour market grew impressively in the past decade. In China employment increased 2.2% a year in 1987–96—outpacing labour force growth of 1.5%. The corresponding rates in India were 2.4% and 2.2%.

• Employment opportunities in developing countries have broadened through expansion of informal sector enterprises, microfinance and NGO activities.

• Each of the four conventions prohibiting forced labour or discrimination in employment and occupation has been ratified by more than 140 countries.

Yet serious problems remain:

• At least 150 million of the world's workers were unemployed at the end of 1998. Unemployment varies by ethnic group—in South Africa unemployment among African males in 1995 was 29%, seven times the 4% rate among their white counterparts.

Thanks to impressive struggles, most of these ugly regimes have given way to democracies

- In developing countries there are some 250 million child labourers—140 million boys and 110 million girls.

The 21st century opens with new threats to human freedoms.

History is moving fast at the start of the 21st century. Recent events have unleashed waves of change, with the new information and communications technologies, the new global rules and institutions and the accelerating global economic integration. With the end of the cold war, the political, economic and social landscape is changing rapidly and radically. This new context opens unparalleled new opportunities. But it also gives rise to new threats to human security and human freedom.

Conflicts within national borders. The number of major armed conflicts peaked at 55 in 1992 and, contrary to many impressions, later declined. Even so, there were 36 major conflicts in 1998. An estimated 5 million people died in intrastate conflicts in the 1990s. Globally in 1998, there were more than 10 million refugees and 5 million internally displaced persons. The number of deaths and displacements alone greatly understates the human rights violations in these conflicts, with widespread rape and torture.

Economic and political transitions. Transitions to democracy brought advances in many human rights, advances now under threat as a result of ethnic conflict, rising poverty, growing inequality and social strain. Stable structures of government are not yet in place or have been greatly weakened. Transition and economic collapse dismantled many previous guarantees of social and economic rights.

Global inequalities and the marginalization of poor countries and poor people. Global inequalities in income increased in the 20th century by orders of magnitude out of proportion to anything experienced before. The distance between the incomes of the rich-est and poorest country was about 3 to 1 in 1820, 35 to 1 in 1950, 44 to 1 in 1973 and 72 to 1 in 1992.

A recent study of world income distribution among households shows a sharp rise in inequality—with the Gini coefficient deteriorating from 0.63 in 1988 to 0.66 in 1993 (a value of 0 signifies perfect equality, a value of 1 perfect inequality). Gaps between rich and poor are widening in many countries—in the Russian Federation the Gini coefficient rose from 0.24 to 0.48 between 1987–88 and 1993–95. In Sweden, the United Kingdom and the United States it rose by more than 16% in the 1980s and early 1990s. It remains very high in much of Latin America—0.57 in Ecuador, 0.59 in Brazil and Paraguay. Meanwhile, economic growth has stagnated in many developing countries. The average annual growth of income per capita in 1990–98 was negative in 50 countries, only one of them an OECD country.

Bold new approaches are needed to achieve universal realization of human rights in the 21st century—adapted to the opportunities and realities of the era of globalization, to its new global actors and to its new global rules.

All rights for all people in all countries should be the goal of the 21st century. The Universal Declaration had that vision more than 50 years ago. The world today has the awareness, the resources and the capacity to achieve this goal on a worldwide scale.

Human freedoms have never advanced automatically. And as in earlier times, advances in the 21st century will be won by human struggle against divisive values—and against the opposition of entrenched economic and political interests. People's movements and civil society groups will be in the vanguard, raising public awareness of rights violations and pressing for changes in law and policy. Today's technologies and today's more open societies present great opportunities for networking and for building alliances.

Seven key features are needed for a broader approach to securing human rights.

As in earlier times, advances in the 21st century will be won by human struggle against divisive values—and against the opposition of entrenched economic and political interests

1. Every country needs to strengthen its social arrangements for securing human freedoms—with norms, institutions, legal frameworks and an enabling economic environment. Legislation alone is not enough.

Laws alone cannot guarantee human rights. Institutions to support the legal process are also needed—as is a culture of social norms and ethics to reinforce the legal structures, not threaten them. An enabling economic environment is essential, too. Many groups in society, as well as governments, can strengthen all these social arrangements.

Norms. Community leaders, religious leaders, business leaders, parents, teachers—all have a role in building norms and upholding the values of respect for human dignity, freedom and equality. And they all have rights and duties. The state also has to promote awareness. Many countries have introduced human rights education in all schools. And awareness of rights is spreading in many other ways. The media have often made the difference in documenting violations—police brutality, disappearances, corporate failures to respect labour standards. More positively, police training in human rights to prevent brutality has been successful in many countries, such as El Salvador.

Institutions. Children's rights cannot be guaranteed without strong and effective institutions—not only schools and health centres, but courts that function and specialized services for registering births. The state has the responsibility to ensure that such institutions are in place, and international cooperation can help in strengthening essential institutions and in building capacity.

New institutions are being established to promote human rights and tackle complaints:
• Independent national commissions for human rights ensure that human rights laws and regulations are being effectively applied. Many are playing a vigorous role, as in New Zealand and South Africa.
• Ombudsmen, pioneered in Sweden, help protect people against rights abuses by public officials.

• Parliamentary human rights bodies now exist in half of all parliaments, mobilizing support and setting standards to guarantee rights.

Legal recognition and enforcement. Recognition under the law lends legal weight to the moral imperative of human rights—and mobilizes the legal system for enforcement. Unless a woman's claim to equal treatment is legally recognized, she cannot demand a remedy against discrimination. States have the first obligation to participate in the international rights regime and to establish national legal frameworks. But human rights activists and movements can also press for legal reforms—to give people access to legal processes, with institutional barriers removed.

An enabling economic environment. The economic environment needs to facilitate access to many rights, not threaten it. Economic resources are needed to pay teachers and health workers, support judges and meet a host of other needs. A growing economy is thus important for human rights, especially for poor countries. But that growth must be pro-poor, pro-rights and sustainable.

2. The fulfilment of all human rights requires democracy that is inclusive—protecting the rights of minorities, providing separation of powers and ensuring public accountability. Elections alone are not enough.

The past two decades have seen breakthroughs with the shift to multiparty democratic regimes—as more than 100 countries ended rule by military dictatorships or single parties. But multiparty elections are not enough. The democratic transition, still young, risks reversals. A broader view of democracy needs to be pursued, incorporating five features:
• *Inclusion of minorities.* To secure human rights for all requires inclusive democracies, not just majoritarian democracies. Many "democracies" hold multiparty elections but exclude minorities from many aspects of political participation—in the legislature, in the cabinet, in the army. Recent history—and research—show that such exclusion and horizontal inequality incited

Laws alone cannot guarantee human rights

many conflicts of the 1980s and 1990s. Greater attention to equity can prevent conflict and build peace.

• *Separation of powers.* When the independence of the judiciary is not ensured, people cannot enjoy legal protection from injustice and abuses of their rights. In young democracies a well-functioning independent judiciary is vital for inclusive democracy.

• *Open civil society and free and independent media.* Public scrutiny and state accountability are essential, yet civil society and the media are still institutionally weak in many countries. The media are state controlled in 5% of countries. Some 1,500 attacks on journalists are reported each year by the Toronto International Freedom of Expression Exchange.

• *Transparent policy-making.* Economic policy-making behind closed doors violates the right to political participation—and is susceptible to the corrupting influences of political power and big money. It creates a disabling environment, ripe for human rights failures. This democratic deficit is widespread in local, national and global economic policy-making—reflected in slum clearances that wantonly deprive people of housing, dams that flood houses and farms, budget allocations that favour water for middle-class suburbs rather than slums, logging that destroys the environment, oil wells that pollute fields and rivers from which people draw livelihoods.

• *Containment of the corrupting power of big money.* All countries—rich, poor, stagnant, dynamic and in transition—face the challenge of ensuring that the voices of the people are heard above the whir of spin doctors and the lobbying power of corporations and special interests.

3. Poverty eradication is not only a development goal—it is a central challenge for human rights in the 21st century.

The torture of a single individual rightly raises public outrage. Yet the deaths of more than 30,000 children every day from mainly preventable causes go unnoticed. Why? Because these children are invisible in poverty.

Poverty eradication is a major human rights challenge of the 21st century. A decent standard of living, adequate nutrition, health care, education, decent work and protection against calamities are not just development goals—they are also human rights.

Of the many failures of human rights, the denial of these economic, social and cultural rights is particularly widespread. Some 90 million children are out of primary school. About 790 million people are hungry and food insecure, and about 1.2 billion live on less than $1 a day (1993 PPP US$). Even in OECD countries some 8 million people are undernourished. In the United States alone, some 40 million people are not covered by health insurance, and one adult in five is functionally illiterate.

Three priorities for human rights and development policies:

• *Ensuring civil and political rights—freedom of speech, association and participation—to empower poor people to claim their social, economic and cultural rights.* Given the causal links among the many human rights, they can be mutually reinforcing and can empower poor people to fight poverty. Guaranteeing civil and political rights is not only an end in itself—it is a good means to poverty eradication. Ensuring freedom for NGOs, the media and workers organizations can do much to give poor people the political space to participate in decision-making on policies that affect their lives.

A major development of the 1990s was the flourishing of NGOs and their global networks—rising in number from 23,600 in 1991 to 44,000 in 1999. From Guyana to Zambia, from India to Russia, people are organizing civil society groups and NGOs, getting experience defending people's rights against evictions, holding government accountable for building schools, for community development and for human rights education and engaging in countless other struggles.

• *For the state, meeting its human rights obligations to implement policies and policy-making processes that do the most to secure economic, social and cultural rights for the most deprived and to ensure their participation in decision-making.* Rights to housing, health care and the like do not mean a claim to free services or a state handout.

A decent standard of living, adequate nutrition, health care, education, decent work and protection against calamities are not just development goals—they are also human rights

Instead, they are claims to social arrangements and policies that promote access to these rights through both the market (housing) and the state (free primary education).

• *Investing economic resources in promoting human rights.* Human rights measures range from the virtually cost-free to those demanding substantial resources—for public budgets to provide schools, teachers and judges, for corporations to put in place working conditions that respect core labour standards. There is no automatic link between resources and rights. High incomes do not guarantee that rich countries are free of serious human rights violations any more than low incomes prevent poor countries from making impressive progress.

Worldwide, public spending on economic and social rights is inadequate and badly distributed. In Ethiopia in the 1990s, annual spending on basic health services was only $3 a person, only 25% of the level required for the minimum health package. The global shortfall for achieving universal provision of basic services in developing countries amounts to $70–80 billion a year. The 20:20 compact calls for 20% of national budgets and 20% of aid budgets to be allocated to universal provision of basic needs. But spending is often much lower—12–14% on average for 30 countries in a recent study, and 4% in Cameroon, 7.7% in the Philippines, 8.5% in Brazil. Bilateral donors on average allocate only 8.3%.

Poor countries need faster growth to generate the resources to finance the eradication of poverty and the realization of human rights. But economic growth alone is not enough. It needs to be accompanied by policy reforms that channel funds into poverty eradication and human development—and into building institutions, shaping norms and reforming laws to promote human rights.

The neglect of economic and social rights can undermine civil and political liberties, just as the neglect of civil and political rights can undermine economic and social rights in times of calamities and threats.

4. Human rights—in an integrated world—require global justice. The state-centred model of accountability must be extended to the obligations of non-state actors and to the state's obligations beyond national borders.

Global integration is shrinking time, shrinking space and eroding national borders. People's lives are more interdependent. The state's autonomy is declining as new global rules of trade bind national policies and as new global actors wield greater influence. And as privatization proceeds, private enterprises and corporations have more impact on the economic opportunities of people. As the world becomes more interdependent, both states and other global actors have greater obligations.

• *States*—decisions of states, whether on interest rates or arms sales, have significant consequences for the lives of people outside national boundaries.

• *Global actors*—the World Trade Organization, the Bretton Woods institutions, global corporations, global NGO networks and the global media—all have significant impacts on the lives of people around the world.

• *Global rules*—more global rules are being developed in all areas, from human rights to environment and trade. But they are developing separately, with the potential for conflict. Human rights commitments and obligations need to be reflected in trade rules—the only ones now truly binding on national policy—because they have enforcement measures.

But little in the current global order binds states and global actors to promote human rights globally. Many least developed countries are being marginalized from the expanding opportunities of globalization. As world exports more than doubled, the share of least developed countries declined from 0.6% in 1980 to 0.5% in 1990 to 0.4% in 1997. And these countries attracted less than $3 billion in foreign direct investments in 1998. The global online community is growing exponentially—reaching 26% of all people in the United States but fewer than 1% in all developing regions.

The present global order suffers from three gaps—in incentives, jurisdiction and participation.

Poor countries need faster growth to generate the resources to finance the eradication of poverty and the realization of human rights

The system of global
governance needs to be
transparent and fair,
giving voice to small and
poor countries

• *Incentive gaps.* Governments are charged in trade negotiations to pursue national interests, not global interests.

• *Jurisdictional gaps.* Human rights treaties have weak enforcement mechanisms, while the trade agreements are backed by the "teeth" of enforcement. So there is pressure to include human rights—such as labour rights—in trade agreements. But sanctions are a blunt instrument. They pressure government policy but do little to change the behaviour of employers.

Global corporations can have enormous impact on human rights—in their employment practices, in their environmental impact, in their support for corrupt regimes or in their advocacy for policy changes. Yet international laws hold states accountable, not corporations. True, many corporations have adopted codes of conduct and policies of social responsibility, especially in response to public pressure—a good first step. But many fail to meet human rights standards, or lack implementation measures and independent audits.

• *Participation gaps.* Small and poor countries generally participate little in global economic rule-making for a host of reasons, starting with the costs of participation and policy research.

Just as nations require an inclusive democracy to guarantee respect for human rights, so the system of global governance needs to be transparent and fair, giving voice to small and poor countries and releasing them from their marginalization from the benefits of the global economy and technology.

5. Information and statistics are a powerful tool for creating a culture of accountability and for realizing human rights. Activists, lawyers, statisticians and development specialists need to work together with communities. The goal: to generate information and evidence that can break down barriers of disbelief and mobilize changes in policy and behaviour.

The constant struggle to realize rights is benefiting tremendously from the information age. Civil society networks provide new sources of information. The Internet disseminates their findings as never before. Greater attention is going to collecting and using high-quality information to put across messages and call for change.

Data are helping some governments make better policies. Data are enhancing public understanding of constraints and trade-offs and creating social consensus on national priorities and performance expectations. Data are also drawing attention to neglected human rights issues—the release of statistics on domestic violence, hate crimes and homelessness in many countries has turned silence into debate. And data are helping identify which actors are having an impact on whether a right is being realized—and creating a need for them to be accountable.

The emerging framework of international human rights law provides a strong foundation for deriving indicators on the legal obligations of the state. Bringing quantitative assessment to this legal framework is empowering governments to understand their obligations and the actions needed to meet them. It is also empowering civil society to stand up in court and provide advocacy.

The use of indicators needs to be focused more on revealing the roles and impacts of other actors in addition to the government. At the local level analysis needs to focus on the important influences, both positive and negative, that households, communities, the media, the private sector, civil society and government have on the realization of rights.

At the international level data are needed not only on the role of the state, but on the roles of corporations and multilateral institutions. Also needed are indicators on the impacts that states have beyond the impacts on their citizens—states as donors and lenders, states as traders and negotiators, states as arms dealers and peace-makers.

Four priorities for strengthening the use of indicators in human rights:

• Collecting new and better official data and ensuring greater public access to the data—an effort spearheaded by the right to information movement.

• Diversifying the sources of information—from national human rights institutions to civil

society and community organizations—and building the reliability and credibility of the information they provide.
- Setting benchmarks for assessing performance. All countries need to build social consensus on priorities and the rate of progress possible in their context.
- Strengthening the procedures that hold actors accountable—from state reports to treaty bodies and NGO "shadow reports" to independent monitoring of multinational corporations.

6. Achieving all rights for all people in all countries in the 21st century will require action and commitment from the major groups in every society—NGOs, media and businesses, local as well as national government, parliamentarians and other opinion leaders.

In every country five priorities will help advance national action:
- *Assessing nationally the existing human rights situation to set priorities for action.* Such assessments were recommended at the Vienna Conference—though only 10 countries have prepared such plans, Australia and Brazil among them. In their place, many assessments are made by international NGOs and institutions based in industrialized countries. Not surprising, reports from outside often generate hostility and tension.

Rather than react to criticisms from foreign governments and international NGOs, it is time for countries to produce their own national assessments—reviewing their performance in relation to the full set of core rights, looking at operational requirements for advance, identifying next steps in the context of the country's resources and realities. Such assessments can best be prepared by a group that includes civil society, not just government—the annual reports of the Pakistan human rights commission are a good example. Many countries have already prepared national human development reports, and a national assessment of human rights could be combined with updates of these reports.
- *Reviewing national legislation against core international human rights to identify areas where action is needed to deal with gaps and contradictions.* Many countries have already undertaken such reviews for CEDAW and the Convention on the Rights of the Child. The process now should be extended—to remove other laws that discriminate against women or violate the rights of other groups. Jordan is reviewing legislation to stop "honour" killings of women. In Argentina people and politicians are collaborating to review laws and institutional barriers to justice, especially to promote access to justice for poor people and women.
- *Using education and the media to promote the norms of human rights throughout society.* The challenge is to build a culture of human rights awareness and commitment. Many countries have been highly creative in incorporating rights within the school system. In Cambodia 25,000 teachers have been trained in human rights, and they have already taught more than 3 million children. Ecuador devoted a week of television to explaining the rights of the child and then made it possible for children to use the electoral machinery to vote on which rights they thought most important for themselves. Several Latin American countries have incorporated human rights in training courses for the police and for social workers.
- *Building alliances for support and action.* Alliances for advancing human rights are going global. Many such alliances have formed to press for progress in the rights of women, children, minorities and groups with special needs, such as the disabled or people with HIV/AIDS. The Disabled People's International, now covering 158 countries, has contributed to changes in law and policy from Uganda to Zimbabwe to the European Union. Alliances are also building on issues—such as the FoodFirst Information and Action Network. And Indian farmers are joining Brazilian struggles for land rights.
- *Promoting an enabling economic environment.* The state has the primary responsibility for ensuring that growth is pro-poor, pro-rights and sustainable—by implementing appropriate policies and ensuring that human rights commitments and goals are incorporated as objectives in economic policy-making. There is a need for open and transparent

The challenge is to build a culture of human rights awareness and commitment public debate—in politics, in the media—that presses for accountability in public policy decisions.

7. Human rights and human development cannot be realized universally without stronger international action, especially to support disadvantaged people and countries and to offset growing global inequalities and marginalization.

A global change in attitude is needed, moving to a positive approach of support for human rights in place of punitive approaches

Growing global interdependence and the desperate scarcity of resources and capacity in poor countries underline the need for the international community to take much stronger action to promote human rights. A global change in attitude is needed, moving to a positive approach of support for human rights in place of punitive approaches that emphasize "naming and shaming" and conditions for aid.

Five priority areas for international action:
• *Strengthening a rights-based approach in development cooperation, without conditionality*. Development cooperation can contribute directly to realizing human rights in poor countries in three ways. The first is to increase support to capacity building for democracy and the promotion of civil and political rights. The second is to increase support for the eradication of income and human poverty. And the third is to introduce an explicit rights-based approach to programming.

Important elements of this approach have already been successfully adopted by Australia, Sweden and the United Kingdom, and by UNDP and the United Nations Children's Fund (UNICEF). Norway recently reviewed its support to human rights efforts in the United Republic of Tanzania, Zambia and Zimbabwe. This experience makes clear the effectiveness of a positive and supportive approach. Finger-pointing engenders hostility and distrust, while conditionality often is ineffective and leads to counterproductive confrontation.

Aid, debt relief, access to markets, access to private financial flows and stability in the global economy are all needed for the full realization of rights in the poorest and least developed countries.

• *Mobilizing the support of international corporations for human rights*. People's movements have mobilized public opinion against multinational corporations that flout human rights. In many cases the firms that were earlier criticized—Shell, Nike, General Motors—have responded by developing codes of conduct. Consumer demand and labelling schemes, such as the United Kingdom's Ethical Trading, are creating incentives for better social and environmental practices. Some corporations, such as Benetton, are engaging in public advocacy on rights issues. The Secretary-General's Global Compact is seeking to mobilize corporate engagement to promote respect for human rights as a norm and a value in the corporate sector. These diverse approaches can build even greater momentum for raising corporate commitments to higher standards for human rights and developing new tools of accountability.

• *Strengthening regional approaches*. Many regional initiatives for human rights have built on shared concerns and shared values of neighbouring countries—the African Charter on Human and Peoples' Rights, the African Human Rights Commission, the European Social Charter, the Inter-American Court of Human Rights. These initiatives need to be strengthened and carried forward to fulfil their potential for sharing experience, political commitment and financial support.

• *Embarking on new efforts for peace-making, peace-building and peacekeeping*. Conflict and war lead to the worst of human rights abuses—not only mass slaughter but rape, torture, the destruction of housing and schools and the unspeakable violence that scars human memories for life. Many new ideas are afoot in the aftermath of the tragedies of the 1990s. Early warning and early preventive action. Stronger legal protection for civilians, including legal status for the displaced. International efforts to bring perpetrators to account. And a broad agenda of peace-making, peace-building, peacekeeping and reconstruction. Prevention is always more cost-effective than later intervention. Governments need to hammer home this fact of experience to generate the political support needed to resolve conflicts before they escalate.

- *Strengthening the international human rights machinery.* Procedures in the existing machinery need to be simplified and speeded up. Proposals are on the table to increase efficiency and effectiveness, to ease the reporting burden on countries and to achieve greater policy attention. The UN system, including the International Labour Organization (ILO), provides a framework for information but lacks enforcement measures.

Recent innovations to strengthen legal enforcement—such as the International Criminal Court, the optional protocol permitting individual complaints and the use of international law in national cases—are promising avenues for the application of human rights law. The experience of UNICEF and the United Nations Development Fund for Women (UNIFEM) in supporting the work of the Convention on the Rights of the Child and of CEDAW illustrates the importance of operational support to countries in participating in these international procedures.

Some specific initiatives could mobilize people around the world to:

- Embark on a global campaign to achieve universal ratification of the core human rights conventions.
- Press all Fortune 500 companies to recognize and support human rights and core labour standards—and join in support of the Secretary-General's Global Compact.
- Achieve the guarantee of compulsory primary education in all constitutions by 2010.
- Achieve the 20:20 compact for all least developed countries by 2010.
- Set up a global commission on human rights in global governance with a mandate to review proposals for strengthening the international human rights machinery and human rights safeguards in global economic agreements and secure a fair global economic system.

• • •

Human rights could be advanced beyond all recognition over the next quarter century. The progress in the past century justifies bold ambitions. But for the globally integrated, open societies of the 21st century, we need stronger commitments to universalism combined with respect for cultural diversity. This will require six shifts from the cold war thinking that dominated the 20th century:

- From the state-centred approaches to pluralist, multi-actor approaches—with accountability not only for the state but for media, corporations, schools, families, communities and individuals.
- From the national to international and global accountabilities—and from the international obligations of states to the responsibilities of global actors.
- From the focus on civil and political rights to a broader concern with all rights—giving as much attention to economic, social and cultural rights.
- From a punitive to a positive ethos in international pressure and assistance—from reliance on naming and shaming to positive support.
- From a focus on multiparty elections to the participation of all through inclusive models of democracy.
- From poverty eradication as a development goal to poverty eradication as social justice, fulfilling the rights and accountabilities of all actors.

The world community needs to return to the audacious vision of those who dreamed of the Rights of Man and of the Citizen and drafted the Universal Declaration of Human Rights. A new millennium is just the occasion to reaffirm such a vision—and to renew the practical commitments to make it happen.

The world community needs to return to the audacious vision of those who drafted the Universal Declaration of Human Rights

UNIVERSAL DECLARATION OF HUMAN RIGHTS

ARTICLE 1

All human beings are born free and equal in dignity and rights. They are endowed with reason and conscience and should act towards one another in a spirit of brotherhood.

ARTICLE 2

Everyone is entitled to all the rights and freedoms set forth in this Declaration, without distinction of any kind, such as race, colour, sex, language, religion, political or other opinion, national or social origin, property, birth or other status. Furthermore, no distinction shall be made on the basis of the political, jurisdictional or international status of the country or territory to which a person belongs, whether it be independent, trust, non-self-governing or under any other limitation of sovereignty.

ARTICLE 3

Everyone has the right to life, liberty and security of person.

ARTICLE 4

No one shall be held in slavery or servitude; slavery and the slave trade shall be prohibited in all their forms.

ARTICLE 5

No one shall be subjected to torture or to cruel, inhuman or degrading treatment or punishment.

ARTICLE 6

Everyone has the right to recognition everywhere as a person before the law.

ARTICLE 7

All are equal before the law and are entitled without any discrimination to equal protection of the law. All are entitled to equal protection against any discrimination in violation of this Declaration and against any incitement to such discrimination.

ARTICLE 8

Everyone has the right to an effective remedy by the competent national tribunals for acts violating the fundamental rights granted him by the constitution or by law.

ARTICLE 9

No one shall be subjected to arbitrary arrest, detention or exile.

ARTICLE 10

Everyone is entitled in full equality to a fair and public hearing by an independent and impartial tribunal, in the determination of his rights and obligations and of any criminal charge against him.

ARTICLE 11

(1) Everyone charged with a penal offence has the right to be presumed innocent until proved guilty according to law in a public trial at which he has had all the guarantees necessary for his defence.

(2) No one shall be held guilty of any penal offence on account of any act or omission which did not constitute a penal offence, under national or international law, at the time when it was committed. Nor shall a heavier penalty be imposed than the one that was applicable at the time the penal offence was committed.

ARTICLE 12

No one shall be subjected to arbitrary interference with his privacy, family, home or correspondence, nor to attacks upon his honour and reputation. Everyone has the right to the protection of the law against such interference or attacks.

ARTICLE 13

(1) Everyone has the right to freedom of movement and residence within the borders of each state.

(2) Everyone has the right to leave any country, including his own, and to return to his country.

ARTICLE 14

(1) Everyone has the right to seek and to enjoy in other countries asylum from persecution.

(2) This right may not be invoked in the case of prosecutions genuinely arising from non-political crimes or from acts contrary to the purposes and principles of the United Nations.

ARTICLE 15

(1) Everyone has the right to a nationality.

(2) No one shall be arbitrarily deprived of his nationality nor denied the right to change his nationality.

ARTICLE 16

(1) Men and women of full age, without any limitation due to race, nationality or religion, have the right to marry and to found a family. They are entitled to equal rights as to marriage, during marriage and at its dissolution.

(2) Marriage shall be entered into only with the free and full consent of the intending spouses.

(3) The family is the natural and fundamental group unit of society and is entitled to protection by society and the State.

ARTICLE 17

(1) Everyone has the right to own property alone as well as in association with others.

(2) No one shall be arbitrarily deprived of his property.

ARTICLE 18

Everyone has the right to freedom of thought, conscience and religion; this right includes freedom to change his religion or belief, and freedom, either alone or in community with others and in public or private, to manifest his religion or belief in teaching, practice, worship and observance.

ARTICLE 19

Everyone has the right to freedom of opinion and expression; this right includes freedom to hold opinions without interference and to seek, receive and impart information and ideas through any media and regardless of frontiers.

ARTICLE 20

(1) Everyone has the right to freedom of peaceful assembly and association.
(2) No one may be compelled to belong to an association.

ARTICLE 21

(1) Everyone has the right to take part in the government of his country, directly or through freely chosen representatives.
(2) Everyone has the right of equal access to public service in his country.
(3) The will of the people shall be the basis of the authority of government; this will shall be expressed in periodic and genuine elections which shall be by universal and equal suffrage and shall be held by secret vote or by equivalent free voting procedures.

ARTICLE 22

Everyone, as a member of society, has the right to social security and is entitled to realization, through national effort and international co-operation and in accordance with the organization and resources of each State, of the economic, social and cultural rights indispensable for his dignity and the free development of his personality.

ARTICLE 23

(1) Everyone has the right to work, to free choice of employment, to just and favourable conditions of work and to protection against unemployment.
(2) Everyone, without any discrimination, has the right to equal pay for equal work.
(3) Everyone who works has the right to just and favourable remuneration ensuring for himself and his family an existence worthy of human dignity, and supplemented, if necessary, by other means of social protection.
(4) Everyone has the right to form and to join trade unions for the protection of his interests.

ARTICLE 24

Everyone has the right to rest and leisure, including reasonable limitation of working hours and periodic holidays with pay.

ARTICLE 25

(1) Everyone has the right to a standard of living adequate for the health and well-being of himself and of his family, including food, clothing, housing and medical care and necessary social services, and the right to security in the event of unemployment, sickness, disability, widowhood, old age or other lack of livelihood in circumstances beyond his control.
(2) Motherhood and childhood are entitled to special care and assistance. All children, whether born in or out of wedlock, shall enjoy the same social protection.

ARTICLE 26

(1) Everyone has the right to education. Education shall be free, at least in the elementary and fundamental stages. Elementary education shall be compulsory. Technical and professional education shall be made generally available and higher education shall be equally accessible to all on the basis of merit.
(2) Education shall be directed to the full development of the human personality and to the strengthening of respect for human rights and fundamental freedoms. It shall promote understanding, tolerance and friendship among all nations, racial or religious groups, and shall further the activities of the United Nations for the maintenance of peace.
(3) Parents have a prior right to choose the kind of education that shall be given to their children.

ARTICLE 27

(1) Everyone has the right freely to participate in the cultural life of the community, to enjoy the arts and to share in scientific advancement and its benefits.
(2) Everyone has the right to the protection of the moral and material interests resulting from any scientific, literary or artistic production of which he is the author.

ARTICLE 28

Everyone is entitled to a social and international order in which the rights and freedoms set forth in this Declaration can be fully realized.

ARTICLE 29

(1) Everyone has duties to the community in which alone the free and full development of his personality is possible.
(2) In the exercise of his rights and freedoms, everyone shall be subject only to such limitations as are determined by law solely for the purpose of securing due recognition and respect for the rights and freedoms of others and of meeting the just requirements of morality, public order and the general welfare in a democratic society.
(3) These rights and freedoms may in no case be exercised contrary to the purposes and principles of the United Nations.

ARTICLE 30

Nothing in this Declaration may be interpreted as implying for any State, group or person any right to engage in any activity or to perform any act aimed at the destruction of any of the rights and freedoms set forth herein.

Human rights

Human rights are the rights possessed by all persons, by virtue of their common humanity, to live a life of freedom and dignity. They give all people moral claims on the behaviour of individuals and on the design of social arrangements—and are universal, inalienable and indivisible. Human rights express our deepest commitments to ensuring that all persons are secure in their enjoyment of the goods and freedoms that are necessary for dignified living.

Universality of human rights

Human rights belong to all people, and all people have equal status with respect to these rights. Failure to respect an individual's human right has the same weight as failure to respect the right of any other—it is not better or worse depending on the person's gender, race, ethnicity, nationality or any other distinction.

Inalienability of human rights

Human rights are inalienable: they cannot be taken away by others, nor can one give them up voluntarily.

Indivisibility of human rights

Human rights are indivisible in two senses. First, there is no hierarchy among different kinds of rights. Civil, political, economic, social and cultural rights are all equally necessary for a life of dignity. Second, some rights cannot be suppressed in order to promote others. Civil and political rights may not be violated to promote economic, social and cultural rights. Nor can economic, social and cultural rights be suppressed to promote civil and political rights.

Realization of human rights

A human right is realized when individuals enjoy the freedoms covered by that right and their enjoyment of the right is secure. A person's human rights are realized if and only if social arrangements are in place sufficient to protect her against standard threats to her enjoyment of the freedoms covered by those rights.

Duties and obligations

The terms *duties* and *obligations* are used interchangeably in this Report. Duties and obligations are norms. Norms provide people and other actors with reasons for conducting themselves in certain ways. Some duties and obligations require only that a person refrain from a certain course of conduct. Others require that the person undertake a course of conduct or one of a range of permissible courses of conduct.

Human rights and the correlate duties of duty bearers

Human rights are correlated with duties. Duty bearers are the actors collectively responsible for the realization of human rights. Those who bear duties with respect to a human right are accountable if the right goes unrealized. When a right has been violated or insufficiently protected, there is always someone or some institution that has failed to perform a duty.

Perfect and imperfect duties

Perfect duties specify both how the duty is to be performed and to whom it is owed. Imperfect duties, by contrast, leave open both how the duty can be performed and how forceful the duty is that must be carried out.

International human rights treaties, covenants and conventions

Used interchangeably, *treaty*, *covenant* and *convention* refer to legally binding agreements between states. These agreements define the duties of states parties to the treaty, covenant or convention.

States parties

States parties to an international agreement are the countries that have ratified it and are thereby legally bound to comply with its provisions.

Ratification of a treaty (covenant, convention)

Ratification of an international agreement represents the promise of a state to uphold it and adhere to the legal norms that it specifies.

Signing of a treaty (covenant, convention)

Signing a treaty, covenant or convention represents a promise of the state to adhere to the principles and norms specified in the document without creating legal duties to comply with them. Signing is the first step that states undertake towards ratifying and thus becoming states parties to an agreement. Presidential signature of an agreement must be ratified by parliament for the agreement to become legally binding.

Reservation to a treaty (covenant, convention)

A reservation to a treaty indicates that a state party does not agree to comply with one or more of its provisions. Reservations are, in principle, intended to be used only temporarily, when states are unable to realize a treaty provision but agree in principle to do so.

Treaty bodies

Treaty bodies are the committees formally established through the principal international human rights treaties to monitor states parties' compliance with the treaties. Treaty bodies have been set up for the six core UN human rights treaties to monitor states parties' efforts to implement their provisions.

Human rights declarations

Human rights declarations enunciate agreed upon principles and standards. These documents are not in themselves legally binding. But some declarations, most notably the Universal Declaration of Human Rights, have been understood as having the status of common law, since their provisions have been so widely recognized as binding on all states.

Human development

Human development is the process of enlarging people's choices, by expanding human functionings and capabilities. Human development thus also reflects human outcomes in these functionings and capabilities. It represents a process as well as an end.

At all levels of development the three essential capabilities are for people to lead a long and healthy life, to be knowledgeable and to have access to the resources needed for a decent standard of living. But the realm of human development extends further: other areas of choice highly valued by people include participation, security, sustainability, guaran-

teed human rights—all needed for being creative and productive and for enjoying self-respect, empowerment and a sense of belonging to a community. In the ultimate analysis, human development is development of the people, for the people and by the people.

Functionings, capabilities and freedom

The functionings of a person refer to the valuable things that the person can do or be (such as being well nourished, living long and taking part in the life of a community). The capability of a person stands for the different combinations of functionings the person can achieve. Capabilities thus reflect the freedom to achieve functionings. In that sense, human development is freedom.

Human poverty and income poverty

Human poverty is defined by impoverishment in multiple dimensions—deprivations in a long and healthy life, in knowledge, in a decent standard of living, in participation. By contrast, income poverty is defined by deprivation in a single dimension—income—because it is believed either that this is the only impoverishment that matters or that any deprivation can be reduced to a common denominator. The concept of human poverty sees lack of adequate income as an important factor in human deprivation, but not the only one. Nor, according to this concept, can all impoverishment be reduced to income. If income is not the sum total of human lives, lack of income cannot be the sum total of human deprivation.

Human development index (HDI)

The HDI measures the average achievements in a country in three basic dimensions of human development—a long and healthy life, knowledge and a decent standard of living. A composite index, the HDI thus contains three variables—life expectancy at birth, educational attainment (adult literacy and the combined gross primary, secondary and tertiary enrolment ratio) and GDP per capita (PPP US$). Income enters the HDI as a proxy for a decent standard of living and as a surrogate for all human choices not reflected in the other two dimensions.

Gender-related development index (GDI)

The GDI measures the achievements in the same dimensions and using the same variables as the HDI does, but takes into account inequality in achievement between women and men. The greater is the gender disparity in basic human development, the lower is a country's GDI compared with its HDI. The GDI is simply the HDI discounted, or adjusted downwards, for gender inequality.

Gender empowerment measure (GEM)

The GEM indicates whether women are able to actively participate in economic and political life. It measures gender inequality in key areas of economic and political participation and decision-making. The GEM, focusing on women's opportunities in economic and political arenas, thus differs from the GDI, an indicator of gender inequality in basic capabilities.

Human poverty index (HPI)

The HPI measures deprivations in human development. Thus while the HDI measures the overall progress in a country in achieving human development, the HPI reflects the distribution of progress and measures the backlog of deprivations that still exists. The HPI is constructed for developing countries (HPI-1) and for industrialized countries (HPI-2). A separate index has been devised for industrialized countries because human deprivation varies with the social and economic conditions of a community, and to take advantage of the greater availability of data for these countries.

HPI-1

The HPI-1 measures deprivation in the same basic dimensions of human development as the HDI. The variables used are the percentage of people born today expected to die before age 40, the percentage of adults who are illiterate and deprivation in overall economic provisioning—public and private—reflected by the percentage of people without access to health services and safe water and the percentage of underweight children.

HPI-2

The HPI-2 focuses on deprivation in the same three dimensions as the HPI-1 and an additional one, social exclusion. The variables are the percentage of people born today expected to die before age 60, the percentage of people whose ability to read and write is not adequate to be functional, the proportion of people who are income poor (with disposable incomes of less than 50% of the median disposable household income) and the proportion of the long-term unemployed (12 months or more).

CHAPTER 1

Human rights and human development

The basic idea of human development—that enriching the lives and freedoms of ordinary people is fundamental—has much in common with the concerns expressed by declarations of human rights. The promotion of human development and the fulfilment of human rights share, in many ways, a common motivation, and reflect a fundamental commitment to promoting the freedom, well-being and dignity of individuals in all societies. These underlying concerns have been championed in different ways for a long time (the French Declaration of the Rights of Man and of the Citizen came in 1789), but the recent literatures on Human Development and on Human Rights have given new shape to old aspirations and objectives.

Extensive use of these two distinct modes of normative thinking, respectively invoking human development and human rights, encourages the question of whether the two concepts can be viewed together in a more integrated way, gaining something through being combined in a more comprehensive vision. To answer this question, it is important not only to have a clear understanding of what the two concepts—human development and human rights—mean, but also to examine their commonalities and their differences. Indeed, it is necessary to undertake two basic diagnostic inquiries:

• How compatible are the normative concerns in the analyses of human development and human rights? Are they *harmonious enough*—to be able to complement rather than undermine each other?

• Are the two approaches sufficiently distinct so that each can add something substantial to the other? Are they *diverse enough*—to enrich each other?

The answers to both of these foundational questions are definitely in the affirmative.

Human development and human rights are close enough in motivation and concern to be compatible and congruous, and they are different enough in strategy and design to supplement each other fruitfully. A more integrated approach can thus bring significant rewards, and facilitate in practical ways the shared attempts to advance the dignity, well-being and freedom of individuals in general.

COMMON MOTIVATION AND BASIC COMPATIBILITY

The idea of human development focuses directly on the progress of human lives and well-being. Since well-being includes living with substantial freedoms, human development is also integrally connected with enhancing certain capabilities—the range of things a person can do and be in leading a life. We value the freedom of being able to live as we would like and even the opportunity to choose our own fate.

CAPABILITIES AND FREEDOMS

Capabilities can vary in form and content, though they are also often closely interrelated. They include, of course, the basic freedoms of being able to meet bodily requirements, such as the ability to avoid starvation and undernourishment, or to escape preventable morbidity or premature mortality. They also include the enabling opportunities given by schooling, for example, or by the liberty and the economic means to move freely and to choose one's abode. There are also important "social" freedoms, such as the capability to participate in the life of the community, to join in public discussion, to participate in political decision-making and even the elementary ability "to

The promotion of human development and the fulfilment of human rights share a common motivation

appear in public without shame" (a freedom whose importance was well discussed by Adam Smith in *The Wealth of Nations*).

The human development approach is concerned, ultimately, with all the capabilities that people have reason to value. The human development index (HDI) incorporates the most elementary capabilities, such as living a long and healthy life, being knowledgeable and enjoying a decent standard of living, and the various indices, tables and more elaborate discussions in the body of the *Human Development Report*s provide information on many other valuable capabilities. Indeed, longevity is itself an important means to other capabilities, since one does not have the freedom to do much unless one is alive.

What about human rights? The idea of an individual right must involve, directly or indirectly, a claim that one person has over others—individuals, groups, societies or states. The claims can take different forms, as has been analysed by legal theorists, from John Austin and Jeremy Bentham to H. L. A. Hart and Stig Kanger. Some rights take the form of immunity from interference by others; libertarians have tended to take a particular interest in such rights. Others take the form of a claim on the attention and assistance of others to be able to do certain things; champions of social security have tended to emphasize such rights.

But diverse as these rights are, they share the characteristic of entailing some entitlements to help from others in defence of one's substantive freedoms. The claim to help may involve a demand for positive support and facilitation, or take only the negative form of assurance that there will be no hindrance from others. But all of these claims are aimed at securing the freedoms of the persons involved—to do this or be that—in one way or another. In this way, human rights are also ultimately grounded in the importance of freedoms for human lives.

SOCIAL, POLITICAL AND ECONOMIC CONCERNS

Given this founding connection between human development and human rights—

particularly the involvement of each in guaranteeing the basic freedoms that people have reason to value—the ideas of human development and those of human rights are linked in a compatible and complementary way. If human development focuses on the enhancement of the capabilities and freedoms that the members of a community enjoy, human rights represent the claims that individuals have on the conduct of individual and collective agents and on the design of social arrangements to facilitate or secure these capabilities and freedoms.

Despite the compatibility of the two approaches, their strategic form and focus are rather different. It is sometimes presumed that these approaches differ because they are concerned with different kinds of freedoms. The human rights literature has often focused primarily or exclusively on political liberties, civil rights and democratic freedoms. But these rights have not figured in some of the aggregate human development indicators, such as the HDI, for example, which concentrates on longevity, literacy and other socio-economic concerns. The domain of interest of the human development approach goes much beyond what is measured by the HDI, however. Political and civil rights and democratic freedoms also have their place in the human development perspective, though they are much harder to quantify, having resisted attempts in earlier *Human Development Report*s to measure them with composite indicators.

An adequate conception of human development cannot ignore the importance of political liberties and democratic freedoms. Indeed, democratic freedom and civil rights can be extremely important for enhancing the capabilities of people who are poor. They can do this directly, since poor people have strong reason to resist being abused and exploited by their employers and politicians. And they can do this indirectly, since those who hold power have political incentives to respond to acute deprivations when the deprived can make use of their political freedom to protest, criticize and oppose. The fuller human development approach does not ignore these concerns that figure so prominently in the human rights literature.

An adequate conception of human development cannot ignore the importance of political liberties and democratic freedoms

Similarly, the human rights literature is concerned not only with political and civil liberties, but also with the rights to education, to adequate health care and to other freedoms that have received systematic investigation in *Human Development Report*s. Indeed, recent documents, such as the Declaration on the Right to Development and the Vienna Declaration and Programme of Action, emphasize that economic, social and cultural rights are no less weighty than civil and political rights. The contrast between the two concepts of human rights and human development does not, therefore, lie in any basic difference in their subject matter.

WHAT HUMAN RIGHTS ADD TO HUMAN DEVELOPMENT

Since there are substantive differences between these two approaches that share common motivations and aims, it is important to investigate whether they are sufficiently distinct to complement and enrich each other. Even more important, what do practitioners of each approach stand to gain from the analyses of the other? How can the aims of each be better promoted by an integration of these approaches?

To have a particular right is to have a claim on other people or institutions that they should help or collaborate in ensuring access to some freedom. This insistence on a claim on others takes us beyond the idea of human development. Of course, in the human development perspective, social progress of the valued kind is taken to be a very good thing, and this should encourage anyone who can help to do something to preserve and promote it. But the normative connection between laudable goals and reasons for action does not yield specific duties on the part of other individuals, collectivities or social institutions to bring about human development— or to guarantee the achievement of any specified level of human development, or of its components.

This is where the human rights approach may offer an additional and very useful perspective for the analysis of human development. It links the human development approach to the idea that others have duties to facilitate and enhance human development. What precise form the link between rights and duties should take is, of course, a different— and, in some ways, later—question (to be addressed shortly).

The first step is to appreciate that assessments of human development, if combined with the human rights perspective, can indicate the duties of others in the society to enhance human development in one way or another. And with the invoking of duties comes a host of related concerns, such as accountability, culpability and responsibility. For example, to assert a human right to free elementary education is to claim much more than that it would be a good thing for everyone to have an elementary education—or even that everyone *should* have an education. In asserting this right we are claiming that all are *entitled* to a free elementary education, and that, if some persons avoidably lack access to it, there must be some culpability somewhere in the social system.

This focus on locating accountability for failures within a social system can be a powerful tool in seeking remedy. It certainly broadens the outlook beyond the minimal claims of human development, and the analysis of human development can profit from it. The effect of a broader outlook is to focus on the actions, strategies and efforts that different duty bearers undertake to contribute to the fulfilment of specified human rights and to the advancement of the corresponding human development. It also leads to an analysis of the responsibilities of different actors and institutions when rights go unfulfilled.

Consider further the example of the right to a free elementary education. If a girl is not schooled because her parents refuse to send her to school, then the responsibility for the failure—and the corresponding blame—can be placed on the parents. But if she cannot be sent to school because the government forbids her going there (as, regrettably, some governments have excluded girls), then the blame can come down not on the parents but on the government. The failure may be more complex when the girl cannot go to school for one, or some combination, of the following reasons:

The human rights approach may offer an additional and very useful perspective for the analysis of human development

- The parents cannot afford the school fees and other expenses.
- The school facilities are inadequate. For example, the school may be unable to guarantee that teachers will be regularly present, so that the parents think that it would be unsafe for the young girl to go there.
- The parents can afford the school expenses but at the cost of sacrificing something else that is also important (such as continuing the medical treatment of one of their other children).

The attribution or sharing of blame can be quite important here, and it is important to recognize how the effects of different inadequacies in a social system tend to aggravate one another. The willingness of parents to make sacrifices for their children's schooling will often be diminished when they have reason to doubt that this schooling will significantly benefit their children. The sacrifice of human development is much the same in all these cases, but the analysis of rights, duties and responsibilities must be quite different. In this respect, concern with duties enhances the ways of judging the nature and demands of progress. Since the process of human development often involves great struggle, the empowerment involved in the language of claims can be of great practical importance.

There are other substantial ways in which ideas of human rights contribute tools to the analysis of social progress offered by the human development approach. Development thinking has traditionally focused on the outcomes of various kinds of social arrangements. And although human development thinking has always insisted on the importance of the process of development, many of the tools developed by the human development approach measure the outcomes of social arrangements in a way that is not sensitive to *how* these outcomes were brought about. Human rights thinking offers tools that amplify the concern with the process of development in two ways:

- Individual rights express the limits on the losses that individuals can permissibly be allowed to bear, even in the promotion of noble social goals. Rights protect individuals and minorities from policies that benefit the com-

Human rights thinking offers tools that amplify the concern with the process of development

munity as a whole but place huge burdens on them.
- Rights thinking incorporates a distinction between how institutions and officials treat citizens and how they affect them. Human rights monitoring has traditionally focused on the conduct of public officials and the institutional structure within a society. This focus may be unduly narrow, but it reflects something important. Even if arbitrarily harsh police procedures such as torture and execution without trial minimize the number of violent deaths within a society overall by creating fear and disincentives to crime, they are not celebrated as promoting the human rights to life, liberty and security of the person. Human rights thinking gives special weight to threats from certain official sources, capturing the idea that there is something particularly wrong about harm to people carried out by those responsible for ensuring justice.

Finally, human rights analysis can enrich our assessments of social progress by helping us to become more attuned to features of a society that might not be adequately emphasized in pure human development accounting. Human rights are fulfilled when individuals enjoy certain goods and freedoms and when there are measures in place to secure these goods and freedoms. Human rights analysis thus involves assessments of the extent to which institutions and social norms are in place that provide security to the human development achievements within a society.

Gains in human development are not always attended by gains in human rights fulfilment, and subsequently a pure human development accounting may fail to pick up on the vulnerability of individuals and groups within a society. The East Asian financial crisis vividly illustrates how societies that have fared extremely well in terms of composite human development indicators were overly dependent on a buoyant market. The instability of the market combined with inadequate social security provisions exposed the insecurity of East Asia's human development gains.

Human rights assessment involves a reorientation of factual concentration which can broaden and enrich human development accounting. Assessments of human rights fulfilment would, for example, focus not only on what progress has been made so far, but also on the extent to which the gains are socially protected against potential threats. The profound concern of the human rights literature with the duties of others in helping each human being live a better and less unfree life is thus quite relevant in considering both the ways and the means of promoting human development.

WHAT HUMAN DEVELOPMENT ADDS TO HUMAN RIGHTS

Just as human rights contribute something important to human development, so human development helps to augment the reach of the human rights approach. First, there is a tradition of articulation and definiteness in the analysis of human development which can add something to the literature of human rights. Human development analysis has been undertaken at various levels, qualitative and quantitative, and has made use of both inclusive tables and exclusive composite indicators. These different types of investigation, used discriminatingly, can help to give concreteness to human rights analysis. This can be significant, but there are also other advantages—more than clarificatory and presentational—that human development can bring to human rights.

Second, promoting the fulfilment of a right often requires an assessment of how different policy choices will affect the prospects for fulfilling the right. Assessing the human rights impact of various policies will involve both an analysis of the probable human achievement outcomes of the policy and a balancing of claims to different types of achievements—not all of which may be at once attainable. Such an exercise in the evaluation of achievement can sensibly be characterized as an exercise much like human development analysis. For example, the government of a non-affluent country may find it impossible to guarantee the fulfilment of all the identified human rights—including social and economic rights. The alternative scenarios of accomplishment and

failure to safeguard the different human rights can be seen as alternative human development achievements, related particularly to each set of policy decisions and the related patterns of rights fulfilment and non-fulfilment.

Human rights advocates have often asserted the indivisibility and importance of all human rights. This claim makes sense if it is understood as denying that there is a hierarchy of different kinds of rights (economic, civil, cultural, political and social). But it cannot be denied that scarcity of resources and institutional constraints often require us to prioritize concern for securing different rights for the purposes of policy choice. Human development analysis helps us to see these choices in explicit and direct terms.

Third, while human rights are ultimately matters of individual entitlement, their fulfilment depends on appropriate social conditions. The goal of human development is to create an enabling environment in which people's capabilities can be enhanced and their range of choices expanded. By attending to this process of human development, human rights analysis can get a fuller assessment of what is feasible given the resource and institutional constraints that prevail within a society, and a clearer understanding of the ways and means of making a more attractive set of policy choices feasible. While the human rights literature has been concerned with the analysis of duties, the human development literature has constantly emphasized the importance of institutional complementarity and resource constraints and the need for public action to address them. Focusing on causally important institutional and operational variables, the human development literature brings to discussion and analysis of human rights some additional understanding of policies that will best promote human rights in a world that is inescapably pluralist in terms of causal influences and interactive impacts.

Fourth, the idea of human development involves change, and in this sense it has an inescapable dynamism that the specification of a given set of human rights may lack. Human development includes an abiding concern with progress, with things moving on

Human development helps to augment the reach of the human rights approach

from where they were earlier. The insistence on a dynamic view can be particularly useful in considering human rights over time. When a country is very poor, it may not be capable of achieving the fulfilment of every right that is judged important. But this is not an argument for giving priority to economic rights over civil and political rights. Economic entitlements complement rather than outweigh the importance of civil and political rights. But regardless of which kind of right is at issue, varying extents of crucial freedoms may be incorporated in different formulations of each right. Within the right to health, for example, the freedom to receive standard or primary medical care must be taken to be more basic than the freedom to receive costly surgical procedures. A poor country must insist on providing the former, but may have to wait until it is much richer to guarantee the second.

In this way, there may be a progression (indeed, "development") in the human rights that receive priority, even though all such rights ultimately have value and importance. By adding the perspective of change and progress in conceptual and practical reasoning about human rights, human development can help to deepen the understanding and broaden the usefulness of the human rights approach. Indeed, the dynamic view inherent in human development analysis has already been partially integrated into human rights thinking, most obviously in the appreciation that some rights must be progressively realized. Human development analysis can give more structure and concreteness to this idea.

THE NATURE OF DUTIES ASSOCIATED WITH HUMAN RIGHTS

What form should the nature of duties associated with human rights take? To whom do they apply? With what degree of compulsion? In many writings on rights—geared rather rigidly to legal rights—it is assumed that rights make no sense unless they are combined with exact duties imposed—without fail—on specified persons or agents who would make sure that these rights are fulfilled. A person's right

to something must, then, be inflexibly coupled with another person's (or another agent's) duty to provide the first person with that something. This corresponds to what the great 18th-century philosopher Immanuel Kant called "perfect duty," strictly linking rights perfectly to prespecified exact duties of particular agents (in form, perfect duties in an ethical system are rather close to legal duties). In contrast, imperfect duties—also a concept explored by Kant—are general and non-compulsive duties of those who can help. This is a far less rigid system (as Amartya Sen explained in 1999 in "Consequential Evaluation and Practical Reason"), since imperfect duties leave open both *how* the duty can be discharged, and how forceful the duty is. Nevertheless, the neglect of the demands of an imperfect duty also involves a serious moral— or political—failure.

Those who insist on the rigid linkage of rights and duties, in the form of perfect duties, tend typically to be rather impatient with invoking the rhetoric of "rights" without exactly specifying particular agents whose precisely defined (and inescapable) duty it is to ensure the fulfilment of those rights. Not surprisingly, they are often very critical of the use of the concept of "human rights" without exact specification of responsible agents and their precise duties to bring about the fulfilment of these rights. Demands for human rights may then appear, in this line of reasoning, as largely "loose talk".

They are not loose talk. Indeed, if this view were to be fully accepted, the human development literature would need to be kept analytically delinked from the approach of human rights—even if the rhetorical and agitprop merits of the language of human rights may be readily conceded when it comes to exposition or to "consciousness raising". But to divorce the rhetoric from the substance of an approach goes entirely against the tradition of the human development literature, which has been committed, right from the beginning, to standing on articulated concepts and exacting argumentation, rather than concentrating on moving language and stirring phrases not matched by explicit defence.

Human development can help to deepen the understanding and broaden the usefulness of the human rights approach

LEGAL RIGHTS AND HUMAN RIGHTS

The issue of the relationship between rights and duties must be seized at a critical level. It has already been argued that rights and duties must be linked in some form, but why the insistence on exactly matching rights with prespecified duties that apply rigidly to particular agents? It can be argued that the insistence on a rights-duties tie-up in this rigid form is simply a hangover from the empire of law, making all invoking of rights—even in ethics and politics—ultimately parasitic on the concepts and ideas that apply specifically to legal rights.

This rather severe view tallies with Jeremy Bentham's argument that a "declaration of rights would be but a lop-sided job without a declaration of duties". It tallies also with Bentham's rejection of the ethical claims of "natural rights" as "nonsense" and the concept of "natural and imprescriptible rights" as "nonsense on stilts" (presumably, artificially elevated nonsense). It refers to this sense of illegitimacy in taking the idea of rights beyond what Bentham, along with many others, thought to be the proper use of an essentially legal concept.

This way of seeing rights—essentially in legal or quasi-legal terms—does, however, militate against the basic idea that people have some claims on others and on the design of social arrangements regardless of what laws happen to be enforced. Indeed, it is a commitment to common fellowship and solidarity, quite well expressed in Article 1 of the Universal Declaration, that inspires the idea that all persons have duties both to refrain from harming others and to help them. The Universal Declaration demands protection from unjust laws and practices on the ground that no matter what the laws may be, individuals have certain rights by virtue of their humanity, not on the basis of their citizenship or contingent facts about the legal reality of the country of which they are citizens. Human rights are moral claims on the behaviour of individual and collective agents, and on the design of social arrangements. Human rights are fulfilled when the persons involved enjoy secure access to the freedom or resource (adequate health protec-

tion, freedom of speech) covered by the right. In many contexts, establishing legal rights may be the best means of furthering the fulfilment of human rights. Nevertheless, legal rights should not be confused with human rights—nor should it be supposed that legal rights are sufficient for the fulfilment of human rights.

This is indeed the approach to rights invoked by such general political theorists as Tom Paine, in his *Rights of Man*, Mary Wollstonecraft, in *A Vindication of the Rights of Woman* (both published in 1792), and also by earlier writers in the social contract tradition such as John Locke and Jean-Jacques Rousseau. All of them asserted that all human beings are endowed with rights prior to the formation of social institutions that constrain both the design of institutions and the conduct of other individuals. The insistence that the discourse of rights cannot go beyond the limits of legal demands does less than justice to the sense of solidarity and fairness in social living, commitments that are not parasitic on the exact laws that may have been enacted in a society.

HUMAN RIGHTS AND IMPERFECT DUTIES

There is, however, a different kind of rationale for insisting on the rigid rights-duties linkage in the form of perfect duties. It can be asked how we can be sure that rights are, in fact, realizable unless they are matched by corresponding duties that ensure their fulfilment. This argument is invoked to suggest that to be effective, any real right must be matched by a specific duty of a particular agent, who will see to the actual fulfilment of that right.

It is certainly plausible to presume that the performance of perfect duties would help a great deal towards the fulfilment of rights. But why cannot there be *unfulfilled* rights? There is no contradiction involved in saying (indeed lamenting): "These individuals have these rights, but alas the rights were not fulfilled". The question of the fulfilment of rights must be distinguished (as Amartya Sen has argued) from the issue of their existence. We need not jump from regretting the *non-fulfilment* of rights all the way to the denial of the existence—or the cogency—of the rights

> Human rights are fulfilled when the persons involved enjoy secure access to the freedom or resource covered by the right

themselves. Often, rights are unfulfilled precisely because of the failure of duty bearers to perform their duties.

In normative discussions human rights are often championed as entitlements, powers or immunities that benefit all who have them. But even when universal and unblemished fulfilment of human rights for all may be very hard to achieve, the articulation of these rights can help to mobilize support from a great many people in their defence. Even though no particular person or agency may be charged with bringing about the fulfilment of the rights involved, the articulation of imperfect duties may be both an assertion of normative importance and a call for responsible action to be undertaken by others. For example, we can argue that women had a human right to be free from discrimination on the basis of gender independent of whether this right was protected by laws and social arrangements. Gender discrimination is not merely a crime practised by individuals who are violating their perfect duties to particular women. Gender discrimination is an injustice entrenched in the social norms and institutions of all societies. This injustice is expressed both in laws and in other social norms and informal practices of discrimination against women.

Women's human rights give them a claim that male-only suffrage and many other practices be ended through social, legal and institutional reforms. The duties correlated with this right cannot easily be allocated to particular duty bearers because the task of reforming these unjust practices falls on the group as a whole. Yet individuals surely have imperfect duties correlative to this right, and speaking of this right clearly expresses something of great normative importance.

Even if it were to be the case that a particular government does not, right now, have the resources (or the possibility of raising the resources) needed to bring about the fulfilment of specified rights for all, it is essential to encourage the government to work towards making their fulfilment feasible. Credit can still be given for the extent to which these alleged rights are fulfilled. This can help to focus attention on these human rights—and to promote their fulfilment. It can also enrich the understanding of processes that lead to successes and failures in human development. The combination of the two perspectives gives us something that neither can provide alone.

The ongoing global struggle for human rights

Struggles and historical events	Conferences, documents and declarations	Institutions

Through the 17th century
Many religious texts emphasize the importance of equality, dignity and responsibility to help others
Over 3,000 years ago Hindu Vedas, Agamas and Upanishads; Judaic text the Torah
2,500 years ago Buddhist Tripitaka and Anguttara-Nikaya and Confucianist Analects, Doctrine of the Mean and Great Learning
2,000 years ago Christian New Testament, and 600 years later, Islamic Qur'an

Codes of conduct—Menes, Asoka, Hammurabi, Draco, Cyrus, Moses, Solon and Manu
1215 Magna Carta signed, acknowledging that even a sovereign is not above the law
1625 Dutch jurist Hugo Grotius credited with birth of international law
1690 John Locke develops idea of natural rights in *Second Treatise of Government*

18th–19th centuries
1789 The French Revolution and the Declaration of the Rights of Man and of the Citizen
1815 Slave revolts in Latin America and in France
1830s Movements for social and economic rights—Ramakrishna in India, religious movements in the West
1840 In Ireland the Chartist Movement demands universal suffrage and rights for workers and poor people
1847 Liberian Revolution
1861 Liberation from serfdom in Russia

1792 Mary Wollstonecraft's *A Vindication of the Rights of Woman*
1860s In Iran Mirza Fath Ali Akhundzade and in China Tan Sitong argue for gender equality
1860s Rosa Guerra's periodical *La Camelia* champions equality for women throughout Latin America
1860s In Japan Toshiko Kishida publishes an essay, *I Tell You, My Fellow Sisters*
1860–80 More than 50 bilateral treaties on abolition of the slave trade, in all regions

1809 Ombudsman institution established in Sweden
1815 Committee on the International Slave Trade Issue, at the Congress of Vienna
1839 Antislavery Society in Britain, followed in 1860s by Confederação Abolicionista in Brazil
1863 International Committee of the Red Cross
1864 International Working Men's Association
1898 League of Human Rights, an NGO, in response to the Dreyfus Affair

---

The 20th century
1900–29
1900–15 Colonized peoples rise up against imperialism in Asia and Africa
1905 Workers movements in Europe, India and the US; in Moscow 300,000 workers demonstrate
1910 Peasants mobilize for land rights in Mexico
1914–18 First World War
1914 onward Independence movements and riots in Europe, Africa and Asia
1915 Massacres of Armenians by the Turks
1917 Russian Revolution
1919 Widespread protests against the exclusion of racial equality from the Covenant of the League of Nations
1920s Campaigns for women's rights to contraceptive information by Ellen Key, Margaret Sanger, Shizue Ishimoto
1920s General strikes and armed conflict between workers and owners in industrialized world

1900 First Pan-African Congress in London
1906 International convention prohibiting night work for women in industrial employment
1907 Central American Peace Conference provides for aliens' right to appeal to courts where they reside
1916 Self-determination addressed in Lenin's *Imperialism, the Highest Stage of Capitalism*
1918 Self-determination addressed in Wilson's "Fourteen Points"
1919 Versailles Treaty stresses right to self-determination and minority rights
1919 Pan-African Congress demands right to self-determination in colonial possessions
1923 Fifth Conference of the American Republics, in Santiago, Chile, addresses women's rights
1924 Geneva Declaration of the Rights of the Child
1924 US Congress approves Snyder Act, granting all Native Americans full citizenship
1926 Geneva Conference adopts Slavery Convention

1902 International Alliance for Suffrage and Equal Citizenship
1905 Trade unions form international federations
1910 International Ladies' Garment Workers' Union
1919 League of Nations and Court of International Justice
1919 International Labour Organization (ILO), to advocate human rights embodied in labour law
1919 Women's International League for Peace and Freedom
1919 NGOs devoted to women's rights start addressing children's rights; Save the Children (UK)
1922 Fourteen national human rights leagues establish International Federation of Human Rights Leagues
1920s National Congress of British West Africa in Accra, to promote self-determination
1925 Representatives of eight developing countries found Coloured International to end racial discrimination
1928 Inter-American Commission on Women, to ensure recognition of women's civil and political rights

---

1930–49
1930 In India Gandhi leads hundreds on long march to Dandi to protest salt tax
1939–45 Hitler's Nazi regime kills 6 million Jews and forces into concentration camps and murders Gypsies, Communists, labour unionists, Poles, Ukrainians, Kurds, Armenians, disabled people, Jehovah's Witnesses and homosexuals

1930 ILO Convention Concerning Forced or Compulsory Labour
1933 International Convention for the Suppression of the Traffic in Women of Full Age
1941 US President Roosevelt identifies four essential freedoms—of speech and religion, from want and fear

1933 Refugee Organization
1935–36 International Penal and Penitentiary Commission, to promote basic rights of prisoners
1945 Nuremberg and Tokyo trials
1945 United Nations
1946 UN Commission on Human Rights

Struggles and historical events	Conferences, documents and declarations	Institutions
1942 René Cassin of France urges creation of an international court to punish war crimes **1942** US government interns some 120,000 Japanese-Americans during Second World War **1942–45** Antifascist struggles in many European countries **1949** Chinese Revolution	**1945** UN Charter, emphasizing human rights **1948** Universal Declaration of Human Rights **1948** ILO Convention on the Freedom of Association and Protection of the Right to Organize **1949** ILO Convention on the Right to Organize and Collective Bargaining	**1948** Organization of American States **1949** Council of Europe
1950–59 **1950s** National liberation wars and revolts in Asia; some African countries gain independence **1955** Political and civil rights movement in US; Martin Luther King Jr. leads the Montgomery bus boycott (381 days)	**1950** European Convention on Human Rights **1951** ILO Equal Remuneration Convention **1957** ILO Convention Concerning Abolition of Forced Labour **1958** ILO Convention Concerning Discrimination in Employment and Occupation	**1950** ILO fact-finding commission deals with violations of trade union rights **1951** ILO Committee on Freedom of Association **1954** European Commission of Human Rights **1959** European Court of Human Rights
1960–69 **1960s** In Africa 17 countries secure right to self-determination, as do countries elsewhere **1962** National Farm Workers (United Farm Workers of America) organizes to protect migrant workers in US **1960s–70s** Feminist movements demand equality	**1965** UN International Convention on the Elimination of All Forms of Racial Discrimination **1966** UN International Covenant on Civil and Political Rights **1966** UN International Covenant on Economic, Social and Cultural Rights **1968** First World Conference on Human Rights, in Tehran	**1960** Inter-American Commission on Human Rights holds its first session **1961** Amnesty International **1963** Organization of African Unity **1967** Pontifical Commission for International Justice and Peace
1970–79 **1970s** Human rights issues attract broad attention—apartheid in South Africa, treatment of Palestinians in occupied territories, torture of political opponents in Chile, "dirty war" in Argentina, genocide in Cambodia **1970s** People protest against Arab-Israeli conflict, Viet Nam war and Nigeria-Biafra civil war **1976** Amnesty International wins Nobel Peace prize	**1973** UN International Convention on Suppression and Punishment of the Crime of Apartheid **1973** ILO Minimum Age Convention **1974** World Food Conference in Rome **1979** UN Convention on the Elimination of All Forms of Discrimination Against Women (CEDAW)	**1970** First commissions on peace and justice in Paraguay and Brazil **1978** Helsinki Watch (Human Rights Watch) **1979** Inter-American Court of Human Rights
1980–89 **1980s** Latin American dictatorships end—in Argentina, Bolivia, Paraguay, Uruguay **1988** In the Philippines peaceful People's Power Movement overthrows Marcos dictatorship **1989** Tiananmen Square **1989** Fall of the Berlin Wall	**1981** African Charter on Human and Peoples' Rights **1984** UN Convention Against Torture and Other Cruel, Inhuman or Degrading Treatment or Punishment **1986** UN Declaration on the Right to Development **1989** UN Convention on the Rights of the Child	**1983** Arab Organization for Human Rights **1985** UN Committee on Economic, Social and Cultural Rights **1988** African Commission on Human and Peoples' Rights
1990–2000 **1990s** Democracy spreads across Africa; Nelson Mandela released from prison and elected president of South Africa **1990s** Ethnic cleansing in former Yugoslavia, and genocide and massive human rights violations in Rwanda **1998** Spain initiates extradition proceedings against General Pinochet of Chile **1999** Doctors without Borders wins Nobel Peace prize **2000** Court in Senegal charges former Chadian dictator Hissene Habre with "torture and barbarity"	**1990–96** Global UN conferences and summits on the issues of children, education, environment and development, human rights, population, women, social development and human settlements **1998** Rome statute for establishing International Criminal Court **1999** CEDAW Optional Protocol for Individual Complaints **1999** ILO Worst Forms of Child Labour Convention	**1992** First Organization for Security and Co-operation in Europe (OSCE) High Commissioner for National Minorities **1993** First UN High Commissioner for Human Rights, appointed at the Vienna Conference **1993–94** International criminal tribunals for former Yugoslavia and Rwanda **1995** South African Truth and Reconciliation Commission **1995–99** Ten countries launch national plans of action for the protection and promotion of human rights

Source: Lauren 1998; Ishay 1997; UN 1997a, 1997b; An-Na'im 2000; Olcott 2000; Mendez 2000; Šilovic 2000; Pinheiro and Baluarte 2000; Vizard 2000; Akash 2000.

CHAPTER 2

Struggles for human freedoms

The history of human rights is the history of human struggles. Yes, people are born with an entitlement to certain basic rights. But neither the realization nor the enjoyment of these rights is automatic.

History tells us how people have had to fight for the rights due them. The cornerstone in this struggle has always been political activism and people's movements—national liberation movements, peasants movements, women's movements, movements for the rights of indigenous people. Often, the burning desire of people to be free and to enjoy their rights started the struggle. Then, building on the people's achievements, the formalization, legalization and institutionalization of those rights came much later.

Struggles for human freedoms have transformed the global landscape. At the beginning of the 20th century a scant 10% of the world's people lived in independent nations. By its end the great majority lived in freedom, making their own choices. The Universal Declaration of Human Rights of 1948 was a breakthrough, ushering in a new era—with the world community taking on realization of human rights as a matter of common concern and a collective goal of humanity.

The global integration of nations and people has been a second breakthrough—as a global movement has entrenched universal human rights in the norms of the world's diverse cultures. Over the past half century an international system of human rights has emerged, with a rapid rise in commitments made to it in the past decade (see the annex). In 1990 only two conventions—the International Convention on the Elimination of All Forms of Racial Discrimination and the Convention on the Elimination of All Forms of Discrimination Against Women (CEDAW)—had been ratified by more than 100 countries. Today five of the six major human rights convenants and conventions have each been ratified by more than 140 countries. (The exception is the Convention Against Torture and Other Cruel, Inhuman or Degrading Treatment or Punishment.) Seven major labour rights conventions have been ratified by 62 countries—nearly a third of the world's countries (annex table A2.1).

Countries have joined together in regional groups to realize human rights, adopt regional charters and establish regional commissions and regional courts. The African Charter on Human and Peoples' Rights, for example, recognizes collective rights and also highlights people's rights to struggle against colonial domination. At the national level, human rights commissions have been set up, 10 countries have formulated national human rights plans, and many more have instituted an ombudsman for human rights.

At the international level, there were two very significant developments in the 1990s. The first was the creation of a system of international justice, with international criminal tribunals for the former Yugoslavia (1993) and Rwanda (1994) for war crimes. The second was the 1998 Rome agreement on the creation of an International Criminal Court. The court, which can establish individual criminal responsibility, complements the existing system to review gross violations of human rights by governments. In addition, an optional protocol to CEDAW now enables individuals and groups to establish cases of gender discrimination.

The new debate on human rights emphasizes their relevance in all policy areas. A rights-based approach to development is making human rights an integral part of development

Struggles for human freedoms have transformed the global landscape

policies and processes. At the national level, the importance of looking at development goals and policies from a human rights perspective is increasingly recognized. The human rights perspective is also assuming growing importance in development cooperation— bilateral and multilateral.

The centrality of human rights in people's lives was reiterated in international conferences in the 1990s. And the 1993 World Conference on Human Rights gave the human rights movement a renewed impetus by defining a comprehensive international agenda for the universal promotion and protection of human rights.

Advances in human development added to this progress. In developing countries today, compared with 1970:

• A newborn can expect to live 10 years longer.
• The infant mortality rate has been cut by more than two-fifths.
• Adult illiteracy is down by nearly half, and combined net primary and secondary enrolment has increased by nearly 50%.
• The share of rural people with safe water has risen more than fourfold, from 13% to about 71%.

Worldwide, 46 countries accounting for more than 1 billion people have achieved high human development. Every region of the world has made progress in human development— but the level and the pace of advance have not been uniform. Sub-Saharan Africa's infant mortality rate of 106 per 1,000 live births is more than three times Latin America and the Caribbean's of 32. And South-East Asia's adult literacy rate of more than 83% is way ahead of South Asia's rate of 54%.

THE STRUGGLE CONTINUES

Gross violations of human rights continue— both loud and silent. They are loud in Rwanda, where a million people died, in Bosnia and Herzegovina, with an estimated death toll of 150,000–250,000. Some of today's grossest violations of human rights are in internal conflicts—giving rise to a conflict between national sovereignty and international interven-

tion. In a major reversal of past practice, the international community has begun to intervene (see the special contribution by Kofi Annan).

There also are silent violations: about 790 million people not adequately nourished, 250 million children used as child labour, 1.2 million women and girls under 18 trafficked for prostitution each year, more than 130 million people living in income poverty in the OECD countries. The world is often aware of loud violations, but not necessarily of the silent.

The indivisibility of human rights has been accepted as a principle, overturning the cold war division of rights into two sets: the civil and political, and the economic, social and cultural. Yet a latent tension remains between some of these rights. And there are other tensions. There is tension between the universality of human rights and cultural specificity. Between national sovereignty and the international community's monitoring of human rights within countries. Between the indivisibility of human rights and the need to establish priorities because of resource constraints. Between the supremacy of international laws and that of national laws. Between international norms and the norms set by regional human rights systems. Between ratifying international treaties and enforcing them nationally.

Many people still see the promotion of human rights for some groups—women, ethnic minorities, immigrants, poor people—as a threat to their own values or interests. This divisiveness in values breeds opposition to human rights for all. Even in times of great prosperity, societies have failed to ensure a life of dignity for all their members—and often displayed indifference or outright hostility to members of other societies.

Serious human deprivations remain. In the developing world 1.2 billion people are income poor, about 1 billion adults illiterate, 1 billion without safe water and more than 2.4 billion without basic sanitation. In the OECD countries, even with an average life expectancy of 76 years, more than 10% of people born today are not expected to survive to age 60. And in some industrialized countries one person in five is functionally illiterate.

There have also been setbacks and reversals. Life expectancy rose steadily in almost all nations in the 1970s and 1980s, only to be slashed by HIV/AIDS in the 1990s. Every minute 11 more people are infected. More than 12 million Africans have died of AIDS, and by 2010 the continent will have 40 million orphans. In many African countries life expectancy has fallen by more than 10 years in the past decade. More than 30 countries accounting for more than half a billion people today have a per capita income lower than that two decades ago. The transition in Eastern Europe and the CIS has reversed some of the big gains in human development. Serious human development setbacks have also been reported in the East Asian countries, as a result of the financial crisis in 1997–98.

Today, with impressive achievements and a significant unfinished agenda in human rights and human development, the struggle continues for realizing and securing human freedoms in seven areas:

- Freedom from discrimination—for equality.
- Freedom from want—for a decent standard of living.
- Freedom for the realization of one's human potential.
- Freedom from fear—with no threats to personal security.
- Freedom from injustice.
- Freedom of participation, expression and association.
- Freedom for decent work—without exploitation.

FREEDOM FROM DISCRIMINATION—FOR EQUALITY

The universalism of life claims demands that all people treat all others equally, without discrimination. This principle of equality has been the driving force for human rights. It is also one of the pillars of human development, which emphasizes equality in opportunity and choices.

SPECIAL CONTRIBUTION

Human rights and intervention in the 21st century

At the dawn of the 21st century the United Nations has become more central to the lives of more people than ever. Through our work in development, peacekeeping, the environment and health, we are helping nations and communities to build a better, freer, more prosperous future. Above all, however, we have committed ourselves to the idea that no individual—regardless of gender, ethnicity or race—shall have his or her human rights abused or ignored. This idea is enshrined in the Charter of the United Nations and the Universal Declaration of Human Rights. It is the source of our greatest inspiration and the impulse for our greatest efforts. Today, we know more than ever that without respect for the rights of the individual, no nation, no community, no society can be truly free. Whether it means advancing development, or emphasizing the importance of preventive action, or intervening—even across state boundaries—to stop gross and systematic violations of human rights, the individual has been the focus of our concerns.

The United Nations' achievements in the area of human rights over the last 50 years are rooted in the universal acceptance of those rights enumerated in the Universal Declaration and in the growing abhorrence of practices for which there can be no excuse, in any culture, under any circumstance. Emerging slowly, but I believe surely, is an international norm against the violent repression of any group or people that must and will take precedence over concerns of state sovereignty. Even though we are an organization of Member States, the rights and ideals the United Nations exists to protect are those of peoples. No government has the right to hide behind national sovereignty in order to violate the human rights or fundamental freedoms of its peoples. Whether a person belongs to the minority or the majority, that person's human rights and fundamental freedoms are sacred.

Our reflections on these critical questions derive from a variety of challenges that confront us today. From Sierra Leone to the Sudan to Angola to the Balkans to Cambodia and to Afghanistan and East Timor, there are a great number of peoples who need more than just words of sympathy from the international community. They need a real and sustained commitment to help end their cycles of violence, and launch them on a safe passage to prosperity. Just as we have learned that the world cannot stand aside when gross and systematic violations of human rights are taking place, so we have also learned that intervention must be based on legitimate and universal principles if it is to enjoy the sustained support of the world's peoples.

Intervention, however, is not just a matter for states. Each one of us—whether as a worker in government, in intergovernmental or non-governmental organizations, in business, in the media, or simply as a human being—has an obligation to do whatever he or she can to defend the human rights of our fellow men and women when they are threatened. Each of us has a duty to halt—or, better, to prevent—the infliction of suffering. Nothing less is required if the noble ideals of our United Nations are to become a reality.

Kofi A. Annan
Secretary-General
of the United Nations

The 20th century's progress towards equality—regardless of gender, race, religion, ethnicity or age—was propelled by social movements. One of the most significant has been the movement for women's rights, with roots back over the centuries (box 2.1).

The struggle against discrimination has also led to civil rights and anti-racism movements the world over. Equality was a driving force in all the major national liberation movements fighting for self-determination in Asia, Africa and Latin America and the Caribbean. Peasants' struggles in Asia and Latin America and the Caribbean also demanded an end to discrimination. The civil rights movement in the United States in the 1950s and 1960s dismantled legal segregation of African Americans. In many cases struggles went beyond national boundaries to become global—as with women's and workers' movements.

All these propelled norms, values, institutions and legal standards towards greater equality and less discrimination. Tolerance of others is now valued more. Diversity is seen as a strength, not a weakness. People appreciate multiculturalism and human solidarity.

There have been institutional changes as well:

• At the international level, 165 countries have ratified CEDAW, and 155 the International Convention on the Elimination of All Forms of Racial Discrimination—thus more than three-quarters of the world's countries have ratified each of these two conventions.

• National institutions and legal standards for affirmative action have emerged in Australia, Canada, India, New Zealand and the United States, where ethnic minorities and indigenous and tribal peoples form a significant part of the population.

• In India affirmative action in economic and political spheres benefit scheduled castes and tribes.

• In Australia and New Zealand there is increasing legal recognition of aboriginal and Maori people's rights.

• In Guatemala development programmes for the indigenous people have been formulated and integrated into the national plan.

Yet discrimination is still part of our lives. Why? Norms may have changed—but not fast enough and not in all important areas. Non-discrimination and equality may be formally recognized in laws, but there is still discrimination in policies, resource allocations and public provisioning of social services.

So, even with new norms, discrimination and inequality remain pervasive in almost all countries. Opportunities for equal wages, equal employment and equal political participation may be formally recognized, but without effective enforcement of laws, gaps remain in these areas for women, ethnic minorities, indigenous peoples and tribal peoples. Minorities everywhere—in democracies or dictatorships, in industrialized or developing countries—face discrimination in rights (figure 2.1).

That is why outcomes in human development are also mixed. In some areas the results are impressive. Between 1992 and 1998 in developing countries, the female adult literacy rate improved from 72% of the male rate to 80% and the share of rural households with access to safe water rose from 61% of the urban share to 78%. In the United States in 1960, the proportion of people finishing four years of high school was 43% for whites and 20% for African Americans—a gap of 23 percentage points. By 1998 the gap was 6 points, with an 82% completion rate for whites and 76% for African Americans. In Guatemala from 1995 to 1999—only four years—the child mortality

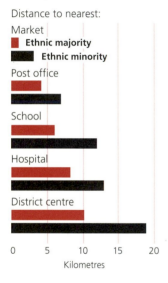

FIGURE 2.1
Ethnic discrimination—services are less accessible to minorities
Vietnam, 1992–93

Distance to nearest:

Market
■ Ethnic majority
■ Ethnic minority

Post office

School

Hospital

District centre

0   5   10   15   20
Kilometres

Source: Van de Walle and Gunewardena 1999.

BOX 2.1

The long struggle for women's rights

In 1792 Mary Wollstonecraft published *A Vindication of the Rights of Woman,* arguing that it is not charity that is wanting in the world—it is justice. The book captures the essence of women's struggle for rights.

The struggle entered a new phase in the 1800s. India abolished *sati* (self-immolation of widows) and legalized intercaste marriage. England reformed laws governing marriage. France recognized women's right to divorce. China allowed women to hold office. New Zealand in 1893 became the first country to extend the right to vote to women.

In the first decade of the 20th century women's movements gathered strength in several countries, including China, Iran, Japan, Korea, the Philippines, Russia, Ceylon, Turkey and Viet Nam. In the first four decades women got the vote in countries ranging from Austria, Germany and the Netherlands to Ceylon, Turkey and Uruguay.

Around the same time Margaret Sanger in the United States, Ellen Key in Sweden and Shizue Ishimoto in Japan launched campaigns for women's right to reproductive health. They demanded that information on contraception be provided to all women.

Source: Human Development Report Office.

rate among Mayans declined by nearly a sixth, from 94 per 1,000 live births to 79.

In other areas the outcomes are deplorable. In Nepal untouchables have a life expectancy of 46 years—15 years less than the Brahmins. In Morocco the adult rural illiteracy rate of 75% is more than twice the urban rate of 37%. In South Africa more than 98% of whites live in formal houses, while more than 50% of Africans live in traditional dwellings and backyard shacks. In the developing world women's economic activity rate is still two-thirds that of men. In the Republic of Korea, the female wage rate is only three-fifths the male rate. Girls in Madagascar, whether or not they go to school, spend three times as many hours as boys collecting water and doing other household chores. And in OECD countries women spend two-thirds of their time on non-market activities, nearly twice what men allocate to these tasks.

There are also disparities in access to services along income and rural-urban lines, perhaps reflecting discrimination in their provision (figures 2.2 and 2.3).

Indigenous peoples are still the most deprived in economic, social and cultural rights—in both developing countries such as India and industrialized countries such as Australia, Canada and the United States. In Canada in 1991, the life expectancy at birth of Inuit males was 58 years and that of registered Indian males 62 years, 17 and 13 years less than that for all Canadian males (figure 2.4). In India in the early 1990s, the adult literacy rate among women of scheduled tribes was 24%, compared with 39% for all Indian women. In Slovakia 80% of Roma children attended kindergarten in 1984, but only 15% do today. Indigenous peoples also are discriminated against in civil and political rights. In Malaysia only two Orang Asli in 10,000 have title to their land.

Discrimination on the basis of sexual orientation continues throughout the world. Civil and political rights of sexual minorities are violated in some countries where they are denied the right to organize into advocacy groups. Economic and social rights are violated where they are, for example, discriminated against in the workplace and in access to housing.

FREEDOM FROM WANT—FOR A DECENT STANDARD OF LIVING

Human poverty is a major obstacle to attaining a decent standard of living and realizing human rights. The Universal Declaration of Human Rights recognized the right to a standard of living adequate for the health and well-being of a person and the right to education. Global conferences have identified poverty elimination as a major goal, reflected in national plans, policies and strategies. And 142 countries have ratified the International Covenant on Economic, Social and Cultural Rights.

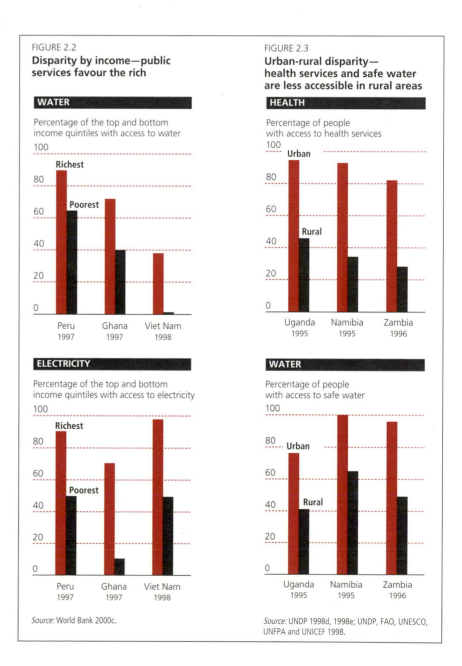

FIGURE 2.2
Disparity by income—public services favour the rich

WATER

Percentage of the top and bottom income quintiles with access to water

ELECTRICITY

Percentage of the top and bottom income quintiles with access to electricity

Source: World Bank 2000c.

FIGURE 2.3
Urban-rural disparity— health services and safe water are less accessible in rural areas

HEALTH

Percentage of people with access to health services

WATER

Percentage of people with access to safe water

Source: UNDP 1998d, 1998e; UNDP, FAO, UNESCO, UNFPA and UNICEF 1998.

FIGURE 2.4
Life expectancy varies by ethnicity
Canada, 1991

Life expectancy at birth (years)

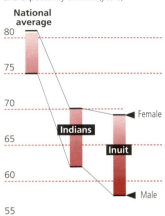

Source: First Nations and Inuit Regional Health Survey National Steering Committee 1999.

FIGURE 2.5
Income poverty varies by region
Brazil, 1991

Percentage of people below national poverty line

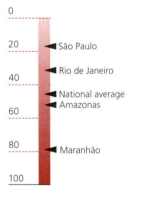

Source: Institute of Applied Economic Research and others 1998.

The world made much progress in reducing human poverty in the 1990s. In developing countries the percentage of people born today not expected to survive to age 40 declined from 20% to 14% between 1990 and 1998. The share of people without access to safe water fell from 32% to 28%. Adult illiteracy went down from 35% to 28%. The income poverty rate, even by the $1 a day yardstick (1993 PPP US$), declined from 29% to 24%. Income poverty is down in every developing region, though the decline ranged from 11 percentage points in East Asia to only 0.3 percentage points in Sub-Saharan Africa.

Some countries made spectacular progress. Malaysia reduced income poverty from 60% in 1960 to 14% in 1993, China from 33% in 1978 to 7% in 1994 and India from 54% in 1974 to 39% in 1994.

Yet widespread income poverty persists. By the $1 a day standard (1993 PPP US$), 1.2 billion people live in income poverty in developing countries, nearly half of them in South Asia. And poverty is no longer a phenomenon of just the South. It has become a Northern phenomenon as well (table 2.1). Even within countries, the incidence of income poverty varies among regions (figure 2.5).

Income inequality, in and across nations, is on the rise. In Brazil, Guatemala and Jamaica the top fifth's share in national income is more than 25 times the bottom fifth's. Poor people also bear a disproportionate burden in such areas as taxes. In Pakistan the combined burden of income taxes, tariffs, excise duties and sales taxes is 10% of income for those with a

monthly salary of less than $12, and –4% for those with more than $40.

Lack of housing is another problem. More than a billion people live in inadequate housing, and about 100 million are estimated to be homeless worldwide. Millions live in shanty towns—in Calcutta, Lagos, Mexico City and Mumbai. In Dublin, Ireland, about 7,000 people become homeless each year. And in the United States about 750,000 people are homeless on any given night.

Poor people lack access to productive resources, such as land and credit. In Zimbabwe the pattern of land distribution is highly skewed, with white farmers owning most of the 4,660 large-scale commercial farms, covering 11 million hectares of land, and 30% of all households practically landless. In Uganda nearly two-thirds of microcredit goes to urban areas, only a third to rural areas. In Kenya less than 5% of institutional credit goes to the informal sector.

FREEDOM FOR THE REALIZATION OF ONE'S HUMAN POTENTIAL

The rights to food, health, education and privacy—as rights to capability building—were fundamental building blocks of the Universal Declaration of Human Rights, reiterated in the International Covenant on Economic, Social and Cultural Rights, CEDAW and the Convention on the Rights of the Child. These rights were also highlighted by international conferences, such as Health for All in Alma-Ata in 1978 and Education for All in Jomtien in 1990.

Health, nutrition and education are now valued not only for their intrinsic worth but also for their positive impacts—direct and indirect—on human capital, productivity and capabilities for participation and social interaction. Consider the effects of education. Domestic violence is sensitive not to years of marriage, a woman's age, living arrangements, the husband's education—but to a woman's education. As has been observed in India, if a woman has more than a secondary education, the incidence of such violence falls by more than two-thirds. Yes, education empowers women. But it also changes the dynamics in households and thus changes norms.

Country	Percentage of people living below the poverty line
United States (1997)	17
Italy (1995)	13
Australia (1994)	12
Canada (1994)	11
United Kingdom (1995)	11

TABLE 2.1
Income poverty in selected OECD countries

Note: The poverty line is set at 50% of equivalent median disposable household income.
Source: Smeeding 2000.

Developing countries have achieved much in food and nutrition, health and education. Between 1980 and 1999 malnutrition was reduced: the proportion of underweight children fell in developing countries from 37% to 27% and that of stunted children from 47% to 33%. Over the same period the child mortality rate declined by more than two-fifths—from 168 per 1,000 live births to 93. Today primary enrolment in developing countries is about 86%, and secondary enrolment about 60%.

But these achievements should not mask the huge deprivations that remain in these areas—in both developing and industrialized countries. About a third of children under five suffer from malnutrition. Nearly 18 million people die every year from communicable diseases—nearly 30 million from non-communicable diseases, mostly in OECD countries. About 90 million children are out of primary school, and 232 million out of secondary.

And look at the disparities in outcomes. Infant mortality rates vary significantly by consumption level (figure 2.6). Literacy varies by language groups. In Namibia in 1998, the adult literacy rate for the German-speaking group was 99%, compared with 16% for the San-speaking group. And school enrolment varies by sex (figure 2.7).

Most of the setbacks in health and education have occurred in Africa and Eastern Europe and the CIS. The most devastating setback: AIDS. At the end of 1999 nearly 34 million people were infected with HIV, 23 million in Sub-Saharan Africa. The AIDS epidemic is also moving fast in Asia, with more than a million people newly infected in 1999 in South and South-East Asia and the Pacific alone.

In Eastern Europe and the CIS the transition to democracy has had costs in human development. The life expectancy of males in many countries is down by five years. Several countries face the unusual prospect of illiteracy—school enrolments are lower than in 1989 in many countries, and pockets of illiteracy may emerge. Serious decay in social services and social safety nets has left people without secure access to their entitlements.

FREEDOM FROM FEAR—WITH NO THREATS TO PERSONAL SECURITY

People want to live without fear of others. No other aspect of human security is so vital as security from physical violence. But in poor nations and rich, people's lives are threatened by violence—in several forms:
• Threats from the state (physical torture, arbitrary arrest and detention).
• Threats from other states (war, support for oppressive regimes).
• Threats from other groups of people (ethnic conflicts, crime, street violence).
• Threats directed at women (rape, domestic violence).
• Threats directed at children (child abuse).

For years civil society movements have mobilized public opinion to eliminate such threats, and international groups have also contributed much. At the global level, the Conventions Against Torture, on the Elimination of All Forms of Discrimination Against Women and on the Rights of the Child—ratified by 119, 165 and 191 countries—protect against torture and ensure the security of women and children. The appointment of a Special Rapporteur on Violence against Women has also contributed. The right of habeas corpus, vital as a tool against arbitrary detention, now prevails in many more countries. Laws relating to rape are stricter. In many countries in the mid-1990s, the average sentence served for rape was at least five years (table 2.2). In Brazil children's rights were legislated in 1986 through the Children's and Adolescents' Act, and the constitution now protects street children.

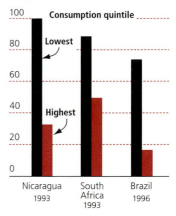

FIGURE 2.6
Infant mortality rate varies between rich and poor

Per 1,000 live births

Source: Wagstaff 2000.

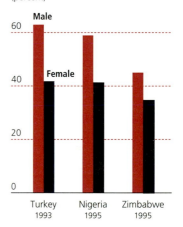

FIGURE 2.7
School enrolment varies by sex

Net secondary enrolment ratio (percent)

Source: UNDP 1996a, 1996b; UNDP, Poverty Reduction Forum, Institute of Development Studies and University of Zimbabwe 1998.

TABLE 2.2
Average sentence served for rape in selected countries, 1990–94

Country	Months
Kuwait	120
Mauritius	96
Samoa (Western)	84
Jamaica	64
Switzerland	64
United States	64

Note: Data refer to any year from 1990 to 1994.
Source: UNCJIN 1999.

Significant advances are being seen in respect for human rights and in freedom from fear. The incidence of torture is lower in many countries. In Honduras the number of torture cases reported to the Committee for the Defence of Human Rights, a major NGO, fell from 156 in 1991 to 7 in 1996. In 1993–96 the number of murders declined in Estonia, Latvia and the Netherlands, and drug-related crimes fell in Denmark and Sweden. Worldwide, the number of major armed conflicts declined by more than a third in 1990–98.

Yet the personal security of people all over the world is still under threat—from conflicts, political oppression, and, in some countries, increasing crime and violence. War and internal conflicts in the 1990s forced 50 million people to flee their homes—1 person of every 120 on earth. In the past decade civil wars have killed 5 million people worldwide. At the end of 1998 more than 10 million people were refugees, 5 million were internally displaced and another 5 million were returnees.

Instruments of political oppression still threaten many thousands of people. The number believed to be incarcerated without a fair trial is quite high in some countries. In many cases oppressive states use the police and military to repress people in their struggles for rights and freedoms. With global as well as regional military expenditures showing a downward trend, the military spending of low-income countries—those with per capita incomes of $765 or less in 1998—rose from $36 billion to $43 billion (all expressed in 1995 constant dollars) in the three years from 1995 to

1998. The objectives of such expenditures need scrutiny by the people of these countries. Sometimes such increases in expenditures—and support to oppressive regimes—come from external sources.

In many countries in Eastern Europe and the CIS increases in such crimes as murder, robbery and theft have made people's lives insecure. Worldwide, the circulation of an estimated 500 million small arms, 100 million of them assault rifles, has contributed to crime and violence. In the Bahamas there are more than 80 recorded homicides per 100,000 people annually, and in Colombia nearly 80. Annual recorded drug offenses are 574 per 100,000 people in Switzerland, 351 in Sweden and 301 in Denmark.

Among the worst personal threats are those to women. Rape has been used as a weapon of war, as in Yugoslavia and Rwanda. Trafficking of women and girls for prostitution has increased with globalization, with 500,000 women a year trafficked out of countries in Eastern Europe and the CIS. In Asia about 250,000 people, mostly women and children, are estimated to be trafficked every year. Between 85 million and 115 million girls and women have undergone some form of female genital mutilation and suffer from its adverse physiological and psychological effects. And every year an estimated 2 million more young girls undergo genital mutilation.

Domestic violence is a serious human rights threat to women in every society—rich and poor, developing and industrialized (table 2.3). Around the world on average, one in every three women has experienced violence in an intimate relationship. Women also face what is known as "honour" killings. In Pakistan the human rights commission reported that in 1999 more than 1,000 women were victims of honour killings, and in Jordan the Public Security Department reported 20 such killings in 1997.

The personal security of children is also at stake. Worldwide, about 100 million children live or work on the street—more than 15,000 in Mexico City, 5,000 in Guatemala City. In the 1990s more than 300,000 children were soldiers, and 6 million were injured in armed conflicts. And in sample surveys in the later part of the 1990s, children and teenagers reported sexual abuse—with nearly 20% of girls reporting

---

TABLE 2.3

Women physically assaulted by an intimate partner

Country	Percentage ever assaulted
Bangladesh (1992)	47
New Zealand (1994)	35
Barbados (1990)	30
Nicaragua (1997)	28
Switzerland (1994–96)	21
Colombia (1995)	19
Moldova, Rep. of (1997)	14
South Africa (1998)	13
Philippines (1993)	10

Source: Johns Hopkins University 1999a.

it in Switzerland, 17% in Oslo, Norway, and more than 14% in New Zealand.

Hate crimes threaten the personal security of ethnic, racial, religious and sexual minorities. The United States in 1998 had 7,755 reported hate crimes, 4,321 related to race. Assaults against non-heterosexual people increased from 11% of hate crimes in 1993 to 16% in 1998.

FREEDOM FROM INJUSTICE

The rule of law is deeply interconnected with freedom from fear and all other freedoms. Without the rule of law and fair administration of justice, human rights laws are no more than paper. Justice is something that people dearly value. As one poor farmer in Bangladesh put it, "I can tolerate poverty, but not to get justice in the eye of the law in my own country just because I am poor, that I cannot accept."

There has been much progress on the legal front. The Universal Declaration of Human Rights inspired many constitutions in the newly independent countries of Asia and Africa during the 1950s and 1960s. And in recent times Cambodia, South Africa, Thailand and most countries in Eastern Europe and the CIS have incorporated its articles in their constitutions.

The outcome: first, recognition of human rights in their legal systems, and second, the rendering of international human rights standards and legal norms supreme over domestic laws. And the constitutions enshrine the separation of powers among the executive, the judiciary and the legislature. All these developments have led to various legal reforms. Egypt recently became the second of the Arab States, after Tunisia, to grant equal divorce rights to women. Some 66 countries have abolished the death penalty for all crimes.

To improve protection of women's rights, many domestic laws have been changed. In doing so, legislatures have often drawn on CEDAW and overruled domestic laws in favour of international ones. In 1995 an amendment to the Citizenship Act in Botswana, citing the commitment of the government to CEDAW, granted the children of women married to foreigners the right to assume their mother's citizenship. In Thailand a new law ensures gender equality in obtaining citizenship.

There has also been progress in institutions. Human rights ombudsmen are working in Bosnia and Herzegovina, Croatia, Hungary, the former Yugoslav Republic of Macedonia, Poland, Romania and Slovenia. More people are taking recourse to their legal and constitutional rights. When a local government in South Africa cut a community's water supply, the community, with the help of the Legal Resources Centre, an NGO, took the matter to court, citing the South African constitution. The local government had to concede that the community had a constitutional right to a water supply, and the community won the case. The judicial system in many countries has done much to protect human rights and freedoms. In India public interest litigation cases in education and environment have been important milestones in securing people's economic and social rights.

But there is a long way to go. In some societies administration of justice remains elusive because of changing norms and inadequate institutional capacity. And although justice is supposed to be blind and absolute, in many societies money and power undermine the independence of the judicial system. In Bangladesh a national survey of corruption by the local chapter of Transparency International in the 1990s showed that 63% of those involved in litigation paid bribes to court officials. In the United Republic of Tanzania 32% of those surveyed in the 1990s reported payments to persons (supposedly) administering justice. Justice has become a commodity that often only the rich and powerful can afford.

The judicial system's fairness is in question in many countries. Unfairness leads to discrimination in process and disparity in outcome. In some countries women still face discrimination in inheritance laws. In many countries the judiciary is little more than an extension of the executive, driving out people's trust. In many others the executive interferes with the judiciary, sometimes arbitrarily dismissing judges, sometimes preventing due process. Not a framework to safeguard people's basic rights.

The efficiency and adequacy of the judicial system are also in question in many societies.

In some societies administration of justice remains elusive because of changing norms and inadequate institutional capacity

Shortages of judges and overwhelming backlogs of cases strangle the rule of law in many countries. In India in 1996, there were more than 5,000 pending cases per judge, and in Bangladesh more than 2,000. In Indonesia and Zambia there are fewer than 2 judges per 100,000 people. In Panama 157 people per 100,000 await trial or adjudication, in Estonia 115 and in Madagascar 100. In 1994 the average custody while awaiting trial, for all offences, was 60 weeks in Mexico, 40 in Hungary and 30 in the Czech Republic. The poor salaries and inadequate legal training for judges, including in human rights law, are major constraints. So is the inadequacy of court facilities.

In many countries those responsible for administering justice are violators of law, not its guardians. Police are viewed with hostility because of their brutality, their involvement in the drug business, their mistreatment of prisoners and their failure to protect the people who need their protection most. Rapes by prison guards have been reported in many countries—in prisons and outside. Prison conditions are often inadequate. In Nicaragua in 1998, only $3 was available per inmate per day to provide food and maintenance and cover the wages of prison officials.

FREEDOM OF PARTICIPATION, EXPRESSION AND ASSOCIATION

The 20th century's brutal militaries, fascist regimes and totalitarian one-party states committed some of the worst abuses of human rights. But thanks to impressive struggles, most of these ugly regimes have given way to democracies (box 2.2). These struggles for more open societies—with full freedom of participation, expression and association—have created environments more conducive to advancing human rights. By 1975, 33 countries had ratified the International Covenant on Civil and Political Rights—by 2000, 144 had.

People do not want to be passive participants, merely casting votes in elections. They want to have an active part in the decisions and events that shape their lives. An estimated one in five people participates in some form of civil society organization. The people's power at the Seattle meeting of the World Trade Organization recently shows their involvement in global issues.

People are demanding more transparency and accountability, and in many cases the legal framework and institution building are helping. Thailand's new constitution allows people to demand accountability from public officials for corruption and misdeeds, and 50,000 signatures against any parliamentarian triggers a review. In Brazil the Federal Audit Tribunal, linked to the legislative branch of the government, holds a mandate to audit all expenditures of the central government.

On the institutional side, there are now 50,000 NGOs in Hungary and 45,000 in Poland, unheard of in Soviet times. People are participating in national poverty hearings, peasants associations, indigenous peoples associations, and truth and reconciliation commissions in postconflict situations—and at the local level, in tenants associations, school boards, water users associations and community policing. Press councils and journalists' wage boards have arisen in many countries to protect a free press and to look after the interests of people in the media. International networks—such as the French-based Reporters without Borders and the US-based Committee to Protect Journalists—play an important role in protecting journalists and advancing the freedom of speech.

The legal framework in many countries may be more conducive to freedom of participation, expression and association, but formidable restrictions remain. Political parties formed along ethnic lines were prohibited in Kazakhstan—they can register only as public

People are demanding more transparency and accountability, and in many cases the legal framework and institution building are helping

---

BOX 2.2

Democracy's advance

In 1900 no country had universal adult franchise. All countries excluded significant groups from the right to vote, notably women and minorities. In 2000 the majority of the world's countries have universal adult suffrage and multiparty elections. During 1974–99 multiparty electoral systems were introduced in 113 countries. The past 25 years have been dubbed by some as the "third wave" of democracy.

Democratization has travelled from region to region. First was Southern Europe in the mid-1970s, then Latin America and the Caribbean in the late 1970s and the late 1980s, then Eastern Europe and the former Soviet republics and East, South-East and South Asia and Central America in the late 1980s and 1990s.

Source: Human Development Report Office.

organizations and thus cannot take part in elections. The Bulgarian, Croatian and Romanian constitutions explicitly limit the right to use minority languages—this, despite these countries having signed the European Charter for Regional and Minority Languages. Almost the entire Arab world bans strikes.

There is an increasing realization that laws are necessary to remove barriers to freedom of participation, expression and association, but that to implement them effectively will require resources. Thus ending press censorship is a necessary step towards freedom of expression, but the infrastructure for an effective system of free media must also be built.

Political activism has been important in winning rights. In Brazil, through the landless rural workers movement, more than 250,000 families won title to more than 15 million acres. In the United States poor and homeless people have mobilized themselves to fight for realization of their economic rights (box 2.3). NGOs are demanding more transparency and accountability, and public officials are responding. In India the Mazdoor Kisan Sangrash Samiti holds regular public hearings on public resources, disbursements and development projects. People can demand copies of official documents on these issues at any time, and public officials must oblige.

What of political participation more broadly? In the past 25 years multiparty electoral systems were introduced in more than 100 countries. In all but a few countries women have the right to vote and to stand for election—a right unrecognized in 1970 even in Switzerland. Voter turnout varies, but it is difficult to identify the reasons why (indicator table 25).

In many formerly colonial countries the disturbing legacy of a district commissioner combining judicial and executive functions is giving way to participatory and elected grass-roots institutions. In India more than 1 million women have been elected in *panchayat* elections, reflecting the broad participation in local government.

Freedom of expression and association has also advanced. Today the state retains its monopoly on the media in only 5% of countries. Speech is now freer in the formerly one-

party states of Eastern Europe and the CIS—with independent newspapers, non-state television and radio stations and open access to the world media.

People also have more access to the tools of information and communication. East Asia had 158 television sets per 1,000 people in 1990—275 in 1996-98. The Arab States over the same period went from 35 telephone mainlines per 1,000 people to 65. And the world went from only 213 Internet host computers in 1981 to 36 million in 1998. Nearly 30,000 NGOs use the Internet. And there are more than 10 million Internet users in China.

All impressive testimony to the advance of freedom, but many setbacks and dangers need to be addressed. Today about 40 countries do not have a multiparty electoral system. Democracies remain fragile. In the 1990s several countries reverted to non-electoral regimes. The validity of many elections is in serious doubt, calling into question the legitimacy of the winners. In some countries non-governmental action is being restricted. As is evident from the gender empowerment measure, women still face discrimination in political and economic opportunities (indicator table 3). Women hold only about 14% of parliamentary seats—and in

There is an increasing realization that laws are necessary to remove barriers to freedom of participation, expression and association, but that to implement them effectively will require resources

BOX 2.3

Empowering poor people—political activism and people's mobilization

The Kensington Welfare Rights Union (KWRU), founded in the United States in April 1991 when six women began meeting weekly in the basement of the Kensington Congregational Church in Philadelphia, describes itself as a multiracial organization of, by and for poor and homeless people. About 4,000 people now see themselves as members of this growing movement for economic rights. Using the language of human rights in its fight against poverty, the KWRU has sparked activity all around the country, similar to the civil rights movement.

The union has developed five strategies based on its experience in organizing: teams of local organizers, a base of operations, lines of communication, mutual support networks and a core of people with commitment, understanding of strategy

and political education. It has also developed six tools: programme, protest, projects of survival, press work, political education and plans not personalities. And it has perfected the tool of establishing tent cities.

The KWRU believes that its main success has been the development of an estimated 3,000 leaders among the ranks of poor people. These leaders network with some 40 poor people's groups, and share experience with groups in Canada and Latin America. In 1997 the KWRU organized a "Freedom Bus", which travelled through 25 US states, getting the message out and mobilizing new leaders. The event, which involved thousands of people, culminated in New York at the United Nations. The union plans a summit on poverty in India in 2000.

Source: Hijab 2000.

the Arab States, as few as 4%. And many countries deny political participation to members of ethnic minorities and specific races.

In many parts of the world journalists have been harassed, arrested, beaten and even murdered for trying to uncover the truth. In 1999, according to the International Press Institute, 87 journalists and media people were killed while doing their job.

FREEDOM FOR DECENT WORK—WITHOUT EXPLOITATION

Productive and satisfying livelihoods give people the means to buy goods and services. They empower people socially by enhancing their dignity and self-esteem. And they can empower people politically by enabling them to influence decision-making in the workplace and beyond. In industrialized countries most workers are employed in the formal labour market—in developing countries most are outside the formal labour market.

The Universal Declaration of Human Rights recognizes the right to work, to freely choose employment and to have just and favourable working conditions. All these rights are reiterated in the International Covenant on Economic, Social and Cultural Rights, which also emphasizes the obligation of parties to the covenant to safeguard the right to work—so that everyone has the opportunity to earn a living.

International Labour Organization (ILO) conventions have been adopted to secure workers' rights and to ensure their safety and non-exploitation (table 2.4; annex table A2.2). Of the seven major labour rights conventions, all but the convention on minimum age have each been ratified by more than 125 countries. And of these, the conventions prohibiting forced labour or discrimination in employment and occupation have each been ratified by more than 140 countries.

Employment in the formal labour market has grown impressively in the past decade. In China in 1987–96, employment increased 2.2% a year—outpacing labour force growth at 1.5%. The corresponding rates in India were 2.4% and 2.2%. In OECD countries in 1987–97, employment and the labour force grew at the same pace, 1.1% a year. Labour productivity has increased in both OECD and developing countries. In 1990–95 labour productivity in Singapore increased 14% a year, in Chile nearly 10% a year. Employment opportunities in developing countries have broadened through expansion of informal sector enterprises, microfinance and NGO activities.

Even so, at least 150 million of the world's workers were unemployed at the end of 1998, and as many as 900 million were underemployed. About 35 million people were unemployed in OECD countries alone. Insecure jobs have become a fact of life in many countries. In the United Kingdom in 1997, 25% of all jobs were part time. Informal sector employment has become dominant in many countries. In the 1990s in Bolivia, it accounted for 57% of urban employment, in the United Republic of Tanzania 56%, in Thailand 48%. Much of this employment is low productivity, low wage and precarious. Unemployment varies among ethnic groups. In South Africa unemployment among African males in 1995 was 29%, more than seven times the 4% rate for their white counterparts.

Labour rights focus not only on ensuring a livelihood, but also on protecting against discrimination in work and benefits and against exploitation. Equal pay for equal work is spreading in principle, the result of a long

TABLE 2.4
Ratification of core International Labour Organization conventions
(as of 4 April 2000)

Principle	Conventions	Number of countries ratifying
Freedom of association and protection of the right to organize and collective bargaining	Convention 87 (1948)	128
	Convention 98 (1949)	146
Minimum working age	Convention 138 (1973)	88
Prohibition of forced labour	Convention 29 (1930)	152
	Convention 105 (1957)	144
Rights to equal remuneration and prohibition of discrimination in employment and occupation	Convention 100 (1951)	145
	Convention 111 (1958)	142

Source: ILO 2000.

struggle. So is recourse to the law. In October 1999, after a court case, the Canadian government agreed to pay $1.8 billion in back salaries and interest to 230,000 past and current federal workers, overwhelmingly women, under the Equal Pay for Work of Equal Value Act.

The struggle against inhumane working conditions has taken different forms—revolutions to overturn an economic system or, more commonly, struggles to protect the rights of workers by securing better wages and other benefits, ensuring workers' safety, providing acceptable working conditions and outlawing discrimination. Different institutions and events have shaped workers' rights over time (box 2.4). People's concerns about exploitation of workers are reflected in their support for ethical trading and insistence on codes of conduct for business. At the national level the tripartite system—government, employer and worker—has been effective in settling labour disputes.

Yet serious problems remain in labour rights and in the human rights of workers. With globalization and the pressure for a flexible labour market, workers' incomes, rights and protections are being compromised. The social welfare system protecting workers is decaying. Trade union membership in the non-agricultural labour force has declined in many countries—both developing and OECD (figure 2.8). Of the 27 million workers in the world's 845 export processing zones, many are not allowed to join unions, a clear violation of workers' rights and human rights. In some cases female workers in garment industries are put under lock and key at the job, another clear violation—and when hundreds of women die in a fire because they cannot get out, a human tragedy. In many societies trade unions and union activities are often suppressed, to undermine workers' struggles for their rights.

In recent years the industrialized world has attracted many migrants—in 1995 an estimated 26–30 million to Europe alone. In many cases migrant workers not only face discrimination in wages, they also live in poor conditions. In Germany Turkish migrant workers earn on average only 73% as much as German workers. In the Middle East and the Persian Gulf region 1.2 million women work as domes-

tic servants without labour protections, facing inhuman working hours, assaults and abuse and other discrimination. Malaysia, home of many migrant workers employed abroad as domestic servants, recently had a national soul-searching when these abuses were revealed.

Worldwide, there are some 250 million child labourers—140 million boys, 110 million girls. Asia accounts for 153 million, Africa for 80 million. And millions of children are domestic workers—often suffering physical and psychological abuse (table 2.5).

TABLE 2.5
Child domestic workers in selected countries, 1990s

Country or city	Thousands
Philippines	766
Jakarta, Indonesia	700
Dhaka, Bangladesh	300
Haiti	250
Lima, Peru	150
Sri Lanka	100

Note: Data refer to the latest year available.
Source: UNICEF, International Child Development Centre, 1999.

FIGURE 2.8
Declining membership in trade unions

Trade union membership as a percentage of non-agricultural workers

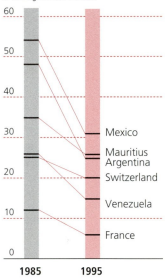

Source: ILO 1997c.

BOX 2.4

Evolution of international workers' rights

Workers movements were established in Great Britain and the United States in the late 18th and early 19th centuries. The harsh working conditions in the industrial age gave rise to demands for international regulation to reduce the poverty of workers. Industrialists and governments feared losing out to competitors if they took unilateral protective action that raised the costs of production. That, too, led to calls for international regulation, through which protective measures could be adopted simultaneously by many countries.

The Welsh industrialist Robert Owen was the first to raise the idea of international action, proposing the creation of a labour commission in 1818. The initial proposals for international legislation came from an Englishman, Charles Hindley, a Belgian, Edouard Ducpétiaux, and three Frenchmen, J. A. Blanqui, Louis René Villarmé and, above all, the industrialist Daniel Le Grand. Le Grand issued a series of appeals beginning in 1844, and drafted proposals to "protect the working class from early and heavy labour" that he sent to various governments.

Proposals for international labour regulation were made in the French parliament and in Austria, Belgium and Germany, especially by the socialists and by Christian social movements. Germany convened an intergovernmental conference in Berlin in 1890, the first official forum to explore the possibility of adopting international labour legislation.

During the First World War trade union organizations from several countries agreed on the need for a mechanism for international legislation. A number of governments, especially France and Great Britain, proposed that international labour legislation be adopted at the peace conference.

During negotiations for the Treaty of Versailles a decision was made to create the International Labour Organization, whose main duty would be to establish an international standard-setting mechanism. The Treaty of Versailles, finally adopted by the peace conference in 1919, included "workers' clauses" to form the basic principles of international labour legislation.

Source: Bartolomei de la Cruz, von Potobsky and Swepston 1996.

We live in an era of dramatic change and transition. The world is being transformed by new rules, new tools and new actors into a vast global marketplace. Human freedoms face new threats from transition, conflicts, xenophobia, human trafficking and religious fundamentalism. And all over the world people with HIV/AIDS face serious threats to their human rights (box 2.5). Along with these new issues, persistent poverty and widening inequality are now treated as a denial of human rights and thus emerge as continuing human rights challenges.

- *Poverty and growing inequalities in income, human development and socioeconomic opportunities.* Human poverty is pervasive, affecting a quarter of the people in the developing world. Worse, inequalities are increasing in many instances—not only in income and wealth, but also in social services and productive resources. These growing inequalities threaten to erode hard-won gains in civil and political liberties, especially in Latin America and in the transition economies of Eastern Europe and the CIS. Poverty and inequality disempower people and open them to discrimination in many aspects of life and to additional violations of their rights (chapter 4).

- *Gross human rights violations in internal conflicts.* Conflicts are hotbeds of gross human rights violations, clearly illustrating the indivisibility and interdependence of all human rights. Past efforts to ensure respect for human rights even during war led to the four Geneva Conventions on the treatment of prisoners and the protection of civilians during international conflict. But most of today's wars are fought within national boundaries. True, Protocol II to the Geneva Conventions, ratified by 149 states, applies solely to non-international armed conflicts, and Common Article 3 of the conventions applies to internal conflicts. But some of today's grossest violations of human rights are in these situations, and an urgent challenge for the international community is to develop principles, institutions, standards and quicker responses for tackling these violations (chapter 6).

- *The transition to democracy and market economies.* The transition to democracy is fraught with fragility. The new formal democracies did not end discrimination against minorities or women—and in many instances such discrimination is growing. The transition in Eastern Europe and the CIS brought major reversals of economic and social rights—those of women to equality in employment, those of children to education and those of all to health care were seriously undermined. Institutions and norms are needed to prevent reversals. The democratic transition does not guarantee freedoms, nor is it sustainable without institutional and social capacity building.

What is needed is not elusive democracy but inclusive democracy, which best protects human rights (chapter 3).

- *Economic globalization and its new rules and actors.* Creating new patterns of interaction among people and states, globalization promises

---

BOX 2.5

Respecting human rights—crucial in dealing with HIV/AIDS

Protection and fulfilment of human rights is essential for an effective response to HIV/AIDS. Respect for human rights helps to reduce vulnerability to HIV/AIDS, to ensure that those living with or affected by HIV/AIDS live a life of dignity without discrimination and to alleviate the personal and societal impact of HIV infection. Conversely, violations of human rights are primary forces in the spread of HIV/AIDS.

Disrespect for civil and political rights makes society-wide mobilization against HIV/AIDS and open dialogue about prevention impossible. And poverty and deprivation contribute to the spread of HIV/AIDS. Where people lack access to information about the risks of HIV/AIDS and are denied adequate education, prevention efforts are bound to fail and the epidemic will spread more quickly. HIV/AIDS is also likely to spread more quickly in countries where the right to health is neglected. Marginalization and disempowerment of women make them more vulnerable to infection and exacerbate the effects of the epidemic. Discrimination against people affected by HIV/AIDS leads to shame, silence and denial, fuelling the epidemic.

In 1998 the United Nations High Commissioner for Human Rights and the Joint United Nations Programme on HIV/AIDS (UNAIDS) together issued the *International Guidelines on HIV/AIDS and Human Rights.* The guidelines provide a framework for supporting both human rights and public health, emphasizing the synergy between the two, and offer concrete measures for protecting human rights in order to deal effectively with HIV/AIDS. They emphasize the government's responsibility for multisectoral coordination and accountability. They call for reforming laws and legal support services to help ensure non-discrimination, protect public health and improve the status of women, children and marginalized groups. And they recommend supporting increased private sector and community participation in the response to HIV/AIDS.

The United Nations Commission on Human Rights, at its session in 1999, passed a resolution asking governments to report on steps taken to promote and implement the guidelines for its 2001 session. South Africa has set a good example. Its human rights commission has endorsed the guidelines and recommended that the parliament adopt a charter on HIV/AIDS. Implementing a human rights approach is an essential step in dealing with this catastrophic threat to human development.

Source: Human Development Report Office; Mann and Tarantola 1996; UNHCR and UNAIDS 1998.

---

unprecedented opportunities for progress in larger freedoms. But it also threatens to compound many challenges for the international community. Developed in a state-centred world, the international system of human rights protection is suited to the post-war era, not the era of globalization. New actors—global corporations, multilateral organizations, global NGOs—wield great influence in social, economic, even political outcomes. What are the duties and obligations of these new actors? How should human rights be ensured in the World Trade Organization's agenda of continuing trade liberalization? How can corporations be held accountable? What are the duties and obligations of the UN agencies, the International Monetary Fund and the World Bank (chapters 4 and 6)?

Dealing with human rights and human development—and with both old and emerging issues—requires a clear understanding of the mutually reinforcing links between the two (chapter 1). It also requires indicators that empower people to identify violations of human rights, assess progress and hold critical actors to account (chapter 5). Most important, it requires action—legal, political, social, economic. And that action must be on all fronts—local, national, regional, global. But enhancing human development and respecting human rights calls above all for one basic action—pursuing a human rights approach to development. And that requires a fundamental shift in development strategies at all levels (chapter 6).

Principal human rights instruments

Milestones in the adoption of major human rights instruments

1948 Universal Declaration of Human Rights

1965 International Convention on the Elimination of All Forms of Racial Discrimination

1966 International Covenant on Civil and Political Rights

1966 International Covenant on Economic, Social and Cultural Rights

1979 Convention on the Elimination of All Forms of Discrimination Against Women

1984 Convention Against Torture and Other Cruel, Inhuman or Degrading Treatment or Punishment

1989 Convention on the Rights of the Child

Countries ratifying the 6 major human rights conventions and covenants

Number of countries

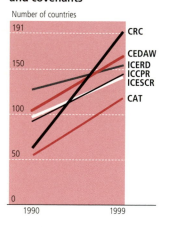

Source: Office of the United Nations High Commissioner for Human Rights.

International Bill of Rights

The International Bill of Rights consists of the Universal Declaration of Human Rights, the International Covenant on Civil and Political Rights and its two optional protocols and the International Covenant on Economic, Social and Cultural Rights. The Universal Declaration of Human Rights recognizes the indivisibility of human rights. Nevertheless, separate covenants evolved on civil and political rights and economic, social and cultural rights, reflecting the legacy of the cold war.

Universal Declaration of Human Rights
Building on the principles of the UN Charter, the Universal Declaration of Human Rights, adopted by the United Nations on 10 December 1948, is the primary document proclaiming human rights standards and norms. The declaration recognizes the universality, indivisibility and inalienability of the rights of all people as the foundation of equality, freedom, justice and peace in the world.

International Covenant on Civil and Political Rights (ICCPR)
Adopted in 1966 and entered into force in 1976, the ICCPR defines a broad range of civil and political rights for all people. This major codification of human rights and fundamental freedoms in civil and political areas has been ratified by 144 states parties.

International Covenant on Economic, Social and Cultural Rights (ICESCR)
Also adopted in 1966 and entered into force in 1976, the ICESCR defines the economic, social and cultural rights of people. It introduced a new way of looking at development, the rights-based perspective. There are 142 states parties to this covenant.

International Convention on the Elimination of All Forms of Racial Discrimination (ICERD)

The ICERD was adopted in 1965 and entered into force in 1969, in the aftermath of decolonization, a period characterized by apartheid and racial and ethnic conflicts. It deals with a particular form of discrimination—that based on race, colour, descent or national or ethnic origin. The convention has been ratified by 155 countries.

Convention on the Elimination of All Forms of Discrimination Against Women (CEDAW)

Adopted in 1979 and entered into force in 1981, CEDAW represents the first comprehensive, legally binding international instrument prohibiting discrimination against women and obligating governments to take affirmative action to advance gender equality. The convention, ratified by 165 countries, is often referred to as the International Bill of Rights for Women.

Convention Against Torture and Other Cruel, Inhuman or Degrading Treatment or Punishment (CAT)

The CAT, adopted in 1984 and entered into force in 1989, added an important pillar to the international protection of human rights. The convention, which deals with the right not to be subjected to torture, lays out the steps to be taken by states to prevent torture and other cruel, inhuman or degrading treatment or punishment. It has been ratified by 119 countries.

Convention on the Rights of the Child (CRC)

Adopted in 1989 and entered into force in 1990, the CRC recognizes the need for specific attention to protecting and promoting the rights of children, to support their growth, development and becoming worthy citizens of the world. It has been ratified by 191 countries, making it almost universal.

The United Nations system for monitoring implementation of human rights

PROCEDURES BASED ON THE UN CHARTER

United Nations Human Rights Commission (1946)
Functions:
- Setting human rights standards.
- Holding an annual public debate on human rights violations.
- Appointing special rapporteurs, special representatives, experts and working groups to study themes or country situations. Today 16 country and more than 20 thematic procedures are in place.

PROCEDURES BASED ON THE SIX UN HUMAN RIGHTS TREATIES

Treaty bodies for monitoring the treaties
- Human Rights Committee (ICCPR).
- Committee on Economic, Social and Cultural Rights (ICESCR).
- Committee on the Elimination of Racial Discrimination (ICERD).
- Committee on the Elimination of Discrimination Against Women (CEDAW).
- Committee against Torture and Other Cruel, Inhuman or Degrading Treatment or Punishment (CAT).
- Committee on the Rights of the Child (CRC).

Functions:
- Receiving and discussing country reports on the status of human rights by engaging in constructive dialogue with states parties.
- Receiving shadow, or alternative, reports from civil society institutions.
- Providing concluding country observations on human rights in states parties.
- Providing general comments or recommendations on treaty rights.
- Providing procedures for hearing individual complaints.
- Providing inquiry procedures for gross or systemic human rights violations.
- Hearing complaints from one state party against another.

TRIPARTITE MECHANISM FOR ILO CONVENTION FOR THE PROTECTION OF WORKERS' RIGHTS
- Government, employers and trade unions.

OTHER BODIES

International Court of Justice (1946)
Functions:
- To settle in accordance with international law the legal disputes submitted to it by states.
- To give advisory opinions on legal questions referred to it by duly authorized international organs and agencies.

International Criminal Court
(agreement to set it up adopted in 1998; court has yet to come into existence)
Proposed functions:
- Bringing cases against individuals for war crimes, genocide and crimes against humanity.
- Increasing state responsibility for infringement of human rights.
- Contributing to an international order that demands respect for human rights.

Office of the High Commissioner for Human Rights (1993)
Functions:
- Providing states with advisory services and technical assistance on request.
- Enhancing international cooperation in human rights.
- Engaging in dialogues with governments aimed at securing respect for all human rights.
- Supporting the existing UN human rights machinery.
- Promoting the effective implementation of human rights standards.

Ratification of treaties by states parties
Number of countries (as of 16 February 2000)

ICCPR
Ratification 144
Signature not followed by ratification 3
Not ratified and not signed 46

ICESCR
Ratification 142
Signature not followed by ratification 5
Not ratified and not signed 46

ICERD
Ratification 155
Signature not followed by ratification 5
Not ratified and not signed 33

CEDAW
Ratification 165
Signature not followed by ratification 3
Not ratified and not signed 25

CAT
Ratification 119
Signature not followed by ratification 9
Not ratified and not signed 65

CRC
Ratification 191
Signature not followed by ratification 1
Not ratified and not signed 1

Regional human rights instruments and institutions

INTER-AMERICAN HUMAN RIGHTS SYSTEM

The inter-American human rights system coexists with the UN treaty-based and non-treaty-based mechanisms.

Main instruments

American Declaration of the Rights and Duties of Man (1948)
- Has a preamble explicitly linking rights and duties.
- Covers a roster of economic and social rights, most relating to labour, contained in a social charter.
- Links human rights and democracy.
- Is legally non-binding and thus has led to the adoption of the American Convention on Human Rights.

American Convention on Human Rights (1969)
- Is fundamentally a civil and political rights treaty.
- Provides progressive treatment of freedom of expression.
- Makes explicit the conditions under which guaranteed rights can be overridden in times of public danger.
- Has been ratified by 24 of the 35 members of the Organization of American States.

Other instruments

Inter-American Convention on Forced Disappearance (1994)

Inter-American Convention to Prevent and Punish Torture (1985)

Convention on the Prevention, Punishment and Eradication of Violence against Women (1994)

Implementing institutions and mechanisms

Inter-American Commission on Human Rights (1959)
- Is made up of members elected by the General Assembly of the Organization of American States.
- Combines promotion and adjudication functions.
- Advises governments on legislation affecting human rights.

Inter-American Court of Human Rights (1979)
- Has two types of jurisdiction—advisory and contentious.
- Issues advisory opinions on correct interpretation of treaty obligations.
- Contentious jurisdiction encompasses cases submitted by the commission against states parties and vice versa.

EUROPEAN HUMAN RIGHTS SYSTEM

The European human rights system is by far the most developed of the regional systems. Distinguished by its preference for judicial approaches, it has gone the furthest in developing judicial processes. The European system also enjoys the highest rate of state compliance with its decisions.

Main instruments

European Convention for the Protection of Human Rights and Fundamental Freedoms (1950)
- Convention provides for collective enforcement of certain civil and political rights.
- European Court of Human Rights rules in cases alleging that individuals have been denied their human rights.
- Contracting states undertake to secure the rights defined by the convention for all.
- Subsequent protocols have extended the initial set of rights.
- Most countries that have ratified the convention have incorporated the provisions into their own national law.

European Social Charter (1961, revised in 1996)
- Guarantees a series of rights relating to conditions of employment and social cohesion.
- Has a system of supervision that includes the Committee of Independent Experts, the Governmental Committee and the Committee of Ministers.
- Provides for collective complaints.

Other instruments

European Convention for the Prevention of Torture and Inhuman or Degrading Treatment or Punishment (1987)

Framework Convention on National Minorities (1995)

Implementing institutions and mechanisms

European Court of Human Rights (1959)
- Has as many judges as there are contracting states.
- Hears cases from individuals and contracting states.
- Uses a procedure that is adversarial and public.
- Issues advisory opinions on legal issues relating to conventions and protocols.

AFRICAN HUMAN RIGHTS SYSTEM

The African system of human rights is relatively recent. It prefers judicial and quasi-judicial approaches.

Instrument

African Charter on Human and Peoples' Rights (1981)
- Covers both civil and political and economic, social and cultural rights.
- Provides for collective rights and for state and individual duties.
- Includes claw-back clauses restricting human rights to the maximum extent allowed by domestic law.

Implementation institutions and mechanisms

African Human Rights Commission (1987)
- Serves more promotional and less protective functions.
- Examines state reports.
- Considers communications alleging violations.
- Expounds the African charter.

African Human Rights Court
(decision to establish it made in 1998; court has yet to start functioning)
- Consists of 11 judges appointed in their personal capacity.
- Complements the work of the African Human Rights Commission.
- Serves more protective and less promotional functions.
- Has a jurisdiction not limited to cases or disputes arising out of the African charter.

ARAB HUMAN RIGHTS SYSTEM

The Arab human rights system came into formal existence with the adoption in 1994 of the Arab Charter of Human Rights by the Arab League. The charter:
- Provides for a Committee of Human Rights Experts to examine reports submitted by the states parties and to report on them to the Permanent Commission of Human Rights of the Arab League.
- Prohibits denial of any of the fundamental human rights, but provides for limitations and restrictions on all rights for reasons of national security, the economy, public order, the rights of others and the like.
- Includes no requirements for a valid declaration of a state of emergency, and during a state of emergency provides for only a few rights, such as prohibition of torture and safeguards for a fair trial.
- Provides for no right to political organization and participation.

	International Convention on the Elimination of All Forms of Racial Discrimination 1965	International Covenant on Civil and Political Rights 1966	International Covenant on Economic, Social and Cultural Rights 1966	Convention on the Elimination of All Forms of Discrimination Against Women 1979	Convention Against Torture and Other Cruel, Inhuman or Degrading Treatment or Punishment 1984	Convention on the Rights of the Child 1989
Afghanistan	●	●	●	○	●	●
Albania	●	●	●	●	●	●
Algeria	●	●	●	●	●	●
Andorra				●		●
Angola		●	●			●
Antigua and Barbuda	●			●	●	●
Argentina	●	●	●	●	●	●
Armenia	●	●	●	●	●	●
Australia	●	●	●	●	●	●
Austria	●	●	●	●	●	●
Azerbaijan	●	●	●	●	●	●
Bahamas	●			●		●
Bahrain	●				●	●
Bangladesh	●		●	●	●	●
Barbados	●	●	●	●		●
Belarus	●	●	●	●	●	●
Belgium	●	●	●	●	●	●
Belize		●		●	●	●
Benin	○	●	●	●	●	●
Bhutan	○			●		●
Bolivia	●	●	●	●	●	●
Bosnia and Herzegovina	●	●	●	●	●	●
Botswana	●			●		●
Brazil	●	●	●	●	●	●
Brunei Darussalam						●
Bulgaria	●	●	●	●	●	●
Burkina Faso	●	●	●	●	●	●
Burundi	●	●	●	●	●	●
Cambodia	●	●	●	●	●	●
Cameroon	●	●	●	●	●	●
Canada	●	●	●	●	●	●
Cape Verde	●	●	●	●	●	●
Central African Republic	●	●	●	●	●	●
Chad	●	●	●	●	●	●
Chile	●	●	●	●	●	●
China	●	○	○	●	●	●
Colombia	●	●	●	●		●
Comoros						●
Congo	●	●	●	●		●
Congo, Dem. Rep. of the	●	●	●	●		●
Cook Islands						●
Costa Rica	●	●	●	●	●	●
Côte d'Ivoire	●	●	●	●	●	●
Croatia	●	●	●	●	●	●
Cuba	●			●	●	●
Cyprus	●	●	●	●	●	●
Czech Republic	●	●	●	●	●	●
Denmark	●	●	●	●	●	●
Djibouti				●		●
Dominica		●	●	●		●

A2.1 Status of major international human rights instruments	International Convention on the Elimination of All Forms of Racial Discrimination 1965	International Covenant on Civil and Political Rights 1966	International Covenant on Economic, Social and Cultural Rights 1966	Convention on the Elimination of All Forms of Discrimination Against Women 1979	Convention Against Torture and Other Cruel, Inhuman or Degrading Treatment or Punishment 1984	Convention on the Rights of the Child 1989
Dominican Republic	●	●	●	●	○	●
Ecuador	●	●	●	●	●	●
Egypt	●	●	●	●	●	●
El Salvador	●	●	●	●	●	●
Equatorial Guinea		●		●		●
Eritrea				●		●
Estonia	●	●	●	●	●	●
Ethiopia	●	●	●	●	●	●
Fiji	●			●		●
Finland	●	●	●	●	●	●
France	●	●	●	●	●	●
Gabon	●	●	●	●	○	●
Gambia	●	●	●	●	○	●
Georgia	●	●	●	●	●	●
Germany	●	●	●	●	●	●
Ghana	●			●		●
Greece	●	●	●	●	●	●
Grenada	○	●	●	●		●
Guatemala	●	●	●	●	●	●
Guinea	●	●	●	●		●
Guinea-Bissau			●	●		●
Guyana	●	●	●	●	●	●
Haiti	●	●		●		●
Holy See	●					●
Honduras		●	●	●	●	●
Hungary	●	●	●	●	●	●
Iceland	●	●	●	●	●	●
India	●	●	●	●	○	●
Indonesia	●			●	●	●
Iran, Islamic Rep. of	●	●	●			●
Iraq	●	●	●	●		●
Ireland	○	●	●	●	○	●
Israel	●	●	●	●	●	●
Italy	●	●	●	●	●	●
Jamaica	●	●	●	●		●
Japan	●	●	●	●		●
Jordan	●	●	●	●		●
Kazakhstan	●			●	●	●
Kenya		●	●	●		●
Kiribati						●
Korea, Dem. People's Rep. of		●	●			●
Korea, Rep. of	●	●	●	●	●	●
Kuwait	●			●	●	●
Kyrgyzstan	●			●	●	●
Lao People's Dem. Rep.	●			●		●
Latvia	●	●	●	●	●	●
Lebanon	●	●	●	●		●
Lesotho	●	●	●	●		●
Liberia	●	○	○	●		●
Libyan Arab Jamahiriya	●	●	●	●	●	●

	International Convention on the Elimination of All Forms of Racial Discrimination 1965	International Covenant on Civil and Political Rights 1966	International Covenant on Economic, Social and Cultural Rights 1966	Convention on the Elimination of All Forms of Discrimination Against Women 1979	Convention Against Torture and Other Cruel, Inhuman or Degrading Treatment or Punishment 1984	Convention on the Rights of the Child 1989
Liechtenstein		●	●	●	●	●
Lithuania	●	●	●	●	●	●
Luxembourg	●	●	●	●	●	●
Macedonia, TFYR	●	●	●	●	●	●
Madagascar	●			●		●
Malawi	●	●	●	●	●	●
Malaysia				●		●
Maldives	●			●		●
Mali	●	●	●	●	●	●
Malta	●	●	●	●	●	●
Marshall Islands						●
Mauritania	●					●
Mauritius	●	●	●	●	●	●
Mexico	●	●	●	●	●	●
Micronesia, Fed. Sts. of						●
Moldova, Rep. of	●	●	●	●	●	●
Monaco	●	●	●		●	●
Mongolia	●	●	●	●		●
Morocco	●	●	●	●	●	●
Mozambique	●	●		●	●	●
Myanmar				●		●
Namibia	●	●	●	●	●	●
Nauru						●
Nepal	●	●	●	●	●	●
Netherlands	●	●	●	●	●	●
New Zealand	●	●	●	●	●	●
Nicaragua	●	●	●	●	○	●
Niger	●	●	●	●		●
Nigeria	●	●	●	●	○	●
Niue						●
Norway	●	●	●	●	●	●
Oman						●
Pakistan	●			●		●
Palau						●
Panama	●	●	●	●	●	●
Papua New Guinea	●			●		●
Paraguay		●	●	●	●	●
Peru	●	●	●	●	●	●
Philippines	●	●	●	●	●	●
Poland	●	●	●	●	●	●
Portugal	●	●	●	●	●	●
Qatar	●				●	●
Romania	●	●	●	●	●	●
Russian Federation	●	●	●	●	●	●
Rwanda	●	●	●			●
Saint Kitts and Nevis				●		●
Saint Lucia	●			●		●
Saint Vincent and the Grenadines	●	●	●	●		●
Samoa (Western)				●		●
San Marino		●		●		●

A2.1 Status of major international human rights instruments

	International Convention on the Elimination of All Forms of Racial Discrimination 1965	International Covenant on Civil and Political Rights 1966	International Covenant on Economic, Social and Cultural Rights 1966	Convention on the Elimination of All Forms of Discrimination Against Women 1979	Convention Against Torture and Other Cruel, Inhuman or Degrading Treatment or Punishment 1984	Convention on the Rights of the Child 1989
São Tomé and Principe		○	○	○		●
Saudi Arabia	●				●	●
Senegal	●	●	●	●	●	●
Seychelles	●	●	●	●	●	●
Sierra Leone	●	●	●	●	○	●
Singapore				●		●
Slovakia	●	●	●	●	●	●
Slovenia	●	●	●	●	●	●
Solomon Islands	●		●	●		
Somalia	●	●		●	●	
South Africa	●	●	○	●	●	●
Spain	●	●	●	●	●	●
Sri Lanka	●	●	●	●	●	●
Sudan	●	●	●	●	○	●
Suriname	●	●	●	●		●
Swaziland	●					●
Sweden	●	●	●	●	●	●
Switzerland	●	●	●		●	●
Syrian Arab Republic	●	●	●			●
Tajikistan	●	●	●	●	●	●
Tanzania, U. Rep. of	●	●	●	●		●
Thailand		●	●	●		●
Togo	●	●	●	●	●	●
Tonga	●					●
Trinidad and Tobago	●	●	●	●		●
Tunisia	●	●	●	●	●	●
Turkey	○			●	●	●
Turkmenistan	●	●	●	●	●	●
Tuvalu				●		●
Uganda	●	●	●	●	●	●
Ukraine	●	●	●	●	●	●
United Arab Emirates	●					●
United Kingdom	●	●	●	●	●	●
United States	●	●	○	○	●	○
Uruguay	●	●	●	●	●	●
Uzbekistan	●			●		●
Vanuatu				●		●
Venezuela	●	●	●	●	●	●
Viet Nam	●	●	●	●		●
Yemen	●	●	●	●	●	●
Yugoslavia	●	●	●	●	●	●
Zambia	●	●	●	●		●
Zimbabwe	●	●	●	●		●
Total states parties	155	144	142	165	119	191
Signatures not followed by ratification	5	3	5	3	9	1
States that have not ratified and signed	33	46	46	25	65	1

● Ratification, accession, approval, notification or succession, acceptance or definitive signature.

○ Signature not yet followed by ratification.

Note: Status as of 16 February 2000.

Source: UN 2000e.

	Freedom of association and collective bargaining		Elimination of forced and compulsory labour		Elimination of discrimination in respect of employment and occupation		Abolition of child labour	
	Convention 87 [a]	Convention 98 [b]	Convention 29 [c]	Convention 105 [d]	Convention 100 [e]	Convention 111 [f]	Convention 138 [g]	Convention 182 [h]
Afghanistan				●	●	●		
Albania	●	●	●	●	●	●	●	
Algeria	●	●	●	●	●	●	●	
Angola		●	●	●	●			
Antigua and Barbuda	●	●	●	●		●	●	
Argentina	●	●	●	●	●	●	●	
Armenia					●	●		
Australia	●	●	●	●	●	●		
Austria	●	●	●	●	●	●		
Azerbaijan	●	●	●		●	●	●	
Bahamas		●	●	●				
Bahrain			●	●				
Bangladesh	●	●	●	●	●	●		
Barbados	●	●	●	●	●	●	●	
Belarus	●	●	●	●	●	●	●	
Belgium	●	●	●	●	●	●	●	
Belize	●	●	●	●	●	●	●	●
Benin	●	●	●	●	●	●		
Bolivia	●	●		●	●	●	●	
Bosnia and Herzegovina	●	●	●		●	●	●	
Botswana	●	●	●	●	●	●	●	●
Brazil		●	●	●	●	●		●
Bulgaria	●	●	●	●	●	●	●	
Burkina Faso	●	●	●	●	●	●	●	
Burundi	●	●	●	●	●	●		
Cambodia	●	●	●	●	●	●	●	
Cameroon	●	●	●	●	●	●		
Canada	●			●	●	●		
Cape Verde	●	●	●	●	●	●		
Central African Republic	●	●	●	●	●	●		
Chad	●	●	●	●	●	●		
Chile	●	●	●	●	●	●	●	
China					●		●	
Colombia	●	●	●	●	●	●		
Comoros	●	●	●	●	●			
Congo	●	●	●	●	●	●	●	
Congo, Dem. Rep. of the		●						
Costa Rica	●	●	●	●	●	●	●	
Côte d'Ivoire	●	●	●	●	●	●		
Croatia	●	●	●	●	●	●	●	
Cuba	●	●	●	●	●	●	●	
Cyprus	●	●	●	●	●	●	●	
Czech Republic	●	●	●	●	●	●		
Denmark	●	●	●	●	●	●	●	
Djibouti	●	●	●	●	●			
Dominica	●	●	●	●	●	●	●	
Dominican Republic	●	●	●	●	●	●	●	
Ecuador	●	●	●	●	●	●	●	
Egypt	●	●	●	●	●	●	●	
El Salvador			●	●		●	●	

	Freedom of association and collective bargaining		Elimination of forced and compulsory labour		Elimination of discrimination in respect of employment and occupation		Abolition of child labour	
	Convention 87 [a]	Convention 98 [b]	Convention 29 [c]	Convention 105 [d]	Convention 100 [e]	Convention 111 [f]	Convention 138 [g]	Convention 182 [h]
Equatorial Guinea					●		●	
Eritrea	●	●	●	●	●	●		
Estonia	●	●	●	●	●			
Ethiopia	●	●		●	●	●	●	
Fiji		●	●	●				
Finland	●	●	●	●	●	●	●	●
France	●	●	●	●	●	●	●	
Gabon	●	●	●	●	●	●		
Gambia								
Georgia	●	●	●	●	●	●	●	
Germany	●	●	●	●	●	●	●	
Ghana	●	●	●	●	●	●	●	
Greece	●	●	●	●	●	●	●	
Grenada	●	●	●	●	●	●		
Guatemala	●	●	●	●	●	●	●	
Guinea	●	●	●	●	●	●		
Guinea-Bissau		●	●	●	●	●		
Guyana	●	●	●	●	●	●	●	
Haiti	●	●	●	●	●	●		
Honduras	●	●	●	●	●	●	●	
Hungary	●	●	●	●	●	●	●	
Iceland	●	●	●	●	●	●	●	
India			●		●	●		
Indonesia	●	●	●	●	●	●	●	●
Iran, Islamic Rep. of			●	●	●	●		
Iraq		●	●	●	●	●	●	
Ireland	●	●	●	●	●	●	●	●
Israel	●	●	●	●	●	●	●	
Italy	●	●	●	●	●	●	●	
Jamaica	●	●	●	●	●	●		
Japan	●	●	●		●			
Jordan		●	●	●	●	●	●	
Kazakhstan						●		
Kenya		●	●	●			●	
Korea, Rep. of					●	●	●	
Kuwait	●		●	●		●	●	
Kyrgyzstan	●	●	●	●	●		●	
Lao People's Dem. Rep.			●					
Latvia	●	●	●	●	●	●		
Lebanon		●	●	●	●	●		
Lesotho	●	●	●		●	●		
Liberia	●	●	●	●				
Libyan Arab Jamahiriya		●	●	●	●	●	●	
Lithuania	●	●	●	●	●	●		
Luxembourg	●	●	●	●	●	●		
Macedonia, TFYR	●	●	●		●	●	●	
Madagascar	●	●	●		●	●		
Malawi	●	●	●	●	●	●		●
Malaysia		●	●	■	●		●	
Mali	●	●	●	●	●	●		

	Freedom of association and collective bargaining		Elimination of forced and compulsory labour		Elimination of discrimination in respect of employment and occupation		Abolition of child labour	
	Convention 87[a]	Convention 98[b]	Convention 29[c]	Convention 105[d]	Convention 100[e]	Convention 111[f]	Convention 138[g]	Convention 182[h]
Malta	●	●	●	●	●	●	●	
Mauritania	●		●	●		●		
Mauritius		●	●	●			●	
Mexico	●		●		●	●		
Moldova, Rep. of	●	●		●		●		
Mongolia	●	●			●	●		
Morocco		●	●	●	●	●	●	
Mozambique	●	●		●	●	●		
Myanmar	●		●					
Namibia	●	●						
Nepal		●			●	●	●	
Netherlands	●		●	●	●	●	●	
New Zealand			●	●	●	●		
Nicaragua	●	●	●	●	●	●		
Niger	●	●	●	●	●	●	●	
Nigeria	●	●	●	●	●			
Norway	●	●	●	●	●	●	●	
Oman			●					
Pakistan	●	●	●	●		●		
Panama	●	●	●	●	●	●		
Papua New Guinea		●	●	●				
Paraguay	●	●	●	●	●	●		
Peru	●	●	●	●	●	●		
Philippines	●	●		●	●	●	●	
Poland	●	●	●	●	●	●	●	
Portugal	●	●	●	●	●	●	●	
Qatar			●			●		
Romania	●	●	●	●	●	●	●	
Russian Federation	●	●	●	●	●	●	●	
Rwanda	●	●		●	●	●	●	
Saint Kitts and Nevis								
Saint Lucia	●	●	●	●	●	●		
Saint Vincent and the Grenadines		●	●	●				
San Marino	●	●	●	●	●	●	●	●
São Tomé and Principe	●	●			●	●		
Saudi Arabia			●	●	●	●		
Senegal	●	●	●	●	●	●	●	
Seychelles	●	●	●	●	●	●	●	●
Sierra Leone	●	●	●	●	●	●		
Singapore		●	●	■				
Slovakia	●	●	●	●	●	●	●	●
Slovenia	●	●	●	●	●	●	●	
Solomon Islands			●					
Somalia			●	●				
South Africa	●	●	●	●	●	●	●	
Spain	●	●	●	●	●	●	●	
Sri Lanka	●	●	●		●	●		
Sudan		●	●	●	●	●		
Suriname	●	●	●	●				
Swaziland	●	●	●	●	●	●		

A2.2 Status of fundamental labour rights conventions

	Freedom of association and collective bargaining		Elimination of forced and compulsory labour		Elimination of discrimination in respect of employment and occupation		Abolition of child labour	
	Convention 87 [a]	Convention 98 [b]	Convention 29 [c]	Convention 105 [d]	Convention 100 [e]	Convention 111 [f]	Convention 138 [g]	Convention 182 [h]
Sweden	●	●	●	●	●	●	●	
Switzerland	●	●	●	●	●	●	●	
Syrian Arab Republic	●	●	●	●	●	●		
Tajikistan	●	●	●	●			●	
Tanzania, U. Rep. of		●	●	●			●	
Thailand			●	●	●		●	
Togo	●	●	●	●	●	●	●	
Trinidad and Tobago	●	●	●	●	●	●		
Tunisia	●	●	●	●	●	●	●	●
Turkey	●	●	●	●	●	●	●	
Turkmenistan	●	●	●	●	●			
Uganda		●	●	●		●		
Ukraine	●	●	●		●	●	●	
United Arab Emirates			●		●	●	●	
United Kingdom	●	●	●	●	●	●		●
United States				●				●
Uruguay	●	●	●	●	●	●	●	
Uzbekistan		●	●	●	●	●		
Venezuela	●	●	●	●	●	●	●	
Viet Nam					●	●		
Yemen	●	●	●	●	●	●	●	
Yugoslavia	●	●	●	●	●	●	●	
Zambia	●	●	●	●	●	●	●	
Zimbabwe		●	●	●	●	●		
Total of 174	128	146	152	144 [i]	145	142	88	13

● Ratification.

■ Ratification denounced.

Note: Information as of 4 April 2000.

a. Freedom of Association and Protection of the Right to Organize Convention (1948). b. Right to Organize and Collective Bargaining Convention (1949). c. Forced Labour Convention (1930). d. Abolition of Forced Labour Convention (1957). e. Equal Remuneration Convention (1951). f. Discrimination (Employment and Occupation) Convention (1958). g. Minimum Age Convention (1973). h. Worst Forms of Child Labour Convention (1999). Has not yet entered into force. i. Excludes denounced ratifications.

Source: ILO 2000.

CHAPTER 3

 Inclusive democracy secures rights

The primary meaning of democracy is that all who are affected by a decision should have the right to participate in making that decision, either directly or through chosen representatives . . . . to exclude the losing groups from participation in decision-making clearly violates the primary meaning of democracy.
—*Arthur Lewis, first Nobel Prize winner in the economics of development*

Democracy is the only form of political regime compatible with respecting all five categories of rights— economic, social, political, civil and cultural

The democratic liberalization sweeping the world is making transitions more civil. One of the more remarkable transitions: in Senegal President Abdou Diouf's loss in an open election in February 2000 ended four decades of one-party rule. Senegal became part of the refreshing trend in Africa of leaders leaving office through the ballot, a rare occurrence until recently. Yet despite undoubted benefits, the transition to democracy in many countries remains imperilled, insecure, fragile. The spread of democracy is important, but we must not overlook the challenges and dangers.

THE LINK BETWEEN HUMAN RIGHTS AND DEMOCRACY

Democracy is the only form of political regime compatible with respecting all five categories of rights—economic, social, political, civil and cultural. But it is not enough to establish electoral democracy. Several policy interventions are required to realize a range of rights under democratic government.

DEMOCRACY IS DEFINED BY HUMAN RIGHTS

Some rights require mechanisms that ensure protection from the state. Others need active promotion by the state.

Four defining features of a democracy are based on human rights:
• Holding free and fair elections contributes to fulfilment of the right to political participation.
• Allowing free and independent media contributes to fulfilment of the right to freedom of expression, thought and conscience.
• Separating powers among branches of government helps protect citizens from abuses of their civil and political rights.

• Encouraging an open civil society contributes to fulfilment of the right to peaceful assembly and association. An open civil society adds an important participatory dimension, along with the separation of powers, for the promotion of rights.

These rights are mutually reinforcing, with progress in one typically linked with advances in others. Openness of the media, for example, is usually correlated with the development of civil society institutions.

But democracy is not homogeneous. From the several forms of democracy, countries choose different institutional mixes depending on their circumstances and needs. For simplicity, it helps to distinguish two broad categories of democracies—majoritarian and inclusive. In a majoritarian democracy government is by the majority, and the role of minorities is to oppose. The danger is that many minorities in plural societies may be permanently excluded, discriminated against and marginalized—since this would not affect the electoral prospects of majority-based political parties. That can lead to violence, the case under several democracies.

In the liberal democratic model all individuals are autonomous in displaying public loyalty to the state, while their various private loyalties— religious, ethnic or regional—are ignored. This puts the emphasis on a majority's right to decide. And when collectives of unequal size live together in a democracy and do not have identical or cross-cutting interests, conflicts become likely.

These dangers are evident in Nigeria, which has experienced much violence since its return to democratic rule. These concerns are emphasized in the special contribution by President Olusegun Obasanjo.

Majoritarian democracies have frequently been undermined by a minority's fear of repression. In 1947 the South Asian subcontinent split into two nations in part because the Muslims of India felt that Westminster-style majoritarian democracy would mean rule by the overwhelming Hindu majority. These fears echoed those of Catholics in Northern Ireland, who lived under a Protestant-elected government from 1921 to 1972. Both situations led to widespread violence.

Now consider an inclusive democracy built on the principle that political power is dispersed and shared in a variety of ways—to protect minorities and to ensure participation and free speech for all citizens. Inclusive democracy emphasizes the quality of representation by striving for consensus and inclusion, not the brute electoral force of the majority. An inclusive democracy also appreciates the need to promote civil society organizations, open media, rights-oriented economic policy and separation of powers. It thus creates mechanisms for the accountability of the majority to the minorities.

After the first elections in a free South Africa, President Nelson Mandela asked a prominent leader of the opposition to join his cabinet, even though the African National Congress had a comfortable majority. Mandela's accommodation of a threatened—and potentially violent—minority is an important lesson for other democracies. Having an opposition is important, and coalitions can make governments unwieldy. But the price of exclusion is often higher, especially when it leads to civil war.

HOLDING FREE ELECTIONS TO ENSURE PARTICIPATION AND NON-DISCRIMINATION

When individuals are acknowledged as an important part of a system, they tend to take responsibility for it and make efforts to maintain and improve it. Voting is the opportunity to choose the government, and faith in the process of electing representatives confers legitimacy on the institutions of government. This basic right of participation, along with related rights, has been extended recently in the once colonized or satellite regimes of Africa, Europe and Asia. The initial progress in democratization has been impressive in parts of Central Asia, such as Kyrgyzstan and Mongolia. In sharp contrast are neighbouring Turk-

---

SPECIAL CONTRIBUTION

Transition to democracy and human rights

A main feature of Nigerian sociopolitical life of the recent dark years is the extent to which it spawned human rights activism. The more tyrannical the regime got, the more people became aware of what they were losing by way of freedom of expression and the right to determine how they were to be governed. In fact, human rights activism became the only form of political expression. It's thus hardly surprising that the protests all became generically known as pro-democracy movements.

The human rights groups aligned themselves into forces that were determined to force General Sani Abacha out of power. And, looking back, they had a strong chance of scoring a unique victory for the nation, had there not been the divine intervention that offered an opportunity for transition without the disadvantages of violent confrontation.

In the immediate years before the transition Nigerian society experienced evil governance. Nigerians were so traumatized by the experience that transition alone was not an ade-

quate palliative. In recognition of this, our administration immediately set up a commission to look into all complaints of human rights abuses in the past. The commission has yet to conclude its findings, but already we seem to be achieving some of the desired effect: namely, that many people have felt a sense of relief simply because they have had the chance to air their grievances and put their cases before someone who is willing and prepared to listen.

By all standards, the transition in Nigeria has been most rapid, and we thank God that it has so far been without any major crises. However, the speed of liberalization is analogous to the sudden release of the lid from a boiling kettle. After years of oppression and suppression, many conflicts have suddenly found voices for public expression. Besides this, there are those forces of activism that are yet to lose their confrontational habits from the days of less sympathetic and undemocratic regimes. Some of these forces have even been hijacked by people with criminal intentions.

We fully accept the challenge of persuading all Nigerians to accept that transition is a process and not a one-off event that was concluded on 29 May 1999. In that process all Nigerians should feel free to bring their legitimate grievances to the dialogue table, where they will be heard rationally, justly and constitutionally. That is the beauty of the unique advantage of democracy over other forms of government.

Our administration is not only fully committed to democratic rule, but our battle cry in the transition process is "Never again will this country sink into the abyss of the recent past when human rights abuse was the order of the day!"

Obasanjo

President Olusegun Obasanjo
President of Nigeria

menistan, which has a president for life, and Uzbekistan, where the Inter-Parliamentary Union and other observers raised concerns about the electoral process.

There are other stirring developments. In the Islamic Republic of Iran the February 2000 parliamentary elections—a democratic path to revolutionary change—is an example of people's power contributing to systemic structural changes.

INDEPENDENT MEDIA—FOR FREEDOM OF EXPRESSION

The freedom of individuals to openly debate and criticize policies and institutions guards against abuses of human rights. Openness of the media not only advances civil and political liberties—it often contributes to economic and social rights. Pricking the public conscience and pressuring for action have worked in several cases (box 3.1).

In many cases the media have raised awareness of rights violations. Child labour in making carpets and soccer balls and poor working conditions in the factories of multinational firms received extensive coverage. In most of these cases NGOs formed an alliance with the media—to mobilize the power of shame to protect the rights of the vulnerable.

THE SEPARATION OF POWERS—FOR THE RULE OF LAW

The state is omnipresent in any discussion of human rights, as culprit and protector, as judge, jury and defendant. It often has to be ready to act against itself—if, say, extrajudicial killing or torture is carried out by its police. A democratic state can fulfil its human rights obligations only if it ensures the rule of law. The institutions that curb the arbitrary exercise of power are a democratically elected legislature, an independent judiciary and an executive that can retain a reasonable professional independence in implementing laws and policies. These key elements of democratic governance are embodied in the separation of powers. And their existence enhances the accountability of the state.

Little noticed by the world, reforms are taking place in this direction in a number of countries, with profound implications for the civil and political rights of people. Not least of these developments has been in China, where a series of fundamental reforms have been introduced into the constitution. A major revision of the penal code introduces the principle of habeas corpus, and a new civil code incorporates the principle of rights and dignity of the individual. Reforms have moved towards greater independence of the judiciary from the executive, and within the judiciary, the functions of judge, prosecutor and legal counsel have been separated, and each of these professional groups has a code of conduct.

AN OPEN CIVIL SOCIETY—FOR DEEPENING PARTICIPATION, EXPRESSION AND ACCOUNTABILITY

The state is accountable to its citizens—but a neutral public space is needed as an intermediary for the citizens to make the state fulfil its

---

BOX 3.1

The power of shame—a weapon for human rights NGOs

For many civil society agencies, shame is their only weapon. And it can be quite powerful.

Brazil
In February 1989, 50 prisoners were locked in an unventilated maximum security cell at the 42nd police station in São Paulo. Eighteen died of asphyxiation. To protest, NGOs filed a petition with the Inter-American Commission on Human Rights. This pressure prompted the federal government and São Paulo state government to pay compensation to the prisoners' families in 1997, and to close down the maximum security cells in São Paulo police stations. And partly as a result of this incident, Brazil has produced guidelines for the treatment of prisoners closely based on the UN framework.

Hungary
In 1997 municipal authorities in the town of Szekesfehervar began to relocate predominantly Roma families from a rundown building on "Radio Street" to a row of containers used to house soldiers stationed in Hungary during the Bosnian war. The containers were placed outside city limits. A number of NGOs banded together to form an ad hoc Anti-Ghetto Committee, which held public demonstrations and lobbied the national government. Municipal authorities finally agreed to purchase flats in the city.

Nigeria
To resist human rights violations by Shell Oil in 1990, the Ogoni people formed the Movement for Survival of Ogoni People, a peaceful movement led by Ken Saro-Wiwa. Although Shell Oil suspended its activities in Ogoniland in 1993, it continued to pump more than 250,000 barrels of oil a day in Nigeria, nearly 12 percent of its international output. In the wake of Saro-Wiwa's execution in 1994, many NGOs and fair trade organizations started campaigning against Shell. The damage to the company's public image and profits compelled it to publicly admit its errors and adopt a human rights code.

Source: Neve and Affonso 1995; Cahn 1999; CAD 1995; Shell Report 1999.

obligations. There may be independent auditing by citizens groups, such as the People's Union for Civil Liberties in India—or by international NGOs, such as Amnesty International or Human Rights Watch. Such pressure is aimed at advancing freedoms of press, of speech, of association. A state may have signed all human rights treaties—but without an open civil society it may be under little pressure to honour its commitments.

In sum, democratic governance provides the ideal political framework for the realization of human rights—because it is based on the extension of civil and political rights, notably the right to participate in political life. And by allowing a voice in political decisions, it can be instrumental in realizing other rights. Democracy builds the institutions needed for the fulfilment of human rights.

HOW AND WHY SOME "DEMOCRACIES" HARM HUMAN RIGHTS

Many democracies nevertheless fail to protect or promote human rights. Although the global transition to democratic regimes is undoubtedly progress, problems of human rights are not resolved simply because an electoral system has replaced an authoritarian regime. The transition to a new order involves complex issues of human rights. In extreme cases of illiberal majoritarian democracy, the human rights of several groups have worsened. In other cases the world community has been too tolerant of human rights abuses under democracies.

Countries in the transition to democracy generally face four challenges in promoting human rights.
• A critical challenge is to integrate minorities and address horizontal inequality between ethnic groups or geographic regions. Perhaps the most persistent weakness of majoritarian democracies is discrimination against minorities and worsening of horizontal inequalities.
• A second key weakness is the arbitrary exercise of power. Elected governments frequently lose legitimacy and popular support when they behave in an authoritarian manner. When elite groups act as if they are above the

law or when elected representatives arbitrarily remove judges, civil servants and others, faith in democratic institutions weakens.
• A third weakness is neglecting the economic dimension of human rights. Many democracies fail to address the economic and social rights of significant groups, typically because this neglect does not hurt the electoral outcomes for those in power.
• Finally, failing to deal adequately with the legacy of an authoritarian past can lead to the recurrence of violence and the reversal of democratic rule.

In each case human rights are seriously affected. Minorities are punished. Children remain uneducated and hungry. Journalists are intimidated, judges threatened, political opponents tortured and human rights activists eliminated. These violations continue under many elected governments.

EXCLUSION AND MARGINALIZATION OF MINORITIES

The Achilles' heel of majoritarian democracies: the exclusion and marginalization of minorities. The scale and extent of discrimination differ, but the histories of India, Israel, Nigeria, Russia, Spain, Sri Lanka, Turkey, Uganda, the United Kingdom, the United States, to name a few, show that minorities suffer serious discrimination.

Rights are protections against the harms that people are likely to suffer. Minority rights protect groups against threats from majoritarian decision-making procedures. The threats typically include:
• *Exclusion from participation*—manipulating political rights and the media to increase the power of the majority in politics, such as through gerrymandering of constituencies.
• *Bypassing of the rule of law*—setting aside the rule of law in times of great social stress, often targeting minorities whose loyalty the majority questions. In assessing the rights of minorities in a democratic society, two questions are relevant. What rights for the protection of minorities are in the constitution? How well does the political system protect these rights in practice?

Many democracies fail to protect or promote human rights

• *Oppression*—imposing social practices on minorities, a recurrent theme in many societies. The languages and cultures of minorities have often been banned or marginalized. Today the rise of religious intolerance in several countries is imposing alien cultural practices on minorities. And in some societies intolerance towards those wishing to practise their religion is a denial of the right to freedom of expression.

• *Impoverishment*—actions of the majority to further its economic interests at the expense of minorities, through, say, forced relocations from resource-rich areas.

Violence against minorities is a burning political issue the world over. Even with constitutional protection, minorities can face large threats. In Western Europe immigrant minorities are constantly exposed to violence and racism (box 3.2).

Violence against minorities is a burning political issue the world over

THE FAILURE TO INTEGRATE MINORITIES— THE EXTREME OF CIVIL WARS

An estimated 5 million people perished in civil wars in the past decade. The breakdown of trust and failure of internal political accommodation often occur because of horizontal inequalities and the absence of democratic processes for settling disputes. The paradox of the former Yugoslavia and Sri Lanka—two countries with reasonable progress in incomes alongside human rights violations, though there are many other examples—is at one level due to civil war. But why are these societies in civil war? The answer relates to the quality of democracy, particularly the way minorities have been excluded.

Yugoslavia in the 1980s was a multi-ethnic, multi-faith federation with much local autonomy for minority ethnic groups, as in Kosovo. But the country—once considered a model of dynamic workers' cooperatives, ethnic integration and non-Soviet socialism—imploded into vicious ethnic cleansing of minorities, which resulted in the first genocide in Europe since Nazi Germany.

In Sri Lanka two large communities—the Sinhalese and Tamil—started out as citizens in a liberal democratic framework with guaranteed rights. In this multi-ethnic society the Sinhalese speakers far outnumbered the Tamil speakers. But in 1956 the Sinhalese majority started imposing a single-language national identity, and had the numbers to force it through parliament.

After decades of troubles the majority has recognized that some form of recognition of the parity of the two communities is a prerequisite for reconstructing the Sri Lankan nation. But the assassination of a well-known human rights activist and lawyer in July 1999, a few months before attempts on the life of the president of Sri Lanka, is a gruesome reminder of the continuing obstacles (box 3.3).

So, despite reasonable progress in income, the failure to integrate minorities can lead to violations of human rights and to war. The spirit of democracy has to be inclusive, embracing the principle that power must be dispersed and shared. The multiple layers of people's identity and loyalty—to their ethnic group, their religion, their region and their state—have to be recognized and given fair play in democratic institutions—or explode into conflict (box 3.4).

ARBITRARY EXERCISE OF POWER

Democracy suffered reversals in Ecuador, Pakistan and Sierra Leone, where elected regimes changed through unconstitutional mechanisms. In other, less extreme cases elected leaders have become more authoritarian.

BOX 3.2

Racism against immigrants and other minorities in Western Europe

The European Monitoring Centre on Racism and Xenophobia, in a comprehensive survey in 1998, confirmed that racism and xenophobia exist in all 15 member countries of the European Union, though the situation varies across countries.

The centre documented vicious attacks, intimidation and discrimination against foreigners, immigrants and racial groups in several countries in 1998—while recognizing just how few cases are ever reported. In Germany there were 430 officially reported cases of xenophobic violence; in Spain 143 cases, mostly against "gypsies"; in France 191 cases, most of them anti-Semitic; in Sweden 591

"acts against ethnic groups"; and in Finland 194 reported racial crimes, most against immigrants and Roma. The study observed that racism is not always linked to social marginalization. Hate crimes are perpetrated in many cases by members of far-right organizations and parties, but also by other citizens and by police officers.

Such uncivil society poses threats to the human rights of minorities in many parts of the world. Refusing to keep silent, by documenting cases and reporting on them in the media, is the first step towards combating racism—bringing it to collective awareness and mobilizing a response.

Source: European Monitoring Centre on Racism and Xenophobia 1998.

An economic crisis might contribute to an elected regime's unpopularity, but a deeper disillusionment comes from the arbitrary exercise of power. In many countries suffering reversals, civilian governments behaved like their military predecessors. Elected to power in an institutional collapse, they did not institute any separation of powers. Instead, the judiciary, legislature and civil service were effectively merged into an instrument of arbitrary power, concentrated in the office of the chief executive. There was no effective check on the exercise of power, a legacy of long periods of military and colonial rule. Rather than undertaking major institutional reforms—which would introduce checks and balances and thereby protect rights—successive civilian governments continued to exercise arbitrary power. Rights to participate, as well as many other rights, have suffered in fragile democracies.

PERSISTENT POVERTY AND GROWING INEQUALITY

Despite half a century of elected governments, India has failed to provide universal primary education. There is no provision in the constitution for mandatory primary education as a right of all citizens. Resources are not the critical constraint. Countries with similar resources, such as China, have legal guarantees for this economic right, and have delivered it.

Mass poverty, particularly when combined with growing vertical or horizontal inequality, often leads to social instability. The resulting law and order problems have an economic base but undermine civil and political rights. Persistent poverty and growing inequality lead to social strife, which has often undermined civil liberties. The fact that progress in human rights is unlikely to be sustainable without balanced development of economic and political rights is explored in detail in chapter 4.

THE TROUBLED LEGACY OF AN AUTHORITARIAN REGIME

Cambodia, Chile, Guatemala, Indonesia, Nigeria, Russia, South Africa—to name a few—have to build democracies on the ashes of a brutal past. Healing deep wounds, taming repressive institutions, changing violent attitudes born of conflict and creating a culture of consensus are vital to the process of democratization.

How best to convert militaristic or fascist states into democracies? There have been three types of responses:

• A country accepts externally imposed democratic institutions because of military defeat and the promise of major financial assistance. This was the case in Germany and Japan after the Second World War—ironically, outsiders "imposed" democratic institutions, which have nonetheless taken root and grown for the past five decades.

• A country has an internal consensus on democracy as the system for the future, often supported by incentives from regional institutions—and by features of the past that provide a symbol of unity during radical institutional change. Spain chose not to rake up a

---

BOX 3.3

A murder that didn't silence a message

Dr. Neelan Tiruchelvam, human rights activist, member of the Sri Lankan parliament, scholar and constitutional lawyer, was brutally assassinated on 29 July 1999. He was a critical link in the discourse on ethnic politics and human rights in Sri Lanka, bringing his intellectual strength, activist inspiration and mediation skills to the peace effort. His contributions, both locally and internationally, to democratization and conflict resolution are most clearly visible in his efforts to mediate a negotiated settlement and his work in drafting constitutional amendments and legislation on equal opportunity and non-discrimination and establishing civil society institutions for human rights.

The politics of ethnicity and the politics of war require people with the commitment and capacity to confront the perpetrators of all forms of discrimination, extreme nationalism, human rights violations and injustices—and to do so at all levels, legal, constitutional, political, intellectual and moral.

Neelan, who belonged to one of the minority communities of Sri Lanka, advocated tolerance and celebration of diversity and pluralism in an environment where both the state and the people could be held accountable for their actions. His life's work was committed to these ideals and practice. The void he leaves behind is great in a world where the voices of moderation, negotiation, self-determination and liberalism are frequently threatened by violence.

On what would have been his 56th birthday, 31 January 2000, human rights activists, academicians, lawyers, political leaders and friends gathered from around the world to pay tribute to his memory and his work. Kofi Annan and Mary Robinson added their messages to this gathering. To quote from Neelan's last address to parliament on 15 June 1999:

We cannot glorify death, whether in the battlefield or otherwise. We, on the other hand, must celebrate life, and are fiercely committed to protecting and securing the sanctity of life, which is the most fundamental value without which all other rights and freedoms become meaningless.

We can only hope that all those individuals and institutions he engaged and inspired, both in Sri Lanka and around the world, will advance his work and his vision.

Source: Wignaraja 2000.

difficult past in human rights, in part because of the consensus across the political spectrum on democracy and the lack of any serious threat of reversion to a militaristic, authoritarian government. As part of this consensus, the major political parties agreed to a symbolic role for the monarchy in consolidating the transition to democratic governance.

• A country uses a truth and reconciliation commission to heal deep wounds. Many countries have felt the need to openly discuss human rights abuses—to recognize suffering and to put the perpetrators of such abuses on the defensive.

Formal truth and reconciliation commissions were first established in Latin America in the 1980s (annex table A3.1). They have since proved, in some countries, to be an ingenious device for balancing the divergent needs of healing and justice. Elsewhere, they have been superficial exercises in futility.

In 1983 the newly elected president of Argentina, Raúl Alfonsín, appointed a National Commission on the Disappearance of Persons, chaired by the writer Ernesto Sabato. In 1984 the commission produced *Nunca Más* (Never Again), a chilling account of the machinery of death created by the military dictatorship. Immediately thereafter, the Argentine courts heard the historic case against the members of the three successive military juntas that governed between 1976 and 1982. The process resulted in the sentencing of powerful figures, omnipotent only a few years before. Restlessness in the armed forces over continued prosecutions later led to presidential pardons for the convicted officers.

Following this experience, the democratic government in Chile also created a truth and reconciliation commission, with members representing a wide political spectrum. Rather than describe the patterns and structure of repression, as the Argentine commission had done, the Chilean commission gave each victim's family an account of what had happened—to the extent that it could reconstruct the facts.

Truth and reconciliation commissions gained global visibility with their adoption in Africa. The deep physical and psychological wounds of apartheid in South Africa were bared in an intensely emotional, participatory process. Victims confronted perpetrators, recalling inhumane acts, but generously expressing forgiveness for unforgivable crimes.

Suddenly Africa, so defamed by its dictators, was leading the world through the wisdom of Nobel Prize winners such as President Mandela and Archbishop Desmond Tutu. The South African Truth and Reconciliation Commission was preceded by one President Yoweri Museveni established in Uganda to come to terms with the terrors of Idi Amin and Milton Obote. Rwanda created an NGO-led commission. The most recent significant example is

---

BOX 3.4

Horizontal inequality and conflict

Africa
Politics in several African countries are dominated by conflict among groups (horizontal conflict) rather than classes. The usual form is majority exclusion of minorities from political and economic resources. This has led to conflict in Nigeria, Rwanda, Uganda and others. South Africa and Zimbabwe face the opposite challenge: protecting minorities previously associated with repressive rule over the majority. Such complexities need to be addressed within the framework of inclusive democracy being pursued by some African countries.

Eastern Europe and the CIS
Threats to the Albanian minority in Serbia evoked memories of the massacre of Muslims in Bosnia and Herzegovina and led to international intervention in Kosovo. The form of the intervention, through the North Atlantic Treaty Organization (NATO), raised complex new issues of international law and sovereignty related to the rights of minorities and the obligations of the international community.

Other minorities face discrimination in the new democracies. The Roma, of Asian descent, have encountered violence, legal discrimination and prejudice in such countries as Bulgaria, the Czech Republic, Hungary and Romania. Estonia and Slovakia face the challenge of integrating Hungarian and Russian minorities. Armenia, Azerbaijan and Georgia face intense ethnic conflict, frequently involving other countries.

Latin America
Constitutions recently adopted in Latin America include provisions on the protection and promotion of the rights of indigenous communities. They are an attempt to clear away the legacy left by the indigenism that was formally instituted following the Inter-American Indigenous Congress in Patzcuaro, Mexico, in 1940.

Indigenism had two main objectives: to speed up and consolidate the national integration of Latin American states, and to promote economic and social development in order to overcome the "centuries-long backwardness" of indigenous communities and assimilate them into the nation-state model. These nationalistic societies, dominated by the white and mestizo urban middle class, rejected cultural diversity and did not recognize the indigenous elements of their culture. Indigenism, which in practice assigned indigenous people the same legal status as minors, exacerbated rather than solved the problems of extreme poverty, marginalization and recognition of ancestral lands.

Political liberalization has begun to reverse formal legal discrimination against indigenous peoples. But in some Latin American countries such progress has been accompanied by growing economic inequality and social marginalization.

Source: Mendez 2000; Oloka-Onyango 2000; Šilovic 2000; Stewart forthcoming.

---

that of Nigeria, whose return to democratic rule in 1999 was accompanied by President Obasanjo's announcement of a truth and reconciliation commission.

Advancing the human rights agenda during the transition to democracy does not always require a truth and reconciliation commission, particularly when there is a consensus in society about the direction of transition, and no perceived threat of a reversal. This was evident in many transitions from one-party to multiparty states (box 3.5).

Truth and reconciliation commissions have not only exposed sordid details of the past, however—they have also put the perpetrators to shame in the public eye. But some have been meek, tokenistic failures. Sceptics note that in proportion to the enormity of the crimes, truth commissions have often achieved very little justice and disclosed too little truth.

Countries that have already suffered a return to military government or fear the resurgence of authoritarian forces may well consider the utility of a truth and reconciliation commission to put such forces on the defensive. An open discussion of their role in brutalizing society and destroying institutions is preferable to appeasing unrepentant authoritarian forces by hiding ugly truths under the carpet. Some countries that protected their armies, by avoiding an open discussion of their human rights abuses, have paid a heavy price in the return to military rule.

Experience with truth and reconciliation commissions suggests, ironically, that the key to their success is to be forward-looking. Commissions should not be seen as an alternative to creating judicial institutions for the future—but as part of a policy of accountability for the past that helps the process of creating independent and just institutions. Truth commissions succeed if society sees them as an effort not only to respect and acknowledge the plight of victims but also to ensure that state-sponsored abuses of human rights are not repeated.

POLICY RESPONSES—ADVANCING HUMAN RIGHTS THROUGH AN INCLUSIVE DEMOCRACY

The solution to the many dilemmas of democracy is not to return to authoritarian government. Nor are civil society organizations by themselves the answer. Reasonable progress requires a political framework conducive to human rights. And there is far more to that framework than elections, which can still produce governments that tolerate or are directly responsible for serious human rights violations.

The rights way forward is a four-part policy agenda for creating an inclusive democracy.

PROTECTING RIGHTS OF MINORITIES AND ADDRESSING HORIZONTAL INEQUALITIES

International comparative analysis studies have emphasized that acute horizontal inequalities in access to political and economic resources lead to conflict. They have also identified 267 minorities particularly at risk across the world.

Horizontal inequalities typically translate into discrimination and marginalization for minority groups. The lack of belonging spurs alienation from the political and economic sys-

BOX 3.5

The importance of laughter and forgetting

In *The Book of Laughter and Forgetting*, Milan Kundera noted that "the past is full of life, eager to irritate us, provoke and insult us, tempt us to destroy or repaint it. The only reason people want to be masters of the future is to change the past." The link between past and future had a twisted logic in the totalitarianism that suffocated Czechoslovakia. Many communist regimes used the past as an ever-changing tool to justify the present—most crudely by obliterating figures in disrepute from historical photographs. That was the fate of Leon Trotsky in the USSR. And in Czechoslovakia, Foreign Minister Vladimir Clementis was airbrushed out of a famous photograph of communist leader Klement Gottwald making a historic speech in Prague in February 1948.

There was a particular irony to the airbrushing of Comrade Clementis. It was freezing, and the foreign minister had had the generosity to lend his hat to his bareheaded leader. So Clementis's hat remained in the photograph and became a symbol—for men such as Vaclav Havel—of the distortion of the past that was so much a part of totalitarian societies. The democratic Czech Republic of the 1990s, under Havel's leadership, has come to terms with its past in a remarkably open way. This attitude contributed to perhaps the most amicable divorce in history, Czechoslovakia's voluntary split into two countries.

Countries such as the Czech Republic and Slovakia illustrate how much wider human development and human rights are than some of the indicators used to measure them. Even a composite indicator such as the human development index, while a broader measure of progress than gross national product, does not pretend to measure civil and political rights. Czechoslovakia had ranked higher in the human development index than in gross national product, indicating a fairer distribution of economic resources than that in many other countries at the same income level. But the index does not measure the political dimension of rights—an area in which many one-party states were seriously deficient.

Source: Kundera 1978; Human Development Report Office.

tem controlled by the majority. Incorporating minority groups requires a more enlightened view of sharing economic and political resources than simple majoritarian democracy. The institutional framework and values of inclusive democracy need to be promoted to prevent violence and civil war.

This does not mean that minorities are better off under authoritarian governments. The recent ethnic cleansings have not occurred under democracies. Some of the worst abuses of minorities have been by dictatorships. But the transition to democracy will improve matters only if there is public policy intervention in favour of minority protection—and that goes far beyond the assumption that the ballot box is an automatic protector.

Several countries have recognized the need for additional measures to incorporate groups that may be left out from a narrowly defined majoritarian democracy. Belgium and Switzerland have taken policy and institutional measures to incorporate groups within representative institutions (box 3.6). Similar efforts have been undertaken by other countries. Germany has cross-party representation in parlia-

ment, with many parliamentary committees chaired by the opposition. And when the second chamber of parliament blocks legislation, conciliation committees work out an acceptable compromise.

Two large new democracies facing major challenges with minorities and horizontal inequalities are Indonesia and Nigeria. They may have something to learn from Malaysia's experience in addressing horizontal inequalities, while Malaysia has much to learn about expanding other human rights from such neighbouring countries as Thailand, where the new constitution and supporting measures represent impressive gains for human rights (box 3.7). Much of East Asia is not only recovering from the economic crisis but doing so under greater political freedom than before.

Malaysia's policies on horizontal inequalities in the 1970s, inevitably contentious, have been admired by many. Race riots shook the nation in 1969. In response, Malaysia embarked on an ambitious programme to address the severe horizontal inequalities underlying the racial violence. The key elements of Malaysia's response are captured in box 3.8.

Other countries' experiences of promoting majorities have been less benevolent. But instituting affirmative action is unavoidable in any country where inherited horizontal inequalities favour a minority, and the majority acquires power—the dilemma in South Africa and Zimbabwe. In such situations public policy has to tackle inequities while maintaining the dynamism of markets historically dominated by the minority.

Much has been learned about the need to address horizontal economic inequalities to prevent political conflict. Governments should avoid nationalizing the economic assets of relatively prosperous minorities. And they should stimulate growth in the assets and incomes of impoverished minorities through such targeted measures as small business promotion and measures to end discrimination in the labour market. Job quotas in the public sector are likely to work only in a rapidly growing economy. Economic stagnation and an overstaffed public sector are a poor environment for affirmative action in the labour market.

BOX 3.6

Minority rights and horizontal inequality— the parliamentary responses in Belgium and Switzerland

Switzerland's political system has tried to incorporate the country's three major ethnic groups—German, French and Italian. The national executive—the Federal Council—has had representation of all three groups since 1959. While the Swiss have an informal criterion of ethnic representation, the 1970 Belgian constitution has a formal requirement of equal representation for the two ethnic groups—Dutch and French. This regulation must be honoured whether the government is formed by one or several parties.

Inclusiveness is also ensured by giving minorities special representation in the second chamber. In Switzerland the national council is the lower chamber, with freely elected members. The upper house, the Council of States, has a representational formula that favours smaller cantons and has real decision-making power. The

cantons have extensive self-governing powers.

While Swiss federalism is territorial, Belgium introduced "non-territorial" federalism to protect some cultural rights. The Dutch and the French each have a cultural council, with members from both houses of the legislature, that acts as a legislature for cultural and educational issues affecting its ethnic group.

Political parties in these countries have naturally tended to reflect a multitude of ethnic, religious and socio-economic cleavages. Such a complex weave of horizontal and vertical divisions could easily lead to neglect and alienation of minorities. The political systems created have tried to address this challenge. Other countries, such as Germany, have also established institutional mechanisms that encourage consensus rather than two-party, adversarial politics.

Source: Donnelly 1989; Lijphart 1999.

A precondition for building an inclusive democracy is ensuring the right to elect representatives. Tampering with the ballot has often undermined the legitimacy of elected governments. In Bangladesh doubts about the independence of the election commission led to an agreement among political parties that elections would always be held under a temporary interim regime. This prevents the military's control over electoral politics, while ensuring that the results of elections are considered legitimate, an important advance in a new democracy. An independent election commission and international election monitors provide other tools for protecting the sanctity of the ballot where trust and autonomous institutions are lacking.

A key element in deepening inclusive democracy is a legal framework that protects the right to participation and free expression. Civil society organizations and open media are vital for monitoring violations of rights. People's participation in local institutions, including school boards, is as important a feature of democracy as participation in elections or in formal political parties.

Jordan shows how civil society organizations can lead in advancing rights in a country undergoing a gradual transition to democracy. Several members of the royal family have not only helped establish human rights NGOs directly but also supported an environment that promotes grass-roots civil society organizations struggling for human rights, including those fighting for women's rights.

An important element of the participatory principle is internal democracy in political parties. Too often, the organizational structure of parties engaged in democratic politics is anything but participatory. Parties that are not open and transparent are unlikely to be democratic in their policy commitments. Without internal democracy, parties become individual or family fiefdoms. Creating a culture of democracy in political parties is thus vital. At the very least, this should involve open, competitive elections for the party leadership.

In Panama the military was abolished as part of wide-ranging structural political reform. The democratic features of the reform included an electoral code, adopted in 1995,

BOX 3.7

The values of Asia

The signs of economic revival in Asia—so soon after the 1997–98 East Asian financial crisis—appear to provide further evidence of the deep structural foundations for economic development laid by the region. But perhaps the most positive outcome has been the remarkable change in civil and political rights, whose neglect the crisis exposed.

There has been a major change in Thailand, where the main safeguard of human rights and human development is the 1997 constitution, the country's first democratic one. The constitution stipulates that "human dignity" is the basis of human rights, which include equality between people and genders, the presumption of innocence, freedom of religion, association and expression, the rights to life, to privacy, to 12 years' education, to property and to health care, the right of children against violence and injustice, the right to access to public information and the rights to take action against public authorities and to use peaceful means against those who subvert the constitution.

Violations of the constitution can be contested in the courts. Unlike rights in past constitutions, many of which had no force unless enacted into law, many of the new provisions are immediately applicable. And while earlier constitutions subordinated rights to interests such as national security, the new constitution does not allow such interests to undermine the substance of rights.

Other Asian societies have made similar gains. Indonesia, the Republic of Korea and Taiwan (province of China) have become more open, with greater recognition of the need to advance civil and political rights. Indonesia, a complex case, has moved to civilian rule, although the new regime is having to grapple with the troubled legacy of East Timor.

The new talk of Asia advancing the cause of human rights and democracy is a far cry from earlier false claims that "Asian values" justified neglect of civil and political rights.

Source: de Barry 1998; Saravanamuttu 2000; Muntarbhorn 2000.

BOX 3.8

Malaysia's response to race riots—addressing horizontal inequality

Unlike many other countries, Malaysia refrained from nationalizing the assets of the richer minority community. This restraint ensured adherence to an efficient, market-led economic framework and reassured the Chinese minority. Political power rested in the hands of the Malay majority, the *bumiputras*. Their legitimate grievances were addressed largely through extensive intervention in the public sector, including programmes for affirmative action in education, technology and employment.

In 1969, around the time of the race riots, the per capita income of the Chinese was twice that of the Malays. Two decades later both communities were substantially richer. But while the average incomes of both communities rose, the gap between

them narrowed—the Malay income was half of Chinese income in 1970, but nearly two-thirds by 1990. This outcome was made possible by an enabling economic environment that generated rapid growth—and more equal sharing of the pie.

Critics of the Malaysian system point to its extensive network of controls on the press, political parties and the judiciary. Others point to Malaysia's practical good sense in many areas—including the unfashionable imposition of temporary capital controls in the midst of the East Asian financial crisis. This pragmatic ethos, it is claimed, will lead to a deepening of democracy, as evidenced by the recent open presidential elections.

Source: Yoke and Leng 1992.

that requires political parties to democratically elect their presidential candidates.

In addition to internal democracy, political parties in new democracies need to exemplify tolerant behaviour. The Institute for Democracy and Electoral Assistance, a policy institute based in Stockholm, has proposed a code of conduct for political parties to promote a public atmosphere of tolerance.

The code sets out principles of behaviour for political parties and their supporters relating to their participation in a democratic election campaign. Ideally, parties would agree voluntarily to this code and negotiate towards consensus on the text, which might later be incorporated in law.

The core prescriptions of such a code generally include:
- *Campaign management*—the right of all parties to campaign and to disseminate political ideas, and respect for the freedom of the press.
- *Election process*—peaceful polling, co-operation with election observers and acceptance of the outcome of the election.
- *Fair conduct*—avoiding defamatory language, destruction of the symbols of other parties or intimidation of voters and election officials.
- *Legal penalties*—for example, disqualification for corrupt practices, such as offering money to induce people to vote, or to stand or not stand.

Efforts to extend participation should also involve special measures to incorporate groups that are underrepresented because of a history of prejudice and discrimination. All over the world, social and structural barriers impede women from participating in politics. In many countries women have enhanced their participation by increasing gender sensitivity and awareness, by lobbying for party and parliamentary electoral quotas for women and by providing support services to women legislators. Gender-balanced local elections often represent the first step, enabling greater political participation at all levels.

In Trinidad and Tobago a network of NGOs conducted workshops to train 300 women to run as candidates in the 1999 local government elections. Of the 91 women contesting the elections, 28 won, virtually doubling the number of seats held by women since the 1996 election.

Sweden has the largest proportion of women in parliament. Although this cannot be attributed to any single factor, the quota system used by the majority party—the Green Party in 1983–90, the Left Party in 1990–93 and the Social Democratic Party since 1993—has undoubtedly contributed.

In South Africa after the end of apartheid, the African National Congress expanded women's political participation in parliament by adopting a quota. According to the Inter-Parliamentary Union, the country now ranks ninth in the world in the proportion of women in parliament, with 119 women in its 399-member National Assembly (in 1994 it was 141st).

India reserves seats for women in local government institutions known as *panchayats,* challenging the traditional structures of policy-making. In 1993 the federal government passed the Panchayat Raj Act, reserving 33% of the three-tiered *panchayats* for women. The *panchayat* elections of 1998 showed that the reservation policy worked in most states: women won 33–40% of the seats.

In the Philippines improving the quality of women legislators' participation in policy-making is as important as increasing the number of elected women. The Centre for Legislative Development provides elected women, particularly at the local level, with the technical skills they need for their job—through training on legislative agenda setting and on the development of legislative proposals and deliberations. To sustain advocacy initiatives, the centre also helps build links between elected women and women's groups.

Widening the participation of those discriminated against—whether minorities, women or others—is linked to the process of changing norms and values. Instilling a democratic culture at all levels of society is a radical process—threatening existing values, inequities and injustices. The task is complicated further by a recent history of violence. Two societies struggling to create a culture of

Too often, the organizational structure of parties engaged in democratic politics is anything but participatory

democracy on the ashes of violence are Cambodia and South Africa (box 3.9).

An independent press has been a vital ally in the recent advances in Eastern Europe. The Network of Independent Journalists, run by the Croatian-based Stina press agency, has campaigned vigorously for extension of freedoms long denied in the region.

Widening participation has several other dimensions. Even well-established democracies face the need for continual reform to adapt to changing circumstances and to correct deficiencies. Recent reforms in the United Kingdom are aimed at addressing the shortcomings of the Westminster model, the subject of debate in the country for decades.

While Thailand was forming its first democratic constitution, the United Kingdom's Labour government began to enact a series of wide-ranging reforms to the country's customary unwritten constitution. These include devolving power to regional assemblies, enhancing the powers of the Scottish parliament in particular. Apart from excessive centralization, another deficiency was the hereditary principle governing membership in the House of Lords, the upper chamber—a symbol of privilege rather than inclusion. The reforms changed its composition and the criteria for selection to reduce the power of inherited privilege. Other changes include a move towards a freedom of information act.

These reforms, linked to the expanded framework of the European Union's human rights legislation, have modernized British democracy. Many of the changes are in line with the EU principle of subsidiarity and decentralization—that power is more accountable when it is close to the beneficiaries. Some decision-making is retained at regional or central levels of authority, where justified for consistency and enforcement of common standards across national boundaries.

IMPLEMENTING THE SEPARATION OF POWERS

When elected leaders behave like military rulers, arbitrary power undermines a basic principle of democracy, violating the checks and balances at the heart of democratic government. Human rights are most vulnerable when the exercise of power is not rule based. An elected leader must face institutional curbs to restrict arbitrary action. Most countries making the transition from authoritarian to democratic government still face this challenge.

There is tension in restricting arbitrary power. A newly elected leader typically inherits an environment in which arbitrary power has been part of authoritarian rule. The elected leader and party are entrusted with building institutions that place checks on their power. Visionary leadership is rare in such situations. Civilians carry on behaving in much the same way as their military and colonial predecessors. That is why a coalition of forces is required to create a culture of accountability for civilian rule—a coalition of an independent press, opposition parties, national civil society institutions and international human rights organizations.

BOX 3.9

Transition from a brutal past to an open society in South Africa and Cambodia

This Constitution provides a historic bridge between the past of a deeply divided society characterized by strife, conflict, untold suffering and injustice, and a future founded on the recognition of human rights, democracy and peaceful co-existence and opportunities for all South Africans, irrespective of colour, race, class, belief or sex.

This quotation from the 1993 interim South African constitution provides a framework of values and institutions for advancing human rights and development. The constitution includes civil, political, economic, social and cultural rights.

But the wide gap between the constitutional promises and the lived realities of millions of poor South Africans remains a challenge. The constitution and new laws are means to overcome that challenge, and South Africa's national action plan for human rights provides a framework for doing so. The plan enables the government to evaluate its human rights performance, set goals and priorities within achievable time frames, devise strategies and allocate resources for promoting human rights. It can also be used as a tool by NGOs and the media to hold the government accountable for its human rights commitments—by monitoring the human rights impact of government policies, legislation and programmes.

Cambodia's recent past was even more violent than South Africa's. And it too has adopted a constitution respectful of human rights, after the Paris peace accords of 1991. But the gap between the constitution's ideals and reality led to heated exchanges in 1997 between the United Nations Human Rights Envoy Thomas Hammerberg and Cambodian leaders.

Over the past three years, however, there have been signs of progress. A coalition of 17 NGOs formed the Human Rights Action Committee, and another group of NGOs won prominence as the Coalition for Free and Fair Elections. The establishment of the Khmer Institute for Democracy, the widespread revival of Buddhism and the appearance of reasonably independent newspapers are all advances, although inevitably many acute problems remain as Cambodia continues its slow climb back from the heart of darkness.

Source: Neou 2000; Liebenberg 2000.

Such a coalition needs to build opposition to arbitrary power. It has to exert pressure for the institutionalized separation of powers. If disputes cannot be settled in court, if corruption undermines the legal process and if the elite is above the law, a country is in no position to fulfil the rights of its citizens. Establishing a sound and supportive institutional framework is thus essential for any serious implementation of rights.

An important aspect of the separation of powers is the role of the judiciary. Argentina and El Salvador provide important examples of promising judicial reform (box 3.10).

Besides independent judiciaries, democracies need a civil service protected from arbitrary instructions from the political leadership. But the actions of civil servants also have to be under public scrutiny. Several institutional mechanisms can curb bureaucratic arrogance. An increasingly popular one is the office of the ombudsman, typically created to examine abuses of authority by public officials. The protection of civil servants against arbitrary political intervention lies in genuinely independent civil service commissions responsible for recruitment, promotion and discipline. These need to be supplemented by open procedures for bureaucrats to take elected representatives to court if asked to do anything illegal.

These open procedures in turn require an independent judiciary, reinforcing the point that an effective separation of powers requires rule-based interaction between institutions. The US constitution and subsequent civil rights reforms provide a classic model for effective separation of powers.

Within the civil service, the police are particularly important for human rights. Recent shootings by the police in New York City, for example, have raised apprehensions among the African American minority, some of whom have called for federal monitoring of the city's police.

Investigative reporters across the world have exposed rape in prisons, extrajudicial killings, torture and many other human rights violations by the police and security forces. Such journalists have played a vital role in raising awareness and contributing to a culture of public outrage at abuses.

Recognizing the importance of police reform for advancing human rights, several countries have taken important steps. Luxembourg is training police to combat racism and xenophobia. In Honduras the police reform has been inspired by an integrated set of principles on demilitarization, subordination to civil authority, respect for human rights, citizen control and accountability. The government created a new Ministry of Security to inculcate a new ethos in what was considered a volatile and dangerous police force.

As with other separations of powers, there is a dual nature to police reform. The police have to be protected from arbitrary orders from the political system. At the same time, the people have to be protected from rights abuses by the police. An ombudsman can monitor police abuses and hear complaints. In addition, human rights NGOs should have the political space to monitor prisons and any abuses by the police system.

BOX 3.10

Strengthening the rule of law in Argentina and El Salvador

Access to justice is an important part of the rule of law. Partnerships of governments, civil society and international development organizations are implementing judicial reform programmes bringing timely and tangible results. Two promising examples, symbolic of similar initiatives being undertaken across the world: Buenos Aires and El Salvador.

Under the 1996 constitution of Buenos Aires, politicians and the people are collaborating on new institutions that will improve access to justice. All laws used by the courts are to be compiled and analysed. Experts, judges and citizens are to confer about the institutional barriers to justice and propose solutions. New laws are to be drafted, new institutions designed and judges retrained. In the words of the president of Argentina, Fernando De la Rua, who started the process when he was mayor of Buenos Aires, "the key objective of the new justice system is to promote and facilitate access to justice, mainly for poor people and women."

In El Salvador judicial reform, a product of the 1992 peace agreement, is a joint effort by government, civil society and international development agencies. Since its inception during the war years, judicial reform has been led and "owned" by Salvadorans working in partnership with international experts sponsored by bilateral and multilateral donors and the development banks. They have rewritten laws, reorganized the judiciary, retrained police and prosecutors and carried out public awareness campaigns.

These examples suggest some lessons:
• An efficient, high-quality justice system entails a social, economic and political commitment. Setting up institutions that protect rights, particularly where public opinion of political parties and the justice system is poor, involves serious resource commitments and substantial political risks
• Countries need international advisory services as well as national political will and social participation to succeed.
• The reform should be holistic to avoid setbacks and obstacles. Legal institutions must be made credible. Laws must fit with the constitution and international human rights conventions. To ensure access to justice, institutional barriers must come down, information about rights and how to exercise them must be freely available and the quality of the public service of justice must be increased.

Source: Yujnovsky 2000.

Such measures as public interest litigation, often involving an appeal to the supreme court, have advanced people's involvement in mechanisms of accountability. People's organizations have used similar instruments to appeal to other branches of government. In Hungary citizens groups representing the Roma have regularly filed discrimination complaints against employers with the Office of the Parliamentary Ombudsman for Minority Rights, including for refusal to hire them because of their ethnicity. After an investigation, the ombudsman recommended that the Ministry of Social and Family Protection compile a brochure informing prospective employees of their rights and that employment centres report all cases of discrimination. It also requested that the Ministry of Justice simplify the procedures for discrimination cases and recommended that the Ministry of Internal Affairs require officials to report such cases.

In Italy in 1993, the Federation of the Association of Haemophiliacs filed a case against the Ministry of Health on behalf of 385 haemophiliac patients infected with HIV by contaminated blood transfusions. No action was taken on the case, and in May 1998 some of the patients filed an appeal with the European human rights commission against the Italian government for violating Article 6 of the European human rights convention. The article asserts entitlement to a fair and public hearing "within a reasonable time". In November 1998 the case filed in 1993 was concluded in favour of the plaintiffs. And in July 1999 the European Commission ordered the Italian government to compensate the victims for its negligent behaviour.

INCORPORATING HUMAN RIGHTS INTO ECONOMIC POLICY

The process of economic policy-making for human development should honour the rights of participation and freedom of expression. These rights imply that economic policy formulation must be open and transparent, allowing debate on the options and conferring the authority for the final decision on elected representatives.

Economic policies have large effects on the rights of people. Those hurt by decisions have the right to know—and to participate in debate and discussion. That does not mean that they have veto power, since many economic policies can hurt a few people justifiably, on grounds of efficiency in resource allocation, reduction of horizontal inequality or, indeed, improvements in human development. But those adversely affected must be heard and, if appropriate, compensated.

The importance of process for sustaining ownership of structural economic policy change is shown by India. Open debate helped embed the decision-making in the national discourse (box 3.11). Opposition remains and is desirable, but India debated the options far more openly than have most countries undergoing similar reforms.

The typical process for international policy-based lending often suffers from a democratic deficit of broad participatory debate, for example, lacking parliamentary debate. It is therefore ironic, but not surprising, that a constant refrain in the international community is "lack of ownership" of the agreed policy programme (box 3.12). And it was one of the weaknesses of adjustment policies in the 1980s, when international financial agencies and national finance ministries often agreed to policies behind closed doors.

Participatory processes can increase efficiency and economic sustainability, particularly for projects requiring community

The process of economic policy-making for human development should honour the rights of participation and freedom of expression

---

BOX 3.11

Ownership of structural adjustment—the rights approach in India

By the late 1980s there was wide consensus that India's economy had performed below potential since independence and recognition of the need for major policy change. Most, if not all, international agencies agreed.

Rather than signing a secretive agreement on a structural adjustment programme with international financial institutions, India engaged in an open policy discussion. There were, and remain, vociferous critics of the reform path being suggested. But the process of open participation and expression of opinion has led to two important results.

First, despite persistent political instability and fragile coalition governments, the broad consensus on economic policy reform has survived. All the major political parties have adhered to the programme. National ownership has not been at issue.

Second, India's economic reforms have produced the most rapid growth in its history—twice the average annual rate before the reforms. That has underscored the importance of the reforms—and led to public debate on how the benefits of the growth should be shared among regions, groups and classes.

Source: Human Development Report Office.

involvement. Many evaluations confirm that community participation in project design increases the efficiency and viability of projects in water and sanitation and in education and health. So, due process can do more than fulfil important participatory rights.

The other side of incorporating rights in economic policy-making relates to the outcome. Individuals have economic and social rights, not all of which can be immediately realized because of resource and institutional constraints. The first step in a rights-oriented approach to economic policy is to recognize these rights. This implies that citizens have a claim to have these rights realized—and may have certain duties to perform to have them fulfilled.

Many human rights are subject to progressive realization. Rights-oriented economic policy-making would force a national debate on choices and on the priority given to fulfilling some rights before others. For example, the citizens of a poor country may find that the government can meet its obligations to fulfil the right to basic education more easily than the right of each individual to housing.

Difficult choices are inherent in economic decision-making, involving complex trade-offs due to scarce resources. Incorporating human rights into economic policy-making does not make these constraints vanish. But it honours certain rights in due process. It also recognizes that choices must produce outcomes that reflect the claims that individuals have to levels of human development—and honour the economic dimension of their human rights.

• • •

Implementing these four interconnected institutional reforms will go a long way towards creating a rights-based, inclusive democracy. But it will not be a technocratic, depoliticized exercise. The agenda will face strong internal opposition, for there are groups whose power, values and interests are threatened by such change. Implementation will require a committed coalition of the media, people's movements and civil society organizations, including professional bodies of lawyers and human rights advocates. Such reforms are possible only with the active involvement of democratic political parties.

Other reforms accompanying these four, such as decentralization, would deepen democracy by extending participation. Decentralization on its own may not further rights—but when allied to these four pillars of reform, it can strengthen democratic governance.

All this can be summarized in a 10-point policy agenda for inclusive democracy:

• An independent judiciary is the pillar in a system of checks and balances against arbitrary power. Judicial appointments, training and the court system have to curb executive authority—not succumb to it. Direct recourse of people's organizations to the judicial system, through public interest litigation, also helps protect rights.

• There are two dimensions to police reform. The police have to be protected from arbitrary orders from the political system. And the people have to be protected from rights abuses inflicted by the police. This requires monitoring of police actions and other measures to

BOX 3.12

The John Le Carré approach to economic policy— structural adjustment by stealth

Structural adjustment has aroused strong passions. Its proponents have argued that poor performance was due to poor policy, pointing to the futility of huge project investments in a perverse policy environment. Its critics point to adverse social consequences and the lack of fine-tuning of a blunt "cookie cutter" approach.

This debate has often ignored a vital shortcoming in the process for negotiating and implementing these programmes—a level of secrecy of which the finest spy novelists, including John Le Carré himself, would be proud. Economic policies that will profoundly affect the lives of many citizens were often agreed in closed-door meetings between finance ministers and international financial institutions. Such secrecy would be considered scandalous in the countries of many of the representatives of these international institutions.

This process is fundamentally contrary to a rights-based approach to economic policy. Regardless of the merits of the programme, the process undermined accountability. This was a particularly serious neglect, since the citizens barred from debating the options are often those who must bear the burden of paying back the debts incurred.

But representatives of international financial institutions are increasingly recognizing this need for greater transparency. Joseph Stiglitz, chief economist of the World Bank from 1996 to 2000, has expressed concerns over a process that has left "a legacy of suspicion and doubt. Opponents see in development conditionality an echo of colonial bonds…the process of negotiating policy conditionality is widely perceived to have undermined transparency and participation".

Getting the policy environment right, and honouring conditions linked to project loans consistent with this objective, are important aspects of economic management. But the process has to respect important rights if governments and nations are to be held accountable through national ownership of programmes.

Source: Stiglitz 1999a; Human Development Report Office.

promote human rights norms in the police force.

- Ensuring non-discrimination against women in politics requires various interventions, including quotas—for the national parliament and at other levels of representation, particularly local.

- Minority participation in decision-making structures should be promoted by giving minorities special weight in legislative procedures and by having opposition and minority representatives chair parliamentary committees.

- Reducing horizontal inequalities requires economic measures. Countries need to consider what to do and what not to do. They should avoid nationalizing the private economic assets of priviledged minorities, instead using targeted economic measures to promote asset accumulation and income opportunities for poor minorities.

- The sanctity of the vote must be guarded by autonomous election commissions, international monitors and, if necessary, interim regimes for the sole purpose of transferring power from one elected regime to another.

- Political parties must be internally democratic. Party leaders should be elected and replaced through open, competitive processes. Political parties should adopt codes of conduct for internal democracy and for tolerant behaviour during the electoral process.

- Countries that have already suffered a return to military government—or fear the resurgence of authoritarian forces—might well consider the utility of a truth and reconciliation commission to create an environment conducive to democracy and respect for human rights.

- Governments should create the political space, and encourage partnerships, for monitoring and promoting human rights. Ultimately, governments and the people benefit when the media are open and civil society institutions free—conditions conducive to partnerships for creating norms and accountability for human rights.

- Pro-poor human development policies—and a reasonable distribution of the resources from economic growth—are vital companions to legal and institutional advances in human rights. The process of economic policy-making has to respect rights of participation and expression. And the content of pro-poor economic policies has to be aimed at increasing resources and targeting programmes to the vulnerable (see chapter 4).

Democracy, as noted earlier, is not homogeneous. Developing a framework of institutions that fit a country's structure and circumstances requires measures that celebrate diversity. Happily, nations no longer face the choice between authoritarianism and democracy. Their challenge for the 21st century is to deepen and enrich fragile democracies.

Truth and reconciliation commissions—a selected list

Country	Year commission was established	Main features
Bolivia	1982	This commission focused on unearthing and documenting disappearances under military rule, a major issue in the Latin American transitions to democracy.
Argentina	1983	Established by President Raúl Alfonsín, this commission consisted of writers, judges, journalists and legislators. Its report focused on 9,000 disappearances under military rule.
Philippines	1986	Established by President Corazon Aquino with a broad mandate and powers to probe the Marcos era, this commission did not produce a final report.
Chile	1990	Led by Senator Raul Rettig, this commission documented two decades of human rights abuses during the Pinochet era.
Chad	1992	Headed by Chad's chief prosecutor, this commission examined human rights violations and corruption.
El Salvador	1992	A distinctive feature of this commission was its international membership, including a former president of Colombia, a former foreign minister of Venezuela and a law professor from George Washington University. Its report, "From Madness to Hope", was released at the United Nations in 1993.
Germany	1992	This commission, headed by an eastern German member of parliament, covered 40 years of human rights violations under communist rule in East Germany.
Rwanda	1993	A unique model for truth commissions, this commission was created, funded and fully sponsored by international NGOs in response to a request by a coalition of Rwandan human rights organizations. The commission covered the civil war period, from 1990 to 1993. Its report was widely circulated in Rwanda.
Guatemala	1994	This famous commission was established in the wake of a peace accord, after 36 years of civil war. Its report, "Memory of Silence", was given to the government and international agencies at a public ceremony in Guatemala City. The commission had a mix of foreign and national lawyers.
Haiti	1994	Established by President Jean-Bertrand Aristide, this commission also contained a mix of international and national members, headed by a sociologist. The commission took 14 months to complete its findings.
Uganda	1994	President Yoweri Museveni's six-member commission, established a year before South Africa's, had an explicit forward-looking mandate. Its clearly stated objective is to prevent a recurrence of the events that traumatized Uganda under Milton Obote and Idi Amin.
South Africa	1995	This most well-known truth and reconciliation commission was established by parliament and chaired by Archbishop Desmond Tutu. The 17-member commission covered 25 years of human rights violations. One of its most significant features was its extensive series of public hearings. The commission submitted its report to President Nelson Mandela in 1998.
Nigeria	1999	This commission, established in June 1999 by President Olusegun Obasanjo, is headed by a senior judge and covers nearly two decades. Soon after its formation, the commission was inundated with submissions.
Sierra Leone	1999	Established a month after the Nigerian commission, this commission has strong amnesty provisions, allowing it to grant pardons and immunity from prosecution to perpetrators. The commission provides a public forum for victims and perpetrators to discuss a brutal past.

Source: Hayner 1994; United States Institute of Peace 2000; Garton Ash 1998.

CHAPTER 4

Rights empowering people in the fight against poverty

It is justice, not charity, that is wanting in the world.
—*Mary Wollstonecraft,* A Vindication of the Rights of Woman, *1792*

The torture of a single individual raises unmitigated public outrage. Yet the deaths of more than 30,000 children a day from mainly preventable causes go almost unnoticed. Why? Because these children are invisible in poverty. As chapter 2 shows, eradicating poverty is more than a major development challenge—it is a human rights challenge.

Of the many human rights failures today, those in economic, social and cultural areas are particularly widespread across the world's nations and people. These include the rights to a decent standard of living, to food, to health care, to education, to decent work, to housing, to a share in scientific progress and to protection against calamities.

Although poor people are also denied a wide range of human rights in civil and political areas, this chapter focuses on the economic, social and cultural rights, of central concern in eradicating poverty (box 4.1). The chapter has two main messages.

• First, the diverse human rights—civil, political, economic, social and cultural—are causally linked and thus can be mutually reinforcing. They can create synergies that contribute to poor people's securing their rights, enhancing their human capabilities and escaping poverty. Because of these complementarities, the struggle to achieve economic and social rights should not be separated from the struggle to achieve civil and political rights. And the two need to be pursued simultaneously.

• Second, a decent standard of living, adequate nutrition, health care and other social and economic achievements are not just development goals. They are human rights inherent in human freedom and dignity. But these rights do not mean an entitlement to a handout. They are claims to a set of social

arrangements—norms, institutions, laws, an enabling economic environment—that can best secure the enjoyment of these rights. It is thus the obligation of governments and others to implement policies to put these arrangements in place. And in today's more interdependent world, it is essential to recognize the obligations of global actors, who in the pursuit of global justice must put in place global arrangements that promote the eradication of poverty.

With this as perspective, the chapter examines:

• *The causal links among diverse rights.* How can different rights be mutually reinforcing?

BOX 4.1

Poverty, human rights and human development

Poverty limits human freedoms and deprives a person of dignity. The Universal Declaration of Human Rights, the Declaration on the Right to Development and a large body of other human rights instruments make this clear. The Vienna Declaration adopted at the 1993 World Conference on Human Rights affirms that "extreme poverty and social exclusion constitute a violation of human dignity".

Human Development Reports take the view that poverty is broader than lack of income—that it is deprivation across many dimensions. If income is not the sum total of human lives, a lack of income cannot be the sum total of human deprivation. Indeed, *Human Development Report 1997*, on poverty, defined it as deprivation in the valuable things that a person can do or be. The term *human poverty* was coined to distinguish this broad deprivation from the narrower *income poverty*, a more con-

ventional definition limited to deprivation in income or consumption.

Human development focuses on expanding capabilities important for all people, capabilities so basic that their lack forecloses other choices. Human poverty focuses on the lack of these same capabilities—to live a long, healthy and creative life, to be knowledgeable, to enjoy a decent standard of living, dignity, self-respect and the respect of others.

How does a person escape poverty? The links between different dimensions of poverty—different capabilities or different rights—can be mutually reinforcing in a downward spiral of entrapment. But they can also be mobilized to create a virtuous circle and an upward spiral of escape. Expanding human capabilities and securing human rights can thus empower poor people to escape poverty.

Source: Human Development Report Office.

- *The obligations and accountabilities associated with these rights.* Who is accountable and for what? How are accountabilities moving beyond the state-centred model in the context of global economic integration with its new actors and new rules?
- *The need for expanding resources and removing injustices.* What does it take to build the social arrangements necessary to secure rights?
- *The need for global justice.* How can the global order create a better enabling environment for global poverty eradication?

RIGHTS AND CAPABILITIES AS ENDS AND MEANS OF ESCAPING POVERTY

Human rights have intrinsic value as ends in themselves. They also have instrumental value. There are causal links between the realization of one right and that of another—rights to food, rights to free speech, rights to education and so on. These rights directly expand human freedoms and human development. They can also supplement and reinforce one another. And when human rights are guaranteed by law, poor people can use legal instruments to secure them.

In a similar way, human development that builds capabilities, such as being knowledgeable, has intrinsic value. But knowledge also has instrumental value as a means to building

other capabilities, such as being healthy. And the two reinforce each other in lifting a person from poverty.

These links are not automatic, but they can be mobilized strategically. Investing in basic capabilities and securing rights in law are a powerful combination—to empower poor people in their fight to escape poverty.

There are important links between the two broad sets of rights—civil and political, and economic, social and cultural—as well as among economic, social and cultural rights.

CIVIL AND POLITICAL RIGHTS— EMPOWERING PEOPLE TO ACHIEVE THEIR ECONOMIC, SOCIAL AND CULTURAL RIGHTS

Studies have shown some important causal links between such rights as freedom of participation and expression and freedom from discrimination and poverty. There can be no better illustration of these links than the effect of the right of free expression and participation in political life on avoiding major social calamity. Amartya Sen pointed to this effect in his classic analysis, an examination of famines all over the world. His and other studies have shown that no famine continued unabated in modern times in any country—poor or rich—with a democratic government and a relatively free press (box 4.2). Loud popular demands, through political processes and the media, push governments to act to stop famine and other social calamities.

There are other illustrations of causal links between civil and political rights and economic, social and cultural rights. Discrimination against women can cause deprivations for them in nutrition and health. Analysis of cross-country data shows that the exceptionally high levels of malnutrition and low-birthweight babies in South Asia cannot be fully explained by such usual determinants as income, health care, female education, female literacy and female age at first marriage. Part of the explanation is the discrimination against women in intrahousehold allocation of food and health care—discrimination due to the weaker sociocultural rights of women in patriarchal society.

BOX 4.2

Democracy—and action to avoid famine

In India famines were frequent during colonial rule—and the Bengal famine killed 2–3 million people in 1943. Famines stopped abruptly after independence with the installation of a democratic form of government.

Policies had been devised to protect vulnerable groups from famine during colonial times, but the people had no political voice to demand that they be activated. A democratic India has been able to pull back from the brink of famine because popular pressures—through the media, an active civil society and democratic multiparty political processes—do not allow government to remain inactive.

Some of the worst famines of modern times, including those in Africa, occurred when there was no catastrophic decline in the aggregate supply of food. Instead, specific groups of people lost their entitlement to food for various reasons, while large segments of the population remained unscathed. A democratic polity—buttressed by a free press and an active civil society in which vulnerable groups have a voice—and the prospects of a coming election make it almost impossible for governments and others not to take quick action.

Source: Sen 1999b; Osmani 2000.

The absence of civil and political rights can block access to social, economic and cultural rights. For example, without workers' right to free association and expression, other labour rights can be inaccessible. Workers interviewed in a study of corporate codes of conduct in six countries in Asia and six in Latin America consistently said that they thought codes were useful only in the context of proper employment contracts and rights to organize. Otherwise, they would only be laid off for complaining.

The same is true for registering births. Without a birth certificate a person may be unable to gain access to education and health services even when available and constitutionally guaranteed. UNICEF estimates that each year some 40 million births worldwide are not registered. It is often children in poor and marginalized families who enter the world deprived of this basic civil right and thus of many other social and economic rights. Regional disparities can be stark—in Turkey the registration rate is 84% in the western region but only 56% in the eastern region. In Indonesia birth certificates are needed for school enrolment and marriage, yet 30–50% of births go unregistered. Similarly, in Kenya children need birth certificates for immunization and school enrolment, but fewer than half the births are registered. South Africa has no data on birth registration, even though certificates are needed for health care and school enrolment. In some countries registration rates have been falling, especially where administrative capacity has declined, as in Tajikistan.

STRATEGIC USE OF CIVIL AND POLITICAL RIGHTS AND LEGAL INSTRUMENTS IN EMPOWERING POOR PEOPLE

Civil action groups in all regions of the world are using civil and political rights—of participation, association, free speech and information—to enlarge the political space and press for economic and social rights.

The strength of such action is growing locally and nationally, often with global support networks. In India a group defending the interests of tribal peoples and forest workers is using the right to information to demand better budget allocations. In Thailand an NGO is using the right of assembly to draw attention to the human costs of dams, land and forest development, slum clearance and private investments. In Russia a regional women's group is demanding action on the devastating health consequences of 50 years of nuclear mismanagement. How? By using methods more traditionally used to fight for political and civil rights—protests, media advocacy, public assembly and legal action (box 4.3).

NGOs have propelled much of this civic action. Their growth and their networking across the globe are part of the wave of transition

BOX 4.3

Mobilizing civil and political rights for economic, social and cultural rights

Social movements around the world are capitalizing on freedom of speech and association and exercising the right to participation—to secure economic, social and cultural rights and advance human development.

The Concerned Citizens of Abra for Good Governance in the Philippines, begun as an election monitoring group in 1986, grew into a public action programme to expose corruption in public works projects. It uses advocacy and human rights education to empower communities to claim their rights.

In India the right to access public documents and budget information has been important in demanding higher budget allocations for the disadvantaged and in fighting corruption that takes scarce public resources away from poverty priorities. Representatives of tribal peoples and forest workers in Gujarat formed Development Initiatives for Social Action and Human Action—and questioned why there was little development in their local communities. Though lacking formal training in budget analysis, they thoroughly analysed the government's books and presented a report to the state parliament on underspending for the benefit of tribal peoples. Allocations for tribal peoples then increased from 12% of the total to 18%.

In Thailand the Assembly of the Poor brings together people affected by dam projects, land and forest conflicts, government

infrastructure projects, slum problems and exploitation by employers. The assembly has organized non-violent rallies to demand government accountability at national and local levels, with solid results. Many unacceptable government projects—such as dam construction and hazardous waste treatment projects—have been cancelled. Forest communities took part in drafting the Community Forest Bill—farmers, in drafting the Eighth Economic and Social Development Plan. The assembly also obtained compensation for workers and an agreement to establish an institute to protect worker safety and health.

In Russia a group of women in Chelyabinsk—site of one of the former Soviet Union's nuclear weapons plants—formed the Movement for Nuclear Safety to tackle horrific environmental and health disasters from 50 years of nuclear mismanagement. They used the newly open press to mount a media campaign calling national and international attention to their plight—and to the inadequate official response. They then mounted broad-based legal and developmental action.

In Honduras, when workers at a factory began to organize a union and several organizers were fired, US retailers suspended their orders from the factory in protest. That led to appointment of an independent monitor and a contract between a new union and the firm. And suspended workers returned to work.

Source: Hijab 2000; Pérez 2000.

to democracy, the move to open societies and the spread of global solidarity on human rights—all part of the globalization of the past two decades.

People are also turning more to the law—including international human rights law—to claim their economic and social rights. In many countries the courts have been a driving force in support of housing rights, for example. In a series of celebrated cases the courts of India established housing as a necessary means to the constitutionally guaranteed right to life, giving people protection from forced evictions if no alternative housing was arranged. In Nigeria the Social and Economic Rights Action Centre submitted complaints to the World Bank Inspection Panel to prevent mass evictions in Lagos that would result from the Lagos Drainage and Sanitation Project. In the Dominican Republic more than 70,000 slum dwellers were allowed to remain in their homes in defiance of a presidential decree after the United Nations Committee on Economic, Social and Cultural Rights condemned the planned eviction.

In Argentina an NGO coalition petitioned the Ministry of Health for failing to provide adequate health care and medication for people living with HIV/AIDS. It did so because the constitution establishes citizens' right to seek state protection if denied rights guaranteed by the constitution, a treaty or a national law.

More NGOs that once focused on civil and political rights are extending their activities to economic, social and cultural rights—and to defending the rights of the most deprived. And more development NGOs are adopting the strategies and principles of human rights—from protests to legal actions. These strategies need not be confrontational. In Cambodia NGOs combine human rights education and monitoring with community development activities. Opting for a strategy combining a non-confrontational approach and promotion of the culture of human rights, they emphasize traditional cultural values of Buddhism.

LINKS AMONG ECONOMIC AND SOCIAL RIGHTS—HEALTH, EDUCATION, HOUSING AND NUTRITION

Many studies have documented the causal links between food, nutrition, housing, sanitation, health care and education. For example, good health reduces requirements for food and increases its effective use for nutrition. Higher educational attainment has a similar complementary effect on nutrition.

Building capabilities in one generation is a means to securing social and economic rights in the next—and to eradicating poverty in the long term. A large body of evidence shows that higher levels of maternal education improve the nutritional status of children. Studies in South Asia show that the rate of undernutrition is as much as 20% lower among children of women who have gone no further than primary school compared with the children of illiterate mothers (box 4.4).

Higher education can also spur political action to demand more social and economic rights. In Sri Lanka scholars have pointed out that the welfare state was strengthened in response to an educated electorate after the

---

BOX 4.4

Building capabilities to secure rights for the next generation

A young baby's complete dependence on its mother and others for nutrition, care and well-being underlines the importance of a child's rights and the obligations of others to fulfil them. Human development analysis adds a scientific reinforcement to these rights, by showing how nutrition, education, health care and socialization help build the human capabilities on which a person's human development—and society's—will depend if freedom and choice are to be meaningful and poverty eradicated.

Despite these obligations to build the human foundations of life, the statistics of deprivation show shameful and widespread failures to fulfil them, even in some of the richest countries.
• Of the some 130 million children born each year, about 30 million are born with impaired growth.
• About a third of children under five in developing countries are stunted by malnutrition, with the highest rates in East Africa and South Asia.

• Even more children in developing countries remain constrained in their physical and mental growth by iron, iodine and vitamin A deficiencies.
• In developed countries children are often at special risk: in Italy, Russia, the United Kingdom and the United States one in five children lives below the poverty line.

Poverty thus has many serious long-term consequences—with early childhood deprivation carried forward from one generation to the next. Malnutrition of the baby in the womb results in low birth-weight—which in turn leads to higher rates of infant and child mortality, increased likelihood of underweight and stunting and weaker mental and social development. Recent research has shown other serious long-term effects for both women and men. Those malnourished in the womb and during the first two years suffer significantly higher rates of heart disease, diabetes and cancer later in life, even in their sixties and seventies.

Source: Bradbury and Jäntti 1999; Human Development Report Office.

Donoughmore Constitution granted universal adult suffrage in 1931. In the Indian state of Kerala higher education and political awareness made a crucial difference in health achievements, which surpassed those even in states that had higher per capita spending on health and more hospital beds per person.

The complementarities among these capabilities show how the rights to food, health care, housing and education reinforce one another.

OBLIGATIONS AND ACCOUNTABILITIES OF THE STATE—AND BEYOND

The notion of rights that people have is that they lay claims to help from others to realize those rights—help from individuals, groups, enterprises, the community and the state. Chapter 1 explains the nature of these obligations. The claims to such rights as food, housing or health care impose obligations on others. These obligations may be imperfect obligations for which the blame for a rights failure cannot be precisely apportioned among several agents. But these are nonetheless rights that all individuals and society should make the best effort to realize and secure—and for which duty bearers are accountable. Some claims take the form of immunity from interference—some the form of attention and assistance from others. For the many economic, social and cultural rights most central to poverty eradication—rights to food, education, health care, housing, work—claims to support, facilitation and promotion are particularly pressing and important.

Sometimes this has been (wrongly) assumed to mean that the state has to resort to simple handout solutions, distributing food, housing and other necessities. That clearly is not an economically sustainable approach to securing people's well-being in the long term. Instead, the right to such necessities is an entitlement to the social arrangements needed to facilitate access to them.

Take housing. The 1995 report of the Special Rapporteur on Housing Rights provides clear guidance: the state is not required to build housing for the entire population free of charge and immediately, and neither total

reliance on a free, unregulated market nor total reliance on state provision is an appropriate approach. A UN Expert Group in 1996 proposed core areas for the state in housing: providing security of tenure, preventing discrimination in housing, forbidding illegal and mass evictions, eliminating homelessness and promoting participatory processes for individuals and families in need of housing. It also recognized that in some cases direct assistance may be needed—as for victims of man-made and natural disasters and for the most vulnerable in society.

Full realization of all social and economic rights is not a goal that can be attained here and now, especially in countries with low human development and low incomes. Required instead is progressive realization through long-term social and economic progress. Mali, for example, cannot immediately reduce its under-five mortality rate of 237 per 1,000 live births to the 142 in the United Republic of Tanzania or the 19 in Sri Lanka—for a host of financial, institutional and social reasons.

But it can and must move in that direction. The obligations of duty bearers, then, are to make the best possible effort to promote progress, as rapidly as possible. Their accountability is to be judged not only by whether a right has been realized, but by whether effective policies have been designed and implemented and whether progress is being made. Ronald Dworkin makes a useful distinction between "abstract rights" and "concrete rights". In this context a person has concrete rights to the appropriate policies—not to food, housing and the like, which are abstract rights.

STATE OBLIGATIONS—TO IMPLEMENT POLICIES THAT HELP REALIZE SOCIAL AND ECONOMIC RIGHTS FOR THE MOST DEPRIVED

The state, as a primary duty bearer, has the responsibility to do its utmost to eliminate poverty by adopting and implementing appropriate policies. And the accountability of the state needs to be defined in terms of implementation of policies.

The accountability of duty bearers is to be judged by whether effective policies have been implemented and whether progress is being made

FIGURE 4.1
**Discrimination by income—
the poorest receive less in public
spending and subsidies**

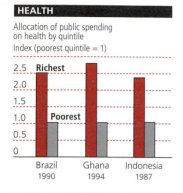

HEALTH

Allocation of public spending
on health by quintile
Index (poorest quintile = 1)

Brazil 1990 · Ghana 1994 · Indonesia 1987

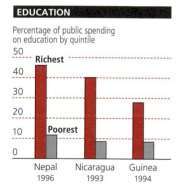

HEALTH SUBSIDY

Percentage of public subsidy
for health by quintile

Guinea 1994 · Ghana 1992 · Côte d'Ivoire 1995

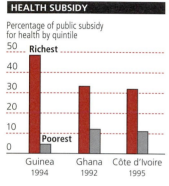

EDUCATION

Percentage of public spending
on education by quintile

Nepal 1996 · Nicaragua 1993 · Guinea 1994

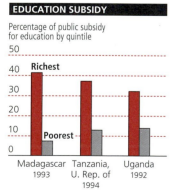

EDUCATION SUBSIDY

Percentage of public subsidy
for education by quintile

Madagascar 1993 · Tanzania, U. Rep. of 1994 · Uganda 1992

Source: Filmer, Hammer and Pritchett 1998;
Castro-Leal and others 1999; Li and others 1999.

The exact mix of policies to eradicate poverty and safeguard human rights depends on a country's circumstances at a particular point in time. Analyses by earlier *Human Development Report*s on strategies for human development, poverty eradication and pro-poor economic growth (in 1992, 1993, 1996 and 1997), along with human rights concerns, point to six elements of policy that are central to accelerating poverty eradication and realizing human rights:

1. *Pursuing pro-poor economic growth.* Low-income countries need to accelerate their growth, but the pattern should be pro-poor, to benefit those in both income and human poverty.

2. *Restructuring budgets.* To provide adequate and non-discriminatory expenditures for primary human concerns, especially basic social services, requires a review of priorities and removal of discrimination against the most deprived.

3. *Ensuring participation.* Poor people have a right to be consulted on decisions that affect their lives. This requires processes that expand political space—to give voice to poor people and their advocates, including NGOs, free media and workers associations.

4. *Protecting environmental resources and the social capital of poor communities.* The natural environment and social networks are resources poor people draw on for their livelihoods and to escape poverty.

5. *Removing discrimination*—against women, ethnic minorities, racial groups and others. Social reforms are needed to remove all forms of discrimination.

6. *Securing human rights in law.* Legislation is a critical aspect of human rights, and these legal obligations need to be reflected in economic and other policies.

Most countries have scope for adopting more pro-poor and pro-rights policies that would accelerate the eradication of poverty and the realization of rights. In many countries serious reforms of economic policy are required—to remove an anti-poor bias, despite entrenched political and economic interests. Expenditure policies may need reform to increase the allocation for priority

social spending and improve its distribution and to remove discriminatory bias against disadvantaged groups (figure 4.1; box 4.5).

STATE DUTIES—TO PUT IN PLACE A PARTICIPATORY PROCESS OF POLICY-MAKING

Many of today's social movements defending economic, social and cultural rights arise as protests against government decisions that hurt the livelihoods of poor people—displacement by dams, environmental damage from clearing forests. Often people have little information about decisions by the government or large businesses that have profound effects on their lives—about building schools, roads, water supplies and irrigation systems or about setting up businesses that would create employment or pollute the environment.

Poor people are dependent on public provisioning, natural environmental resources and employment for their livelihoods. But they are also least able to get information about important public policy and planning decisions—and least able to express their views. States thus have an obligation to put in place decision-making processes that are transparent and open to dialogue, especially with poor people and poor communities. In the commitment to holding itself accountable, the state must *accept* responsibility for its impact on people's lives, *cooperate* by providing information and hearing people's views on policy proposals and *respond* adequately to those views—as described further in chapter 5.

As UNDP's *Poverty Report 2000* points out, "holding governments accountable is a bottom-line requirement for good governance." This requires that people be organized, informed and able to claim political space. It also calls for devolution of authority to local governments and transparency in use of public funds.

Many countries are taking initiatives to facilitate participation and accountability. The Philippines National Economic Development Authority selects civil society groups to monitor government programmes. And agencies in India make public records available and hold public hearings to institutionalize cooperation.

NON-STATE ACTORS—ESPECIALLY GLOBAL ACTORS

The state can never relinquish its responsibility for adopting policies to eradicate poverty. But it is not the sole duty bearer. In a market economy and open society, socio-economic progress that leads to poverty eradication depends on actions of private agents in business and civil society— communities, families, trade unions, employers, the media, NGOs, religious groups and others. This is apparent in the rise in private investment as a share of gross domestic investment in low- and middle-income developing countries. According to World Bank data, in 1980–97 it rose from 54% to 72% in South Asia, 70% to 84% in Latin America and the Caribbean, 52% to 68% in Sub-Saharan Africa and 51% to 55% in East Asia and the Pacific.

And as global economic integration proceeds, the autonomy of the state in policy-making dwindles, constrained by multilateral agreements, by the need to maintain competitive economies in the global marketplace and, for many poor countries dependent on external financing, by agreements with creditors. Global actors—and states acting collectively in global institutions—have greater responsibilities today to help realize economic and social rights of poor people in both rich and poor countries:

• The World Trade Organization (WTO) can set global trade policies that open export opportunities and reduce import costs for poor countries.

• The international financial institutions— the International Monetary Fund, the World Bank and other multilateral banks and donors—can foster pro-poor macroeconomic policies through their lending conditions.

• Global corporations—through investment decisions with huge effects on economic growth, employment conditions and the environment— can help open opportunities for work and for developing skills for poor people. Transnational corporations and their foreign affiliates produced 25% of global output in 1998, and the top 100 (ranked by foreign assets) had sales totalling $4 trillion. Global corporations also have the potential to do great damage—by destroying livelihoods through environmental practices

that lay forests bare, deplete fishing stocks, dump hazardous materials and pollute rivers and lakes that were once a source of water and fish. They can also disempower poor people and rob them of their dignity through hazardous and inhumane working conditions. And their influence can inevitably go further—in supporting repressive regimes or, alternatively, in supporting political reforms (box 4.6).

• Global media, information and entertainment industries—with their tremendous reach in all corners of the world—can be powerful agents in either helping or detracting from poverty eradication. They shape not just information and entertainment but also new values and cultures. Needed are values that tolerate cultural diversity and respect the dignity of poor people—to reinforce solidarity with poor people and mobilize individuals, communities, employers and others to take responsibility for eradicating poverty.

• Global NGO networks—one of the major developments of the 1990s—can shape policies on global poverty issues, such as reducing the debt of poor countries. The number of global NGOs rose from 23,600 in 1991 to almost 44,000 in 1999. Under authoritarian regimes, NGOs have often been a force of political opposition. In open democracies they can be more constructive as mediators building trust between the state and the people. And in many countries they are taking over services that the state is unable or unwilling to provide.

All these actors have an ethical obligation, rooted in human rights, to do the best they can to implement policies that are pro-poor and to facilitate poor people's realization of social and economic rights. At the same time, the state has an obligation to ensure that all global actors at least respect human rights. States negotiate multilateral agreements within the framework of the WTO, and states make up the governing bodies of the Bretton Woods institutions. They must act more cooperatively in the common interest.

RESOURCES AND ECONOMIC GROWTH— MEANS TO REALIZING HUMAN RIGHTS

Economic growth is a means to human well-being—and to the expansion of human free-

doms. It is not an end in itself, with intrinsic value. The ends are realizing human rights and advancing human development.

NO AUTOMATIC LINK BETWEEN ECONOMIC RESOURCES AND HUMAN RIGHTS

Lack of economic resources is often invoked to justify lack of progress in achieving human rights. But the links between economic resources and human rights are far more complex—and by no means automatic.

1. *Measures to promote realization of human rights span the spectrum—from the cost-free to the unaffordable.* Many measures place little burden on the resources of the state or any other actor. Legislation to prohibit labour abuses or discrimination in access to housing requires modest resources. But to enforce these laws and change behaviour is more costly. To secure rights, societies need norms, institutions, a legal framework and an enabling economic environment—all of which require resources. And while it was long assumed that it was economic and social rights that required resources, it is now recognized that civil, political and cultural rights also require resources. Human rights for all need not cost a fortune, but substantial additional resources are needed to support free elementary education for all, reproductive health services for all women, reasonable salaries for judges and support for the court system sufficient to deter corruption. Many countries lack not just the financial resources to secure human rights in law—they also lack the capacity. Even so, many opportunities for action could be mobilized with greater political will.

2. *Resources do not guarantee rights.* There is a broad correlation between income and achievements in economic and social rights. But the range is enormous, and countries with similar incomes can have sharply different achievements in eliminating such basic deprivations as illiteracy and avoidable infant mortality. Consider the stark contrast between South Africa, with a per capita income of $3,310, and Viet Nam, with a per capita income of $350. Infant mortality is 60 per 1,000 live births in South Africa, 31 in Viet Nam. The

---

BOX 4.6

Human rights accountability of global corporations

Society no longer accepts the view that the conduct of global corporations is bound only by the laws of the country they operate in. By virtue of their global influence and power, they must accept responsibility and be accountable for upholding high human rights standards—respecting rights of workers, protecting the environment, refraining from supporting or condoning regimes that abuse human rights.

Global corporations can cause human rights violations indirectly by relying on repressive regimes to create secure business conditions. But they can also be agents of positive change for human rights—they have a track record of policy lobbying on economic issues.

Voluntary codes of corporate conduct have proliferated—but they tend to be weak on two fronts. First, they rarely refer to internationally agreed human rights standards. For example, most apparel industry codes refer to national standards

rather than the higher International Labour Organization standards. Second, they lack mechanisms for implementation and external monitoring and audit.

Some important initiatives go beyond self-imposed voluntary codes to develop a more coherent set of global standards. They include a civil society initiative—SA8000 of the Council for Economic Priorities, an independent certification and audit on systematically defined standards, based on ILO conventions and detailed procedures for enforcement—the European Parliament's call for a European code for global corporations and the OECD guidelines. The Secretary-General's Global Compact calls on corporations to assume leadership in the commitment to basic human rights principles.

Lest we forget: nation states have the responsibility to regulate the conduct of private agents and to ensure respect for human rights.

Source: Human Development Report Office.

---

adult literacy rate is 84.6% in South Africa, but 92.9% in Viet Nam.

Human rights abuses continue in the most prosperous countries today, not only in civil and political rights but also in economic and social rights. The booming economy in the United States has not ended homelessness, malnutrition or lack of access to health care. Gender gaps across the world in health, education, employment and political participation show a wide range of discrimination at similar levels of income.

3. *There is no automatic link between economic growth and progress in human development and human rights.* Economic growth provides important resources for achieving economic and social rights and for building basic human capabilities. But as the analysis of the relationship between economic growth and human development in *Human Development Report 1996* shows, there is no automatic link between economic growth and progress in human development. Some countries have had fast growth with little impact on improvement in human development. Others have had low growth with better performance in improving human development. Similarly, *Human Development Report 1997* shows that the impact of economic growth on poverty eradication depends not only on the rate but also on the pattern of economic growth.

Policies are needed to ensure that the pattern of growth benefits the poor and that the resources generated are invested in building human capabilities. Growth alone is not enough. It can be *ruthless,* leaving losers to abject poverty. *Jobless,* creating little employ-

ment. *Voiceless,* failing to ensure participation of people. *Futureless,* destroying the environment for future generations. And *rootless,* destroying cultural traditions and history.

4. *Tough choices need to be made in resource allocation.* Poor countries face tight resource constraints, and they have to make tough choices to establish priorities. But that does not justify neglecting resource allocations to institutions for protecting human rights. Further, many countries spend substantial resources on the wrong kind of institutions—such as intelligence services for censoring the press and suppressing political opposition and labour unions. Human rights and the legal commitments associated with them should command the highest priority, whatever the resource constraints.

TWO FALLACIES AND TWO IMPERATIVES

It is tempting to seek an economist explanation for lack of respect for human rights. But neither the level nor the growth of per capita income determines the level of achievement in human rights. With the same income, different outcomes are possible across the range of economic, social and cultural rights—but also the civil and political.

It is also tempting to neglect the importance of resources for the full realization of rights. Economic resources and economic growth are important means. Although there is scope for taking measures that have modest costs and for restructuring budgets, additional resources are also needed. And the lack of economic growth in poor countries has been an

FIGURE 4.2
Slow growth in incomes

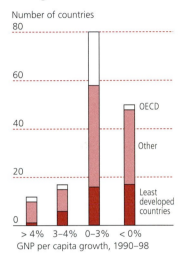

Number of countries

GNP per capita growth, 1990–98

Source: World Bank 2000b.

TABLE 4.1
Countries by average annual growth in GNP per capita, 1990–98

GNP per capita growth rate	Total number of countries	OECD	Least developed countries	Low human development countries	Low-income countries	Arab States	East Asia	Eastern Europe and the CIS	Latin America and the Caribbean	South Asia	South-East Asia and the Pacific	Sub-Saharan Africa
> 4%	12	2	1	0	2	1	2	0	4	0	2	1
3–4%	17	2	6	5	6	1	0	1	4	4	3	3
0–3%	80	22	16	15	22	6	1	1	21	4	5	20
< 0%	50	2	17	13	25	4	1	18	3	0	4	19
Total	159	28	40	33	55	12	4	20	32	8	14	43

Note: Rows do not sum to totals because some countries fall in more than one category. Not all countries in all categories are included in the table because of lack of data.
Source: Indicator table 13.

enormous obstacle to the realization of all rights. A review of 159 countries for which GNP per capita growth data are available for the period 1990–98 shows that of the 33 low human development countries with data, only 5 achieved average annual per capita growth of more than 3%. For 13 of them, per capita growth was in fact negative (table 4.1; figure 4.2).

That is why accelerating economic growth in poor countries is essential to progress in securing all rights for all people. But as we have seen, growth is not enough. Policies are needed to link growth and rights. The allocation of resources and the pattern of economic growth must be pro-poor, pro-human development and pro-human rights. Resources generated by growth need to go to poverty eradication, human development and securing human rights. And as noted, implementing such policies and achieving growth depend not only on the actions of the state but on an international enabling environment.

GLOBAL JUSTICE—OBLIGATIONS AND RESPONSIBILITIES OF STATE AND NON-STATE ACTORS TO DESIGN A PRO-POOR GLOBAL ORDER

As the world becomes increasingly interdependent, both states—in their policies that affect other states—and other global actors have greater obligations to create a better enabling environment for the realization of economic and social rights. Increasingly, people's lives are threatened by "global bads" over which no single nation can have control—surges of financial volatility, global climate change, global crime. Decisions of states—whether on interest rates or arms sales—have significant consequences for the lives of people outside national boundaries. Despite mutual self-interest as well as ethical obligations to design pro-poor global economic and social policies, little binds or encourages national governments, corporations, the media and other global actors to do so under current arrangements for global governance. Today's marginalization of poor countries from global trade and investment surely reflects the failure of global policies (box 4.7).

If global poverty eradication is both a moral obligation and a global public good, why is not enough of it being provided? Because of an incentives gap, a jurisdictional gap and a participation gap—the sources of many public goods failures, according to a recent UNDP study, *Global Public Goods*.

THE INCENTIVES GAP

As governments negotiate global policies, they are charged primarily with pursuing national

---

BOX 4.7

Marginalization of poor countries from the bounty of the world economy

Global economic integration is creating opportunities for people around the world, but there is wide divergence among countries in expanding trade, attracting investment and using new technologies. Many of the poorest countries are marginalized from these growing global opportunities. The income gaps between the poorest and richest countries are widening.

Trade. World exports of goods and services expanded rapidly between 1990 and 1998, from $4.7 trillion to $7.5 trillion (constant 1995 prices). And 25 countries had export growth averaging more than 10% a year (including Bangladesh, Mexico, Mozambique, Turkey and Viet Nam), but exports declined in Cameroon, Jamaica and Ukraine. In 1998 least developed countries, with 10% of the world population, accounted for only 0.4% of global exports, down from 0.6% in 1980 and 0.5% in 1990. Sub-Saharan Africa's share declined to 1.4%, down from 2.3% in 1980 and 1.6% in 1990 (see figure 4.3). Although average tariffs are higher in developing than in developed countries, many poor nations still face tariff peaks and tariff escalation in such key sectors as agriculture, footwear and leather goods.

Foreign direct investment. Foreign direct investment flows have boomed, reaching more than $600 billion in 1998. But these flows are highly concentrated, with just 20 countries receiving 83% of the $177 billion going to developing and transition economies, mainly China, Brazil, Mexico and Singapore. The 48 least developed countries attracted less than $3 billion in 1998, a mere 0.4% of the total.

Communications and information technology. The global online community has grown rapidly—from about 16 million Internet users in 1995 to an estimated 304 million users in March 2000. But access to the Internet varies between regions. In 1998 more than 26% of all people living in the United States were surfing the Internet, compared with 0.8% of all people in Latin America and the Caribbean, 0.1% in Sub-Saharan Africa and 0.04% in South Asia.

Income inequalities. Among 159 countries with available data, 50 had negative average annual growth in GNP per capita in 1990–98, and only four Sub-Saharan countries and seven least developed countries had growth rates above 3%, the minimum rate for doubling incomes in a generation (see figure 4.2; table 4.1).

A recent World Bank study by Milanovic examines world income distribution using household survey data for the first time—from 91 countries. It shows a sharp rise in world income inequality between 1988 and 1993—from a Gini coefficient of 0.63 to 0.66 (a value of 0 indicates perfect equality, a value of 1.0 perfect inequality). The increase was driven more by rising differences in mean incomes between countries than by rising inequalities within countries.

The super-rich. Meanwhile, the super-rich get richer. The combined wealth of the top 200 billionaires hit $1,135 billion in 1999, up from $1,042 billion in 1998. Compare that with the combined incomes of $146 billion for the 582 million people in all the least developed countries.

Source: Milanovic 1999; UNCTAD 1999b; UNDP 1999b; World Bank 1999b; *Forbes Magazine* 2000; NUA 2000.

---

interests, not the collective global interest, so they fail to produce pro-poor policies (box 4.8). After the Uruguay Round, it was estimated that the new trade agreements would lead to an increase in global income of some $212–510 billion, but a net loss of $600 million a year for the least developed countries, and $1.2 billion a year for Sub-Saharan Africa. A recent UNCTAD study estimates that more favourable conditions of market access for major export items of developing countries, such as textiles, clothing and leather products, could offer the potential for $700 billion in additional exports by 2005 for these countries, four times the average annual private capital inflows in the 1990s. Global market integration is proceeding apace, but the benefits are accruing to the more dynamic and powerful countries of both the North and the South (figure 4.3). Smaller, low-income countries share little in these global gains, and many are marginalized from the competitive global economy.

Global technology could have a huge impact on poverty eradication—by giving poor people access to seeds for high-yielding food crops or to life-saving medicines. Yet the 1994 agreement on Trade-Related Aspects of Intellectual Property Rights—TRIPS—tightens patent and copyright protection, favouring

those who develop and market technology rather than society's interest in liberal diffusion of new technology. The agreement has raised concerns about the consequences for protecting the traditional and collective knowledge of indigenous peoples and for public health (box 4.9).

And although promoting poverty reduction may be in the collective interest of corporations, there is no individual corporate interest. Strategies that target corporate reputations, such as media campaigns exposing human rights violations, and those that target corporate profit, such as consumer boycotts and labelling schemes, can help fill the incentives gap. These strategies help shape social norms and create profit motives to promote realization of human rights.

THE JURISDICTIONAL GAP

Human rights obligations are codified in international human rights treaties. Most of these conventions have been ratified by the majority of the world's states, but the enforcement mechanisms remain weak. Treaty bodies merely recommend actions by states parties without any enforcement measures. Part of the problem is that international human rights laws apply only to states, to corporations as

FIGURE 4.3
Rapid export growth, shifting shares

Total exports (US$ trillions)

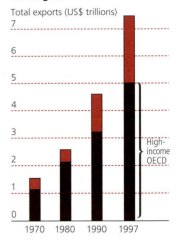

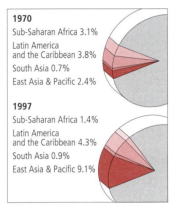

1970
Sub-Saharan Africa 3.1%
Latin America and the Caribbean 3.8%
South Asia 0.7%
East Asia & Pacific 2.4%

1997
Sub-Saharan Africa 1.4%
Latin America and the Caribbean 4.3%
South Asia 0.9%
East Asia & Pacific 9.1%

Note: Regional classifications are those used in World Bank 2000b.
Source: World Bank 2000b.

BOX 4.8

Global justice—reconciling conflicting values of impartiality and self-interest

Human rights express the bold idea that all persons have claims that human affairs be arranged so as to secure them from the worst abuses and deprivations—and to ensure the freedoms necessary for a life of dignity.

The challenge of changing norms to promote human rights is among the oldest. We are inescapably drawn to viewing the world in two ways:
- Each of us can recognize that we are but one among many—and that our well-being and that of those close to us is of no greater intrinsic importance than the well-being of others. This draws us to view the world impartially, granting equal worth to all people and showing equal concern for abuses and deprivations, regardless of who suffers them.
- We also view the world from within the web of our own interests, identifications and commitments. This is to some extent unobjectionable: each of us has a life to live, and it is often families, friends, causes and commitments that give us a reason to go on living.

While compatible, these perspectives have tension between them. This tension is often reflected in metaphors—such as the level playing field—used to reconcile the perspectives by insisting that individual and

collective interests must be pursued within fair social arrangements.

Development studies have long emphasized the importance of constraining individual and collective self-concern. Poor governance and corruption—often rooted in the excessive self-concern of public officials—are now seen as significant obstacles to development. But excessive partiality also exists at the international level, where it is often openly supported rather than condemned.

Many people—in developed and developing countries alike—view a predominant concern for preserving and enlarging their own collective advantage as legitimate and even praiseworthy. But if we condemn those who seek to turn domestic policies to their advantage, how can we applaud those who do much the same thing at the international level, pursuing almost exclusively their compatriots' interests in international negotiations and in constructing laws and institutions?

Among the most important challenges of the 21st century will be to design and reform international institutions to reflect shared moral values, not bargains between conflicting national interests.

Source: Nagel 1991; Pogge 1993; Human Development Report Office.

---

well. Furthermore, they focus on states' domestic efforts, not international impacts. And in many states national laws do not reflect standards of international human rights conventions. No wonder that pressures are mounting to link human rights to trade so that the stronger enforcement mechanisms of trade rules can be applied. But such an approach could distort the effect of what might be well-intentioned laws. Trade sanctions are a blunt instrument, penalizing the country as a whole, not just those responsible for rights violations. It may be the workers who end up losing their jobs, and the people of the country who suffer the consequences of economic decline. Moreover, sanctions do not attack the root causes of rights violations. Child labour, for example, is rooted in poverty, which trade sanctions could worsen (box 4.10).

More attention needs to be paid to the potential impact of international economic agreements on the realization of economic and social rights. In WTO negotiations, government delegations should ask three questions:
- What are the potential benefits of the legislation on growth and equity?
- What are the safeguards against negative impacts on human rights?

BOX 4.9

Building human rights safeguards into the TRIPS agreement

Intellectual property rights manage two conflicting social concerns. One is protecting the rights of creators of technology by restricting conditions of diffusion for commercial use. The other is permitting open access to and sharing of scientific progress.

The agreement on Trade-Related Aspects of Intellectual Property Rights, or TRIPS, is one of the pillars of the Uruguay Round agreements, and also one of the most contentious. It tightens intellectual property rights protection for the creator. It introduces an enforceable global standard by linking intellectual property rights with trade, making them binding and enforceable through the World Trade Organization processes.

Are society's interests—the rights to health and the rights of indigenous peoples—adequately protected?
- *Access to health care.* Provisions restrain many public policies that promote wider access to health care. National laws of many developing countries have intentionally excluded pharmaceuticals from product patent protection (allowing only process patents) to promote local manufacturing capacity for generic drugs and to make drugs available at lower prices. The move from process to product patents introduced under the TRIPS agreement dramatically reduces the possibilities for local companies to produce cheaper versions of important life-saving drugs, such as those for cancer and HIV/AIDS. Local production in India had kept prices at a fraction of the levels in neighbouring countries. For example, in 1998 the anti-AIDS drug flucanazole cost $55 in India for 100 tablets (150 milligrams) but $697 in Malaysia, $703 in Indonesia and $817 in the Philippines.
- *Traditional knowledge and resource rights of indigenous peoples.* Biotechnology for plant breeding and pharmaceuticals has given enormous economic value to genetic materials, plant varieties and other biological resources. Life forms—plants and animals—have traditionally been excluded from patents. But the TRIPS agreement requires all WTO member countries to permit patents on micro-organisms and microbiological and non-biological processes. So "bioprospecting" has mushroomed—with scientists "reinventing" and patenting products and processes using traditional knowledge that communities have held for centuries. Patents have been awarded for using the healing properties of turmeric, for the pesticide properties of the neem tree and other plant properties—all part of traditional knowledge. In a number of such cases the patents were challenged and reversed.

The TRIPS agreement benefits technologically advanced countries. It is estimated that industrialized countries hold 97% of all patents, and global corporations 90% of all technology and product patents. Developing countries have little to gain from the stronger patent protection from the TRIPS agreement because they have little research and development capacity. Research and development for a new drug is estimated to cost around $150–200 million, but no developing country has a pharmaceutical sales volume of even $400 million. There is little evidence so far that patent protection has stimulated research and development in or for poor countries or that it offers the potential to do so.

There are also questions about the compatibility of the TRIPS agreement with human rights law and environmental agreements. The Universal Declaration of Human Rights, the International Covenant on Economic, Social and Cultural Rights and the International Covenant on Civil and Political Rights recognize the human right to share in scientific progress. The Convention on Biodiversity requires states to protect and promote the rights of communities, farmers and indigenous peoples in their use of biological resources and knowledge systems. It also requires equitable sharing of the benefits arising from the commercial use of communities' biological resources and local knowledge.

Stronger human rights safeguards can be built into the TRIPS agreement and its implementation. The African Group of WTO Members has proposed a review of the agreement, particularly for provisions to protect indigenous knowledge. And India has suggested amendments to promote transfer of environmentally sound technology.

Stronger national policies are needed to protect society's interests within the realities of the new global regime. Compulsory licensing and parallel imports, provided for under the TRIPS agreement, can make essential medicines more affordable. They should be built into national legislation, as Argentina, India, South Africa and Thailand have done. Indigenous knowledge can be protected by such means as national gene banks and regulation of exports of germ plasm, as India is doing.

Source: Correa 1999; WHO 1999e; Dutfield 2000; Ghosh 2000.

- Is the agreement consistent with obligations under international human rights law?

The same questions should be asked by the WTO dispute settlement body. And there is a need for serious review of the compatibility and consistency between provisions of WTO agreements and international human rights laws, including the human rights provisions of multilateral environmental agreements (box 4.11; table 4.2).

THE PARTICIPATION GAP

Just as inclusive democracy is needed to ensure minority participation at the national level (chapter 3), inclusive global democracy is needed in which all countries—small and weak as well as large and powerful—have a voice in decisions. Participation is needed as a matter of right, and to create a global economy with fair and just rules. Global economic policy-making occurs in a world of grossly unequal economic and political power. The playing field is not level when the "teams" have vastly different resources, expertise and negotiating power. Poor and small countries can ill afford the high costs of participating in the WTO, for example. Fourteen of them have either a one-person delegation in Geneva or none at all. They lack access to well-researched legal and economic policy advice. And they cannot afford top legal representation in dispute settlements.

The community of states has an obligation to put in place procedures for greater participation and transparency in global decision-making. The WTO, for example, has been heavily criticized for its non-transparent and non-participatory decision-making, depending more on informal consensus than formal procedures. A major review of decision-making in international bodies should focus on two issues. One is the participation of small and weak countries in the processes of negotiation and dispute settlement. The second is the participation of civil society—including corporations, trade unions and global networks of NGOs—in a forum for open debate rather than in behind-the-scenes lobbying and on-the-street demonstrations.

HUMAN RIGHTS TO EMPOWER POOR PEOPLE IN THEIR FIGHT AGAINST POVERTY

History shows that even without the full set of civil and political rights, rapid progress is possible in economic, social and cultural rights. But withholding civil and political rights in no way helps achieve these rapid advances. Quite the reverse, for civil and political rights empower poor people to claim their economic and social rights—to food, to housing, to education, to

---

BOX 4.10

The social clause—no panacea for workers' rights

The good news of increased flows of North-South trade and investments has also raised concerns. Some workers in the North fear a race to the bottom, with production relocating in search of cheap labour. Consumers have begun to worry about the conditions in which the goods they buy are being produced. But as the pressure to include a social clause in multilateral trade agreements has mounted, strong opposition has built from governments of developing countries and many civil society groups, which see such a clause as a thinly veiled protectionist measure. Governments of developed countries have varied and nuanced positions.

A social clause is far from likely to be a panacea for protecting labour rights in the North or the South. The issues are complex, and the impacts uncertain.
- Economic analysis and evidence of the links between trade and labour standards are inconclusive.
- Trade sanctions could be counterproductive, hurting rather than helping workers in poor countries. Sanctions and other penalties would further constrain these countries' access to global markets.
- Social clauses apply only to export sectors. These sectors provide only a fraction of employment in most countries—for example, less than 5% of child labour is employed in export industries. And they are not always where the worst violations occur.
- Sanctions would not help attack poverty, a root cause of many workers' rights issues, such as families sending children out to work.
- A social clause can be a powerful instrument for a large, rich country but not for a small, poor one. Trade penalties can have a much more devastating effect on a small country exporting only a few commodities, because the dispute settlement process is extremely costly, requiring international legal expertise. And poor countries are unlikely to take a large country on for fear of consequences in areas beyond trade, such as aid, debt relief and export credits.

Ultimately, what is needed to improve workers' rights in developing countries are investments and economic growth that create jobs, stronger national laws and their implementation, and adoption of higher standards by the domestic private sector and foreign corporate investors. Sanctions or even threats of a social clause may turn government policies around. But workers' rights depend on the behaviour of individual employers—from a multinational corporation such as Nike or Rio Tinto to a family with domestic servants—and that depends on the enforcement of laws.

What are some alternatives to trade sanctions?
- Measures to give teeth to the enforcement of core labour standards of the International Labour Organization.
- Programmes involving employers and governments to improve workers' rights. The ILO programmes against child labour, which build on successful initiatives that provide education in Bangladesh and Pakistan, are an example.
- Initiatives to tighten the accountability of corporations, including corporate codes of conduct that respect core labour standards, with independent monitoring and implementation.
- Consumer action such as labelling and boycotts to create market incentives for higher labour standards.

Source: Belser 1999; Khor 1999; Panayotou 1999; Ghosh 2000; Rodas-Martini 2000.

---

health care, to decent work and to social security. These rights empower them to demand accountability—for good public services, for pro-poor public policies, for a transparent participatory process open to hearing their views. This propels dynamic public policy for equitable development and accelerated human development.

Moreover, neglect of economic and social rights can undermine civil and political liberties, reversing recent progress. Economic stagnation, high unemployment, scant economic opportunities for urban youth, growing gaps between rich and poor, inflows of the international Mafia—all are sources of enormous strain on fragile transition democracies, in many parts of Africa, Latin America, Eastern Europe and the former Soviet Union.

Consider the fear and insecurity in the streets, felt across the globe from Bogotá to Nairobi, from Moscow to Manila. Economic and social policies that increase inequalities, particularly in the context of economic stagnation and unemployment, often lead to crime and put pressure on the judicial system. The ensuing failures in the administration of justice lead to quasilegal investigative methods, violations of constitutional guarantees and the use of coercive powers by the police. Communities end up facing a false dichotomy—a supposed choice between respecting human rights and fighting crime. That sets in motion a downward spiral pitting communities, especially poor communities, against the police and judiciary.

In sum: progress towards a democratic society that respects human rights will be consolidated if laws and institutions to protect civil and political rights are accompanied by investments in accelerating human development and poverty eradication. Economic revival and an equitable distribution of the

---

BOX 4.11

International trade, human rights and environmental agreements

The international system for governing trade, human rights and environmental issues reveals a patchwork of different legal regimes that have evolved separately (table 4.2). The scope for conflict between these regimes has been thrown into sharpest relief in the heated debates about potential incompatibility between World Trade Organization rules and multilateral environmental agreements.

Multilateral trade agreements and multilateral environmental agreements

There is widespread concern among environmental and human rights activists that the WTO dispute settlement system might deal with trade and environmental issues as purely trade matters, rather than as environmental issues with broader public interests. That is similar to what is perceived to have happened in the beef growth hormones case brought by Canada and the United States against the European Union at the WTO. In this case, arguably about food safety and human health concerns, the WTO ruled in favour of the complainants, treating the case as a market access issue.

Twenty of the some 200 multilateral environmental agreements in existence contain some form of trade measure. Although no complaint has arisen at the WTO about these trade measures, both trade and environmental analysts recognize the potential for conflict, particularly with regard to such agreements as the Kyoto Protocol and the Convention on Biological Diversity. With the uncertainty about whether trade or environmental rules will prevail, many have called for clarity rather than waiting for a WTO dispute to settle the matter irrevocably. Among the options proposed are an agreement not to bring any trade cases relating to multilateral environmental agreements before the WTO dispute settlement body, and an agreement that in the event of a conflict environmental provisions will take precedence over WTO rules.

The recently concluded Biosafety Protocol negotiations in Montreal (January 2000) represent a major step forward in developing a more consistent approach. The protocol, which will govern movement and trade of living modified organisms, contains the most sophisticated elaboration yet of the precautionary principle, which suggests that in the face of a scientific uncertainty and potentially great environmental harm, policy-makers should skew their actions so that errors of too much protection are more likely than errors of too little. The protocol also states that its provisions will not be subordinated to any other international agreements, although some ambiguity remains. Most significant, it provides an operational framework for the WTO dispute process to interpret the precautionary principle as it applies to trade.

Need for consistency in international legal regimes and norms and standards

Globalization has made it vital to work towards a harmonious set of international legal regimes, norms and standards on trade, human rights and the environment. If trade is recognized as a means to enhancing human well-being, commercial interests must not override protection of fundamental human rights and freedoms. The legal regime for trade, embodied by such organizations as the WTO, will have to develop in tune with its social and environmental counterparts. The evolving relationship between the WTO and multilateral environmental agreements is beginning to show the way—especially through joint interpretive agreements—to a more coordinated system.

The human rights community has remained untouched by these discussions, but soon it too will face potential conflicts with trade agreements (such as forced labour). It must not be caught napping.

Source: Mehra 1999.

---

economic gains are a vital companion to constitutional advance.

Four challenges that public policy must recognize:

• Equitable economic and social policies have direct connections to sustaining civil and political liberties. One policy priority all countries can consider deserves priority attention—meeting the 20:20 compact target of increasing expenditures for human priorities, including primary health and education, by restructuring national and aid budgets or protecting them in balancing budgets.

• Civil and political liberties empower poor people—advancing social and economic progress, reducing economic and social poverty and inequality. Promoting the work of civil society organizations—including NGOs, workers organizations and the free media—will help vibrant societies

TABLE 4.2

Comparing and contrasting three sets of international laws

	Trade	Human rights	Environment
Applicability and jurisdiction	Agreements applicable to contracting parties (for GATT/WTO agreements, WTO member states)	Agreements applicable only to countries that have ratified them (ICESCR, ICCPR, CEDAW, CAT, CRC), except for Universal Declaration of Human Rights, which is regarded as international customary law and the embodiment of human rights norms and standards	Agreements applicable only to countries that have ratified them (Montreal Protocol, Basel Convention, Kyoto Protocol, Convention on Biodiversity). The Rio Declaration and Agenda 21 of the United Nations Conference on Environment and Development are non-binding but expressions of internationally accepted environmental norms and standards
Principles	Centred on states	Centred on states and individuals	Centred on states, individuals and communities
	Most favoured nation (non-discrimination between trading nations)	Primacy of human rights	Precautionary principle
		Non-retrogression (states cannot remove, weaken or withdraw from human rights obligations or policies in fulfilment thereof)	Polluter-pays principle
	Non-discrimination between goods considered "like products" on the basis of their process or production methods		Common but differentiated responsibilities of states
		Right to an effective remedy in an appropriate forum	Responsibility to future generations
		Right of participation of affected individuals and groups	
		Positive discrimination/affirmative action	
Enforcement and monitoring bodies	Legally binding, with trade sanctions and monetary fines (compensation) as potential penalties	Legally binding where adopted under national laws or, in the case of the European Union, regional laws	Mix of legally binding (Kyoto and Montreal Protocols) and non-binding (Agenda 21)
			Enforcement mechanisms weak or non-existent at international level
		Monitoring mechanisms for the UN Charter and treaty-based agreements	Trade bans on such products as hazardous chemicals and endangered species permitted under Convention on Trade in Endangered Species, Basel Convention and Montreal Protocol
			Treaty secretariats act as ad hoc monitoring bodies but with no clear mandate
Conflict resolution	Dispute settlement mechanism for WTO conflicts	None	None

Source: Mehra 2000.

secure human rights. Lifting archaic regulations that restrict activities of NGOs and censor the media is a priority.

- The human rights obligations of public institutions—and other important actors—are to implement pro-poor policies and policy-making processes that guarantee the right to participation by the poor.

- The human rights obligations of global actors—state and non-state—are to put in place global institutional and legal arrangements that promote the eradication of poverty.

Societies across the globe are becoming more open and more plural. The move to democracy and the emergence of NGOs were the key developments of the 1990s. Building on the mutually reinforcing rights—to free expression, assembly, participation, food, housing, health care and many others—is essential in empowering poor people to lift themselves from poverty.

CHAPTER 5

Using indicators for human rights accountability

Statistical indicators are a powerful tool in the struggle for human rights. They make it possible for people and organizations—from grassroots activists and civil society to governments and the United Nations—to identify important actors and hold them accountable for their actions. That is why developing and using indicators for human rights has become a cutting-edge area of advocacy. Working together, governments, activists, lawyers, statisticians and development specialists are breaking ground in using statistics to push for change—in perceptions, policies and practices. Indicators can be used as a tool for:

• Making better policies and monitoring progress.

• Identifying unintended impacts of laws, policies and practices.

• Identifying which actors are having an impact on the realization of rights.

• Revealing whether the obligations of these actors are being met.

• Giving early warning of potential violations, prompting preventive action.

• Enhancing social consensus on difficult trade-offs to be made in the face of resource constraints.

• Exposing issues that had been neglected or silenced.

BUILDING ACCOUNTABILITY

Over the past two decades growing demands for influential actors to acknowledge their accountability in all spheres of public life have led to the creation of new procedures. Through many routes, formal accountability is being created: for actors to *accept* responsibility for the impacts of their action and inaction on human rights, to *cooperate* by providing information

and entering into dialogue and to *respond* adequately to claims made.

Nationally, accountability procedures have been greatly strengthened in many countries through the constitutional recognition of human rights and the establishment of national human rights institutions and related arrangements such as ombudsman offices and antidiscrimination commissioners. And internationally, states have increasingly been held to account under both UN and regional mechanisms, on the basis of treaties ratified by countries and of generally applicable special procedures—such as special rapporteurs—under the UN Charter.

But accountability is not exacted only through such formal mechanisms. A diverse range of techniques is gradually coming together to ensure greatly increased acknowledgement of accountability from other actors, including corporations, NGOs and such multilateral actors as the World Bank, the World Trade Organization, the International Monetary Fund and the agencies of the United Nations.

As procedures of accountability are developed, they create important opportunities to collect information. By ratifying the human rights treaties, states make a commitment to submit reports on how much the rights addressed in each treaty are being realized in their country. For all six major treaties, NGOs are invited to submit alternative reports, giving them a valuable opportunity to present data supplementing the perspectives of official reports. When corporations sign on to codes of conduct and admit independent monitors onto their premises, they create a unique opportunity to collect detailed data on their practices.

Beyond the procedures of accountability, human rights are increasingly being used as criteria for designing and evaluating policy, creat-

Developing and using indicators for human rights has become a cutting-edge area of advocacy

ing a growing demand for indicators. Some governments—such as that of South Africa—have brought human rights to the centre of their national policy strategies and require tools to direct and assess the impact of their policies. Similarly, some donor countries—such as Australia and Norway—are using human rights as criteria for development assistance and need to assess their impact. And international organizations are declaring commitments to specific goals—such as the commitments arising from the UN conferences of the 1990s. If these are to be met, information is needed on progress towards their realization—and on whether those committed are doing enough to ensure progress.

WHY STATISTICS?

Rights can never be fully measured merely in statistics: the issues go far beyond what can be captured in numbers (box 5.1). But this is true of all uses of statistics. Nevertheless, as a tool for analysis, statistics can open the questions behind the generalities and help reveal the broader social challenges.

Data collection and analysis is a time-consuming process, demanding attention to detail and accuracy—making it seem academic and removed from the front line of advocacy. But when data are carefully collected, analysed and interpreted, when the findings are released and turned into messages, they become an important means for promoting human rights. And in an information age of networking and lobbying, creating and disseminating accurate information is a fast way of drawing widespread attention to an issue.

The task of assessing rights is not confined to expert opinion and international discussion. The rise of civil society has extended the possibilities of analysis, especially at local levels, and civil society organizations are often at the frontier of generating new approaches. In the absence of data, rankings and ratings of human rights performance by legal and political experts have sometimes been used instead—but often creating dispute rather than opening a dialogue between those advocating change and those being assessed (box 5.2). Today information is demanded that empowers people with facts, not opinion.

Now, as the fields of human rights and human development draw closer together, the quantitative techniques of statistics are getting greater attention. This brings a new level of professionalism and credibility to the information collected—and shows that many of the earlier qualitative ratings can be replaced by more detailed quantitative data that can stand up to scrutiny and break down barriers of disbelief.

CREATING INDICATORS: FROM DEVELOPMENT TO RIGHTS

Statistical indicators have been used in development for many years, for advocacy and for focusing policy. The earlier preoccupation with economic indicators has been considerably broadened since the launch of the *Human Development Report*s in 1990. These Reports have presented composite indices—the HDI,

---

BOX 5.1

Handle with care

Statistics come with strings attached. They provide great power for clarity, but also for distortion. When based on careful research and method, indicators help establish strong evidence, open dialogue and increase accountability. But they need to be:

• *Policy relevant*—giving messages on issues that can be influenced, directly or indirectly, by policy action.
• *Reliable*—enabling different people to use them and get consistent results.
• *Valid*—based on identifiable criteria that measure what they are intended to measure.
• *Consistently measurable over time*—necessary if they are to show whether progress is being made and targets are being achieved.
• *Possible to disaggregate*—for focusing on social groups, minorities and individuals.
• *Designed to separate the monitor and the monitored where possible*—minimizing the conflicts of interest that arise when an actor monitors its own performance.

Getting the facts straight is serious when rights are at risk. The powerful impact of statistics creates four caveats in their use:
• *Overuse*—Statistics alone cannot capture the full picture of rights and should not be the only focus of assessment. All statistical analysis needs to be embedded in an interpretation drawing on broader political, social and contextual analysis.
• *Underuse*—Data are rarely voluntarily collected on issues that are incriminating, embarrassing or simply ignored. One European social worker in the 1980s, complaining about the lack of data on homeless people, remarked, "Everything else is counted—every cow and chicken and piece of butter." Even when data are collected, they may not be made public for many years—and then there may be political pressure on the media not to publicize the findings.
• *Misuse*—Data collection is often biased towards institutions and formalized reporting, towards events that occur, not events prevented or suppressed. But lack of data does not always mean fewer occurrences. Structural repression is invisible when fear prevents people from protesting, registering complaints or speaking out.
• *Political abuse*—Indicators can be manipulated for political purposes to discredit certain countries or actors. And using them as criteria for trade or aid relationships would create new incentives to manipulate reporting.

Source: Human Development Report Office; Jabine and Claude 1992; Spirer 2000.

HPI, GDI and GEM—that have captured policy-makers' attention and created debates on strategies for human development.

Human development indicators and human rights indicators have three common features. They both share the goal of producing information that will give policy signals on how to better realize human freedoms—such as freedom from want, freedom from fear and freedom from discrimination. They both rely on measures of outcomes and inputs to tell the story—not only literacy and infant mortality rates, but also teacher-pupil ratios and immunization rates. And they both use measures of averages and disaggregations, the global and the local, to reveal information at many different levels. But there are three important contrasts in approach:

• *Conceptual foundations.* Human development indicators assess the expansion of people's capabilities. Human rights indicators assess whether people are living with dignity and freedom—and also the extent to which critical actors have fulfilled their obligations to create and uphold just social arrangements to ensure this.

• *Focus of attention.* Human development indicators focus primarily on human outcomes and inputs, drawing attention to unacceptable disparities and suffering. Human rights indicators also focus on these human outcomes but bring additional attention to the policies and practices of legal and administrative entities and the conduct of public officials.

• *Additional information.* A human rights assessment needs additional data—not only on violations, such as torture and disappearances, but also on the processes of justice, such as data on judicial institutions and legal frameworks and opinion poll data on social norms. Further, there is even greater emphasis on data that are disaggregated—by gender, ethnicity, race, religion, nationality, birth, social origin and other relevant distinctions.

The human development indices have long revealed that economic and social rights are far from being realized for millions of people. The human poverty index focuses on deprivations in the most basic of economic and social necessities: leading a long and healthy life, being knowledgeable, having the resources for a decent standard of living and being included in social and community life.

Adjusted to the different contexts of developing and industrialized countries, the components of the HPI reveal not only the extent of human deprivation worldwide, but also that deprivation exists in every country, no matter its level of development (see What do the human development indices reveal?). By creating summary measures of deprivation, the human development indices play a vital role in drawing attention to the gross deprivations of so many people in the world and have provided important advocacy tools for promoting human rights.

Yet to capture the additional features of human rights—and to create policy and advocacy tools—indicators are needed that can help create a culture of accountability. Building such a culture means exploring the impact that different actors have on the realization of rights—and assessing whether or not they are meeting their obligations to address them. For the state, these obligations are set out in inter-

---

BOX 5.2

The freedom indices: were they tools for the times?

The human development index, launched in *Human Development Report 1990,* drew instant attention to how well countries were doing in achieving social and economic outcomes. But many asked why it missed out on political and civil freedoms, also inherent in the concept of human development. To balance the focus, the next two Reports proposed to complement the HDI with indices of civil and political freedoms.

Human Development Report 1991 introduced the human freedom index, derived from 40 criteria rated in Professor Charles Humana's *World Human Rights Guide.* Following a critical review and debate of this source and method, *Human Development Report 1992* launched the political freedom index, which focused on five freedoms and drew on the judgements of a range of experts, scoring each country from 1 to 10. Why has neither of these indices been continued?

• The human freedom index and the political freedom index were based on qualitative judgements, not quantifiable empirical data.

• Both indices were aimed at analysing complex issues with summary answers—either yes or no or a rating of 1–10. But because no data and examples were provided, the indices did not empower readers to understand the judgements.

• The HDI shows clearly where change is needed through data on its components. But neither the human freedom index nor the political freedom index could reveal why a country scored yes rather than no, or 4 rather than 5. So, the assessments could not be translated into policy advocacy.

Assessing human freedoms is inevitably contentious—all the more reason to make the method transparent and repeatable by others, to channel differences of opinion into debate rather than inflaming dispute. The lessons learned from the freedom indices must be a clear guide in creating indicators of human rights.

Source: Humana 1992; Human Development Report Office.

national law, which provides a framework for developing indicators of legal accountability. But the need to take into account the complex impacts of other actors—locally and globally—calls for developing indicators that extend beyond current legal obligations.

A wide array of information is needed for exploring rights through statistics, reaching, like a pyramid, from summary aggregate measures—such as the human development indices and national average outcomes—to detailed data specific to a particular context. Raising national life expectancy or average calorie consumption is an important step towards realizing rights—but at the same time, far greater detail and disaggregation of data are needed to show whether the rights of all people are being realized. Using statistics to go

deeper into the issues can help reveal the disparities behind average outcomes and help focus attention on what needs to be done to address the situation (box 5.3).

Many actors are contributing to creating these pyramids of data. The Office of the High Commissioner for Human Rights is encouraging efforts to devise globally relevant indicators. The human rights treaty bodies have produced guidelines for statistical information that states parties should provide in their reports to show how they are respecting, protecting and fulfilling rights. Some corporations are making more data available on their practices and impacts—although there is still great resistance to such transparency. And civil society organizations—from grass-roots advocacy groups to research institutes—are collecting and analysing locally specific data to understand the obstacles in the context of their own countries, municipalities and communities.

Despite many similarities, human rights and human development indicators have different emphases—making it clear that a high human development ranking is not a guarantee of a faultless human rights record. Realizing rights goes far beyond average national performance—and the highest human development performers are as accountable as the rest for their commitments to rights (box 5.4).

Indicators for human rights need to be explored for four interlocking objectives:
- *Asking whether states respect, protect and fulfil rights*—the overriding framework of accountability for the role of the state.
- *Ensuring that key principles of rights are met*—asking whether rights are being realized without discrimination, and with adequate progress, people's participation and effective remedies.
- *Ensuring secure access*—through the norms and institutions, laws and enabling economic environment that turn outcomes from needs met into rights realized.
- *Identifying critical non-state actors*—highlighting which other actors have an impact on realizing rights and revealing what that impact is.

It is often said that civil and political rights need a different approach to developing indi-

---

BOX 5.3

Using statistics to look behind the questions

Imagine a country in which 87% of children are enrolled in secondary school. What does this reveal about the right of a child to an education? Certainly, the final goal—secondary education for all—has not been reached. But have all the obligations of those involved been met? Answering means looking beyond this one statistic, deeper into the issues.

If we discover that only 77% of girls are enrolled and 97% of boys, then much of the failure is due to discrimination. Do opinion polls reveal that parents discount the importance of girls' education? Then parents are failing to respect the rights of their daughters to a literate future and the government is failing to raise awareness and change that norm. Or do surveys reveal inadequate provision of school facilities, such as a lack of separate classrooms for girls or very few female teachers? Then the government is failing to promote the rights of girls to real access to an education.

Perhaps there is gender equity—but discriminatory legislation enforces apartheid and grossly underprovides for schools for children of the oppressed ethnic group, with only 40% of them in school. That would be a failure of the government to respect the rights of all people without discrimination, calling for an immediate change in legislation, but also for changes in institutions and norms.

Or perhaps there is no discrimination—but all schools lack resources and cannot provide quality education. Is the government giving enough priority to education? It depends on resource availability. In a country spending twice as much on military power and presidential palaces as on secondary education, the answer would be no—and the government would be failing to adequately fulfil rights. But in a country spending 0.5% of revenues on national security and 8% on secondary education, the answer would be quite different: a lack of resources, not a lack of priority, would be the constraint.

And what about progress? If a country had raised enrolments from 50% to 87% in five years, it would be making strong progress in realizing rights—but if the country had let enrolments fall from 95% to 87%, it would be headed backwards.

If resources are lacking, what are donors and the international community doing? How much development assistance are they providing? What percentage is allocated to the education sector?

Clearly, statistics alone cannot give conclusive answers—but they do help open key questions. They need to be embedded in a deeper analysis of the actors involved and their range of obligations. But if statistics can reveal whether or not those obligations are being met, they help to create accountability and, ultimately, to realize rights.

Source: Human Development Report Office.

---

cators than that for economic, social and cultural rights—but most of the differences are myths (box 5.5). The same framework can be adapted to developing indicators for all human rights.

RESPECTING, PROTECTING AND FULFILLING RIGHTS

Assessing the state's legal accountability means asking whether it is respecting, protecting and fulfilling rights, taking into account resource constraints, historical background and natural conditions.

- *Respecting rights*—refraining from interfering with people's pursuit of their rights, whether through torture or arbitrary arrest, illegal forced housing evictions or the introduction of medical fees that make health care unaffordable for poor people.
- *Protecting rights*—preventing violations by other actors, whether ensuring that private employers comply with basic labour standards, preventing monopoly ownership of the media or preventing parents from keeping their children out of school.
- *Fulfilling rights*—taking legislative, budgetary, judicial and other measures, whether creating legislation requiring equal pay for equal work or increasing budgetary allocations to the most deprived regions.

RESPECTING RIGHTS

Statistics can highlight violations of respect for rights. Data on torture, forced housing evictions, rigged elections and food blockades causing famines are powerful in calling for the accountability of those responsible. Collecting statistical evidence is a tremendous challenge in such cases because of the strong implications that such data bring—and official statistics are often the weakest source. Few states would voluntarily and intentionally document such despicable acts for all to see. This predictable bias against reporting official failure to respect rights calls for caution in making comparisons among countries or in the same country over time.

Such statistics are notoriously uncertain and often missing. Data showing the number

---

BOX 5.4

Uses and abuses of the human development index

In Canada, Ontario is the only province that provides full public funding for the religious schools of just one group—Roman Catholics. Although 8% of the provincial population is from other religious minorities—mostly Jewish, Sikh and Muslim—there is no public funding for them to establish schools. In the absence of public funding, 42,000 of Ontario's students attend private religious schools at an average cost per pupil of more than $5,000 a year.

Canada ratified the International Covenant on Civil and Political Rights in 1976, which includes a commitment to non-discrimination on religious grounds. One parent from a minority religion took his case to the United Nations Human Rights Committee, challenging Ontario's policy of publicly funding schools of only one religion. In 1999 the committee decided that this was a case of religious discrimination, giving Canada 90 days in which to provide an effective and enforceable remedy.

In February 2000 the Canadian government replied to the committee, saying that no remedy would be provided because education is a provincial affair and the government of Ontario refused to comply. One reason given by the premier of the Ontario government was Canada's top ranking in the human development index: "When [the United Nations] says we're the best country in the world to live in...I assume this means our education system as well, and it means how we treat minority religious groups as well."

But ranking in the HDI promises no such thing. The HDI simply captures average national achievements in the most basic outcomes, including adult literacy rates and school enrolments. Canada's high scores in adult literacy and combined gross enrolments do not disprove religious discrimination in access to public education—and in no way waive the need for Ontario to provide a remedy.

Source: Bayefsky 2000; Human Development Report Office; Ontario Parents for Equality in Education Funding 2000; CFRB 1010 1999.

BOX 5.5

Dispelling the myths of difference

Contrasts are often drawn between civil and political rights and economic, social and cultural rights—and then used to justify taking very different approaches to their assessment. Yet many of these contrasts are myths.

Myth 1: Civil and political rights are all negative rights—economic, social and cultural rights all positive. Not so. There are positive and negative duties to respect, protect and fulfil both kinds of rights. Ensuring the right to a fair trial includes taking steps to set up an independent judiciary with adequate training and salaries to preserve the judges' independence. Ensuring the right to housing includes not interfering with people's access to housing by refraining from forced evictions.

Myth 2: Civil and political rights are realized immediately—economic, social and cultural rights gradually. Not true. Even though acts of torture must be ended immediately, in some countries it can take time and resources to ensure that they will never be repeated, by training police officers, setting up monitoring systems for prisoners and reviewing cases brought

before the court. In contrast, even though raising secondary school enrolments often depends on resources, laws that discriminate between boys and girls or between religions and races in education must be removed immediately.

Myth 3: Civil and political rights are all free—economic, social and cultural rights all need resources. Not the case. Holding free and fair elections can be expensive. And simply removing discriminatory housing or health legislation is costless.

Myth 4: Civil and political rights indicators are all qualitative descriptions—economic, social and cultural rights indicators all quantitative statistics. Untrue. Statistics are important for gauging the extent of torture, conditions in prisons and political participation. And qualitative descriptions may be useful to, say, gauge the adequacy of a law to protect tenants' rights.

Dispelling these myths reveals the underlying similarities of civil, cultural, economic, political and social rights and calls for a common approach to creating indicators.

Source: Green 2000; Human Development Report Office.

---

of recorded cases of torture can condemn the activities of a state—but their absence in no way condones them. In fact, sometimes the lack of data is itself revealing data (box 5.6). Secretly held official sources occasionally come to light that reveal more than ever expected—and certainly more than intended by the violators. In Guatemala a recently discovered dossier has produced data revealing clear policy control behind the terror campaign of the early 1980s, pushing accountability for the deaths and disappearances up to the highest levels (box 5.7).

When collecting data, separating the monitor from the monitored helps to remove this bias—but often endangers those trying to document the violations. International and local human rights organizations have bravely confronted the risks of compiling information on such violations as torture, media repression, electoral manipulation and disappearances for many years, always recognizing that the resulting picture is incomplete.

Completing the picture often becomes possible only many years later. The South African Truth and Reconciliation Commission put great emphasis on data collection and analysis, gathering 21,300 statements and identifying 37,700 gross violations of human rights—the result is one of the largest structured databases on human rights abuses ever compiled. By providing details on the age and gender of the victims, their political affiliation and the type and date of abuse suffered, the database enabled the researchers to make powerful statements about the human rights violations that occurred. The results underpinned the findings of the commission, by dramatically highlighting the scale and extent of past violence, and helped shape the rehabilitation and reparation policies.

PROTECTING RIGHTS

If states are to protect individuals' rights from being violated by private actors, they must identify those actors. Corporations may pollute the environment and harm the health of the community. The practices of unscrupulous landlords threaten the right to adequate housing for vulnerable tenants. Domestic violence threatens personal security and health, especially for women and children. What measures can capture the extent to which states protect people against such threats?

BOX 5.6

When lack of data is revealing data

Incriminating data on the most extreme violations of rights are hardly likely to be provided freely and openly by governments. Argentine statisticians and economists were among the first to "disappear" in 1976–77—a hint of the military government's fears of revealing data being leaked. But even when there are no data there may be clues. A sudden break or change in a data series can speak volumes. Violators of rights often leave data footprints and strong grounds for suspicion. Statisticians analysing human rights data can find predictable and systematic patterns in the silence between the numbers.

No data on a known phenomenon. After the Chernobyl reactor disaster in the Soviet Union, many informal reports revealed that doctors had been ordered not to diagnose any radiation-related illnesses, including cancer, leukaemia and anaemia. While the data should reflect an increase in such cases, this silencing would cause a clear—and suspicious—decline.

Sudden cessation of a series. Kwashiorkor is a serious childhood disease caused by long-term malnutrition. In 1968, under the apartheid government of South Africa, data collected showed that its incidence in the country was 300 times as high among Africans as among whites. Rather than tackle the underlying issues, the South African government chose instead to collect no more data on kwashiorkor—a clear decision to hide the issue.

Too close for comfort. All raw data have random variations and fluctuations. When these disappear and data series become highly regular, showing even improvements over time or closely matching the targeted levels, there are strong grounds to suspect that invented data are disguising reality.

Sudden jumps in other data categories. During Argentina's repressive military rule of the 1970s, the bodies of those killed in detention were statistically hidden in the category of *nigun nombre*—no name—burials. One study tracking such burials from 1970 to 1984 found statistically significant leaps in the number of *nigun nombre* burials at the height of the repression, revealing the true location of those who disappeared.

Source: Samuelson and Spirer 1992.

BOX 5.7

Statistics that reveal chilling policy—and create accountability

Nobody in Guatemala could say that they didn't know about the disappearances in the early 1980s: several highly respected NGOs and the Guatemalan human rights commission had documented as much as they knew of the fate of many scientists, students, doctors and engineers.

But a military archive discovered in 1998 revealed that the military forces had kept detailed records of their death squad operations. Data reconstructed from those records produced clear evidence of an incisive policy initiative in late 1983: a switch in strategy from indiscriminate terror in the countryside, killing mostly rural peasants, to highly targeted disappearances of individual people mainly in the capital.

The implications? The shift between these two modes of terror—captured so clearly in data—was so dramatic, complete and rapid that it must have been highly coordinated. Who had the power to switch off the massacres and turn on selective urban assassinations? Only the Guatemalan military high command had that authority. Accountability does not stop at those who pulled the trigger or typed the death squad dossier. Statistical evidence can force it up the ranks to reach those who used murder as an optimal policy strategy.

Source: Ball 1999.

• *Direct measurement of the harmful activity*, such as the volume of chemical pollution a commercial enterprise is dumping into a river, subminimum wages paid in a factory, physical abuse of women in the home and significant patterns in local crime rates.

• *Measurement of state action to prevent or stop it.* Creating law is a primary tool for the state for preventing other actors from violating rights—but how much effort does the state make to enforce those laws? This could be gauged by, for example, the frequency of inspections for enterprises that pollute or create substandard working conditions and the size of the penalties imposed. Similarly, what obstacles are blocking children from school—such as parental attitudes or employers' rules—and what measures is the government taking to overcome them?

FULFILLING RIGHTS

Fulfilling rights calls for designing and implementing policies that ensure that the standards of rights are met for all—and that access to them is made as secure as possible. Such policies apply to all rights, but there is no simple formula for all contexts. Every country must create the policies and social arrangements needed for ensuring that the rights of all its people are fulfilled.

The implications? Assessing whether states are meeting their obligations to fulfil rights—or not—calls for a close focus on the context. Development analysis—including the findings of the *Human Development Reports*—is an important means for this. It aims to understand the links between different policy choices and the resulting economic and social outcomes in widely differing contexts and at different levels of development. Across all contexts, however, indicators are needed to ensure that:

• Policies embody the key principles of rights —non-discrimination and true participation.

• Action is taken to ensure adequate progress and the provision of effective remedies.

• Rights are made secure by building social norms, institutions, laws and an enabling economic environment.

ENSURING KEY PRINCIPLES AND ADEQUATE ACTION

Running through every right are key principles that must be met and actions that must be taken:

• No discrimination—ensuring equitable treatment for all.

• Adequate progress—committing resources and effort to the priority of rights.

• True participation—enabling people to be involved in decisions that affect their well-being.

• Effective remedy—ensuring redress when rights are violated.

Deeply rooted in concepts of social justice, these principles and calls to action are strongly reinforced by international human rights law, creating powerful legal tools for advocacy (box 5.8). It is often through assessing whether they are being met in policies and practices that civil society organizations have had greatest success in using indicators to claim rights.

NO DISCRIMINATION

Discrimination can be de jure, embedded in the purpose of policy through legislation or institutions that favour some and marginalize

---

BOX 5.8

Legal norms running through rights

The major documents of international human rights law emphasize principles and obligations of action ensuring that the process of realizing rights involves:

• *Non-discrimination.* "Each state party to the present covenant undertakes to respect and ensure to all individuals within its territory and subject to its jurisdiction the rights recognized in the present covenant without distinction of any kind, such as race, colour, sex, language, religion, political or other opinion, national or social origin, property, birth or other status" (International Covenant on Civil and Political Rights, Article 2[1]).

• *Adequate progress.* "While full realization of the relevant rights may be achieved progressively, steps towards that goal must be taken within a reasonably short time

after the Covenant's entry into force for the States concerned. Such steps should be deliberate, concrete and targeted as clearly as possible towards meeting the obligations recognized in the Covenant" (Committee on Economic, Social and Cultural Rights, General Comment 3, para. 2).

• *True participation.* "States should encourage popular participation in all spheres as an important factor in development and in the full realization of all human rights" (Declaration on the Right to Development, Article 8[2]).

• *Effective remedy.* "Everyone has the right to an effective remedy by the competent national tribunals for acts violating the fundamental rights granted him by the constitution or by law" (Universal Declaration of Human Rights, Article 8).

Source: UN 1948, 1966a, 1966b, 1986, 1990.

others. It can also be de facto, found in the effects of policy—a result of historical injustice that may no longer be visible itself. Both kinds of discrimination must be overcome to realize rights. Purposeful discrimination, as in discriminatory legislation, can be changed relatively fast—and there is no justification for it to remain standing. Discrimination in the effects of policy takes time and extra effort to eradicate—but is no less important because historical injustice easily becomes present and future injustice if it is not addressed.

Data are among the most powerful tools for revealing de facto discrimination, often where people did not realize or believe that it existed. It is here that statistics can explode myths, reveal unknown biases and expose the status quo as unacceptable. Discrimination by race and gender has been widely revealed through statistics, creating greater national awareness of the issues.

The discrimination in education spending and achievement in South Africa under apartheid was a particularly clear example (fig-ure 5.1). Though the gap remains wide, current government policies are focused on reducing it. Measures of gender disparities, such as the GDI and GEM, reveal discrimination against women in every country. In developing countries there are still 80% more illiterate women than illiterate men, and worldwide, women occupy only 14% of seats in parliaments. Time use and employment surveys have repeatedly shown that women are paid less for equal work and work many more hours in unpaid labour.

At the national level, disaggregating the human development indices by region, gender and ethnic group gives a striking initial picture of who is deprived or discriminated against in economic and social rights. The disaggregated human development index can give a broad impression of average outcomes in life expectancy, literacy, school enrolments and resources for a decent standard of living. But it is the human poverty index that more directly captures deprivation and discrimination through its focus not on average progress but on the proportion of people failing to reach a minimum threshold.

In national human development reports many countries are now using national data to disaggregate these indicators by district, gender, ethnicity and income group. The stark contrast in outcomes is immediately clear (figure 5.2). In Brazil two government think tanks together with UNDP created a detailed database of human development statistics showing different human development outcomes across municipalities—with tremendous consequences for public awareness and a direct impact in reshaping government policies (box 5.9).

Governments need to take action to counter the accumulated effects of these discriminatory outcomes. Yet many countries continue to focus resources and opportunities on those already privileged. Across a range of countries, public health and education spending is routinely concentrated on providing services for the better off, reinforcing the divide. By the principles of rights, it is an imperative to reorient resources towards the marginalized so that long-standing and systemic discrimination is overcome.

BOX 5.9

The power of statistics to create national debate

The human development index cannot capture the full complexity and richness of the concept of human development—but it does give a powerful picture of the basic conditions of people's lives, informing the public, empowering debate and focusing policy.

In Brazil two leading government think tanks—the Institute of Applied Economic Research (IPEA) and the João Pinheiro Foundation—with the support of UNDP, produced *The Atlas of Human Development* in Brazil in 1998. By disaggregating the human development index at the local level, they created a CD-ROM database for all 4,500 municipalities in 27 states, giving detailed data on education, survival and health, housing and income throughout the country—by municipality, state and region.

By focusing locally, the atlas caught the attention of national and local press, igniting media debates and local politics, asking why neighbouring communities had such disparate human development rankings.

Installing the database in local libraries helped to generate tremendous interest among local communities.

At the state level the data shaped policies. In the state of Minas Gerais the government used the data to redistribute sales tax revenues among municipalities, boosting the municipalities with low human development outcomes and also the investing in health, education, sanitation, food security and environmental conservation.

At the federal level the data revealed that although most deprivation is in the northeast of the country, human poverty can be found even in São Paulo, the richest state. The Ministry for National Integration used the atlas to ensure better targeting of assistance throughout Brazil.

The impact of the atlas shows the potential of statistics—for empowering communities, creating accountability and reshaping policy. Such success is strong motivation for improving the collection and use of data.

Source: Libanio 2000; Institute of Applied Economic Research and others 1998.

FIGURE 5.1
Discrimination by race—education in South Africa

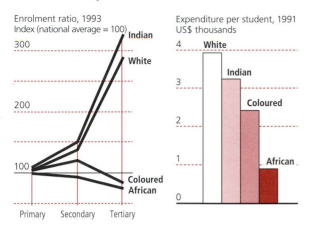

Enrolment ratio, 1993
Index (national average = 100)

- Indian
- White
- Coloured
- African

Primary Secondary Tertiary

Expenditure per student, 1991
US$ thousands

- White
- Indian
- Coloured
- African

Percentage of adults with at least
7 years of schooling

- White
- Indian
- Coloured
- African

Source: Castro-Leal 1996; Buckland and Fielden 1994; South Africa, Central Statistical Services 1994.

FIGURE 5.2
Disaggregating the average can reveal discrimination

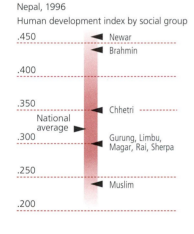

Nepal, 1996
Human development index by social group

- Newar
- Brahmin
- Chhetri
- National average
- Gurung, Limbu, Magar, Rai, Sherpa
- Muslim

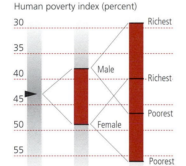

Cambodia, 1997
Human poverty index (percent)

Average   Gender   Income quintile

- Richest
- Male
- Richest
- Female
- Poorest
- Poorest

Source: UNDP 1998a, 1998b.

FIGURE 5.3
Resources and human poverty—industrialized country contrasts

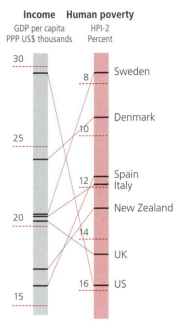

Income | Human poverty

GDP per capita
PPP US$ thousands | HPI-2
Percent

- Sweden — 8
- Denmark — 10
- Spain — 12
- Italy
- New Zealand — 14
- UK
- US — 16

Source: Human Development Report Office.

FIGURE 5.4
Giving priority to basic health and education in Nepal

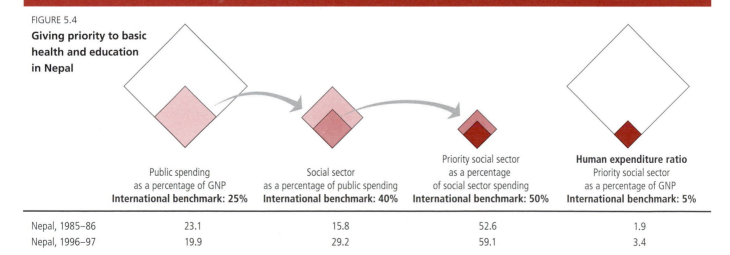

	Public spending as a percentage of GNP International benchmark: 25%	Social sector as a percentage of public spending International benchmark: 40%	Priority social sector as a percentage of social sector spending International benchmark: 50%	Human expenditure ratio Priority social sector as a percentage of GNP International benchmark: 5%
Nepal, 1985–86	23.1	15.8	52.6	1.9
Nepal, 1996–97	19.9	29.2	59.1	3.4

Source: UNDP 1998b.

In many countries civil society organizations are increasingly focusing their advocacy efforts on monitoring national and local budgetary processes to assess how public money is allocated to the needs of different social groups—and then to check on how it is actually used. By analysing national and state-level budgets, they demystify the process, create debate in the media and even help their political representatives better understand the impact of the decisions they are making (box 5.10).

ADEQUATE PROGRESS

There is no justification for not respecting rights. Torture and disappearances, food blockades and forced housing evictions cannot be tolerated at any level of development. But protecting and fulfilling rights requires resources and time. Changing legislation may be costless—but to turn law into reality calls for investing in public institutions—to extend their services and strengthen their capacity—and educating the public and training officials. International human rights law requires states parties to the International Covenant on Economic, Social and Cultural Rights to dedicate the maximum of available resources to realizing these rights in order to make adequate progress. But there is also a need to dedicate adequate resources to protecting and fulfilling civil and political rights—to build institutional capacity that ensures that violations do not occur or recur.

Countries clearly have different amounts of resources available to secure rights in these ways: worldwide, national per capita incomes range from $30,000 to just $500 (PPP US$). The same level of spending per pupil could be the maximum commitment of available resources in a low-income country, yet reflect a clear lack of commitment in a high-income country. How can importance differences between these cases be distinguished?

Making assessments is easier when informed by what has been possible elsewhere—raising questions about why an achievement possible in one place has not been possible in another. The human development indices have long made such resource comparisons. The human poverty index ranks industrialized countries by the extent to which illiteracy, short life expectancy, social exclusion and income poverty are still found in the midst of their thriving societies. Per capita national income can be used as a broad proxy for available resources, since it is from this resource base that governments may raise revenues for eradicating human poverty. Comparing countries' human poverty index with their average income per capita reveals that some industrialized countries give greater resource priority than others to minimizing human poverty (figure 5.3).

Are countries making progress towards realizing rights? This can be assessed in two ways:
• Tracking changes in inputs, such as education spending or teacher-pupil ratios.
• Tracking changes in outcomes, such as falling illiteracy rates or declining child malnutrition.

Tracking changes in such inputs as budgetary allocations can reveal how priorities are being reshaped. *Human Development Report 1991* explored the four key ratios of public spending that determine how much priority is given to essential issues. Data on budgetary

---

BOX 5.10

Demystifying budgets

To my surprise, I found the state and district budget documents fascinating. These documents are not just numbers. They speak about the expressed intention of the government, its policies, its allocation of financial resources, which create the rich and poor regions and groups within the state.

—M. D. Mistry,
founder of Development Initiatives for Social and Human Action (DISHA)

DISHA is an NGO founded in Gujarat, India, to promote development for tribal areas and forest, mine and construction workers. The NGO quickly realized that central to assessing the development of tribal areas was to focus on the budget—the most powerful way of understanding the government's priorities, monitoring whether objectives are turned into reality and ensuring that resources are allocated to reduce, not exacerbate, disparities between communities. By producing summaries on how budgetary allocations affect different issues—from education, policing, rural housing and minimum wages to the situation of women and tribal groups—DISHA has made public knowledge of the priorities and focus of the budget—how revenue is allocated, whether it is actually spent that way and who stands to gain.

Its work has rallied media attention and increased public interest in the budgetary process. As one member of DISHA said, "Through budget analysis, I want to assert the right of poor and tribal people to know what the government is doing with public resources and to judge its performance year to year." Through its analyses, the NGO questioned inadequate allocations to deprived areas and people and why promised allocations had never actually been spent.

Source: Foundation for Public Interest 1997; Mistry 1999; International Budget Project 1999.

restructuring in Nepal, for example, show increasing priority being given to basic health and education spending (figure 5.4). Between 1985–86 and 1996–97 public spending fell as a percentage of GNP, but social sector spending allocated to priorities—primary health and education, water supply and local development—increased, rising towards 20% of public spending—the international standard proposed by the 20:20 initiative.

Tracking changes in outcomes is the focus of the human development indices. Yet aggregated national averages—especially adult literacy and life expectancy—change very slowly and are not sensitive to short-term progress, or to how different groups benefit from average progress. A new approach to assessing progress in human development is needed, one that more fully reflects the principles of rights—disaggregating across social groups to give special attention to how those worst off are affected (see annex).

When a country is making progress, who is to say whether or not its rate of progress is adequate? What can be achieved depends on the context—on resources, historical constraints, policy options and competing priorities. At the same time, agreed standards are needed: recognizing that making progress takes time is by no means an excuse to make no progress at all.

One useful tool for agreeing on an adequate rate of progress is the benchmark. Governments have often declared general goals—say, ending female illiteracy as soon as possible. Far better, they can work with civil society and agree to set a benchmark of, say, reducing female illiteracy from 30% to 15% by 2010. That turns a worthy but unassessable goal into a clear target that can be monitored. In Bolivia, for example, the government consulted with civil society and opposition political parties to create an action plan for 1997–2002, setting annual benchmarks for 17 easily monitored indicators, including the proportion of births attended by trained personnel and of girls who stay in primary school (figure 5.5).

Setting benchmarks enables civil society and government to reach agreement about what rate of progress would be adequate (box

5.11). The stronger is the basis of national dialogue, the more national commitment there will be to the benchmark. The need for democratic debate and widely available public information is clear. If benchmarks are to be a tool of accountability—not just the rhetoric of empty promises—they must be:

- Specific, time bound and verifiable.
- Set with the participation of the people whose rights are affected, to agree on what is an adequate rate of progress and to prevent the target from being set too low.
- Reassessed independently at their target date, with accountability for performance.

To strengthen the benchmarking process, several actors can take a lead. Government agencies can use benchmarks as the intermediate goals of their policy-making. Governments, policy institutes and national NGOs can assess what has been achieved in similar countries, as a guide for agreeing on what targets are feasible domestically. National human rights institutions can use those benchmarks to monitor progress—not only in realizing economic, social and cultural rights but also in, say, eliminating discriminatory gaps, improving the efficiency of the judicial process and increasing participation. The Office of the High Commissioner for Human Rights could provide assistance to

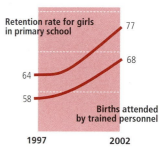

FIGURE 5.5

Setting benchmarks for progress in Bolivia

Percent

Retention rate for girls in primary school — 77

64

68

58

Births attended by trained personnel

1997   2002

Source: UDAPE 2000.

BOX 5.11

Benchmarking—to agree on an adequate rate of progress

Benchmarks have the potential to bring statistical precision into national debates—and they are increasingly being used to set specific, time-bound targets for making progress. In Thailand more than 30 benchmarks for realizing children's rights in 1992–96 were set as part of the Seventh National Social and Economic Development Plan, including:

- Reduce maternal mortality to 30 per 100,000 live births and infant and child mortality to 23 and 35 per 1,000 live births by 1996.
- Ensure that at least 70% of newborn infants weigh more than 3 kilograms, and at least 93% more than 2.5 kilograms, by 1996.
- Expand basic education from six to nine years and ensure that not less than

73% of those who complete the sixth grade continue with secondary education by 1996.

These benchmarks took into account proposals from the National Youth Bureau and civil society and also reflected the global goals set at the World Summit for Children in 1990. Setting goals through participation adds legitimacy—and encourages the NGOs involved to actively monitor the results.

Like any tool, benchmarking has its weaknesses. The pressure to meet targets can sometimes lead to results being manipulated to report what people want to see. The lesson? Separate the monitor from the monitored, or benchmarks will have their biggest impact on recorded statistics, not on reality.

Source: Hunt 1998; Muntarbhorn and Taylor 1994.

countries in developing national approaches to setting and monitoring benchmarks.

TRUE PARTICIPATION

Participation plays an important role in realizing rights. States are legally obliged to enable people to take part in the decisions that affect their welfare—by providing data, allowing others to collect and use data and providing opportunities for people to be involved in policy-making. Indicators are needed to assess whether this is taking place.

First, to what extent are people aware of their rights? Public opinion polls reveal much about what is known and what is not. And the commitment to raising awareness can be assessed by the extent and impact of human rights education—whether by the state through schools and public facilities or by corporations making their workers aware of their labour rights and the corporate code of conduct.

Second, how much information is actually collected and made publicly available? The public availability of data on human rights is a telling indication of the commitment to accountability. To what extent are influential actors willing to record and publicize data on their behaviour and impact? Not only governments but also corporations, donors and multilateral institutions are under more pressure to

collect more data—and to put more data in the public domain. But how much data are collected? And how much are made publicly available? Every example mentioned in this Report—whether good or bad—is at least one step ahead of silence because data have drawn public attention to it, helping to build momentum for change. All countries face the issues illustrated here, but without the data to identify them, the challenge to realize rights is all the greater.

Third, are there opportunities for people to be involved in consultations? Participation comes in many forms—town hall meetings, referendums, media debates, public hearings. FACTUS, a database on trends and practices in European cultural policies, collates information on towns in 37 European countries. Questions reveal how policies of decentralizing resources and consulting the public differ across municipalities (table 5.1). Of course, such a rough indicator cannot capture the quality and extent of participation, but it is a first sign of the local government's attitude towards actively involving people in promoting cultural rights. More detailed data—on the percentage of the budget decentralized, the number of organizations and individuals consulted and the budget for those policies, for example—would begin to present a fuller picture of the quality of participation.

EFFECTIVE REMEDY

If a right is violated, there must be an entitlement to a remedy. Remedies are not only judicial, reached through the courts. They can be administrative, or even an official guarantee that the violation will not happen again. Indicators are needed to assess whether effective remedies are provided. An assessment of judicial remedies can be made by studying the efficacy of the justice system designed to provide them. How many cases come to court—and what is the average time that it takes? What is the current backlog of cases per judge? Such data from South Asia reveal a serious inability of the courts to provide timely remedies (table 5.2). Of all cases filed, how many are never con-

---

TABLE 5.1

Do municipalities have policies enabling participation in promoting culture?

Municipality	Policies to transfer responsibility and resources between levels of public authority?	Policies to empower consumers, artists and voluntary organizations to take part in decision-making for cultural provision?
Prague, Czech Republic	●	●
Catalonia, Spain	●	●
Timis, Romania	◐	◐
Naples, Italy	◐	◐
Istria, Croatia	●	◐
Cork, Ireland	●	●
Helsinki, Finland	●	○
Nicosia, Cyprus	○	◐
Mafra, Portugal	○	○
Göteborg, Sweden	○	○

Municipal responses, 1996–99
● Official policy
◐ Informal policy
○ No policy

Source: Interarts Observatory 1999.

cluded? And of the cases brought to court, what percentage are won by the alleged victim? Statistics can reveal patterns in judicial outcomes that raise important questions. Casa Alianza, a Central American NGO, has carefully documented data on trials to show that there is little, if any, remedy for street children who are abused, tortured and murdered by civilians or officials (box 5.12).

All these aspects of realizing rights can be brought together to assess the extent to which a state is meeting its legal obligations to respect, protect and fulfil rights—with no discrimination, adequate progress, true participation and effective remedy. Civil society organizations are leading the way in making such analyses, proving just how rich the resulting picture can be—as a 1998 analysis by the Centre for Economic and Social Rights showed for the right to health in Ecuador (table 5.3).

ENSURING SECURE ACCESS

Securing rights goes far beyond attention to human outcomes. The absence of poverty and torture does not, alone, ensure that the related rights are being realized. These outcomes need to be secured through social norms, institutions, laws and an enabling economic environment. Statistics on each of these areas can help assess the extent to which this secure access is being ensured—and raise questions in every country.

SOCIAL NORMS

If social norms are to create secure access, they must support human rights, not threaten them. Opinion polls can gauge this reality—despite the possible gap between stated and actual opinions. Survey data from around the world on attitudes towards violence against women show the importance of changing norms and perceptions—of both men and women—to protect women's right to personal security. In India a 1996 study of primary education found that 98% of parents believed it important for boys to be educated, but only 89% for girls. In 1998 more than 7,700 hate crimes were reported in the United States, reflecting a continued intolerance of difference—a threat

familiar to people in many countries (figure 5.6). Such data not only reveal the threats of intolerance and discrimination embedded in social norms—they also indicate where action is needed to transform norms through education, empowerment and awareness.

INSTITUTIONS

Is the quality of institutions adequate to create secure access to the goods and services they are set up to provide? A tough and complex question that shifts the focus of indicators from outcomes to access to services—for example, from maternal mortality ratios to the availability and accessibility of prenatal health services and the proportion of births attended by medical personnel.

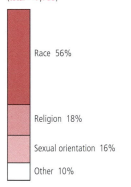

FIGURE 5.6
Intolerance of difference— hate crimes in the United States

Object of reported hate crimes, 1998 (total = 7,755)

Race 56%

Religion 18%

Sexual orientation 16%

Other 10%

Source: Human Rights Campaign 1998.

TABLE 5.2
Justice delayed, justice denied?
1996

Country	Cases pending per 1,000 persons	Persons per judge	Cases pending per judge
Bangladesh	53	95,000	5,150
India	23	91,000	2,150
Pakistan	5	85,000	450
Nepal	4	85,000	300

Source: Mahbub ul Haq Human Development Centre 1999.

BOX 5.12
No remedy for the violence done—the street children of Guatemala

More than 15,000 street children live in the urban centres of Guatemala and its neighbour Honduras—either runaways or outcasts, but often viewed by the public as "vermin", bad for the neighbourhood. Governmental and social indifference to their plight has left them unprotected from abuse and, at times, torture and murder at the hands of officials and civilians alike.

To expose the violations of these children's rights, Casa Alianza/Convent House Latin America—an NGO dedicated to defending and rehabilitating street children—documented every known case, creating a shocking report of undeniable evidence. But Casa Alianza has gone further, pushing for justice through the courts—and documenting the results to create data revealing a startling lack of remedy.

In Guatemala 392 cases involving street children were taken to court between March 1990 and September 1998. By the end of that period 47% had been filed for lack of investigation and 44% more were in danger of the same; 4% were closed for lack of evidence. Only 5% of cases—17 in total—had been heard and concluded. Of those, Casa Alianza won 15.

What of the people involved? Some 220 members of the security forces were charged in the cases brought, yet only 10% have ever received a sentence.

Documenting these cases drew public attention to an issue previously ignored. But Casa Alianza believes that the inability of the judicial system to provide a remedy for the violence done to street children is a failure to protect their rights—and an unspoken endorsement of continuing violence and impunity.

Source: Casa Alianza 1999; Harris 2000.

TABLE 5.3

Realizing the right to health in Ecuador—assessing the state's obligations

State obligation	Assessment	Available or desirable indicators
Respecting rights Is there direct interference with people's ability to realize their rights? Is there avoidable regression in the existing levels of health or access to health care?	State petroleum operations dump heavy metals and carcinogens into water sources of communities in the Ecuadoran Amazon. Avoidable cuts are made in programmes without adequate contingency plans for the most vulnerable.	*Desired data: annual volume of chemical pollution by state operations.* In 1990 an estimated 50% of children under five were malnourished. Between 1990 and 1994 the coverage of nutrition programmes fell from 11% to 4%.
Protecting rights Do people suffer systematic, harmful effects on their health from actions by private actors? What measures does the state take to protect them?	The abuse of women and children by partners and family members is a grave threat to their health. Despite the recent Law against Violence against Women and the Family, the state has not adequately protected victims through the judicial system. The private petroleum industry is not prevented from dumping heavy metals and carcinogens into community water sources in the Ecuadoran Amazon	In 1998, 88% of women in Guayaquil, the largest city, said they had suffered some form of intrafamilial violence. Between 1989 and 1992, of 1,920 complaints relating to sex crimes against women and girls in Guayaquil, only 2% resulted in convictions. In the late 1980s private oil companies were dumping almost 4.4 million gallons of toxic waste into the Amazon daily.
Fulfilling rights Has the state taken adequate measures to tackle the roots of national health problems?	In 1996 government research concluded that more than 80% of deaths could be avoided by giving priority to primary and secondary preventive care. Nutrition programmes have limited coverage compared with those in other Latin American countries.	In 1995 only 17% of the health budget was allocated to primary care, and just 7% to preventive care. In the mid-1990s programme coverage was just 4%—compared with 40% in Bolivia and 85% in Peru.
Non-discrimination Is there discrimination—in the state's efforts or in outcomes?	Despite high inequality and extreme deprivation of rural, poor and indigenous populations, the government devotes most expenditures and resources to urban and better-off groups.	In 1997, 84% of urban people had access to health services—compared with only 10% of rural people—and 80% of health personnel were in urban areas. *Desired data: health care access disaggregated by ethnicity, income level and education level.*
Adequate progress Has the state made adequate progress—both in outcomes and in inputs—towards meeting its obligations?	In 1970 the state set benchmarks: • Safe water for 80% of the urban population and 50% of the rural. • Sanitation for 70% of the urban population and 50% of the rural. Since the late 1980s successive governments have cut health spending—to pay off debt and to increase military spending.	In 1982–90 the share of households with access to safe water fell from 88% to 78% in urban areas, and remained below 25% in rural. The share with access to sanitation fell from 46% to 38% in urban areas, and from 15% to 10% in rural. In 1998, 4% of the national budget went to health, and 45% to debt servicing.
Participation Are people educated about and aware of their rights?	There are no government programmes for public education on the right to health, and public information on personal health is very limited.	*Desired data: percentage of people aware of their right to health; percentage of people aware of basic health norms.*
Are there mechanisms aimed at ensuring communities greater influence on and participation in policies concerning their health?	The system for allocating resources is very centralized and bureaucratic, undermining opportunities for participation.	*Desired data: percentage of the health budget allocated locally; percentage of health programmes designed with popular consultation.*
Effective remedy Has the state provided effective remedies for violations of the right to health?	Inefficiency, corruption and a lack of resources create many barriers to effective lawsuits.	After 25 years of massive damage to the health of Amazonian communities by state and private oil companies, only a handful of claims have been filed—and none successfully.

Note: The table is based on a 1998 case study by the Centre for Economic and Social Rights.
Source: CESR 1998.

Assessments are needed both of the institutions that create the framework for all rights—such as the judiciary, ombudsmen and national human rights institutions—and of institutions that deliver on specific rights—health services and schools, electoral commissions and prisons.

Asking what secure access would mean points to the data needed. For example:
• Do health posts provide secure access to health services? To find out, start by asking how many people are served by one health post and from what distance. How capable are the medical staff of treating the illnesses they encounter? Track the stock levels of essential medicines to reveal the extent and frequency of shortages—and the vulnerabilities they entail.
• Is an ombudsman's office really capable of resolving complaints? Ask whether its budget is adequate and whether its staff is qualified. Analyse the number of cases brought, their type, the time taken to process them—and their outcomes.

Laws

Assessing whether a law threatens or reinforces rights can be difficult. The perfect law may be enshrined in the national constitution—but never actually used in practice, or used consistently for or against only one social group. So, should the assessment be of the law as written or the law as applied? Both.

Does an adequate law exist? In many states, for example, the right to adequate shelter is not enshrined in domestic law; clearly, the right is not legally secured. If there is a law, how is it applied? Has it ever been invoked—and has it ever been successful? Do outcomes indicate a bias in its use? A report by Amnesty International on capital punishment in the United States points to just one example. Blacks and whites in the United States are victims of murder in almost equal numbers, yet 82% of prisoners executed since 1977 were convicted of the murder of a white person. How well is the law known? Is the relevant statute easily accessible? Available in local languages? Summarized in non-legal language so that the average person can understand it?

How accessible and available is legal advice? Is there legal aid for those who cannot afford to take a case to court? Are facilities providing legal advice accessible and close to major population centres?

Enabling economic environment

The importance of resources recurs at all levels of analysis of securing access to rights. From the macro focus on the stability of the economy to the micro focus on the vulnerability of household expenses, data can be used to ask whether the structure of the economic environment helps or hinders the realization of the right. An economy may be booming and lifting incomes at all levels—yet if there is neither an official nor a community-based system of social security, an adequate standard of living is not being best secured. At the micro level, examining the cost of food as a percentage of household budgets can reveal the high vulnerability of low-income households to fluctuations in food prices. From the opportunity cost of taking time off work to vote—if the polling station is very far—to the rising costs of equipping a child for school that is supposed to be free, data on costs can reveal how financially insecure any right can be for those who need to pay for it.

Identifying actors

The traditional focus on the state as the responsible actor is strongly reinforced by legal obligations. But improvements in human rights require the partnership of governments and families, corporations, communities and international agencies. Social arrangements are created and supported ultimately by people, acting individually or through communities, associations, companies, institutions and governments. Changes in the human rights situation of a country—both good and bad—may be caused not only by the state, but also by these other critical actors. Their roles and obligations are increasingly being brought under scrutiny.

More than 50 years ago the Universal Declaration of Human Rights recognized the need

Improvements in human rights require the partnership of governments and families, corporations, communities and international agencies

to focus on international impacts on rights. Article 28 declared, "Everyone is entitled to a social and international order in which the rights and freedoms set forth in this Declaration can be fully realized." Today the interaction of actors, locally and globally, calls for analyses of the increasingly complex local and international orders, which are stretching the bounds of legal obligations. Indicators are needed that explore this complexity. They can identify which actors have a critical impact on the realization of rights—from the community to the global level—revealing where problems lie and signalling the action to alleviate them.

Locally, assessing the roles and impacts of different actors can give a far richer picture of why rights are not being realized. It can also point to needed interventions—which may call for community initiative, not just state action. In India in 1992, 30% of all children aged 6–14—about 23 million boys and 36 million girls—were out of school. In 1996 an independent Indian research team undertook a study in the north of the country to find out why. Surveying villages and households, the team created a rich database that uncovered some hidden reasons behind the problems of primary education. Most actors—from parents and teachers to politicians and the media—had not fulfilled their roles, a collective social failure that called not only for state policies but also for local community solutions (table 5.4).

At the international level, globalization and market liberalization have created an unprecedented interdependence that expands the influence of actors over human rights outcomes around the world. The more actors, the more complex the question. For a corporation with domestic employees, the assessment is relatively straightforward, since control over their safety and pay is directly under the company. But for many global corporations, subcontracting makes workers' rights increasingly difficult to monitor, let alone ensure. Mattel, a global corporation producing toys, has established a code of conduct and an independent

TABLE 5.4

Realizing the right to primary education in India—are actors meeting their obligations?

Actor	Obligation	Measure	Result
Parents	Must be willing to send children to school.	Proportion of parents who think it is important for children to be educated.	• 89% for girls, 98% for boys.
Government	Must provide schools that are accessible.	Distance of school from house.	• 92% of rural population had a primary school within 1 kilometre. • 49% of rural population had an upper-primary school within 1 kilometre.
	Must provide adequate facilities.	Number of teachers.	• 12% of primary schools had only one teacher appointed. • 21% had only a single teacher present at the time of the survey.
		State of facilities.	• 58% of schools had at least two rooms. • 60% had a leaking roof. • 89% did not have a functioning toilet. • 59% did not have drinking water.
		Head teacher attendance and activity.	On the day of the survey visit to the school: • 25% of head teachers were engaged in teaching activities. • 42% were engaged in non-teaching activities. • 33% were absent.
Community	Must support school, teachers and parents.	Public discussions.	• 49% of village education committees had not met in the past year.
Media	Must report on neglect of basic education.	Proportion of newspaper articles on basic education.	In one year's newspaper articles: • 8,550 on foreign investment. • 3,430 on foreign trade. • 2,650 on defence. • 990 on education. • 60 on rural primary education.

Note: The sample consisted of 188 villages, 1,200 households and 236 schools in four northern states of India in 1996.
Source: PROBE Team 1999.

council to monitor its implementation (box 5.13). Beyond corporations, indicators are needed for assessing the impacts of the actions or inaction of multilateral actors on the realization of rights—including the international financial institutions, the World Trade Organization and many UN agencies.

Also needed are indicators for the impacts of states beyond their own citizens—states as donors and lenders, traders and negotiators, arms dealers and peace-makers. The crimes of dictators are widely acknowledged, but foreign support for their regimes usually escapes the scrutiny it deserves. Foreign policies affect human rights through arms sales, insurgency and counterinsurgency training, sanctions, patterns of foreign aid and tariffs and quotas on imports. Powerful non-state actors and representatives of states shape laws and policies at both the national and the international level, through lobbying, funding of political candidates and other forms of pressure.

Overlooking these tremendously influential practices would produce a narrow picture of human rights and of the information relevant to assessing their realization. Explanations of national human rights problems may focus on domestic factors, but there is still a need to examine how international interactions help shape those domestic factors in the first place. It will be a major challenge to create indicators—and first to collect the data—that reveal the complex human rights impacts of these different actors.

THE WAY FORWARD

Collecting good statistical data on human rights is a tremendous challenge—but it is being tackled:
- *Rise of new actors*. The rise of civil society organizations and locally based human rights documentation centres has spread awareness and understanding of rights and created thousands of new potential data collection points around the world.
- *More access to information*. Greater freedom of expression and information and more transparency in many countries are allowing a wider group of people—and a

greater degree of truth—to be involved in the process. From Guatemala and Indonesia to South Africa and the former Soviet republics, the freer voices of civil society organizations and the media have greatly informed and broadened public dialogue.
- *Rise of information technology*. The phenomenal expansion of access to technology—especially the Internet—has simplified and speeded up data management to an incredible degree. Data can be recorded, collated and publicly posted far more quickly and widely.
- *More professional documentation of rights*. Many efforts have been made to improve the reliability of information being recorded. Through training courses, standardized formats and guidelines posted online, the expertise of people documenting human rights is being strengthened.

How can these opportunities be used to strengthen accountability through indicators? Four routes: collecting more and better official data, diversifying sources of information for the community, increasing access to official

---

BOX 5.13

Monitoring Mattel—no toying with statistics

Mattel is the largest toy manufacturer in the world, with large production plants in China, Indonesia, Malaysia, Mexico and Thailand. This global corporation has recognized the importance of reputation. Widely publicized attacks on the Nike Corporation in 1996 for substandard labour conditions in its Asian plants prompted Mattel to take steps to ensure that it would not face similar accusations. In 1997 the company set itself a code of conduct—with standards exceeding the industry average—and founded MIMCO, the Mattel Independent Monitoring Council, to monitor its compliance with the code.

Monitoring is a four-stage process, with each stage verifying and supplementing the information gathered in the previous one. Managers of each plant prepare dossiers on wages, working conditions, environment and safety. These are checked for consistency with financial data. Confidential on-site interviews with employees give insights into child labour,

wages, safety, harassment, workers associations and penalties. Finally, the monitors make on-site visits to see the work environment for themselves. MIMCO compares the results across plants and makes recommendations to the Mattel board of directors—and the team returns to each plant six months later to assess their implementation.

The council emphasizes the importance of translating the principles of the code of conduct—such as good air quality and working conditions—into quantifiable standards. Even if there is no agreement on exactly what the standards should be, at least it is possible to know what is being measured. Finally, MIMCO insists on publishing its findings without restrictions from Mattel and welcomes scrutiny of those findings by other NGOs.

As the most influential corporation in children's toys, Mattel took a brave step in adopting this approach, one that many other influential corporations would do well to follow.

Source: MIMCO 2000; Sethi 2000.

information and strengthening the procedures of accountability.

COLLECTING MORE AND BETTER OFFICIAL DATA

Assessing rights calls for data that reveal failures of duties and insecurity of the rights—and data on all people. These include data on the marginalized and deprived, who are often missed by official statistics, data collected by alternative sources in order to separate actors from monitors and data disaggregated by region, gender, ethnicity, income level and other categories of discrimination. Assessing rights thus calls for a new approach to data collection. Statistical capacity building is rarely given priority—but information is an essential tool for designing and assessing policy. National statistical offices and UN agencies need to work together much more closely to make this possible. Even today, many of the most basic development indicators are still incomplete data sets.

DIVERSIFYING SOURCES OF INFORMATION

Official statistics are important for a government's self-monitoring and assessment, but the picture that they present can be enriched—or sometimes contradicted—by alternative sources. Violence against women is severely underreported when statistics are collected only through police reports, especially in countries where women are afraid of the police or fearful of public judgement (figure 5.7). Supplementing these data with information from women's groups and shelters would help. Similarly, when corporate practices are being assessed, the evaluation is far more likely to be accepted as valid when conducted by an independent monitor.

What can be done in the community? Sample surveys can check the reliability of official data—and go further into the underlying local problems. Schools, hospitals, libraries and the local marketplace can all be rich sources of information on people's lives, opinions and awareness. But if civil society organizations are to provide new sources of information, their data must have credibility—often lacking in the past, making for easy dismissal of their

claims by officials. The Human Rights Information and Documentation Systems, International (HURIDOCS) project has been strengthening the reliability of non-official data for many years by creating standardized definitions and formats to be used in gathering data and by providing training for data collectors and analysts.

Care is also needed to ensure that sensitive data are stored securely. When organizations take on the ethical obligation of serving the victims, survivors and witnesses of violations, they also take on the obligation of dealing with the data safely, separating identities from evidence given and using widely available, low-cost computer encryption programmes to reassure witnesses about the safety of giving evidence.

REALIZING THE RIGHT TO INFORMATION

Providing information on national needs and government priorities can enhance public understanding of difficult trade-offs, creating a greater social consensus in the face of limited resources and multiple demands. But when people lack access to information on policies and practices that affect their well-being, there are many additional costs:
• Away from the torchlight of public scrutiny, corruption flourishes.
• Press freedom is compromised when journalists choose to turn a blind eye to the misdemeanours of some officials in return for special access to leaks and secret information.
• Powerful private actors can effectively buy secrecy—even for information that reveals serious threats to public health and safety.

Legislated access to information is not enough. Policies encouraging openness in public life are also needed to ensure that the data are within reach of all. Official data may be made public—but available only in offices in major cities, accessible only to those with the knowledge, time and determination to find them. The Internet greatly widens these possibilities—but only for those who can get on line. The right to information movement has proved that the focus, quality and outcomes of policy-making can be transformed when people demand that information be made public and then put it to use.

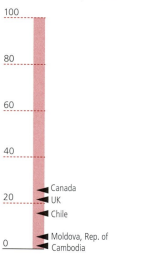

FIGURE 5.7
Abuse of women usually goes unreported

Percentage of abused women who contacted the police, 1993–97

100

80

60

40

20 — Canada
— UK
— Chile

— Moldova, Rep. of
0 — Cambodia

Note: Data refer to any year from 1993 to 1997.
Source: Johns Hopkins University 1999b.

The call to acknowledge accountability is touching all influential actors—pushing for them to accept responsibility, cooperate with monitors and respond to recommendations. Non-state actors need to strengthen their commitments. Corporate codes of conduct need to be translated into quantifiable standards, with independent monitors to collect data on their implementation. Multilateral agencies need similar scrutiny of their impacts. The World Bank has set an important example by setting up an inspection panel to allow civil society to present alternative assessments of the impact of projects. Other multilaterals need to follow suit, including the World Trade Organization, the International Monetary Fund and many UN agencies.

Under Article 55 of the UN Charter, all UN members make a commitment to promote "universal respect for, and observance of, human rights and fundamental freedoms for all without distinction." And by ratifying the human rights treaties, they make additional legal commitments. But to what extent do they put these commitments into practice? An index can be created to assess the extent to which UN members can be held internationally accountable. The data are available and verifiable—but it is only now, with such a significant leap in participation in the international human rights regime, that such an index would be meaningful (box 5.14).

• • •

Recalling the difference that a focus on statistics made to its work promoting rights, one Indian NGO reported, "We were not merely a struggle-oriented and slogan-shouting organization. We had the intellectual ability to put our case across solidly in the government's own terminology. The government had no alternative but to accept our conclusions, since they were based on its own facts and figures." Such empowerment is invaluable—and is needed by all actors intent on promoting the realization of human rights. Holding actors to account for the human impacts of their policies and practices is central to the pursuit of justice—and using indicators is increasingly recognized as a tool central to that process.

BOX 5.14

Towards a human rights international accountability index

Members of the United Nations are held accountable for human rights through three routes:

• *Accept.* All countries ratifying or acceding to the major international human rights treaties commit themselves, in that act, to international scrutiny of their human rights record.

• *Cooperate.* All states ratifying a human rights treaty are committed to submitting an initial report within one to two years on the status of rights addressed in the treaty and periodic reports thereafter—yet many do not. For the six major treaties, almost 250 initial reports were overdue on 1 January 1999. Even states that have not ratified treaties are called upon to cooperate with requests made by special rapporteurs and other special procedures by inviting them to visit the country.

• *Respond.* By becoming a party to a treaty, a state undertakes to cooperate with the treaty body concerned by responding to its concluding observations and final views. Equally, by joining the United Nations, states agree to cooperate with the organization, and these days that includes its human rights special procedures.

An index can be constructed to capture the commitments in each of these areas (box table 5.14).

Source: Alston 2000.

BOX TABLE 5.14

Indicators for a human rights international accountability index

Dimension	Basis for indicators

Accept: fundamental acknowledgement of international accountability	• Ratification or accession to:
	  • International Covenant on Civil and Political Rights (ICCPR)
	  • International Covenant on Economic, Social and Cultural Rights (ICESCR)
	  • International Convention on the Elimination of All Forms of Racial Discrimination (ICERD)
	  • Convention on the Elimination of All Forms of Discrimination Against Women (CEDAW)
	  • Convention Against Torture and Other Cruel, Inhuman or Degrading Treatment or Punishment (CAT)
	  • Convention on the Rights of the Child
	  • The four Geneva Conventions of 1949
	• Ratification of the individual complaints procedures for the ICCPR, ICERD, CEDAW, CAT and the Geneva Conventions

Cooperate: participation in established international procedures	• Submission of reports due to treaty bodies in good time • Provision of requested information to special rapporteurs and thematic missions • Cooperation with monitoring missions • Cooperation with UN-sponsored election monitors • Cooperation with the International Committee of the Red Cross in relation to prison visits
Respond: extent of adequate replies to requests	• Adequate response to recommendations by treaty bodies • Adequate response to final views adopted in connection with communications procedures • Adequate response to recommendations by country rapporteurs and thematic mechanisms

---

Since I came to office three years ago, I have adopted pro–human development policies
and implemented a wide range of new programmes.
Why, then, are we still the same rank in the human development index?
—An elected president, 1999

Since its launch in 1990, the HDI has captured the attention of governments, the media and civil society. They compare their country's ranking with their neighbours', often asking why achievements made elsewhere have not been made at home. This use of the HDI gives it additional appeal as a tool for assessing progress in realizing some social and economic rights.

But the high profile of the HDI can lead to misuse. When a country's ranking rises from one year to the next, governments may be tempted to claim credit, pointing to recent policies. And when the ranking falls or stays the same, the media and political opposition may be tempted to blame recent policies. The HDI cannot reflect such short-term impacts of policies. Two of its indicators are slow to change: adult literacy and life expectancy. And although combined gross enrolments and average incomes may vary more year to year, when expressed as national averages they still do not respond much to policies that raise enrolments among illiterate communities or tackle income poverty among the most deprived.

Human Development Report 1999 produced the first long-term trend data for the HDI, for 1975-97. Even across 22 years, progress is gradual at every level of development, as shown in the figure below.

Framework for assessing progress

Period	Average perspective	Deprivation perspective	Inequality perspective
One period	What is the national average?	Who are the most deprived? By: • Income quintile • Gender • Region • Rural or urban • Ethnic group • Education level	What is the disparity? Between: • Bottom and top income quintiles • Females and males • Worst-off and best-off regions • Rural and urban • Worst-off and best-off ethnic groups • No education and higher education
Over time	How has the national average changed?	How have the most deprived social groups progressed?	How have disparities between social groups changed—have they widened or narrowed?

Neither governments nor the public can wait 20 years to find out whether policies have promoted human development and helped realize human rights. Indicators are needed that capture the shorter-term impacts of policies and that reflect the priorities and principles of rights—indicators that:

• Reveal who are the most deprived—and how their lives are affected by policies. This calls for disaggregation to identify social groups with the worst outcomes so that their progress can be tracked.

• Reflect disparities between groups—such as by gender, ethnicity, region and urban or rural dwelling—to help identify current or historical discrimination and to show whether policies are reducing or exacerbating the gaps.

• Respond to policy measures—so that the findings help in assessing governments' performance. This calls for using variables that respond in the short term—for example, the literacy rate among 15- to 19-year olds rather than the adult literacy rate—but lack of data is a common problem. Responsiveness also calls for using data that are available frequently—at least every five years, for example—but this, too, is still often not possible.

To reflect these demands, three perspectives need to be used simultaneously:
1. *Average perspective*—showing overall progress in the country.
2. *Deprivation perspective*—showing the progress by the most deprived groups.
3. *Inequality perspective*—showing the progress in narrowing inequalities.

This framework, shown in the table above, can be applied in every country, using variables most relevant to each country's most pressing issues. But disaggregated data are needed to make it possible. More and more such data are being collected at the national level, disaggregated by gender, ethnicity, urban or rural dwelling, district, income level, education level and other relevant characteristics.

Examples from Benin, Egypt, Guatemala and India show that when data are available for more than one period, the combination of the three perspectives provides new insights. By revealing who are the most deprived—and whether they benefit from national progress—these analyses help in making assessments of the realization of human rights and the achievement of human development.

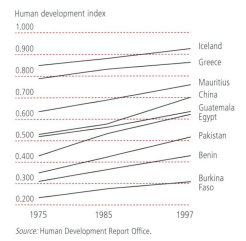

Human development index

1.000

0.900 — Iceland
0.800 — Greece
0.700 — Mauritius / China
0.600 — Guatemala / Egypt
0.500 — Pakistan
0.400 — Benin
0.300 — Burkina Faso
0.200

1975   1985   1997

Source: Human Development Report Office.

THREE PERSPECTIVES ON PROGRESS: APPLYING THE FRAMEWORK

*This example on immunization of infants in Egypt clearly illustrates
the depth that can be revealed by combining three perspectives
on the data: average, deprivation and inequality.*

Average perspective

In 1992 only 67% of all 12- to 23-month-old infants were fully immunized. By 1998 coverage had risen to 93%, as shown in the figure at right. Impressive progress overall—but how did coverage differ across social groups? Who were the most deprived groups, and how much did they benefit?

**Egypt
Immunization rate**
Percentage of 12- to 23-month-old infants fully immunized

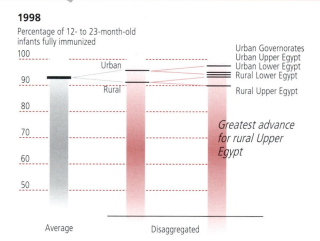

1992
Percentage of 12- to 23-month-old infants fully immunized

Rural Upper Egypt most deprived

Urban Lower Egypt
Urban Governorates
Rural Lower Egypt
Urban Upper Egypt
Rural Upper Egypt

Average Disaggregated

1998
Percentage of 12- to 23-month-old infants fully immunized

Urban
Rural

Urban Governorates
Urban Upper Egypt
Urban Lower Egypt
Rural Lower Egypt
Rural Upper Egypt

Greatest advance for rural Upper Egypt

Average Disaggregated

Deprivation perspective

Disaggregating the national average in 1992 reveals the initial disparities across the country—between rural and urban areas and among three regions, the Urban Governorates, Upper Egypt and Lower Egypt. The figures above show the stark contrast: coverage ranged from 83% in urban Lower Egypt to just 52% in rural Upper Egypt.

By 1998, how had the most deprived areas—rural and urban Upper Egypt—benefited from national progress?

Coverage rose to 90% or more in every area, with particularly strong progress in the two most deprived areas. Rural Upper Egypt made especially fast progress in coverage, from 52% to 90%.

Inequality perspective

What was the impact on inequality? Faster progress among those worst off dramatically reduced inequality between regions. The figure at right shows that the gap between the bottom and top regions was reduced by three-quarters between 1992 and 1998, from 31 percentage points to just 7 points.

Inequality declines dramatically

Best-off region
Worst-off region

31   7

1992   1998

WHO ARE THE MOST DEPRIVED? FIRST FOCUS FOR REALIZING RIGHTS

*Progress in realizing human rights calls for particular emphasis
on ensuring that the most deprived social groups benefit. The first step is to identify them.
Data revealing differences between social groups—as far as data availability allows—
enable policy-makers to design programmes directly targeting the worse-off.*

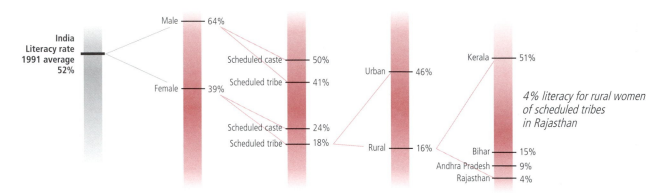

In India this approach could help address the challenge of achieving literacy for all. In 1991, 52% of the population aged seven and above was literate. But breaking data down by gender, some castes and urban or rural dwelling reveals especially extreme deprivation among rural women of scheduled tribes—with a literacy rate of just 16% in 1991. Focusing further on this social group—by disaggregating across all states—reveals widely differing outcomes. In Kerala in 1991, the literacy rate for rural women of scheduled tribes was 51%, almost the national average. But in several states it was below 15%—and in Rajasthan just 4%. The principles of human rights call for policy measures to tackle the extreme deprivation of these groups.

MAKING PROGRESS: HOW MUCH FOR THE MOST DEPRIVED?

*Once the most deprived groups have been identified, data can reveal whether they benefit
from national progress—or are excluded from it.*

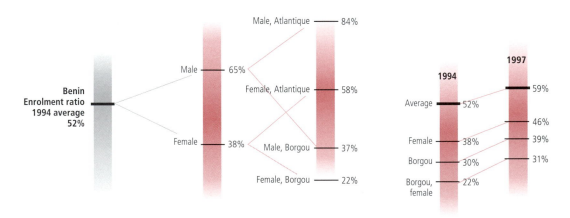

In Benin in 1994, there were wide disparities in school enrolments, by gender and by district. National average net enrolment in primary education was 52%—but it was just 38% for girls, compared with 65% for boys. And there were large differences across districts, with 71% of all children enrolled in Atlantique but only 30% in Borgou. The policy implications? Particular focus was needed on raising female enrolments across the country and raising all enrolments in the most deprived districts. By 1997 national average enrolment had risen 7 percentage points to 59%. How much progress was made for the most deprived? Female enrolment across the country rose 8 percentage points to 46%, total enrolment in Borgou rose 9 points to 39% and female enrolment in Borgou also rose 9 points to 31%. The most deprived groups made slightly faster progress than the national average and so were not left behind—but did not catch up enough to reduce their deprivation compared with achievements in other groups.

TACKLING INEQUALITIES AND OVERCOMING DISCRIMINATION

How does the progress made by different social groups affect overall inequality in a country?
Reducing disparities among groups can counteract historical discrimination that may have been due
to earlier policies and prejudices.

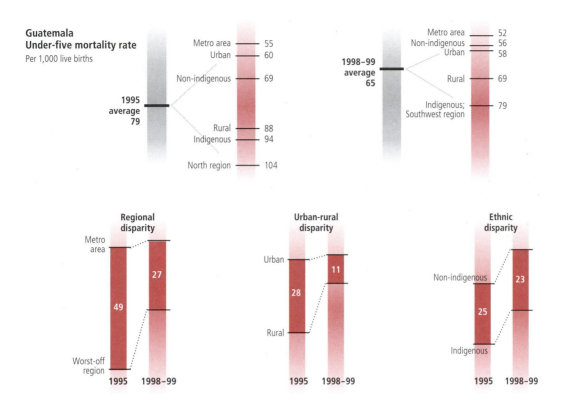

Guatemala
Under-five mortality rate
Per 1,000 live births

1995 average 79

Metro area 55
Urban 60
Non-indigenous 69
Rural 88
Indigenous 94
North region 104

1998–99 average 65

Metro area 52
Non-indigenous 56
Urban 58
Rural 69
Indigenous; Southwest region 79

Regional disparity

Metro area
49 (1995)
27 (1998–99)
Worst-off region

Urban-rural disparity

Urban
28 (1995)
11 (1998–99)
Rural

Ethnic disparity

Non-indigenous
25 (1995)
23 (1998–99)
Indigenous

Changes in under-five mortality in different social groups in Guatemala reveal diverse impacts on inequality. In 1995 the national average rate—for the 10 years prior to the survey—was 79 deaths per 1,000 live births. But there was great inequality among social groups—between urban and rural, between indigenous and non-indigenous and among regions.

By 1998–99 progress had been made by all groups. But how had inequalities changed? The gap between the worst- and best-performing regions was reduced most—from 49 to 27—but remained wide and in need of continued effort. The rural-urban gap was more than halved—from 28 to 11. But the gap between ethnic groups was reduced only slightly, from 25 to 23—emphasizing the need for increased effort to tackle such disparities.

These studies highlight three priorities:
• *Use disaggregated data for assessing progress in human development and human rights.* Producing statistics that reveal differences by gender, region, ethnicity and other social characteristics is the first step in identifying where progress is needed most and is central to an approach based on the principles of human rights.
• *Focus on the most deprived.* Data on progress by those initially worst-off can create a picture quite unlike the impression that national averages alone give.
• *Focus on inequality gaps.* Data on progress for the top and bottom groups can reveal whether disparities and historical discrimination are being eliminated or exacerbated.

Governments and civil society in every country can assess progress in these ways, with national statistical offices increasingly recognizing the importance of collecting data disaggregated by social group. Making such data available is an essential step forward in assessing progress in human development, monitoring the realization of rights and devising policies targeting those most in need. In every country national human development reports can lead by integrating such detailed studies of progress into their analysis.

Source: Osman and El Leithy 2000; Shiva Kumar 2000; Rodas-Martini and Pira 2000; Benin National Institute of Statistics and Economic Analysis 1999; Sori-Coulibaly 2000.

CHAPTER 6

Promoting rights in human development

We shall have to repent in this generation, not so much for the evil deeds of the wicked people, but for the appalling silence of the good people.
—*Martin Luther King Jr.*

It is time to move from the rhetoric of universal commitment to the reality of universal achievement

All rights for all people in every country should be the goal of this century. The Universal Declaration of Human Rights set out this global vision more than 50 years ago. The world today has the awareness, the resources and the capacity to achieve this goal on a worldwide scale. It is time to move from the rhetoric of universal commitment to the reality of universal achievement. Much action is already under way—in countries and internationally.

Progress will be neither easy nor straightforward. Human rights may be universal, but they are not universally accepted. Huge advances have been made almost everywhere in the decades since the Universal Declaration of Human Rights, but new threats lurk on the horizon. The nature of the struggle depends on the right and the opponent. The fight against exploitation by individuals, groups or firms defines one domain of struggle. The opponents can also be governments, whose agencies have violated rights of citizens across the world.

Those who oppose human rights do so for a mix of reasons. And they often camouflage their denial of rights with distorted claims of cultural relativism and political necessity—or make lack of resources an excuse for inaction.

Indeed, human rights are seen as a threat by many groups, including many in positions of power or superiority. Rights challenge entrenched interests, just as equitable development threatens those in privileged positions. But in the longer run all can gain. Human rights and human development help build law-abiding, prosperous and stable countries.

Individual commitment and community struggle will be the critical factors for advancing rights and human development in the future—just as they have been in the past. But governments and many other actors also have

vital roles. Governments have a special responsibility to lead—but NGOs, the private sector, professionals and many others in civil society have an important part to play, including making government accountable for human rights.

PRIORITIES FOR NATIONAL ACTION

All rights cannot be fulfilled simultaneously, and a refusal to establish priorities runs the risk of making the rights approach synonymous with a "wish list". The importance of universality and the need to establish priorities for action are emphasized in the special contribution by the High Commissioner for Human Rights, Mary Robinson.

Applying the NILE principles—of norms, institutions, laws and an enabling economic environment (outlined in the overview)—to any country situation implies five steps for developing priorities for national action:
* Launch independent national assessments of human rights.
* Align national laws with international human rights standards and commitments.
* Promote human rights norms.
* Strengthen a network of human rights institutions.
* Promote a rights-enabling economic environment.

LAUNCH INDEPENDENT NATIONAL ASSESSMENTS OF HUMAN RIGHTS

Countries differ, and any analysis of policy and institutions in a country needs to be based on a factual account of the extent to which rights have been realized and what the key shortfalls are. Such a diagnosis will reveal whether torture is an ongoing practice, whether the judicial system promotes or obstructs rights, whether the burning issue is lack of freedom of expression or lack of food.

Rather than react to criticisms from outsiders, countries need to take the initiative and produce their own national annual assessments. Important in itself, this would also reduce the tension generated by annual human rights assessments of developing countries by organizations based in the North, whether official or non-governmental. For many countries now bristle at external assessments, for a variety of reasons—some bad, some good.

Despite the end of the cold war and the supposed adoption of an approach integrating all human rights, the external reports deal almost exclusively with civil and political rights, ignoring economic and social rights. These reviews can distort the reality of human rights struggles by groups, institutions and individuals across the world by making human rights appear to be an issue of the "West versus the rest". That is clearly not the intention of these reports, many of which involve extensive collaboration with national institutions. But the world needs to move to the next stage— independent national assessments.

National reviews should go beyond the narrow human rights focus of today's assessments. They can improve both the knowledge of human rights and the process of monitoring progress and setbacks. And they should adopt the framework of advancing rights for human development—covering all rights, not just the civil and political.

An important feature of these annual assessments must be independence. Democratically elected governments should encourage these reports, not fear them. Lack of independent reports on human rights can be a most telling indicator.

Independent national assessments are already being undertaken in several countries. The annual reports of Pakistan's human rights commission have not only documented violations of civil, cultural and political rights but have also covered economic and social rights. The commission's chairwoman, Asma Jehangir, has emphasized the links between extreme poverty, sectarian clashes and civil rights abuses. Successive Pakistani governments in the 1990s have provided the space for these independent assessments, which are widely reported on by the print media. Brazil

SPECIAL CONTRIBUTION

Universality and priorities

Simply stated, universality of human rights means that human rights must be the same everywhere and for everyone. By virtue of being human, every individual is entitled to inalienable rights and freedoms. These rights ensure the dignity and worth of the human person and guarantee human well-being.

Some ask whether human rights are truly universal. The implication is that the rights contained in the Universal Declaration of Human Rights (UDHR) may not apply to some countries and societies. But the text of the UDHR is written in universal terms. "All human beings" are born free and equal in dignity and rights. "Everyone" is entitled to rights without distinction of race, sex or other status. "Everyone" has the right to food, health, housing, education. The record shows that the UDHR is a distillation of many different cultural, legal and religious beliefs. In the 50 years since it was written, its ideals have been repeatedly reasserted. The 1993 World Conference on

Human Rights affirmed that all human rights are universal, indivisible and interdependent.

Does universality negate cultural diversity? Are human rights at odds with religious beliefs? Are they a Western conception that is being imposed to advance global markets? Who can deny that we all seek lives free from fear, discrimination, starvation, torture? When have we ever heard a free voice demand an end to freedom? When has a slave ever argued for slavery? The 1993 World Conference noted that "it is the duty of States, regardless of their political, economic and cultural systems, to promote and protect all human rights."

Human rights are also indivisible. This means that civil and political rights, on the one hand, and economic, social and cultural rights, on the other, must be treated equally. Neither set has priority over the other. Although every country must set priorities for the use of its resources at any given time, this is not the same as choosing between specific rights. We must

not be selective, for these rights are interrelated and interdependent. Freedom from fear and want are inextricably linked to freedom of speech and belief. The right to education is linked to health, and there is a clear connection between a mother's literacy and the health of her very young children.

Every moment spent debating the universality of human rights is one more opportunity lost to achieve effective implementation of all human rights. Universality is, in fact, the essence of human rights: all people are entitled to them, all governments are bound to observe them, all state and civil actors should defend them. The goal is nothing less than all human rights for all.

Mary Robinson
United Nations High Commissioner for Human Rights

recently produced a national human rights report that profiles each state using human development indicators, analyses of progress in human rights and documentation of human rights violations. Brazil is also launching local human rights observatories, monitoring instruments that are part of a network among NGOs, a university and the national human rights secretariat. Country examples such as these provide the stimulus for the global spread of independent national assessments.

REMOVE "BLACK" LAWS TO ALIGN NATIONAL LAWS WITH INTERNATIONAL STANDARDS

Many countries have "black" laws—laws that violate the human rights of particular individuals, minorities, women or other groups. Some laws are blatantly discriminatory. Institutions allied in struggles against discrimination, such as national human rights commissions and pol-

icy institutes, should publish a list of black laws. These laws should be presented to parliament, debated in the media—and changed.

Action against black laws has been successful in many cases. Egypt shows how a creative alliance can end gender discrimination in divorce (box 6.1). Similar progress is being made in the Arab States on other family-related human rights abuses, such as in Jordan, where legislation has been proposed to stop killings of women in the name of honour (box 6.2).

Other actions also are needed to remove discriminatory laws and to improve the judicial system's effectiveness in promoting human rights.

• *Integrating human rights into national constitutions.* Including universal human rights in the constitution—and thus making them enforceable in court—has given people the legal ammunition needed to take action when their rights are violated. The political power of a strong legal judgement against discrimination should not be underestimated. In Israel an Arab family appealed against legal discrimination that had prevented them from moving into a Jewish neighbourhood. In March 2000 the Israeli supreme court agreed: "We do not accept the conception that the values of the State of Israel as a Jewish state justify discrimination between citizens on the basis of religion or nationality."

Following decisions of the United Nations Human Rights Committee to recognize discrimination on the basis of sexual orientation, first South Africa, and later Ecuador and Fiji, included sexual orientation in the non-discrimination provisions of their constitutions.

• *Using public interest litigation.* Delays in the judicial system are being overcome in some instances by recourse to public interest litigation, often heard by a special bench of the court, to address discriminatory and arbitrary administrative actions violating rights. Public interest litigation has been used in the supreme court of India, for example, when rights such as that to education have been violated.

• *Providing resources for an efficient judiciary.* Increased litigation for human rights can create problems if there are too few courts or if judges, magistrates and lawyers are poorly paid. And if people have to wait for years or even decades before their case is heard, disen-

---

BOX 6.1

Ending gender discrimination in divorce—legal gains in Egypt

The start of the 21st century witnessed a major victory for women's rights in Egypt—the passage of a law in February 2000 enabling a woman to divorce without her husband's consent. The law also authorizes the courts to deduct alimony from his wages if he fails to pay. "Every society needs a shock. . . .this was a necessary and overdue shock", said the progressive assistant justice minister who drafted the law.

The law was the product of a dynamic and persistent alliance of civil court judges,

women's groups, lawyers and progressive Muslim clerics. They won in part because they argued their case in the context of their culture, emphasizing aspects of Islam that confer equal rights on women and aspects of Muslim history, such as the instance when the Prophet Mohammad permitted an unhappy woman to leave her husband.

The alliance of government agencies, civil society institutions and private firms defeated a fierce assault from traditionalists.

Source: Human Development Report Office.

BOX 6.2

Legislation against "honour" killings in Jordan

According to the *Jordan Times,* 22 women were killed in Jordan in the name of family honour in 1998, and more than 14 by mid-1999. A coalition of women's groups, journalists, lawyers, NGOs and other advocates circulated a petition calling for the repeal of Article 340 of the Penal Code, which provides a reduced penalty for men who murder their female relatives in cases of "honour" killings. In July 1999 a legal committee of the Justice

Ministry recommended abolishing the article.

The February 2000 review of Jordan by the Committee on the Elimination of Discrimination against Women noted that "several provisions of the penal code continue to discriminate against women. In particular, the committee is concerned that article 340 of the penal code provides a defence to a man who kills or injures his wife, or his female kin, caught in the act of adultery."

Source: Equality Now 1999; Hamdan 1999; Hijab 2000.

---

chantment is inevitable. While chapter 3 emphasized the vital importance of an independent judiciary, efficiency is also essential. Making an independent judiciary efficient requires resources and a decentralized judicial system that brings justice close to the people.

PROMOTE HUMAN RIGHTS NORMS

With deep-seated prejudices and injustices embodied in teaching materials, values and norms, changing attitudes can be the hardest thing to do.

Three ways to influence norms: educating people, sensitizing officials and mobilizing public opinion through the media.
• *Educating people about human rights*. As the Universal Declaration of Human Rights makes clear, human rights should be taught in every school as universal rights that all people possess. Cambodia emphasizes changing social norms through early education. Since 1994, 25,000 Cambodian teachers have been trained in the human rights curriculum. The curriculum, already taught to more than 3 million children, may turn out to be a vital investment in the country's future.

Using radio, television, video—and traditional songs, skits, dramas and puppet shows—to highlight different aspects of human rights is also an important part of an education strategy, especially for illiterate citizens. In 1995 the Cambodian Institute of Human Rights adopted an innovative approach to teaching people human rights—using television quiz shows. In 1997 the contestants were members of the military and the police force. The programmes were also broadcast on the national radio, the primary source of information. In Bulgaria a parliamentary committee has started working with television programmes, using popular entertainment to influence human rights norms.
• *Sensitizing officials to human rights issues*. Educating policy-makers, the army, the police and other groups about human rights is essential for creating a human rights culture. Ecuador was one of the first countries to ratify the Convention on the Rights of the Child. Soon after, it used the national electoral machinery to give children the opportunity to vote on the pro-

visions that mattered most to them. A week of television programmes explaining the convention preceded the vote. Nearly 200,000 children voted. One result: the share of adults knowing about the convention jumped to more than 90%. Other countries have begun to bring awareness of the rights of children and women into training for social and family case workers. In Guatemala Conavigua, a national council of Guatemalan women widowed by war, works to educate and raise awareness about the peace agreements.
• *Mobilizing public opinion through the media*. The media can mobilize public opinion by spreading awareness of human rights policies and highlighting violations. In many countries the media already are a major force for reporting and demanding accountability, as examples in this Report have shown. A related tool for influencing norms: the Internet. Cyber networks have brought attention to rights, disseminating information on good practices and on rights violations.

A coalition of African NGOs working for the right to food and food security uses the Internet to exchange experiences and lessons. The Third World Network uses it to disseminate information and good practices on human rights. The Dalit and Tribal People's Electronic Resource Site in India brings attention to the exclusion of 250 million low-caste people.

STRENGTHEN A NETWORK OF HUMAN RIGHTS INSTITUTIONS

Many institutions that work on rights do not see themselves as human rights institutions. Building a wide alliance of public agencies, civil society organizations, the media and the private sector increases the efficacy of efforts for advocacy and accountability.
• *Creating partnerships around causes*. Forging partnerships with other groups fighting for the same cause can provide strength and solidarity. The Convention on the Rights of the Child has stimulated broad alliances in a wide range of countries (box 6.3). Similar alliances have been built at the national level to promote women's rights (box 6.4). In any society some groups have special needs because of who they are or because of their situation—people with

The media can mobilize public opinion by spreading awareness of human rights policies and highlighting violations

BOX 6.3

The rights of the child—turning words into actions

The Convention on the Rights of the Child, adopted unanimously by the UN General Assembly in 1989, entered into force as international human rights law less than a year later. It has quickly become the most ratified human rights treaty in history, with 191 countries—all but Somalia and the United States—ratifying it in less than a decade. And in many countries around the world, it is already making an impact.

The convention built on earlier declarations:
• The first Declaration of the Rights of the Child, drafted in 1923 by Eglantyne Jebb, founder of Save the Children. One year later it was elaborated and adopted by the League of Nations, declaring that "mankind owes to the child the best it has to give".
• The Universal Declaration of Human Rights, adopted in 1948, applying equally to all children as well as adults.
• The Declaration on the Rights of the Child, adopted unanimously in 1959 by the UN General Assembly, providing a fuller and more precise definition of the rights of the child.
• The International Year of the Child—1979—during which it was recommended that the United Nations draft a comprehensive treaty binding on states.

The 1989 convention provides a comprehensive approach by incorporating all human rights—civil and political as well as economic, social and cultural. The "soul" of the convention is four articles setting out its overarching principles:
• No discrimination against children.
• In all matters concerning children, the best interests of the child shall be primary.
• The right of the child to life, survival and development.
• The right of the child to express views freely in all matters affecting him or her.

The convention requires states to adopt all appropriate measures—legislative, administrative, social, economic, budgetary, educational or other—and to allocate the resources necessary to ensure effective implementation. The convention recognizes the obligations of other parties—parents and families, civil society and the international community. The fact that a child depends completely on others over the early years underlines the importance of obligations. The needs of very young children cannot wait—whether for care, food and warmth or for loving stimulus, basic education and health care.

Norms

The convention has encouraged children to speak out and defend their rights. In Colombia the Children's Movement for Peace, nominated for the Nobel Peace prize, organized a national movement when 2.7 million children voted in a symbolic referendum on the human rights of minors. In Ecuador and Mexico, too, millions of children went to the polls and voted on their rights.

Children's rights became a principal item in all the major UN conferences of the 1990s. The convention formed the basis for other international legal instruments, such as the Hague Convention on Protection of Children and Cooperation in Respect of Inter-Country Adoption. The new ILO convention on the worst forms of child labour is another example. And several regional instruments are based on the convention, such as the African Charter on the Rights and Welfare of the Child.

The convention has led to a process for formulating two optional protocols—to raise the minimum age of military recruitment and participation in armed conflicts, and to enhance the protection of children from sexual exploitation, including through greater international cooperation.

Institutions

Many states have appointed an ombudsman or commissioner for children, as a new independent institution or as part of an existing human rights mechanism. Norway was first to take such a step, followed by Costa Rica, Austria, Russia and Australia. Honduras has set up mechanisms to promote an integrated policy approach to children, to ensure coordination between relevant bodies and departments and to monitor progress in implementing the convention.

Laws

The convention paved the way for recognizing and safeguarding children's rights at the national level:
• Today at least 22 countries have incorporated children's rights in their constitutions—including Brazil, Ecuador, Ethiopia and South Africa.
• More than 50 countries have a process of law review to ensure compatibility with the convention's provisions.
• Bolivia, Brazil and Nicaragua have promoted the adoption of a code on the rights of children and adolescents.
• Other countries have given consideration to major areas requiring legislative changes, from child labour (India, Pakistan, Portugal) to protection from sexual exploitation (Australia, Belgium, Germany, Sweden, Thailand), juvenile justice (Brazil, Costa Rica, El Salvador) and inter-country adoption (Paraguay, Romania, the United Kingdom).
• In addition, countries have taken important legislative steps to promote changes in behaviour and forbid practices incompatible with the convention's spirit and provisions—the ban on female genital mutilation (in several West African states, including Burkina Faso and Senegal), the prohibition of corporal punishment of children in schools and in the family (as in Austria, Cyprus and the Nordic countries).

An enabling economic environment

• Parliaments in Brazil, South Africa and Sri Lanka have enacted legislation and national budgets to more clearly identify allocations for children.
• Norway now publishes a "children's annex" to its annual budget, which is regularly submitted to the parliament.
• In Belgium the parliament produced an impact report on children, monitoring government policy for respect for the rights of the child.
• In Sweden the parliament adopted a bill to ensure visibility of the child's perspective in decision-making and called for an analysis of the impact of budgetary decisions and legislation on children.

Source: Human Development Report Office.

HIV/AIDS, people with disabilities, refugees, homosexuals and so on. Realizing their human rights often requires alliances, such as the Disabled People's International (box 6.5).

One global alliance fights for the right to food—the FoodFirst Information and Action Network (FIAN), which takes on advocacy of complex issues of land tenure and agricultural policy. Rather than focus on government responsibility for directly delivering food to the poorest, FIAN and similar groups press for policy change to create a more conducive economic environment for providing food to the poor. In an act of global solidarity, landless Indian farmers joined FIAN at the Brazilian embassy in New Delhi to support land rights for the rural landless in Brazil. In a rapidly globalizing world such dynamic alliances can create national and international solidarity for promoting specific rights.

- *Using national human rights commissions.* In some countries national human rights commissions try to ensure that the laws and regulations for realizing human rights are effectively applied. Such commissions receive and investigate complaints of human rights abuses, resolve them through conciliation and arbitration and review the government's human rights policies and the implementation of ratified human rights treaties. For example, the Mexican human rights commission is extremely active in the rights of people with disabilities, the New Zealand commission in human rights education and the South African commission in economic and social rights.
- *Appointing an ombudsman for human rights.* Protecting individuals from rights abuses by public officials or institutions is a vital role of human rights ombudsmen around the world. In Slovenia the ombudsman files an annual report on the observance of human rights with parliament. According to the 1998 report, the ombudsman has received increasing complaints against public officials, with the number rising from 2,352 in 1995 to 3,448 in 1998. In 1998 the largest share related to court and police procedures, but the biggest increases were for labour relations and restrictions on personal freedoms.
- *Instituting parliamentary human rights bodies.* According to the Inter-Parliamentary Union, of the 120 national parliaments today,

nearly half have formal bodies dealing with human rights. Their mandates reflect the national context, but these bodies share the goal of ensuring that the standards set out in the Universal Declaration of Human Rights and the other human rights covenants and instruments are translated into law—and realized in practice.

In the Republic of Moldova the parliament appointed three parliamentary advocates to

---

BOX 6.4

Alliances for achieving women's human rights

The Convention on the Elimination of All Forms of Discrimination Against Women (CEDAW), adopted in 1979, has helped realize women's rights the world over. Women's human rights are violated in three main areas:
- Discrimination in economic, political and social opportunities.
- Inequality in family life, including in marriage and in reproductive decision-making.
- Gender-based violence, ranging from violence at home to violence in the community, by the state and during armed conflict.

Through solidarity and struggle, the environment that has sanctioned violations of women's rights is changing in many parts of the world. New policies and laws are recognizing and advancing women's human rights. But reality lags far behind rhetoric.

A strategy to address the abuses of women's human rights must rest on women's empowerment—ensuring that they have greater control over their economic resources, bodies and lives. And it must include the following:
- *Changing social norms.* Among the greatest challenges to recognition of women's human rights are patriarchal attitudes and traditions. On grounds of cultural relativism, some governments and religious groups justify female genital mutilation, stoning of women and self-immolation of widows. To counter this requires human rights education, partnerships and persuasion from within. A coalition of progressive NGOs in the occupied Palestine territory has mounted a successful challenge to religious orthodoxy. In Cambodia and Kyrgyzstan NGOs are training journalists to recognize and change distorted media depictions of women that contribute to gender-based violence.
- *Changing laws and reforming the criminal justice system.* Rights can be

established by redress of law—national and international. Using the United Republic of Tanzania's ratification of CEDAW, courts there nullified customary law denying women the right to sell inherited land. But in many cases national laws must be changed or written—especially for security against violence, for equal economic and social opportunity and for rights to land and inheritance. In Brazil special police forces have been trained to respond to victims of gender abuse, contributing to changes in attitudes and practices.
- *Implementing international agreements.* CEDAW brought changes to constitutions in Colombia, South Africa and Uganda. It brought new laws to China, Costa Rica and Japan. And it has been held binding in court cases in Australia, Nepal and Zambia. While CEDAW does not explicitly address violence against women, a new general recommendation was appended in 1991 prohibiting gender violence by the state and by private persons or groups. The Vienna Declaration of 1993 was the first UN document to state that women's human rights are an indivisible and integral part of universal human rights.

CEDAW's new optional protocol, introduced in 1994, contains unique procedures enabling individuals to claim remedies for violations of convention rights. In addition, NGOs can submit "shadow" reports—alternative statements to supplement state submissions. A coalition of Croatian women's NGOs presented a shadow report in 1998—and subsequently forged a new alliance with the Croatian Commission for Equality.

Though CEDAW has many ratifications, it also has many reservations. These reservations must be removed to allow this valuable document to come to life at the national level everywhere.

Source: Coomaraswamy 2000; Womenwatch 2000; Landsberg-Lewis 1998.

---

examine individual claims and to institute legal procedures. They are also expected to improve the legislative framework for human rights through analysis and policy recommendations. Consistent with this mission, the advocates in 1998 established an independent institution for protecting human rights. The Centre for Human Rights reports to the legislature each year on the observance of human rights.

In Nicaragua the Committee for Human Rights and Peace, set up in 1981, works with NGOs in seeking information and documentation on the performance of state officials. In Brazil the Committee on Human Rights receives, assesses and investigates complaints about threats to human rights. Each year the committee organizes a national conference on human rights, with more than 400 representatives of civil society groups. It has also helped prepare the national human rights plan and monitor and evaluate its implementation (box 6.6).

All these national institutions need to be harnessed in an alliance for promoting human rights. With each having a different comparative advantage and mandate, collaboration among them is needed to realize rights and fight against coalitions opposing progress.

PROMOTE A RIGHTS-ENABLING ECONOMIC ENVIRONMENT

In all countries a critical task for public policy is to build an enabling environment that empowers people, ensures them opportunities to fulfil their human rights and, where necessary, provides support for them to do so. This is where many policies for human rights and human development come together.

To generate the resources and the opportunities for fulfilling human rights, public policy has to foster a growing, efficient and sustainable economy. But public policy has an additional responsibility—it has to ensure that part of the bigger pool of resources goes to advance people's political and economic rights.

How to create an enabling economic environment in which public policy can most effectively provide resources for advancing human rights? Through four sets of actions. First, the public sector must focus on what it can do and leave for others what it should not do, a lesson reinforced by global developments of the past quarter century. Running banks and industrial enterprises is, by and large, better suited to the private sector. Leaving that task to private initiative not only increases the efficiency of the economy but also enables the public sector to focus on providing the institutions and services that the private sector will not.

Second, with this division of labour, the state can focus on the direct provision of many economic, social and civil rights. Building human capabilities of the poor, through basic health care, nutrition and education, is a primary responsibility of the government. Financ-

---

BOX 6.5

An alliance for the rights of individuals with special needs— the Disabled People's International

A good example of effective action to protect people with special vulnerabilities in human rights is the Disabled People's International (DPI). The DPI is a grassroots cross-disability network set up in 1980 to give people with disabilities a voice. From the start it has dealt with human rights. Today the DPI has member organizations in 158 countries, more than half of them in the developing world.

The DPI's main strategy is to raise awareness of disability issues and of the human rights of people with disabilities, but it also supports development projects. The organization played an important part in developing standard rules on disability. These served as a blueprint for a convention adopted by the Organization of American States in July 1998 to eliminate all forms of discrimination against people with disabilities.

The DPI has also contributed to changes in law or policy in such places as South Africa, Uganda, Zimbabwe and the European Union.

Source: Hijab 2000.

BOX 6.6

Putting pressure on the government— the national human rights action plan of Brazil

The Brazilian national action plan for human rights, published in 1996 by a partnership of civil society organizations, was the first Latin American programme for protecting and promoting human rights. In partnership with civil society organizations, the government has published maps of human rights violations, established programmes to protect witnesses and victims and started training courses on human rights for 5,000 military police. In December 1999 Brazil recognized the jurisdiction of the Inter-American Court of Human Rights.

In 1997–99 the implementation of the action plan was evaluated at local, state and national levels. With the federal government beginning to support human rights, rather than neglecting them or supporting violations, tension has arisen with state governments and agencies that do not respect rights.

In January 2000 the Centre for the Study of Violence at the University of São Paulo published a national report on the status of human rights in Brazil. One of its criticisms of the action plan was that it concentrated too much on civil and political rights, at the expense of economic, social and cultural rights.

Source: Pinheiro and Baluarte 2000.

---

ing the judicial system to protect rights and improving prison conditions are among its responsibilities for advancing civil rights.

Third, the major economic ministries, such as finance and planning, need to integrate rights into the economic policy-making process. By reflecting ministries' obligations on economic and social rights in economic policy-making, the government can assess the shortfalls in meeting these rights and ways to reduce them within resource constraints. Such a process would also clarify the resource requirements for providing, say, mandatory primary education. The concept of imperfect obligation, defined in chapter 1, is relevant here. Governments must recognize the economic and social rights of the people they serve, but it is meaningless to assert that those in poor countries must fulfil all of them immediately.

Finally, the private sector also has responsibilities in creating an enabling economic environment. Chambers of commerce and other business organizations should contribute to efforts to further improve rights—not only at the workplace but also in advocating policies to address human rights violations. Many companies have advocated reducing child labour through mandatory primary education (box 6.7). Firms should be engaged in a dialogue, to learn what businesses across the world are doing about human rights. And they should be encouraged, through prestigious national awards, to suggest and implement practices to advance rights.

The private sector should also cooperate with public agencies in incorporating human rights concerns into the "principles of market supervision", especially to avoid discrimination in the job market, to prohibit child labour and to ensure free association and collective bargaining. Consumer rights and protection from market abuses are best handled by non-profit organizations.

PRIORITIES FOR INTERNATIONAL ACTION

Enlightened, responsible international policy action is needed to help poor countries move towards realization of all rights. The focus cannot be on simple transfers of resources. There must also be a global environment that facilitates the development of poor nations.

This implies an international agenda with five main actions:
- Reduce global inequality and marginalization.
- Prevent deadly conflicts through early warning systems.
- Strengthen the international system for promoting human rights.
- Support regional institutions in their promotion of human rights.
- Get commitment from global corporations.

REDUCE GLOBAL INEQUALITY AND MARGINALIZATION

Many proud civilizations are wounded by deepening poverty and marginalization—and many feel ostracized from the world community because of their lack of participation in new knowledge and global institutions.

Several actions are critical for creating a conducive global environment for promoting human rights.
- *Adopting a rights ethos for aid.* Aid, in its early phases, was not concerned with an integrated vision of human rights. Indeed, much of it was dictated by foreign policy concerns. Sometimes it flowed—with cynical disregard—to dictators who repressed civil and political rights. But the days are over when this could be justified by arguing that aid was at least promoting some economic and social rights.

BOX 6.7

A private firm's advocacy for mandatory primary education

South Asia has more children out of school than the rest of the world together—a poisonous environment for the spread of child labour. Pakistan has been a focus of global attention, for using child labour for the production of soccer balls in Sialkot and bonded labour in the brick kilns industry. Firms that have come under scrutiny have typically responded—if they have responded—by educating children or removing those below a certain age from their plants.

Sayyed Engineers went further—joining an advocacy campaign for mandatory primary education. Working with the Economic Policy Research Unit, an independent policy think tank, Sayyed Engineers and other firms undertook a national survey on child labour and primary education, later publishing a policy-oriented report. Author of the report's foreword: Imran Khan, the immensely popular captain of the national cricket team. The survey, the report and the production of calendars spotlighting the issue were financed entirely by private firms.

Source: Human Development Report Office.

Many examples of misallocation build public cynicism about the aid bureaucracy. The people in donor countries need to speak directly to the people in poor countries—by engaging in debates and decisions about the use of aid to promote economic, social and civil rights.

Some donor countries are now taking the lead in focusing on civil and political rights in their efforts to promote good governance. Australia, Germany, Norway, Sweden, Switzerland and the United Kingdom are among those taking a rights-based approach to development assistance. Norway recently reviewed its support to human rights efforts in the United Republic of Tanzania, Zambia and Zimbabwe. The review noted that "naming and shaming" is typically done more effectively by civil society institutions and the media, which have a clear comparative advantage in this. Technical cooperation was more helpful for support to human rights institutions.

• *Forging compacts for progressive realization of rights.* Global compacts for meeting basic rights targets can also help, financed through national budget restructuring and increased international support. These global compacts call for open and accountable commitments to meeting some basic economic and social rights, such as access to education and health care.

Such proposals are similar to the 20:20 initiative, first suggested in *Human Development Report 1992.* Some developing countries are now fulfilling their side of the 20:20 proposal—allocating 20% of public spending to basic social services. No donors are living up to their side—allocating 20% of their aid budgets to basic social services. Doing so would help mobilize the additional $70–80 billion a year needed from national and international sources to ensure basic social services for all.

• *Writing off debt.* Debt continues to constrain human development and realization of human rights. Bilateral donors such as France have cancelled some of their debt, but others need to follow suit. The initiative for debt relief for heavily indebted poor countries (HIPCs) has had limited impact so far. By December 1999, of 40 HIPCs, only Bolivia, Burkina Faso,

Côte d'Ivoire, Guyana, Mali, Mozambique and Uganda had completed debt relief negotiations. New measures introduced in 1999 seek to provide faster, deeper debt relief with links to poverty reduction. But debt relief still lags far behind intentions and promises. Needed is accelerated implementation for all countries, and new initiatives to link debt reduction to human development.

• *Accelerating action to develop technologies for human poverty reduction.* Today's international arrangements constrain the ability of poor countries to use, adapt and develop the findings of recent research for advancing their economies and raising the living standards of their people. Why? Because distorted research priorities focus on the problems of the rich—part of the underprovision of public goods.

Some private foundations, such as the Bill and Melinda Gates Foundation, have recently given support to vaccine research for the diseases facing poor people. In the United States a tax credit scheme for pharmaceutical companies, proposed in early 2000, would use market incentives to redirect research efforts. The credits would stimulate vaccine research on tuberculosis, malaria and AIDS—diseases that take more than 5 million lives a year in poor countries. The expected spending of $1 billion over the next decade is similar to what UNICEF spends on its vaccination programmes. Such public-private partnerships are the stimulus needed for other research and technology programmes aimed at the problems of poor people.

There are also proposals to establish regional centres of technology, and to bring research results to poor people through the Internet and other cost-reducing telecommunications technology. Some poor countries have made major advances in adopting new technology in some sectors. China, India and several other Asian countries have become vibrant players in the technology revolution.

Such promising developments need to be built on—by the international community and by "South-South" collaboration—to address dryland agriculture, environmental degradation and the health hazards consuming the lives of poor people.

- *Accelerating access to markets for the exports of developing countries*. For many developing countries, better access to trade opportunities will spur growth in incomes and employment, as occurred for much of East Asia. But some of the most marginalized countries still produce agricultural products with declining terms of trade. They continue to need policy reform, technical assistance and aid inflows to diversify their economies.

While globalization shrinks the world, the distance between its richest and poorest people grows. Those who are integrated live in a charmed circle of prosperity. But for those outside, the turbulence of continued marginalization and poverty is creating a volcano of despair.

Viewing global justice as a right for the poorest and the marginalized requires a moral commitment and calls for fundamental changes in attitudes and perspectives, internationally and nationally. Our view of common humanity must extend beyond the borders of the nation state to where fulfilling human rights in any one part of the world is given the same seriousness and the same support as fulfilling rights in any other.

The cost of inaction is high—as leaders of both rich and poor countries have recognized. US President Bill Clinton has referred to the "widening gulf between the world's haves and have-nots" and urged that we "work harder to treat the sources of despair before they turn into the poison of hatred". President Mandela, no stranger to hatred, has underlined "the scale of global inequity as we exit the century, as well as the opportunity and rewards".

PREVENT DEADLY CONFLICTS

Some of the modern concern with human rights grew out of the struggle to protect people and their rights during war. The Universal Declaration of Human Rights was inspired in part by outrage over the tragedy of the holocaust and the killing and destruction of the Second World War. Recent violence in Afghanistan, Angola, Bosnia and Herzegovina, Chechnya, East Timor, Kashmir, Kosovo, Rwanda, Sierra Leone, Somalia and other places has stirred new thinking about preventing conflict—and about building peace.

Preventing and reducing conflicts has two important implications for human rights. The first is the *direct* effect of reducing a primary source of gross human rights violations. The second is the *indirect* effect of freeing up resources, so that the world community can shift its focus away from peacekeeping operations and towards human development. Initiatives to bring diverse national actors together and diagnose the causes of conflict have been effective in some countries and show promise for replication elsewhere.

The Carnegie Commission on Preventing Deadly Conflicts estimated that the cost to the international community of the seven major wars in the 1990s, not including Kosovo, was $200 billion—four times the development aid in any single year. Not too surprising, then, that the volume of development aid went down substantially in the 1990s. The shift of resources away from development may even be contributing to future conflicts—as assistance is withdrawn just when needed to prevent escalation.

With so much money thrown at problems after they explode, the current allocation of resources for international assistance is far from rational. The key challenge is to gear international institutions—particularly the United Nations, formed with this intent—to preventing conflict. The rewards in lives saved and human development promoted are too high for continued procrastination.

With global resource flows doing so little to create an enabling environment for human rights, poor people must be bewildered. Poor countries send huge amounts to rich countries to service debt. Meanwhile, rich nations spend huge sums on "peacekeeping" missions after conflicts break out, at the same time reducing resources for development assistance.

The biggest change needed is to shift the mandate—and resources—to preventing conflicts by addressing their underlying causes. Promoting a global democracy also requires eschewing the militaristic path and focusing on global human development. Two types of policy instruments are needed: early warning systems and disarmament for development.

Our view of common humanity must extend beyond the borders of the nation state

- *Deploying early warning systems*. If the world community is serious about shifting to preventive measures, it has to make more creative use of early warning systems.

The deployment of a preventive force in the former Yugoslav Republic of Macedonia appears to be a successful example. The Organization of African Unity has also emphasized the importance of more effective early warning systems to avoid deadly conflict. Early warning systems are being used in Africa for the prevention of famine or natural disasters, as in Botswana, South Africa and Zimbabwe.

Implementing early warning systems for manmade disasters is a complex challenge, but deserves support in the shift to preventive actions (box 6.8).

Early warning requires early response. A broad range of political, economic and social—not just military—measures are needed for quick response. Negotiating missions with distinguished international leadership can go a long way in preventive diplomacy.

- *Disarming for development*. Civil wars can last for decades—witness the recent histories of Afghanistan, Guatemala, Lebanon, Mozambique, Somalia and Sudan. The fuel for destruction in these civil wars is not nuclear bombs and chemical warfare, which attract attention, but the more mundane mines and light weapons. The abundance of supply can be gauged by the price: in some African countries an AK-47 sells for $6, the price of a meal at McDonald's.

When weapons circulate, so do fear and the expectation of conflict, undermining investment and markets. Disarming for development can help restore an enabling environment for economic revival. During Albania's civil disturbances in 1997 civilians stormed government arms depots. Alarmed by the prospect of 600,000 weapons in circulation, the Albanian government, the United Nations and several international donors financed a "weapons in exchange for development" project in the Gramsch district. In return for 6,000 weapons and ammunition, the district received assistance for rebuilding physical and social infrastructure destroyed during conflict.

Bilateral aid agencies should raise concerns about the harmful effects of actions by other ministries of their governments—a protest in which the media and NGOs can participate. In particular, they should point to the damage to human rights from agreements for sales of the small arms and mines used so widely in civil wars. And companies that sell instruments of torture could be classified as rogue firms.

The Economic Community of West African States is working with the United Nations and other agencies to reduce the proliferation of light weapons. Economic revival is likely if weapons-for-development swaps

---

BOX 6.8

FEWER conflicts—a network for early warning systems

The Forum for Early Warning and Early Response (FEWER) is an independent consortium of intergovernmental and nongovernmental organizations and academic institutions whose aim is to provide decision-makers with information and analyses for early warning of conflict and with options for early response.

FEWER is working with the United Nations, the Organization for Security and Co-operation in Europe (OSCE) and other organizations to implement a strategy for early warning and response involving the Caucasus, Central Asia, South-East Asia, West Africa and the Great Lakes region of Central Africa.

An early warning system requires an analysis of many sources of information and a built-in quality assurance system. The core analysis requires not only a factual understanding, but also an understanding of perceptions—often as important as facts—and of cultural sensitivities. And it should use a comprehensive methodology and standard formats for reporting and corroboration. Rigorous analysis, involving national, regional and international specialists, led to reasonably accurate predictions for the Democratic Republic of the Congo and the Daghestan-Chechen conflict.

This approach surveys the conflict prevention capacities of different actors in the region and brings together a coalition of the "willing"—governments, intergovernmental and non-governmental organizations, local communities. It then has them agree on four things: what is generating the conflict, what are the long-term peace objectives, what and who are the potential spoilers and what tools are available to outline a programme for conflict prevention and resolution.

For the former Yugoslav Republic of Macedonia, early warning of conflict allowed an intervention in response. In 1999 the OSCE High Commissioner for National Minorities issued a powerful and effective early warning signal about the fallout in the country due to tensions in Kosovo. The warning led to a reasonably swift donor response, in a conflict region of high political visibility.

To provide effective support to the international community in preventing conflicts and related human rights abuses, early warning systems must take the following into account:
- Political will and early warning are interdependent. Without political will—as in the two years preceding the Zaire crisis—early warning is irrelevant. But without proper early warning—based on accurate and adequate information, systematic and comprehensive analysis and real and effective options—all the political will in the world is unlikely to lead to effective action. And proper early warning is essential in developing political will, which takes time and trust. Proper early warning of the genocide in Rwanda might have made it possible to mobilize political will for effective intervention.
- Early warning information and analysis often reflect the interests of the stakeholder doing the collecting and analysing. There is a need for an independent early warning capacity with solely a peace agenda.

Source: Adelman 1999; FEWER 1999; van der Stoel 1999.

---

reduce tension and the expectation of conflict. Such swaps can also misfire. But when they work, as the aftermath of previous conflicts across the world has shown, the repairs and public works create a framework for economic revival.

Can anything be done to protect human rights while civil wars rage? Cynicism about the value of doing so is misplaced. The laws of war grew out of the vision of the founder of the Red Cross, and these laws have made an enormous difference. Now these rules of international engagement need to be extended to internal conflicts. How? No easy answers—but step by step, despite caution and differences, the international community is struggling to find some solutions. The Security Council is seeking consensus for strengthening the legal protection of civilians. Some countries still have not ratified the basic international instruments. Many can do much more to ensure that their military and police force are trained to work within the international standards applying to war.

STRENGTHEN THE INTERNATIONAL SYSTEM OF HUMAN RIGHTS

The modern international human rights machinery was established with the Universal Declaration of Human Rights. In the first two or three decades there was some action, much inaction and only limited achievements, in part because of the cold war. In the past decade implementation of international standards has gathered pace (see chapter 2).

The reporting procedures and monitoring strategies of treaty bodies have been strengthened over the past two decades. NGOs are participating more in reporting, often by providing "shadow" (alternative) reports that complement the information provided by governments. The treaty bodies, working through constructive dialogue, assist governments in implementing their treaty commitments. Although lacking real implementation power, they often raise sensitive questions and identify the most pressing human rights issues needing remedial action.

But the review process is slow and seriously under-resourced—a result of the number of countries represented, the range of issues and factual detail on which countries are asked to provide information and the limited time available to the independent experts elected to the committees.

Proposed solutions include changes to expedite reporting and greater public involvement. Proposals have also been made for consolidating the six supervisory committees into a single treaty body, with more financial and staff resources to give it more teeth. Removing the inefficiencies is a priority. Without major reform and additional resources, it will be difficult to create a treaty-based culture of compliance.

The Rome statute to establish an International Criminal Court represents a vision of a new era—one of effective action against the most extreme violations of individual human rights within nation states. The court should reinforce the responsibility of states for protecting human rights and contribute to an international order that demands respect for human rights.

A new precedent for accountability in human rights was set by the Pinochet case. In this pioneering case one state, Spain, requested extradition from another, the United Kingdom, of someone accused of torture and related crimes while head of state of a third, Chile. Some African governments have used the International Criminal Court's provisions in ways that provide impressive illustrations of the actions made possible by an increasingly supportive international human rights framework (box 6.9). Still, much remains to be done. For example, all the crimes of the wars in Bosnia and Herzegovina and Croatia and of Kosovo are still to be accounted for.

Future advances should focus not on creating new institutions but on consolidating and integrating the mandates of existing agencies. UNICEF, for example, has incorporated a rights-based approach in its programmes and is working with many states to implement them. It is working with civil society organizations and joining forces with others to secure the rights of children. And its campaign to change social norms that "validate" honour killings of women continues its emphasis on

A new precedent for accountability in human rights was set by the Pinochet case

discrimination leading to adverse economic, social and political outcomes for women.

UNIFEM's work on aspects of CEDAW and related areas is pioneering and wide ranging. UNESCO has a procedure for filing individual complaints for alleged infringements of rights to education, information, language and culture. The International Labour Organization, from its inception, has set standards and put in place mechanisms for protecting workers' rights and promoting their welfare. Its monitoring procedures provide an opportunity for partnerships for human rights and workers' welfare between the government, employers and trade unions.

UNDP is integrating human rights concerns into its work on human development, and its network of country offices is using an imaginative mix of advocacy and technical assistance programmes to build institutions in support of human rights. UNDP is also creating a unique advocacy asset—a network built around the global and national human development reports. Written by national institutions, many of the national reports have already assessed the human rights situation in the country and offered policy recommendations. Thus where feasible, these reports can be the initial independent national assessments of human rights. UNDP's technical assistance programmes provide support for institutions of governance and organize training programmes and workshops. In all these endeavours the country offices and regional bureaux work closely with the Office of the High Commissioner for Human Rights.

With most UN agencies working on different aspects of human rights, a more coordinated and integrated approach could offer big gains in efficiency and efficacy.

SUPPORT REGIONAL INSTITUTIONS IN THEIR PROMOTION OF HUMAN RIGHTS

Most regions have taken human rights initiatives, encouraging action from allies and peers. The advantage of these initiatives is that they embed the advance of universal human rights in a culturally sensitive discourse. The danger is that in the name of pragmatism, they water down international standards and visions in order to reach agreement.

The regional human rights bodies reflect both achievements and shortcomings (box 6.10). Initiated in 1949, the Council of Europe devotes major efforts to protecting human rights and fundamental freedoms. From the beginning it included in its aims "the maintenance and further realization of human rights and fundamental freedoms". A core principle is universality of human rights, backed by promotion of "common standards throughout all member states, to the benefit of all, no matter who they are or where they are from".

The Arab human rights charter has sparked debate on whether it represents progress—and whether its provisions water down international commitments. Nonetheless, it is an important advance in the regional recognition of rights, embodying them within the cultural traditions that define people's lives.

In Asia NGOs have taken the initiative in developing a regional human rights charter—

BOX 6.9

African countries take the initiative in implementing the International Criminal Court's provisions

The agreement to create the International Criminal Court as a permanent mechanism of international criminal justice advances the principle of individual accountability in the world community for such crimes as genocide, crimes against humanity and serious violations of the laws and customs of war. The statute for establishing the court, adopted at a conference of the international community in Rome in 1998, achieved several important goals. It extended the court's jurisdiction to internal as well as international conflicts. And it affirmed the modern definition of crimes against humanity, recognizing that constraints on gross abuse of a population should not be limited to events during a state of war. This broad definition warns all governments of the possible consequences of violence directed towards their own people.

For many countries making the transition to democracy, the legal and political framework that the International Criminal Court represents has immediate practical importance. Some African countries are leading the way. On 3 February 2000 a court in Senegal charged the former Chadian dictator Hissene Habre with "torture and barbarity". Habre, who ruled Chad for eight years starting in 1982, has lived comfortably in a smart suburb of Senegal's capital, Dakar, since fleeing his own country in 1990.

Senegal is one of the first countries to take advantage of the international conventions allowing crimes against humanity to be tried in countries other than those in which they were committed. It also has the admirable record of being the first country to ratify the Rome statute, in February 1999.

Ghana soon followed suit. In November 1999 its parliament voted unanimously to ratify the Rome statute, strongly affirming the importance of familiarity with its provisions by other African states as a safeguard for the wave of democratization on the continent. The parliament's actions received widespread support from the country's civil society organizations.

Source: Parliamentarians for Global Action 2000; Bassiouni 1999; *Economist* 2000.

complicated, since the region is the world's most populous and diverse. No other continent has such a mix of major religions, side by side with explicitly secular governments—nor such a mix of wealthy and poor nations. The Asian charter does not have the support of governments, and is meant more to mobilize civil society institutions within a framework of shared humane values.

GET COMMITMENT FROM GLOBAL CORPORATIONS

People's movements have galvanized public opinion against multinational corporations that flout human rights. Well-targeted campaigns have severely damaged their public image, and consumer boycotts have reduced their profits. In many cases the maligned firms have responded by developing codes of conduct to provide common human rights guidelines for global operations.

Critics of voluntary codes point to the need for mandatory actions monitored by a regulatory body—by the industry, an international NGO or a government body. Supporters point to the need for the codes to constrain the behaviour of subcontractors to the principal firm, as well as of national firms, where many of the rights violations occur.

Benetton, the Italian-based garment manufacturer, has gone beyond voluntary codes and expanded into public advocacy of rights issues—advocacy that has nothing to do with its operations. One of its campaigns pushes for the end of the death penalty.

Such campaigns mark an important and possibly decisive shift in private corporations' involvement in rights issues—an entirely different role in advocating issues that affect rights beyond their working environment. This socially conscious advocacy could offer a more effective force for change than project interventions related to a firm's operations. An interesting example is that of a private corporation that has pledged to refuse diamond sales for financing conflict (box 6.11).

Another interesting innovation is the partnership between firms and civil society organizations, to recognize violations of certain rights.

Liz Claiborne, Bell Atlantic and American Express have joined with labour unions, government agencies and non-profit agencies, such as Victim Services in Manhattan, that deal with domestic violence. These firms encourage their staff to report violations and provide counselling to employees who are victims of abuse.

Many firms are trying to rectify poor past performance. Take the Coca-Cola Company, being sued by minority employees for institutional bias. In response to the legal cases and

---

BOX 6.10

European regional initiatives for promoting human rights

Several European initiatives have extended the mechanisms for promoting human rights beyond the boundaries of the nation state.

Council of Europe
Genocide and suffering of people in Europe led to the creation of regional institutions aimed at preventing similar events by recognizing and realizing human rights and freedoms. Now with 41 member states, the Council of Europe continues to work towards democratic ideals, ensuring universality of human rights by promoting common standards throughout all member states.

The structures of the council include the European Court of Human Rights, which has dealt with about 4,000 cases since its founding. The court has passed judgements against nation states in several cases—secret surveillance using telephone taps without adequate security grounds, failure to protect children abused by their parents, expulsion of foreigners in circumstances violating their right to family life.

The Council of Europe has adopted resolutions on a range of human rights issues. These have included regulating the use of personal data in police records, ensuring the rights of conscientious objectors and of foreign prisoners and ensuring education on human rights in European schools. It has also adopted recommendations on many areas of human rights, such as AIDS and the abolition of capital punishment.

European Union
The European Union also plays an important part in making and implementing human rights policies. One EU institution that appears to be acquiring greater importance is the European Court of Justice, based in Luxembourg. In 1989 an offshoot of the court, the Court of First Instance, was created to hear cases brought by firms and individuals, usually involving commercial disputes. The European Court of Justice has since then dealt with legal issues among member states.

Organization for Security and Co-operation in Europe
In January 1993 Max van der Stoel took up his duties as the first High Commissioner for National Minorities for the Organization for Security and Co-operation in Europe (OSCE), a post established as "an instrument of conflict prevention at the earliest possible stage". This mandate was created largely in response to the situation in the former Yugoslavia, which some feared would be repeated elsewhere in Europe, especially among the countries in transition to democracy.

Three sets of recommendations have been elaborated to serve as references for nation states to respect the human rights of minorities and thereby reduce the chances of conflict—the Hague recommendation on education rights of national minorities (1996), the Oslo recommendation on their linguistic rights (1998) and the Lund recommendations on their effective participation in public life (1999).

An area where the European multilateral institutions failed, however, was in the prevention of massive human rights violations in Bosnia and Herzegovina.

Source: Council of Europe 2000; European Court of Justice and Court of First Instance 2000; OSCE 1996, 1998 and 1999.

---

media attention, Coca-Cola established quantitative targets for promoting diversity. "What gets measured gets done", noted chief executive Douglas Daft. "Employee diversity is a clear business imperative. . . .my own salary will be tied to achieving these diversity goals."

A SUMMARY OF ACTIONS TO REALIZE A VISION FOR THE 21ST CENTURY

Defining the comparative advantage of different institutions is the starting point of any implementation strategy (figure 6.1). Many institutions have multiple and overlapping roles. But each has comparative advantages, and concentrating on strengths can increase their effectiveness, particularly when partnerships recognize that other institutions are focusing on other elements of advocacy and implementation.

How useful is it to engage in finger-pointing on violations of human rights? Is it better to support countries by acknowledging progress and providing assistance for strengthening institutions? The answer, of course, is to do both. Finger-pointing is a necessary part of invoking

---

BOX 6.11

A diamond in the rough—global witness to sanctions busting in Angola's civil war

In Angola Jonas Savimbi and his rebel group UNITA, refusing to accept the results of an election they participated in and lost, went back to fighting in 1992, in arguably the world's longest ongoing civil war. The United Nations later imposed sanctions on Angolan diamonds under the control of UNITA, which was selling them to finance purchases of arms and spare parts. But the sanctions were busted through support from some governments and the complicity of businesses operating through Antwerp, the major trading centre for diamonds.

A human rights group, Global Witness, exposed the complicity of de Beers, the South African conglomerate that effectively controls the world diamond market. The finger-pointing led de Beers to announce a commitment not to purchase any diamonds from the Angolan rebels. It also took related measures, which human rights groups have welcomed.

A UN report published in March 2000 calls for strong measures against governments or private parties that are busting sanctions aimed at preventing diamonds from financing landmines.

Source: UN Secretary-General 2000; Global Witness 1998.

FIGURE 6.1

Building a network for NILE: comparative advantages for human rights actions

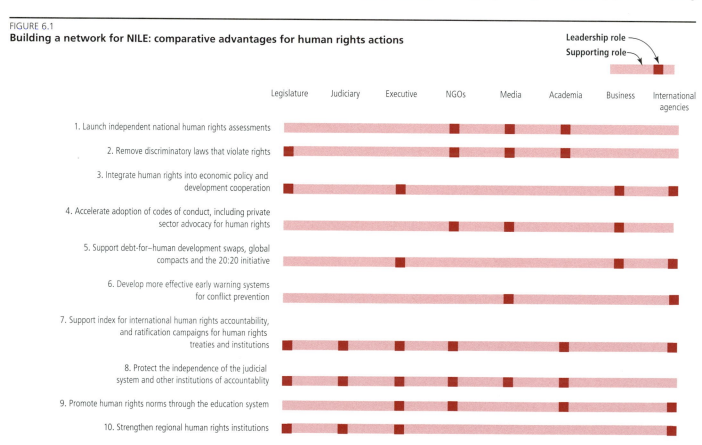

Note: For an analysis of NILE—norms, institutions, legal frameworks and enabling economic environment—see the overview.

Source: Human Development Report Office.

accountability. And supporting good intentions requires pragmatic interventions for changing laws and building the implementation capacity of institutions. Some actors, such as NGOs, are better placed than others for finger-pointing. And the comparative advantage of intergovernmental agencies is implementing programmes that promote human rights and development.

The conceptual integration of human rights and human development, articulated in chapter 1, advances the common goal of political, economic and social freedom. Just as individuals have the right not to be tortured, they have the right not to die from hunger. Social arrangements must not only ensure the freedom of expression but also prevent severe malnutrition. Political and civil freedoms are vitally important—but so is the right to a standard of living that gives people dignity. Economic rights are as important as political rights, though the strategies and instruments to advance each may differ substantially.

A VISION FOR THE 21ST CENTURY

The 21st should be the century for the worldwide spread of freedoms. All people have the right to enjoy seven freedoms—from discrimination, from want, for personal development, from threats to personal security, for participation, from injustice and for productive work. Each of these freedoms requires a vision worthy of collective effort by the nations of the world. And the universality of human rights provides the foundation for this global vision.

• Women and racial and ethnic groups have suffered violent discrimination. Their struggles against deep prejudices have brought many gains in freedom. But with many battles won, the war is not yet over for the billions still suffering from discrimination. The human rights and human development movements will struggle for the changes in laws, norms and institutions that must liberate those remaining shackled by discrimination.

• Famines wiped millions from the earth during the 20th century, mostly because of inhumanity, not nature. Such violent deprivations are now rare, but freedom from want remains a distant dream for millions of people. In the 21st century national and global economic systems have to honour obligations to those humiliated by want. The ultimate purpose of global economic growth is to provide people the dignity of being free from want, a point emphasized by the human development perspective.

• The frequency of torture in history provides a tragic indicator of the evil that lurks in the hearts of men. The elimination of torture, and the national and international prosecution of those who engage in it, are central to the continuing struggle for the freedom for personal security. There are other important dimensions to personal security. Many women who have been raped feel ashamed and face legal systems that reflect patriarchal prejudices. Freedom for personal security requires global coalitions for changing the laws, institutions and values that deny dignity and protection to women.

• The global gains in democracy are still very recent. The 21st century should give all people—for the first time in history—the right to choose their government and the freedom to participate in the decisions that affect their lives. Active involvement in civic institutions and unprecedented access to information and knowledge will enhance fundamental political freedoms.

• The arbitrary exercise of power has traditionally reinforced the helplessness of the powerless. When governments operated on the principle of the divine right of kings, rulers did not seek legitimacy for their power in any notion of justice. The struggle against such injustice demanded that social institutions be based on legitimacy, consent and rule of law. In the 21st century securing freedom against injustice will require institutions that protect people through transparent rules applied equally to all.

• All adults deserve the freedom to work without humiliation and exploitation. And children should be at school, not at work. Much has been achieved in protecting children and improving the working conditions of adults. Many enjoy the freedom for productive work. But millions toil in inhumane con-

The 21st should be the century for the worldwide spread of freedoms. All people have the right to enjoy seven freedoms

ditions, while others feel socially excluded by lack of work. In the 21st century dignity demands a commitment to including the ostracized and abolishing oppressive working conditions.

These are ambitious goals—yet there is nothing new in these aspirations. These are the freedoms that have motivated people throughout history. The fight for these freedoms, across all cultures and races, has been the bond holding the human family together. What is unique to the 21st century is the possibility that these aspirations can become a reality for all people.

References

Background papers, country and regional studies and background notes for Human Development Report 2000

Background papers

Akash, M.M. 2000. "Right-Based Approach to Development and Right to Land."

Alston, Philip. 2000. "Towards a Human Rights Accountability Index."

Anand, Sudhir, and Amartya Sen. 2000. "Human Development Progress Indicators."

Coomaraswamy, Radhika. 2000. "Women's International Human Rights."

Desai, Meghnad. 2000. "Rights and Obligations: A Framework for Accountability."

Dias, Ayesha. 2000. "Human Rights, Environment and Development: with Special Emphasis on Corporate Accountability."

Flinterman, Cees, and J. Gutter. 2000. "The United Nations and Human Rights: Achievements and Challenges."

Ghosh, Jayati. 2000. "Rules of Economic Integration and Human Rights."

Goonesekere, Savitri. 2000. "Human Rights Systems in the UN."

Green, Maria. 2000. "Human Rights Indicators: An Overview of the Field."

Häusermann, Julia, and Emma Morely. 2000a. "Successful Grass-roots Strategies and Multi-Agency Initiative."

———. 2000b. "TNC's, Codes of Conduct, Self-Imposed Codes and Human Rights."

Hijab, Nadia. 2000. "Human Rights and Human Development: Learning from Those Who Act."

Leckie, Scott. 2000. "Housing Rights."

Muntarbhorn, Vitit. 2000. "Child Rights: A Decade of the Convention on the Rights of the Child and Beyond."

Normand, Roger. 2000. "Separate and Unequal: Trade and Human Rights Regimes."

Osmani, Siddiq R. 2000. "Human Rights to Food, Health and Education."

Pinheiro, Paulo Sergio, and David Carlos Baluarte. 2000. "Study on National Strategies—Human Rights Commissions, Ombudsmen, Specialized Agencies and National Action Plans."

Rodas-Martini, Pablo. 2000. "The Debate on Labour Standards and International Trade: Technically Inconclusive and Politically Explosive."

Rodas-Martini, Pablo, Fabriola Rivera and Luis Gerardo Cifuentes. 2000. "Labour Conditions in the EPZ's: A Brief Survey and a Case Study."

Sen, Amartya, and Sudhir Anand. 2000. "Human Rights and Human Development."

Shiva Kumar, A.K. 2000. "Measuring Progress in Human Development: Tracking Inputs, Assessing Efforts, Evaluating Outcomes."

Vizard, Polly. 2000. "The Evolution of the Idea of Human Rights in Western and Non-Western Thought."

Country and regional studies

An-Na'im, Abdullahi A. 2000. "Human Rights in the Arab World—A Regional Perspective."

Hassan, Bahey El-Din. 2000. "Egypt Human Rights Report."

Khader, Asma. 2000. "Human Development and Human Rights—A Country Study of Jordan."

Liebenberg, Sandra. 2000. "A Country Study of South Africa—Human Development and Human Rights."

Mendez, Juan E. 2000. "Human Rights in Latin America and the Caribbean—A Regional Perspective."

Muntarbhorn, Vitit. 2000. "Human Rights and Human Development: Thailand—A Country Study."

Mutua, Makau. 2000. "The African Human Rights System: A Critical Evaluation."

Neou, Kassie. 2000. "Country Study—Cambodia."

Olcott, Martha Brill. 2000. "Regional Study on Human Development and Human Rights—Central Asia."

Oloka-Onyango, Joseph. 2000. "Human Rights and Sustainable Development in Contemporary Africa—A New Dawn or Retreating Horizon?"

Pérez, Andres E. 2000. "Honduras: The Birth of Citizenship and State Conscience."

Rosero, Rocio. 2000. "Human Rights and Human Development in Ecuador."

Rubaduka, Jean, and Noël Twagiramungu. 2000. "Human Rights and Human Development in Rwanda: Assessments and Prespectives, 1984–1999" (Droits de la Personne et Developpement au Rwanda: 1984–1999. Bilan et Perspectives).

Saidov, Akmal. 2000. "Regional Study on Human Development and Human Rights in Uzbekistan."

Saravanamuttu, Johan. 2000. "Country Study—Report of Human Rights in Malaysia."

Sarkar, Lotika. 2000. "Country Study—India."

Šilovic, Darko. 2000. "Regional Study on Human Development and Human Rights in Central and Eastern Europe."

Sutil, Jorge Correa, and Felipe González Morales. 2000. "Human Development and Human Rights in Chile" (Desarrollo Humano y Derechos Humanos en Chile).

Background notes

Goldstone, Leo. 2000. "Proposals for Human Rights Benchmarks."

Mehra, Malini. 2000. "A Comparison of International Trade, Human Rights and Environmental Agreements."

Mirza, Zafar. 2000. "A Note on TRIPS."

Osman, Osman M., and Heba El Leithy. 2000. "Human Development Progress: The Case of Egypt."

Rodas-Martini, Pablo, and Juan Pablo Pira. 2000. "Short-Term Indicators: The Guatemalan Experience."

Sori-Coulibaly, Rosine. 2000. "Taking into Account Short-Term Changes in Measuring Human Development: Case Study of the HDI of Benin."

Transparency International. 2000. "Justice and Corruption."

Bibliographic note

Chapter 1 draws on the following: Bentham 1996, Dworkin 1978, Hart 1961, Kanger 1985, Kant 1956, Nussbaum and Sen 1991, O'Neill 1996, Pogge 1992, Sen 1985, 1999a, 1999b and 1999c, Sen and Anand 2000, Sengupta 1999 and Shue 1980.

Chapter 2 draws on the following: Amnesty International 1998, An-Na'im 2000, Bartolomei de la Cruz, von Potobsky and Swepston 1996, Brooke 1998, Brown, Renner and Flavin 1998, Brown and others 2000, Cairncross 2000, Coomaraswamy 2000, Donnelly 1999, First Nations and Inuit Regional Health Survey National Steering Committee 1999, Flinterman and Gutter 2000, Goldberg, Mourinho and Kulke 1996, Goonesekere 2000, Hamblin and Reid 1993, Hassan 2000, Häusermann and Morley 2000a, Hijab 2000, ILO 1997c and 1998c, International Gay and Lesbian Human Rights Commission 1999, International IDEA 1997, Korea Institute for Health and Social Affairs and UNDP 1998, Lauren 1998, Leckie 2000, Liebenberg 2000, Lowry 1997, Mahbub ul Haq Human Development Centre 1999, Mann and Tarantola 1996, Mendez 2000, Muntarbhorn 2000, Mutua 2000, National Alliance to End Homelessness 1998, Neou 2000, Neubeur 1998, Olcott 2000, Oloka-Onyango 2000, Osmani 2000, Pérez 2000, Pinheiro and Baluarte 2000, Prusher 1998, SAPES 1998, Saravanamuttu 2000, Sarkar 2000, Shelter 1998, Shiva Kumar 2000, _ilovic 2000, Simon Community of Ireland 1995, Smeeding 2000, Transparency International 2000, UN 1996a, UNAIDS 2000, UNAIDS and UNDP 1998, UNAIDS and WHO 2000a and 2000b, UNCJIN 1999, UNDP 1996a, 1996b, 1997a, 1998b, 1998c, 1998d, 1998e and 1999a, UNDP, Poverty Reduction Forum, Institute of Development Studies and University of Zimbabwe 1998, UNDP, FAO, UNESCO, UNFPA and UNICEF 1998, UNHCHR 1996, 1997, 1999a and 1999b, UNHCHR and UNAIDS 1998, UNICEF 1997b and 1998, UNICEF, International Child Development Centre 1999, USAID 1999, US Census Bureau 2000, van de Walle and Gunewardena 1999, Vizard 2000, Wagstaff 2000 and World Bank 2000c.

Chapter 3 draws on the following: An-Na'im 2000, CAD 1995, Cahn 1999, de Barry 1998, Desai 2000, Diamond 1999, Donnelly 1989, ECRI 2000, European Monitoring Centre on Racism and Xenophobia 1998, Federazione Italiana delle Associazioni Emofilici 2000, Garton Ash 1998, Gurr and others 1999, Hassan 2000, Hayner 1994, International IDEA 1999, Khader 2000, Kundera 1980, Liebenberg 2000, Lijphart 1999, Mendez 2000, Muntarbhorn 2000, Mutua 2000, Neou 2000, Neve and Affonso 1995, Olcott 2000, Oloka-Onyango 2000, Pérez 2000, Reyes 2000, Roma Rights 1999a, 1999b and 1999c, Saravanamuttu 2000, Sarkar 2000, Shell Report 1999, _ilovic 2000, Stewart forthcoming, Stiglitz 1999a, United States Institute of Peace 2000, Wignaraja 2000, Yoke and Leng 1992 and Yujnovsky 2000.

Chapter 4 draws on the following: Belser 1999, Bradbury and Jäntti 1999, Cameron and Campbell 1998, Cancado-Trindade 1995 and 1999, Correa 1999, Dias 2000, Dreze and

Sen 1995, Dumoulin 1997, Dutfield 2000, FAO 1998, Finger and Schuknecht 2000, Forbes Magazine 2000, Ghosh 2000, Häusermann and Morely 2000a, Hijab 2000, Holmes and Sunstein 1999, ICFTU 1999, ILO 1997c, Khader 2000, Khor 1999, Leckie 2000, Lobo and Velasquez 1998, Mehra 1999, Mehrotra, Vandemoortele and Delamonica forthcoming, Mirza 2000, Michalopoulos 1999, Milanovic 1999, Nagel 1991, Neou 2000, Normand 2000, OECD 1996 and 1999a, OECD, Development Assistance Committee 1999, Osmani 2000, Panayotou 1999, Pérez 2000, Pogge 1993, Posey 1996, Rodas-Martini 2000, Rodas-Martini, Rivera and Cifuentes 2000, Sen 1999b and 1999c, Tansey 1999, UNCTAD 1999a and 1999b, UNDP 1999b, UNEP 1999, UNICEF and UNDP 1998, US Census Bureau 2000, WHO 1999e, WIPO 1998, Women Working Worldwide 1999, World Bank 2000b and WTO 1999.

Chapter 5 draws on the following: Alston 2000, Amnesty International 1998, Ball 1999, Bayefsky 2000, Benin, National Institute of Statistics and Economic Analysis 1999, Buckland and Fielden 1994, Casa Alianza 1999, Castro-Leal 1996, CESR 1998, CFRB 1010 Toronto 1999, FFC 1998, Foundation for Public Interest 1997, Green 2000, Harris 2000, Humana 1992, Human Rights Campaign 1998, Hunt 1998, HURIDOCS 2000, Interarts Observatory 1999, International Budget Project 1999, Institute of Applied Economic Research and others 2000, Jabine and Claude 1992, Leckie 1998, Libanio 2000, Mahbub ul Haq Human Development Centre 1999, MIMCO 2000, Mistry 1999, Muntarbhorn and Taylor 1994, O'Sullivan forthcoming, Ontario Parents for Equality in Education Funding 2000, Osman and El Leithy 2000, PROBE Team 1999, Rodas-Martini and Pira 2000, Samuelson and Spirer 1992, Sethi 2000, Shiva Kumar 2000, Sori-Coulibaly 2000, South Africa, Central Statistical Services 1994, Tomasevski 1995, UDAPE 2000, UN 1948, 1966a, 1966b, 1986, 1987, 1990 and 1991, UNDP 1991, 1992, 1998a and 1998b and UNHCHR 1999a and 1999b.

Chapter 6 draws on the following: Adelman 1999, An-Na'im 2000, Asian Human Rights Charter 1998, Bassiouni 1999, Brown and Rosencrance 1999, Coomaraswamy 2000, Council of Europe 2000, DFID 2000, *Economist* 2000, Equity Now 1999, European Court of Justice and Court of First Instance 2000, FEWER 1999, Flinterman and Gutter 2000, Global Witness 1998, Hassan 2000, Häusermann and Morely 2000a, Hamdan 1999, Hijab 2000, Human Rights Watch 1997, 1998 and 1999, ILO 1998c, IPU 1998, Mendez 2000, Muntarbhorn 2000, Mutua 2000, Neou 2000, Noman 1999, Oloka-Onyango 2000, Parliamentarians for Global Action 2000, Pinheiro and Baluarte 2000, OSCE 1996, 1998 and 1999, Sarkar 2000, Selbervik 1999, Slovenia, Human Rights Ombudsman 1998, UN Secretary-General 1999 and 2000, UNDP, Regional Bureau for Europe and the CIS 1998, UNICEF 1997a, 1998 and 1999a, UNIFEM 1997, 1998 and 1999, van der Stoel 1999, Wallensteen and Sollenberg 1999, Weiner and Noman 1995 and WHO 1997, 1998 and 1999a.

References

Adelman, H. 1999. "Early Warning and Humanitarian Intervention in Zaire: March–December 1996." Forum on Early Warning and Early Response. [http://www.fewer.org/pubs/index.htm]. 15 March 2000.

Alston, Philip. 1999. "Governance, Human Rights, and the Normative Areas." Background paper for UNDP, *Human Development Report 1999*. United Nations Development Programme, Human Development Report Office, New York.

Amnesty International. 1998. "USA: Selected Statistics on Human Rights Violations in USA." [http://www.amnesty-usa.org/news/1998/25106398.htm]. 9 February 2000.

Asian Human Rights Charter. 1998. "Asian Human Rights Charter—A People's Charter." [http://www.ahrchk.net/charter/declaration.htm]. 11 November 1999.

Austin, John. 1954. *The Province of Jurisprudence Determined.* New York: Noonday Press.

Ball, Patrick. 1999. "Statement by the American Association for the Advancement of Science on the Release of the Guatemalan Death Squad Dossier." [http://hrdata.aaas.org/gdsd]. 1 February 2000.

Bardhan, Kalpana, and Stephen Klasen. 1999. "UNDP's Gender-Related Indices: A Critical Review." *World Development* 27 (6): 985–1010.

Bartolomei de la Cruz, Héctor, Geraldo von Potobsky and Lee Swepston, eds. 1996. *The International Labour Organization: The International Standards System and Basic Human Rights.* Boulder, Colo.: Westview Press.

Bassiouni, Cherif, ed. 1999. *ICC Ratification and National Implementing Legislation.* Bordeaux: Association International de Droit Penale.

Bayefsky, Anne. 2000. Personal correspondence on Waldman v. Canada. 25 February. Ontario.

Beitz, Charles. 1989. *Political Equality.* Princeton, N.J.: Princeton University Press.

Belser, Patrick. 1999. "Globalisation, International Labour Standards, and Multilateral Institutions." Background paper for UNDP, *Human Development Report 1999.* United Nations Development Programme, Human Development Report Office, New York.

Benin, National Institute of Statistics and Economic Analysis. 1999. "Analysis of Social Conditions: Social Profile and Human Development Indicators" (Tableau de Bord Social: Profil Social et Indicateurs du Developpement Humain). Projet BEN/96/001/PRCIG. Cotonou.

Bentham, Jeremy. 1996. *Works.* Oxford: Clarendon Press.

Bhagwati, Jagdish. 1998. *A Stream of Windows: Unsettling Reflections on Trade, Immigration, and Democracy.* Cambridge, Mass.: MIT Press.

Bradbury, Bruce, and Markus Jäntti. 1999. "Child Poverty across Industrialized Nations." Innocenti Occasional Papers, Economic and Social Policy Series, no. 71. Paper presented at the 15th General Conference of the International Association for Research in Income and Wealth, 23–29 August, Cambridge.

Brooke, James. 1998. "Equity Cases in Canada as Redress for Women." *New York Times.* 19 November.

Brown, Lester R., Michael Renner and Christopher Flavin. 1998. *Vital Signs 1998.* The Worldwatch Institute. New York: W.W. Norton and Company.

Brown, Lester R., Christopher Flavin, Hilary French, Janet Abramovitz, Seth Dunn, Gary Gardner, Ashley Mattoon, Anne Platt, Molly O'Meara, Michael Renner, Chris Bright, Sandra Postel, Brian Halweil and Linda Starke. 2000. *The State of the World.* The Worldwatch Institute. New York: W.W. Norton and Company.

Brown, Michael, and Richard Rosencrance, eds. 1999. *The Costs of Conflict: Prevention and Cure in the Global Arena.* New York: Carnegie Commission on Preventing Deadly Conflicts.

Buckland, P., and J. Fielden. 1994. *Public Expenditure on Education in South Africa, 1987/8 to 1991/2: An Analysis of the Data.* Johannesburg: Centre for Education Policy Development and the World Bank.

CAD (Coalition against Dictatorship). 1995. "Nigerian Casefile: The Ken Saro-Wiwa-Ogoni Handbook." Committee Report, Paris. [http://www.hartford-hwp.com/archives/34a/023.html]. 12 April 2000.

Cahn, Claude. 1999. Correspondence on examples of struggles that have achieved goals for Roma rights and the use of shame by a national NGO. European Roma Rights Center. 12 December. Budapest.

Cairncross, Sandy. 2000. "Access to Water and Sanitation." London School of Hygiene and Tropical Medicine Note. London.

Camargo, Jose Marcio, and Francisco H.G. Ferreira. 1999. "The Poverty Reduction Strategy of the Government of Brazil: A Rapid Appraisal." A contribution to UNDP, *Poverty Report 2000: Overcoming Human Poverty.* Draft. New York.

Cameron, James, and Karen Campbell, eds. 1998. *Dispute Resolution in the World Trade Organization.* London: Cameron May-Elster.

Cancado-Trindade, A.A. 1995. "Relations between Sustainable Development and Economic, Social and Cultural Rights: Recent Developments." In A. Al Naouimi and R. Meese, eds., *International Legal Issues Arising under the UN Decade of International Law.* The Hague: Kluwer Law International.

———. 1999. "Sustainable Human Development and Conditions of Life as a Matter of Legitimate International Concern: The Legacy of the UN World Conferences." In Nisuke Ando, ed., *Japan and International Law Past, Present and Future.* The Hague: Kluwer Law International.

Casa Alianza. 1999. "Guatemala: Graphical Data about Criminal Cases." [http://www.casa-alianza.org/EN/index-en.shtml]. 14 February 2000.

Castro-Leal, F. 1996. "The Impact of Public Health Spending on Poverty and Inequality in South Africa." PSP Discussion Paper Series. World Bank, Washington, D.C.

Castro-Leal, F., Julia Dayton, Lionel Demery and Kalpana Mehra. 1999. "Public Social Spending in Africa: Do the Poor Benefit?" *World Bank Research Observer* 14 (1): 49–72.

CDIAC (Carbon Dioxide Information Analysis Center). 1999. "CO_2 Emissions." [http://cdiac.esd.ornl.gov/ftp/ndp030/global96.ems]. February 1999.

Central Information and Statistical Office and UNDP (United Nations Development Programme). 1999. *Report on: Index and Human Development Experience in Venezuela, 1999* (Informe Sobre: Indice y entorno del desarrallo humano en Venezuela 1999). Caracas: CDB Publications.

CESR (Centre for Economic and Social Rights). 1998. *From Needs to Rights: Realising the Right to Health in Ecuador.* Quito: Genesis Ediciones.

CFRB 1010 Toronto. 1999. Transcript of "Free For All." 15 November 1999.

Child Info. 2000. "Child Mortality: Mongolia." [http://www.childinfo.org/cmr/cmrmgl.html]. March 2000.

Correa, Charles. 1999. "Intellectual Property Rights and the Use of Compulsory Licenses: Options for Developing Countries." South Centre, Geneva.

Council of Europe. 2000. "Protecting Human Rights and Fundamental Freedoms." [http://www.dhdirhr.coe.fr/Intro/eng/GENERAL/intro.htm]. 14 April 2000.

Danieli, Yael, Elsa Stamatopoulou and Clarence J. Dias. 1999. *The Universal Declaration of Human Rights: Fifty Years and Beyond.* Amityville, N.Y.: Baywood.

de Barry, Theodore. 1998. *Asian Values and Human Rights.* Cambridge, Mass.: Harvard University Press.

DFID (Department for International Development). 2000. "Strategies for Achieving the International Development Targets: Human Rights for Poor People." Consultation document. Strategies for Achieving the International Development Targets Series. London.

Diamond, Larry. 1999. *Developing Democracy: Toward Consolidation.* Baltimore, Md.: Johns Hopkins University Press.

Donnelly, Jack. 1989. *Universal Human Rights in Theory and Practice.* Ithaca, N.Y.: Cornell University Press.

———. 1998. *International Human Rights.* Boulder, Colo.: Westview Press.

———. 1999. "Non-Discrimination and Sexual Orientation: Making a Place for Sexual Minorities in the Global Human Rights Regime." In Peter Baehr, Cees Flintermann and Mignon Senders, eds., *Innovation and Inspiration: Fifty Years of the Universal Declaration of Human Rights.* Amsterdam: Royal Netherlands Academy of Arts and Sciences.

Dreze, Jean, and Amartya Sen. 1995. *Political Economy of Hunger.* Oxford: Clarendon Press.

Dumoulin, Jerome. 1997. "Assessing the Economic Impacts of the 1999 GATT Agreement on the Pharmaceutical Sector of Developing Countries" (La Mesure des Consequences Economiques des Accords du GATT de 1994 sur le Secteur Pharmaceutique des Pays en Developpement). Paper presented at the Centre International de l'Enfance et de la Famille Seminar, 12–14 November, Paris.

Dutfield, Graham. 2000. *Intellectual Property Rights, Trade and Biodiversity.* World Conservation Union. London: Earthscan Publications.

Dworkin, Ronald. 1978. *Taking Rights Seriously.* Cambridge, Mass.: Harvard University Press.

Economist. 2000. "Africa's Many Pinochets-in-Waiting." 12 February.

ECRI (European Commission against Racism and Intolerance). 2000. "Combating Racism and Intolerance: A Basket of Good Practices." [http://www.ecri.coe.int/en/04/01/e04010001.htm]. 14 April 2000.

Elster, Jon. 1992a. "On Doing What One Can: An Argument against Restitution and Retribution as a Means of Overcoming the Communist Legacy." *East European Constitutional Review.* [http://home.sol.no/~hmelberg/elarticb.htm]. 10 February 2000.

———. 1992b. "On Majoritarianism and Rights." *East European Constitutional Review.* [http://home.sol.no/~hmelberg/elarticb.htm]. 10 February 2000.

EMEP (Co-operative Programme for Monitoring and Evaluation of the Long-Range Transmission of Air Pollutants in Europe). 1999. "Tables of Anthropogenic Emissions in the ECE Region." [http://www.emep.int/emis_tables/tab1.html]. November 1999.

Equality Now. 1999. "Words and Deeds: Holding Governments Accountable in the Beijing + 5 Review Process." [http://www.equalitynow.org/action_eng_16_3.html]. 10 April 2000.

European Court of Justice and Court of First Instance. 2000. "A Court for Europe." [http://curia.eu.int/en/pres/jeu.htm]. 12 March 2000.

European Monitoring Centre on Racism and Xenophobia. 1998. *Annual Report 1998: Part 2—Looking Reality in the Face.* Vienna. [http://www.eumc.at/publications/anualreport/report1998.html]. 14 April 2000.

FAO (Food and Agriculture Organization of the United Nations). 1998. *The Right to Food.* Rome.

———. 1999. "Food Balance Sheets." [http://apps.fao.org/lim500/nph-rap.pl?foodBalanceSheet&Domain=FoodBalanceSheet]. October 1999.

———. 2000. "Food Aid." [http://www.fao.org]. February 2000.

Federazione Italiana delle Associazioni Emofilici. 2000. "Cosa dicono i Giornali." [http://www.espero.it/emofilia/attualita'/news.htm]. 15 April 2000.

FEWER (Forum on Early Warning and Early Response). 1999. "Conflict and Peace Analysis/Response Manual." [http://www.fewer.org/pubs/index.htm]. 10 March 2000.

Filmer, Deon, Jeffrey Hammer and Lant Pritchett. 1998. "Health Policy in Poor Countries: Weaker Links in the Chain." Policy Research Working Paper 1878. World Bank, Development Research Group, Washington, D.C.

FFC (Financial and Fiscal Commission Secretariat). 1998. *Public Expenditure on Basic Social Services in South Africa.* Report for United Nations Children's Fund and United Nations Development Programme. Johannesburg: Financial and Fiscal Commission.

Finger, Michael, and Ludger Schuknecht. 2000. "Market Access Advances and Retreats: The Uruguay Round and Beyond." Policy Research Working Paper 2232. World Bank, Development Research Group, Washington, D.C. [http://www.worldbank.org/research/workingpapers]. 7 February 2000.

First Nations and Inuit Regional Health Survey National Steering Committee. 1999. *First Nations and Inuit Regional Health Survey: National Report 1999.* St. Regis, Quebec.

Forbes Magazine. 2000. "A Decade of Wealth." [http://www.forbes.com]. 15 March 2000.

Foundation for Public Interest. 1997. *Budget Analysis and Advocacy Work of DISHA.* Ahmedabad.

Freeman, Kathleen. 1965. *If Any Man Build: The History of the Save the Children Fund.* London: Hodder and Stoughton.

Garton Ash, Timothy. 1998. "The Truth about Dictatorship." *New York Review of Books* 45 (3). [http://www.nybooks.com/nyrev/WWWarchdisplay.cgi?19980219035F]. 12 April 2000.

Global Witness. 1998. *A Rough Trade: The Role of Companies and Governments in the Angolan Conflict.* London. [http://www.oneworld.org/globalwitness/reports/Angola/title.htm]. 8 January 2000.

Goldberg, A., D. Mourinho and U. Kulke. 1996. *Labour Market Discrimination against Foreign Workers in Germany.* IMP 7. Geneva: International Labour Organization.

Goldschmidt-Clermont, Luisella, and Elisabetta Pagnossin Aligisakis. 1995. "Measures of Unrecorded Economic Activities in Fourteen Countries." Background paper for UNDP, *Human Development Report 1995.* United Nations Development Programme, Human Development Report Office, New York.

Gurr, Ted Robert, Betty Brown, Pamela L. Burke, Michael Dravis, Jonathan Fox, Michael L. Haxton, Mizan Khan, Deepa Khosla, Monty G. Marshall, Beáta Kovás Nás, Anne Pitsch and Marion Recktenwald. 1999. *Peoples versus States: Minorities at Risk in the New Century.* College Park, Md.: University of Maryland. [http://www.bsos.umd.edu/cidcm/mar/trgpvs.html]. 10 March 2000.

Hamblin, Julie, and Elizabeth Reid. 1993. *Women, the HIV Epidemic and Human Rights: A Tragic Imperative.* Issues Paper 8. United Nations Development Programme, HIV and Development Programme, New York.

Hamdan, Dima. 1999. "Amendment to Article 340 on Honour Crimes Faces Opposition in Parliament." *Jordan Times.* 17 November.

Harris, Bruce. 2000. Correspondence on Casa Alianza and street children in Central America. 9 March. San Jose, Costa Rica.

Hart, H.L.A. 1961. *The Concept of Law.* Oxford: Clarendon Press.

Harvey, Andrew S. 1995. "Market and Non-Market Productive Activity in Less Developed and Developing Countries: Lessons from Time Use." Background paper for UNDP, *Human Development Report 1995.* United Nations Development Programme, Human Development Report Office, New York.

Hayner, Priscilla. 1994. "Fifteen Truth Commissions—1974 to 1994: A Comparative Study." *Human Rights Quarterly* 16 (4): 597–655.

Held, David. 1995. *Democracy and the Global Order: From the Modern State to Cosmopolitan Governance.* Stanford, Calif.: Stanford University Press.

Heston, Alan, and Robert Summers. 1999. Correspondence on data on GDP per capita (PPP US$). University of Pennsylvania, Department of Economics, Philadelphia. March.

Holmes, Stephen, and Cass Sunstein. 1999. *The Cost of Rights.* New York: W.W. Norton and Company.

Humana, Charles. 1992. *World Human Rights Guide.* New York: Oxford University Press.

Human Rights and Equal Opportunity Commission. 2000. "Aboriginal and Torres Strait Islander Social Justice." [http://www.hreoc.gov.au/social_justice/statistics/index.html]. 9 February 2000.

Human Rights Campaign. 1998. "Gays, Lesbians and Bisexuals Rank Third in Reported Hate Crimes—1998." [http://www.hrc.org/issues/hate/stats98.html]. 10 February 2000.

Human Rights Watch. 1997. *Human Rights Watch World Report 1997.* New York.

———. 1998. *Human Rights Watch World Report 1998.* New York.

———. 1999. *Human Rights Watch World Report 1999.* New York.

Hunt, Paul. 1998. "State Obligations, Indicators, Benchmarks and the Right to Education." *Human Rights Law and Practice* 4: 109–15.

HURIDOCS (Human Rights Information and Documentation Systems, International). 2000. "General Information Brochure." [http://www.huridocs.org/brocheng.htm]. 20 February 2000.

Hurley, Susan, and Stephen Shute, eds. 1993. *On Human Rights.* New York: Basic Books.

ICFTU (International Confederation of Free Trade Unions). 1999. *Building Workers' Human Rights into the Global Trading System.* Brussels.

IISS (International Institute for Strategic Studies). 1999. *The Military Balance 1999–2000.* Oxford: Oxford University Press.

ILO (International Labour Organization). 1996. *Estimates and Projections of the Economically Active Population, 1950–2010.* 4th ed. Diskette. Geneva.

———. 1997a. *Annual Report.* Geneva.

———. 1997b. *Children at Work—Health and Safety Risks.* Geneva.

———. 1997c. *World Labour Report 1997/98—Industrial Relations, Democracy and Social Stability.* Geneva.

———. 1997d. *Yearbook of Labour Statistics 1997.* Geneva.

———. 1998a. *Annual Report.* Geneva.

———. 1998b. "Protecting the Most Vulnerable of Today's Workers." [http://www.ilo.org/public/english/protection/migrant/papers/protvul/index.htm]. 14 April 2000.

———. 1998c. *World Employment Report 1998–99.* Geneva.

———. 1999a. *Annual Report.* Geneva.

———. 1999b. "Ratification of ILO Conventions." [http://www.ilo.org/public/english/dialogue/actrav/enviro/backgrnd/raticore.htm]. 14 April 2000.

———. 1999c. *Yearbook of Labour Statistics 1999.* Geneva.

———. 2000. ILO database on international labour standards (ILOLEX). [http://ilolex.ilo.ch:1567/public/english/50normes/infleg/iloeng/index.htm]. April 2000.

Institute of Applied Economic Research, João Pinheiro Foundation, Brazilian Bureau of Statistics and UNDP (United Nations Development Programme) Brazil. 1998. *Atlas of Human Development in Brazil.* Brasilia: United Nations Development Programme Brazil.

Interarts Observatory. 1999. *FACTUS.* Barcelona.

International Budget Project. 1999. "A Guide to Budget Work. Appendix 2: Sample History of the Work of Two Groups: DISHA, India and the Budget Information Service of IDASA, South Africa." [http://www.internationalbudget.org/resources/guide/guide-07.htm]. 7 March 2000.

International Gay and Lesbian Human Rights Commission. 1999. "Sexual Orientation and the Human Rights Mechanisms of the United Nations: Examples and Approaches." San Francisco.

International IDEA (Institute for Democracy and Electoral Assistance). 1997. *Voter Turnout from 1945 to 1997: A Global Report.* Stockholm.

———. 1998. *Democracy and Deep-Rooted Conflict: Options for Negotiators.* Stockholm.

———. 1999. *Code of Conduct: Political Parties Campaigning in Democratic Elections.* Stockholm.

IPU (Inter-Parliamentary Union). 1995. *Women in Parliaments 1945–1995: A World Statistical Survey.* Geneva.

———. 1998. *Parliamentary Human Rights Bodies, World Directory.* Geneva.

———. 2000a. Correspondence on date of latest elections, political parties represented and voter turnout. March. Geneva.

———. 2000b. Correspondence on year women received the right to vote and stand for election, and the year the first woman was elected or appointed to parliament. March. Geneva.

———. 2000c. "Parline Database." [http://www.ipu.org/parline-e/parlinesearch.asp]. March 2000.

———. 2000d. "Women in Parliament." [http://www.ipu.org/wmn-e/classif.htm]. February 2000.

Ishay, Micheline R., ed. 1997. *The Human Rights Reader. Major Political Writings, Essays, Speeches, and Documents—From the Bible to the Present.* New York: Routledge.

ITU (International Telecommunication Union). 1998. *World Telecommunication Indicators.* Database. Geneva.

Jabine, Thomas B., and Richard P. Claude. 1992. *Human Rights and Statistics: Getting the Record Straight.* Philadelphia: University of Pennsylvania Press.

Johns Hopkins University. 1999a. "Physical Assault on Women by an Intimate Partner." Tables compiled for *Population Reports.* Center for Health and Gender Equality. [http://www.jhuccp.org/pr/l11/l11tables.stm]. 27 January 2000.

———. 1999b. *Population Reports.* School of Hygiene and Public Health, Center for Communication Programs. Series L, no. 11. [http://www.jhuccp.org/pr/]. 27 January 2000.

Kaldor, Mary. 1999. *New and Old Wars: Organized Violence in a Global Era.* Stanford, Calif.: Stanford University Press.

Kanger, Stig. 1985. "On Realization of Human Rights." *Acta Philosophica Fennica* 38.

Kant, Immanuel. 1956. *Critique of Practical Reason.* Translated by L.W. Beck. New York: Bobbs-Merrill.

Kaul, Inge, Isabelle Grunberg and Marc A. Stern, eds. 1999. *Global Public Goods: International Cooperation in the 21st Century.* New York: Oxford University Press.

Khor, Martin. 1999. *A Comment on Attempted Linkages between Trade and Non-Trade Issues in the WTO.* Penang, Malaysia: Third World Network.

Korea Institute for Health and Social Affairs and UNDP (United Nations Development Programme). 1998. *Korea: Human Development Report 1998.* Seoul.

Kundera, Milan. 1980 [1978]. *The Book of Laughter and Forgetting.* New York: Penguin Books.

Landsberg-Lewis, Ilana, ed. 1998. *Bringing Equality Home—Implementing the Convention on the Elimination of All Forms of Discrimination Against Women.* New York: United Nations Development Fund for Women.

Lauren, Gordon Paul. 1998. *The Evolution of International Human Rights: Visions Seen.* Philadelphia: University of Pennsylvania Press.

Leckie, Scott. 1998. "Another Step towards Indivisibility: Identifying the Key Features of Violations of Economic, Social, and Cultural Rights." *Human Rights Quarterly* 20: 81–124.

Li and others. 1999. "Distribution of Government Education Expenditures in Developing Countries—Preliminary Estimates." World Bank, Education Sector Thematic Group, Washington, D.C.

Libanio, Jose Carlos. 2000. Email correspondence on the *Atlas of Human Development in Brazil*. 1 February 2000. Rio de Janeiro.

Lijphart, Arend. 1999. *Patterns of Democracy: Government Forms and Performance in Thirty-Six Countries.* New Haven, Conn.: Yale University Press.

LIS (Luxembourg Income Study). 2000. "Population below Income Poverty Line." [http://lissy.ceps.lu/lim.htm]. January 2000.

Lobo, Felix, and Manuel G. Velasquez. 1998. *Medicines and the New Economic Environment.* Madrid: Civitas.

Lowry, Christopher. 1997. "Street Children in the Developing World: Political and Social Policies Division." Ottawa: Canadian International Development Agency.

Mahbub ul Haq Human Development Centre. 1999. *Human Development in South Asia: The Crisis of Governance.* Karachi: Oxford University Press.

Mann, Jonathan, and Daniel Tarantola, eds. 1996. *AIDS in the World II.* New York: Oxford University Press.

Mazdoor Kisan Shakti Sangathan. 1996. *The Right to Know, the Right to Live: People's Struggle in Rajasthan and the Right to Information.* Rajasthan.

Mehra, Malini, ed. 1999. *Human Rights and Economic Globalisation—Directions for the WTO.* Uppsala, Sweden: Global Publications Foundation.

Mehrotra, Santosh, Jan Vandemoortele and Enrique Delamonica. Forthcoming. "Basic Services for All? Public Spending and the Social Dimensions of Poverty." United Nations Children's Fund, New York.

Michalopoulos, Constantine. 1999. "Trade Policy and Market Access Issues for Developing Countries: Implications for the Millennium Round." Policy Research Working Paper 2214. World Bank, Development Research Group, Washington, D.C. [http://www.worldbank.org/research/workingpapers]. 28 January 2000.

Milanovic, Branko. 1998. *Income, Inequality and Poverty during the Transition from Planned to Market Economy.* Washington, D.C.: World Bank.

———. 1999. "True World Income Distribution, 1988 and 1993: First Calculations Based on Household Surveys Alone." Policy Research Working Paper 2244. World Bank, Development Research Group, Washington, D.C.

MIMCO (Mattel Independent Monitoring Council). 2000. "Audit Report 1999: Executive Summary." [http://www.mattel.com/corporate/company/responsibility/index.asp?section=mim]. 1 March 2000.

Mistry, M.D. 1999. "The Beginnings of DISHA and Its Budget Training Work in India." [http://www.internationalbudget.org]. 7 March 2000.

Muntarbhorn, Vitit, and Charles Taylor. 1994. *Roads to Democracy: Human Rights and Democratic Development in Thailand.* Montreal: International Centre for Human Rights and Democratic Development.

Nagel, Thomas. 1977. "Poverty and Food: Why Charity Is Not Enough." In Peter Brown and Henry Shue, eds., *Food Policy: The Responsibility of the United States in Life and Death Choices.* New York: Free Press.

———. 1991. *Equality and Partiality.* New York: Oxford University Press.

National Alliance to End Homelessness. 1998. "Facts about Homelessness in Washington, D.C." [http://www.endhomelessness.org/back/factsdc.htm]. 14 April 2000.

Neubeur, Rita. 1998. "Justice behind Bars." *Choices.* (December): 24–25.

Neve, Cristina, and Beatriz Affonso. 1995. "Report on a Mass Murder: Death of 18 Prisoners at the 42nd Police Station, Parada de Lucas, São Paulo" (Relato de uma chacina. Morte de 18 detentos na 42a DP, Parada de Lucas, São Paulo). In Center for the Study of Violence and University of São Paulo and Teotônio Vilela Commission, *Human Rights in Brazil* (Os Direitos Humanos no Brasil), São Paulo.

Noman, O. 1999. *Democracy and Human Development in Asia.* New York: Oxford University Press.

NUA. 2000. "How Many On Line?" [http://www.nua.ie]. 14 April 2000.

Nussbaum, Martha, and Amartya Sen, eds. 1991. *The Quality of Life.* Oxford: Oxford University Press.

O'Neill, Onora. 1986. *Faces of Hunger.* London: Allen Unwin.

———. 1989. *Constructions of Reason.* Cambridge: Cambridge University Press.

———. 1996. *Towards Justice and Virtue.* Cambridge: Cambridge University Press.

O'Sullivan, Gerald. Forthcoming. "The South African Truth and Reconciliation Commission: Database Representation." In P. Ball, Herbert Spirer and Louise Spirer, eds., *Making the Case: Information Management Systems and Analysis for Human Rights—Case Histories of Information Management Systems for Large-Scale Violations of Human Rights.* Washington, D.C.: American Association for the Advancement of Science.

OECD (Organisation for Economic Co-operation and Development). 1996. *Trade, Employment and Labour Standards: A Study of Core Workers' Rights and International Trade.* Paris.

———. 1999a. *Economic Outlook.* Paris.

———. 1999b. *Employment Outlook 1999.* Paris.

———. 1999c. *Environmental Data Compendium 1999.* Paris.

OECD (Organisation for Economic Co-operation and Development), Development Assistance Committee. 1999. *Development Co-operation 1998 Report.* Paris.

———. 2000. *Development Co-operation 1999 Report.* Paris.

OECD (Organisation for Economic Co-operation and Development) and Statistics Canada. 2000. *Literacy in the Information Age—Final Report on the IALS.* Paris.

OFDA (Office of US Foreign Disaster Assistance) and CRED (Centre for Research on the Epidemiology of Disasters). 2000. "EM-DAT: The OFDA/CRED International Disaster Database." Université Catholique de Louvain, Brussels, Belgium. [http://www.md.ucl.ac.be/cred]. March 2000.

Ontario Parents for Equality in Education Funding. 2000. "Press Release on Fair Funding Rally, February 5, 2000." [http://www.jpeef.org/opeef.htm]. 25 February 2000.

OSCE (Organization for Security and Co-operation in Europe). 1996. "The Hague Recommendation Regarding the Education Rights of National Minorities." [http://www.osce.org/inst/hcnm/]. 14 April 2000.

———. 1998. "The Oslo Recommendation Regarding the Linguistic Rights of National Minorities." [http://www.osce.org/inst/hcnm/]. 14 April 2000.

———. 1999. "The Lund Recommendations on the Effective Participation of National Minorities in Public Life." [http://www.osce.org/inst/hcnm/]. 14 April 2000.

Panayotou, Theodore. 1999. "Globalisation and Environment." Background paper for UNDP, *Human Development Report 1999.* United Nations Development Programme, Human Development Report Office, New York.

Parliamentarians for Global Action. 2000. *Dossier on the Ratification of Ghana of the Statute of the International Criminal Court.* New York. [http://www.pgaction.org/]. 14 April 2000.

Pogge, Thomas. 1989. *Realizing Rawls.* Ithaca, N.Y.: Cornell University Press.

———. 1992. "O'Neill on Rights and Duties." *Grazer Philosophische Studien* 43: 223–47.

———. 1993. "The Bounds of Nationalism." *Canadian Journal of Philosophy* 22 (supplement).

———. 1995. "How Should Human Rights Be Conceived?" *Jahrbuch für Recht und Ethik* 3: 103–20.

Posey, Darrell. 1996. *Traditional Resource Rights.* World Conservation Union, Biodiversity Programme, Gland, Switzerland.

PROBE (Public Report on Basic Education in India) Team. 1999. *Public Report on Basic Education in India.* New Delhi: Oxford University Press.

Prusher, Ilene R. 1998. "Brutality in the Name of Honour." In *Choices* (December).

Psacharopoulos, George, and Zafiris Tzannatos, eds. 1992. *Case Studies on Women's Employment and Pay in Latin America.* Washington, D.C.: World Bank.

Reyes, Socorro. 2000. "Seeking Gender Balance: Women Strategize for Change." Women's Environment and Development Organization, New York.

Roma Rights. 1999a. "Bulgarian Roma Rights Organisation Scores Political Victory." *Roma Rights Quarterly.* [http://errc.org/rr_nr1_1999/snap02.shtml]. 12 March 2000.

———. 1999b. "Local Government in Hungary Taken to Court by Roma." [http://errc.org/rr_nr1_1999/snap11.shtml] 12 March 2000.

———. 1999c. "Ombudsman Investigates Discrimination in Employment in Hungary." [http://errc.org/rr_nr1_1999/snap23.shtml]. 12 March 2000.

Samuelson, Douglas A., and Herbert F. Spirer. 1992. "Use of Incomplete and Distorted Data in Inference about Human Rights Violations." In Thomas B. Jabine and Richard P. Claude, eds., *Human Rights and Statistics: Getting the Record Straight.* Philadelphia: University of Pennsylvania Press.

SAPES (South African Political Economy Series Trust). 1998. *SADC Human Development Report 1998: Governance and Human Development in Southern Africa.* South African Regional Institute for Policy Studies. Harare: United Nations Development Programme.

Selbervik, Hilde. 1999. "Aid and Conditionality, The Role of the Bilateral Donor: A Case Study of the Norwegian-Tanzanian Aid Relationship." Evaluation Report 6.99. Norwegian Ministry of Foreign Affairs, Oslo. [http://odin.dep.no/ud]. 14 April 2000.

Sen, Amartya. 1985. *Commodities and Capabilities.* Amsterdam: North Holland.

———. 1992. *Inequality Reexamined.* Cambridge, Mass.: Harvard University Press.

———. 1999a. "Consequential Evaluation and Practical Reason." Trinity College, Department of Economics, Cambridge.

———. 1999b. *Development as Freedom.* New York: Alfred Knopf.

———. 1999c. "Human Rights and Economic Achievements." In Joanne Bauer and Daniel Bell, eds., *The East Asian Challenge for Human Rights.* Cambridge: Cambridge University Press.

Sengupta, Arjun. 1999. "Study on the Current State of Progress in the Implementation of the Right to Development Pursuant to Commission Resolution 1998/72 and General Assembly Resolution 53/155." United Nations document E/CN.4/1999/WG.18/2. New York.

Sethi, Prakash. 2000. Personal correspondence on Mattel Independent Monitoring Council. 17 February. New York.

Shell Report. 1999. "People, Planet and Profits—An Act of Commitment." Houston, Tex. [http://www.shell.com/royal-en/]. 14 April 2000.

Shelter. 1998. "National Campaign for Homeless People." London. [http://www.shelter.org.uk/]. 14 April 2000.

Shue, Henry. 1980. *Basic Rights: Subsistence, Affluence, and U.S. Foreign Policy.* Princeton, N.J.: Princeton University Press.

Simon Community of Ireland. 1995. "Homeless in Dublin." [http://indigo.ie/~simonnat/homeless.html]. 4 April 2000.

SIPRI (Stockholm International Peace Research Institute). 2000. *SIPRI Yearbook 2000—Armaments, Disarmament and International Security.* Oxford: Oxford University Press.

Slovenia, Human Rights Ombudsman. 1998. *Annual Report 1998.* [http://www.varuh-rs.si/index-eng.html]. 1 March 2000.

Smeeding, Tim. 1997. "Financial Poverty in Developed Countries: The Evidence from the Luxembourg Income Study." In UNDP, *Human Development Papers 1997: Poverty and Human Development.* New York.

———. 2000. Correspondence on income poverty in industrialized countries. 20 January. New York.

South Africa, Central Statistical Services. 1994. *October Household Survey.* Pretoria: Government Printer.

Spirer, Herbert. 2000. Correspondence on properties of human rights indicators. 18 March. New York.

Standard & Poor's. 2000. "Sovereign Long-Term Debt Ratings." [http://www.standardandpoors.com/ratings/sovereigns/index.htm]. February 2000.

Stewart, Frances. Forthcoming. "The Root Causes of Humanitarian Emergencies." In E. Wayne Nafziger, Frances Stewart and Raimo Vayrynen, eds., *The Origins of Humanitarian Emergencies: War and Displacement in Developing Countries.* New York: Oxford University Press.

Stiglitz, Joseph. 1998. "The Role of International Financial Institutions in the Current Global Economy." [http://www.worldbank.org/knowledge/chiefecon/stiglitz.htm]. 19 October 1999.

———. 1999a. "Democratic Development as the Fruits of Labor." [http://www.worldbank.org/knowledge/chiefecon/stiglitz.htm]. 2 December 1999.

———. 1999b. "On Liberty, the Right to Know, and Public Discourse: The Role of Transparency in Public Life." [http://www.worldbank.org/knowledge/chiefecon/stiglitz.htm]. 2 December 1999.

———. 1999c. "Participation and Development Perspectives from the Comprehensive Development Paradigm." [http://www.worldbank.org/knowledge/chiefecon/stiglitz.htm]. 2 December 1999.

Tansey, Geoff. 1999. "Trade, Intellectual Property, Food and Biodiversity." Quaker Peace and Service, London.

Tomasevski, Katarina. 1995. "Indicators." In Asbjorn Eide, Catarina Krause and Allan Rosas, eds., *Economic, Social and Cultural Rights: A Textbook.* Dordrecht: Martinus Nijhoff Publishers.

Tuck, Richard. 1979. *Natural Rights Theories.* Cambridge: Cambridge University Press.

UDAPE (Unidad de Analisis de Political Sociales y Economicas). 2000. "Internal Aide Memorandum." La Paz.

UN (United Nations). 1948. *The Universal Declaration of Human Rights.* [http://www.unhchr.ch/html/intlinst.htm]. 4 May 2000.

———. 1966a. *International Covenant on Civil and Political Rights.* [http://www.unhchr.ch/html/intlinst.htm]. 4 May 2000.

———. 1966b. *International Covenant on Economic, Social and Cultural Rights.* [http://www.unhchr.ch/html/intlinst.htm]. 4 May 2000.

———. 1986. *The Declaration on the Right to Development.* [http://www.unhchr.ch/html/intlinst.htm]. 4 May 2000.

———. 1987. *Limburg Principles.* UN document E/CN.4/1987/17. [http://www.unhchr.ch/html/intlinst.htm]. 4 May 2000.

———. 1990. *The Nature of States Parties Obligations (Art. 2, par. 1) General Comment 3.* [http://www.unhchr.ch/html/intlinst.htm]. 4 May 2000.

———. 1991. *Revised General Guidelines Regarding the Form and Contents of Reports to Be Submitted by States Parties under Articles 16 and 17 of the International Covenant on Economic, Social and Cultural Rights.* UN document E/C.12/1001/1. [http://www.unhchr.ch/html/intlinst.htm]. 4 May 2000.

———. 1995a. "Impact of Armed Conflict on Children—Report of Graca Machel, Expert of the Secretary-General of the

United Nations." [http://www.unicef.org/graca/]. 14 April 2000.

———.1995b. *World Urbanization Prospects: The 1994 Revision.* Database. Population Division. New York.

———.1996a. *Second International Consultation on HIV/AIDS and Human Rights.* Economic and Social Council, Commission on Human Rights, 53rd session, item 9 (a) of the provisional agenda, 23–25 September, Geneva.

———.1996b. *World Urbanization Prospects: The 1996 Revision.* Database. Population Division. New York.

———. 1997a. *Human Rights. A Compilation of International Instruments.* Vol. 1, *Universal Instruments.* New York.

———. 1997b. *Human Rights. A Compilation of International Instruments.* Vol. 2, *Regional Instruments.* New York.

———. 1998a. "Human Rights and Conflicts." *Human Rights Today.* UN Briefing Papers. [http://www.un.org/rights/HRToday]. 14 April 2000.

———.1998b. "Principles and Recommendations for Population and Housing Censuses. (Revision 1)." Statistical Papers Series M, No. 67/Rev. 1. Statistics Division. New York.

———.1998c. *World Population Prospects 1950–2050: The 1998 Revision.* Database. Population Division. New York.

———. 2000a. Correspondence on births to mothers under 20. Statistics Division. January. New York.

———. 2000b. Correspondence on women in government. UN Secretariat and Department for Economic and Social Affairs, Division for the Advancement of Women. March. New York.

———. 2000c. *Energy Statistics Yearbook 1997.* New York.

———. 2000d. *Fifth United Nations Survey of Crime Trends and Operations of Criminal Justice Systems.* United Nations Office at Vienna, Crime Prevention and Criminal Justice Division. Vienna. [http://www.uncjin.org/]. March 2000.

———. 2000e. "Multilateral Treaties Deposited with the Secretary-General." [http://untreaty.un.org]. February 2000.

UN (United Nations) Secretary-General. 1999. *Annual Report of the Secretary-General on the Work of the Organization.* [A/54/1][http://www.un.org/Docs/SG/Report99/toc.htm]. 14 April 2000.

———. 2000. *"We the Peoples": The Role of the United Nations in the 21st Century.* New York: United Nations. [http://www.un.org/millennium/sg/report/full.htm]. 10 March 2000.

UNAIDS (Joint United Nations Programme on HIV/AIDS). 2000. "AIDS Now Greatest Threat to Development, Says UNAIDS Chief." Press release, 11 February. [http://www.unaids.org/whatsnew/press/eng/stockholm110200.html]. 14 April 2000.

UNAIDS (Joint United Nations Programme on HIV/AIDS) and UNDP (United Nations Development Programme). 1998. *HIV/AIDS and Human Development: South Africa.* Pretoria: Amabukha Publications.

UNAIDS (Joint United Nations Programme on HIV/AIDS) and WHO (World Health Organization). 2000a. "AIDS Epidemic Update: December 1999." UNAIDS/99.53E; WHO/CDS/CSR/EDC/99.9; WHO/FCH/HSI99.6. Geneva.

———. 2000b. *Report on the Global HIV/AIDS Epidemic.* [http://www.who.int/emc-hiv/global_report/index.html]. March 2000.

UNCJIN (United Nations Crime and Justice Information Network). 1999. "Data on Crime and Justice." [http://www.uncjin.org/Statistics/WCTS/WCTS5/wcts5.html]. 14 April 2000.

UNCTAD (United Nations Conference on Trade and Development). 1999a. *Trade and Development Report.* Geneva.

———. 1999b. *World Investment Report 1999—Foreign Direct Investment and the Challenge of Development.* Geneva.

UNDP (United Nations Development Programme). 1991. *Human Development Report 1991.* New York: Oxford University Press.

———. 1992. *Human Development Report 1992.* New York: Oxford University Press.

———. 1996a. *Human Development Report 1996: Turkey.* Ankara.

———.1996b. *Nigerian Human Development Report 1996.* Lagos.

———. 1997a. *Ghana Human Development Report 1997.* Accra.

———. 1997b. *Human Development Report for Peru: Indices and Indicators* (Informe Sobre El Desarrollo Humano del Peru: Indices e Indicatores). Lima.

———.1997c. *Swaziland Human Development Report 1997— Sustainable Human Development: The Road Ahead.* Mbabane.

———. 1998a. *Cambodia National Human Development Report.* Phnom Penh.

———.1998b. *Human Development Report of Nepal 1998.* Kathmundu.

———.1998c. *National Human Development Report of Sri Lanka 1998: Regional Dimensions of Human Development.* Colombo.

———. 1998d. *Uganda Human Development Report 1998.* Kampala.

———. 1998e. *Zambia Human Development Report 1998.* Lusaka.

———.1999a. *China Human Development Report 1999: Transition and the State.* Beijing: China Finance and Economic Publishing House.

———.1999b. *Human Development Report 1999.* New York: Oxford University Press.

———. 2000. *Poverty Report 2000: Overcoming Human Poverty.* New York.

UNDP (United Nations Development Programme), Regional Bureau for Europe and the CIS. 1998. *The New Yalta: Commemorating the 50th Anniversary of the Declaration of Human Rights in RBEC Region.* Ankara.

UNDP (United Nations Development Programme) and Government of Botswana. 1997. *Botswana Human Development Report 1997: Challenges for a Sustainable Human Development— A Long-Term Perspective.* Gaborone: TA Publications.

UNDP (United Nations Development Programme) and Lithuania Social Policy Unit. 1999. *Lithuanian Human Development Report 1999.* Vilnius.

UNDP (United Nations Development Programme) and UNHCR (United Nations High Commissioner for Refugees). 1998. "Humanitarian Assistance and Assistance to Refugees." [http://www.un.org/ha/general.htm]. 14 April 2000.

UNDP (United Nations Development Programme), Poverty Reduction Forum, Institute of Development Studies and University of Zimbabwe. 1998. *Human Development Report 1998: Zimbabwe.* Harare.

UNDP (United Nations Development Programme), FAO (Food and Agriculture Organization of the United Nations), UNESCO (United Nations Educational, Scientific and Cultural Organization), UNFPA (United Nations Population Fund) and UNICEF (United Nations Children's Fund). 1998. *Namibia Human Development Report 1998.* Windhoek.

UNECE (United Nations Economic Commission for Europe). 1999a. Correspondence on injuries and deaths from road accidents. March. Geneva.

———.1999b. *Trends in Europe and North America 1998–99.* Geneva.

———. 2000. Correspondence on secretariat estimates of unemployment based on national statistics. March. Geneva.

UNEP (United Nations Environment Programme). 1999. "The Relationship between Intellectual Property Rights and the Relevant Provisions of the Trade-Related Aspects of Intellectual Property Rights (TRIPS agreement) and the Convention on Biological Diversity." Convention on Biodiversity. 11 October. Montreal.

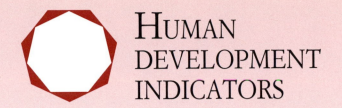

HUMAN DEVELOPMENT INDICATORS

Statistics provide objective information on trends in human development and inputs for the analysis of critical policy issues. Thus although the *Human Development Report* is not a statistical publication, it presents data on a wide array of indicators in diverse areas of human development.

The Report's primary purpose is to assess the state of human development across the globe and provide a critical analysis of a specific theme each year. Readers find it useful to have a report that focuses on human well-being rather than on economic trends, and that combines thematic policy analysis with detailed country data in a user-friendly presentation.

The indicators in the *Human Development Report* reflect the rich body of information available internationally. As a secondary user of data, the Report presents statistical information that has been built up through the collective effort of many people and organizations. The original sources range from national censuses and surveys to international data series collected and harmonized by international organizations. The Human Development Report Office gratefully acknowledges the collaboration of the many agencies that made publication of the latest data on human development possible (box 1).

To allow comparisons across countries and over time, all the statistical tables in the Report are based on internationally standardized data, collected and processed by sister agencies in the international system or, in a few cases, by other bodies. These organizations, whether collecting data from national sources or through their own surveys, harmonize definitions and collection methods to make their data as internationally comparable as possible. The data produced by these agencies may sometimes differ from data produced by national sources, often because of adjustments to harmonize data. In a few cases, where data are not available from international organizations—particularly for the human development indices—other sources have been used. These sources are clearly referenced in the relevant tables.

The text of the Report draws on a much wider variety of sources—commissioned papers, journal articles and other scholarly publications, government documents, reports of NGOs, reports of international organizations, national human development reports. Where such information is used in boxes or tables in the text, the source is shown and the full citation is given in the references.

THE NEED FOR BETTER HUMAN DEVELOPMENT STATISTICS

The need to strengthen data collection and reporting at the national and international levels cannot be overstated. Despite the considerable efforts of international organizations to collect, process and disseminate social and economic statistics and to standardize definitions and data collection methods, many problems remain in the coverage, consistency and comparability of data across countries and over time. These limitations are a major constraint in monitoring human development nationally and globally.

While the data in the Report demonstrate the wealth of information available, they also show many gaps in data on critical human development issues. For example, data are often unavailable for the 57 core indicators selected in the UN Common Country Assessment (CCA). For more than 90 countries no data are available on youth literacy. For 66 developing countries there are no recent data on the incidence of income poverty using the standard $1 a day measure (1993 PPP US$). And for only 117 countries are there data on underweight children under five. Many of these CCA indicators are also being used to monitor progress towards the international development goals.

Lack of data is a particular constraint in monitoring gender disparity and poverty. Coverage of the gender-related development index (GDI) is limited to 143 countries, the gender empowerment measure (GEM) to 70 countries and the human poverty index (HPI-1 and HPI-2) to 103 countries. Wage data disaggregated by gender are available from the International Labour Organization for only 46 countries. Coverage of critical aspects of human poverty is also limited. UNICEF reports estimates of population

Major sources of data used in the *Human Development Report*

By generously sharing data, the following organizations made it possible for the *Human Development Report* to publish the important human development statistics appearing in the indicator tables.

Carbon Dioxide Information Analysis Center (CDIAC) CDIAC, a data and analysis centre of the US Department of Energy, focuses on the greenhouse effect and global climate change. It is the source of the data on carbon dioxide emissions.

Co-operative Programme for Monitoring and Evaluation of the Long-Range Transmission of Air Pollutants in Europe (EMEP) This specialized agency of the United Nations Economic Commission for Europe (UNECE) collects and analyses data on air pollution for UNECE member countries. It is the source of the data on sulphur dioxide emissions.

Food and Agriculture Organization (FAO) The FAO collects, analyses and disseminates information and data on food and agriculture. It is the source of the data on food aid and food production and supply.

Inter-Parliamentary Union (IPU) This organization provides data on trends in political participation and structures of democracy. The *Human Development Report* relies on the IPU for information on women's political representation and other election-related data.

International Institute for Strategic Studies (IISS) An independent centre for research, information and debate on the problems of conflicts, the IISS maintains an extensive military database. The data on armed forces are from its publication *The Military Balance*.

International Labour Organization (ILO) The ILO maintains an extensive programme of statistical publications, with the *Yearbook of Labour Statistics* its most comprehensive collection of labour force data. The ILO is the source of the employment and wage data, projections of economic activity rates and information on the ratification status of labour rights conventions.

International Monetary Fund (IMF) The IMF has an extensive programme for developing and compiling statistics on international financial transactions and balance of payments. Much of the economic data provided to the Human Development Report Office by other agencies originate from the IMF.

International Telecommunication Union (ITU) This specialized UN agency maintains an extensive collection of statistics on communications and information. The data on trends in communications are from its database *World Telecommunications Indicators*.

Joint United Nations Programme on HIV/AIDS (UNAIDS) and World Health Organization (WHO) This joint UN programme monitors the spread of HIV/AIDS. Its *Report on the Global HIV/AIDS Epidemic* is the primary source of HIV/AIDS data for the Report.

Luxembourg Income Study (LIS) A cooperative research project with 25 member countries, the LIS focuses on poverty and policy issues. The income poverty estimates for many OECD countries are from the LIS.

Office of US Foreign Disaster Assistance/Center for Research on the Epidemiology of Disasters (OFDA/CRED) OFDA/CRED maintains the *International Disaster Database*, with data on more than 12,000 mass disasters and their effects from 1900 to the present. This source provides the estimates of people killed in natural and technological disasters.

Organisation for Economic Co-operation and Development (OECD) The OECD publishes data on social and economic trends in its member countries as well as data on aid flows. It is the source of data on aid, employment and functional illiteracy.

United Nations Children's Fund (UNICEF) UNICEF monitors the well-being of children and provides a wide array of data. Its *State of the World's Children* provides data for the Report.

United Nations Conference on Trade and Development (UNCTAD) UNCTAD provides trade and economic statistics through a number of publications, including the *World Investment Report*, a source of investment flows data for the Report. UNCTAD also contributes to trade data that the Human Development Report Office receives from other agencies.

United Nations Crime Prevention and Criminal Justice Division This UN office, the source of data on crime and judicial systems for the Report, maintains and develops the UN database on such issues through surveys of crime trends and the operations of criminal justice systems.

United Nations Economic Commission for Europe (UNECE) This regional UN agency collects and publishes a wide range of social and economic data on its member countries. UNECE data in this year's Report include indicators on unemployment and personal distress.

United Nations Educational, Scientific and Cultural Organization (UNESCO) This specialized UN agency is the source of education data. The Report draws on its *Statistical Yearbook* and *World Education Report* as well as data received directly from UNESCO.

United Nations High Commissioner for Refugees (UNHCR) This UN organization provides data on refugees through its *Refugees and Others of Concern to UNHCR (Statistical Overview)*.

United Nations Multilateral Treaties Deposited with the Secretary-General (UN Treaty Section) The Human Development Report Office compiles information on the status of major international human rights instruments based on the database maintained by this UN office.

United Nations Population Division (UNPOP) This specialized UN office produces international data on population trends. The *Human Development Report* relies on two of its publications, *World Population Prospects* and *World Urbanization Prospects*, for demographic estimates.

United Nations Statistics Division (UNSD) The United Nations Statistics Division provides a wide range of statistical outputs and services for producers and users of statistics worldwide. It also contributes to many statistical data series that the Human Development Report Office receives from other agencies. This year's Report uses UNSD data on electricity consumption and personal distress.

World Bank The World Bank produces data on economic trends as well as a broad array of other data. Its *World Development Indicators* is the primary source for a number of the indicators presented in the Report.

World Health Organization (WHO) This specialized agency maintains a large number of data series on health issues, the sources for the health-related indicators in the Report.

World Resources Institute This non-governmental organization maintains a large database on environmental issues. It presents comprehensive data in its biannual publication *World Resources*, the source for some of the data on environmental protection and resources in the Report.

without access to safe water for 130 countries, but no estimates for 58 others.

The data on adult literacy illustrate the consistency and comparability problems (box 2). So do the crime data supplied by the United Nations Crime Prevention and Criminal Justice Division. These data come from the Fifth United Nations Survey of Crime Trends and Operations of Criminal Justice Systems (1990–94), and their availability and reliability depend heavily on a country's law enforcement and reporting system. These factors must be considered when making comparisons, even with internationally standardized data.

Also causing comparability problems are the significant shifts and breaks in statistical series that often occur when statistical bodies and research institutions update or improve their estimates using new data sources, such as censuses and surveys. The transition in the countries of Eastern Europe and the CIS has led to a break in most of their statistical series, so data for recent years pose problems of reliability, consistency and international comparability and are often subject to revisions.

Data availability suffers when there is a war or civil strife. In such cases reporting of data in the main statistical tables of the Report is interrupted, and any available data on basic human development indicators are presented in a special table following the main statistical tables. That has been the case for Afghanistan, the Democratic People's Republic of Korea, Liberia and Somalia. When data again become available, as they have for such countries as Rwanda, the country is re-introduced in the main tables.

The state of human development statistics is ultimately an issue of priorities. Why should trade balance data be available soon after the end of every month, while data on child malnutrition or school enrolments often take years to produce—years that excluded children may never recover?

Improving human development statistics is a complex undertaking. But there are three general priorities. First, national statistical capacity needs to be improved. Second, better coordination is needed between national and international statistical agencies. National statistical offices often offer the Human Development Report Office data that differ from those provided by international agencies. While the office is not in a position to use or comment on such data, the differences point to a need for better communication between national and international statistical bodies. Finally, improved communication is needed between international statistical bodies to ensure efficiency in collecting statistics and in building national statistical capacity.

All these improvements would enhance international statistics, but particular emphasis needs to be placed on improving human development statistics.

BOX 2

The challenges of measuring literacy

Literacy involves a continuum of reading and writing skills, often extending to basic arithmetic skills (numeracy) and life skills. The literacy rate reflects the accumulated achievement of primary education and adult literacy programmes in imparting basic literacy skills to the population. Because of the need to collect internationally comparable data, the concept of literacy is usually reduced to the standard definition—the ability to read and write, with understanding, a simple statement related to one's daily life.

Countries collect literacy statistics in different ways. Most rely on national population censuses that take place every 5 or 10 years, or household, labour force or other demographic surveys. Some use literacy surveys to collect more detailed data. Additional data from national publications and reports and from ad hoc surveys are used to supplement literacy statistics at the international level.

Literacy ideally should be determined by measuring the reading, writing and numeracy skills of each person within a social context. Organizing such measurements during national population censuses may be too time-consuming, costly and complex. However, some countries do require census enumerators to administer a simple test by asking each person in a household to read a simple, preselected text. But enumerators usually determine literacy status on the basis of self-declaration or a declaration by the head of the household. That sometimes gives rise to concerns about data reliability and thus comparability.

Some countries may equate never having attended school with illiteracy—or having attended school or completed grade 4 with literacy. But the latest UN recommendations on censuses advise against assuming any links between school attendance and literacy or educational attainment (UN 1998b).

The most recent UNESCO literacy estimates and projections come from its February 2000 assessment, covering 134 countries, 116 of them developing. Many developed countries, having attained high levels of literacy, no longer collect literacy statistics during national population censuses and thus are not included in the UNESCO data. For 78 countries that provided literacy statistics from the 1990 round of population censuses, the quality and reliability of the estimates are relatively high. For 30 countries statistics from the 1980 censuses have produced estimates and projections of acceptable quality. These are supplemented by estimates of lower quality based on statistics collected before 1980 or derived from correlated indicators.

Source: UNESCO 2000a.

DATA USED IN THE HUMAN DEVELOPMENT INDEX

The human development index (HDI) is calculated using international data available at the time the Report is prepared.

Life expectancy at birth. The life expectancy estimates used in the Report are from the 1998 revision of the United Nations Population Division database *World Population Prospects* (UN 1998c). The United Nations Population Division derives population estimates and projections biannually from population censuses, supplemented with information from national survey data. In the 1998 revision it made significant adjustments to further incorporate the demographic impact of HIV/AIDS, which has led to substantial changes in life expectancy estimates for a number of countries, particularly in Sub-Saharan Africa. Adjustments were also made to reflect extensive migration, the growth in the number of refugees in Africa and other parts of the world and the demographic changes in Eastern Europe and the CIS (UN 1998c).

The life expectancy estimates published by the United Nations Population Division are five-year averages. The life expectancy estimates for 1998 shown in table 1 (on the HDI) were obtained through linear interpolation based on these five-year averages. While the human development indices require yearly estimates, other tables showing data of this type, such as table 9 (on survival), present the unaltered five-year averages. Estimates for years after 1995 refer to medium-variant projections.

Adult literacy. The adult literacy rates presented in the Report are new estimates and projections from UNESCO's February 2000 literacy assessment. UNESCO has incorporated new population estimates from the United Nations Population Division and new literacy statistics collected through national population censuses. It has also recently refined its estimation procedures.

Gross primary, secondary and tertiary enrolment. The 1998 gross enrolment ratios presented in the Report are preliminary estimates from UNESCO. Gross enrolment ratios are calculated by dividing the number of children enrolled in each level of schooling by the number of children in the age group corresponding to that level. Thus they are affected by the age- and sex-specific population estimates published by the United Nations Population Division, and by the timing and methods of surveys by administrative registries, of population censuses and of national education surveys. Moreover, UNESCO periodically revises its methodology for projecting and estimating enrolment. For 13 countries included in the main statistical tables, UNESCO estimates are not available and estimates by the Human Development Report Office are used.

Gross enrolment ratios can hide important differences among countries because of differences in the age range corresponding to a level of education and in the duration of education programmes. Such factors as grade repetition can also lead to distortions in the data. For the HDI, net enrolment, for which data are collected for single years of age, would be the preferred indicator of access to education as a proxy of knowledge. Because this indicator measures enrolments only of a particular age group, the data could be more easily and reliably aggregated and used for international comparisons. But net enrolment data are available for too few countries to be used in the HDI.

GDP per capita (PPP US$). The GDP per capita (PPP US$) data used in the Report are provided by the World Bank and are based on the latest International Comparison Programme (ICP) surveys. The surveys cover 118 countries, the largest number ever in a round of ICP surveys. The World Bank also provided estimates based on these surveys for another 44 countries.

The surveys were carried out separately in different regions. As regional data are expressed in different currencies and may be based on different classification schemes or aggregation formulas, the data are not strictly comparable across regions. Price and expenditure data from the regional surveys were linked using a standard classification scheme to compile internationally comparable purchasing power parity (PPP) data. The base year for the PPP data is 1996; data for the reference year 1998 were extrapolated using relative price movements over time between each country and the United States, the base country. For countries not covered by the World Bank, PPP estimates provided by Alan Heston and Robert Summers (1999) of the University of Pennsylvania are used.

DATA, METHODOLOGY AND PRESENTATION OF THE HUMAN DEVELOPMENT INDICATORS

The data in this year's Report reflect the continuous efforts over the years to publish the best available data and to improve their presentation and transparency. Building on improvements made in 1999, this year's Report has, for several more indicators, reduced to two years the time lag between the reference date of indicators and the date of release of the Report.

The definitions of statistical terms have been revised and expanded to include more indicators for which short, meaningful definitions can be given. In addition, the transparency of sources has been further improved. When an agency provides data it has collected from another source, both sources are credited. But when international statistical organizations build on the work of many other contributors, only the ultimate source is given. The sources also show the original data components used in any calculations by the Human Development Report Office to ensure that all calculations can be easily replicated.

COUNTRY CLASSIFICATIONS

Countries are classified in four ways in this year's Report: in major world aggregates, by region, by human development level and by income (see the classification of countries).

These designations do not necessarily express a judgement about the development stage reached by a particular country or area. Instead, they are classifications used by different organizations for operational purposes. The term *country* as used in the text and the tables refers, as appropriate, to territories or areas.

Major world classifications. This year the classification *industrialized countries* is replaced by *OECD,* which is more clearly defined. The other global groups are *all developing countries* and *Eastern Europe and the CIS.* These groups are not mutually exclusive. The classification *world* represents the universe of 174 countries covered by the Report.

Regional classifications. Developing countries are further classified into the following regions: Arab States, East Asia, Latin America and the Caribbean (including Mexico), South Asia, South-East Asia and the Pacific, Southern Europe and Sub-Saharan Africa. These regional classifications are consistent with the Regional Bureaux of UNDP. An additional classification is *least developed countries*, as defined by the United Nations.

Human development classifications. All countries are classified into three clusters by achievement in human development: high human development (with an HDI of 0.800 or above), medium human development (0.500–0.799) and low human development (less than 0.500).

Income classifications. All countries are grouped by income based on World Bank classifications (valid through July 2000): high income (GNP per capita of $9,361 or more in 1998), middle income ($761–9,360) and low income ($760 or less).

AGGREGATES AND GROWTH RATES

Aggregates. Aggregates are presented at the end of most tables, for the classifications described above. Aggregates that are the total for the classification (such as for population) are indicated by a T. All other aggregates are weighted averages.

Unless otherwise indicated, an aggregate is shown for a classification only when data are available for two-thirds of the countries and represent two-thirds of the available weight in that classification. The Human Development Report Office does not fill in missing data for the purpose of aggregation. Therefore, aggregates for each classification represent only the countries for which data are available and are shown in the tables.

Aggregates are not shown where appropriate weighting procedures were unavailable. Aggregates for indices and growth rates are based only on countries for which data exist for all necessary points in time. For the world classification, which refers only to the universe of 174 countries, aggregates are not always shown where no aggregate is shown for one or more regions. Aggregates in the *Human Development Report* will not always conform to those in other publications because of differences in country classifications and methodology.

Growth rates. Multiyear growth rates are expressed as average annual rates of change. Only the beginning and end points are used in their calculation. Year-to-year growth rates are expressed as annual percentage changes.

PRESENTATION

In the indicator tables countries and areas are ranked in descending order by their HDI value. To locate a country in the tables, refer to the key to countries on the back cover flap, which lists countries alphabetically with their HDI rank.

Short citations of sources are given at the end of each table. These correspond to full references in the primary statistical references, which follow the indicator tables and technical note. Where appropriate, definitions of indicators appear in the definitions of statistical terms. All other relevant information appears in the footnotes at the end of each table.

Owing to lack of comparable data, not all countries have been included in the indicator tables. For UN member countries not included in the main indicator tables, basic human development indicators are presented in a separate table.

In the absence of the words *annual, annual rate* or *growth rate*, a hyphen between two years indicates that the data were collected during one of the years shown, such as 1993–97. A slash between two years indicates an average for the years shown, such as 1996/97. The following signs have been used:

.. Data not available.
(.) Less than half the unit shown.
< Less than.
– Not applicable.
T Total.

What do the human development indices reveal?

Since first being published in 1990, the *Human Development Report* has developed and constructed several composite indices to measure different aspects of human development.

The human development index (HDI), constructed every year since 1990, measures average achievements in basic human development in one simple composite index and produces a ranking of countries.

The gender-related development index (GDI) and the gender empowerment measure (GEM), introduced in *Human Development Report 1995*, are composite measures reflecting gender inequalities in human development. The GDI measures achievements in the same dimensions and using the same variables as the HDI does, but taking account of inequality in achievement between men and women. The GEM measures gender inequality in economic and political opportunities.

Human Development Report 1997 introduced the concept of human poverty and formulated a composite measure of it—the human poverty index (HPI). While the HDI measures average achievements in basic dimensions of human development, the HPI measures deprivations in those dimensions.

Table 1 presents the basic dimensions of human development captured in the indices and the indicators used to measure them.

The concept of human development is much deeper and richer than what can be captured in any composite index or even by a detailed set of statistical indicators. Yet simple tools are needed to monitor progress in human development. The HDI, GDI, GEM and HPI all provide summary information about human development in a country.

TABLE 1

HDI, GDI, HPI-1, HPI-2—same dimensions, different indicators

Index	Longevity	Knowledge	Decent standard of living	Participation or exclusion
HDI	Life expectancy at birth	1. Adult literacy rate 2. Combined enrolment ratio	Adjusted per capita income in PPP US$	–
GDI	Female and male life expectancy at birth	1. Female and male adult literacy rates 2. Female and male combined enrolment ratios	Female and male per capita incomes (PPP US$) based on female and male earned income shares	–
HPI-1 For developing countries	Probability at birth of not surviving to age 40	Adult illiteracy rate	Deprivation in economic provisioning, measured by: 1. Percentage of people without access to safe water 2. Percentage of people without access to health services 3. Percentage of children under five who are underweight	–
HPI-2 For industrialized countries	Probability at birth of not surviving to age 60	Adult functional illiteracy rate	Percentage of people living below the income poverty line (50% of median disposable household income)	Long-term unemployment rate (12 months or more)

Source: Human Development Report Office.

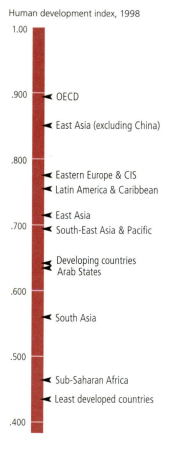

FIGURE 1

Human development varies among regions

Human development index, 1998

Source: Human Development Report Office.

Two major points. First, income is not the sum total of human lives, nor is its lack the sum total of human deprivations. Thus by focusing on areas beyond income and treating income as a proxy for a decent standard of living, both the HDI and the HPI provide a more comprehensive measure of human well-being than income or its lack. Second, the composite indices of human development do not, by themselves, provide a complete picture. They must be supplemented with other indicators of human development.

THE HUMAN DEVELOPMENT INDEX

With normalization of the values of the variables that make up the HDI, its value ranges from 0 to 1 (for a detailed explanation of the method for constructing the HDI see the technical note). The HDI value for a country shows the distance that it has to travel to reach the maximum possible value of 1—or its shortfall—and also allows intercountry comparisons. A challenge for every country is to find ways to reduce its shortfall.

WHAT DOES THE 2000 HDI REVEAL?

The HDI reveals the following state of human development:

• Of the 174 countries for which the HDI is constructed this year, 46 are in the high human development category (with an HDI value equal to or more than 0.800), 93 in the medium human development category (0.500–0.790) and 35 in the low human development category (less than

0.500). Twenty countries have experienced reversals of human development since 1990 as a result of HIV/AIDS, particularly in Sub-Saharan Africa, and economic stagnation and conflict, in Sub-Saharan Africa and Eastern Europe and the CIS.

• Canada, Norway and the United States rank at the top on the HDI, Sierra Leone, Niger and Burkina Faso at the bottom (table 2). Wide disparities in global human development persist. Canada's HDI value of 0.935 is nearly four times Sierra Leone's of 0.252. Thus Canada has to make up a shortfall in human development of only about 7%, Sierra Leone one of 75%.

• Disparities between regions can be significant, with some having more ground to cover in making up shortfalls than others (figure 1). Sub-Saharan Africa has more than twice the distance to cover as Latin America and the Caribbean, South Asia nearly three times as much as East Asia without China.

• Disparities within regions can also be substantial. In South-East Asia and the Pacific HDI values range from 0.484 in the Lao People's Democratic Republic to 0.881 in Singapore. Among the Arab States they range from 0.447 in Djibouti to 0.836 in Kuwait.

• The link between economic prosperity and human development is neither automatic nor obvious. Two countries with similar incomes can have very different HDI values; countries with similar HDI values can have very different incomes (figure 2; table 3). Of the 174 countries, 97 rank higher on the HDI than on GDP per capita (PPP US$), suggesting that they have converted income into human development very effectively. For 69 countries, the HDI rank is lower than the GDP per capita (PPP US$) rank. These countries have been less successful in translating economic prosperity into better lives for their people.

TRENDS IN HUMAN DEVELOPMENT, 1975–98

Of the 101 countries for which HDI trends between 1975 and 1998 are available, all but Zambia had a higher HDI in 1998 than in 1975. Zambia managed to improve its HDI from 1975 to 1985, but then slid back, largely because of the effects of HIV/AIDS on life expectancy.

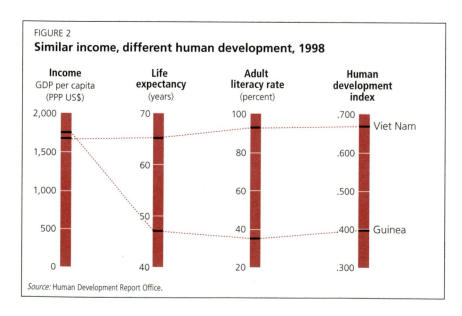

FIGURE 2

Similar income, different human development, 1998

Source: Human Development Report Office.

TABLE 2
HDI ranks, 1998

1	Canada	45	United Arab Emirates	89	Maldives	133	Papua New Guinea
2	Norway	46	Estonia	90	Azerbaijan	134	Cameroon
3	United States	47	Saint Kitts and Nevis	91	Ecuador	135	Pakistan
4	Australia	48	Costa Rica	92	Jordan	136	Cambodia
5	Iceland	49	Croatia	93	Armenia	137	Comoros
6	Sweden	50	Trinidad and Tobago	94	Albania	138	Kenya
7	Belgium	51	Dominica	95	Samoa (Western)	139	Congo
8	Netherlands	52	Lithuania	96	Guyana	140	Lao People's Dem. Rep.
9	Japan	53	Seychelles	97	Iran, Islamic Rep. of	141	Madagascar
10	United Kingdom	54	Grenada	98	Kyrgyzstan	142	Bhutan
11	Finland	55	Mexico	99	China	143	Sudan
12	France	56	Cuba	100	Turkmenistan	144	Nepal
13	Switzerland	57	Belarus	101	Tunisia	145	Togo
14	Germany	58	Belize	102	Moldova, Rep. of	146	Bangladesh
15	Denmark	59	Panama	103	South Africa	147	Mauritania
16	Austria	60	Bulgaria	104	El Salvador	148	Yemen
17	Luxembourg	61	Malaysia	105	Cape Verde	149	Djibouti
18	Ireland	62	Russian Federation	106	Uzbekistan	150	Haiti
19	Italy	63	Latvia	107	Algeria	151	Nigeria
20	New Zealand	64	Romania	108	Viet Nam	152	Congo, Dem. Rep. of the
21	Spain	65	Venezuela	109	Indonesia	153	Zambia
22	Cyprus	66	Fiji	110	Tajikistan	154	Côte d'Ivoire
23	Israel	67	Suriname	111	Syrian Arab Republic	155	Senegal
24	Singapore	68	Colombia	112	Swaziland	156	Tanzania, U. Rep. of
25	Greece	69	Macedonia, TFYR	113	Honduras	157	Benin
26	Hong Kong, China (SAR)	70	Georgia	114	Bolivia	158	Uganda
27	Malta	71	Mauritius	115	Namibia	159	Eritrea
28	Portugal	72	Libyan Arab Jamahiriya	116	Nicaragua	160	Angola
29	Slovenia	73	Kazakhstan	117	Mongolia	161	Gambia
30	Barbados	74	Brazil	118	Vanuatu	162	Guinea
31	Korea, Rep. of	75	Saudi Arabia	119	Egypt	163	Malawi
32	Brunei Darussalam	76	Thailand	120	Guatemala	164	Rwanda
33	Bahamas	77	Philippines	121	Solomon Islands	165	Mali
34	Czech Republic	78	Ukraine	122	Botswana	166	Central African Republic
35	Argentina	79	Saint Vincent and the Grenadines	123	Gabon	167	Chad
36	Kuwait	80	Peru	124	Morocco	168	Mozambique
37	Antigua and Barbuda	81	Paraguay	125	Myanmar	169	Guinea-Bissau
38	Chile	82	Lebanon	126	Iraq	170	Burundi
39	Uruguay	83	Jamaica	127	Lesotho	171	Ethiopia
40	Slovakia	84	Sri Lanka	128	India	172	Burkina Faso
41	Bahrain	85	Turkey	129	Ghana	173	Niger
42	Qatar	86	Oman	130	Zimbabwe	174	Sierra Leone
43	Hungary	87	Dominican Republic	131	Equatorial Guinea		
44	Poland	88	Saint Lucia	132	São Tomé and Principe		

Source: Human Development Report Office.

Even though virtually all countries for which data are available enhanced the basic capabilities of their people in 1975–98, the dynamics varied.

• The rate of advancement differed among countries (table 4). In every human development category—high, medium and low—there were cases of fast progress and slow. Advancement in human development is not only an issue of long-term progress. There is also a need, for policy-making and for advocacy, to monitor short-term progress, an issue discussed in chapter 5.

• Countries that started from similar HDI values in 1975 may have ended up with very different ones in 1998. And countries with very

TABLE 3
Similar HDI, different incomes, 1998

Country	HDI value	GDP per capita (PPP US$)
Luxembourg	0.908	33,505
Ireland	0.907	21,482
Saudi Arabia	0.747	10,158
Thailand	0.745	5,456
South Africa	0.697	8,488
El Salvador	0.696	4,036

Source: Human Development Report Office.

different starting points in 1975 may have ended up with similar HDI values in 1998 (figure 3). These differences result from a combination of factors, but the policies countries pursued are a major determinant.

FIGURE 3
Different human progress

Same starting point, different outcomes
Human development index

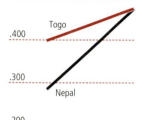

Same outcome, different paths
Human development index

Source: Human Development Report Office.

TABLE 4
Fastest and slowest progress in human development, 1975–98
For 101 countries with available data

	Country	1975 HDI	1998 HDI	Absolute change 1975–98
Starting from high human development (0.800–1.000)				
Fastest progress	Ireland	0.805	0.907	0.102
	Luxembourg	0.818	0.908	0.090
	Australia	0.841	0.929	0.088
Slowest progress	New Zealand	0.843	0.903	0.060
	Denmark	0.859	0.911	0.052
	Switzerland	0.870	0.915	0.045
Starting from medium human development (0.500–0.799)				
Fastest progress	Tunisia	0.511	0.703	0.192
	China	0.518	0.706	0.188
	Algeria	0.508	0.683	0.175
Slowest progress	Zimbabwe	0.519	0.555	0.036
	Guyana	0.676	0.709	0.033
	Romania	0.750	0.770	0.020
Starting from low human development (0–0.499)				
Fastest progress	Indonesia	0.456	0.670	0.214
	Egypt	0.430	0.623	0.193
	Nepal	0.291	0.474	0.183
Slowest progress	Central African Republic	0.332	0.371	0.039
	Congo, Dem. Rep. of the	0.416	0.430	0.014
	Zambia	0.444	0.420	0.024

Source: Human Development Report Office.

• Seven countries in Sub-Saharan Africa—Botswana, Burundi, Congo, the Democratic Republic of the Congo, Kenya, Zambia and Zimbabwe—saw a reversal in 1985–98 in the progress they had made in building basic human capabilities in the previous decade (1975–85). The reversal is explained largely by the drop in life expectancy due to HIV/AIDS. Similar effects can be seen for the Central African Republic, Namibia and South Africa in 1990–98. Uganda is the only country that managed to turn around such a reversal. Its HDI value declined in 1985–90 because of HIV/AIDS, but then improved by 1998 to surpass the value in 1985.

• Six countries in Eastern Europe and the CIS—Bulgaria, Estonia, Latvia, the Republic of Moldova, Romania and the Russian Federation—saw a decline in their HDI in 1985–98, a reflection of the costs of transition for human development. Seven countries in the region—Armenia, Belarus, Lithuania, Kazakhstan, Tajikistan, Ukraine and Uzbekistan—for which data are available only for 1990 and 1998, registered a decline in their HDI during those eight years. Economic stagnation played a part in the decline in most of these countries. In some, such as Tajikistan, conflicts were also responsible.

HUMAN POVERTY AND DEPRIVATION

The human poverty index is a multidimensional measure of poverty. It brings together in one composite index the deprivation in four basic dimensions of human life—a long and healthy life, knowledge, economic provisioning and social inclusion. These dimensions of deprivation are the same for both developing and industrialized countries. Only the indicators to measure them differ, to reflect the realities in these countries and because of data limitations.

For developing countries the HPI-1 measures human poverty. Deprivation in a long and healthy life is measured by the percentage of people born today not expected to survive to age 40, deprivation in knowledge by the adult illiteracy rate and deprivation in economic provisioning by the percentage of people lacking access to health services and safe water and the percentage of children under five who are moderately or severely underweight.

Two points. First, for economic provisioning in developing countries, public provisioning is more important than private income. At the same time, more than four-fifths of private income is spent on food. Thus in developing countries lack of access to health services and safe water and the level of malnutrition capture the deprivation in economic provisioning more practically than other variables. Second, the absence of a suitable indicator and lack of data prevent the human poverty index from reflecting the deprivation in social inclusion in developing countries.

For industrialized countries the HPI-2 measures human poverty. Deprivation in a long and healthy life is measured by the percentage of people born today not expected to survive to age 60, deprivation in knowledge by the adult functional illiteracy rate, deprivation in economic provisioning by the incidence of income poverty (since private income is the larger source of economic provisioning in industrialized countries) and deprivation in social inclusion by long-term unemployment.

The components and the results of the HPI-1 and HPI-2 are presented in indicator tables 4 and 5. The technical note presents a detailed discussion of the methodology for constructing the two indices.

WHAT DOES THE HPI-1 REVEAL?

Calculated for 85 countries, the HPI-1 reveals the following (table 5):

- The HPI-1 ranges from 3.9% in Uruguay to 64.7% in Niger. Nine countries have an HPI-1 of less than 10%: Bahrain, Chile, Costa Rica, Cuba, Fiji, Jordan, Panama, Trinidad and Tobago and Uruguay. These developing countries have overcome severe levels of poverty.

- For 29 countries—more than a third of those for which the HPI-1 was calculated—the HPI-1 exceeds 33%, implying that at least a third of their people suffer from human poverty. Others have further to go. The HPI-1 exceeds 50% in Burkina Faso, the Central African Republic, Ethiopia, Guinea-Bissau, Mali, Mozambique, Nepal and Niger.

- A comparison of HDI and HPI-1 values shows the distribution of achievements in human progress. Human development can be distributed more equitably—as in countries with a relatively low HPI-1 for a given HDI value—or less equitably—as in those with a relatively low HDI value for a given HPI-1 (figure 4). Policies play a big part in determining how achievements in human progress are distributed.

WHAT DOES THE HPI-2 REVEAL?

The HPI-2 values show that human poverty is not confined to developing countries.

FIGURE 4
No automatic link between HDI and HPI-1, 1998

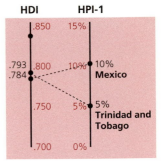

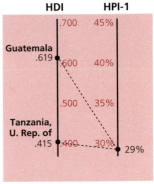

Source: Human Development Report Office.

TABLE 5
HPI-1 ranking, 1998

1 Uruguay	23 Paraguay	45 Swaziland	67 Uganda
2 Costa Rica	24 Turkey	46 Indonesia	68 Pakistan
3 Cuba	25 Peru	47 Viet Nam	69 Malawi
4 Chile	26 Ecuador	48 Botswana	70 Bangladesh
5 Trinidad and Tobago	27 Bolivia	49 Guatemala	71 Haiti
6 Fiji	28 United Arab Emirates	50 Tanzania, U. Rep. of	72 Côte d'Ivoire
7 Jordan	29 Thailand	51 Kenya	73 Senegal
8 Panama	30 China	52 Zimbabwe	74 Benin
9 Bahrain	31 Iran, Islamic Rep. of	53 Myanmar	75 Gambia
10 Guyana	32 Syrian Arab Republic	54 Congo	76 Yemen
11 Colombia	33 South Africa	55 Egypt	77 Mauritania
12 Mexico	34 El Salvador	56 Iraq	78 Guinea-Bissau
13 Lebanon	35 Sri Lanka	57 Comoros	79 Mozambique
14 Mauritius	36 Tunisia	58 India	80 Nepal
15 Venezuela	37 Cape Verde	59 Ghana	81 Mali
16 Jamaica	38 Oman	60 Sudan	82 Central African Republic
17 Qatar	39 Honduras	61 Rwanda	83 Ethiopia
18 Malaysia	40 Lesotho	62 Nigeria	84 Burkina Faso
19 Libyan Arab Jamahiriya	41 Nicaragua	63 Togo	85 Niger
20 Dominican Republic	42 Algeria	64 Zambia	
21 Brazil	43 Maldives	65 Morocco	
22 Philippines	44 Namibia	66 Cameroon	

Source: Human Development Report Office.

• Among the 18 industrialized countries for which the HPI-2 was calculated, Norway has the lowest level of human poverty, at 7.3%, followed by Sweden and the Netherlands, at 7.6% and 8.2% (table 6). Those with the highest human poverty are the United States (15.8%), Ireland (15.0%) and the United Kingdom (14.6%).

• For some rich countries adult functional illiteracy and income poverty are significant. In Ireland, the United Kingdom and the United States more than one in five adults are functionally illiterate. More than 17% of people in the United States and more than 10% in Australia, Canada, Italy, Japan and the United Kingdom are income-poor, with the income poverty line set at 50% of the median disposable household income.

• A high HDI value does not automatically mean low human deprivation. All 18 countries for which the HPI-2 was calculated have an HDI of at least 0.899, suggesting that they have achieved high human development. Yet their levels of human poverty vary. Sweden and the United Kingdom have very similar HDI values—0.926 and 0.918. But while Sweden's HPI-2 value is only 7.6%, the United Kingdom's is 14.6%.

DISPARITIES WITHIN COUNTRIES

Differences in human development exist not only between countries and between the devel-oping and developed worlds. National human development data, disaggregated by region, gender, ethnic group or rural and urban areas, reveal significant disparities within countries too. And disparities of all kinds are interrelated and overlapping.

. . . BETWEEN RURAL AND URBAN AREAS. . .

When the HDI and the HPI are disaggregated along the rural-urban divide, they document more progress in human development and less deprivation for people in urban areas than for those in rural areas. The rural-urban divides in Uganda and Swaziland provide good examples of such disparity.

In 1996 the HPI-1 in rural Uganda, at 43%, was more than twice that in urban Uganda, at 21% (table 7). In Swaziland in 1999, the rural HDI at 0.525 was less than two-thirds the urban HDI at 0.812.

. . . BETWEEN REGIONS OR DISTRICTS. . .

• In China the disaggregated HDI shows strong disparities in basic human capabilities between provinces (figure 5). Qinghai lags behind Shanghai in every indicator used in the HDI, and its HDI value is only three-fifths that of Shanghai.

• Federal District and Delta Amacuro, two provinces in Venezuela, are far apart in human

---

TABLE 6
HPI-2 ranking, 1998

1	Norway	6	Germany	11	Canada	16	United Kingdom
2	Sweden	7	Luxembourg	12	Italy	17	Ireland
3	Netherlands	8	France	13	Australia	18	United States
4	Finland	9	Japan	14	Belgium		
5	Denmark	10	Spain	15	New Zealand		

Source: Human Development Report Office.

TABLE 7
Rural-urban disparities in human poverty in Uganda, 1996
Percent

	People born today not expected to survive to age 40	Adult illiteracy rate	People without access to safe water	People without access to health services	Children under five who are malnourished	HPI-1
Rural	38	43	57	57	27	43
Urban	27	16	23	5	15	21

Source: UNDP 1998d.

WHAT DO THE HUMAN DEVELOPMENT INDICES REVEAL?

development. In 1996 life expectancy in the Federal District was 72 years, 8 years more than the 64 years in Amacuro. And the adult literacy rate in the Federal District was 96%, compared with 74% in Amacuro. As a result of such disparities, the HDI in the Federal District was 0.823, while that in Amacuro was only 0.506.

• In Zimbabwe the 1990s, the HPI-1 in Mashonaland Central province at 26% is more than three times that in Bulawayo province at 8%. In Mashonaland Central 21% of people born today are not expected to survive to age 40—more than twice the 10% in Bulawayo. About 33% of adults are illiterate—more than five times the 6% in Bulawayo. And 17% of children under five are malnourished—more than four times the 4% in Bulawayo.

. . . BETWEEN ETHNIC AND LANGUAGE GROUPS. . .

• In Guatemala in 1995–96, the HDI values for the four principal Mayan communities—Kakchikel, Mam, K'iche' and Q'eqchi—were 0.419, 0.368, 0.366 and 0.356, only 60–70% of the overall HDI for Guatemala at 0.596.

• In South Africa in 1995, the unemployment rate among African males at 29% was more than seven times that among white males at 4%.

• In India the illiteracy rate among the scheduled tribes is 70%, compared with 48% for India as a whole.

• In Namibia in 1998, the HPI-1 of the San-speaking group at nearly 60% was more than six times those of the English- and German-speaking groups at less than 10%.

. . . BETWEEN MEN AND WOMEN. . .

The HDI is a measure of average achievements and thus masks the differences in human development between men and women. So additional measures are needed to capture gender inequalities.

The gender-related development index captures achievement in the same set of basic capabilities as the HDI does—life expectancy, educational attainment and income—but adjusts the results for gender inequality (for a detailed discussion of the methodology for the

GDI and its components, see the technical note). This year the GDI has been calculated for 143 countries (table 8).

• For every country the GDI value is lower than the HDI value. Thus when adjusted for gender, HDI values decline, indicating the presence of gender inequality in every society. With gender equality in human development, the HDI and GDI values would be the same.

• Of the 143 countries, as many as 30 have a GDI value of less than 0.500, showing that women in these countries suffer the double deprivation of low overall achievement in human development and lower achievement than men.

• For 39 of the 143 countries, the GDI rank is lower than the HDI rank. In these societies the average achievements in human development have not been equally distributed between men and women. But for 55 countries, the GDI rank is higher than the HDI rank, suggesting a more equitable distribution.

• Some countries show a marked improvement in their GDI ranks relative to their HDI ranks. These countries are fairly diverse. They include industrialized countries (Denmark, France and New Zealand), countries in Eastern Europe and the CIS (Estonia, Hungary and Poland) and developing countries (Jamaica, Sri Lanka and Thailand). This shows that gender equality in human development can be achieved at different income levels and stages of development—and across a range of cultures.

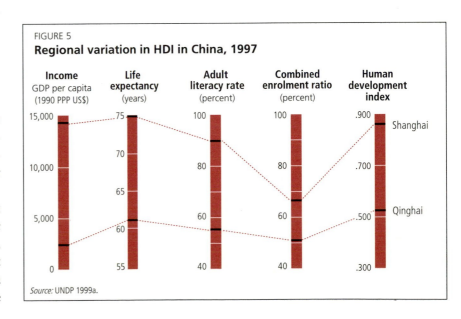

FIGURE 5
Regional variation in HDI in China, 1997

Source: UNDP 1999a.

TABLE 8
GDI ranking, 1998

1	Canada	37	Uruguay	73	Dominican Republic	109	Equatorial Guinea
2	Norway	38	Hungary	74	Lebanon	110	Papua New Guinea
3	Australia	39	Chile	75	Armenia	111	Cameroon
4	United States	40	Poland	76	Saudi Arabia	112	Kenya
5	Iceland	41	Qatar	77	Albania	113	Comoros
6	Sweden	42	Bahrain	78	Ecuador	114	Congo
7	Belgium	43	Estonia	79	China	115	Pakistan
8	Netherlands	44	United Arab Emirates	80	Guyana	116	Madagascar
9	Japan	45	Croatia	81	Moldova, Rep. of	117	Lao People's Dem. Rep.
10	United Kingdom	46	Costa Rica	82	Oman	118	Sudan
11	France	47	Lithuania	83	El Salvador	119	Nepal
12	Finland	48	Trinidad and Tobago	84	Iran, Islamic Rep. of	120	Togo
13	Switzerland	49	Belarus	85	South Africa	121	Bangladesh
14	Denmark	50	Mexico	86	Tunisia	122	Mauritania
15	Germany	51	Latvia	87	Uzbekistan	123	Haiti
16	Austria	52	Panama	88	Cape Verde	124	Nigeria
17	New Zealand	53	Bulgaria	89	Viet Nam	125	Congo, Dem. Rep. of the
18	Ireland	54	Russian Federation	90	Indonesia	126	Zambia
19	Italy	55	Romania	91	Algeria	127	Tanzania, U. Rep. of
20	Luxembourg	56	Venezuela	92	Tajikistan	128	Senegal
21	Spain	57	Malaysia	93	Swaziland	129	Côte d'Ivoire
22	Israel	58	Colombia	94	Honduras	130	Uganda
23	Cyprus	59	Fiji	95	Syrian Arab Republic	131	Eritrea
24	Singapore	60	Belize	96	Bolivia	132	Benin
25	Greece	61	Mauritius	97	Nicaragua	133	Yemen
26	Hong Kong, China (SAR)	62	Thailand	98	Namibia	134	Gambia
27	Portugal	63	Ukraine	99	Egypt	135	Rwanda
28	Slovenia	64	Philippines	100	Guatemala	136	Malawi
29	Malta	65	Libyan Arab Jamahiriya	101	Botswana	137	Mali
30	Korea, Rep. of	66	Brazil	102	Myanmar	138	Central African Republic
31	Brunei Darussalam	67	Jamaica	103	Morocco	139	Mozambique
32	Bahamas	68	Sri Lanka	104	Lesotho	140	Guinea-Bissau
33	Czech Republic	69	Turkey	105	Ghana	141	Ethiopia
34	Kuwait	70	Peru	106	Zimbabwe	142	Burkina Faso
35	Argentina	71	Paraguay	107	Iraq	143	Niger
36	Slovakia	72	Maldives	108	India		

Source: Human Development Report Office.

TABLE 9
GEM ranking

1	Norway	19	Spain	37	Colombia	55	Ukraine
2	Iceland	20	Venezuela	38	Singapore	56	Mauritius
3	Sweden	21	Ireland	39	Dominican Republic	57	Paraguay
4	Denmark	22	Trinidad and Tobago	40	Belize	58	Romania
5	Finland	23	Israel	41	Japan	59	Eritrea
6	Germany	24	Costa Rica	42	Hungary	60	Tunisia
7	Netherlands	25	Latvia	43	Ecuador	61	Fiji
8	Canada	26	Czech Republic	44	Philippines	62	Swaziland
9	New Zealand	27	Estonia	45	Uruguay	63	Korea, Rep. of
10	Belgium	28	Slovakia	46	Panama	64	Turkey
11	Australia	29	Lithuania	47	Malaysia	65	Syrian Arab Republic
12	Austria	30	El Salvador	48	Honduras	66	Sri Lanka
13	United States	31	Italy	49	Greece	67	Bangladesh
14	Switzerland	32	Botswana	50	Peru	68	Egypt
15	United Kingdom	33	Slovenia	51	Chile	69	Jordan
16	Bahamas	34	Croatia	52	Suriname	70	Niger
17	Barbados	35	Mexico	53	Russian Federation		
18	Portugal	36	Poland	54	Bolivia		

Source: Human Development Report Office.

• The achievement in basic capabilities for women relative to men also varies within countries. In Sri Lanka the GDI for the district of Anuradhapura at 0.558 is 1.5 times that for the district of Puttalam.

. . . INCLUDING IN POLITICAL AND
PROFESSIONAL LIFE

The gender empowerment measure captures gender inequality in key areas of economic and political participation and decision-making. It thus focuses on women's opportunities rather than their capabilities (for a discussion of the methodology of the GEM and its components see the technical note). The GEM has been calculated for 70 countries (table 9).

• The top three countries are Norway (0.825), Iceland (0.802) and Sweden (0.794). These countries are not only good at strengthening the basic capabilities of women relative to men's. They have also opened many opportunities for them to participate in economic and political life. The GEM values are lowest in Niger (0.119), Jordan (0.220) and Egypt (0.274). In these societies opportunities for women are much more constrained.

• Only 2 of the 70 countries have achieved a GEM value of more than 0.800. Thirty-nine countries have a GEM value of more than 0.500, and 31 countries a value of less than 0.500. Clearly, many countries have much further to go in extending broad economic and political opportunities to women.

• Some developing countries outperform much richer industrialized countries in gender equality in political, economic and professional activities. The Bahamas and Barbados are ahead of Spain and Portugal. Venezuela outperforms Ireland. Costa Rica and Trinidad and Tobago do better than Italy. And El Salvador, the Dominican Republic and Mexico outrank Greece and Japan. Japan's GEM value at 0.490 is less than four-fifths that of the Bahamas, at 0.633. The crucial message of the GEM: high income is not a prerequisite for creating opportunities for women.

• Different regions of the same country allow women different roles in public life. The disaggregated GEM for Peru shows disparities between two provinces—Lima and Cajamarca (figure 6).

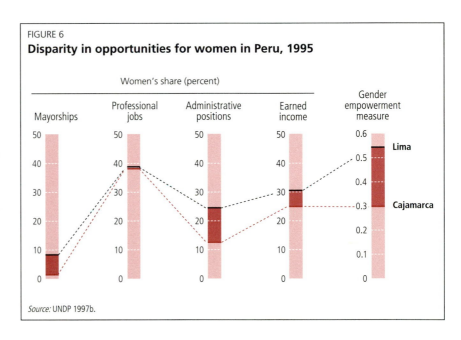

FIGURE 6
Disparity in opportunities for women in Peru, 1995

Source: UNDP 1997b.

HDI rank	Life expectancy at birth (years) 1998	Adult literacy rate (% age 15 and above) 1998	Combined primary, secondary and tertiary gross enrolment ratio (%) 1998[a]	GDP per capita (PPP US$) 1998	Life expectancy index	Education index	GDP index	Human development index (HDI) value 1998	GDP per capita (PPP US$) rank minus HDI rank[b]
High human development									
1 Canada	79.1	99.0 [c]	100	23,582	0.90	0.99	0.91	0.935	8
2 Norway	78.3	99.0 [c]	97	26,342	0.89	0.98	0.93	0.934	1
3 United States	76.8	99.0 [c]	94	29,605	0.86	0.97	0.95	0.929	-1
4 Australia	78.3	99.0 [c]	114 [d]	22,452	0.89	0.99	0.90	0.929	9
5 Iceland	79.1	99.0 [c]	89	25,110	0.90	0.96	0.92	0.927	1
6 Sweden	78.7	99.0 [c]	102 [d]	20,659	0.90	0.99	0.89	0.926	15
7 Belgium	77.3	99.0 [c]	106 [d]	23,223	0.87	0.99	0.91	0.925	4
8 Netherlands	78.0	99.0 [c]	99	22,176	0.88	0.99	0.90	0.925	6
9 Japan	80.0	99.0 [c]	85	23,257	0.92	0.94	0.91	0.924	1
10 United Kingdom	77.3	99.0 [c]	105 [d]	20,336	0.87	0.99	0.89	0.918	13
11 Finland	77.0	99.0 [c]	101 [d]	20,847	0.87	0.99	0.89	0.917	8
12 France	78.2	99.0 [c]	93	21,175	0.89	0.97	0.89	0.917	5
13 Switzerland	78.7	99.0 [c]	80	25,512	0.90	0.93	0.92	0.915	-9
14 Germany	77.3	99.0 [c]	90	22,169	0.87	0.96	0.90	0.911	1
15 Denmark	75.7	99.0 [c]	93	24,218	0.85	0.97	0.92	0.911	-8
16 Austria	77.1	99.0 [c]	86	23,166	0.87	0.95	0.91	0.908	-4
17 Luxembourg	76.8	99.0 [c]	69 [e]	33,505	0.86	0.89	0.97	0.908	-16
18 Ireland	76.6	99.0 [c]	91	21,482	0.86	0.96	0.90	0.907	-2
19 Italy	78.3	98.3	83	20,585	0.89	0.93	0.89	0.903	3
20 New Zealand	77.1	99.0 [c]	96	17,288	0.87	0.98	0.86	0.903	7
21 Spain	78.1	97.4	94	16,212	0.89	0.96	0.85	0.899	9
22 Cyprus	77.9	96.6	81 [f]	17,482	0.88	0.92	0.86	0.886	3
23 Israel	77.9	95.7	81	17,301	0.88	0.91	0.86	0.883	3
24 Singapore	77.3	91.8	73	24,210	0.87	0.86	0.92	0.881	-16
25 Greece	78.2	96.9	81	13,943	0.89	0.91	0.82	0.875	9
26 Hong Kong, China (SAR)	78.6	92.9	64	20,763	0.89	0.83	0.89	0.872	-6
27 Malta	77.3	91.5	79	16,447	0.87	0.87	0.85	0.865	2
28 Portugal	75.5	91.4	93	14,701	0.84	0.92	0.83	0.864	3
29 Slovenia	74.6	99.6 [g]	81	14,293	0.83	0.93	0.83	0.861	4
30 Barbados	76.5	97.0 [h, i]	80	12,001 [i, j]	0.86	0.91	0.80	0.858	9
31 Korea, Rep. of	72.6	97.5	90	13,478	0.79	0.95	0.82	0.854	4
32 Brunei Darussalam	75.7	90.7	72	16,765	0.84	0.84	0.85	0.848	-4
33 Bahamas	74.0	95.5	74	14,614	0.82	0.88	0.83	0.844	-1
34 Czech Republic	74.1	99.0 [c]	74	12,362	0.82	0.91	0.80	0.843	3
35 Argentina	73.1	96.7	80	12,013	0.80	0.91	0.80	0.837	3
36 Kuwait	76.1	80.9	58	25,314 [i, j]	0.85	0.73	0.92	0.836	-31
37 Antigua and Barbuda	76.0 [h]	95.0 [h, i]	78 [c]	9,277	0.85	0.89	0.76	0.833	9
38 Chile	75.1	95.4	78	8,787	0.83	0.90	0.75	0.826	9
39 Uruguay	74.1	97.6	78	8,623	0.82	0.91	0.74	0.825	9
40 Slovakia	73.1	99.0 [c]	75	9,699	0.80	0.91	0.76	0.825	5
41 Bahrain	73.1	86.5	81	13,111	0.80	0.85	0.81	0.820	-5
42 Qatar	71.9	80.4	74	20,987 [i, j]	0.78	0.78	0.89	0.819	-24
43 Hungary	71.1	99.3 [g]	75	10,232	0.77	0.91	0.77	0.817	-1
44 Poland	72.7	99.7 [g]	79	7,619	0.80	0.92	0.72	0.814	10
45 United Arab Emirates	75.0	74.6	70	17,719	0.83	0.73	0.86	0.810	-21
46 Estonia	69.0	99.0 [c]	86	7,682	0.73	0.95	0.72	0.801	7
Medium human development									
47 Saint Kitts and Nevis	70.0 [h]	90.0 [h, i]	79 [c]	10,672	0.75	0.86	0.78	0.798	-7
48 Costa Rica	76.2	95.3	66	5,987	0.85	0.85	0.68	0.797	18
49 Croatia	72.8	98.0	69	6,749	0.80	0.88	0.70	0.795	7
50 Trinidad and Tobago	74.0	93.4	66	7,485	0.82	0.84	0.72	0.793	5

HDI rank	Life expectancy at birth (years) 1998	Adult literacy rate (% age 15 and above) 1998	Combined primary, secondary and tertiary gross enrolment ratio (%) 1998[a]	GDP per capita (PPP US$) 1998	Life expectancy index	Education index	GDP index	Human development index (HDI) value 1998	GDP per capita (PPP US$) rank minus HDI rank[b]
51 Dominica	76.0 [h]	94.0 [i, k]	74 [c]	5,102	0.85	0.87	0.66	0.793	27
52 Lithuania	70.2	99.5 [g]	77	6,436	0.75	0.92	0.70	0.789	8
53 Seychelles	71.0 [h]	84.0 [h, i]	76 [c]	10,600	0.77	0.81	0.78	0.786	-12
54 Grenada	72.0 [h]	96.0 [h, i]	76 [c]	5,838	0.78	0.89	0.68	0.785	13
55 Mexico	72.3	90.8	70	7,704	0.79	0.84	0.73	0.784	-3
56 Cuba	75.8	96.4	73	3,967 [l]	0.85	0.89	0.61	0.783	40
57 Belarus	68.1	99.5 [g]	82	6,319	0.72	0.93	0.69	0.781	6
58 Belize	74.9	92.7	73	4,566	0.83	0.86	0.64	0.777	25
59 Panama	73.8	91.4	73	5,249	0.81	0.85	0.66	0.776	14
60 Bulgaria	71.3	98.2	73	4,809	0.77	0.90	0.65	0.772	19
61 Malaysia	72.2	86.4	65	8,137	0.79	0.79	0.73	0.772	-10
62 Russian Federation	66.7	99.5 [g]	79	6,460	0.69	0.92	0.70	0.771	-3
63 Latvia	68.7	99.8 [g]	75	5,728	0.73	0.91	0.68	0.771	6
64 Romania	70.2	97.9	70	5,648	0.75	0.88	0.67	0.770	6
65 Venezuela	72.6	92.0	67	5,808	0.79	0.84	0.68	0.770	3
66 Fiji	72.9	92.2	81	4,231	0.80	0.88	0.63	0.769	23
67 Suriname	70.3	93.0 [h, i]	80	5,161 [i, j]	0.76	0.89	0.66	0.766	9
68 Colombia	70.7	91.2	71	6,006	0.76	0.85	0.68	0.764	-3
69 Macedonia, TFYR	73.2	94.6 [i, m]	69	4,254	0.80	0.86	0.63	0.763	19
70 Georgia	72.9	99.0 [h, i]	72	3,353	0.80	0.90	0.59	0.762	29
71 Mauritius	71.6	83.8	63	8,312	0.78	0.77	0.74	0.761	-21
72 Libyan Arab Jamahiriya	70.2	78.1	92	6,697 [i, j]	0.75	0.83	0.70	0.760	-15
73 Kazakhstan	67.9	99.0 [c]	77	4,378	0.72	0.92	0.63	0.754	11
74 Brazil	67.0	84.5	84	6,625	0.70	0.84	0.70	0.747	-16
75 Saudi Arabia	71.7	75.2	57	10,158	0.78	0.69	0.77	0.747	-32
76 Thailand	68.9	95.0	61	5,456	0.73	0.84	0.67	0.745	-5
77 Philippines	68.6	94.8	83	3,555	0.73	0.91	0.60	0.744	17
78 Ukraine	69.1	99.6 [g]	78	3,194	0.73	0.92	0.58	0.744	26
79 Saint Vincent and the Grenadines	73.0 [h]	82.0 [h, i]	68 [c]	4,692	0.80	0.77	0.64	0.738	2
80 Peru	68.6	89.2	79	4,282	0.73	0.86	0.63	0.737	7
81 Paraguay	69.8	92.8	65	4,288	0.75	0.84	0.63	0.736	5
82 Lebanon	70.1	85.1	77	4,326	0.75	0.82	0.63	0.735	3
83 Jamaica	75.0	86.0	63	3,389	0.83	0.78	0.59	0.735	15
84 Sri Lanka	73.3	91.1	66	2,979	0.81	0.83	0.57	0.733	25
85 Turkey	69.3	84.0	61	6,422	0.74	0.76	0.69	0.732	-24
86 Oman	71.1	68.8	58	9,960 [i, j]	0.77	0.65	0.77	0.730	-42
87 Dominican Republic	70.9	82.8	70	4,598	0.76	0.79	0.64	0.729	-5
88 Saint Lucia	70.0 [h]	82.0 [i, k]	68 [c]	5,183	0.75	0.77	0.66	0.728	-14
89 Maldives	65.0	96.0	75	4,083	0.67	0.89	0.62	0.725	1
90 Azerbaijan	70.1	99.0 [c]	72	2,175	0.75	0.90	0.51	0.722	29
91 Ecuador	69.7	90.6	75	3,003	0.75	0.85	0.57	0.722	17
92 Jordan	70.4	88.6	69 [c]	3,347	0.76	0.82	0.59	0.721	8
93 Armenia	70.7	98.2	72	2,072	0.76	0.90	0.51	0.721	29
94 Albania	72.9	83.5	69	2,804	0.80	0.78	0.56	0.713	17
95 Samoa (Western)	71.7	79.7	65	3,832	0.78	0.75	0.61	0.711	-3
96 Guyana	64.8	98.3	66	3,403	0.66	0.88	0.59	0.709	1
97 Iran, Islamic Rep. of	69.5	74.6	69	5,121	0.74	0.73	0.66	0.709	-20
98 Kyrgyzstan	68.0	97.0 [h, i]	70	2,317	0.72	0.88	0.52	0.706	19
99 China	70.1	82.8	72	3,105	0.75	0.79	0.57	0.706	7
100 Turkmenistan	65.7	98.0 [h, i]	72 [c]	2,550 [i]	0.68	0.89	0.54	0.704	14

HDI rank	Life expectancy at birth (years) 1998	Adult literacy rate (% age 15 and above) 1998	Combined primary, secondary and tertiary gross enrolment ratio (%) 1998[a]	GDP per capita (PPP US$) 1998	Life expectancy index	Education index	GDP index	Human development index (HDI) value 1998	GDP per capita (PPP US$) rank minus HDI rank[b]
101 Tunisia	69.8	68.7	72	5,404	0.75	0.70	0.67	0.703	-29
102 Moldova, Rep. of	67.8	98.6	70	1,947	0.71	0.89	0.50	0.700	22
103 South Africa	53.2	84.6	95	8,488	0.47	0.88	0.74	0.697	-54
104 El Salvador	69.4	77.8	64	4,036	0.74	0.73	0.62	0.696	-13
105 Cape Verde	69.2	72.9	78	3,233	0.74	0.75	0.58	0.688	-3
106 Uzbekistan	67.8	88.0	77	2,053	0.71	0.84	0.50	0.686	17
107 Algeria	69.2	65.5	69	4,792	0.74	0.67	0.65	0.683	-27
108 Viet Nam	67.8	92.9	63	1,689	0.71	0.83	0.47	0.671	24
109 Indonesia	65.6	85.7	65	2,651	0.68	0.79	0.55	0.670	4
110 Tajikistan	67.5	99.0	69	1,041	0.71	0.89	0.39	0.663	43
111 Syrian Arab Republic	69.2	72.7	59	2,892	0.74	0.68	0.56	0.660	-1
112 Swaziland	60.7	78.3	72	3,816	0.60	0.76	0.61	0.655	-19
113 Honduras	69.6	73.4	58	2,433	0.74	0.68	0.53	0.653	2
114 Bolivia	61.8	84.4	70	2,269	0.61	0.80	0.52	0.643	4
115 Namibia	50.1	80.8	84	5,176	0.42	0.82	0.66	0.632	-40
116 Nicaragua	68.1	67.9	63	2,142	0.72	0.66	0.51	0.631	4
117 Mongolia	66.2	83.0 [h, i]	57	1,541	0.69	0.74	0.46	0.628	10
118 Vanuatu	67.7	64.0 [h, i]	47	3,120	0.71	0.58	0.57	0.623	-12
119 Egypt	66.7	53.7	74	3,041	0.69	0.60	0.57	0.623	-11
120 Guatemala	64.4	67.3	47	3,505	0.66	0.61	0.59	0.619	-24
121 Solomon Islands	71.9	62.0 [h, i]	46	1,940	0.78	0.57	0.49	0.614	5
122 Botswana	46.2	75.6	71	6,103	0.35	0.74	0.69	0.593	-57
123 Gabon	52.4	63.0 [h, i]	63 [c]	6,353	0.46	0.63	0.69	0.592	-60
124 Morocco	67.0	47.1	50	3,305	0.70	0.48	0.58	0.589	-22
125 Myanmar	60.6	84.1	56	1,199 [i, j]	0.59	0.75	0.41	0.585	25
126 Iraq	63.8	53.7	50	3,197 [i, j]	0.65	0.52	0.58	0.583	-22
127 Lesotho	55.2	82.4	57	1,626	0.50	0.74	0.47	0.569	6
128 India	62.9	55.7	54	2,077	0.63	0.55	0.51	0.563	-7
129 Ghana	60.4	69.1	43	1,735	0.59	0.60	0.48	0.556	0
130 Zimbabwe	43.5	87.2	68	2,669	0.31	0.81	0.55	0.555	-18
131 Equatorial Guinea	50.4	81.1	65	1,817 [i, j]	0.42	0.76	0.48	0.555	-4
132 São Tomé and Principe	64.0 [h]	57.0 [h, i]	49 [c]	1,469	0.65	0.54	0.45	0.547	7
133 Papua New Guinea	58.3	63.2	37	2,359	0.55	0.54	0.53	0.542	-17
134 Cameroon	54.5	73.6	46	1,474	0.49	0.64	0.45	0.528	4
135 Pakistan	64.4	44.0	43	1,715	0.66	0.44	0.47	0.522	-4
136 Cambodia	53.5	65.0 [h, i]	61	1,257	0.48	0.64	0.42	0.512	1
137 Comoros	59.2	58.5	39	1,398	0.57	0.52	0.44	0.510	5
138 Kenya	51.3	80.5	50	980	0.44	0.70	0.38	0.508	18
139 Congo	48.9	78.4	65	995	0.40	0.74	0.38	0.507	16
Low human development									
140 Lao People's Dem. Rep.	53.7	46.1	57	1,734	0.48	0.50	0.48	0.484	-9
141 Madagascar	57.9	64.9	40	756	0.55	0.56	0.34	0.483	23
142 Bhutan	61.2	42.0 [h, i]	33 [m]	1,536	0.60	0.39	0.46	0.483	-4
143 Sudan	55.4	55.7	34	1,394	0.51	0.48	0.44	0.477	0
144 Nepal	57.8	39.2	61	1,157	0.55	0.46	0.41	0.474	7
145 Togo	49.0	55.2	62	1,372	0.40	0.57	0.44	0.471	0
146 Bangladesh	58.6	40.1	36	1,361	0.56	0.39	0.44	0.461	0
147 Mauritania	53.9	41.2	42	1,563	0.48	0.41	0.46	0.451	-11
148 Yemen	58.5	44.1	49	719	0.56	0.46	0.33	0.448	18
149 Djibouti	50.8	62.3	21	1,266 [i, j]	0.43	0.49	0.42	0.447	-2
150 Haiti	54.0	47.8	24	1,383	0.48	0.40	0.44	0.440	-7

HDI rank	Life expectancy at birth (years) 1998	Adult literacy rate (% age 15 and above) 1998	Combined primary, secondary and tertiary gross enrolment ratio (%) 1998[a]	GDP per capita (PPP US$) 1998	Life expectancy index	Education index	GDP index	Human development index (HDI) value 1998	GDP per capita (PPP US$) rank minus HDI rank[b]
151 Nigeria	50.1	61.1	43	795	0.42	0.55	0.35	0.439	10
152 Congo, Dem. Rep. of the	51.2	58.9	33	822	0.44	0.50	0.35	0.430	8
153 Zambia	40.5	76.3	49	719	0.26	0.67	0.33	0.420	12
154 Côte d'Ivoire	46.9	44.5	41	1,598	0.36	0.43	0.46	0.420	-20
155 Senegal	52.7	35.5	36	1,307	0.46	0.36	0.43	0.416	-9
156 Tanzania, U. Rep. of	47.9	73.6	33	480	0.38	0.60	0.26	0.415	17
157 Benin	53.5	37.7	43	867	0.47	0.40	0.36	0.411	0
158 Uganda	40.7	65.0	41	1,074	0.26	0.57	0.40	0.409	-6
159 Eritrea	51.1	51.7	27	833	0.43	0.44	0.35	0.408	0
160 Angola	47.0	42.0 [h, i]	25	1,821	0.37	0.36	0.48	0.405	-34
161 Gambia	47.4	34.6	41	1,453	0.37	0.37	0.45	0.396	-21
162 Guinea	46.9	36.0 [h, i]	29	1,782	0.37	0.34	0.48	0.394	-34
163 Malawi	39.5	58.2	75	523	0.24	0.64	0.28	0.385	9
164 Rwanda	40.6	64.0	43	660 [i, n]	0.26	0.57	0.31	0.382	4
165 Mali	53.7	38.2	26	681	0.48	0.34	0.32	0.380	2
166 Central African Republic	44.8	44.0	26	1,118	0.33	0.38	0.40	0.371	-15
167 Chad	47.5	39.4	32	856	0.38	0.37	0.36	0.367	-9
168 Mozambique	43.8	42.3	25	782	0.31	0.37	0.34	0.341	-6
169 Guinea-Bissau	44.9	36.7	34	616	0.33	0.36	0.30	0.331	0
170 Burundi	42.7	45.8	22	570	0.30	0.38	0.29	0.321	1
171 Ethiopia	43.4	36.3	26	574	0.31	0.33	0.29	0.309	-1
172 Burkina Faso	44.7	22.2	22	870	0.33	0.22	0.36	0.303	-16
173 Niger	48.9	14.7	15	739	0.40	0.15	0.33	0.293	-9
174 Sierra Leone	37.9	31.0 [h, i]	24 [c]	458	0.22	0.29	0.25	0.252	0
All developing countries	64.7	72.3	60	3,270	0.66	0.68	0.58	0.642	–
Least developed countries	51.9	50.7	37	1,064	0.45	0.46	0.39	0.435	–
Arab States	66.0	59.7	60	4,140	0.68	0.60	0.62	0.635	–
East Asia	70.2	83.4	73	3,564	0.75	0.80	0.60	0.716	–
East Asia (excluding China)	73.1	96.3	85	13,635	0.80	0.93	0.82	0.849	–
Latin America and the Caribbean	69.7	87.7	74	6,510	0.74	0.83	0.70	0.758	–
South Asia	63.0	54.3	52	2,112	0.63	0.54	0.51	0.560	–
South Asia (excluding India)	63.4	50.5	47	2,207	0.64	0.49	0.52	0.550	–
South-East Asia and the Pacific	66.3	88.2	66	3,234	0.69	0.81	0.58	0.691	–
Sub-Saharan Africa	48.9	58.5	42	1,607	0.40	0.53	0.46	0.464	–
Eastern Europe and the CIS	68.9	98.6	76	6,200	0.73	0.91	0.69	0.777	–
OECD	76.4	97.4	86	20,357	0.86	0.94	0.89	0.893	–
High human development	77.0	98.5	90	21,799	0.87	0.96	0.90	0.908	–
Medium human development	66.9	76.9	65	3,458	0.70	0.73	0.59	0.673	–
Low human development	50.9	48.8	37	994	0.43	0.45	0.38	0.421	–
High income	77.8	98.6	92	23,928	0.88	0.96	0.91	0.920	–
Medium income	68.8	87.8	73	6,241	0.73	0.83	0.69	0.750	–
Low income	63.4	68.9	56	2,244	0.64	0.65	0.52	0.602	–
World	66.9	78.8	64	6,526	0.70	0.74	0.70	0.712	–

Note: The human development index has been calculated for UN member countries with reliable data in each of its components, as well as for two non-members, Switzerland and Hong Kong, China (SAR). For data on the remaining 16 UN member countries see table 32.

a. Preliminary UNESCO estimates, subject to further revision. b. A positive figure indicates that the HDI rank is higher than the GDP per capita (PPP US$) rank, a negative the opposite. c. Human Development Report Office estimate. d. For purposes of calculating the HDI, a value of 100.0% was applied. e. The ratio is an underestimate, as many secondary and tertiary students pursue their studies in nearby countries. f. Not including Turkish students or population. g. For purposes of calculating the HDI, a value of 99.0% was applied. h. UNICEF 1999c. i. Data refer to a year or period other than that specified in the column heading, differ from the standard definition or refer to only part of the country. j. Heston and Summers 1999. k. UNICEF 1996. l. As GDP per capita (PPP US$) is not available for Cuba, the sub-regional weighted average for the Caribbean was used. m. Human Development Report Office estimate based on national sources. n. World Bank 1999a.

Source: Column 1: unless otherwise noted, interpolated on the basis of life expectancy data from UN 1998c; *column 2:* unless otherwise noted, UNESCO 2000a; *column 3:* unless otherwise noted, UNESCO 2000c; *column 4:* unless otherwise noted, World Bank 2000a; *columns 5-9:* Human Development Report Office calculations; see the technical note for details.

2 Gender-related development index

HDI rank	Gender-related development index (GDI) 1998		Life expectancy at birth (years) 1998		Adult literacy rate (% age 15 and above) 1998		Combined primary, secondary and tertiary gross enrolment ratio (%) 1997		GDP per capita (PPP US$) 1998 [a]		HDI rank minus GDI rank [b]
	Rank	Value	Female	Male	Female	Male	Female	Male	Female	Male	
High human development											
1 Canada	1	0.932	81.9	76.2	99.0 [c]	99.0 [c]	101 [d]	98	17,980 [e]	29,294 [e]	0
2 Norway	2	0.932	81.3	75.4	99.0 [c]	99.0 [c]	98	93	22,400 [f]	30,356 [f]	0
3 United States	4	0.927	80.2	73.5	99.0 [c]	99.0 [c]	97	91	22,565 [e]	36,849 [e]	-1
4 Australia	3	0.927	81.2	75.6	99.0 [c]	99.0 [c]	114 [d]	111 [d]	17,974	26,990	1
5 Iceland	5	0.925	81.4	76.9	99.0 [c]	99.0 [c]	89	86	22,062	28,127	0
6 Sweden	6	0.923	81.0	76.4	99.0 [c]	99.0 [c]	108 [d]	95	18,605 [f]	22,751 [f]	0
7 Belgium	7	0.921	80.7	74.0	99.0 [c]	99.0 [c]	107 [d]	104 [d]	15,951	30,801	0
8 Netherlands	8	0.919	80.8	75.1	99.0 [c]	99.0 [c]	96	99	14,902	29,600	0
9 Japan	9	0.916	83.0	76.9	99.0 [c]	99.0 [c]	83	86	14,091	32,794	0
10 United Kingdom	10	0.914	80.0	74.7	99.0 [c]	99.0 [c]	109 [d]	99	15,290	25,575	0
11 Finland	12	0.913	80.8	73.2	99.0 [c]	99.0 [c]	104 [d]	95	17,063 [f]	24,827 [f]	-1
12 France	11	0.914	82.1	74.4	99.0 [c]	99.0 [c]	94	91	16,437	26,156	1
13 Switzerland	13	0.910	81.9	75.5	99.0 [c]	99.0 [c]	76	83	16,802	34,425	0
14 Germany	15	0.905	80.3	74.1	99.0 [c]	99.0 [c]	88	90	15,189 [f]	29,476 [f]	-1
15 Denmark	14	0.909	78.4	73.1	99.0 [c]	99.0 [c]	95	90	19,965	28,569	1
16 Austria	16	0.901	80.3	73.8	99.0 [c]	99.0 [c]	85	86	14,432 [f]	32,190 [f]	0
17 Luxembourg	20	0.895	80.1	73.5	99.0 [c]	99.0 [c]	70	68	18,967	48,628 [g]	-3
18 Ireland	18	0.896	79.4	73.8	99.0 [c]	99.0 [c]	92	87	11,847 [f]	31,260 [f]	0
19 Italy	19	0.895	81.3	75.2	97.9	98.8	83	80	12,665 [e]	28,982 [e]	0
20 New Zealand	17	0.900	79.9	74.3	99.0 [c]	99.0 [c]	99	92	13,646	21,040	3
21 Spain	21	0.891	81.6	74.7	96.5	98.4	96	90	9,636 [e]	23,078 [e]	0
22 Cyprus	23	0.877	80.1	75.6	94.7	98.6	81	79	9,981	25,009	-1
23 Israel	22	0.877	79.9	75.8	93.7	97.7	81	79	11,660 [e]	23,034 [e]	1
24 Singapore	24	0.876	79.5	75.1	87.6	96.0	71	74	15,966	32,334	0
25 Greece	25	0.869	80.8	75.7	95.5	98.4	80	80	8,963 [f]	19,079 [f]	0
26 Hong Kong, China (SAR)	26	0.864	81.5	76.0	89.1	96.3	67	64	10,768	29,775	0
27 Malta	29	0.848	79.5	75.1	92.0	90.9	77	78	7,066 [e]	26,006 [e]	-2
28 Portugal	27	0.858	78.9	72.0	89.0	94.2	94	88	10,215	19,538	1
29 Slovenia	28	0.857	78.3	70.7	99.6 [h]	99.7 [h]	82	77	10,941 [e]	17,841 [e]	1
30 Barbados	..	..	78.8	73.8	..	..	81	80	..	..	..
31 Korea, Rep. of	30	0.847	76.2	69.0	95.9	99.0 [h]	84	94	8,342	18,529	0
32 Brunei Darussalam	31	0.843	78.3	73.6	86.7	94.1	73	71	10,135 [e]	22,790 [e]	0
33 Bahamas	32	0.842	77.3	70.7	96.2	94.8	77	71	11,577 [e]	17,755 [e]	0
34 Czech Republic	33	0.841	77.7	70.6	99.0 [c]	99.0 [c]	74	73	9,713 [e]	15,153 [e]	0
35 Argentina	35	0.824	76.9	69.8	96.6	96.7	82	77	5,553 [i]	18,724 [i]	-1
36 Kuwait	34	0.827	78.4	74.3	78.5	83.2	59	56	13,347 [e, j]	36,466 [e, j]	1
37 Antigua and Barbuda	..	..	..	..	..	..	..	..	..	..	..
38 Chile	39	0.812	78.4	72.4	95.2	95.6	76	78	4,011 [i]	13,660 [i]	-3
39 Uruguay	37	0.821	78.2	70.7	98.0	97.2	81	74	5,791 [i]	11,630 [i]	0
40 Slovakia	36	0.822	76.9	69.4	99.0 [c]	99.0 [c]	75	73	7,701 [e]	11,800 [e]	2
41 Bahrain	42	0.803	75.5	71.3	81.2	90.2	82	78	4,799 [e]	19,355 [e]	-3
42 Qatar	41	0.807	75.6	70.2	81.7	79.8	75	72	6,624 [e, j]	28,508 [e, j]	-1
43 Hungary	38	0.813	75.1	67.1	99.1 [h]	99.4 [h]	75	73	7,452	13,267	3
44 Poland	40	0.811	77.1	68.4	99.7 [h]	99.7 [h]	79	78	5,821 [e]	9,519 [e]	2
45 United Arab Emirates	44	0.793	76.7	74.1	77.1	73.4	72	66	5,398 [e]	24,758 [e]	-1
46 Estonia	43	0.798	74.7	63.4	99.0 [c]	99.0 [c]	87	82	6,076 [e]	9,492 [e]	1
Medium human development											
47 Saint Kitts and Nevis	..	..	..	..	..	..	..	..	..	..	..
48 Costa Rica	46	0.789	79.1	74.4	95.4	95.3	65	66	3,126	8,768	-1
49 Croatia	45	0.790	76.7	69.0	96.9	99.3 [h]	69	68	4,835 [e]	8,795 [e]	1
50 Trinidad and Tobago	48	0.784	76.4	71.7	91.5	95.3	66	67	4,131 [e]	10,868 [e]	-1

HDI rank	Gender-related development index (GDI) 1998		Life expectancy at birth (years) 1998		Adult literacy rate (% age 15 and above) 1998		Combined primary, secondary and tertiary gross enrolment ratio (%) 1997		GDP per capita (PPP US$) 1998 [a]		HDI rank minus GDI rank [b]
	Rank	Value	Female	Male	Female	Male	Female	Male	Female	Male	
51 Dominica	..	..	..	..	..	..	..	..	..	..	..
52 Lithuania	47	0.785	75.7	64.7	99.4 [h]	99.6 [h]	78	74	5,037	7,998	1
53 Seychelles	..	..	..	..	..	..	..	..	..	..	..
54 Grenada	..	..	..	..	..	..	..	..	..	..	..
55 Mexico	50	0.775	75.7	69.7	88.7	92.9	69	71	4,112	11,365	-1
56 Cuba	..	..	78.2	74.3	96.3	96.5	73	70	..	..	..
57 Belarus	49	0.778	74.0	62.3	99.4 [h]	99.7 [h]	83	79	4,973 [e]	7,839 [e]	1
58 Belize	60	0.754	76.3	73.5	92.5	92.9	72	72	1,704 [e]	7,368 [e]	-9
59 Panama	52	0.770	76.5	71.9	90.8	92.1	74	72	3,034 [e]	7,421 [e]	0
60 Bulgaria	53	0.769	74.9	67.8	97.6	98.9	75	69	3,691	5,984	0
61 Malaysia	57	0.762	74.5	70.1	82.0	90.7	66	64	4,501 [f]	11,674 [f]	-3
62 Russian Federation	54	0.769	72.9	60.7	99.3 [h]	99.7 [h]	81	75	5,072 [e]	8,039 [e]	1
63 Latvia	51	0.770	74.5	62.8	99.8 [h]	99.8 [h]	76	73	4,951 [f]	6,655 [f]	5
64 Romania	55	0.767	74.1	66.5	96.9	98.9	69	69	4,169 [e]	7,178 [e]	2
65 Venezuela	56	0.763	75.9	70.2	91.4	92.6	68	66	3,281 [e]	8,302 [e]	2
66 Fiji	59	0.755	75.1	70.8	89.9	94.4	79	81	2,047 [e]	6,344 [e]	0
67 Suriname	..	..	72.9	67.7	..	..	82	76	..	..	..
68 Colombia	58	0.760	74.5	67.6	91.2	91.3	71	70	4,079 [i]	7,979 [i]	2
69 Macedonia, TFYR	..	..	75.4	71.1	..	..	68	69	..	..	..
70 Georgia	..	..	76.9	68.7	..	..	71	70	..	..	..
71 Mauritius	61	0.750	75.3	68.1	80.3	87.3	63	62	4,375 [e]	12,266 [e]	0
72 Libyan Arab Jamahiriya	65	0.738	72.4	68.5	65.4	89.6	92	92	2,452 [e, j]	10,634 [e, j]	-3
73 Kazakhstan	..	..	72.7	63.2	..	..	79	73	..	..	..
74 Brazil	66	0.736	71.2	63.3	84.5	84.5	82	78	3,830	9,483	-3
75 Saudi Arabia	76	0.715	73.7	70.2	64.4	82.8	54	58	2,663 [e]	16,179 [e]	-12
76 Thailand	62	0.741	72.1	65.9	93.2	96.9	59	58	4,159	6,755	3
77 Philippines	64	0.739	70.5	66.8	94.6	95.1	85	80	2,512	4,580	2
78 Ukraine	63	0.740	73.9	64.2	99.4 [h]	99.7 [h]	80	74	2,327	4,191	4
79 Saint Vincent and the Grenadines	..	..	..	..	..	..	..	..	..	..	..
80 Peru	70	0.723	71.2	66.2	84.3	94.2	77	79	2,104 [e]	6,493 [e]	-2
81 Paraguay	71	0.723	72.2	67.7	91.5	94.0	64	65	2,058	6,481	-2
82 Lebanon	74	0.718	71.9	68.3	79.1	91.5	77	76	1,985 [e]	6,777 [e]	-4
83 Jamaica	67	0.732	77.0	73.0	89.9	81.9	63	62	2,629 [e]	4,163 [e]	4
84 Sri Lanka	68	0.727	75.6	71.1	88.3	94.1	67	65	1,927	4,050	4
85 Turkey	69	0.726	72.0	66.8	75.0	92.9	54	67	4,703 [f]	8,104 [f]	4
86 Oman	82	0.697	73.5	69.1	57.5	78.0	57	60	2,651 [e, j]	16,404 [e, j]	-8
87 Dominican Republic	73	0.720	73.3	69.2	82.8	82.9	72	68	2,333 [e]	6,787 [e]	2
88 Saint Lucia	..	..	..	..	..	..	..	..	..	..	..
89 Maldives	72	0.720	63.8	66.1	96.0	96.0	75	74	3,009 [e]	5,100 [e]	4
90 Azerbaijan	..	..	74.3	65.8	..	..	71	71	..	..	..
91 Ecuador	78	0.701	72.7	67.5	88.7	92.5	72	75	1,173 [i]	4,818 [i]	-1
92 Jordan	..	..	71.8	69.1	82.6	94.2	..	..	..	..	..
93 Armenia	75	0.718	73.8	67.4	97.3	99.2 [h]	68	75	1,667 [e]	2,501 [e]	3
94 Albania	77	0.708	76.0	70.1	76.2	90.5	68	67	1,977 [e]	3,594 [e]	2
95 Samoa (Western)	..	..	73.9	69.6	78.2	81.1	66	64	..	..	..
96 Guyana	80	0.698	68.2	61.5	97.8	98.8	66	65	1,852 [e]	4,994 [e]	0
97 Iran, Islamic Rep. of	84	0.691	70.4	68.7	67.4	81.7	67	73	2,137 [e]	8,019 [e]	-3
98 Kyrgyzstan	..	..	72.2	63.7	..	..	71	68	..	..	..
99 China	79	0.700	72.3	68.1	74.6	90.7	67	71	2,440 [e]	3,732 [e]	3
100 Turkmenistan	..	..	69.2	62.3	..	..	..	..	..	..	..

2 Gender-related development index

HDI rank	Gender-related development index (GDI) 1998		Life expectancy at birth (years) 1998		Adult literacy rate (% age 15 and above) 1998		Combined primary, secondary and tertiary gross enrolment ratio (%) 1997		GDP per capita (PPP US$) 1998[a]		HDI rank minus GDI rank[b]
	Rank	Value	Female	Male	Female	Male	Female	Male	Female	Male	
101 Tunisia	86	0.688	71.0	68.6	57.9	79.4	68	74	2,772[e]	7,982[e]	-3
102 Moldova, Rep. of	81	0.697	71.7	63.8	97.9	99.5[h]	71	69	1,548[e]	2,381[e]	3
103 South Africa	85	0.689	56.2	50.3	83.9	85.4	94	93	5,205[e]	11,886[e]	0
104 El Salvador	83	0.693	72.7	66.7	75.0	80.8	63	64	2,779[f]	5,343[f]	3
105 Cape Verde	88	0.675	71.6	65.8	64.6	83.7	76	79	1,931[e]	4,731[e]	-1
106 Uzbekistan	87	0.683	70.9	64.6	83.4	92.7	74	78	1,613[e]	2,499[e]	1
107 Algeria	91	0.661	70.6	67.7	54.3	76.5	64	71	2,051[e]	7,467[e]	-2
108 Viet Nam	89	0.668	70.0	65.3	90.6	95.3	59	64	1,395[e]	1,991[e]	1
109 Indonesia	90	0.664	67.5	63.7	80.5	91.1	61	68	1,780[e]	3,526[e]	1
110 Tajikistan	92	0.659	70.4	64.5	98.6	99.5[h]	65	73	777[e]	1,307[e]	0
111 Syrian Arab Republic	95	0.636	71.5	66.9	58.1	87.2	56	63	1,218[e]	4,530[e]	-2
112 Swaziland	93	0.646	63.0	58.4	77.3	79.5	70	74	2,267[e]	5,485[e]	1
113 Honduras	94	0.644	72.5	67.7	73.5	73.4	59	57	1,252[e]	3,595[e]	1
114 Bolivia	96	0.631	63.6	60.2	77.8	91.3	64	75	1,217[i]	3,334[i]	0
115 Namibia	98	0.624	50.6	49.5	79.7	81.9	84	80	3,513[e]	6,852[e]	-1
116 Nicaragua	97	0.624	70.9	66.1	69.3	66.3	65	61	1,256[e]	3,039[e]	1
117 Mongolia	..	..	67.7	64.7	..	..	62	50	..	..	..
118 Vanuatu	..	..	69.9	65.8	..	..	44	49	..	..	..
119 Egypt	99	0.604	68.3	65.1	41.8	65.5	66	77	1,576	4,463	0
120 Guatemala	100	0.603	67.6	61.7	59.7	74.9	43	51	1,614[e]	5,363[e]	0
121 Solomon Islands	..	..	74.1	69.9	..	..	44	48	..	..	..
122 Botswana	101	0.584	47.1	45.1	78.2	72.8	71	70	3,747[f]	8,550[f]	0
123 Gabon	..	..	53.7	51.1	..	..	..	..	..	..	..
124 Morocco	103	0.570	68.9	65.2	34.0	60.3	43	56	1,865[e]	4,743[e]	-1
125 Myanmar	102	0.582	62.3	59.0	79.5	88.7	54	55	1,011[f, j]	1,389[f, j]	1
126 Iraq	107	0.548	65.3	62.3	43.2	63.9	44	57	966[e, j]	5,352[e, j]	-3
127 Lesotho	104	0.556	56.4	54.0	92.9	71.0	61	53	982[e]	2,291[e]	1
128 India	108	0.545	63.3	62.5	43.5	67.1	46	61	1,105[e]	2,987[e]	-2
129 Ghana	105	0.552	62.2	58.7	59.9	78.5	38	48	1,492[e]	1,980[e]	2
130 Zimbabwe	106	0.551	44.0	43.1	82.9	91.7	66	71	1,990[e]	3,359[e]	2
131 Equatorial Guinea	109	0.542	52.0	48.8	71.5	91.4	60	69	1,033[e, j]	2,623[e, j]	0
132 São Tomé and Principe	..	..	..	..	..	..	..	..	..	..	..
133 Papua New Guinea	110	0.536	59.1	57.6	55.1	70.9	33	40	1,714[e]	2,966[e]	0
134 Cameroon	111	0.518	55.8	53.3	67.1	80.3	41	52	902[e]	2,054[e]	0
135 Pakistan	115	0.489	65.6	63.3	28.9	58.0	28	56	776[e]	2,594[e]	-3
136 Cambodia	..	..	55.2	51.5	..	..	54	68	..	..	..
137 Comoros	113	0.503	60.6	57.8	51.6	65.5	35	42	974[e]	1,822[e]	0
138 Kenya	112	0.503	52.2	50.5	73.5	87.6	49	50	764[e]	1,195[e]	2
139 Congo	114	0.499	51.1	46.7	71.5	85.7	58	71	706[e]	1,297[e]	1

Low human development

HDI rank	Rank	Value	Female	Male	Female	Male	Female	Male	Female	Male	
140 Lao People's Dem. Rep.	117	0.469	55.0	52.5	30.2	61.9	48	62	1,390[e]	2,073[e]	-1
141 Madagascar	116	0.478	59.4	56.4	57.8	72.2	39	39	562[e]	953[e]	1
142 Bhutan	..	..	62.5	60.0	..	..	..	..	..	..	..
143 Sudan	118	0.453	56.8	54.0	43.4	68.0	31	37	645[e]	2,139[e]	0
144 Nepal	119	0.449	57.6	58.1	21.7	56.9	49	69	783[e]	1,521[e]	0
145 Togo	120	0.448	50.3	47.8	38.4	72.5	47	75	883[e]	1,870[e]	0
146 Bangladesh	121	0.441	58.7	58.6	28.6	51.1	30	40	744[f]	1,949[f]	0
147 Mauritania	122	0.441	55.5	52.3	31.0	51.7	36	45	1,130[e]	2,003[e]	0
148 Yemen	133	0.389	58.9	57.9	22.7	65.7	27	70	311[e]	1,122[e]	-10
149 Djibouti	..	..	52.4	49.1	51.4	74.0	17	24	..	..	..
150 Haiti	123	0.436	56.4	51.5	45.6	50.1	24	25	976[e]	1,805[e]	1

HDI rank	Gender-related development index (GDI) 1998		Life expectancy at birth (years) 1998		Adult literacy rate (% age 15 and above) 1998		Combined primary, secondary and tertiary gross enrolment ratio (%) 1997		GDP per capita (PPP US$) 1998 [a]		HDI rank minus GDI rank [b]
	Rank	Value	Female	Male	Female	Male	Female	Male	Female	Male	
151 Nigeria	124	0.425	51.5	48.7	52.5	70.1	38	48	477 [e]	1,118 [e]	1
152 Congo, Dem. Rep. of the	125	0.418	52.7	49.6	47.1	71.3	27	38	590 [e]	1,060 [e]	1
153 Zambia	126	0.413	41.0	39.9	69.1	84.0	46	53	540 [e]	903 [e]	1
154 Côte d'Ivoire	129	0.401	47.5	46.3	35.7	52.8	32	48	856 [e]	2,313 [e]	-1
155 Senegal	128	0.405	54.6	50.9	25.8	45.4	31	40	917 [e]	1,698 [e]	1
156 Tanzania, U. Rep. of	127	0.410	49.0	46.8	64.3	83.3	32	33	400 [e]	561 [e]	3
157 Benin	132	0.391	55.3	51.8	22.6	53.8	31	53	715 [e]	1,024 [e]	-1
158 Uganda	130	0.401	41.5	39.9	54.2	76.1	36	44	865 [e]	1,285 [e]	2
159 Eritrea	131	0.394	52.6	49.6	38.2	65.7	24	30	568	1,102	2
160 Angola	..	..	48.6	45.4	..	..	23	28	..	..	..
161 Gambia	134	0.388	49.0	45.8	27.5	41.9	35	48	1,085 [e]	1,828 [e]	0
162 Guinea	..	..	47.4	46.4	..	..	19	36	..	..	..
163 Malawi	136	0.375	39.8	39.2	44.1	73.2	70	79	432 [e]	616 [e]	-1
164 Rwanda	135	0.377	41.7	39.5	56.8	71.5	42	44	535 [e, k]	788 [e, k]	1
165 Mali	137	0.371	55.0	52.4	31.1	45.8	20	31	524 [e]	843 [e]	0
166 Central African Republic	138	0.359	46.8	42.9	31.7	57.5	20	33	856 [e]	1,395 [e]	0
167 Chad	..	..	49.0	46.0	..	..	20	41	..	..	..
168 Mozambique	139	0.326	45.0	42.6	27.0	58.4	20	29	647 [e]	921 [e]	0
169 Guinea-Bissau	140	0.298	46.4	43.5	17.3	57.1	24	43	401 [e]	837 [e]	0
170 Burundi	..	..	44.0	41.3	37.5	54.8	20	25	..	..	..
171 Ethiopia	141	0.297	44.4	42.5	30.5	42.1	19	32	383 [e]	764 [e]	0
172 Burkina Faso	142	0.290	45.5	43.9	12.6	32.0	16	25	712 [e]	1,028 [e]	0
173 Niger	143	0.280	50.5	47.3	7.4	22.4	11	19	541 [e]	941 [e]	0
174 Sierra Leone	..	..	39.4	36.5	..	..	..	..	..	..	..
All developing countries	–	0.634	66.4	63.2	64.5	80.3	55	63	2,169	4,334	–
Least developed countries	–	0.427	52.9	51.2	41.0	61.4	32	42	771	1,356	–
Arab States	–	0.612	67.5	64.6	47.3	71.5	54	65	1,837	6,341	–
East Asia	–	0.710	72.5	68.2	75.5	91.1	67	71	2,788	4,297	–
East Asia (excluding China)	–	0.846	76.4	69.7	95.1	98.6	81	88	9,414	17,744	–
Latin America and the Caribbean	–	0.748	73.2	66.7	86.7	88.7	73	72	3,640	9,428	–
South Asia	–	0.542	63.6	62.6	42.3	65.7	44	59	1,147	3,021	–
South Asia (excluding India)	–	0.533	64.2	62.7	38.8	61.7	38	55	1,263	3,108	–
South-East Asia and the Pacific	–	0.688	68.3	64.2	85.0	92.4	63	66	2,316	4,154	–
Sub-Saharan Africa	–	0.459	50.3	47.6	51.6	68.0	37	46	1,142	2,079	–
Eastern Europe and the CIS	–	0.774	73.8	64.1	98.2	99.1	78	74	4,807	7,726	–
OECD	–	0.889	79.6	73.2	96.7	98.2	86	86	14,165	26,743	–
High human development	–	0.903	80.3	73.8	98.3	98.7	91	88	15,361	28,448	–
Medium human development	–	0.665	68.9	65.0	69.7	83.7	60	67	2,319	4,566	–
Low human development	–	0.411	51.9	50.1	38.9	59.9	31	42	693	1,294	–
High income	–	0.916	81.0	74.6	98.4	98.7	93	90	16,987	31,100	–
Medium income	–	0.743	72.2	65.8	85.0	90.4	72	73	3,948	8,580	–
Low income	–	0.594	64.7	62.2	59.6	78.1	50	60	1,549	2,912	–
World	–	0.706	69.1	64.9	73.1	84.6	60	67	4,435	8,587	–

a. Data refer to the latest available year. b. The HDI ranks used in this column are those recalculated for the universe of 143 countries. A positive figure indicates that the GDI rank is higher than the HDI rank, a negative the opposite. c. Human Development Report Office estimate. d. For purposes of calculating the GDI, a value of 100.0% was applied. e. No wage data available. An estimate of 75% was used for the ratio of the female non-agricultural wage to the male non-agricultural wage. f. The manufacturing wage was used. g. For purposes of calculating the GDI, a value of $40,000 was applied. h. For purposes of calculating the GDI, a value of 99.0% was applied. i. Wage data based on Psacharopoulos and Tzannatos 1992. j. Heston and Summers 1999. k. World Bank 1999a.

Source: Columns 1 and 2: Human Development Report Office calculations; see the technical note for details; *columns 3 and 4:* interpolated on the basis of life expectancy data from UN 1998c; *columns 5 and 6:* UNESCO 2000a; *columns 7 and 8:* UNESCO 2000c; *columns 9 and 10:* unless otherwise noted, calculated on the basis of the following: for GDP per capita (PPP US$), World Bank 2000a; for wages, wage data from ILO 1999c; for economic activity rate, data on economically active population from ILO 1996; for population shares, population data from UN 1998c; for details on the calculation of GDP per capita (PPP US$) by gender see the technical note; *column 11:* Human Development Report Office calculations.

HDI rank	Gender empowerment measure (GEM)		Seats in parliament held by women (as % of total) [a]	Female administrators and managers (as % of total) [b]	Female professional and technical workers (as % of total) [b]	Women's GDP per capita (PPP US$) [b]
	Rank	Value				
High human development						
1 Canada	8	0.739	22.7	37.3	52.2	17,980 [c]
2 Norway	1	0.825	36.4	30.6	58.5	22,400 [d]
3 United States	13	0.707	12.5	44.4	53.4	22,565 [c]
4 Australia	11	0.715	25.1	24.0	44.4	17,974
5 Iceland	2	0.802	34.9	25.4	52.8	22,062
6 Sweden	3	0.794	42.7	27.4	48.6	18,605 [d]
7 Belgium	10	0.725	24.9	30.2	47.1	15,951
8 Netherlands	7	0.739	32.9	22.8	45.7	14,902
9 Japan	41	0.490	9.0	9.5	44.0	14,091
10 United Kingdom	15	0.656	17.1	33.0	44.7	15,290
11 Finland	5	0.757	36.5	25.6	62.7	17,063 [d]
12 France	..	..	9.1	..	..	..
13 Switzerland	14	0.683	22.4	20.1	39.9	16,802
14 Germany	6	0.756	33.6	26.6	49.0	15,189 [d]
15 Denmark	4	0.791	37.4	23.1	49.7	19,965
16 Austria	12	0.710	25.1	27.3	47.3	14,432 [d]
17 Luxembourg	..	..	16.7	..	..	..
18 Ireland	21	0.593	13.7	26.2	46.2	11,847 [d]
19 Italy	31	0.524	10.0	53.8	17.8	12,665 [c]
20 New Zealand	9	0.731	29.2	36.6	51.5	13,646
21 Spain	19	0.615	18.0	32.4	43.8	9,636 [c]
22 Cyprus	..	..	7.1	..	..	..
23 Israel	23	0.555	12.5	22.4	52.9	11,660 [c]
24 Singapore	38	0.505	4.3	20.5	42.3	15,966
25 Greece	49	0.456	6.3	22.0	44.9	8,963 [d]
26 Hong Kong, China (SAR)	..	..	..	20.8	36.2	..
27 Malta	..	..	9.2	..	..	..
28 Portugal	18	0.618	18.7	32.2	51.1	10,215
29 Slovenia	33	0.519	10.0	25.0	52.9	10,941 [c]
30 Barbados	17	0.629	20.4	38.7	51.2	9,037 [c, e]
31 Korea, Rep. of	63	0.323	4.0	4.7	31.9	8,342
32 Brunei Darussalam	..	..	..	..	..	..
33 Bahamas	16	0.633	19.6	31.0	51.4	11,577 [c]
34 Czech Republic	26	0.537	13.9	23.2	54.1	9,713 [c]
35 Argentina	..	..	21.3	..	..	..
36 Kuwait	..	..	0.0	..	..	..
37 Antigua and Barbuda	..	..	8.3	..	..	..
38 Chile	51	0.440	8.9	22.4	50.5	4,011 [f]
39 Uruguay	45	0.472	11.5	24.0	63.1	5,791 [f]
40 Slovakia	28	0.533	14.0	29.7	59.7	7,701 [c]
41 Bahrain	..	..	..	7.3	20.1	..
42 Qatar	..	..	..	..	..	..
43 Hungary	42	0.487	8.3	35.3	60.4	7,452
44 Poland	36	0.512	12.7	33.6	60.3	5,821 [c]
45 United Arab Emirates	..	..	0.0	..	..	..
46 Estonia	27	0.537	17.8	33.5	70.3	6,076 [c]
Medium human development						
47 Saint Kitts and Nevis	..	..	13.3	..	..	..
48 Costa Rica	24	0.553	19.3	29.9	45.1	3,126
49 Croatia	34	0.517	16.1	25.4	51.2	4,835 [c]
50 Trinidad and Tobago	22	0.583	19.4	39.7	50.5	4,131 [c]

HDI rank	Gender empowerment measure (GEM)		Seats in parliament held by women (as % of total) [a]	Female administrators and managers (as % of total) [b]	Female professional and technical workers (as % of total) [b]	Women's GDP per capita (PPP US$) [b]
	Rank	Value				
51 Dominica	..	..	..	..	..	..
52 Lithuania	29	0.531	17.5	35.7	69.7	5,037
53 Seychelles	..	..	23.5	..	..	..
54 Grenada	..	..	17.9	..	..	..
55 Mexico	35	0.514	18.0	20.7	40.2	4,112
56 Cuba	..	..	27.6	18.5	..	..
57 Belarus	..	..	13.4	..	..	..
58 Belize	40	0.493	13.5	36.6	38.8	1,704 [c]
59 Panama	46	0.470	9.9	33.6	48.6	3,034 [c]
60 Bulgaria	..	..	10.8	28.9	..	..
61 Malaysia	47	0.468	12.2	19.5	43.9	4,501 [d]
62 Russian Federation	53	0.426	5.7	37.9	65.6	5,072 [c]
63 Latvia	25	0.540	17.0	41.0	64.1	4,951 [d]
64 Romania	58	0.405	5.6	26.4	56.3	4,169 [c]
65 Venezuela	20	0.597	28.6 [g]	24.3	57.6	3,281 [c]
66 Fiji	61	0.384	10.7	48.3 [h]	10.5 [h]	2,047 [c]
67 Suriname	52	0.428	15.7	13.3	69.0	2,735 [c, e]
68 Colombia	37	0.510	12.2	40.4	44.6	4,079 [f]
69 Macedonia, TFYR	..	..	7.5	..	..	..
70 Georgia	..	..	7.2	..	..	2,542 [c]
71 Mauritius	56	0.420	7.6	22.6	38.4	4,375 [c]
72 Libyan Arab Jamahiriya	..	..	..	..	..	..
73 Kazakhstan	..	..	11.2	..	..	..
74 Brazil	..	..	5.9	..	62.0	..
75 Saudi Arabia	..	..	..	..	..	..
76 Thailand	..	..	..	21.6	55.8	..
77 Philippines	44	0.479	12.9	33.7	64.6	2,512
78 Ukraine	55	0.421	7.8	36.9	64.9	2,327
79 Saint Vincent and the Grenadines	..	..	4.8	..	..	..
80 Peru	50	0.446	10.8	26.9	41.6	2,104 [c]
81 Paraguay	57	0.406	8.0	22.6	54.1	2,058
82 Lebanon	..	..	2.3	..	..	..
83 Jamaica	..	..	16.0	..	..	..
84 Sri Lanka	66	0.309	4.9	17.3 [h]	27.2 [h]	1,927
85 Turkey	64	0.321	4.2	11.5	33.9	4,703 [d]
86 Oman	..	..	..	..	..	..
87 Dominican Republic	39	0.505	14.5	30.6	49.4	2,333 [c]
88 Saint Lucia	..	..	13.8	..	..	..
89 Maldives	..	..	6.0	..	..	..
90 Azerbaijan	..	..	12.0	..	..	..
91 Ecuador	43	0.481	14.6	27.5	46.6	1,173 [f]
92 Jordan	69	0.220	2.5	4.6 [i]	28.7 [i]	1,463
93 Armenia	..	..	3.1	..	..	..
94 Albania	..	..	5.2	..	..	..
95 Samoa (Western)	..	..	8.2	..	..	..
96 Guyana	..	..	18.5	..	..	..
97 Iran, Islamic Rep. of	..	..	..	..	..	..
98 Kyrgyzstan	..	..	..	..	..	..
99 China	..	..	21.8	..	..	..
100 Turkmenistan	..	..	26.0	..	..	..

3 Gender empowerment measure

	Gender empowerment measure (GEM)		Seats in parliament held by women (as % of total) [a]	Female administrators and managers (as % of total) [b]	Female professional and technical workers (as % of total) [b]	Women's GDP per capita (PPP US$) [b]
HDI rank	Rank	Value				
101 Tunisia	60	0.398	11.5	12.7 [i]	35.6 [i]	2,772 [c]
102 Moldova, Rep. of	..	..	8.9	..	..	..
103 South Africa	..	..	28.0 [j]	..	..	..
104 El Salvador	30	0.527	16.7	34.9	44.3	2,779 [d]
105 Cape Verde	..	..	11.1	..	..	..
106 Uzbekistan	..	..	6.8	..	..	..
107 Algeria	..	..	4.0	..	..	..
108 Viet Nam	..	..	26.0	..	..	..
109 Indonesia	..	..	8.0	..	..	..
110 Tajikistan	..	..	..	..	..	..
111 Syrian Arab Republic	65	0.315	10.4	2.9	37.0	1,218 [c]
112 Swaziland	62	0.381	6.3	24.1 [h]	61.2 [h]	2,267 [c]
113 Honduras	48	0.460	9.4	54.4	48.5	1,252 [c]
114 Bolivia	54	0.422	10.2	24.9	42.6	1,217 [f]
115 Namibia	..	..	20.4	..	..	..
116 Nicaragua	..	..	9.7	..	..	..
117 Mongolia	..	..	7.9	..	..	..
118 Vanuatu	..	..	0.0	..	..	..
119 Egypt	68	0.274	2.0	16.4	28.4	1,576
120 Guatemala	..	..	8.8	..	..	..
121 Solomon Islands	..	..	2.0	..	..	..
122 Botswana	32	0.521	17.0	25.7	52.8	3,747 [d]
123 Gabon	..	..	9.5	..	..	..
124 Morocco	..	..	0.7	..	..	..
125 Myanmar	..	..	.. [k]	..	..	..
126 Iraq	..	..	6.4	..	..	..
127 Lesotho	..	..	10.7	..	..	..
128 India	..	..	8.9	..	20.5	..
129 Ghana	..	..	9.0	..	..	..
130 Zimbabwe	..	..	14.0	..	..	..
131 Equatorial Guinea	..	..	5.0	..	26.8	..
132 São Tomé and Principe	..	..	9.1	..	..	..
133 Papua New Guinea	..	..	1.8	..	..	..
134 Cameroon	..	..	5.6	..	..	..
135 Pakistan	..	..	.. [k]	8.0	25.1	..
136 Cambodia	..	..	9.3	..	..	..
137 Comoros	..	..	.. [k]	..	..	..
138 Kenya	..	..	3.6	..	..	..
139 Congo	..	..	12.0	..	..	..
Low human development						
140 Lao People's Dem. Rep.	..	..	21.2	..	..	..
141 Madagascar	..	..	8.0	..	..	..
142 Bhutan	..	..	2.0	..	..	..
143 Sudan	..	..	.. [k]	..	..	..
144 Nepal	..	..	6.4	..	..	..
145 Togo	..	..	4.9	..	..	..
146 Bangladesh	67	0.305	9.1	4.9	34.7	744 [d]
147 Mauritania	..	..	2.2	..	..	..
148 Yemen	..	..	0.7	..	..	..
149 Djibouti	..	..	0.0	..	..	..
150 Haiti	..	..	..	..	..	..

HDI rank	Gender empowerment measure (GEM)		Seats in parliament held by women (as % of total) [a]	Female administrators and managers (as % of total) [b]	Female professional and technical workers (as % of total) [b]	Women's GDP per capita (PPP US$) [b]
	Rank	Value				
151 Nigeria	..	..	3.3	..	..	..
152 Congo, Dem. Rep. of the	..	..	.. [k]	..	..	..
153 Zambia	..	..	10.1	..	..	..
154 Côte d'Ivoire	..	..	.. [k]	..	..	..
155 Senegal	..	..	14.0	..	..	..
156 Tanzania, U. Rep. of	..	..	16.4	..	..	..
157 Benin	..	..	6.0	..	..	..
158 Uganda	..	..	17.9	..	..	..
159 Eritrea	59	0.402	14.7	16.8	29.5	568
160 Angola	..	..	15.5	..	..	..
161 Gambia	..	..	2.0	..	..	..
162 Guinea	..	..	8.8	..	..	..
163 Malawi	..	..	8.3	..	..	..
164 Rwanda	..	..	17.1	..	..	..
165 Mali	..	..	12.2	..	..	..
166 Central African Republic	..	..	7.3	..	..	..
167 Chad	..	..	2.4	..	..	..
168 Mozambique	..	..	30.0	..	..	..
169 Guinea-Bissau	..	..	7.8	..	..	..
170 Burundi	..	..	6.0	..	..	..
171 Ethiopia	..	..	..	..	..	..
172 Burkina Faso	..	..	10.5	..	..	..
173 Niger	70	0.119	1.2	8.3 [h]	8.0 [h]	541 [c]
174 Sierra Leone	..	..	8.8	..	..	..
All developing countries	–	..	13.6	..	..	..
Least developed countries	–	..	10.7	..	..	..
Arab States	–	..	3.5	..	..	..
East Asia	–	..	21.2	..	..	..
East Asia (excluding China)	–	..	4.2	..	..	..
Latin America and the Caribbean	–	..	12.9	..	..	..
South Asia	–	..	8.8	..	..	..
South Asia (excluding India)	–	..	..	..	..	..
South-East Asia and the Pacific	–	..	12.7	..	..	..
Sub-Saharan Africa	–	..	11.0	..	..	..
Eastern Europe and the CIS	–	..	8.4	..	..	..
OECD	–	..	15.1	..	..	..
High human development	–	..	15.5	..	..	..
Medium human development	–	..	13.7	..	..	..
Low human development	–	..	9.2	..	..	..
High income	–	..	16.3	..	..	..
Medium income	–	..	9.9	..	..	..
Low income	–	..	14.5	..	..	..
World	–	..	13.6	..	..	..

a. Data are as of 29 February 2000. (A value of 0 was converted to 0.001 for purposes of calculating the GEM.) b. Data refer to the latest available year. c. No wage data available. An estimate of 75% was used for the ratio of the female non-agricultural wage to the male non-agricultural wage. d. The manufacturing wage was used. e. Heston and Summers 1999. f. Wage data based on Psacharopoulos and Tzannatos 1992. g. Data refer to the Legislative National Commission of Venezuela. h. Data refer to employees only. i. Calculated on the basis of occupational data from ILO 1997d. j. The figures on the distribution of seats do not include the 36 special rotating delegates appointed on an ad hoc basis, and the percentage given was therefore calculated on the basis of the 54 permanent seats. k. The parliament has been suspended.

Source: Columns 1 and 2: Human Development Report Office calculations; see the technical note for details; *column 3:* IPU 2000d; *columns 4 and 5:* unless otherwise noted, calculated on the basis of occupational data from ILO 1999c; *column 6:* unless otherwise noted, calculated on the basis of the following: for GDP per capita (PPP US$), World Bank 2000a; for wages, wage data from ILO 1999c; for economic activity rate, data on economically active population from ILO 1996; for population shares, population data from UN 1998c; for details on the calculation of women's GDP per capita (PPP US$) see the technical note.

HDI rank	Human poverty index (HPI-1) 1998 Rank	Value (%)	People not expected to survive to age 40 [†] (%) [a] 1998	Adult illiteracy rate [†] (% age 15 and above) 1998	Population without access — To safe water [†] (%) 1990-1998 [b]	To health services [†] (%) 1981-1993 [b]	To sanitation (%) 1990-1998 [b]	Under-weight children under age five [†] (%) 1990-1998 [b]	Share of income or consumption — Poorest 20% (%) 1987-1998 [b]	Richest 20% (%) 1987-1998 [b]	Richest 20% to poorest 20% 1987-1998 [b]	Population below income poverty line (%) — $1 a day (1993 PPP US$) 1989-1998 [b]	National poverty line 1987-1997 [b]
High human development													
22 Cyprus	..	..	3.2	3.4	0	0	..	..	..	..	..	..	..
24 Singapore	..	..	2.2	8.2	0 [c]	0	..	..	..	..	..	..	..
26 Hong Kong, China (SAR)	..	..	2.2	7.1	..	..	..	..	..	..	..	..	..
30 Barbados	..	..	3.1	..	0	0	0	5 [c]	..	..	..	..	..
31 Korea, Rep. of	..	..	4.6	2.5	7	0	0	..	7.5	39.3	5.2	..	..
32 Brunei Darussalam	..	..	3.1	9.3	..	4	..	..	..	..	..	..	..
33 Bahamas	..	..	5.7	4.5	6	0	18	..	..	..	..	..	..
35 Argentina	..	..	5.5	3.3	29	..	32	..	..	..	..	..	25.5
36 Kuwait	..	..	2.8	19.1	..	0	..	6 [c]	..	..	..	..	..
37 Antigua and Barbuda	..	..	..	..	..	0	4	10 [c]	..	..	..	..	..
38 Chile	4	4.7	4.4	4.6	9	5	..	1	3.5	61.0	17.4	4.2	20.5
39 Uruguay	1	3.9	5.0	2.4	5 [c, d]	0 [c]	..	5	5.4	48.3	8.9	6.6 [e]	..
41 Bahrain	9	9.6	4.6	13.5	6	0	3	9	..	..	..	..	..
42 Qatar	17	13.7	4.8	19.6	0 [f]	0	3	6	..	..	..	..	..
45 United Arab Emirates	28	17.9	3.0	25.4	3	10	8	14	..	..	..	..	..
Medium human development													
47 Saint Kitts and Nevis	..	..	..	..	0	0	0	..	..	..	..	..	..
48 Costa Rica	2	4.0	3.9	4.7	4	3	16	2	4.0	51.8	13.0	9.6	..
50 Trinidad and Tobago	5	5.1	4.0	6.6	3	1	..	7 [c]	5.5	45.9	8.3	12.4	21.0
51 Dominica	..	..	..	..	4	0	20	5 [c]	..	..	..	..	..
53 Seychelles	..	..	..	..	..	1	..	6 [c]	..	..	..	..	..
54 Grenada	..	..	..	..	..	..	..	..	..	..	..	..	..
55 Mexico	12	10.4	8.2	9.2	15	9	28	14 [c]	3.6	58.2	16.2	17.9	10.1
56 Cuba	3	4.6	4.4	3.6	7	0	34	9	..	..	..	..	..
58 Belize	..	..	6.0	7.3	32	0	..	..	..	..	..	..	..
59 Panama	8	8.9	6.3	8.6	7	18	17	7	3.6	52.8	14.7	10.3	..
61 Malaysia	18	14.0	4.7	13.6	22	12	6	19	4.5	53.8	12.0	..	15.5
65 Venezuela	15	12.4	6.4	8.0	21	.. [g]	41	5	..	..	..	14.7	31.3
66 Fiji	6	8.4	4.9	7.8	23	1	8	8	..	..	..	..	..
67 Suriname	..	..	7.2	..	..	9	..	..	..	..	..	..	..
68 Colombia	11	10.4	9.8	8.8	15	13	15	8	3.0	60.9	20.3	11.0	17.7
71 Mauritius	14	11.6	4.8	16.2	2	1	0	16	..	..	..	..	10.6
72 Libyan Arab Jamahiriya	19	15.3	6.3	21.9	3	0	2	5	..	..	..	..	..
74 Brazil	21	15.6	11.3	15.5	24	.. [g]	30	6	2.5	63.8	25.5	5.1	17.4
75 Saudi Arabia	..	..	5.6	24.8	5 [c]	2	14 [c]	..	..	..	..	..	..
76 Thailand	29	18.7	10.4	5.0	19	41	4	19	6.4	48.4	7.6	28.2 [e]	13.1
77 Philippines	22	16.1	8.9	5.2	15	.. [g]	13	28	5.4	52.3	9.7	18.7 [e]	37.5
79 Saint Vincent and the Grenadines	..	..	..	..	11	20	2	..	..	..	..	..	..
80 Peru	25	16.5	11.3	10.8	33	.. [g]	28	8	4.4	51.2	11.6	15.5	49.0
81 Paraguay	23	16.4	8.6	7.2	40	.. [g]	59	4	2.3	62.4	27.1	19.4	21.8
82 Lebanon	13	10.8	7.3	14.9	6	5	37	3	..	..	..	..	..
83 Jamaica	16	13.4	5.0	14.0	14	.. [g]	11	10	1.9	83.7	44.1	3.2	34.2
84 Sri Lanka	35	20.3	5.2	8.9	43	10	37	34	8.0	42.8	5.4	6.6	35.3
85 Turkey	24	16.4	9.3	16.0	51	0	20	10	5.8	47.7	8.2	2.4	..
86 Oman	38	22.7	6.2	31.2	15	11	22	23	..	..	..	..	..
87 Dominican Republic	20	15.4	8.8	17.2	21	.. [g]	15	6	4.3	53.7	12.5	3.2	20.6
88 Saint Lucia	..	..	..	..	15	0	..	..	5.2	48.3	9.3	..	..
89 Maldives	43	25.4	13.0	4.0	40	25	56	43	..	..	..	..	..
91 Ecuador	26	16.8	10.9	9.4	32	20	24	17 [c]	5.4	49.7	9.2	20.2	35.0
92 Jordan	7	8.8	6.9	11.4	3	10	1	5	7.6	44.4	5.8	7.4 [e]	15.0
95 Samoa (Western)	..	..	5.3	20.3	32	0	..	..	..	..	..	..	..

4 Human poverty in developing countries

HDI rank	Human poverty index (HPI-1) 1998 Rank	Human poverty index (HPI-1) 1998 Value (%)	People not expected to survive to age 40 † (%) a 1998	Adult illiteracy rate † (% age 15 and above) 1998	Population without access To safe water † (%) 1990-1998 b	Population without access To health services † (%) 1981-1993 b	Population without access To sani-tation (%) 1990-1998 b	Under-weight children under age five † (%) 1990-1998 b	Share of income or consumption Poorest 20% (%) 1987-1998 b	Share of income or consumption Richest 20% (%) 1987-1998 b	Share of income or consumption Richest 20% to poorest 20% 1987-1998 b	Population below income poverty line (%) $1 a day (1993 PPP US$) 1989-1998 b	Population below income poverty line (%) National poverty line 1987-1997 b
96 Guyana	10	10.0	13.4	1.7	9	4	12	12	6.3	46.9	7.4	..	..
97 Iran, Islamic Rep. of	31	19.2	9.4	25.4	5	27	36	16	..	..	..	..	..
99 China	30	19.0	7.7	17.2	33	.. g	76	16	5.9	46.6	7.9	..	6
101 Tunisia	36	21.9	7.5	31.3	2	10	20	9	5.9	46.3	7.8	1.3	19.9
103 South Africa	33	20.2	25.9	15.4	13	.. g	13	9	2.9	64.8	22.3	11.5	..
104 El Salvador	34	20.2	10.7	22.2	34	.. g	10	11	3.4	56.5	16.6	25.3	48.3
105 Cape Verde	37	22.0	10.1	27.1	35	18	73	14	..	..	..	..	..
107 Algeria	42	24.8	8.8	34.5	10	.. g	9	13	7.0	42.6	6.1	15.1 e	22.6
108 Viet Nam	47	28.2	11.2	7.1	55	.. g	71	41	8.0	44.5	5.6	..	50.9
109 Indonesia	46	27.7	12.3	14.3	26	57	47	34	8.0	44.9	5.6	26.3	15.1
111 Syrian Arab Republic	32	19.3	8.2	27.3	14	1	33	13	..	..	..	..	..
112 Swaziland	45	27.4	20.2	21.7	50	45	41	10 c	2.7	64.4	23.9	..	..
113 Honduras	39	23.3	11.3	26.6	22	38	26	18	3.4	58.0	17.1	40.5	50.0
114 Bolivia	27	17.4	18.0	15.6	20	.. g	35	10	5.6	48.2	8.6	11.3	..
115 Namibia	44	26.6	33.5	19.2	17	.. g	38	26	..	..	..	34.9	..
116 Nicaragua	41	24.2	12.2	32.1	22	.. g	15	12	4.2	55.2	13.1	3.0	50.3
117 Mongolia	..	..	10.9	..	32	0	..	..	7.3	40.9	5.6	..	..
118 Vanuatu	..	..	9.6	..	23	20	72	20 c	3.7	53.1	14.4	..	..
119 Egypt	55	32.3	9.9	46.3	13	1	12	12	9.8	39.0	4.0	3.1	..
120 Guatemala	49	29.2	15.3	32.7	32	40	13	27	2.1	63.0	30.0	39.8	..
121 Solomon Islands	..	..	5.6	..	..	20	..	21 c	..	..	..	..	..
122 Botswana	48	28.3	37.1	24.4	10	14	45	17	..	..	..	33.3 c	..
123 Gabon	..	..	30.7	..	33	13	..	..	..	..	..	..	..
124 Morocco	65	38.4	11.3	52.9	35	38	42	9	6.6	46.3	7.0	7.5 e	26.0
125 Myanmar	53	31.4	17.6	15.9	40	52	57	39	..	..	..	..	..
126 Iraq	56	32.9	15.8	46.3	19	2	25	23	..	..	..	..	..
127 Lesotho	40	23.3	26.0	17.6	38	20	62	16	2.8	60.1	21.5	43.1	49.2
128 India	58	34.6	15.8	44.3	19	25	71	53	8.1	46.1	5.7	44.2	35.0
129 Ghana	59	35.4	20.6	30.9	35	75	68	27	8.4	41.7	5.0	78.4	31.4
130 Zimbabwe	52	30.0	41.0	12.8	21	29	48	15	4.0	62.3	15.6	36.0	25.5
131 Equatorial Guinea	..	..	33.2	18.9	5	..	46	..	..	..	..	..	..
132 São Tomé and Principe	..	..	..	..	18	12	65	16	..	..	..	..	..
133 Papua New Guinea	..	..	18.3	36.8	32	0	..	..	4.5	56.5	12.6	..	..
134 Cameroon	66	38.5	27.4	26.4	46	85	11	22	..	..	..	..	..
135 Pakistan	68	40.1	14.3	56.0	21	15	44	38	9.5	41.1	4.3	31.0	34.0
136 Cambodia	..	..	27.7	..	32	0	..	..	6.9	47.6	6.9	..	..
137 Comoros	57	33.0	20.1	41.5	47	18	77	26	..	..	..	..	..
138 Kenya	51	29.5	30.6	19.5	56	.. g	15	22	5.0	50.2	10.0	26.5	42.0
139 Congo	54	31.9	34.4	21.6	66	.. g	31	17 c	..	..	..	..	..

Low human development

HDI rank	Human poverty index (HPI-1) 1998 Rank	Human poverty index (HPI-1) 1998 Value (%)	People not expected to survive to age 40 † (%) a 1998	Adult illiteracy rate † (% age 15 and above) 1998	Population without access To safe water † (%) 1990-1998 b	Population without access To health services † (%) 1981-1993 b	Population without access To sani-tation (%) 1990-1998 b	Under-weight children under age five † (%) 1990-1998 b	Share of income or consumption Poorest 20% (%) 1987-1998 b	Share of income or consumption Richest 20% (%) 1987-1998 b	Share of income or consumption Richest 20% to poorest 20% 1987-1998 b	Population below income poverty line (%) $1 a day (1993 PPP US$) 1989-1998 b	Population below income poverty line (%) National poverty line 1987-1997 b
140 Lao People's Dem. Rep.	..	..	28.9	53.9	32	0	..	..	9.6	40.2	4.2	..	..
141 Madagascar	..	..	21.8	35.1	32	0	..	..	5.1	52.1	10.2	..	..
142 Bhutan	..	..	19.6	..	42	20	30	38 c	..	..	..	..	..
143 Sudan	60	35.5	26.6	44.3	27	30	49	34	..	..	..	..	..
144 Nepal	80	51.3	21.9	60.8	29	90	84	47	7.6	44.8	5.9	37.7	42.0
145 Togo	63	37.8	34.2	44.8	45	.. g	63	25	..	..	..	..	32.3
146 Bangladesh	70	43.6	20.8	59.9	5	26	57	56	8.7	42.8	4.9	29.1	35.6
147 Mauritania	77	49.7	28.7	58.8	63	70	43	23	6.2	45.6	7.4	3.8	57.0
148 Yemen	76	49.4	21.2	55.9	39	84	34	46	6.1	46.1	7.6	5.1	19.1
149 Djibouti	..	..	32.8	37.7	32	0	..	..	..	..	..	..	..
150 Haiti	71	45.2	26.5	52.2	63	55	75	28	..	..	..	..	65.0

4 Human poverty in developing countries

HDI rank	Human poverty index (HPI-1) 1998 Rank	Value (%)	People not expected to survive to age 40[†] (%)[a] 1998	Adult illiteracy rate[†] (% age 15 and above) 1998	Population without access — To safe water[†] (%) 1990-1998[b]	To health services[†] (%) 1981-1993[b]	To sanitation (%) 1990-1998[b]	Under-weight children under age five[†] (%) 1990-1998[b]	Share of income or consumption — Poorest 20% (%) 1987-1998[b]	Richest 20% (%) 1987-1998[b]	Richest 20% to poorest 20% 1987-1998[b]	Population below income poverty line (%) — $1 a day (1993 PPP US$) 1989-1998[b]	National poverty line 1987-1997[b]
151 Nigeria	62	37.6	33.3	38.9	51	33	59	36	4.4	55.7	12.7	70.2	43
152 Congo, Dem. Rep. of the	..	..	31.7	41.1	32	0	..	..	..	..	..	..	..
153 Zambia	64	37.9	46.2	23.7	62	25	29	24	4.2	54.75	13.0	72.6	86.0
154 Côte d'Ivoire	72	45.8	37.0	55.5	58	40	61	24	7.1	44.3	6.2	12.3	..
155 Senegal	73	47.9	28.0	64.5	19	60	35	22	6.4	48.2	7.5	26.3	33.4
156 Tanzania, U. Rep. of	50	29.2	35.4	26.4	34	7	14	27	6.8	45.5	6.7	19.9	51.1
157 Benin	74	48.8	28.9	62.3	44	58	73	29	..	..	..	..	33.0
158 Uganda	67	39.7	45.9	35.0	54	29	43	26	6.6	46.1	7.0	36.7	55.0
159 Eritrea	..	..	31.4	48.3	32	0	..	..	..	..	..	..	..
160 Angola	..	..	37.7	..	69	76	60	42	..	..	..	..	..
161 Gambia	75	49.0	37.2	65.4	31	..[g]	63	26	4.4	52.8	12.0	53.7	64.0
162 Guinea	..	..	37.8	..	54	55	69	..	6.4	47.2	7.4	..	..
163 Malawi	69	41.9	47.5	41.8	53	20	97	30	..	..	..	..	54.0
164 Rwanda	61	37.5	45.9	36.0	21[h]	..[g]	..	27	9.7	39.1	4.0	35.7[c]	51.2
165 Mali	81	51.4	33.1	61.8	34	80	94	40	4.6	56.2	12.2	72.8	..
166 Central African Republic	82	53.0	40.4	56.0	62	88	73	27	2.0	65.0	32.5	66.6	..
167 Chad	..	..	36.9	60.6	32	0	..	..	..	..	..	..	..
168 Mozambique	79	50.7	41.9	57.7	54	70	66	26	6.5	46.5	7.2	37.9	..
169 Guinea-Bissau	78	50.2	40.6	63.3	57	36	54	23[c]	2.1	58.9	28.0	..	48.8
170 Burundi	..	..	..	54.2	48	20	49	37	7.9	41.6	5.3	..	36.2
171 Ethiopia	83	55.3	42.1	63.7	75	45	81	48	7.1	47.7	6.7	31.3	..
172 Burkina Faso	84	58.4	39.9	77.8	58	30	63	30	5.5	55.0	10.0	61.2	..
173 Niger	85	64.7	35.2	85.3	39	70	81	50	2.6	53.3	20.5	61.4	63.0
174 Sierra Leone	..	..	50.0	..	66	64	89	29	1.1	63.4	57.6	57.0	68.0
All developing countries	–	..	14.3	27.6	28	..	56	31	..	..	..	..	..
Least developed countries	–	..	30.3	49.0	36	..	60	40	..	..	..	..	..
Arab States	–	..	12.2	40.3	17	..	23	19	..	..	..	..	..
East Asia	–	..	7.5	16.6	32	..	..	..	..	..	..	..	..
East Asia (excluding China)	–	..	4.6	3.1	8	..	..	..	..	..	..	..	..
Latin America and the Caribbean	–	..	9.7	12.3	22	..	29	10	..	..	..	..	..
South Asia	–	..	15.7	45.7	18	..	65	49	..	..	..	..	..
South Asia (excluding India)	–	..	15.6	49.5	15	..	49	41	..	..	..	..	..
South-East Asia and the Pacific	–	..	12.0	11.3	29	..	..	..	..	..	..	..	..
Sub-Saharan Africa	–	..	34.6	40.6	46	..	52	31	..	..	..	..	..
Eastern Europe and the CIS	–	..	8.1	..	..	..	..	..	..	..	..	..	..
OECD	–	..	3.9	..	..	..	..	..	..	..	..	..	..
High human development	–	..	3.3	..	..	..	..	..	..	..	..	..	..
Medium human development	–	..	11.4	23.3	26	..	56	29	..	..	..	..	..
Low human development	–	..	31.9	50.8	39	..	59	39	..	..	..	..	..
High income	–	..	3.0	..	..	..	..	..	..	..	..	..	..
Medium income	–	..	9.4	12.6	20	..	..	..	..	..	..	..	..
Low income	–	..	15.7	31.0	30	..	67	36	..	..	..	..	..
World	–	..	12.3	24.8	27	..	..	30[i]	..	..	..	..	..

† Denotes indicators used to calculate the human poverty index (HPI-1).

a. Data refer to the probability at birth of not surviving to age 40, times 100. b. Data refer to the most recent year available during the period specified in the column heading. c. Data refer to a year or period other than that specified in the column heading, differ from the standard definition or refer to only part of the country. d. Human Development Report Office estimate based on national sources. e. Data refer to the percentage of the population living below a poverty line defined as $2 a day (1993 PPP US$). f. Data refer to the urban population without access to safe water. g. For purposes of calculating the HPI-1, an estimate of 25%, the unweighted average for the 97 countries with data, was applied. h. Data refer to the rural population without access to safe water. i. Aggregate as calculated in UNICEF 1999c.

Source: Columns 1 and 2: Human Development Report Office calculations; see the technical note for details; column 3: interpolated on the basis of survival data from UN 1998c; column 4: UNESCO 2000a; columns 5 and 7: calculated on the basis of access data from UNICEF 1999c; column 6: World Bank 1998; column 8: UNICEF 1999c; columns 9 and 10: World Bank 2000b; column 11: calculated on the basis of income or consumption data from World Bank 2000b; columns 12 and 13: World Bank 2000b.

5 Human poverty in OECD, Eastern Europe and the CIS

HDI rank	Human poverty index (HPI-2) 1998 Rank	Value (%)	People not expected to survive to age 60 † (%) [a] 1998	People who are functionally illiterate † (% age 16-65) [b] 1994-98	Long-term unemployment † (as % of labour force) [c] 1998	Share of income or consumption — Poorest 20% (%) 1987-98 [d]	Richest 20% (%) 1987-98 [d]	Richest 20% to poorest 20% 1987-98 [d]	Population below income poverty line (%) — 50% of median income † 1987-97 [d,e]	$14.40 a day (1985 PPP US$) 1989-95 [d,f]	$4 a day (1990 PPP US$) 1989-95 [d]
High human development											
1 Canada	11	11.8	9.2	16.6	0.8	7.5	39.3	5.2	10.6	5.9	..
2 Norway	1	7.3	8.9	8.5	0.3	9.7	35.8	3.7	5.8	2.6	..
3 United States	18	15.8	12.4	20.7	0.4	5.2	46.4	8.9	17.3	14.1	..
4 Australia	13	12.2	8.8	17.0	2.7	5.9	41.3	7.0	11.9	7.8	..
5 Iceland	..	..	8.3	..	0.4	..	..	..	..	..	..
6 Sweden	2	7.6	8.5	7.5	2.7	9.6	34.5	3.6	8.7	4.6	..
7 Belgium	14	12.4	9.9	18.4 [g]	5.5	9.5	34.5	3.6	5.5	12.0	..
8 Netherlands	3	8.2	9.2	10.5	1.9	7.3	40.1	5.5	6.2	14.4	..
9 Japan	9	11.2	8.1	.. [h]	0.8	10.6	35.7	3.4	11.8 [i]	3.7	..
10 United Kingdom	16	14.6	9.6	21.8	2.1	6.6	43.0	6.5	10.6	13.1	..
11 Finland	4	8.6	11.1	10.4	3.1	10.0	35.8	3.6	3.9	3.8	..
12 France	8	11.1	11.1	.. [h]	5.2	7.2	40.2	5.6	8.4	12.0 [j]	..
13 Switzerland	..	..	9.7	..	1.5 [k]	6.9	40.3	5.8	..	..	..
14 Germany	6	10.4	10.5	14.4	4.9	8.2	38.5	4.7	5.9 [i]	11.5	..
15 Denmark	5	9.3	12.7	9.6	1.5	9.6	34.5	3.6	6.9	7.6	..
16 Austria	..	..	10.7	..	1.4	10.4	33.3	3.2	..	8.0	..
17 Luxembourg	7	10.5	10.4	.. [h]	0.9	9.4	36.5	3.9	4.1	4.3 [j]	..
18 Ireland	17	15.0	9.8	22.6	4.4	6.7	42.9	6.4	9.4	36.5 [j]	..
19 Italy	12	11.9	8.9	.. [h]	8.1	8.7	36.3	4.2	12.8	2.0	..
20 New Zealand	15	12.8	10.9	18.4	1.5	2.7	46.9	17.4	9.2 [i]	..	..
21 Spain	10	11.6	9.9	.. [h]	10.2	7.5	40.3	5.4	9.1	21.1	..
23 Israel	..	..	9.2	..	..	6.9	42.5	6.2	..	..	..
25 Greece	..	..	8.8	..	5.3 [k]	7.5	40.3	5.4	..	..	..
27 Malta	..	..	8.3	..	..	..	..	..	..	..	..
28 Portugal	..	..	12.3	48.0	2.2	7.3	43.4	5.9	..	..	..
29 Slovenia	..	..	14.4	42.2	..	8.4	35.4	4.2	..	..	<1.0
34 Czech Republic	..	..	13.9	15.7	2.0	10.3	35.9	3.5	..	..	<1.0
40 Slovakia	..	..	16.1	..	..	11.9	31.4	2.6	..	..	<1.0
43 Hungary	..	..	21.1	33.8	4.0	8.8	39.9	4.5	11.0	..	4.0
44 Poland	..	..	16.9	42.6	4.0	7.7	40.9	5.3	11.2	..	20.0
46 Estonia	..	..	23.3	..	..	6.2	41.8	6.7	..	..	37.0
Medium human development											
49 Croatia	..	..	16.1	..	..	9.3	36.2	3.9	..	..	..
52 Lithuania	..	..	22.9	..	..	7.8	40.3	5.2	..	..	30.0
57 Belarus	..	..	25.9	..	..	11.4	33.3	2.9	..	..	22.0
60 Bulgaria	..	..	18.0	..	..	8.5	37.0	4.4	..	..	15.0
62 Russian Federation	..	..	29.5	..	..	4.4	53.7	12.2	19.3	..	50.0
63 Latvia	..	..	24.6	..	..	7.6	40.3	5.3	..	..	22.0
64 Romania	..	..	20.3	..	..	8.9	37.3	4.2	..	..	59.0
69 Macedonia, TFYR	..	..	13.8	..	..	..	..	..	..	..	..
70 Georgia	..	..	17.2	..	..	..	..	..	..	..	..
73 Kazakhstan	..	..	25.2	..	..	6.7	42.3	6.3	..	..	65.0
78 Ukraine	..	..	23.6	..	..	8.6	41.2	4.8	..	..	63.0
90 Azerbaijan	..	..	21.7	..	..	..	..	..	..	..	..
93 Armenia	..	..	19.5	..	..	..	..	..	..	..	..
94 Albania	..	..	13.7	..	..	..	..	..	..	..	..
98 Kyrgyzstan	..	..	24.9	..	..	6.3	47.4	7.5	..	..	88.0
100 Turkmenistan	..	..	27.0	..	..	6.1	47.5	7.8	..	..	61.0
102 Moldova, Rep. of	..	..	25.3	..	..	6.9	41.5	6.0	..	..	66.0
106 Uzbekistan	..	..	24.7	..	..	7.4	40.9	5.5	..	..	63.0
110 Tajikistan	..	..	24.9	..	..	..	..	..	..	..	..

MONITORING HUMAN DEVELOPMENT: ENLARGING PEOPLE'S CHOICES . . .

HDI rank	Human poverty index (HPI-2) 1998		People not expected to survive to age 60 [†] (%) [a] 1998	People who are functionally illiterate [†] (% age 16-65) [b] 1994-98	Long-term unemploy-ment [†] (as % of labour force) [c] 1998	Share of income or consumption			Population below income poverty line (%)		
	Rank	Value (%)				Poorest 20% (%) 1987-98 [d]	Richest 20% (%) 1987-98 [d]	Richest 20% to poorest 20% 1987-98 [d]	50% of median income [†] 1987-97 [d, e]	$14.40 a day (1985 PPP US$) 1989-95 [d, f]	$4 a day (1990 PPP US$) 1989-95 [d]
All developing countries	–	..	..	..	..	..	..	..	..	..	..
Eastern Europe and the CIS	–	..	24.3	..	..	..	..	..	..	..	..
OECD	–	..	12.3	..	..	..	..	..	..	..	..
World	–	..	..	..	..	..	..	..	..	..	..

† Denotes indicators used to calculate the human poverty index (HPI-2).

Note: This table includes Israel and Malta, which are not OECD member countries, but excludes Mexico, the Republic of Korea and Turkey, which are. For the human poverty index and indicators for these three countries see table 4.

a. Data refer to the probability at birth of not surviving to age 60, times 100. b. Based on level 1 prose. Data refer to the most recent year available during 1994-98. c. Data refer to unemployment lasting 12 months or more. d. Data refer to the most recent year available during the period specified in the column heading. e. Poverty is measured at 50% of equivalent median disposable household income. f. Based on the US poverty line. g. Data refer to Flanders. h. For purposes of calculating the HPI-2, an estimate of 15.1%, the unweighted average for countries with available data, was applied. i. Smeeding 1997. j. Data refer to a year or period other than that specified in the column heading. k. Data refer to 1997.

Source: Columns 1 and 2: Human Development Report Office calculations; see the technical note for details; *column 3:* interpolated on the basis of survival data from UN 1998c; *column 4:* OECD and Statistics Canada 2000; *column 5:* calculated on the basis of data on long-term unemployment (as percentage of unemployment) and unemployment (as percentage of the labour force) from OECD 1999b; *columns 6 and 7:* World Bank 2000b; *column 8:* calculated on the basis of data on income or consumption shares from World Bank 2000b; *column 9:* unless otherwise noted, LIS 2000; *column 10:* Smeeding 1997; *column 11:* Milanovic 1998.

6 Comparisons of human development indices

HDI rank	Human development index (HDI) 1998	Gender-related development index (GDI)[a]	Gender empower-ment measure (GEM)[a]	Human poverty index (HPI)[b] (%) 1998	HDI as % of highest value in group 1998	GDI as % of highest value in group[a]	GEM as % of highest value in group[a]	HPI as % of lowest value in group[b] 1998
All developing countries	0.642	0.634	..	..	–	–	–	–
Arab States	0.635	0.612	..	..	–	–	–	–
36 Kuwait	**0.836**	**0.827**	..	..	100	100	..	..
41 Bahrain	0.820	0.803	..	9.6	98	97	..	109
42 Qatar	0.819	0.807	..	13.7	98	97	..	156
45 United Arab Emirates	0.810	0.793	..	17.9	97	96	..	204
72 Libyan Arab Jamahiriya	0.760	0.738	..	15.3	91	89	..	175
75 Saudi Arabia	0.747	0.715	..	..	89	86	..	..
82 Lebanon	0.735	0.718	..	10.8	88	87	..	124
86 Oman	0.730	0.697	..	22.7	87	84	..	259
92 Jordan	0.721	..	0.220	**8.8**	86	..	55	100
101 Tunisia	0.703	0.688	**0.398**	21.9	84	83	100	250
107 Algeria	0.683	0.661	..	24.8	82	80	..	283
111 Syrian Arab Republic	0.660	0.636	0.315	19.3	79	77	79	220
119 Egypt	0.623	0.604	0.274	32.3	75	73	69	368
124 Morocco	0.589	0.570	..	38.4	70	69	..	438
126 Iraq	0.583	0.548	..	32.9	70	66	..	375
143 Sudan	0.477	0.453	..	35.5	57	55	..	404
148 Yemen	0.448	0.389	..	49.4	54	47	..	564
149 Djibouti	0.447	..	..	..	53	..	..	..
East Asia	0.716	0.710	..	..	–	–	–	–
26 Hong Kong, China (SAR)	**0.872**	**0.864**	..	..	100	100	..	..
31 Korea, Rep. of	0.854	0.847	**0.323**	..	98	98	100	..
99 China	0.706	0.700	..	**19.0**	81	81	..	100
117 Mongolia	0.628	..	..	..	72	..	..	..
Latin America and the Caribbean	0.758	0.748	..	..	–	–	–	–
30 Barbados	**0.858**	..	0.629	..	100	..	99	..
33 Bahamas	0.844	**0.842**	0.633	..	98	100	100	..
35 Argentina	0.837	0.824	..	..	98	98	..	..
37 Antigua and Barbuda	0.833	..	..	..	97	..	..	..
38 Chile	0.826	0.812	0.440	4.7	96	96	70	121
39 Uruguay	0.825	0.821	0.472	**3.9**	96	97	75	100
47 Saint Kitts and Nevis	0.798	..	..	..	93	..	..	..
48 Costa Rica	0.797	0.789	0.553	4.0	93	94	87	103
50 Trinidad and Tobago	0.793	0.784	0.583	5.1	92	93	92	132
51 Dominica	0.793	..	..	..	92	..	..	..
54 Grenada	0.785	..	..	..	92	..	..	..
55 Mexico	0.784	0.775	0.514	10.4	91	92	81	269
56 Cuba	0.783	..	..	4.6	91	..	..	118
58 Belize	0.777	0.754	0.493	..	91	90	78	..
59 Panama	0.776	0.770	0.470	8.9	90	91	74	229
65 Venezuela	0.770	0.763	0.597	12.4	90	91	94	320
67 Suriname	0.766	..	0.428	..	89	..	68	..
68 Colombia	0.764	0.760	0.510	10.4	89	90	81	268
74 Brazil	0.747	0.736	..	15.6	87	87	..	403
79 Saint Vincent and the Grenadines	0.738	..	..	..	86	..	..	..
80 Peru	0.737	0.723	0.446	16.5	86	86	70	426
81 Paraguay	0.736	0.723	0.406	16.4	86	86	64	424
83 Jamaica	0.735	0.732	..	13.4	86	87	..	347
87 Dominican Republic	0.729	0.720	0.505	15.4	85	86	80	398
88 Saint Lucia	0.728	..	..	..	85	..	..	..

HDI rank	Human development index (HDI) 1998	Gender-related development index (GDI) [a]	Gender empowerment measure (GEM) [a]	Human poverty index (HPI) [b] (%) 1998	HDI as % of highest value in group 1998	GDI as % of highest value in group [a]	GEM as % of highest value in group [a]	HPI as % of lowest value in group [b] 1998
91 Ecuador	0.722	0.701	0.481	16.8	84	83	76	435
96 Guyana	0.709	0.698	..	10.0	83	83	..	259
104 El Salvador	0.696	0.693	0.527	20.2	81	82	83	524
113 Honduras	0.653	0.644	0.460	23.3	76	76	73	602
114 Bolivia	0.643	0.631	0.422	17.4	75	75	67	450
116 Nicaragua	0.631	0.624	..	24.2	74	74	..	627
120 Guatemala	0.619	0.603	..	29.2	72	72	..	755
150 Haiti	0.440	0.436	..	45.2	51	52	..	1,168
South Asia	**0.560**	**0.542**	..	..	–	–	–	–
84 Sri Lanka	**0.733**	**0.727**	**0.309**	20.3	100	100	100	106
89 Maldives	0.725	0.720	..	25.4	99	99	..	132
97 Iran, Islamic Rep. of	0.709	0.691	..	**19.2**	97	95	..	100
128 India	0.563	0.545	..	34.6	77	75	..	180
135 Pakistan	0.522	0.489	..	40.1	71	67	..	209
142 Bhutan	0.483	..	..	..	66	..	..	..
144 Nepal	0.474	0.449	..	51.3	65	62	..	267
146 Bangladesh	0.461	0.441	0.305	43.6	63	61	99	227
South-East Asia and the Pacific	**0.691**	**0.688**	..	..	–	–	–	–
24 Singapore	**0.881**	**0.876**	**0.505**	..	100	100	100	..
32 Brunei Darussalam	0.848	0.843	..	..	96	96	..	..
61 Malaysia	0.772	0.762	0.468	14.0	88	87	93	165
66 Fiji	0.769	0.755	0.384	**8.4**	87	86	76	100
76 Thailand	0.745	0.741	..	18.7	85	85	..	221
77 Philippines	0.744	0.739	0.479	16.1	84	84	95	191
95 Samoa (Western)	0.711	..	..	..	81	..	..	..
108 Viet Nam	0.671	0.668	..	28.2	76	76	..	334
109 Indonesia	0.670	0.664	..	27.7	76	76	..	329
118 Vanuatu	0.623	..	..	..	71	..	..	..
121 Solomon Islands	0.614	..	..	..	70	..	..	..
125 Myanmar	0.585	0.582	..	31.4	66	66	..	372
133 Papua New Guinea	0.542	0.536	..	..	62	61	..	..
136 Cambodia	0.512	..	..	..	58	..	..	..
140 Lao People's Dem. Rep.	0.484	0.469	..	..	55	54	..	..
Sub-Saharan Africa	**0.464**	**0.459**	..	..	–	–	–	–
53 Seychelles	**0.786**	..	..	..	100	..	..	..
71 Mauritius	0.761	**0.750**	0.420	**11.6**	97	100	81	100
103 South Africa	0.697	0.689	..	20.2	89	92	..	175
105 Cape Verde	0.688	0.675	..	22.0	88	90	..	190
112 Swaziland	0.655	0.646	0.381	27.4	83	86	73	236
115 Namibia	0.632	0.624	..	26.6	80	83	..	230
122 Botswana	0.593	0.584	**0.521**	28.3	75	78	100	245
123 Gabon	0.592	..	..	..	75	..	..	..
127 Lesotho	0.569	0.556	..	23.3	72	74	..	202
129 Ghana	0.556	0.552	..	35.4	71	74	..	306
130 Zimbabwe	0.555	0.551	..	30.0	71	73	..	259
131 Equatorial Guinea	0.555	0.542	..	..	71	72	..	..
132 São Tomé and Principe	0.547	..	..	..	70	..	..	..
134 Cameroon	0.528	0.518	..	38.5	67	69	..	333
137 Comoros	0.510	0.503	..	33.0	65	67	..	285

HDI rank	Human develop-ment index (HDI) 1998	Gender-related develop-ment index (GDI) [a]	Gender empower-ment measure (GEM) [a]	Human poverty index (HPI) [b] (%) 1998	HDI as % of highest value in group 1998	GDI as % of highest value in group [a]	GEM as % of highest value in group [a]	HPI as % of lowest value in group [b] 1998
138 Kenya	0.508	0.503	..	29.5	65	67	..	255
139 Congo	0.507	0.499	..	31.9	65	67	..	276
141 Madagascar	0.483	0.478	..	..	62	64	..	..
145 Togo	0.471	0.448	..	37.8	60	60	..	327
147 Mauritania	0.451	0.441	..	49.7	57	59	..	429
151 Nigeria	0.439	0.425	..	37.6	56	57	..	325
152 Congo, Dem. Rep. of the	0.430	0.418	..	..	55	56	..	..
153 Zambia	0.420	0.413	..	37.9	53	55	..	327
154 Côte d'Ivoire	0.420	0.401	..	45.8	53	54	..	396
155 Senegal	0.416	0.405	..	47.9	53	54	..	414
156 Tanzania, U. Rep. of	0.415	0.410	..	29.2	53	55	..	252
157 Benin	0.411	0.391	..	48.8	52	52	..	422
158 Uganda	0.409	0.401	..	39.7	52	53	..	343
159 Eritrea	0.408	0.394	0.402	..	52	53	77	..
160 Angola	0.405	..	..	..	52	..	..	..
161 Gambia	0.396	0.388	..	49.0	50	52	..	423
162 Guinea	0.394	..	..	..	50	..	..	..
163 Malawi	0.385	0.375	..	41.9	49	50	..	362
164 Rwanda	0.382	0.377	..	37.5	49	50	..	324
165 Mali	0.380	0.371	..	51.4	48	49	..	444
166 Central African Republic	0.371	0.359	..	53.0	47	48	..	458
167 Chad	0.367	..	..	..	47	..	..	..
168 Mozambique	0.341	0.326	..	50.7	43	43	..	438
169 Guinea-Bissau	0.331	0.298	..	50.2	42	40	..	434
170 Burundi	0.321	..	..	..	41	..	..	..
171 Ethiopia	0.309	0.297	..	55.3	39	40	..	478
172 Burkina Faso	0.303	0.290	..	58.4	39	39	..	504
173 Niger	0.293	0.280	0.119	64.7	37	37	23	559
174 Sierra Leone	0.252	..	..	..	32	..	..	..
Eastern Europe and the CIS	**0.777**	**0.774**	..	..	–	–	–	–
29 Slovenia	**0.861**	**0.857**	0.519	..	100	100	96	..
34 Czech Republic	0.843	0.841	0.537	..	98	98	99	..
40 Slovakia	0.825	0.822	0.533	..	96	96	99	..
43 Hungary	0.817	0.813	0.487	..	95	95	90	..
44 Poland	0.814	0.811	0.512	..	94	95	95	..
46 Estonia	0.801	0.798	0.537	..	93	93	99	..
49 Croatia	0.795	0.790	0.517	..	92	92	96	..
52 Lithuania	0.789	0.785	0.531	..	92	92	98	..
57 Belarus	0.781	0.778	..	..	91	91	..	..
60 Bulgaria	0.772	0.769	..	..	90	90	..	..
62 Russian Federation	0.771	0.769	0.426	..	90	90	79	..
63 Latvia	0.771	0.770	**0.540**	..	90	90	100	..
64 Romania	0.770	0.767	0.405	..	89	89	75	..
69 Macedonia, TFYR	0.763	..	..	..	89	..	..	..
70 Georgia	0.762	..	..	..	88	..	..	..
73 Kazakhstan	0.754	..	..	..	88	..	..	..
78 Ukraine	0.744	0.740	0.421	..	86	86	78	..
90 Azerbaijan	0.722	..	..	..	84	..	..	..
93 Armenia	0.721	0.718	..	..	84	84	..	..
94 Albania	0.713	0.708	..	..	83	83	..	..

6 Comparisons of human development indices

HDI rank	Human development index (HDI) 1998	Gender-related development index (GDI) [a]	Gender empowerment measure (GEM) [a]	Human poverty index (HPI) [b] (%) 1998	HDI as % of highest value in group 1998	GDI as % of highest value in group [a]	GEM as % of highest value in group [a]	HPI as % of lowest value in group [b] 1998
98 Kyrgyzstan	0.706	..	..	..	82	..	..	..
100 Turkmenistan	0.704	..	..	..	82	..	..	..
102 Moldova, Rep. of	0.700	0.697	..	..	81	81	..	..
106 Uzbekistan	0.686	0.683	..	..	80	80	..	..
110 Tajikistan	0.663	0.659	..	..	77	77	..	..
OECD [c]	**0.893**	**0.889**	..	..	–	–	–	–
1 Canada	**0.935**	**0.932**	0.739	11.8	100	100	90	163
2 Norway	0.934	0.932	**0.825**	**7.3**	100	100	100	100
3 United States	0.929	0.927	0.708	15.8	99	99	86	218
4 Australia	0.929	0.927	0.715	12.2	99	100	87	168
5 Iceland	0.927	0.925	0.802	..	99	99	97	..
6 Sweden	0.926	0.923	0.794	7.6	99	99	96	104
7 Belgium	0.925	0.921	0.725	12.4	99	99	88	170
8 Netherlands	0.925	0.919	0.739	8.2	99	99	90	113
9 Japan	0.924	0.916	0.490	11.2	99	98	59	154
10 United Kingdom	0.918	0.914	0.656	14.6	98	98	79	201
11 Finland	0.917	0.913	0.757	8.6	98	98	92	119
12 France	0.917	0.914	..	11.1	98	98	..	154
13 Switzerland	0.915	0.910	0.683	..	98	98	83	..
14 Germany	0.911	0.905	0.756	10.4	97	97	92	143
15 Denmark	0.911	0.909	0.791	9.3	97	97	96	129
16 Austria	0.908	0.901	0.710	..	97	97	86	..
17 Luxembourg	0.908	0.895	..	10.5	97	96	..	145
18 Ireland	0.907	0.896	0.593	15.0	97	96	72	206
19 Italy	0.903	0.895	0.524	11.9	97	96	64	164
20 New Zealand	0.903	0.900	0.731	12.8	97	97	89	176
21 Spain	0.899	0.891	0.615	11.6	96	96	74	160
23 Israel	0.883	0.877	0.555	..	94	94	67	..
25 Greece	0.875	0.869	0.456	..	94	93	55	..
27 Malta	0.865	0.848	..	..	93	91	..	..
28 Portugal	0.864	0.858	0.618	..	92	92	75	..
31 Korea, Rep. of	0.854	0.847	0.323	..	91	91	39	..
34 Czech Republic	0.843	0.841	0.537	..	90	90	65	..
43 Hungary	0.817	0.813	0.487	..	87	87	59	..
44 Poland	0.814	0.811	0.512	..	87	87	62	..
55 Mexico	0.784	0.775	0.514	10.4	84	83	62	143
85 Turkey	0.732	0.726	0.321	16.4	78	78	39	226
World	**0.712**	**0.706**	..	..	–	–	–	–

Note: The highest value in a country group is determined on the basis of the fourth decimal place, not shown here. The highest value for each of the indices is presented in bold. For the human poverty index, the bold figure refers to the lowest value in the country group. The regional or group aggregates are as shown in tables 1 and 2.

a. Data refer to the latest available year. b. For the HPI, the lower the value, the better the country's performance. c. Includes Israel and Malta.

Source: Human Development Report Office calculations; see the technical note for details.

HDI rank	Human development index (HDI)					GDP per capita (1995 US$)				
	1975	1980	1985	1990	1998	1975	1980	1985	1990	1998
High human development										
1 Canada	0.865	0.880	0.902	0.925	0.935	14,535	16,423	17,850	19,160	20,458
2 Norway	0.853	0.872	0.883	0.895	0.934	19,022	23,595	27,113	28,840	36,806
3 United States	0.862	0.882	0.894	0.909	0.929	19,364	21,529	23,200	25,363	29,683
4 Australia	0.841	0.858	0.870	0.884	0.929	14,317	15,721	17,078	18,023	21,881
5 Iceland	0.857	0.879	0.888	0.906	0.927	17,445	22,609	23,977	26,510	29,488
6 Sweden	0.860	0.870	0.880	0.889	0.926	21,157	22,283	24,168	26,397	27,705
7 Belgium	0.841	0.858	0.871	0.890	0.925	18,620	21,653	22,417	25,744	28,790
8 Netherlands	0.857	0.869	0.883	0.897	0.925	18,584	20,443	21,256	24,009	28,154
9 Japan	0.849	0.874	0.888	0.904	0.924	23,296	27,672	31,588	38,713	42,081
10 United Kingdom	0.837	0.845	0.854	0.874	0.918	13,015	14,205	15,546	18,032	20,237
11 Finland	0.832	0.852	0.869	0.892	0.917	17,608	19,925	22,347	25,957	28,075
12 France	0.844	0.860	0.872	0.892	0.917	18,730	21,374	22,510	25,624	27,975
13 Switzerland	0.870	0.882	0.889	0.901	0.915	36,154	39,841	41,718	45,951	44,908
14 Germany	..	..	..	..	0.911	..	..	..	..	31,141
15 Denmark	0.859	0.867	0.876	0.883	0.911	22,984	25,695	29,332	31,143	37,449
16 Austria	0.836	0.850	0.863	0.885	0.908	18,857	22,200	23,828	27,261	30,869
17 Luxembourg	0.818	0.833	0.847	0.870	0.908	21,650	23,926	26,914	35,347	46,591
18 Ireland	0.805	0.818	0.833	0.857	0.907	8,605	10,044	10,944	13,907	23,422
19 Italy	0.825	0.843	0.853	0.875	0.903	11,969	14,621	15,707	18,141	19,574
20 New Zealand	0.843	0.851	0.862	0.871	0.903	14,005	13,961	15,416	15,026	16,427
21 Spain	0.814	0.834	0.850	0.870	0.899	10,040	10,512	10,943	13,481	15,644
22 Cyprus	..	..	..	..	0.886	3,619	6,334	7,818	10,405	12,857
23 Israel	0.802	0.823	0.841	0.856	0.883	10,620	11,412	12,093	13,566	15,978
24 Singapore	0.725	0.756	0.785	0.823	0.881	8,722	11,709	14,532	19,967	31,139
25 Greece	0.798	0.819	0.839	0.849	0.875	8,302	9,645	10,005	10,735	12,069
26 Hong Kong, China (SAR)	0.753	0.792	0.819	0.855	0.872	7,404	11,290	13,690	18,813	21,726
27 Malta	0.715	0.750	0.777	0.812	0.865	2,996	4,659	5,362	7,019	18,620
28 Portugal	0.733	0.756	0.783	0.813	0.864	6,024	7,193	7,334	9,696	11,672
29 Slovenia	..	..	..	0.840	0.861	..	..	..	9,659	10,637
30 Barbados	..	..	..	..	0.858	5,497	6,764	6,373	7,340	7,894
31 Korea, Rep. of	0.684	0.722	0.765	0.807	0.854	2,894	3,766	5,190	7,967	11,123
32 Brunei Darussalam	..	0.806	0.811	0.825	0.848	21,758	29,442	21,152	18,716	18,038
33 Bahamas	..	..	..	..	0.844	8,030	12,727	13,835	13,919	..
34 Czech Republic	..	..	0.824	0.830	0.843	..	..	4,884	5,270	5,142
35 Argentina	0.781	0.795	0.801	0.804	0.837	7,317	7,793	6,354	5,782	8,475
36 Kuwait	..	..	..	..	0.836	21,838	16,922	10,736	..	..
37 Antigua and Barbuda	..	..	..	..	0.833	..	4,057	5,164	6,980	8,559
38 Chile	0.702	0.736	0.753	0.780	0.826	1,842	2,425	2,345	2,987	4,784
39 Uruguay	0.753	0.773	0.777	0.797	0.825	4,092	4,962	3,964	4,611	6,029
40 Slovakia	..	..	0.806	0.812	0.825	..	..	3,630	3,825	3,822
41 Bahrain	..	0.749	0.778	0.797	0.820	..	12,022	8,797	8,551	9,260
42 Qatar	..	..	..	..	0.819	..	..	..	..	..
43 Hungary	0.772	0.787	0.799	0.798	0.817	3,581	4,199	4,637	4,857	4,920
44 Poland	..	0.775	0.779	0.785	0.814	..	2,932	2,819	2,900	3,877
45 United Arab Emirates	0.737	0.770	0.781	0.804	0.810	37,520	37,841	24,971	20,989	16,666
46 Estonia	..	0.804	0.812	0.806	0.801	..	4,022	4,451	4,487	3,951
Medium human development										
47 Saint Kitts and Nevis	..	..	..	..	0.798	..	2,569	3,123	4,479	6,716
48 Costa Rica	0.732	0.756	0.756	0.775	0.797	2,231	2,482	2,176	2,403	2,800
49 Croatia	..	..	..	0.786	0.795	..	..	..	5,432	4,846
50 Trinidad and Tobago	0.719	0.752	0.771	0.777	0.793	3,302	4,615	4,731	4,095	4,618

7 Trends in human
development
and per capita
income

		Human development index (HDI)					GDP per capita (1995 US$)				
HDI rank		1975	1980	1985	1990	1998	1975	1980	1985	1990	1998
51	Dominica	..	..	..	..	0.793	..	1,679	2,142	2,862	3,310
52	Lithuania	..	..	..	0.809	0.789	..	..	..	3,191	2,197
53	Seychelles	..	..	..	..	0.786	3,600	4,882	4,957	6,297	7,192
54	Grenada	..	..	..	..	0.785	..	1,709	2,111	2,819	3,347
55	Mexico	0.687	0.731	0.749	0.757	0.784	3,380	4,167	4,106	4,046	4,459
56	Cuba	..	..	..	..	0.783	..	..	..	..	..
57	Belarus	..	..	..	0.804	0.781	..	..	..	2,761	2,198
58	Belize	..	0.706	0.714	0.748	0.777	1,624	2,036	1,822	2,543	2,725
59	Panama	0.707	0.726	0.740	0.741	0.776	2,572	2,709	2,887	2,523	3,200
60	Bulgaria	..	0.760	0.781	0.782	0.772	..	1,329	1,553	1,716	1,372
61	Malaysia	0.620	0.663	0.696	0.725	0.772	1,750	2,348	2,644	3,164	4,251
62	Russian Federation	..	0.804	0.814	0.812	0.771	2,555	3,654	3,463	3,668	2,138
63	Latvia	..	0.785	0.797	0.797	0.771	2,382	2,797	3,210	3,703	2,328
64	Romania	0.750	0.783	0.789	0.771	0.770	1,201	1,643	1,872	1,576	1,310
65	Venezuela	0.714	0.729	0.736	0.755	0.770	4,195	3,995	3,357	3,353	3,499
66	Fiji	0.680	0.702	0.713	0.740	0.769	2,086	2,319	2,102	2,356	2,416
67	Suriname	..	..	..	..	0.766	888	930	801	787	..
68	Colombia	0.657	0.687	0.700	0.720	0.764	1,612	1,868	1,875	2,119	2,392
69	Macedonia, TFYR	..	..	..	..	0.763	..	..	..	..	1,349
70	Georgia	..	..	..	..	0.762	1,788	2,366	2,813	2,115	703
71	Mauritius	0.626	0.652	0.682	0.718	0.761	1,531	1,802	2,151	2,955	4,034
72	Libyan Arab Jamahiriya	..	..	..	..	0.760	..	..	..	..	..
73	Kazakhstan	..	..	..	0.784	0.754	..	..	..	2,073	1,281
74	Brazil	0.639	0.674	0.687	0.706	0.747	3,464	4,253	4,039	4,078	4,509
75	Saudi Arabia	0.588	0.647	0.673	0.709	0.747	9,658	11,553	7,437	7,100	6,516
76	Thailand	0.600	0.643	0.673	0.708	0.745	863	1,121	1,335	2,006	2,593
77	Philippines	0.648	0.682	0.685	0.713	0.744	974	1,166	967	1,064	1,092
78	Ukraine	..	..	..	0.793	0.744	..	..	..	1,979	837
79	Saint Vincent and the Grenadines	..	..	..	..	0.738	..	1,322	1,649	2,168	2,635
80	Peru	0.635	0.664	0.686	0.698	0.737	2,835	2,777	2,452	2,012	2,611
81	Paraguay	0.660	0.695	0.701	0.713	0.736	1,297	1,871	1,754	1,816	1,781
82	Lebanon	..	..	..	0.677	0.735	..	..	..	1,721	2,999
83	Jamaica	0.686	0.690	0.692	0.720	0.735	1,819	1,458	1,353	1,651	1,559
84	Sri Lanka	0.612	0.648	0.676	0.699	0.733	382	452	536	590	802
85	Turkey	0.590	0.614	0.651	0.683	0.732	1,898	1,959	2,197	2,589	3,167
86	Oman	..	..	..	..	0.730	3,516	3,509	5,607	5,581	..
87	Dominican Republic	0.611	0.648	0.678	0.686	0.729	1,179	1,325	1,325	1,366	1,799
88	Saint Lucia	..	..	..	..	0.728	..	2,076	2,150	3,542	3,907
89	Maldives	..	..	0.632	0.677	0.725	..	..	650	917	1,247
90	Azerbaijan	..	..	..	..	0.722	..	..	..	1,067	431
91	Ecuador	0.620	0.665	0.686	0.696	0.722	1,301	1,547	1,504	1,475	1,562
92	Jordan	..	..	..	..	0.721	993	1,715	1,824	1,436	1,491
93	Armenia	..	..	..	0.750	0.721	..	..	..	1,541	892
94	Albania	..	0.670	0.688	0.697	0.713	..	916	915	842	795
95	Samoa (Western)	..	..	0.667	..	0.711	..	974	915	931	998
96	Guyana	0.676	0.679	0.668	0.670	0.709	873	819	626	554	825
97	Iran, Islamic Rep. of	0.566	0.573	0.616	0.653	0.709	1,611	1,129	1,208	1,056	1,275
98	Kyrgyzstan	..	..	..	..	0.706	..	..	..	1,562	863
99	China	0.518	0.548	0.584	0.619	0.706	138	168	261	349	727
100	Turkmenistan	..	..	..	..	0.704	..	..	..	1,154	486

HDI rank	Human development index (HDI)					GDP per capita (1995 US$)				
	1975	1980	1985	1990	1998	1975	1980	1985	1990	1998
101 Tunisia	0.511	0.563	0.610	0.642	0.703	1,373	1,641	1,771	1,823	2,283
102 Moldova, Rep. of	..	0.717	0.739	0.757	0.700	..	1,453	1,572	1,776	614
103 South Africa	0.645	0.659	0.678	0.705	0.697	4,574	4,620	4,229	4,113	3,918
104 El Salvador	0.581	0.581	0.604	0.642	0.696	1,779	1,596	1,333	1,378	1,716
105 Cape Verde	..	..	0.572	0.611	0.688	..	..	1,039	1,120	1,354
106 Uzbekistan	..	..	..	0.690	0.686	..	..	..	1,338	1,007
107 Algeria	0.508	0.556	0.607	0.642	0.683	1,460	1,692	1,860	1,638	1,521
108 Viet Nam	..	..	0.580	0.602	0.671	..	..	183	206	331
109 Indonesia	0.465	0.526	0.578	0.619	0.670	385	504	603	778	972
110 Tajikistan	..	..	..	0.712	0.663	..	..	..	718	345
111 Syrian Arab Republic	0.530	0.571	0.605	0.624	0.660	907	1,071	1,036	956	1,209
112 Swaziland	0.505	0.536	0.564	0.613	0.655	1,073	1,046	1,035	1,446	1,409
113 Honduras	0.520	0.569	0.601	0.624	0.653	614	733	681	682	722
114 Bolivia	0.512	0.546	0.571	0.595	0.643	1,010	1,016	835	836	964
115 Namibia	..	0.607	0.624	0.644	0.632	..	2,384	2,034	1,948	2,133
116 Nicaragua	0.569	0.580	0.588	0.597	0.631	999	690	611	460	452
117 Mongolia	..	..	..	..	0.628	..	..	479	498	408
118 Vanuatu	..	..	..	..	0.623	..	1,426	1,672	1,596	1,403
119 Egypt	0.430	0.478	0.529	0.570	0.623	516	731	890	971	1,146
120 Guatemala	0.504	0.540	0.552	0.577	0.619	1,371	1,598	1,330	1,358	1,533
121 Solomon Islands	..	..	..	..	0.614	419	583	666	784	753
122 Botswana	0.492	0.554	0.611	0.651	0.593	1,132	1,678	2,274	3,124	3,611
123 Gabon	..	..	..	..	0.592	6,480	5,160	4,941	4,442	4,630
124 Morocco	0.426	0.470	0.505	0.537	0.589	956	1,114	1,173	1,310	1,388
125 Myanmar	..	..	..	..	0.585	..	..	..	..	..
126 Iraq	..	..	..	..	0.583	..	..	..	..	..
127 Lesotho	0.466	0.506	0.531	0.561	0.569	220	311	295	370	486
128 India	0.405	0.431	0.470	0.510	0.563	222	231	270	331	444
129 Ghana	0.434	0.465	0.480	0.510	0.556	411	394	328	352	399
130 Zimbabwe	0.519	0.546	0.606	0.599	0.555	686	638	662	706	703
131 Equatorial Guinea	..	..	..	..	0.555	..	..	352	333	1,049
132 São Tomé and Principe	..	..	..	..	0.547	..	..	..	365	337
133 Papua New Guinea	0.438	0.458	0.478	0.496	0.542	1,048	975	936	888	1,085
134 Cameroon	0.406	0.452	0.504	0.519	0.528	616	730	990	764	646
135 Pakistan	0.352	0.383	0.420	0.462	0.522	274	318	385	448	511
136 Cambodia	..	..	..	..	0.512	..	..	..	240	279
137 Comoros	..	0.465	0.488	0.496	0.510	..	499	544	516	403
138 Kenya	0.441	0.487	0.509	0.530	0.508	301	337	320	355	334
139 Congo	0.421	0.470	0.516	0.503	0.507	709	776	1,096	933	821
Low human development										
140 Lao People's Dem. Rep.	..	..	..	0.415	0.484	..	..	..	321	421
141 Madagascar	0.409	0.447	0.449	0.461	0.483	364	344	277	276	238
142 Bhutan	..	..	..	..	0.483	..	232	292	387	493
143 Sudan	0.342	0.368	0.390	0.406	0.477	237	229	210	198	296
144 Nepal	0.291	0.328	0.369	0.414	0.474	149	148	165	182	217
145 Togo	0.400	0.445	0.439	0.456	0.471	411	454	385	375	333
146 Bangladesh	0.329	0.348	0.381	0.412	0.461	203	220	253	274	348
147 Mauritania	0.344	0.372	0.392	0.400	0.451	549	557	511	438	478
148 Yemen	..	..	..	0.399	0.448	..	..	..	266	254
149 Djibouti	..	..	..	..	0.447	..	..	..	..	742
150 Haiti	..	..	..	0.436	0.440	500	607	527	481	370

HDI rank	Human development index (HDI)					GDP per capita (1995 US$)				
	1975	1980	1985	1990	1998	1975	1980	1985	1990	1998
151 Nigeria	0.317	0.373	0.388	0.411	0.439	301	314	230	258	256
152 Congo, Dem. Rep. of the	0.416	0.430	0.447	0.450	0.430	392	313	293	247	127
153 Zambia	0.444	0.456	0.470	0.451	0.420	641	551	483	450	388
154 Côte d'Ivoire	0.366	0.398	0.405	0.406	0.420	1,035	1,045	879	791	823
155 Senegal	0.309	0.327	0.352	0.376	0.416	609	557	561	572	581
156 Tanzania, U. Rep. of	..	..	..	0.406	0.415	..	..	..	175	173
157 Benin	0.285	0.322	0.349	0.358	0.411	339	362	387	345	394
158 Uganda	..	..	0.366	0.361	0.409	..	..	227	251	332
159 Eritrea	..	..	..	..	0.408	..	..	..	..	175
160 Angola	..	..	..	..	0.405	..	698	655	667	527
161 Gambia	0.269	0.301	0.331	0.352	0.396	356	376	378	374	353
162 Guinea	..	..	..	..	0.394	..	..	..	532	594
163 Malawi	0.312	0.336	0.347	0.348	0.385	157	169	161	152	166
164 Rwanda	..	..	..	..	0.382	233	321	312	292	227
165 Mali	0.248	0.277	0.293	0.314	0.380	268	301	271	249	267
166 Central African Republic	0.332	0.350	0.371	0.372	0.371	454	417	410	363	341
167 Chad	0.253	0.253	0.296	0.323	0.367	252	176	235	228	230
168 Mozambique	..	0.302	0.297	0.328	0.341	..	166	115	144	188
169 Guinea-Bissau	0.250	0.252	0.283	0.307	0.331	226	168	206	223	173
170 Burundi	0.281	0.306	0.334	0.339	0.321	162	176	198	206	147
171 Ethiopia	..	..	0.265	0.287	0.309	..	..	91	100	110
172 Burkina Faso	0.227	0.247	0.270	0.280	0.303	196	207	224	225	259
173 Niger	0.236	0.259	0.257	0.273	0.293	298	328	242	235	215
174 Sierra Leone	..	..	..	..	0.252	316	320	279	279	150
All developing countries	..	..	..	..	0.642	720	1,170	1,520	2,170	3,260
Least developed countries	..	..	..	..	0.435	..	..	690	890	1,050
Arab States	..	..	..	..	0.635	1,480	2,670	2,990	3,850	4,520
East Asia	..	..	..	..	0.716	290	540	960	1,670	3,570
East Asia (excluding China)	..	..	..	..	0.849	1,580	3,050	4,870	9,130	13,790
Latin America and the Caribbean	..	..	..	..	0.758	2,200	3,650	4,090	5,040	6,470
South Asia	..	..	..	..	0.560	510	720	990	1,450	2,110
South Asia (excluding India)	..	..	..	..	0.550	740	930	1,260	1,630	2,210
South-East Asia and the Pacific	..	..	..	..	0.691	590	1,070	1,370	2,220	3,150
Sub-Saharan Africa	..	..	..	..	0.464	780	1,070	1,170	1,450	1,520
Eastern Europe and the CIS	..	..	..	..	0.777	..	..	..	7,500	5,620
OECD	..	..	..	..	0.893	5,390	8,690	11,210	16,040	20,360
High human development	..	..	..	..	0.908	5,640	9,130	11,790	16,950	21,770
Medium human development	..	..	..	..	0.673	860	1,430	1,900	2,660	3,460
Low human development	..	..	..	..	0.421	420	580	660	850	980
High income	..	..	..	..	0.920	6,200	10,040	13,060	18,770	23,900
Medium income	..	..	..	..	0.750	2,160	3,590	4,300	5,630	6,110
Low income	..	..	..	..	0.602	350	560	830	1,300	2,220
World	..	..	..	..	0.712	1,880	2,970	3,740	5,150	6,400

Source: Columns 1-5: Human Development Report Office calculations; see the technical note for details; columns 6-10: calculated on the basis of GDP and population data from World Bank 2000b; aggregates calculated for the Human Development Report Office by the World Bank.

8 Trends in human development and economic growth

HDI rank	Change in human development index (HDI)				GDP per capita (1995 US$)						Average annual rate of change (%)
	1975-80	1980-85	1985-90	1990-98	1975	Lowest value during 1975-98[a]	Year	Highest value during 1975-98[a]	Year	1998	1975-98[a]
High human development											
1 Canada	0.016	0.022	0.022	0.010	14,535	14,535	1975	20,458	1998	20,458	1.5
2 Norway	0.019	0.011	0.012	0.039	19,022	19,022	1975	36,806	1998	36,806	2.9
3 United States	0.020	0.013	0.014	0.020	19,364	19,364	1975	29,683	1998	29,683	1.9
4 Australia	0.017	0.012	0.013	0.045	14,317	14,317	1975	21,881	1998	21,881	1.9
5 Iceland	0.022	0.009	0.018	0.020	17,445	17,445	1975	29,488	1998	29,488	2.3
6 Sweden	0.010	0.010	0.009	0.037	21,157	20,889	1977	27,705	1998	27,705	1.2
7 Belgium	0.017	0.013	0.019	0.035	18,620	18,620	1975	28,790	1998	28,790	1.9
8 Netherlands	0.012	0.014	0.014	0.028	18,584	18,584	1975	28,154	1998	28,154	1.8
9 Japan	0.024	0.015	0.016	0.020	23,296	23,296	1975	43,412	1997	42,081	2.6
10 United Kingdom	0.008	0.009	0.020	0.044	13,015	13,015	1975	20,237	1998	20,237	1.9
11 Finland	0.019	0.017	0.023	0.025	17,608	17,473	1977	28,075	1998	28,075	2.0
12 France	0.015	0.012	0.021	0.024	18,730	18,730	1975	27,975	1998	27,975	1.8
13 Switzerland	0.011	0.007	0.012	0.014	36,154	35,977	1976	45,951	1990	44,908	0.9
14 Germany	..	..	..	..	28,594 [b]	28,472	1993	31,141	1998	31,141	1.2
15 Denmark	0.008	0.009	0.007	0.028	22,984	22,984	1975	37,449	1998	37,449	2.1
16 Austria	0.014	0.014	0.022	0.023	18,857	18,857	1975	30,869	1998	30,869	2.2
17 Luxembourg	0.015	0.014	0.023	0.038	21,650	21,650	1975	46,591	1998	46,591	3.4
18 Ireland	0.013	0.015	0.024	0.050	8,605	8,587	1976	23,422	1998	23,422	4.4
19 Italy	0.018	0.010	0.022	0.028	11,969	11,969	1975	19,574	1998	19,574	2.2
20 New Zealand	0.008	0.011	0.009	0.032	14,005	13,504	1977	16,690	1997	16,427	0.7
21 Spain	0.019	0.016	0.020	0.030	10,040	10,040	1975	15,644	1998	15,644	1.9
22 Cyprus	..	..	..	..	3,619	3,619	1975	12,857	1998	12,857	5.7
23 Israel	0.021	0.018	0.015	0.027	10,620	10,288	1977	15,978	1998	15,978	1.8
24 Singapore	0.031	0.029	0.038	0.058	8,722	8,722	1975	31,276	1997	31,139	5.7
25 Greece	0.021	0.020	0.010	0.026	8,302	8,302	1975	12,069	1998	12,069	1.6
26 Hong Kong, China (SAR)	0.039	0.027	0.036	0.017	7,404	7,404	1975	23,554	1997	21,726	4.8
27 Malta	0.035	0.027	0.035	0.053	2,996	2,996	1975	18,620	1998	18,620	8.3
28 Portugal	0.023	0.027	0.030	0.051	6,024	6,024	1975	11,672	1998	11,672	2.9
29 Slovenia	..	..	..	0.021	9,659 [c]	8,331	1992	10,637	1998	10,637	1.2
30 Barbados	..	..	..	..	5,497	5,474	1976	7,894	1998	7,894	1.6
31 Korea, Rep. of	0.038	0.043	0.042	0.047	2,894	2,894	1975	11,925	1997	11,123	6.0
32 Brunei Darussalam	..	0.005	0.014	0.023	21,758	17,654	1994	32,732	1979	18,038	-0.8
33 Bahamas	..	..	..	..	8,030	8,030	1975	14,087	1989	12,444 [d]	2.2
34 Czech Republic	..	..	0.007	0.013	4,861 [e]	4,651	1993	5,335	1989	5,142	0.4
35 Argentina	0.014	0.006	0.003	0.034	7,317	5,782	1990	8,475	1998	8,475	0.6
36 Kuwait	..	..	..	..	21,838	9,913	1988	22,618	1979	16,756 [d]	-1.3
37 Antigua and Barbuda	..	..	..	..	3,296 [f]	3,296	1977	8,559	1998	8,559	4.6
38 Chile	0.034	0.017	0.027	0.046	1,842	1,842	1975	4,784	1998	4,784	4.2
39 Uruguay	0.020	0.005	0.020	0.028	4,092	3,932	1984	6,029	1998	6,029	1.7
40 Slovakia	..	..	0.006	0.013	3,529 [e]	2,912	1993	3,919	1989	3,822	0.6
41 Bahrain	..	0.029	0.019	0.023	12,022 [g]	8,257	1987	12,022	1980	9,260	-1.4
42 Qatar	..	..	..	..	..	..	..	..	..	..	..
43 Hungary	0.016	0.012	-0.001	0.019	3,581	3,581	1975	5,018	1989	4,920	1.4
44 Poland	..	0.004	0.006	0.029	2,932 [g]	2,468	1982	3,877	1998	3,877	1.6
45 United Arab Emirates	0.032	0.011	0.023	0.006	37,520	16,666	1998	37,841	1980	16,666	-3.5
46 Estonia	..	0.008	-0.006	-0.005	4,022 [g]	3,064	1994	4,807	1989	3,951	-0.1
Medium human development											
47 Saint Kitts and Nevis	..	..	..	..	2,074 [f]	2,074	1977	6,716	1998	6,716	5.8
48 Costa Rica	0.024	0.000	0.018	0.022	2,231	2,116	1983	2,800	1998	2,800	1.0
49 Croatia	..	..	..	0.008	5,432 [c]	3,480	1993	5,432	1990	4,846	-1.4
50 Trinidad and Tobago	0.032	0.019	0.006	0.016	3,302	3,302	1975	5,148	1982	4,618	1.5

8 Trends in human development and economic growth

	Change in human development index (HDI)				GDP per capita (1995 US$)						
HDI rank	1975-80	1980-85	1985-90	1990-98	1975	Lowest value during 1975-98[a]	Year	Highest value during 1975-98[a]	Year	1998	Average annual rate of change (%) 1975-98[a]
51 Dominica	..	..	..	..	1,649 [f]	1,482	1979	3,310	1998	3,310	3.4
52 Lithuania	..	..	..	-0.020	2,606 [h]	1,792	1994	3,191	1990	2,197	-1.5
53 Seychelles	..	..	..	..	3,600	3,600	1975	7,192	1998	7,192	3.1
54 Grenada	..	..	..	..	1,517 [f]	1,517	1977	3,347	1998	3,347	3.8
55 Mexico	0.044	0.018	0.008	0.027	3,380	3,380	1975	4,459	1998	4,459	1.2
56 Cuba	..	..	..	..	..	..	..	..	..	..	..
57 Belarus	..	..	..	-0.024	2,545 [h]	1,772	1995	2,831	1989	2,198	-1.3
58 Belize	..	0.008	0.035	0.028	1,624	1,589	1976	2,743	1993	2,725	2.3
59 Panama	0.018	0.014	0.002	0.035	2,572	2,382	1989	3,200	1998	3,200	1.0
60 Bulgaria	..	0.020	0.001	-0.010	1,329 [g]	1,317	1997	1,895	1988	1,372	0.2
61 Malaysia	0.043	0.033	0.028	0.047	1,750	1,750	1975	4,705	1997	4,251	3.9
62 Russian Federation	..	0.010	-0.002	-0.041	2,555	2,138	1998	3,796	1989	2,138	-0.8
63 Latvia	..	0.012	-0.001	-0.026	2,382	1,900	1993	3,731	1989	2,328	-0.1
64 Romania	0.033	0.006	-0.018	-0.001	1,201	1,201	1975	1,909	1986	1,310	0.4
65 Venezuela	0.014	0.008	0.019	0.015	4,195	3,244	1989	4,473	1977	3,499	-0.8
66 Fiji	0.022	0.011	0.027	0.029	2,086	2,045	1987	2,603	1996	2,416	0.6
67 Suriname	..	..	..	..	888	647	1987	1,050	1978	818 [d]	-0.4
68 Colombia	0.030	0.013	0.020	0.044	1,612	1,612	1975	2,423	1997	2,392	1.7
69 Macedonia, TFYR	..	..	..	..	1,350 [i]	1,193	1994	1,350	1993	1,349	0.0
70 Georgia	..	..	..	..	1,788	545	1994	2,813	1985	703	-4.0
71 Mauritius	0.026	0.031	0.036	0.042	1,531	1,531	1975	4,034	1998	4,034	4.3
72 Libyan Arab Jamahiriya	..	..	..	..	..	..	..	..	..	..	..
73 Kazakhstan	..	..	..	-0.030	2,187 [h]	1,240	1995	2,235	1988	1,281	-4.7
74 Brazil	0.034	0.013	0.019	0.041	3,464	3,464	1975	4,562	1997	4,509	1.2
75 Saudi Arabia	0.059	0.026	0.036	0.038	9,658	6,516	1998	11,553	1980	6,516	-1.7
76 Thailand	0.043	0.030	0.036	0.036	863	863	1975	2,957	1996	2,593	4.9
77 Philippines	0.034	0.004	0.027	0.031	974	967	1985	1,195	1982	1,092	0.5
78 Ukraine	..	..	..	-0.049	2,007 [h]	837	1998	2,119	1989	837	-7.6
79 Saint Vincent and the Grenadines	..	..	..	..	1,155 [f]	1,155	1977	2,635	1998	2,635	4.0
80 Peru	0.029	0.022	0.011	0.039	2,835	2,012	1990	2,903	1981	2,611	-0.4
81 Paraguay	0.034	0.006	0.012	0.024	1,297	1,297	1975	1,971	1981	1,781	1.4
82 Lebanon	..	..	..	0.058	2,462 [j]	1,387	1989	2,999	1998	2,999	2.0
83 Jamaica	0.003	0.002	0.028	0.015	1,819	1,353	1985	1,819	1975	1,559	-0.7
84 Sri Lanka	0.036	0.029	0.023	0.034	382	382	1975	802	1998	802	3.3
85 Turkey	0.024	0.037	0.032	0.049	1,898	1,898	1975	3,167	1998	3,167	2.3
86 Oman	..	..	..	..	3,516	3,492	1979	5,668	1995	5,668 [d]	2.4
87 Dominican Republic	0.037	0.030	0.009	0.043	1,179	1,179	1975	1,799	1998	1,799	1.9
88 Saint Lucia	..	..	..	..	2,076 [g]	1,853	1982	3,907	1998	3,907	3.6
89 Maldives	..	..	0.045	0.048	650 [k]	650	1985	1,247	1998	1,247	5.1
90 Azerbaijan	..	..	..	..	1,336 [h]	377	1995	1,336	1987	431	-9.8
91 Ecuador	0.046	0.021	0.010	0.026	1,301	1,301	1975	1,584	1997	1,562	0.8
92 Jordan	..	..	..	..	993	993	1975	1,880	1986	1,491	1.8
93 Armenia	..	..	..	-0.029	1,541 [c]	687	1993	1,541	1990	892	-6.6
94 Albania	..	0.018	0.009	0.017	916 [g]	575	1992	958	1982	795	-0.8
95 Samoa (Western)	..	..	..	..	949 [l]	856	1994	1,045	1979	998	0.3
96 Guyana	0.003	-0.011	0.001	0.039	873	554	1990	882	1976	825	-0.2
97 Iran, Islamic Rep. of	0.007	0.043	0.037	0.056	1,611	953	1988	1,825	1976	1,275	-1.0
98 Kyrgyzstan	..	..	..	..	1,311 [m]	737	1995	1,562	1990	863	-3.4
99 China	0.030	0.036	0.034	0.087	138	134	1976	727	1998	727	7.5
100 Turkmenistan	..	..	..	..	1,162 [h]	469	1997	1,259	1988	486	-7.6

HDI rank	Change in human development index (HDI)				GDP per capita (1995 US$)						Average annual rate of change (%)
	1975-80	1980-85	1985-90	1990-98	1975	Lowest value during 1975-98[a]	Year	Highest value during 1975-98[a]	Year	1998	1975-98[a]
101 Tunisia	0.052	0.047	0.032	0.061	1,373	1,373	1975	2,283	1998	2,283	2.2
102 Moldova, Rep. of	..	0.022	0.018	-0.057	1,453[g]	614	1998	1,825	1989	614	-4.7
103 South Africa	0.014	0.019	0.027	-0.009	4,574	3,788	1993	4,868	1981	3,918	-0.7
104 El Salvador	0.000	0.023	0.037	0.055	1,779	1,313	1982	1,955	1978	1,716	-0.2
105 Cape Verde	..	..	0.040	0.076	792[n]	792	1981	1,354	1998	1,354	3.2
106 Uzbekistan	..	..	..	-0.003	1,263[h]	975	1996	1,343	1989	1,007	-2.0
107 Algeria	0.048	0.051	0.035	0.041	1,460	1,448	1994	1,860	1985	1,521	0.2
108 Viet Nam	..	..	0.022	0.069	180[e]	180	1984	331	1998	331	4.4
109 Indonesia	0.062	0.052	0.040	0.051	385	385	1975	1,139	1997	972	4.1
110 Tajikistan	..	..	..	-0.050	788[m]	321	1996	812	1988	345	-6.7
111 Syrian Arab Republic	0.042	0.034	0.018	0.036	907	907	1975	1,209	1998	1,209	1.3
112 Swaziland	0.031	0.028	0.049	0.042	1,073	975	1979	1,446	1990	1,409	1.2
113 Honduras	0.049	0.032	0.022	0.029	614	614	1975	754	1979	722	0.7
114 Bolivia	0.034	0.026	0.024	0.048	1,010	797	1986	1,073	1978	964	-0.2
115 Namibia	..	0.018	0.020	-0.012	2,384[g]	1,948	1990	2,384	1980	2,133	-0.6
116 Nicaragua	0.011	0.008	0.008	0.035	999	419	1993	1,069	1977	452	-3.4
117 Mongolia	..	..	..	0.018	417[n]	374	1993	525	1989	408	-0.1
118 Vanuatu	..	..	..	..	1,647[o]	1,384	1992	1,683	1984	1,403	-0.8
119 Egypt	0.047	0.051	0.041	0.053	516	516	1975	1,146	1998	1,146	3.5
120 Guatemala	0.036	0.012	0.024	0.042	1,371	1,299	1986	1,598	1980	1,533	0.5
121 Solomon Islands	..	..	..	..	419	419	1975	866	1996	753	2.6
122 Botswana	0.062	0.057	0.040	-0.058	1,132	1,132	1975	3,611	1998	3,611	5.2
123 Gabon	..	..	..	..	6,480	3,798	1987	8,510	1976	4,630	-1.5
124 Morocco	0.044	0.035	0.032	0.052	956	956	1975	1,388	1998	1,388	1.6
125 Myanmar	..	..	..	..	..	..	..	..	..	..	..
126 Iraq	..	..	..	..	..	..	..	..	..	..	..
127 Lesotho	0.040	0.025	0.031	0.008	220	220	1975	515	1997	486	3.5
128 India	0.026	0.039	0.039	0.054	222	221	1976	444	1998	444	3.0
129 Ghana	0.031	0.015	0.031	0.046	411	309	1983	419	1978	399	-0.1
130 Zimbabwe	0.027	0.060	-0.008	-0.044	686	575	1978	725	1991	703	0.1
131 Equatorial Guinea	..	..	..	..	352[k]	322	1991	1,049	1998	1,049	8.8
132 São Tomé and Principe	..	..	..	..	380[m]	337	1997	380	1986	337	-1.0
133 Papua New Guinea	0.019	0.020	0.018	0.046	1,048	888	1990	1,219	1994	1,085	0.2
134 Cameroon	0.046	0.052	0.014	0.010	616	566	1976	1,028	1986	646	0.2
135 Pakistan	0.031	0.037	0.042	0.060	274	274	1975	512	1996	511	2.7
136 Cambodia	..	..	..	0.046	225[h]	225	1987	287	1996	279	2.0
137 Comoros	..	0.022	0.008	0.014	499[g]	403	1998	545	1984	403	-1.2
138 Kenya	0.046	0.022	0.021	-0.023	301	296	1976	355	1990	334	0.5
139 Congo	0.049	0.046	-0.012	0.004	709	615	1977	1,141	1984	821	0.6
Low human development											
140 Lao People's Dem. Rep.	..	..	..	0.069	275[j]	275	1988	421	1998	421	4.3
141 Madagascar	0.038	0.001	0.013	0.022	364	235	1996	364	1975	238	-1.8
142 Bhutan	..	..	..	..	232[g]	232	1980	493	1998	493	4.3
143 Sudan	0.027	0.022	0.016	0.071	237	198	1990	296	1998	296	1.0
144 Nepal	0.038	0.041	0.044	0.060	149	148	1980	218	1997	217	1.6
145 Togo	0.045	-0.005	0.017	0.014	411	271	1993	454	1980	333	-0.9
146 Bangladesh	0.019	0.033	0.031	0.049	203	203	1975	348	1998	348	2.4
147 Mauritania	0.028	0.020	0.008	0.051	549	432	1992	582	1976	478	-0.6
148 Yemen	..	..	..	0.050	266[c]	231	1994	266	1990	254	-0.6
149 Djibouti	..	..	..	..	1,032[b]	742	1998	1,032	1991	742	-4.6
150 Haiti	..	..	..	0.003	500	360	1994	607	1980	370	-1.3

	Change in human development index (HDI)				GDP per capita (1995 US$)						
HDI rank	1975-80	1980-85	1985-90	1990-98	1975	Lowest value during 1975-98 [a]	Year	Highest value during 1975-98 [a]	Year	1998	Average annual rate of change (%) 1975-98 [a]
151 Nigeria	0.056	0.014	0.024	0.028	301	216	1984	328	1977	256	-0.7
152 Congo, Dem. Rep. of the	0.013	0.017	0.004	-0.020	392	127	1998	392	1975	127	-4.8
153 Zambia	0.013	0.014	-0.019	-0.031	641	386	1995	659	1976	388	-2.2
154 Côte d'Ivoire	0.032	0.007	0.001	0.014	1,035	711	1994	1,238	1978	823	-1.0
155 Senegal	0.018	0.026	0.023	0.040	609	528	1993	645	1976	581	-0.2
156 Tanzania, U. Rep. of	..	..	..	0.008	170 [j]	157	1992	177	1991	173	0.2
157 Benin	0.037	0.027	0.009	0.053	339	334	1976	394	1998	394	0.7
158 Uganda	..	..	-0.005	0.047	236 [p]	223	1986	332	1998	332	2.2
159 Eritrea	..	..	..	..	158 [q]	150	1993	175	1998	175	1.8
160 Angola	..	..	..	..	698 [g]	428	1994	708	1988	527	-1.6
161 Gambia	0.032	0.030	0.021	0.044	356	341	1996	395	1984	353	0.0
162 Guinea	..	..	..	..	501 [m]	501	1986	594	1998	594	1.4
163 Malawi	0.024	0.011	0.001	0.037	157	135	1994	173	1979	166	0.2
164 Rwanda	..	..	..	..	233	154	1994	333	1983	227	-0.1
165 Mali	0.028	0.016	0.022	0.066	268	240	1988	322	1979	267	0.0
166 Central African Republic	0.018	0.022	0.001	-0.001	454	317	1993	475	1977	341	-1.2
167 Chad	0.000	0.043	0.027	0.044	252	173	1981	256	1977	230	-0.4
168 Mozambique	..	-0.005	0.031	0.013	166 [g]	111	1986	188	1998	188	0.7
169 Guinea-Bissau	0.002	0.031	0.024	0.024	226	168	1980	246	1997	173	-1.1
170 Burundi	0.025	0.028	0.005	-0.017	162	143	1997	211	1991	147	-0.4
171 Ethiopia	..	..	0.021	0.023	117 [n]	85	1992	121	1983	110	-0.4
172 Burkina Faso	0.020	0.023	0.011	0.023	196	196	1975	259	1998	259	1.2
173 Niger	0.022	-0.002	0.016	0.021	298	205	1997	347	1979	215	-1.4
174 Sierra Leone	..	..	..	..	316	150	1998	320	1980	150	-3.2

a. Data may refer to a period shorter than that specified where data are not available for all years. b. Data refer to 1991. c. Data refer to 1990. d. Data refer to 1995. e. Data refer to 1984. f. Data refer to 1977. g. Data refer to 1980. h. Data refer to 1987. i. Data refer to 1993. j. Data refer to 1988. k. Data refer to 1985. l. Data refer to 1978. m. Data refer to 1986. n. Data refer to 1981. o. Data refer to 1979. p. Data refer to 1982. q. Data refer to 1992.

Source: Columns 1-4: Human Development Report Office calculations; see the technical note for details; columns: 5-11: calculated on the basis of GDP and population data from World Bank 2000b.

HDI rank	Life expectancy at birth (years)		Infant mortality rate (per 1,000 live births)		Under-five mortality rate (per 1,000 live births)		People not expected to survive to age 60 (%)[a]	Maternal mortality ratio reported (per 100,000 live births)[b]
	1970-75	1995-2000	1970	1998	1970	1998	1995-2000	1990-98
High human development								
1 Canada	73.2	79.0	19	6	23	6	9.3	..
2 Norway	74.4	78.1	13	4	15	4	9.1	6
3 United States	71.3	76.7	20	7	26	8	12.6	8
4 Australia	71.7	78.3	17	5	20	5	8.9	..
5 Iceland	74.3	79.0	13	5	14	5	8.4	..
6 Sweden	74.7	78.6	11	4	15	4	8.7	5
7 Belgium	71.4	77.2	21	6	29	6	10.1	..
8 Netherlands	74.0	77.9	13	5	15	5	9.3	7
9 Japan	73.3	80.0	14	4	21	4	8.2	8
10 United Kingdom	72.0	77.2	18	6	23	6	9.8	7
11 Finland	70.7	76.8	13	4	16	5	11.3	6
12 France	72.4	78.1	18	5	24	5	11.3	10
13 Switzerland	73.8	78.7	15	5	18	5	9.8	5
14 Germany	71.0	77.2	22	5	26	5	10.7	8
15 Denmark	73.6	75.7	14	5	19	5	12.8	10
16 Austria	70.6	77.0	26	5	33	5	10.9	..
17 Luxembourg	70.7	76.7	19	5	26	5	10.6	0
18 Ireland	71.3	76.4	20	6	27	7	10.0	6
19 Italy	72.1	78.2	30	6	33	6	9.0	7
20 New Zealand	71.7	76.9	17	5	20	6	11.1	15
21 Spain	72.9	78.0	27	6	34	6	10.1	6
22 Cyprus	71.4	77.8	29	8	33	9	10.0	0
23 Israel	71.6	77.8	24	6	27	6	9.3	5
24 Singapore	69.5	77.1	22	4	27	5	10.6	6
25 Greece	72.3	78.1	38	6	54	7	8.9	1
26 Hong Kong, China (SAR)	72.0	78.5	..	..	..	..	9.2	..
27 Malta	70.6	77.2	25	6	32	7	8.4	..
28 Portugal	68.0	75.3	53	8	62	9	12.6	8
29 Slovenia	69.8	74.5	25	5	29	5	14.6	11
30 Barbados	69.4	76.4	40	13	54	15	11.6	0
31 Korea, Rep. of	62.6	72.4	43	5	54	5	16.7	20
32 Brunei Darussalam	68.3	75.5	58	8	78	9	11.0	0
33 Bahamas	66.6	73.8	38	18	49	21	17.5	..
34 Czech Republic	70.0	73.9	21	5	24	6	14.2	9
35 Argentina	67.1	72.9	59	19	71	22	16.5	38
36 Kuwait	67.3	75.9	49	12	59	13	10.3	5
37 Antigua and Barbuda	..	..	..	17	..	20	..	150
38 Chile	63.4	74.9	77	11	96	12	13.8	23
39 Uruguay	68.7	73.9	48	16	57	19	15.5	21
40 Slovakia	70.0	73.0	25	9	29	10	16.4	9
41 Bahrain	63.5	72.9	67	16	93	20	14.6	46
42 Qatar	62.6	71.7	71	15	93	18	15.6	10
43 Hungary	69.3	70.9	36	10	39	11	21.6	15
44 Poland	70.5	72.5	32	10	36	11	17.3	8
45 United Arab Emirates	62.5	74.9	61	9	83	10	11.0	3
46 Estonia	70.5	68.7	21	18	26	22	23.8	50
Medium human development								
47 Saint Kitts and Nevis	..	..	..	30	..	37	..	130
48 Costa Rica	67.9	76.0	58	14	77	16	11.6	29
49 Croatia	69.6	72.6	34	8	42	9	16.4	12
50 Trinidad and Tobago	65.9	73.8	49	16	57	18	15.0	..

. . . TO LEAD A LONG AND HEALTHY LIFE . . .

HDI rank	Life expectancy at birth (years)		Infant mortality rate (per 1,000 live births)		Under-five mortality rate (per 1,000 live births)		People not expected to survive to age 60 (%) [a]	Maternal mortality ratio reported (per 100,000 live births) [b]
	1970-75	1995-2000	1970	1998	1970	1998	1995-2000	1990-98
51 Dominica	..	..	..	17	..	20	..	65
52 Lithuania	71.3	69.9	23	19	28	23	23.3	18
53 Seychelles	..	..	..	14	..	18	..	..
54 Grenada	..	..	..	23	..	28	..	0
55 Mexico	62.4	72.2	79	28	110	34	18.9	48
56 Cuba	70.7	75.7	34	7	43	8	13.4	27
57 Belarus	71.5	68.0	22	22	27	27	26.1	22
58 Belize	67.6	74.7	56	35	77	43	13.7	140
59 Panama	66.2	73.6	48	18	71	20	15.1	85
60 Bulgaria	71.2	71.1	28	14	32	17	18.3	15
61 Malaysia	63.0	72.0	46	9	63	10	16.1	39
62 Russian Federation	68.2	66.6	29	21	36	25	29.7	50
63 Latvia	70.1	68.4	21	18	26	22	25.0	45
64 Romania	69.0	70.0	46	21	57	24	20.7	41
65 Venezuela	65.7	72.4	47	21	61	25	17.0	65
66 Fiji	65.1	72.7	50	19	61	23	14.6	38
67 Suriname	64.0	70.1	51	28	68	35	19.9	110
68 Colombia	61.6	70.4	70	25	113	30	20.7	80
69 Macedonia, TFYR	67.5	73.1	85	23	120	27	14.0	11
70 Georgia	69.2	72.7	36	19	46	23	17.5	70
71 Mauritius	62.9	71.4	64	19	86	23	18.7	50
72 Libyan Arab Jamahiriya	52.9	70.0	105	20	160	24	19.8	75
73 Kazakhstan	64.4	67.6	50	36	66	43	25.8	70
74 Brazil	59.6	66.8	95	36	135	42	26.8	160
75 Saudi Arabia	53.9	71.4	118	22	185	26	16.8	..
76 Thailand	59.6	68.8	74	30	102	37	25.8	44
77 Philippines	57.8	68.3	60	32	90	44	21.8	170
78 Ukraine	70.1	68.8	22	18	27	22	24.1	25
79 Saint Vincent and the Grenadines	..	..	..	20	..	23	..	43
80 Peru	55.5	68.3	115	43	178	54	23.0	270
81 Paraguay	65.9	69.6	57	27	76	33	19.7	190
82 Lebanon	65.0	69.9	40	29	50	35	19.0	100
83 Jamaica	69.0	74.8	47	10	62	11	13.3	120
84 Sri Lanka	65.0	73.1	65	17	100	19	15.3	60
85 Turkey	57.9	69.0	150	37	201	42	20.1	130
86 Oman	49.0	70.9	126	15	200	18	17.7	19
87 Dominican Republic	59.8	70.6	91	43	128	51	19.0	230
88 Saint Lucia	..	..	..	18	..	21	..	30
89 Maldives	51.4	64.5	157	62	255	87	27.6	350
90 Azerbaijan	69.0	69.9	41	36	53	46	22.1	37
91 Ecuador	58.8	69.5	94	30	140	39	21.5	160
92 Jordan	56.6	70.2	77	30	107	36	19.5	41
93 Armenia	72.5	70.5	24	25	30	30	19.8	35
94 Albania	67.7	72.8	68	30	82	37	13.9	..
95 Samoa (Western)	58.5	71.4	106	22	160	27	17.7	..
96 Guyana	60.0	64.4	81	58	101	79	28.2	190
97 Iran, Islamic Rep. of	55.9	69.2	133	29	208	33	21.3	37
98 Kyrgyzstan	63.1	67.6	111	56	146	66	25.4	65
99 China	63.2	69.8	85	38	120	47	18.0	65
100 Turkmenistan	60.7	65.4	82	53	120	72	27.6	110

HDI rank	Life expectancy at birth (years)		Infant mortality rate (per 1,000 live births)		Under-five mortality rate (per 1,000 live births)		People not expected to survive to age 60 (%) [a]	Maternal mortality ratio reported (per 100,000 live births) [b]
	1970-75	1995-2000	1970	1998	1970	1998	1995-2000	1990-98
101 Tunisia	55.6	69.5	135	25	201	32	19.6	70
102 Moldova, Rep. of	64.8	67.5	46	28	61	35	25.7	42
103 South Africa	53.6	54.7	80	60	115	83	50.5	..
104 El Salvador	58.2	69.1	105	30	160	34	23.4	160
105 Cape Verde	57.5	68.9	87	54	123	73	21.3	55
106 Uzbekistan	64.2	67.5	66	45	90	58	25.1	21
107 Algeria	54.5	68.9	123	35	192	40	18.5	220
108 Viet Nam	50.3	67.4	112	31	157	42	23.9	160
109 Indonesia	49.3	65.1	104	40	172	56	26.7	450
110 Tajikistan	63.4	67.2	78	55	111	74	25.3	65
111 Syrian Arab Republic	57.0	68.9	90	26	129	32	20.7	110
112 Swaziland	47.3	60.2	140	64	209	90	34.5	230
113 Honduras	54.0	69.4	116	33	170	44	22.8	220
114 Bolivia	46.7	61.4	144	66	243	85	32.8	390
115 Namibia	48.7	52.4	104	57	155	74	52.4	230
116 Nicaragua	55.1	67.9	113	39	165	48	24.3	150
117 Mongolia	53.8	65.9	105	64 [c]	150	82 [c]	25.9	150
118 Vanuatu	54.0	67.4	107	38	160	49	23.1	..
119 Egypt	52.1	66.3	157	51	235	69	23.0	170
120 Guatemala	53.7	64.0	115	41	168	52	31.1	190
121 Solomon Islands	62.0	71.7	71	22	99	26	16.2	550
122 Botswana	53.2	47.4	98	38	139	48	68.3	330
123 Gabon	45.0	52.4	140	85	232	144	48.6	600
124 Morocco	52.9	66.6	120	57	187	70	23.0	230
125 Myanmar	49.8	60.1	122	80	179	113	33.4	230
126 Iraq	57.0	62.4	90	103	127	125	31.5	..
127 Lesotho	49.5	56.0	125	94	190	136	43.3	..
128 India	50.3	62.6	130	69	206	105	29.7	410
129 Ghana	50.0	60.0	111	67	186	105	34.9	210
130 Zimbabwe	51.5	44.1	86	59	138	89	74.5	400
131 Equatorial Guinea	40.5	50.0	165	108	281	171	49.4	..
132 São Tomé and Principe	..	..	..	60	..	77	..	..
133 Papua New Guinea	47.7	57.9	90	79	130	112	41.2	370
134 Cameroon	45.8	54.7	127	94	215	153	46.2	430
135 Pakistan	50.6	64.0	118	95	183	136	26.7	..
136 Cambodia	40.3	53.4	155	104	244	163	46.6	470
137 Comoros	48.9	58.8	159	67	215	90	36.8	500
138 Kenya	51.0	52.0	96	75	156	117	56.3	590
139 Congo	46.7	48.6	100	81	160	108	59.4	..
Low human development								
140 Lao People's Dem. Rep.	40.4	53.2	145	96	218	116	44.9	650
141 Madagascar	46.5	57.5	184	95	285	157	38.8	490
142 Bhutan	43.2	60.7	156	84	267	116	33.8	380
143 Sudan	43.7	55.0	107	73	177	115	43.4	550
144 Nepal	43.3	57.3	156	72	234	100	39.1	540
145 Togo	45.5	48.8	128	81	216	144	58.9	480
146 Bangladesh	44.9	58.1	148	79	239	106	37.9	440
147 Mauritania	43.5	53.5	150	120	250	183	44.4	550
148 Yemen	42.1	58.0	194	87	303	121	38.0	350
149 Djibouti	41.0	50.4	160	111	241	156	49.0	..
150 Haiti	48.5	53.8	148	91	221	130	49.6	..

HDI rank	Life expectancy at birth (years)		Infant mortality rate (per 1,000 live births)		Under-five mortality rate (per 1,000 live births)		People not expected to survive to age 60 (%) [a]	Maternal mortality ratio reported (per 100,000 live births) [b]
	1970-75	1995-2000	1970	1998	1970	1998	1995-2000	1990-98
151 Nigeria	43.5	50.1	120	112	201	187	52.2	..
152 Congo, Dem. Rep. of the	46.1	50.8	147	128	245	207	52.4	..
153 Zambia	47.3	40.1	109	112	181	202	79.5	650
154 Côte d'Ivoire	45.4	46.7	160	90	240	150	63.4	600
155 Senegal	41.8	52.3	164	70	279	121	47.0	560
156 Tanzania, U. Rep. of	46.5	47.9	129	91	218	142	61.1	530
157 Benin	44.0	53.4	149	101	252	165	46.2	500
158 Uganda	46.5	39.6	110	84	185	134	76.3	510
159 Eritrea	44.3	50.8	150	70	225	112	51.5	1,000
160 Angola	38.0	46.5	179	170	301	292	54.4	..
161 Gambia	37.0	47.0	183	64	319	82	53.7	..
162 Guinea	37.3	46.5	197	124	345	197	54.4	670
163 Malawi	41.0	39.3	189	134	330	213	72.5	620
164 Rwanda	44.6	40.5	124	105	210	170	70.7	..
165 Mali	42.9	53.3	221	144	391	237	43.2	580
166 Central African Republic	43.0	44.9	149	113	248	173	64.7	1,100
167 Chad	39.0	47.2	149	118	252	198	56.1	830
168 Mozambique	42.5	45.2	163	129	278	206	60.9	1,100
169 Guinea-Bissau	36.5	45.0	186	130	316	205	57.7	910
170 Burundi	44.0	42.4	135	106	228	176	67.8	..
171 Ethiopia	41.0	43.3	159	110	239	173	65.5	..
172 Burkina Faso	40.9	44.4	163	109	278	165	64.3	..
173 Niger	39.0	48.5	197	166	330	280	51.6	590
174 Sierra Leone	35.0	37.2	206	182	363	316	69.5	..
All developing countries	55.6	64.4	110	64	168	93	28.0	..
Least developed countries	44.2	51.6	150	104	242	161	50.1	..
Arab States	52.4	65.6	126	55	193	72	25.2	..
East Asia	63.2	70.0	84	37	118	46	17.9	..
East Asia (excluding China)	63.3	72.8	46	10	59	11	16.2	..
Latin America and the Caribbean	61.1	69.5	86	32	123	39	22.4	..
South Asia	50.1	62.7	130	72	206	106	29.7	..
South Asia (excluding India)	49.8	63.0	132	78	208	108	29.7	..
South-East Asia and the Pacific	52.3	65.9	97	41	149	57	26.2	..
Sub-Saharan Africa	45.0	48.9	138	106	226	172	56.4	..
Eastern Europe and the CIS	68.6	68.7	37	26	47	33	24.6	..
OECD	70.4	76.2	40	12	52	14	12.5	..
High human development	71.2	76.9	25	7	32	8	11.6	..
Medium human development	58.2	66.6	101	51	151	72	24.5	..
Low human development	43.6	50.7	147	105	241	167	52.0	..
High income	72.0	77.7	21	6	26	6	10.6	..
Medium income	62.4	68.6	82	34	118	42	23.3	..
Low income	54.6	63.1	114	72	177	108	29.7	..
World	59.9	66.7	97	58	148	84	25.2	..

a. Data refer to the probability at birth of not surviving to age 60, times 100. b. The maternal mortality data are those reported by national authorities. Periodically, UNICEF and the World Health Organization (WHO) evaluate these data and make adjustments to account for the well-documented problems of underreporting and misclassification of maternal deaths and to develop estimates for countries with no data. Such an exercise is in progress and results are expected soon. c. UNICEF 2000.

Source: Columns 1, 2 and 7: UN 1998c; columns 3 and 5: UNICEF 2000; columns 4 and 6: UNICEF 1999c; column 8: UNICEF 1999c, data from the WHO and UNICEF.

10 Health profile

HDI rank	Infants with low birth-weight (%) 1990-97[a]	One-year-olds fully immunized Against tuber-culosis (%) 1995-98[a]	One-year-olds fully immunized Against measles (%) 1995-98[a]	Oral rehydration therapy use rate (%) 1990-98[a]	Preg-nant women with anaemia (%) 1975-91[a]	Tuber-culosis cases (per 100,000 people) 1997	Malaria cases (per 100,000 people) 1997[b]	People living with HIV/AIDS Total number (age 0-49) 1997[b]	People living with HIV/AIDS Adult rate (% age 15-49) 1997[b]	Cigarette consumption per adult Annual average 1993-97[c]	Cigarette consumption per adult Index (1984-86 = 100) 1993-97[c]	Doctors (per 100,000 people) 1992-95[a]	Nurses (per 100,000 people) 1992-95[a]
High human development													
1 Canada	6	..	96	..	..	6.2 [d]	..	44,000	0.33	1,866	63	221	958
2 Norway	4	..	93 [e]	..	..	4.7	..	1,300	0.06	759	92	..	..
3 United States	7	..	89 [e]	..	..	6.4	..	820,000	0.76	2,372	74	245	878
4 Australia	6	..	86	..	..	6.3	..	11,000	0.14	1,950	72	..	..
5 Iceland	..	98 [e]	98 [e]	..	..	3.6	..	200	0.14	2,234	71	..	..
6 Sweden	5	12 [e]	96 [e]	..	..	5.2	..	3,000	0.07	1,185	69	299	1,048
7 Belgium	6	..	64	..	..	12.7	..	7,500	0.14	1,922	80	365	..
8 Netherlands	..	..	96	..	..	9.5	..	14,000	0.17	1,700	113	..	..
9 Japan	7	91	94	..	..	33.6	..	6,800	0.01	2,857	87	177	641
10 United Kingdom	7	99	95	..	..	10.1	..	25,000	0.09	1,833	86	164	..
11 Finland	4	99	98	..	..	11.1	..	500	0.02	1,222	66	269	2,184
12 France	5	83	97	..	..	11.4	..	110,000	0.37	2,086	89	280	392
13 Switzerland	5	..	..	..	..	10.3	..	12,000	0.32	2,846	116	301	..
14 Germany	..	..	88	..	..	13.6	..	35,000	0.08	2,070	90	319	..
15 Denmark	6	..	84	..	..	10.6	..	3,100	0.12	1,843	88	283	..
16 Austria	6	..	90	..	..	16.5	..	7,500	0.18	2,085	82	327	530
17 Luxembourg	..	58	91	..	..	9.1	..	300	0.14	..	..	399	977
18 Ireland	4	..	..	..	..	12.0	..	1,700	0.09	2,411	94	167	..
19 Italy	5	..	55	..	..	8.5	..	90,000	0.31	1,855	78	..	..
20 New Zealand	6	..	81	..	..	5.0	..	1,300	0.07	1,223	53	210	1,249
21 Spain	4	..	78 [e]	..	..	17.5	..	120,000	0.57	2,428	87	400	..
22 Cyprus	..	..	90	..	..	6.1	..	..	0.26	..	..	231	425
23 Israel	7	..	94	..	..	7.3	..	..	0.07	2,137	86	459	671
24 Singapore	7	98	96	..	..	57.5	..	3,100	0.15	1,275	57	147	416
25 Greece	6	70	90	..	..	7.3	..	7,500	0.14	3,923	111	387	278
26 Hong Kong, China (SAR)	..	..	..	..	..	111.7	..	3,100	0.08	984	..	..	..
27 Malta	..	96	60	..	..	3.0	..	200	0.11	..	..	250	1,189
28 Portugal	5	88	96	..	..	52.1	..	35,000	0.69	2,077	107	291	304
29 Slovenia	..	98	93	..	..	25.0	..	<100	0.01	..	..	219	686
30 Barbados	10	..	92	..	..	2.3	..	4,300	2.89	837	127	113	323
31 Korea, Rep. of	9	75	85	..	..	57.3	3.8	3,100	0.01	2,982	111	127	232
32 Brunei Darussalam	..	96	100	..	..	58.4 [d]	..	..	0.20 [f]	..	..	..	..
33 Bahamas	..	..	93	..	..	30.9	..	6,300	3.77	435	43	141	258
34 Czech Republic	6	99	95	..	23	17.9	..	2,000	0.04	..	..	293	944
35 Argentina	7	99	99	..	26	34.6	1.7	120,000	0.69	1,555	83	268	54
36 Kuwait	7	..	100	..	40	30.5	..	..	0.12	2,524	80	178	468
37 Antigua and Barbuda	8	..	100	..	..	7.6 [d]	..	..	..	..	..	76	233
38 Chile	5	96	93	..	13	26.5	..	16,000	0.20	1,152	112	108	42
39 Uruguay	8	99	92	..	20	22.0	..	5,200	0.33	1,530 [d]	..	309	61
40 Slovakia	..	92	99	..	..	24.3	..	<100	(.)	..	..	325	..
41 Bahrain	6	72	100	39	..	26.5	..	..	0.15	2,821	88	11	289
42 Qatar	..	100	90	54	..	37.3	..	..	0.09	..	..	143	354
43 Hungary	9	100	100	..	..	42.4	..	2,000	0.04	2,499	77	337	..
44 Poland	..	94	91 [e]	..	..	36.2	..	12,000	0.06	3,143	93	..	..
45 United Arab Emirates	6	98	95	42	..	22.4 [d]	4.3	..	0.18	..	..	168	321
46 Estonia	..	100	89	..	..	51.1	..	<100	0.01	1,989	..	312	636
Medium human development													
47 Saint Kitts and Nevis	9	99	99	..	..	7.3 [d]	..	..	..	..	..	89	590
48 Costa Rica	7	87	86	31	27	17.7	125.7	10,000	0.55	690	54	126	95
49 Croatia	..	93	91	5	..	45.7	..	..	0.01	2,674	..	201	470
50 Trinidad and Tobago	10	..	90	..	53	21.1	..	6,800	0.94	685	51	90	168

. . . TO LEAD A LONG AND HEALTHY LIFE . . .

10 Health profile

HDI rank	Infants with low birthweight (%) 1990-97[a]	One-year-olds fully immunized		Oral rehydration therapy use rate (%) 1990-98[a]	Pregnant women with anaemia (%) 1975-91[a]	Tuberculosis cases (per 100,000 people) 1997	Malaria cases (per 100,000 people) 1997[b]	People living with HIV/AIDS		Cigarette consumption per adult		Doctors (per 100,000 people) 1992-95[a]	Nurses (per 100,000 people) 1992-95[a]
		Against tuberculosis (%) 1995-98[a]	Against measles (%) 1995-98[a]					Total number (age 0-49) 1997[b]	Adult rate (% age 15-49) 1997[b]	Annual average 1993-97[c]	Index (1984-86 =100) 1993-97[c]		
51 Dominica	10	99	98	..	..	8.5	..	..	..	..	..	46	263
52 Lithuania	..	99	97	..	..	78.7	..	<100	0.01	..	..	137	366
53 Seychelles	10	100	93	..	..	26.7	..	..	..	..	..	104	417
54 Grenada	9	..	97	..	..	4.3	..	..	..	..	..	50	239
55 Mexico	7	93	89	80	41	25.0	5.4	180,000	0.35	821	69	85	241
56 Cuba	7	99	99	..	47	13.0	..	1,400	0.02	..	..	518	752
57 Belarus	..	98	98	..	..	56.4	..	9,000	0.17	1,434	..	379	1,160
58 Belize	4	93	84	..	..	39.7	1,789.7	2,100	1.89	1,095	101	47	76
59 Panama	8	99	96	94 [e]	..	39.2	18.6	9,000	0.61	..	..	119	98
60 Bulgaria	6	98	95	..	..	40.8	..	..	0.01	2,362	95	333	652
61 Malaysia	8	100	86	..	56	64.4	127.0	68,000	0.62	998	63	43	160
62 Russian Federation	6	95	98	..	30	82.3	..	40,000	0.05	1,369	..	380	659
63 Latvia	..	100	97	..	..	81.0	..	<100	0.01	..	..	303	628
64 Romania	7	100	97	..	31	107.7	..	5,000	0.01	1,681	..	176	430
65 Venezuela	9	80	94	..	29	26.3	98.3	82,000	0.69	1,240 [d]	..	194	77
66 Fiji	12	95	75	..	..	21.1	..	260	0.06	1,022	83	38	215
67 Suriname	13	..	82	..	..	16.2	2,747.8	2,800	1.17	4,075	178	40	227
68 Colombia	9	82	75	53	24	21.7	451.8	72,000	0.36	487	40	105	49
69 Macedonia, TFYR	..	97	98	..	..	31.6	..	<100	0.01	..	..	213	..
70 Georgia	..	91	90	14	..	155.4	..	<100	(.)	..	..	436	863
71 Mauritius	13	87	85	..	29	13.7 [d]	5.7	..	0.08	1,636	86	11	27
72 Libyan Arab Jamahiriya	7	100	92	49	..	22.9 [d]	..	..	0.05	1,443 [d]	..	219	334
73 Kazakhstan	9	99	100	31	27	101.4	..	2,500	0.03	1,622	..	360	874
74 Brazil	8	99	96	54	33	51.1	240.1	580,000	0.63	1,749 [d]	..	134	41
75 Saudi Arabia	7	92	93	53	..	16.1	105.9	..	0.01	1,731	76	166	348
76 Thailand	6	98	91	95	57	51.2	163.3	780,000	2.23	1,120	125	24	99
77 Philippines	9	91	71	64	48	294.5	58.8	24,000	0.06	1,844	99	11	43
78 Ukraine	..	97	96	..	..	52.9	..	110,000	0.43	1,248	..	429	1,211
79 Saint Vincent and the Grenadines	8	99	99	..	..	21.4 [d]	..	..	..		..	46	187
80 Peru	11	96	90	55	53	172.6	754.1	72,000	0.56	208	70	73	49
81 Paraguay	5	83	..	33	44	39.2	11.1	3,200	0.13	1,604 [d]	..	67	10
82 Lebanon	10	..	91	82	49	22.3	..	..	0.09	..	..	191	122
83 Jamaica	10	90	88	..	40	4.7	..	14,000	0.99	789	94	57	69
84 Sri Lanka	25	90	91	34	39	35.7	1,196.0	6,900	0.07	399	73	23	112
85 Turkey	8	73	76	27	74	33.1	55.9	..	0.01	1,664	79	103	151
86 Oman	8	96	98	61	54	9.8	44.5	..	0.11	..	..	120	290
87 Dominican Republic	13	86	95	39	..	69.2	10.1	83,000	1.89	784	78	77	20
88 Saint Lucia	8	85	90	..	..	10.3	..	..	..	..	..	35	177
89 Maldives	13	99	98	18	..	63.4	3.8	..	0.05 [f]	..	..	19	13
90 Azerbaijan	6	96	98	..	36	60.5	129.7	<100	(.)	1,102	..	390	1,081
91 Ecuador	13	98	88	64	17	79.8	137.1	18,000	0.28	269	31	111	34
92 Jordan	10	..	86	29	50	6.9	..	..	0.02	1,315	77	158	224
93 Armenia	7	95	94	30	..	28.9	23.7	<100	0.01	1,181	..	312	831
94 Albania	7	87	89	..	..	19.1	..	<100	0.01	..	..	141	423
95 Samoa (Western)	6	100	100	..	..	19.0	..	..	..	1,497	..	38	186
96 Guyana	15	93	93	..	..	48.1	3,806.4	10,000	2.13	..	..	33	88
97 Iran, Islamic Rep. of	10	98	100	48	17	17.7	59.9	..	(.) [f]	785	66	..	..
98 Kyrgyzstan	6	94	98	98 [e]	..	119.3	..	<100	(.)	..	..	310	879
99 China	9	96	97	85	52	33.7	2.2	400,000	0.06	1,802	114	115	88
100 Turkmenistan	5	98	99	98	..	79.3	..	<100	0.01	..	..	353	1,195

HDI rank	Infants with low birth-weight (%) 1990-97 [a]	One-year-olds fully immunized Against tuber-culosis (%) 1995-98 [a]	Against measles (%) 1995-98 [a]	Oral rehydration therapy use rate (%) 1990-98 [a]	Preg-nant women with anaemia (%) 1975-91 [a]	Tuber-culosis cases (per 100,000 people) 1997	Malaria cases (per 100,000 people) 1997 [b]	People living with HIV/AIDS Total number (age 0-49) 1997 [b]	Adult rate (% age 15-49) 1997 [b]	Cigarette consumption per adult Annual average 1993-97 [c]	Index (1984-86 = 100) 1993-97 [c]	Doctors (per 100,000 people) 1992-95 [a]	Nurses (per 100,000 people) 1992-95 [a]
101 Tunisia	8	91	94	81	38	26.1 [d]	..	..	0.04	1,573	92	67	283
102 Moldova, Rep. of	4	99	99	..	20	65.4	..	2,500	0.11	..	..	107	40
103 South Africa	..	95	76	..	37	242.7	75.2 [d]	2,900,000	12.91	1,618 [d]	..	59	175
104 El Salvador	11	99	98	69	14	28.0	..	18,000	0.58	484	57	91	38
105 Cape Verde	9	84	66	83	..	43.3	5.0	..	..	..	..	29	57
106 Uzbekistan	..	97	96	37	..	54.8	..	<100	(.)	1,220	..	335	1,032
107 Algeria	9	95	75	98 [e]	42	45.8	0.7	..	0.07	1,033	67	83	..
108 Viet Nam	17	98	89	..	52	111.0	86.2	88,000	0.22	..	..	..	..
109 Indonesia	8	83	60	70	64	10.9	79.3	52,000	0.05	1,389	138	12	67
110 Tajikistan	..	98	95	..	50	30.7	507.2	<100	(.)	..	..	4	46
111 Syrian Arab Republic	7	75	97	61	..	33.1	0.9	..	0.01	1,319	61	109	212
112 Swaziland	10	85	62	99 [e]	..	441.9 [d]	..	84,000	18.50	..	..	..	..
113 Honduras	9	96	99	32	14	67.4	1,101.2	43,000	1.46	909 [d]	..	22	17
114 Bolivia	5	85	51	48	54	126.7	662.2	2,600	0.07	270	150	51	25
115 Namibia	16	85	63	100 [e]	16	372.2	26,216.6	150,000	19.94	..	..	23	81
116 Nicaragua	9	96	71	58	36	64.5	915.2	4,100	0.19	1,131 [d]	..	82	56
117 Mongolia	7	95	93	80	45	116.3	..	<100	0.01	..	..	268	452
118 Vanuatu	7	99	94	..	..	103.4	3,441.9	..	..	207	62	..	..
119 Egypt	10	97	98	95	24	21.7	0.0	..	0.03	1,214	78	202	222
120 Guatemala	15	88	81	22	45	28.2	305.1	27,000	0.52	302	64	90	30
121 Solomon Islands	20	72	64	..	..	78.7	16,853.8	..	..	628	287	..	141
122 Botswana	11	66	80	43	..	455.7	..	190,000	25.10	..	..	..	..
123 Gabon	..	72	32	39	..	80.6 [d]	3,152.4	23,000	4.25	540	52	19	56
124 Morocco	9	90	91	29	45	109.8	0.5	..	0.03	816	..	34	94
125 Myanmar	24	91	85	96 [e]	58	36.6	256.1	440,000	1.79	..	..	28	43
126 Iraq	15	76	79	54 [e]	18	125.6	66.1	..	(.) [f]	1,465	93	51	64
127 Lesotho	11	46	43	84 [e]	7	257.2	..	85,000	8.35	..	..	5	33
128 India	33	79	66	67 [e]	88	118.3	275.3	4,100,000	0.82	117	72	48	..
129 Ghana	8	86	62	36	64	58.6	11,940.9	210,000	2.38	235 [d]	..	4	..
130 Zimbabwe	10	73	65	60	..	374.6	..	1,500,000	25.84	311	64	14	164
131 Equatorial Guinea	..	99	82	..	..	76.5 [d]	..	2,400	1.21	..	..	21	34
132 São Tomé and Principe	7	80	59	74 [e]	..	31.5 [d]	..	..	..	..	..	32	..
133 Papua New Guinea	23	33	59	..	16	177.3	847.0	4,500	0.19	..	..	18	97
134 Cameroon	13	72	44	34	44	28.4	4,613.0	320,000	4.89	749 [d]	..	7	..
135 Pakistan	25	66	55	97 [e]	37	3.1 [d]	53.8	64,000	0.09	562	85	52	32
136 Cambodia	..	76	63	48	..	148.6	1,095.5	130,000	2.40	..	..	58	136
137 Comoros	8	84	67	32	..	22.2 [d]	2,422.4 [d]	..	0.14	..	..	10	33
138 Kenya	16	94	71	69	35	139.9	..	1,600,000	11.64	339	66	15	23
139 Congo	16	29	18	41	..	139.4 [d]	350.4	100,000	7.78	428 [d]	..	27	49
Low human development													
140 Lao People's Dem. Rep.	18	56	71	32	62	37.0	1,075.8	1,100	0.04	416	75	..	..
141 Madagascar	5	80	65	23	..	82.8 [d]	..	8,600	0.12	302 [d]	..	24	55
142 Bhutan	..	94	71	85	..	70.1 [d]	464.1	..	(.) [f]	..	..	20	6
143 Sudan	15	81	63	31	36	41.8	5,282.7	..	0.99	70 [d]	..	10	70
144 Nepal	..	86	73	29	65	106.9	29.4	26,000	0.24	628	121	5	5
145 Togo	20	73	32	23	48	39.4 [d]	..	170,000	8.52	453	59	6	31
146 Bangladesh	50	91	62	61	53	52.0	55.9	21,000	0.03	237	87	18	5
147 Mauritania	11	69	20	51	24	158.4	..	6,100	0.52	327	..	356	1,020
148 Yemen	19	77	66	35	..	73.7	8,560.3	..	0.01	763	..	26	51
149 Djibouti	11	35	21	..	..	587.9	699.5	33,000	10.30	1,468 [d]	..	20	..
150 Haiti	15	28	22	31	64	136.8	..	190,000	5.17	230	92	16	13

. . . TO LEAD A LONG AND HEALTHY LIFE . . .

HDI rank	Infants with low birth-weight (%) 1990-97 [a]	One-year-olds fully immunized Against tuber-culosis (%) 1995-98 [a]	One-year-olds fully immunized Against measles (%) 1995-98 [a]	Oral rehydration therapy use rate (%) 1990-98 [a]	Preg-nant women with anaemia (%) 1975-91 [a]	Tuber-culosis cases (per 100,000 people) 1997	Malaria cases (per 100,000 people) 1997 [b]	People living with HIV/AIDS Total number (age 0-49) 1997 [b]	People living with HIV/AIDS Adult rate (% age 15-49) 1997 [b]	Cigarette consumption per adult Annual average 1993-97 [c]	Cigarette consumption per adult Index (1984-86 = 100) 1993-97 [c]	Doctors (per 100,000 people) 1992-95 [a]	Nurses (per 100,000 people) 1992-95 [a]
151 Nigeria	16	27	26	86 [e]	55	14.1	593.3	2,300,000	4.12	187 [d]	..	21	142
152 Congo, Dem. Rep. of the	15	13	10	90 [e]	..	98.3 [d]	..	950,000	4.35	253 [d]	..	..	..
153 Zambia	13	81	69	57	34	488.4 [d]	37,458.2 [d]	770,000	19.07	396 [d]	..	..	..
154 Côte d'Ivoire	12	84	66	29	34	96.5	6,990.1	700,000	10.06	667 [d]	..	..	..
155 Senegal	4	80	65	39	26	94.0	..	75,000	1.77	817 [d]	..	7	35
156 Tanzania, U. Rep. of	14	83	72	50	59	147.4	3,602.1	1,400,000	9.42	196	82	210	738
157 Benin	..	92	82	33	41	33.9	11,918.4	54,000	2.06	..	..	6	33
158 Uganda	13	69	30	49	30	133.4	..	930,000	9.51	173	105	4	28
159 Eritrea	13	71	52	38	..	243.6	..	..	3.17	..	..	2	..
160 Angola	19	71	65	..	29	123.8	..	110,000	2.12	548 [d]	..	..	..
161 Gambia	..	99	91	99 [e]	80	116.1	27,369.4	13,000	2.24	330	74	2	25
162 Guinea	13	69	58	80 [e]	..	56.8	10,951.4	74,000	2.09	211	..	15	3
163 Malawi	20	100	90	70	55	205.0	..	710,000	14.92	176	80	2	6
164 Rwanda	17	79	66	47	..	79.3	20,309.9	370,000	12.75	..	..	..	..
165 Mali	16	84	57	29	58	43.7	3,688.3	89,000	1.67	..	..	4	9
166 Central African Republic	15	53	39	34	67	102.0 [d]	..	180,000	10.77	..	..	6	45
167 Chad	..	43	30	29	37	29.7 [d]	4,843.4	87,000	2.72	158	..	2	6
168 Mozambique	20	99	87	49	58	103.2	..	1,200,000	14.17	..	..	..	..
169 Guinea-Bissau	20	82	51	..	74	158.4 [d]	..	12,000	2.25	82	108	18	45
170 Burundi	..	58	44	38	68	61.0 [d]	..	260,000	8.30	115 [d]	..	6	17
171 Ethiopia	16	74	46	95 [e]	42	97.4	..	2,600,000	9.31	..	..	4	8
172 Burkina Faso	21	72	46	18	24	14.8	..	370,000	7.17	233 [d]	..	..	..
173 Niger	15	46	27	21	41	38.9	10,025.6	65,000	1.45	..	..	3	17
174 Sierra Leone	11	79	68	..	31	71.4	..	68,000	3.17	461 [d]	..	..	..
All developing countries	..	82	72	..	..	68.6	..	28,567,010 T	1.18	..	..	78	98
Least developed countries	..	72	55	..	..	88.4	..	11,425,200 T	4.13	..	..	30	78
Arab States	..	88	84	..	..	49.6	..	..	0.16	..	..	109	179
East Asia	..	95	97	..	..	35.1	..	406,250 T	0.06	..	..	115	94
East Asia (excluding China)	..	77	86	..	..	66.5	..	6,250 T	0.02	..	..	134	243
Latin America and the Caribbean	..	92	89	..	..	47.8	..	1,582,800 T	0.61	..	..	132	100
South Asia	..	79	66	..	..	93.6	..	..	0.62	..	..	44	24
South Asia (excluding India)	..	80	65	..	..	29.8	..	..	0.06	..	..	33	24
South-East Asia and the Pacific	..	88	73	..	..	81.0	..	1,590,960 T	0.58	..	..	19	75
Sub-Saharan Africa	..	63	48	..	..	106.4	..	20,736,100 T	7.58	..	..	32	135
Eastern Europe and the CIS	..	96	96	..	..	67.6	..	185,700 T	0.09	..	..	345	782
OECD	..	..	87	..	..	18.4	..	1,555,800 T	0.32	..	..	222	..
High human development	..	..	90	..	..	18.4	..	1,534,150 T	0.34	..	..	246	..
Medium human development	..	87	80	..	..	68.1	..	14,732,660 T	0.67	..	..	105	177
Low human development	..	65	49	..	..	78.7	..	13,842,800 T	4.44	..	..	27	93
High income	..	..	89	..	..	14.3	..	1,369,450 T	0.37	..	..	252	..
Medium income	..	92	88	..	..	70.1	..	..	0.75	..	..	172	297
Low income	..	79	68	..	..	67.9	..	22,948,700 T	1.23	..	..	70	91
World	..	83	75	..	..	60.4	..	30,109,610 T	0.99	..	..	122	248

a. Data refer to the most recent year available during the period specified in the column heading. b. Data refer to the end of 1997. c. Data refer to a moving average calculated over three years within the period specified in the column heading. d. Data refer to a year other than that specified in the column heading. e. Data refer to a year or period other than that specified in the column heading, differ from the standard definition or refer to only part of the country. f. Data refer to a WHO-UNAIDS estimate using 1994 data on HIV/AIDS prevalence.

Source: Column 1: UNICEF 1999c, data from the WHO and UNICEF; *columns 2-4:* UNICEF 1999c; *column 5:* World Bank 2000b; *column 6:* WHO 1999c; *column 7:* WHO 1999d; *columns 8 and 9:* UNAIDS and WHO 2000b; *column 10:* WHO 2000a; *column 11:* calculated on the basis of cigarette consumption data from WHO 2000a; *columns 12 and 13:* WHO 2000b.

HDI rank	Adult literacy rate (% age 15 and above) 1998	Youth literacy rate (% age 15-24) 1998	Age group enrolment ratios (adjusted)		Children reaching grade 5 (%) 1995-97 [b]	Tertiary students in science (as % of total tertiary) [a] 1995-97 [b]	Public education expenditure			
			Primary age group (% of relevant age group) 1997	Secondary age group (% of relevant age group) 1997			As % of GNP 1995-97 [b]	As % of total government expenditure 1995-97 [b]	Pre-primary, primary and secondary (as % of all levels) 1994-97 [b]	Tertiary (as % of all levels) 1994-97 [b]
High human development										
1 Canada	..	..	99.9	95.2	..	..	6.9 [c]	12.9 [c]	64.7	35.3
2 Norway	..	..	99.9	97.6	100	18	7.4	15.8	61.7	27.9
3 United States	..	..	99.9	96.3	..	..	5.4 [c]	14.4 [c]	74.8	25.2
4 Australia	..	..	99.9	96.0	..	32	5.5	13.5	69.5	30.5
5 Iceland	..	..	99.9	87.5	99	20	5.4	13.6	77.8	17.7
6 Sweden	..	..	99.9	99.9	97	31	8.3	12.2	72.8	27.2
7 Belgium	..	..	99.9	99.9	..	25	3.1 [d]	6.0 [d]	75.4 [d]	21.5 [d]
8 Netherlands	..	..	99.9	99.9	..	20	5.1	9.8	70.7	29.3
9 Japan	..	..	99.9	99.9	100	23	3.6 [c]	9.9 [c]	81.2	12.1
10 United Kingdom	..	..	99.9	91.8	..	29	5.3	11.6	76.3	23.7
11 Finland	..	..	99.9	95.4	100	37	7.5	12.2	69.2	28.9
12 France	..	..	99.9	98.7	..	25	6.0	10.9	80.9	17.9
13 Switzerland	..	..	99.9	83.7	..	31	5.4	15.4	78.6	19.3
14 Germany	..	..	99.9	95.3	..	31	4.8	9.6	72.2	22.5
15 Denmark	..	..	99.9	94.8	100	21	8.1	13.1	72.9	22.0
16 Austria	..	..	99.9	97.3	..	28	5.4	10.4	77.0	21.2
17 Luxembourg	..	..	..	..	..	..	4.0	15.1	95.3	4.7
18 Ireland	..	..	99.9	99.9	100	30	6.0	13.5	73.7	23.8
19 Italy	98.3	99.8	99.9	95.0	99	28	4.9	9.1	81.2	15.1
20 New Zealand	..	..	99.9	92.9	..	21	7.3	17.1	69.0	29.1
21 Spain	97.4	99.8	99.9	91.9	98	31	5.0	11.0	81.3	16.6
22 Cyprus	96.6	99.7	..	..	100	17 [e]	4.5	13.2	87.5	6.5
23 Israel	95.7	99.6	..	..	..	27	7.6 [c]	12.3 [c]	73.5	18.2
24 Singapore	91.8	99.7	91.4	75.6	..	..	3.0	23.4	60.3	34.8
25 Greece	96.9	99.7	99.9	91.4	..	30	3.1	8.2	73.3	25.0
26 Hong Kong, China (SAR)	92.9	99.2	91.3	69.0	100	36	2.9	17.0	56.9	37.1
27 Malta	91.5	98.4	99.9	85.2	100	13	5.1	10.8	54.5	10.9
28 Portugal	91.4	99.8	99.9	89.7	..	31	5.8	11.7	75.8	16.4
29 Slovenia	99.6	99.8	..	..	..	29	5.7	12.6	78.3	16.9
30 Barbados	..	..	97.4	85.7	..	21	7.2	19.0	..	..
31 Korea, Rep. of	97.5	99.8	99.9	99.9	98	34	3.7	17.5	82.0	8.0
32 Brunei Darussalam	90.7	99.3	87.9	81.9	92	6	..	..	..	..
33 Bahamas	95.5	97.3	94.6	84.6	..	..	..	13.2	..	..
34 Czech Republic	..	..	99.9	99.9	..	34	5.1	13.6	81.5	15.8
35 Argentina	96.7	98.5	99.9	76.9	..	30 [c]	3.5	12.6	80.5	19.5
36 Kuwait	80.9	91.6	65.2	63.2	..	23	5.0	14.0	69.8	30.2
37 Antigua and Barbuda	..	..	..	..	..	..	..	..	67.2	12.7
38 Chile	95.4	98.7	90.4	85.2	100	43	3.6	15.5	77.1	16.1
39 Uruguay	97.6	99.3	94.3	83.8	98	24	3.3	15.5	61.6	19.6
40 Slovakia	..	..	..	..	..	43	5.0	..	68.6	12.7
41 Bahrain	86.5	98.0	98.2	87.2	95	39 [c]	4.4	12.0	64.7	..
42 Qatar	80.4	94.1	83.3	73.3	99	..	3.4 [c]	..	..	..
43 Hungary	99.3	99.8	97.5	96.9	..	32	4.6	6.9	83.1	15.5
44 Poland	99.7	99.8	99.4	86.5	97	29	7.5	24.8	52.7	11.1
45 United Arab Emirates	74.6	89.2	82.0	77.8	98	27	1.8	16.7	..	..
46 Estonia	..	..	99.9	86.1	96	32	7.2	25.5	69.2	17.9
Medium human development										
47 Saint Kitts and Nevis	..	..	..	..	..	57	3.8	8.8	80.6	11.4
48 Costa Rica	95.3	98.2	91.8	55.8	90	18 [c]	5.4	22.8	64.5	28.3
49 Croatia	98.0	99.8	99.9	72.4	98	38	5.3	..	..	..
50 Trinidad and Tobago	93.4	97.3	99.9	71.5	97	41	4.4	..	73.5	13.3

...TO ACQUIRE KNOWLEDGE...

11 Education profile

HDI rank	Adult literacy rate (% age 15 and above) 1998	Youth literacy rate (% age 15-24) 1998	Age group enrolment ratios (adjusted) Primary age group (% of relevant age group) 1997	Secondary age group (% of relevant age group) 1997	Children reaching grade 5 (%) 1995-97 [b]	Tertiary students in science (as % of total tertiary) [a] 1995-97 [b]	Public education expenditure As % of GNP 1995-97 [b]	As % of total government expenditure 1995-97 [b]	Pre-primary, primary and secondary (as % of all levels) 1994-97 [b]	Tertiary (as % of all levels) 1994-97 [b]
51 Dominica	..	..	..	..	..	58	..	..	..	..
52 Lithuania	99.5	99.8	..	..	..	38	5.5	22.8	66.0	18.3
53 Seychelles	..	..	..	..	99	45	7.9	24.1	65.7	16.2
54 Grenada	..	..	..	..	..	..	4.7	10.6	..	..
55 Mexico	90.8	96.6	99.9	66.1	86	31	4.9	23.0	82.8	17.2
56 Cuba	96.4	99.7	99.9	69.9	100	21	6.7	12.6	64.8	14.9
57 Belarus	99.5	99.8	..	..	..	33	5.9	17.8	72.5	11.1
58 Belize	92.7	97.7	99.9	63.6	70	..	5.0	19.5	88.6	6.9
59 Panama	91.4	96.6	89.9	71.3	..	27 [c]	5.1	16.3	50.9	26.1
60 Bulgaria	98.2	99.6	97.9	77.6	93	25	3.2	7.0	73.8	18.0
61 Malaysia	86.4	97.1	99.9	64.0	99	..	4.9	15.4	63.3	25.5
62 Russian Federation	99.5	99.8	99.9	87.6	..	49	3.5	9.6	80.7	19.3
63 Latvia	99.8	99.8	99.9	80.6	..	29	6.3	14.1	71.0	12.2
64 Romania	97.9	99.6	99.9	75.8	..	32	3.6	10.5	66.5	16.0
65 Venezuela	92.0	97.7	82.5	48.9	89	..	5.2 [c]	22.4 [c]	29.5	34.7
66 Fiji	92.2	98.9	99.9	84.2	..	..	5.4 [c, f]	..	..	..
67 Suriname	..	..	99.9	..	..	..	3.5	..	..	..
68 Colombia	91.2	96.6	89.4	76.4	73	31	4.4 [f]	19.0 [f]	72.0	19.2
69 Macedonia, TFYR	..	..	..	..	95	38	5.1	20.0	78.0	22.0
70 Georgia	..	..	89.0	75.9	..	48	5.2 [c]	6.9 [c]	67.0	18.5
71 Mauritius	83.8	93.5	96.5	68.0	99	17	4.6	17.4	67.3	24.7
72 Libyan Arab Jamahiriya	78.1	95.8	99.9	99.9	..	..	..	..	..	..
73 Kazakhstan	..	..	..	..	..	42	4.4	17.6	70.2	13.9
74 Brazil	84.5	92.0	97.1	65.9	71	23 [c]	5.1	..	73.8	26.2
75 Saudi Arabia	75.2	92.0	60.1	58.7	89	18	7.5	22.8	84.4	15.6
76 Thailand	95.0	98.8	88.0	47.6	..	21	4.8	20.1	70.3	16.4
77 Philippines	94.8	98.4	99.9	77.8	..	31	3.4	15.7	79.3	18.0
78 Ukraine	99.6	99.9	..	..	..	..	7.3	15.7	73.5	10.7
79 Saint Vincent and the Grenadines	..	..	..	..	..	..	..	..	..	..
80 Peru	89.2	96.4	93.8	83.9	..	..	2.9	19.2	56.4 [f]	16.0 [f]
81 Paraguay	92.8	96.8	96.3	61.1	78	22	4.0 [f]	19.8 [f]	68.1 [f]	19.7 [f]
82 Lebanon	85.1	94.6	76.1	..	..	17	2.5 [f]	8.2 [f]	68.9	16.2
83 Jamaica	86.0	93.5	95.6	69.8	..	20	7.5	12.9	68.7	22.4
84 Sri Lanka	91.1	96.5	99.9	76.0	..	29	3.4	8.9	74.8	9.3
85 Turkey	84.0	95.9	99.9	58.4	95	22	2.2	14.7	65.3	34.7
86 Oman	68.8	96.6	67.7	66.6	96	31	4.5	16.4	92.3	7.0
87 Dominican Republic	82.8	90.4	91.3	78.5	..	25	2.3	13.8	62.0	13.0
88 Saint Lucia	..	..	..	..	..	..	9.8	22.2	69.3	12.5
89 Maldives	96.0	98.9	..	..	..	..	6.4	10.5	..	..
90 Azerbaijan	..	..	..	..	..	38	3.0	18.8	78.6	7.5
91 Ecuador	90.6	96.7	99.9	50.9	85	..	3.5	13.0	74.4	21.3
92 Jordan	88.6	99.3	..	..	98	27 [g]	7.9	19.8	64.5	33.0
93 Armenia	98.2	99.7	..	..	..	33	2.0	10.3	78.8	13.2
94 Albania	83.5	97.6	..	..	82	22	3.1 [c]	..	84.5	10.3
95 Samoa (Western)	79.7	86.2	96.5	..	85	14	..	..	..	..
96 Guyana	98.3	99.8	92.8	74.9	91	25	5.0	10.0	71.3	7.7
97 Iran, Islamic Rep. of	74.6	93.2	90.0	81.2	90	36	4.0	17.8	62.9	22.9
98 Kyrgyzstan	..	..	99.5	77.8	..	28	5.3	23.5	74.6	14.1
99 China	82.8	97.2	99.9	70.0	94	53	2.3	12.2	69.6	15.6
100 Turkmenistan	..	..	..	..	..	..	..	..	..	..

HDI rank	Adult literacy rate (% age 15 and above) 1998	Youth literacy rate (% age 15-24) 1998	Age group enrolment ratios (adjusted) Primary age group (% of relevant age group) 1997	Secondary age group (% of relevant age group) 1997	Children reaching grade 5 (%) 1995-97 [b]	Tertiary students in science (as % of total tertiary) [a] 1995-97 [b]	Public education expenditure As % of GNP 1995-97 [b]	As % of total government expenditure 1995-97 [b]	Pre-primary, primary and secondary (as % of all levels) 1994-97 [b]	Tertiary (as % of all levels) 1994-97 [b]
101 Tunisia	68.7	92.0	99.9	74.3	91	27	7.7	19.9	79.7	18.5
102 Moldova, Rep. of	98.6	99.8	..	..	..	44	10.6	28.1	77.5	13.3
103 South Africa	84.6	90.8	99.9	94.9	..	18 [c]	8.0	23.9	73.1	14.3
104 El Salvador	77.8	87.7	89.1	36.4	77	20	2.5	16.0	69.9	7.2
105 Cape Verde	72.9	87.8	99.9	36.6	..	..	..	..	..	..
106 Uzbekistan	88.0	96.3	..	..	..	..	7.7	21.1	..	..
107 Algeria	65.5	87.3	96.0	68.5	94	50	5.1 [h]	16.4	95.3 [h]	..
108 Viet Nam	92.9	96.7	99.9	55.1	..	..	3.0	7.4	69.0	22.0
109 Indonesia	85.7	97.3	99.2	56.1	88	28	1.4 [i]	7.9 [i]	73.5 [f]	24.4 [f]
110 Tajikistan	99.0	99.8	..	..	..	23	2.2	11.5	86.1	7.1
111 Syrian Arab Republic	72.7	85.9	94.7	42.3	94	31	3.1 [h]	13.6 [h]	71.7	25.9
112 Swaziland	78.3	89.5	94.6	81.5	76	22	5.7	18.1	62.9	26.6
113 Honduras	73.4	82.4	87.5	36.0	60	26 [c]	3.6	16.5	74.0	16.6
114 Bolivia	84.4	95.4	97.4	40.0	..	..	4.9	11.1	60.5	27.7
115 Namibia	80.8	91.0	91.4	80.7	86	4	9.1	25.6	86.9	13.1
116 Nicaragua	67.9	73.1	78.6	50.5	51	31	3.9 [h]	8.8 [h]	82.5 [h]	..
117 Mongolia	61.4	77.8	85.1	55.9	..	25	5.7	15.1	75.9	14.3
118 Vanuatu	..	..	71.3	42.8	..	..	4.8	..	90.8	6.4
119 Egypt	53.7	68.3	95.2	75.1	..	15	4.8	14.9	66.7	33.3
120 Guatemala	67.3	78.4	73.8	34.9	50	..	1.7 [f]	15.8 [f]	75.2 [f]	15.2 [f]
121 Solomon Islands	..	..	..	..	81	29	..	..	..	..
122 Botswana	75.6	87.4	80.1	88.8	90	27	8.6	20.6	..	..
123 Gabon	..	..	..	..	59	..	2.9 [h]	..	..	..
124 Morocco	47.1	65.5	76.6	37.7	75	29	5.3 [f]	24.9 [f]	83.5 [f]	16.5 [f]
125 Myanmar	84.1	90.5	99.3	54.2	..	37	1.2 [c,f]	14.4 [c,f]	88.0 [f]	11.7 [f]
126 Iraq	53.7	70.7	74.6	42.9	..	..	..	..	..	..
127 Lesotho	82.4	89.9	68.6	72.9	80	13	8.4	..	70.4	28.7
128 India	55.7	70.9	77.2	59.7	59	25	3.2	11.6	66.0	13.7
129 Ghana	69.1	89.5	43.4	..	..	..	4.2	19.9	..	..
130 Zimbabwe	87.2	96.7	93.1	59.2	79	23	7.1 [c]	..	78.1	17.3
131 Equatorial Guinea	81.1	96.2	79.3	68.5	..	..	1.7 [c]	5.6 [c]	..	..
132 São Tomé and Principe	..	..	..	..	..	..	..	..	..	..
133 Papua New Guinea	63.2	74.7	78.9	..	73	..	..	..	..	..
134 Cameroon	73.6	92.9	61.7	39.8	..	..	..	..	86.8	13.2
135 Pakistan	44.0	61.4	..	..	..	..	2.7	7.1	79.8	13.0
136 Cambodia	37.4	56.9	99.9	38.8	49	23	2.9	..	..	..
137 Comoros	58.5	66.7	50.1	35.7	79	..	..	..	71.7	17.2
138 Kenya	80.5	94.3	65.0	61.1	..	..	6.5	16.7	..	..
139 Congo	78.4	96.7	78.3	84.1	55	11	6.1	14.7	62.0	28.0
Low human development										
140 Lao People's Dem. Rep.	46.1	67.5	73.0	63.4	55	45	2.1	8.7	78.9	7.4
141 Madagascar	64.9	78.6	58.7	..	40	20	1.9	16.1	63.4	21.1
142 Bhutan	..	..	13.2	..	82	..	4.1	7.0	79.6	20.4
143 Sudan	55.7	75.1	..	..	..	..	1.4	..	..	..
144 Nepal	39.2	57.3	78.4	54.6	52	14	3.2	13.5	64.1	19.0
145 Togo	55.2	71.3	82.3	58.3	71	11	4.5	24.7	72.7	24.7
146 Bangladesh	40.1	49.6	75.1	21.6	..	..	2.2 [f]	..	88.6 [f]	7.9 [f]
147 Mauritania	41.2	50.1	62.9	..	64	8	5.1 [f]	16.2 [f]	74.6 [f]	21.2 [f]
148 Yemen	44.1	62.6	..	..	..	6	7.0	21.6	..	..
149 Djibouti	62.3	82.1	31.9	19.6	79	..	..	..	..	..
150 Haiti	47.8	62.5	19.4	34.2	..	..	..	..	..	..

... TO ACQUIRE KNOWLEDGE ...

HDI rank	Adult literacy rate (% age 15 and above) 1998	Youth literacy rate (% age 15-24) 1998	Age group enrolment ratios (adjusted)		Children reaching grade 5 (%) 1995-97 [b]	Tertiary students in science (as % of total tertiary) [a] 1995-97 [b]	Public education expenditure			
			Primary age group (% of relevant age group) 1997	Secondary age group (% of relevant age group) 1997			As % of GNP 1995-97 [b]	As % of total government expenditure 1995-97 [b]	Pre-primary, primary and secondary (as % of all levels) 1994-97 [b]	Tertiary (as % of all levels) 1994-97 [b]
151 Nigeria	61.1	84.7	..	..	..	41 [c]	0.7	11.5	..	..
152 Congo, Dem. Rep. of the	58.9	79.7	58.2	37.1	64	..	..	..	..	..
153 Zambia	76.3	87.0	72.4	42.2	..	..	2.2	7.1	59.8	23.2
154 Côte d'Ivoire	44.5	62.3	58.3	34.1	75	26	5.0	24.9	81.4	18.6
155 Senegal	35.5	48.7	59.5	19.8	87	..	3.7	33.1	76.8	23.2
156 Tanzania, U. Rep. of	73.6	89.9	47.4	..	81	39	..	..	..	..
157 Benin	37.7	55.3	67.6	28.2	61	18	3.2	15.2	80.8	18.8
158 Uganda	65.0	77.5	..	..	..	15	2.6	21.4	..	..
159 Eritrea	51.7	68.9	29.3	37.9	70	..	1.8	..	62.1 [h]	..
160 Angola	..	..	34.7	31.2	..	..	..	..	..	..
161 Gambia	34.6	54.3	65.9	33.3	80	..	4.9	21.2	80.5	12.9
162 Guinea	..	..	45.6	14.6	54	42	1.9	26.8	64.7	26.1
163 Malawi	58.2	69.5	98.5	72.6	..	18	5.4	18.3	67.7	20.5
164 Rwanda	64.0	81.5	78.3	..	..	..	..	..	..	..
165 Mali	38.2	62.5	38.1	17.9	84	..	2.2	..	67.4	17.7
166 Central African Republic	44.0	64.5	46.2	19.0	..	..	..	..	69.6 [f]	24.0 [f]
167 Chad	39.4	63.0	47.9	17.9	59	14	1.7 [c]	..	67.7	9.0
168 Mozambique	42.3	58.4	39.6	22.4	46	46	..	..	..	..
169 Guinea-Bissau	36.7	54.6	52.3	24.1	..	..	..	..	..	..
170 Burundi	45.8	60.8	35.6	17.1	..	..	4.0	18.3	79.4	17.1
171 Ethiopia	36.3	51.5	35.2	24.8	51	36	4.0	13.7	69.9	15.9
172 Burkina Faso	22.2	32.5	32.3	12.8	79	19	3.6	11.1	81.7	18.3
173 Niger	14.7	21.6	24.4	9.4	73	..	2.3 [h]	12.8 [h]	92.1 [h]	..
174 Sierra Leone	..	..	44.0	..	..	30	..	..	..	..
All developing countries	72.7 [j]	84.1	85.7	60.4	..	..	3.8	..	..	..
Least developed countries	50.0 [j]	62.5	60.4	31.2	..	..	..	..	..	..
Arab States	59.7	77.0	86.4	61.7	..	..	5.4	..	..	..
East Asia	83.4	97.3	99.8	71.0	..	..	2.9	..	..	..
East Asia (excluding China)	96.9 [j]	99.7	97.9	93.7	..	..	3.5	..	..	..
Latin America and the Caribbean	87.7	93.7	93.3	65.3	..	..	4.5	..	..	..
South Asia	54.3	68.9	78.0	..	..	..	3.2	..	..	..
South Asia (excluding India)	50.5	64.3	80.8	..	..	..	3.2	..	..	..
South-East Asia and the Pacific	89.3 [j]	96.9	97.8	58.3	..	..	3.3	..	..	..
Sub-Saharan Africa	59.6 [j]	75.8	56.2	41.4	..	..	6.1	..	..	..
Eastern Europe and the CIS	.. [j]	..	..	..	..	..	4.9	..	..	..
OECD	.. [j]	..	99.9	88.8	..	..	5.0	..	..	..
High human development	.. [j]	..	99.3	94.3	..	..	5.0	..	..	..
Medium human development	76.3 [j]	87.5	90.6	65.0	..	..	4.1	..	..	..
Low human development	48.1 [j]	63.9	56.6	28.3	..	..	2.5	..	..	..
High income	.. [j]	..	99.5	95.6	..	..	5.0	..	..	..
Medium income	87.0 [j]	93.1	94.4	70.9	..	..	4.6	..	..	..
Low income	69.2 [j]	81.4	82.9	57.4	..	..	2.5	..	..	..
World	.. [j]	85.1	87.6	65.4	..	..	4.8	..	..	..

a. Data refer to enrolment in natural and applied sciences. b. Data refer to the most recent year available during the period specified in the column heading. c. Data refer to a year other than that specified in the column heading. d. Data refer to the Flemish community only. e. Not including expenditures on Turkish institutions. f. Data refer to expenditures by the ministry of education only. g. Data refer to the East Bank only. h. Not including expenditure on tertiary education. i. Data refer to the central government only. j. Aggregate is missing or differs from that in table 1 as only literacy data from UNESCO are presented in this table.

Source: Columns 1 and 2: calculated on the basis of data on adult literacy rates from UNESCO 2000a; *columns 3 and 4:* UNESCO 1999a; *columns 5-10:* UNESCO 1999c.

HDI rank	International tourism departures		Main telephone lines (per 1,000 people)		Public telephones (per 1,000 people)		Cellular mobile subscribers (per 1,000 people)		Televisions (per 1,000 people)		Personal computers (per 1,000 people)		Internet hosts (per 1,000 people)
	Thousands 1997-98[a]	Index (1990 = 100) 1997-98[a]	1990	1996-98[a]	1990	1996-98[a]	1990	1996-98[a]	1990	1996-98[a]	1990	1996-98[a]	1998
High human development													
1 Canada	17,648	86	565	634	6.2	6.1	22	176	628	715	107	330	36.94
2 Norway	3,120	117	503	660	3.0	2.8	46	474	422	579	..	373	71.75
3 United States	52,735	118	545	661	7.6	6.5	21	256	772	847	217	459	112.77
4 Australia	3,161	146	456	512	..	4.3	11	288	522	639	150	412	40.09
5 Iceland	227	160	510	646	4.1	3.5	39	331	317	356	39	326	89.83
6 Sweden	11,422	183	681	674	4.3	..	54	464	466	531	105	361	42.86
7 Belgium	7,773	203	393	500	1.3	1.6	4	173	446	510	88	286	20.58
8 Netherlands	12,860	143	464	593	0.5	1.4	5	213	482	543	94	318	39.75
9 Japan	15,806	144	441	503	6.7	6.2	7	374	611	707	60	237	13.34
10 United Kingdom	50,872	163	441	556	6.2	5.7	19	252	433	645	108	263	24.59
11 Finland	4,743	406	534	554	4.0	4.1	45	572	494	640	100	349	89.17
12 France	18,077	93	495	570	3.2	4.0	5	188	539	601	71	208	8.57
13 Switzerland	12,213	127	574	675	7.1	7.7	18	235	396	535	87	422	34.51
14 Germany	82,975	147	441	567	2.2	1.9	4	170	525	580	91	305	17.67
15 Denmark	4,972	127	567	660	1.3	1.5	29	364	535	585	115	377	56.29
16 Austria	13,263	156	418	491	4.1	3.7	10	249	473	516	65	233	21.20
17 Luxembourg	..	..	481	692	0.8	1.2	2	308	346	619	..	732	18.26
18 Ireland	3,053	170	281	435	1.7	2.3	7	257	293	456	86	272	15.17
19 Italy	14,327	89	388	451	7.5	6.6	5	355	420	486	36	173	6.71
20 New Zealand	1,166	163	434	479	1.3	1.3	16	203	443	501	..	282	35.20
21 Spain	13,203	123	316	414	1.1	1.7	1	179	389	506	28	145	7.79
22 Cyprus	417	183	428	585	3.9	2.9	5	168	183	167	9	..	7.94
23 Israel	2,983	338	343	471	3.1	6.9	3	359	259	318	63	217	19.15
24 Singapore	3,745	303	390	562	9.6	6.1	19	346	379	348	74	458	21.20
25 Greece	1,935	117	389	522	5.6	5.9	0	194	194	466	17	52	4.71
26 Hong Kong, China (SAR)	4,197	205	450	558	0.7	1.7	24	475	282	431	47	254	12.38
27 Malta	167	137	360	499	2.1	4.5	0	59	736	518	14	260	4.79
28 Portugal	2,425	107	243	413	2.5	4.0	1	309	186	542	27	81	5.60
29 Slovenia	..	..	211	375	1.2	1.7	0	84	275	356	..	251	11.51
30 Barbados	..	..	281	424	1.6	2.1	0	45	265	283	..	75	0.16
31 Korea, Rep. of	3,067	196	310	433	5.5	13.1	2	302	210	346	37	157	4.01
32 Brunei Darussalam	300	122	136	247	0.1	3.3	7	156	241	638	..	..	3.79
33 Bahamas	..	..	274	352	2.2	4.8	8	27	223	896	..	..	1.63
34 Czech Republic	..	..	158	364	..	3.6	0	94	..	447	12	97	8.41
35 Argentina	5,522	221	95	203	0.7	2.7	(.)	78	249	289	7	39	1.84
36 Kuwait	..	..	247	236	..	0.3	15	138	432	491	7	105	3.44
37 Antigua and Barbuda	..	..	253	468	2.1	4.7	0 [b]	19	364	452	..	..	2.41
38 Chile	1,351	176	66	205	1.3	0.9	1	65	206	232	11	48	2.03
39 Uruguay	654	..	134	250	1.7	2.8	0	60	388	242	..	91	4.68
40 Slovakia	414	..	135	286	1.2	2.7	0	87	..	402	..	65	4.10
41 Bahrain	..	..	192	245	1.0	2.5	14	143	424	419	..	93	0.90
42 Qatar	..	..	190	260	..	1.3	8	114	392	808	..	121	0.02
43 Hungary	12,317	91	96	336	2.5	4.3	(.)	105	417	437	10	59	9.41
44 Poland	49,328	223	86	228	0.7	1.8	0	50	295	413	8	44	3.37
45 United Arab Emirates	..	..	206	389	2.3	11.1	17	210	91	294	..	106	7.61
46 Estonia	1,659	..	204	343	..	1.9	0	170	344	480	..	34	16.62
Medium human development													
47 Saint Kitts and Nevis	..	..	237	418	..	..	0 [c]	11	220	244	..	122	0.12
48 Costa Rica	330	173	101	172	2.2	0.5	0	28	221	387	..	(.)	0.85
49 Croatia	..	..	172	348	0.8	2.6	(.)	41	215	267	..	112	2.12
50 Trinidad and Tobago	250	98	141	206	0.6	1.6	0	20	331	331	..	47	1.52

198

12 Access to information flows

HDI rank	International tourism departures		Main telephone lines (per 1,000 people)		Public telephones (per 1,000 people)		Cellular mobile subscribers (per 1,000 people)		Televisions (per 1,000 people)		Personal computers (per 1,000 people)		Internet hosts (per 1,000 people)
	Thousands 1997-98[a]	Index (1990 = 100) 1997-98[a]	1990	1996-98[a]	1990	1996-98[a]	1990	1996-98[a]	1990	1996-98[a]	1990	1996-98[a]	1998
51 Dominica	..	..	164	252	..	4.2	0	9	70	175	..	..	1.95
52 Lithuania	3,241	..	212	300	2.3	2.0	0	72	353	376	..	54	2.65
53 Seychelles	31	172	124	244	1.9	2.9	0	49	71	190	..	..	0.09
54 Grenada	..	..	177	263	..	2.1	2	13	87	325	..	..	0.03
55 Mexico	9,803	133	65	104	1.0	3.3	1	35	150	261	8	47	1.18
56 Cuba	55	458	31	35	1.0	0.9	0	(.)	206	239	..	..	0.01
57 Belarus	969	..	153	241	..	1.9	0	1	268	314	..	..	0.10
58 Belize	..	..	92	138	0.0[c]	2.8	0	15	164	180	..	..	1.10
59 Panama	211	140	93	134	0.9	1.2	0	6	172	187	..	..	0.27
60 Bulgaria	3,059	128	242	329	1.5	1.9	0	15	250	366	..	..	1.23
61 Malaysia	25,631	172	89	198	1.4	8.2	5	99	149	166	8	59	2.16
62 Russian Federation	11,711	..	140	197	1.5	1.3	0	5	365	420	3	41	1.24
63 Latvia	1,961	..	234	302	..	1.5	0	68	370	593	..	..	5.83
64 Romania	6,893	61	102	167	1.2	1.0	0	29	194	226	(.)	10	1.05
65 Venezuela	524	170	82	117	1.7	3.2	(.)	87	177	185	11	43	0.34
66 Fiji	78	128	57	97	0.5	1.1	0	10	15	97	..	..	0.27
67 Suriname	47	85	92	152	0.4	0.6	0	14	138	217	..	..	(.)
68 Colombia	1,140	146	75	173	1.0	1.4	0	49	118	217	..	28	0.44
69 Macedonia, TFYR	..	..	148	199	..	0.7	0	15	..	250	..	..	0.57
70 Georgia	433	..	99	115	0.9	0.1	0	11	201	472	..	..	0.14
71 Mauritius	143	161	52	214	0.2	2.1	2	53	170	228	4	87	0.50
72 Libyan Arab Jamahiriya	650	153	48	84	..	0.1	0	3	99	143	..	..	(.)
73 Kazakhstan	..	..	80	104	..	0.4	0	2	282	234	..	..	0.09
74 Brazil	4,598	387	65	121	1.6	3.0	(.)	47	213	316	3	30	1.30
75 Saudi Arabia	..	..	77	143	0.4	2.1	1	31	249	260	24	50	0.02
76 Thailand	1,412	160	24	84	0.4	1.9	1	32	108	236	4	22	0.34
77 Philippines	1,817	160	10	37	0.1	0.2	0	22	49	108	3	15	0.13
78 Ukraine	10,326	..	136	191	1.7	1.1	0	3	327	490	..	14	0.39
79 Saint Vincent and the Grenadines	..	..	124	188	0.7	1.5	0	7	142	162	..	..	0.00
80 Peru	577	175	26	67	0.3	1.9	(.)	30	96	144	..	18	0.19
81 Paraguay	498	..	27	55	0.3	0.2	0	41	52	101	..	(.)	0.22
82 Lebanon	1,650	..	118	194	..	..	0	157	349	352	..	39	0.74
83 Jamaica	..	..	45	166	0.5	0.8	0	22	136	323	..	5	0.13
84 Sri Lanka	518	174	7	28	..	0.2	(.)	9	35	92	(.)	4	0.03
85 Turkey	4,601	158	121	254	0.7	1.2	1	53	230	286	5	23	0.73
86 Oman	..	..	60	92	0.3	1.6	2	43	657	595	2	21	0.28
87 Dominican Republic	354	..	48	93	0.4	0.6	(.)	31	84	84	..	..	0.59
88 Saint Lucia	..	..	127	268	..	2.9	0[c]	13	186	211	..	136	0.16
89 Maldives	37	176	29	71	..	1.8	0	6	24	39	..	..	0.38
90 Azerbaijan	232	..	86	89	..	0.3	0	8	195	254	..	..	0.06
91 Ecuador	330	182	48	78	0.4	0.3	0	25	86	293	..	..	0.13
92 Jordan	1,347	118	58	86	..	0.6	(.)	12	76	52	..	9	0.06
93 Armenia	..	..	157	157	..	0.1	0	2	210	217	..	4	0.27
94 Albania	18	..	12	37	0.2	0.1	0	2	86	161	..	..	0.05
95 Samoa (Western)	..	..	26	49	0.2	0.9	0	17	39	69	..	5	0.01
96 Guyana	..	..	16	70	..	..	0	2	35	59	..	..	0.08
97 Iran, Islamic Rep. of	1,354	172	40	112	..	1.3	0	6	66	157	..	32	(.)
98 Kyrgyzstan	32	..	72	76	..	0.4	0	(.)	228	44	..	..	0.33
99 China	8,426	..	6	70	(.)	2.1	(.)	19	156	272	(.)	9	0.01
100 Turkmenistan	357	..	60	82	0.8	0.1	0	1	191	201	..	..	0.06

HDI rank	International tourism departures		Main telephone lines (per 1,000 people)		Public telephones (per 1,000 people)		Cellular mobile subscribers (per 1,000 people)		Televisions (per 1,000 people)		Personal computers (per 1,000 people)		Internet hosts (per 1,000 people)
	Thousands 1997-98[a]	Index (1990 = 100) 1997-98[a]	1990	1996-98[a]	1990	1996-98[a]	1990	1996-98[a]	1990	1996-98[a]	1990	1996-98[a]	1998
101 Tunisia	1,526	88	38	81	0.4	1.5	(.)	4	81	198	3	15	(.)
102 Moldova, Rep. of	35	..	106	150	1.8	1.0	0	2	299	297	..	6	0.14
103 South Africa	3,080	500	87	115	1.1	3.5	(.)	56	97	125	7	47	3.26
104 El Salvador	868	165	24	80	0.5	0.9	0	18	92	250	..	..	0.14
105 Cape Verde	..	..	24	98	..	1.0	0	3	3	45	..	..	(.)
106 Uzbekistan	..	..	69	65	0.8	0.2	0	1	181	273	..	..	0.01
107 Algeria	1,377	36	32	53	0.2	0.2	(.)	1	68	68	1	4	(.)
108 Viet Nam	168	..	1	26	..	(.)	0	2	39	180	..	6	(.)
109 Indonesia	2,200	320	6	27	0.1	1.0	(.)	5	61	136	1	8	0.07
110 Tajikistan	..	..	45	37	..	(.)	0	(.)	189	285	..	..	0.01
111 Syrian Arab Republic	2,750	264	40	95	0.2	0.2	0	0	60	68	..	2	(.)
112 Swaziland	..	..	17	30	0.2	0.9	0	5	19	107	..	..	0.29
113 Honduras	202	103	17	38	0.1	0.4	0	5	72	90	..	..	0.02
114 Bolivia	298	123	28	69	..	0.6	0	27	113	115	..	..	0.08
115 Namibia	..	..	39	69	0.7	1.3	0	12	22	32	..	19	1.60
116 Nicaragua	422	244	13	31	0.1	0.3	0	4	65	190	..	..	0.16
117 Mongolia	..	..	32	37	0.3	0.1	0	1	66	63	..	5	0.01
118 Vanuatu	12	200	18	28	..	..	0	1	9	13	..	..	0.43
119 Egypt	2,921	145	30	60	(.)	0.1	(.)	1	107	127	..	9	0.04
120 Guatemala	391	135	21	41	0.3	..	(.)	10	53	126	..	..	0.08
121 Solomon Islands	..	..	14	19	0.0	0.4	0	2	..	14	..	..	0.05
122 Botswana	460	240	21	56	0.2	1.3	0	15	16	27	..	25	0.42
123 Gabon	..	..	22	33	..	0.7	0	8	45	136	..	9	0.00
124 Morocco	1,359	113	16	54	0.1	1.1	(.)	4	102	160	..	3	0.07
125 Myanmar	..	..	2	5	..	(.)	0	(.)	3	7	..	..	(.)
126 Iraq	..	..	37	31	..	..	0	0	72	82	..	..	0.00
127 Lesotho	..	..	7	10	..	..	0	5	6	24	..	..	0.01
128 India	3,811	167	6	22	0.1	0.4	0	1	32	69	(.)	3	0.01
129 Ghana	..	..	3	8	..	0.1	0	1	15	115	(.)	2	0.01
130 Zimbabwe	123	62	12	17	0.1	0.2	0	4	30	29	(.)	9	0.08
131 Equatorial Guinea	..	..	4	13	..	(.)	0	1	9	162	..	2	0.00
132 São Tomé and Principe	..	..	19	22	..	0.1	0	0	..	227	..	..	0.82
133 Papua New Guinea	63	95	8	11	..	..	0	1	2	24	..	..	0.03
134 Cameroon	..	..	3	5	(.)	(.)	0	(.)	23	81	1	..	(.)
135 Pakistan	..	..	8	19	(.)	0.2	(.)	1	26	88	1	4	0.02
136 Cambodia	41	..	(.)	2	..	(.)	0	6	..	123	..	1	0.01
137 Comoros	..	..	8	9	..	0.2	0	0	2	4	(.)	..	0.01
138 Kenya	350	167	8	9	0.2	0.2	0	(.)	15	21	(.)	3	0.02
139 Congo	..	..	7	8	(.)	..	0	1	6	8	..	..	(.)
Low human development													
140 Lao People's Dem. Rep.	..	..	2	6	..	(.)	0	1	7	4	..	1	0.00
141 Madagascar	35	103	2	3	(.)	(.)	0	1	19	46	..	1	(.)
142 Bhutan	..	..	4	16	0.0	..	0	0	..	19	..	4	0.06
143 Sudan	200	..	3	6	..	0.1	0	(.)	73	141	..	2	0.00
144 Nepal	110	134	3	8	(.)	(.)	0	0	2	4	..	..	0.01
145 Togo	..	..	3	7	(.)	0.1	0	2	6	20	..	7	0.03
146 Bangladesh	992	256	2	3	..	(.)	0	1	5	7	..	..	0.00
147 Mauritania	..	..	3	6	0.1	0.3	0	0	14	91	..	6	0.01
148 Yemen	..	..	11	13	..	..	0	1	274	..	..	1	(.)
149 Djibouti	..	..	11	13	0.1	0.1	0	(.)	44	73	2	..	0.01
150 Haiti	..	..	7	8	..	(.)	0	0	5	5	..	..	0.00

... TO ACQUIRE KNOWLEDGE ...

12 Access to information flows

HDI rank	International tourism departures Thousands 1997-98 [a]	Index (1990=100) 1997-98 [a]	Main telephone lines (per 1,000 people) 1990	Main telephone lines (per 1,000 people) 1996-98 [a]	Public telephones (per 1,000 people) 1990	Public telephones (per 1,000 people) 1996-98 [a]	Cellular mobile subscribers (per 1,000 people) 1990	Cellular mobile subscribers (per 1,000 people) 1996-98 [a]	Televisions (per 1,000 people) 1990	Televisions (per 1,000 people) 1996-98 [a]	Personal computers (per 1,000 people) 1990	Personal computers (per 1,000 people) 1996-98 [a]	Internet hosts (per 1,000 people) 1998
151 Nigeria	..	..	3	4	(.)	..	0	(.)	36	67	..	6	(.)
152 Congo, Dem. Rep. of the	..	..	1	(.)	..	..	0	(.)	1	43	..	..	(.)
153 Zambia	..	..	9	9	0.1	0.1	0	1	34	137	..	..	0.03
154 Côte d'Ivoire	5	250	6	12	(.)	(.)	0	6	62	70	..	4	0.02
155 Senegal	..	..	6	16	..	1.0	0	2	36	41	2	11	0.02
156 Tanzania, U. Rep. of	150	50	3	4	(.)	(.)	0	1	2	21	..	2	(.)
157 Benin	420	..	3	7	..	(.)	0	1	16	91	..	1	(.)
158 Uganda	..	..	2	3	..	0.1	0	1	11	26	..	1	0.01
159 Eritrea	..	..	..	7	..	0.1	..	0	..	14	..	..	0.00
160 Angola	..	..	8	6	..	(.)	0	1	6	124	..	1	(.)
161 Gambia	..	..	7	21	0.1	0.2	0	4	..	4	..	3	0.01
162 Guinea	..	..	2	5	0.0	0.1	0	3	7	41	..	3	0.00
163 Malawi	..	..	3	3	0.1	(.)	0	1	..	2	..	..	(.)
164 Rwanda	..	..	2	2	..	0.1	0	2	(.)	..	..	..	0.00
165 Mali	..	..	1	3	..	0.1	0	(.)	9	11	..	1	(.)
166 Central African Republic	..	..	2	3	(.)	(.)	0	(.)	4	5	..	..	0.00
167 Chad	10	42	1	1	(.)	(.)	0	0	1	2	..	..	0.00
168 Mozambique	..	..	3	4	..	(.)	0	(.)	3	4	..	2	0.01
169 Guinea-Bissau	..	..	6	7	..	0.1	0	0	..	..	..	..	0.01
170 Burundi	16	67	2	3	(.)	(.)	0	(.)	1	10	..	..	0.00
171 Ethiopia	140	157	3	3	(.)	(.)	0	0	2	5	..	..	(.)
172 Burkina Faso	..	..	2	4	..	0.1	0	(.)	5	6	(.)	1	0.02
173 Niger	10	56	1	2	..	(.)	0	(.)	11	26	..	(.)	(.)
174 Sierra Leone	..	..	3	4	(.)	0.1	0	0	10	26	..	..	(.)
All developing countries	..	..	21	58	..	1.3	..	18	95	162	..	..	0.26
Least developed countries	..	..	3	4	..	(.)	..	1	16	29	..	..	(.)
Arab States	..	..	35	65	..	0.7	(.)	10	121	144	..	12	0.13
East Asia	15,690 T	..	19	85	0.2	2.5	(.)	31	158	275	2	15	0.22
East Asia (excluding China)	7,264 T	..	314	431	4.8	11.2	4	310	212	344	38	162	4.85
Latin America and the Caribbean	..	..	62	118	1.1	2.4	(.)	43	170	252	..	..	0.99
South Asia	6,822 T	177	7	24	..	0.4	(.)	2	30	69	..	..	0.01
South Asia (excluding India)	3,011 T	191	11	30	..	0.3	(.)	2	25	69	..	..	0.01
South-East Asia and the Pacific	35,467 T	..	13	43	..	1.1	1	16	61	139	..	..	0.32
Sub-Saharan Africa	..	..	11	14	..	0.5	..	5	24	50	..	..	0.27
Eastern Europe and the CIS	102,985 T	..	125	193	..	1.3	(.)	18	306	379	..	..	1.65
OECD	427,092 T	137	393	490	4.7	4.9	10	223	502	594	94	255	37.86
High human development	434,097 T	140	419	524	5.0	5.2	11	245	531	621	102	277	40.97
Medium human development	..	..	28	68	..	1.3	(.)	15	120	193	..	..	0.24
Low human development	..	..	3	4	..	0.1	..	1	22	37	..	..	(.)
High income	359,785 T	134	470	569	5.5	5.1	13	266	577	674	118	315	48.18
Medium income	186,014 T	..	84	143	1.1	2.1	(.)	39	189	258	..	..	1.09
Low income	..	..	6	36	..	1.0	..	8	80	145	..	..	0.02
World	..	..	99	142	1.3	1.9	..	54	186	253	..	..	7.42

a. Data refer to the most recent year available during the period specified in the column heading. b. Data refer to 1988. c. Data refer to 1989.

Source: *Column 1:* World Bank 2000b, data from World Tourism Organization; *column 2:* calculated on the basis of international tourism data from World Bank 2000b, data from World Tourism Organization; *columns 3 and 4:* calculated on the basis of data on main telephone lines and population from ITU 1998; *columns 5 and 6:* calculated on the basis of data on public telephones and population from ITU 1998; *columns 7 and 8:* calculated on the basis of data on cellular mobile subscribers and population from ITU 1998; *columns 9 and 10:* calculated on the basis of data on television receivers and population from ITU 1998; *columns 11 and 12:* calculated on the basis of data on personal computers and population from ITU 1998; *column 13:* calculated on the basis of data on Internet hosts and population from ITU 1998.

HDI rank	GNP (US$ billions) [a] 1998	GNP annual growth rate (%) [b]		GNP per capita (US$) [a] 1998	GNP per capita annual growth rate (%) [b]		Average annual rate of inflation (%)	
		1975-95	1990-98		1975-90	1990-98	1990-98	1998
High human development								
1 Canada	580.9	2.9	2.0	19,170	1.7	0.9	1.4	-0.6
2 Norway	152.0	3.1	4.0	34,310	2.7	3.4	1.8	-0.5
3 United States	7,903.0	2.8	2.8	29,240	1.8	1.8	1.9	1.0
4 Australia	387.0	2.7	3.9	20,640	1.3	2.7	1.7	0.6
5 Iceland	7.6	3.8	2.6	27,830	2.7	1.6	2.9	1.7
6 Sweden	226.5	1.6	0.9	25,580	1.3	0.5	2.4	0.6
7 Belgium	259.0	2.2	2.0	25,380	2.1	1.7	2.3	0.9
8 Netherlands	389.1	2.3	2.7	24,780	1.7	2.1	2.1	2.9
9 Japan	4,089.1	4.2	1.4	32,350	3.5	1.1	0.2	0.3
10 United Kingdom	1,264.3	2.3	1.9	21,410	2.1	1.6	3.0	2.5
11 Finland	125.1	2.9	1.6	24,280	2.5	1.2	1.7	1.4
12 France	1,465.4	2.6	1.7	24,900	2.1	1.2	1.7	0.2
13 Switzerland	284.1	2.0	0.6	39,980	1.7	-0.2	1.7	1.1
14 Germany	2,179.8	..	..	26,570	..	..	2.2	0.9
15 Denmark	175.2	2.0	2.9	33,040	1.9	2.5	1.6	1.4
16 Austria	216.7	2.6	2.2	26,830	2.5	1.6	2.5	1.0
17 Luxembourg	19.2	4.5	3.3	45,100	4.1	1.9	2.2	1.7
18 Ireland	69.3	3.1	6.7	18,710	2.4	6.0	2.0	2.4
19 Italy	1,157.0	2.9	1.2	20,090	2.7	1.0	4.4	2.9
20 New Zealand	55.4	0.9	2.2	14,600	0.2	1.0	1.6	1.3
21 Spain	555.2	2.5	2.0	14,100	1.9	1.8	4.2	2.2
22 Cyprus	9.0	8.1	3.9	11,920	7.4	2.6	3.7	2.2
23 Israel	96.5	3.8	5.2	16,180	1.7	2.0	11.0	5.4
24 Singapore	95.5	7.7	8.1	30,170	5.7	6.0	2.1	-1.5
25 Greece	123.4	2.5	1.9	11,740	1.7	1.4	11.0	5.2
26 Hong Kong, China (SAR)	158.2	8.3	3.9	23,660	6.4	1.8	6.4	1.1
27 Malta	3.8	6.2	13.0	10,100	5.6	12.1	-5.5	0.5
28 Portugal	106.4	3.7	2.4	10,670	3.2	2.4	5.8	4.2
29 Slovenia	19.4	..	..	9,780	..	..	27.0	7.4
30 Barbados	1.7 [c]	2.1	1.1	6,610 [c]	1.8	0.7	2.4	3.8
31 Korea, Rep. of	398.8	8.4	5.1	8,600	7.0	4.1	6.4	5.3
32 Brunei Darussalam	7.8	..	1.2	24,630	..	-1.4	1.1	-0.2
33 Bahamas	3.5 [d]	6.3	0.8	12,400 [d]	4.2	-0.9	2.9	..
34 Czech Republic	53.0	..	-1.7	5,150	..	-1.6	13.7	11.0
35 Argentina	290.3	-0.1	6.3	8,030	-1.6	4.9	7.8	-2.0
36 Kuwait	32.0 [c]	0.2	..	20,200 [c]	-4.7	..	..	..
37 Antigua and Barbuda	0.6	..	4.1	8,450	..	3.5	2.6	2.8
38 Chile	73.9	4.5	8.3	4,990	2.9	6.6	9.3	5.1
39 Uruguay	20.0	1.2	4.5	6,070	0.6	3.7	40.5	10.7
40 Slovakia	19.9	..	0.1	3,700	..	-0.1	11.4	5.1
41 Bahrain	4.9	..	4.5	7,640	..	1.4	-0.2	-4.9
42 Qatar	7.9 [c]	1.3	..	12,000 [c]	-5.6	..	..	..
43 Hungary	45.7	1.7	-0.1	4,510	1.8	0.2	22.0	14.2
44 Poland	151.3	..	3.9	3,910	..	3.7	26.9	12.0
45 United Arab Emirates	48.7	5.3	2.0	17,870	-3.4	-2.8	2.4	1.6
46 Estonia	4.9	..	-2.8	3,360	..	-1.8	75.4	9.4
Medium human development								
47 Saint Kitts and Nevis	0.3	..	4.1	6,190	..	4.5	2.9	3.3
48 Costa Rica	9.8	3.2	4.2	2,770	0.4	2.0	17.6	12.3
49 Croatia	20.8	..	-2.2	4,620	..	-1.5	131.2	9.0
50 Trinidad and Tobago	5.8	1.8	2.8	4,520	0.6	2.1	6.9	6.7

... TO HAVE ACCESS TO THE RESOURCES NEEDED FOR A DECENT STANDARD OF LIVING ...

	GNP (US$ billions) [a]	GNP annual growth rate (%) [b]		GNP per capita (US$) [a]	GNP per capita annual growth rate (%) [b]		Average annual rate of inflation (%)	
HDI rank	1998	1975-95	1990-98	1998	1975-90	1990-98	1990-98	1998
51 Dominica	0.2	11.0	1.5	3,150	10.9	1.4	3.2	-0.4
52 Lithuania	9.4	..	-4.9	2,540	..	-4.8	111.5	6.6
53 Seychelles	0.5	4.7	2.9	6,420	3.5	1.4	1.4	2.0
54 Grenada	0.3	..	2.6	3,250	..	2.2	2.8	3.6
55 Mexico	368.1	3.5	3.0	3,840	1.1	1.2	19.5	14.0
56 Cuba	..	..	..	..	..	..	..	..
57 Belarus	22.3	..	-2.2	2,180	..	-2.2	449.9	74.2
58 Belize	0.6	6.5	3.5	2,660	3.7	0.5	3.1	0.9
59 Panama	8.3	1.5	4.7	2,990	-0.7	2.9	2.2	1.4
60 Bulgaria	10.1	..	-2.7	1,220	..	-2.0	116.9	22.2
61 Malaysia	81.3	6.7	6.4	3,670	3.9	3.8	5.1	9.1
62 Russian Federation	331.8	..	-7.1	2,260	..	-7.0	230.9	11.6
63 Latvia	5.9	3.5	-6.6	2,420	3.0	-5.5	71.1	11.3
64 Romania	30.6	2.5	-2.9	1,360	1.9	-2.6	113.8	46.6
65 Venezuela	82.1	1.2	2.8	3,530	-1.6	0.5	49.2	21.2
66 Fiji	1.7	2.5	0.8	2,210	0.9	-0.1	3.7	7.3
67 Suriname	0.7	0.1	0.8	1,660	-0.6	0.5	138.0	..
68 Colombia	100.7	3.8	3.5	2,470	1.7	1.5	21.5	17.5
69 Macedonia, TFYR	2.6	..	..	1,290	..	..	17.9	1.0
70 Georgia	5.3	1.8	-11.8	970	1.1	-11.7	709.3	3.4
71 Mauritius	4.3	5.5	5.2	3,730	4.3	4.0	6.2	5.6
72 Libyan Arab Jamahiriya	..	..	..	..	..	..	..	..
73 Kazakhstan	20.9	..	-6.5	1,340	..	-5.9	330.7	4.9
74 Brazil	767.6	2.7	2.7	4,630	0.6	1.3	347.4	3.7
75 Saudi Arabia	143.4	3.9	1.6	6,910	-1.4	-1.8	1.4	-14.0
76 Thailand	131.9	7.8	4.6	2,160	5.7	3.4	4.8	8.7
77 Philippines	78.9	3.1	3.3	1,050	0.6	1.0	8.5	10.5
78 Ukraine	49.2	..	-10.4	980	..	-10.1	440.0	13.2
79 Saint Vincent and the Grenadines	0.3	..	3.3	2,560	..	2.6	2.5	2.3
80 Peru	60.5	-0.3	5.8	2,440	-2.6	4.0	33.7	5.5
81 Paraguay	9.2	5.6	2.3	1,760	2.4	-0.4	14.6	13.8
82 Lebanon	15.0	..	7.2	3,560	..	5.3	24.0	8.0
83 Jamaica	4.5	-0.3	1.5	1,740	-1.5	0.6	29.1	5.0
84 Sri Lanka	15.2	4.6	5.0	810	3.0	3.7	9.7	8.8
85 Turkey	200.5	4.2	4.4	3,160	1.9	2.8	79.4	74.2
86 Oman	10.6 [c]	8.4	..	4,940 [c]	3.8	..	-2.9	..
87 Dominican Republic	14.6	3.0	5.3	1,770	0.7	3.4	10.6	4.9
88 Saint Lucia	0.6	..	3.0	3,660	..	1.4	2.5	2.0
89 Maldives	0.3	..	6.5	1,130	..	3.7	8.2	0.8
90 Azerbaijan	3.8	..	-9.6	480	..	-10.7	322.3	-8.3
91 Ecuador	18.4	3.2	3.4	1,520	0.5	1.3	32.0	25.8
92 Jordan	5.3	..	6.2	1,150	..	1.5	3.3	3.7
93 Armenia	1.7	..	-5.7	460	..	-6.5	349.1	11.2
94 Albania	2.7	..	-0.3	810	..	-0.5	51.5	24.8
95 Samoa (Western)	0.2	..	1.8	1,070	..	1.1	4.3	4.0
96 Guyana	0.7	-4.5	9.8	780	-5.1	8.9	16.0	3.2
97 Iran, Islamic Rep. of	102.2	0.4	4.0	1,650	-2.8	2.3	28.3	15.9
98 Kyrgyzstan	1.8	..	-6.2	380	..	-6.9	157.8	11.5
99 China	923.6	8.4	10.4	750	6.8	9.2	9.7	-1.1
100 Turkmenistan	3.0 [e]	..	..	650 [e]	..	..	663.4	13.5

HDI rank	GNP (US$ billions) [a] 1998	GNP annual growth rate (%) [b] 1975-95	GNP annual growth rate (%) [b] 1990-98	GNP per capita (US$) [a] 1998	GNP per capita annual growth rate (%) [b] 1975-90	GNP per capita annual growth rate (%) [b] 1990-98	Average annual rate of inflation (%) 1990-98	Average annual rate of inflation (%) 1998
101 Tunisia	19.2	4.5	4.5	2,060	1.9	2.7	4.8	3.5
102 Moldova, Rep. of	1.7	..	..	380	..	..	173.9	8.0
103 South Africa	136.9	1.7	1.7	3,310	-0.7	-0.4	10.6	7.9
104 El Salvador	11.2	-0.3	5.2	1,850	-1.7	3.0	8.9	2.6
105 Cape Verde	0.5	..	4.7	1,200	..	2.2	4.4	2.8
106 Uzbekistan	22.9	..	..	950	..	..	356.7	33.2
107 Algeria	46.4	3.6	1.4	1,550	0.6	-0.9	21.1	-4.2
108 Viet Nam	26.5	..	8.0	350	..	6.1	18.5	8.9
109 Indonesia	130.6	6.7	4.1	640	4.6	2.4	12.2	73.1
110 Tajikistan	2.3	..	-10.0	370	..	-11.6	300.0	49.9
111 Syrian Arab Republic	15.5	3.2	3.9	1,020	-0.1	0.9	8.9	7.0
112 Swaziland	1.4	6.0	3.0	1,400	2.7	-0.2	12.4	8.5
113 Honduras	4.6	3.7	4.3	740	0.4	1.4	20.6	13.6
114 Bolivia	8.0	..	4.6	1,010	..	2.1	9.9	7.7
115 Namibia	3.2	..	3.8	1,940	..	1.1	9.5	11.4
116 Nicaragua	1.8	-2.5	3.8	370	-5.2	0.9	38.9	12.9
117 Mongolia	1.0	..	0.1	380	..	-1.8	78.2	11.5
118 Vanuatu	0.2	..	-0.6	1,260	..	-3.3	4.3	3.1
119 Egypt	79.2	7.2	4.6	1,290	4.6	2.6	9.7	3.6
120 Guatemala	17.8	2.5	4.4	1,640	-0.1	1.7	11.4	6.8
121 Solomon Islands	0.3	6.1	2.8	760	2.5	-0.5	9.7	12.0
122 Botswana	4.8	12.3	3.9	3,070	8.5	1.4	10.3	7.9
123 Gabon	4.9	0.0	3.2	4,170	-3.2	0.5	7.2	-8.6
124 Morocco	34.4	4.2	2.6	1,240	1.9	0.7	3.5	0.7
125 Myanmar	..	..	..	..	..	..	25.9	34.0
126 Iraq	..	..	..	..	..	..	..	..
127 Lesotho	1.2	4.6	3.2	570	2.0	0.9	7.7	3.7
128 India	427.4	4.8	5.6	440	2.6	3.8	8.9	8.9
129 Ghana	7.3	1.7	4.3	390	-1.1	1.5	28.6	17.6
130 Zimbabwe	7.2	3.0	1.8	620	-0.2	-0.5	21.9	29.8
131 Equatorial Guinea	0.5	..	17.7	1,110	..	14.8	12.7	-23.6
132 São Tomé and Principe	0.0	..	1.5	270	..	-1.1	57.5	37.1
133 Papua New Guinea	4.1	1.3	4.5	890	-1.0	2.1	7.1	10.3
134 Cameroon	8.7	5.4	0.5	610	2.5	-2.2	6.1	1.1
135 Pakistan	61.5	6.2	4.3	470	3.2	1.7	11.1	7.8
136 Cambodia	2.9	..	4.7	260	..	1.8	32.8	17.0
137 Comoros	0.2	3.8	-0.5	370	..	-3.0	3.9	3.0
138 Kenya	10.2	4.8	2.4	350	1.1	-0.3	15.8	10.6
139 Congo	1.9	3.8	1.5	680	0.9	-1.3	7.1	-16.9
Low human development								
140 Lao People's Dem. Rep.	1.6	..	6.2	320	..	3.5	16.3	84.0
141 Madagascar	3.7	0.6	1.3	260	-2.0	-1.5	22.1	8.8
142 Bhutan	0.4	..	5.1	470	..	2.0	9.7	5.9
143 Sudan	8.2	1.4	5.3	290	-1.3	3.1	74.4	28.9
144 Nepal	4.9	4.0	4.8	210	1.3	2.3	8.9	3.3
145 Togo	1.5	2.2	1.6	330	-0.7	-1.4	8.8	2.7
146 Bangladesh	44.2	4.7	4.9	350	2.2	3.2	3.6	5.3
147 Mauritania	1.0	2.0	4.1	410	-0.6	1.3	5.3	8.8
148 Yemen	4.6	..	2.8	280	..	-1.5	24.2	-4.6
149 Djibouti	..	..	..	..	..	..	4.4	3.0
150 Haiti	3.2	1.6	-1.1	410	-0.3	-3.2	23.3	12.7

HDI rank	GNP (US$ billions) [a] 1998	GNP annual growth rate (%) [b]		GNP per capita (US$) [a] 1998	GNP per capita annual growth rate (%) [b]		Average annual rate of inflation (%)	
		1975-95	1990-98		1975-90	1990-98	1990-98	1998
151 Nigeria	36.4	1.5	3.5	300	-1.5	0.6	38.7	10.5
152 Congo, Dem. Rep. of the	5.4	-0.2	-5.3	110	-3.3	-8.3	1,423.1	15.0
153 Zambia	3.2	0.6	1.4	330	-2.5	-1.3	63.5	23.2
154 Côte d'Ivoire	10.2	1.3	4.1	700	-2.3	1.3	8.7	3.0
155 Senegal	4.7	2.4	3.2	520	-0.4	0.5	5.6	2.2
156 Tanzania, U. Rep. of	7.2	..	3.4	220	..	0.4	24.3	17.3
157 Benin	2.3	3.0	4.8	380	0.0	1.8	10.1	4.2
158 Uganda	6.6	..	7.1	310	..	3.9	15.3	10.7
159 Eritrea	0.8	..	..	200	..	..	10.1	-0.9
160 Angola	4.6	..	-3.3	380	..	-6.4	924.3	60.9
161 Gambia	0.4	3.3	3.6	340	-0.2	0.1	4.4	1.8
162 Guinea	3.8	..	4.7	530	..	2.0	6.7	4.3
163 Malawi	2.2	2.8	3.6	210	-0.5	0.9	33.2	23.2
164 Rwanda	1.9	4.7	-1.4	230	1.5	-3.3	18.1	2.6
165 Mali	2.6	2.1	3.7	250	-0.3	0.8	9.3	4.8
166 Central African Republic	1.1	0.8	1.3	300	-1.6	-0.8	5.4	1.8
167 Chad	1.7	1.6	3.1	230	-0.8	0.1	8.3	4.1
168 Mozambique	3.5	..	5.8	210	..	3.5	41.1	3.8
169 Guinea-Bissau	0.2	2.5	-1.2	160	-0.5	-3.4	41.8	7.7
170 Burundi	0.9	4.4	-1.9	140	1.7	-4.2	11.8	12.1
171 Ethiopia	6.2	..	3.3	100	..	1.0	8.0	9.7
172 Burkina Faso	2.6	3.2	4.1	240	0.8	1.7	6.6	3.1
173 Niger	2.0	1.5	2.4	200	-1.7	-1.0	6.8	3.0
174 Sierra Leone	0.7	0.6	-4.1	140	-1.4	-6.4	32.5	26.9
All developing countries	5,698.5 T	3.9	5.1	1,250	1.7	3.3	..	..
Least developed countries	156.5 T	2.4	3.3	270	-0.3	0.9	..	..
Arab States	564.6 T	3.2	3.0	2,220	0.1	0.5	..	..
East Asia	1,481.6 T	8.7	8.2	1,140	7.1	7.1	..	..
East Asia (excluding China)	558.1 T	8.0	5.6	10,020	6.5	4.4	..	..
Latin America and the Caribbean	1,903.9 T	2.2	3.6	3,830	0.1	1.9	..	..
South Asia	656.0 T	4.0	5.5	490	1.6	3.6	..	..
South Asia (excluding India)	228.6 T	2.7	4.1	630	-0.1	2.1	..	..
South-East Asia and the Pacific	574.2 T	5.6	6.1	1,130	3.4	4.3	..	..
Sub-Saharan Africa	310.8 T	2.0	2.3	530	-0.9	-0.4	..	..
Eastern Europe and the CIS	842.7 T	..	-4.3	2,110	..	-4.3	..	..
OECD	23,008.0 T	2.9	2.2	20,900	2.0	1.5	..	..
High human development	23,338.4 T	2.9	2.3	22,690	2.1	1.7	..	..
Medium human development	4,902.1 T	3.8	3.1	1,200	1.9	1.6	..	..
Low human development	184.8 T	1.8	3.3	280	-1.0	0.8	..	..
High income	22,273.3 T	2.8	2.2	25,870	2.2	1.6	..	..
Medium income	4,319.5 T	3.0	2.1	2,970	1.1	0.8	..	..
Low income	1,830.6 T	6.0	7.3	530	3.9	5.5	..	..
World	28,423.5 T	3.0	2.4	4,910	1.2	1.0	..	..

a. Data refer to GNP calculated using the World Bank Atlas method, in current US dollars. For further details see World Bank 2000b. b. Data are calculated on the basis of constant (1995 US dollar) series. Growth rates over intervals are compound averages. c. Data refer to 1995. d. Data refer to 1996. e. Data refer to 1997.

Source: Columns 1, 4, 7 and 8: World Bank 2000b; aggregates calculated for the Human Development Report Office by the World Bank; *columns 2, 3, 5 and 6:* calculated on the basis of GNP and GNP per capita data from World Bank 2000b; aggregates calculated for the Human Development Report Office by the World Bank.

14 Macroeconomic structure

	GDP (US$ billions)[a] 1998	Agriculture (as % of GDP)[b] 1998	Industry (as % of GDP)[b] 1998	Services (as % of GDP)[b] 1998	Consumption Private (as % of GDP) 1998	Consumption Government (as % of GDP) 1998	Gross domestic investment (as % of GDP) 1998	Gross domestic savings (as % of GDP) 1998	Central government Tax revenue (as % of GDP) 1998	Central government Expenditure (as % of GDP) 1998	Overall budget surplus/ deficit (as % of GDP)[c] 1998
High human development											
1 Canada	580.6	..	..	..	58.7 [d]	20.0 [d]	19.7 [d]	21.3 [d]	18.1 [e]	24.7 [e]	-3.5 [e]
2 Norway	145.9	2.0 [d]	32.1 [d]	65.9 [d]	47.5 [d]	20.2 [d]	25.2 [d]	32.3 [d]	34.1 [d]	35.7 [d]	0.7 [d]
3 United States	8,230.4	1.7 [d]	26.2 [d]	72.0 [d]	67.7 [d]	15.2 [d]	18.5 [d]	17.1 [d]	20.5	21.1	0.9
4 Australia	361.7	3.2 [f]	26.2 [f]	70.6 [f]	62.1 [d]	16.7 [d]	21.8 [d]	21.3 [d]	22.7	24.5	2.8
5 Iceland	7.9	..	25.7 [e]	63.0 [e]	61.1 [d]	20.5 [d]	17.8 [d]	18.5 [d]	25.2 [d]	29.2 [d]	0.4 [d]
6 Sweden	226.5	..	..	..	53.1 [d]	25.8 [d]	14.1 [d]	21.1 [d]	35.8	42.7	-1.6
7 Belgium	248.2	1.1 [d]	27.6 [d]	71.2 [d]	63.3 [d]	14.4 [d]	17.8 [d]	22.3 [d]	43.3 [d]	46.6 [d]	-2.0 [d]
8 Netherlands	381.8	3.1 [e]	26.9 [e]	70.0 [e]	59.1 [d]	13.7 [d]	20.2 [d]	27.2 [d]	42.7 [d]	47.6 [d]	-1.7 [d]
9 Japan	3,783.0	1.7 [d]	37.2 [d]	61.1 [d]	60.3 [d]	9.7 [d]	28.7 [d]	29.9 [d]	..	..	..
10 United Kingdom	1,357.2	1.8 [f]	31.5 [f]	66.7 [f]	64.3 [d]	20.3 [d]	15.9 [d]	15.4 [d]	36.4	37.9	0.6
11 Finland	123.5	4.0 [f]	34.3 [f]	61.7 [f]	52.9 [d]	20.9 [d]	17.3 [d]	26.2 [d]	28.1 [d]	35.3 [d]	-2.5 [d]
12 France	1,427.0	2.3 [d]	26.2 [d]	71.5 [d]	59.9 [d]	19.3 [d]	16.8 [d]	20.7 [d]	39.2 [d]	46.6 [d]	-3.5 [d]
13 Switzerland	263.6	..	..	..	61.2 [d]	14.1 [d]	20.3 [d]	24.8 [d]	22.0 [d]	27.9 [d]	-1.3 [d]
14 Germany	2,134.2	1.1 [d]	..	44.1 [d]	57.8 [d]	19.4 [d]	21.3 [d]	22.8 [d]	26.5	32.9	-0.9
15 Denmark	174.9	4.0 [e]	26.8 [e]	69.2 [e]	50.7 [d]	25.3 [d]	20.6 [d]	24.0 [d]	33.7 [e]	41.4 [e]	-1.9 [e]
16 Austria	211.9	1.4 [f]	30.5 [f]	68.1 [f]	56.2 [d]	19.0 [d]	25.3 [d]	24.8 [d]	34.8 [d]	40.5 [d]	-2.7 [d]
17 Luxembourg	17.4	0.8 [d]	..	..	48.0 [d]	12.4 [d]	23.6 [d]	39.6 [d]	41.9 [d]	41.0 [d]	2.1 [d]
18 Ireland	81.9	5.6 [e]	..	60.6 [e]	49.5 [d]	13.1 [d]	19.6 [d]	37.4 [d]	31.6 [f]	35.5 [f]	-0.4 [f]
19 Italy	1,171.9	2.6 [d]	30.5 [d]	66.9 [d]	61.8 [d]	16.3 [d]	17.5 [d]	21.9 [d]	38.6	44.6	-3.3
20 New Zealand	52.8	..	..	..	63.4 [d]	15.2 [d]	20.8 [d]	21.4 [d]	32.1	33.4	0.5
21 Spain	553.2	3.5 [f]	..	25.1 [f]	62.0 [d]	16.2 [d]	20.7 [d]	21.9 [d]	28.1 [f]	36.1 [f]	-5.5 [f]
22 Cyprus	9.0	..	..	..	63.4 [f]	18.0 [f]	25.1 [f]	18.6 [f]	24.7 [d]	37.0 [d]	-5.3 [d]
23 Israel	100.5	100.0 [e]	..	..	61.3	29.5	20.3	9.2	36.4	49.0	-1.2
24 Singapore	84.4	0.1	35.2	64.6	38.7	10.0	33.5	51.3	16.1 [d]	16.8 [d]	11.7 [d]
25 Greece	120.7	10.6 [e]	17.7 [e]	71.7 [e]	73.4 [d]	14.8 [d]	20.1 [d]	11.8 [d]	20.6 [d]	34.0 [d]	-8.4 [d]
26 Hong Kong, China (SAR)	166.4	0.1 [d]	14.7 [d]	85.2 [d]	60.1	9.4	30.2	30.5	..	..	..
27 Malta	3.5	..	..	..	62.4	20.0	23.0	17.6	29.0 [d]	41.6 [d]	-9.8 [d]
28 Portugal	106.7	3.9 [e]	35.2 [e]	60.9 [e]	64.5 [d]	18.6 [d]	25.6 [d]	16.9 [d]	32.1 [d]	40.8 [d]	-2.1 [d]
29 Slovenia	19.5	4.0	38.6	57.4	55.7	20.6	25.2	23.7	..	..	..
30 Barbados	2.3	6.6 [f]	20.0 [f]	73.4 [f]	66.8 [f]	15.0 [f]	16.4	16.8	..	..	..
31 Korea, Rep. of	320.7	4.9	43.5	51.6	55.3	10.9	20.9	33.8	17.3 [d]	17.4 [d]	-1.3 [d]
32 Brunei Darussalam	4.9	2.8	44.4	52.7	..	..	..	..	..	..	..
33 Bahamas	3.7 [f]	..	..	..	..	..	..	..	16.3	19.3	-1.9
34 Czech Republic	56.4	4.2	39.2	56.6	52.2	19.3	29.9	28.5	31.6	35.0	-1.6
35 Argentina	298.1	5.7	28.7	65.6	70.7	11.9	19.9	17.4	12.4 [d]	15.3 [d]	-1.5 [d]
36 Kuwait	25.2	0.4 [e]	53.5 [e]	46.1 [e]	56.2	31.2	14.3	12.7	1.5	50.9	..
37 Antigua and Barbuda	0.6	4.0	18.9	77.1	..	..	32.2	24.1	..	..	..
38 Chile	78.7	7.4	30.4	62.2	65.0	9.8	26.5	25.2	18.4	21.6	0.4
39 Uruguay	20.6	8.5	27.5	64.0	71.0	13.7	15.8	15.3	30.0	33.3	-0.8
40 Slovakia	20.4	4.4	31.6	64.0	50.2	21.6	39.4	28.2	..	..	..
41 Bahrain	5.3	0.9 [e]	39.9 [e]	59.2 [e]	35.4 [d]	22.5 [d]	6.0 [d]	42.1 [d]	10.1	32.0	-5.8
42 Qatar	9.2 [d]	..	..	..	..	..	..	..	..	..	..
43 Hungary	47.8	6.0 [d]	34.0 [d]	60.0 [d]	61.3	10.3	31.0	28.4	31.4	43.4	-6.1
44 Poland	158.6	..	..	..	62.3	16.4	26.4	21.3	32.7	37.7	-1.0
45 United Arab Emirates	47.2	..	..	..	..	..	..	..	0.7	11.0	-0.3
46 Estonia	5.2	6.3	26.7	67.0	57.7	22.6	29.3	19.7	29.9	32.9	-0.1
Medium human development											
47 Saint Kitts and Nevis	0.3	4.6	24.3	71.1	38.1	42.3	45.4	19.6	..	..	..
48 Costa Rica	10.5	15.2	24.3	60.5	56.6	16.6	28.7	26.8	23.1 [f]	30.1 [f]	-3.8 [f]
49 Croatia	21.8	8.9	32.4	58.7	59.6	26.2	23.2	14.2	43.3	45.6	0.6
50 Trinidad and Tobago	6.4	1.8	47.5	50.7	81.8	11.2	22.1	7.1	23.3 [e]	28.2 [e]	0.2 [e]

206   . . . TO HAVE ACCESS TO THE RESOURCES NEEDED FOR A DECENT STANDARD OF LIVING . . .

HDI rank	GDP (US$ billions) [a] 1998	Agriculture (as % of GDP) [b] 1998	Industry (as % of GDP) [b] 1998	Services (as % of GDP) [b] 1998	Consumption Private (as % of GDP) 1998	Consumption Government (as % of GDP) 1998	Gross domestic investment (as % of GDP) 1998	Gross domestic savings (as % of GDP) 1998	Central government Tax revenue (as % of GDP) 1998	Central government Expenditure (as % of GDP) 1998	Overall budget surplus/ deficit (as % of GDP) [c] 1998
51 Dominica	0.2	20.2	22.5	57.3	58.6	20.9	25.4	20.5	..	..	..
52 Lithuania	10.7	10.4	32.6	57.0	63.2	24.5	24.2	12.3	25.4	30.4	-0.4
53 Seychelles	0.5	4.1	23.6	72.4	46.5	33.2	37.5	20.3	34.3	68.3	1.4
54 Grenada	0.3	8.4	22.2	69.4	65.7	17.2	40.6	17.1	23.1 [e]	28.1 [e]	2.3 [e]
55 Mexico	393.5	4.9	26.6	68.4	68.2	9.4	24.4	22.4	13.0 [d]	16.3 [d]	-1.1 [d]
56 Cuba	..	..	..	..	..	..	..	..	..	..	..
57 Belarus	22.6	13.4	46.1	40.5	60.4	19.5	26.1	20.1	28.7	32.2	-0.9
58 Belize	0.7	18.7	25.5	55.8	67.3	13.8	23.9	18.9	..	..	..
59 Panama	9.1	7.9	18.4	73.8	60.0	16.5	32.8	23.5	18.4 [d]	27.0 [d]	0.2 [d]
60 Bulgaria	12.3	18.7	25.5	55.7	71.2	15.1	14.7	13.7	0.0	0.0	0.0
61 Malaysia	72.5	13.2	43.6	43.3	41.5	10.0	26.7	48.5	18.9 [d]	19.7 [d]	2.9 [d]
62 Russian Federation	276.6	7.3	35.3	57.4	64.9	13.8	16.3	21.2	18.4 [e]	25.4 [e]	-4.7 [e]
63 Latvia	6.4	4.7	29.4	65.9	63.9	26.3	23.0	9.8	28.0	33.0	0.1
64 Romania	38.2	16.4	40.1	43.4	76.1	14.7	17.7	9.2	24.4 [d]	31.9 [d]	-3.9 [d]
65 Venezuela	95.0	5.0	34.0	61.0	72.9	7.5	19.6	19.6	12.8	19.8	-2.8
66 Fiji	1.6	19.5	31.0	49.5	70.7	16.0	12.0	13.3	21.3 [f]	29.6 [f]	-4.9 [f]
67 Suriname	0.3 [e]	..	..	..	..	..	..	..	..	..	..
68 Colombia	102.9	13.5	25.1	61.4	69.6	16.4	19.6	13.9	10.1	16.0	-4.7
69 Macedonia, TFYR	2.5	11.4	28.3	60.3	75.4	17.5	22.8	7.1	..	..	..
70 Georgia	5.1	26.0	15.8	58.2	97.2	8.9	7.8	-6.1	4.6	8.6	-2.5
71 Mauritius	4.2	8.6	33.1	58.3	65.0	11.0	24.1	24.0	17.7	22.4	0.9
72 Libyan Arab Jamahiriya	..	..	..	..	..	..	..	..	..	..	..
73 Kazakhstan	22.0	9.2	31.2	59.6	76.3	10.9	17.3	12.8	..	..	..
74 Brazil	778.2	8.4	28.8	62.8	63.6	17.8	21.3	18.6	..	..	..
75 Saudi Arabia	128.9	7.0	47.6	45.4	41.3	32.5	21.0	26.2	..	..	..
76 Thailand	111.3	11.2	41.2	47.7	47.5	10.7	25.3	41.8	14.5	18.6	-3.5
77 Philippines	65.1	16.9	31.6	51.5	70.4	13.3	20.5	16.3	17.0 [d]	19.3 [d]	0.1 [d]
78 Ukraine	43.6	14.4	34.4	51.2	56.2	26.1	20.7	17.7	..	..	..
79 Saint Vincent and the Grenadines	0.3	10.9	26.9	62.2	70.5	18.8	31.8	10.7	26.6	42.3	-8.2
80 Peru	62.7	7.1	36.8	56.1	71.6	8.9	24.3	19.5	13.7	16.4	-0.2
81 Paraguay	8.6	24.9	26.2	48.9	72.9	10.5	21.0	16.6	..	..	..
82 Lebanon	17.2	12.4	26.5	61.1	98.3	14.5	27.6	-12.8	12.7	32.1	-15.1
83 Jamaica	6.4	8.0	33.7	58.4	60.0	21.6	31.5	18.4	..	..	..
84 Sri Lanka	15.7	21.1	27.5	51.4	71.3	9.8	25.4	18.9	14.5	25.0	-8.0
85 Turkey	198.8	17.6	25.4	57.0	66.3	12.6	24.6	21.1	19.1 [d]	29.9 [d]	-8.4 [d]
86 Oman	15.0	..	..	..	..	..	..	..	6.4	31.6	-6.6
87 Dominican Republic	15.9	11.6	32.8	55.6	74.9	8.2	25.8	16.9	15.5 [d]	16.7 [d]	0.4 [d]
88 Saint Lucia	0.6	8.1	18.9	72.9	68.8	15.2	19.3	16.1	..	..	..
89 Maldives	0.4	16.4	..	..	..	..	..	..	20.6	51.1	-5.3
90 Azerbaijan	3.9	20.3	38.7	41.0	84.2	11.0	39.2	4.8	18.2	25.1	-3.9
91 Ecuador	18.4	12.9	35.2	51.9	68.2	12.5	26.5	19.3	..	..	..
92 Jordan	7.4	3.0	25.7	71.3	69.5	26.7	25.0	3.8	19.8 [d]	34.0 [d]	-3.3 [d]
93 Armenia	1.9	32.9	31.8	35.3	..	11.2	19.0	-14.2	..	..	..
94 Albania	3.0	54.4	24.5	21.0	96.5	10.2	16.0	-6.7	14.8	29.8	-8.5
95 Samoa (Western)	0.2	..	..	..	..	..	..	..	..	..	..
96 Guyana	0.7	34.7	32.5	32.8	65.3	17.6	28.7	17.1	..	..	..
97 Iran, Islamic Rep. of	113.1	24.9 [f]	36.7 [f]	38.4 [f]	65.3	20.2	16.1	14.5	11.2	26.7	0.3
98 Kyrgyzstan	1.7	46.0	23.6	30.4	82.1	15.7	18.3	2.2	..	..	..
99 China	959.0	18.4	48.7	32.9	45.4	11.9	38.3	42.6	5.7 [d]	8.1 [d]	-1.5 [d]
100 Turkmenistan	2.4	24.6	41.8	33.6	..	..	..	..	..	..	..

14 Macroeconomic structure

HDI rank	GDP (US$ billions)[a] 1998	Agriculture (as % of GDP)[b] 1998	Industry (as % of GDP)[b] 1998	Services (as % of GDP)[b] 1998	Consumption Private (as % of GDP) 1998	Consumption Government (as % of GDP) 1998	Gross domestic investment (as % of GDP) 1998	Gross domestic savings (as % of GDP) 1998	Central government Tax revenue (as % of GDP) 1998	Central government Expenditure (as % of GDP) 1998	Overall budget surplus/deficit (as % of GDP)[c] 1998
101 Tunisia	20.0	12.4	28.4	59.1	62.7	13.0	27.5	24.3	24.8 [f]	32.6 [f]	-3.1 [f]
102 Moldova, Rep. of	1.6	28.9	31.3	39.8	84.4	18.4	26.0	-2.8	..	..	..
103 South Africa	133.5	4.0	31.8	64.3	63.0	20.2	15.6	16.9	24.6	29.7	-2.9
104 El Salvador	11.9	12.1	28.0	59.9	86.6	9.5	16.6	4.0	..	..	..
105 Cape Verde	0.5	12.2	19.1	68.7	75.6	16.2	40.2	8.3	..	..	..
106 Uzbekistan	20.4	31.2	27.0	41.9	59.4	21.6	19.2	19.0	..	..	..
107 Algeria	47.3	12.1	47.3	40.6	54.7	18.1	27.2	27.2	30.7 [f]	29.2 [f]	2.9 [f]
108 Viet Nam	27.2	25.7	32.6	41.7	71.1	7.6	28.7	21.3	15.8	20.1	-1.1
109 Indonesia	94.2	19.5	45.3	35.2	70.2	5.8	14.0	24.1	15.6	17.9	-2.4
110 Tajikistan	2.2	5.7	29.7	64.6	75.7 [e]	9.1 [e]	14.7 [e]	15.2 [e]	..	..	..
111 Syrian Arab Republic	17.4	..	..	..	70.3	11.4	29.5	18.3	16.4 [d]	24.6 [d]	-0.2 [d]
112 Swaziland	1.2	16.0	38.7	45.3	60.8	20.0	12.3	19.2	..	..	..
113 Honduras	5.4	20.3	30.9	48.8	66.2	10.3	29.6	23.4	..	..	..
114 Bolivia	8.6	15.4	28.7	55.9	75.2	14.0	20.0	10.8	15.1	21.9	-2.3
115 Namibia	3.1	10.0	34.2	55.9	55.7	25.5	19.0	18.8	..	..	..
116 Nicaragua	2.0	34.1	21.5	44.4	84.7	14.2	33.4	1.1	23.9 [e]	33.2 [e]	-0.6 [e]
117 Mongolia	1.0	32.8	27.6	39.6	62.5	17.5	25.8	20.0	13.5	23.0	-10.8
118 Vanuatu	0.2	24.7 [d]	12.2 [d]	63.2 [d]	..	..	..	..	..	..	..
119 Egypt	82.7	17.5	32.3	50.2	74.0	10.2	22.2	15.8	16.6 [d]	30.6 [d]	-2.0 [d]
120 Guatemala	18.9	23.3	20.0	56.8	86.8	5.6	16.0	7.7	..	..	..
121 Solomon Islands	0.3	..	..	..	..	..	..	..	..	..	..
122 Botswana	4.9	3.6	46.1	50.4	51.8	26.4	20.6	21.8	14.7 [f]	35.3 [f]	8.4 [f]
123 Gabon	5.5	7.3	60.3	32.5	41.9	14.9	32.3	43.2	..	..	..
124 Morocco	35.5	16.6	32.0	51.4	67.2	18.2	22.6	14.7	23.8 [e]	33.3 [e]	-4.4 [e]
125 Myanmar	..	53.2	9.0	37.8	..	..	11.7 [d]	11.1 [d]	4.5 [d]	8.9 [d]	-0.9 [d]
126 Iraq	..	..	..	..	..	..	..	..	..	..	..
127 Lesotho	0.8	11.5	42.0	46.5	..	21.7	48.6	-42.7	38.7	55.8	-4.1
128 India	430.0	29.3	24.7	45.9	68.6	10.5	23.6	20.9	8.6	14.4	-5.2
129 Ghana	7.5	10.4	6.9	82.7	76.5	10.3	22.9	13.2	..	..	..
130 Zimbabwe	6.3	19.5	24.4	56.1	69.0	15.6	17.2	15.4	26.4 [d]	35.7 [d]	-5.0 [d]
131 Equatorial Guinea	0.5	21.8	66.4	11.8	65.9	20.9	84.6	13.2	..	..	..
132 São Tomé and Principe	0.0	21.3	16.7	62.0	90.2	25.6	41.3	-15.9	..	..	..
133 Papua New Guinea	3.7	24.4	42.3	33.3	51.0	20.7	30.3	28.3	..	..	..
134 Cameroon	8.7	42.4	21.6	35.9	71.0	9.2	18.4	19.9	9.4 [e]	12.7 [e]	0.2 [e]
135 Pakistan	63.4	26.4	24.7	48.9	76.3	11.0	17.1	12.7	12.6	21.4	-6.3
136 Cambodia	2.9	50.6	14.8	34.6	85.8	8.7	15.0	5.5	..	..	..
137 Comoros	0.2	38.7	12.8	48.5	93.8	11.6	19.8	-5.4	..	..	..
138 Kenya	11.6	26.1	16.2	57.7	77.2	16.1	14.4	6.7	23.5 [f]	29.0 [f]	-0.9 [f]
139 Congo	2.0	11.5	49.9	38.6	59.4	14.3	35.1	26.4	6.7 [d]	38.4 [d]	-8.6 [d]
Low human development											
140 Lao People's Dem. Rep.	1.3	52.6	22.0	25.4	71.1	5.1	24.9	23.7	..	..	..
141 Madagascar	3.7	30.6	13.6	55.8	88.6	6.1	13.3	5.3	8.5 [f]	17.3 [f]	-1.3 [f]
142 Bhutan	0.4	38.2	36.5	25.4	36.2	25.8	47.3	37.9	7.8	36.9	-0.4
143 Sudan	10.4	39.3	18.2	42.6	..	..	..	..	..	..	..
144 Nepal	4.8	40.5	22.2	37.3	80.3	9.3	21.7	10.5	8.8	17.5	-4.7
145 Togo	1.5	42.1	21.1	36.8	81.2	11.3	14.2	7.5	..	..	..
146 Bangladesh	42.7	22.2	27.9	49.9	78.5	4.4	22.2	17.1	..	..	..
147 Mauritania	1.0	24.8	29.5	45.7	78.2	13.8	21.0	8.0	..	..	..
148 Yemen	4.3	17.6	48.8	33.6	75.7	21.9	21.5	2.4	15.2	42.2	-2.6
149 Djibouti	0.5 [d]	3.6 [d]	20.5 [d]	75.8 [d]	78.3 [d]	27.9 [d]	9.5 [d]	-6.2 [d]	..	..	..
150 Haiti	3.9	30.4	20.1	49.6	..	6.5	10.7	-6.9	..	..	..

... TO HAVE ACCESS TO THE RESOURCES NEEDED FOR A DECENT STANDARD OF LIVING ...

HDI rank	GDP (US$ billions) [a] 1998	Agriculture (as % of GDP) [b] 1998	Industry (as % of GDP) [b] 1998	Services (as % of GDP) [b] 1998	Consumption Private (as % of GDP) 1998	Consumption Government (as % of GDP) 1998	Gross domestic investment (as % of GDP) 1998	Gross domestic savings (as % of GDP) 1998	Central government Tax revenue (as % of GDP) 1998	Central government Expenditure (as % of GDP) 1998	Overall budget surplus/ deficit (as % of GDP) [c] 1998
151 Nigeria	41.4	31.7	41.0	27.3	77.5	10.7	20.0	11.8	..	..	..
152 Congo, Dem. Rep. of the	7.0	57.9 [d]	16.9 [d]	25.2 [d]	82.6 [d]	8.5 [d]	8.1	9.0 [d]	4.3 [d]	10.4 [d]	-0.8 [d]
153 Zambia	3.4	17.3	26.4	56.3	83.8	10.8	14.3	5.3	..	..	..
154 Côte d'Ivoire	11.0	26.0	22.7	51.3	64.8	10.6	18.2	24.5	20.8	24.0	-1.3
155 Senegal	4.7	17.4	24.1	58.5	74.8	10.3	19.6	14.9	..	..	..
156 Tanzania, U. Rep. of	8.0	45.7	14.9	39.4	83.3	8.3	15.0	8.4	..	..	..
157 Benin	2.3	38.6	13.5	47.9	82.1	9.7	17.1	8.3	..	..	..
158 Uganda	6.8	44.6	17.6	37.8	84.7	9.6	15.1	5.7	..	..	..
159 Eritrea	0.6	9.3 [d]	29.5 [d]	61.2 [d]	80.9	48.0	40.9	-29.0	..	..	..
160 Angola	7.5	12.3	51.5	36.3	34.9	34.7	20.2	30.4	..	..	..
161 Gambia	0.4	27.4	13.7	58.9	79.8	12.7	18.4	7.4	..	..	..
162 Guinea	3.6	22.4	35.4	42.1	73.7	6.9	21.1	19.4	10.0	16.9	-4.1
163 Malawi	1.7	35.9	17.8	46.4	85.2	14.4	13.7	0.4	..	..	..
164 Rwanda	2.0	47.4	21.2	31.4	90.3	11.5	15.7	-1.8	..	..	..
165 Mali	2.7	46.9	17.5	35.6	77.0	13.0	20.9	10.1	..	..	..
166 Central African Republic	1.1	52.6	18.6	28.8	83.9	11.7	13.5	4.4	..	..	..
167 Chad	1.7	39.8	14.3	45.9	88.0	9.4	15.0	2.6	..	..	..
168 Mozambique	3.9	34.3	20.8	44.8	89.0	9.3	20.4	1.7	..	..	..
169 Guinea-Bissau	0.2	62.4	12.7	24.9	99.6	9.3	11.3	-8.9	..	..	..
170 Burundi	0.9	54.2	16.4	29.5	89.3	13.2	9.0	-2.5	12.7 [d]	24.0 [d]	-5.5 [d]
171 Ethiopia	6.5	49.8	6.7	43.5	79.4	14.3	18.2	6.3	..	..	..
172 Burkina Faso	2.6	33.3	27.2	39.5	73.0	14.7	28.6	12.4	..	..	..
173 Niger	2.0	41.4	17.0	41.7	83.9	12.7	10.4	3.3	..	..	..
174 Sierra Leone	0.6	44.2	23.9	32.0	92.9	8.4	8.1	-1.3	10.2 [d]	17.7 [d]	-6.0 [d]
All developing countries	5,554.5 T	13.5	34.1	52.5	61.2	13.1	25.0	25.6	68.7	..	..
Least developed countries	145.9 T	32.7	24.1	43.1	78.1	10.4	19.1	10.7	52.3	..	..
Arab States	473.6 T	11.7	39.9	48.4	58.9	21.6	22.6	19.5	70.0	29.6	..
East Asia	1,447.3 T	13.3	43.6	43.0	49.3	11.4	33.5	39.3	71.6	10.4	-1.4
East Asia (excluding China)	488.2 T	3.3	33.7	63.0	57.0	10.4	24.1	32.6	74.7	..	..
Latin America and the Caribbean	1,965.9 T	7.8	28.7	63.6	67.4	13.6	21.9	19.0	70.1	..	..
South Asia	670.5 T	27.7	27.0	45.3	69.5	11.8	21.7	18.7	64.1	17.6	-4.3
South Asia (excluding India)	240.5 T	24.9	31.1	44.0	71.2	14.1	18.2	14.7	66.2	24.7	-2.6
South-East Asia and the Pacific	469.7 T	13.2	39.2	47.5	54.6	9.7	24.2	35.7	70.0	..	..
Sub-Saharan Africa	319.8 T	18.8	29.6	51.6	69.0	16.0	17.6	14.8	51.2	..	..
Eastern Europe and the CIS	806.6 T	9.9	35.0	55.2	63.2	16.5	22.1	20.2	69.8	..	..
OECD	22,938.8 T	2.2	29.6	64.6	62.9	15.5	20.7	21.5	77.5	29.8	-0.7
High human development	23,251.2 T	2.5	29.6	64.7	62.8	15.6	20.8	21.6	77.6	29.9	-0.6
Medium human development	4,779.8 T	14.5	34.8	50.8	61.3	13.9	24.9	24.8	68.0	..	..
Low human development	197.0 T	31.7	27.6	40.7	76.9	10.4	19.0	12.2	51.4	..	..
High income	22,236.5 T	2.4	..	65.0	62.8	15.8	20.7	21.4	77.8	30.2	-0.6
Medium income	4,159.0 T	9.4	32.7	57.9	63.7	14.8	21.9	21.6	69.5	..	..
Low income	1,832.6 T	23.1	38.7	38.2	57.8	11.0	30.2	31.0	65.5	..	..
World	28,228.1 T	4.8	30.6	62.1	62.6	15.3	21.5	22.1	75.8	..	..

Note: The percentage shares of agriculture, industry and services may not sum to 100 because of rounding.

a. Data refer to GDP at market prices (current US dollars). b. Data refer to value added. c. Including grants. d. Data refer to 1997. e. Data refer to 1995. f. Data refer to 1996.

Source: Columns 1-8: World Bank 2000b; *columns 9-11:* World Bank 2000b, data from the IMF.

HDI rank	Exports of goods and services (as % of GDP) 1990	Exports of goods and services (as % of GDP) 1998	Imports of goods and services (as % of GDP) 1990	Imports of goods and services (as % of GDP) 1998	Net foreign direct investment flows (US$ millions) Annual average 1987-92	Net foreign direct investment flows (US$ millions) 1998	Net portfolio investment flows (US$ millions)[a] 1990	Net portfolio investment flows (US$ millions)[a] 1998	Net bank and trade-related lending (US$ millions)[b] 1990	Net bank and trade-related lending (US$ millions)[b] 1998	Sovereign long-term debt rating[c] 1999
High human development											
1 Canada	26.1	40.7[d]	26.0	39.0[d]	5,899	16,500	..	..	..	..	AA+
2 Norway	40.6	41.3[d]	34.1	34.2[d]	320	3,597	..	..	..	..	AAA
3 United States	9.9	12.1[d]	11.3	13.5[d]	46,211	193,375	..	..	..	..	AAA
4 Australia	17.3	20.8[d]	17.1	21.4[d]	6,312	6,568	..	..	..	..	AA+
5 Iceland	34.3	36.4[d]	32.8	35.8[d]	-2	112	..	..	..	..	A+
6 Sweden	29.9	43.8[d]	29.5	36.8[d]	2,070	19,358	..	..	..	..	AA+
7 Belgium	68.1	72.9[d]	65.9	68.4[d]	7,214[e]	20,889[e]	..	..	..	..	AA+
8 Netherlands	54.2	56.0[d]	49.5	48.9[d]	7,147	31,859	..	..	..	..	AAA
9 Japan	10.7	11.1[d]	10.0	9.9[d]	911	3,192	..	..	..	..	AAA
10 United Kingdom	24.4	28.7[d]	27.1	29.2[d]	22,156	63,124	..	..	..	..	AAA
11 Finland	23.1	39.8[d]	24.6	31.0[d]	377	11,115	..	..	..	..	AA+
12 France	22.6	26.6[d]	22.6	22.7[d]	12,092	28,039	..	..	..	..	AAA
13 Switzerland	36.3	39.9[d]	35.7	35.5[d]	2,490	3,707	..	..	..	..	AAA
14 Germany	..	26.8[d]	..	25.3[d]	2,560	19,877	..	..	..	..	AAA
15 Denmark	35.8	36.0[d]	30.8	32.6[d]	897	6,623	..	..	..	..	AA+
16 Austria	40.2	42.3[d]	38.9	42.9[d]	648	5,915	..	..	..	..	AAA
17 Luxembourg	101.9	101.2[d]	96.8	85.2[d]	..	..	..	..	..	..	AAA
18 Ireland	58.7	79.7[d]	52.8	61.9[d]	615	6,820	..	..	..	..	AA+
19 Italy	20.0	27.3[d]	20.0	23.0[d]	4,317	2,611	..	..	..	..	AA
20 New Zealand	27.6	28.9[d]	26.9	28.2[d]	1,625	1,160	..	..	..	..	AA+
21 Spain	17.1	28.4[d]	20.4	27.2[d]	9,943	11,307	..	..	..	..	AA+
22 Cyprus	51.5	..	57.1	..	83	200	..	..	..	..	A
23 Israel	34.7	31.9	45.4	43.1	187	1,839	..	..	..	..	A-
24 Singapore	202.0	152.5	195.0	134.7	3,674	7,218	..	..	..	..	AAA
25 Greece	16.8	15.7[d]	28.1	24.0[d]	938	700	..	..	..	..	..
26 Hong Kong, China (SAR)	134.3	125.1	125.8	124.8	1,886	1,600	..	..	..	..	A
27 Malta	85.2	88.5	98.9	93.9	46	130	..	..	..	..	A
28 Portugal	33.9	31.4[d]	41.2	40.1[d]	1,676	1,711	..	..	..	..	AA
29 Slovenia	..	56.7	..	58.1	37[f]	165	..	..	..	..	A
30 Barbados	49.1	65.4	51.7	65.0	10	16	-44	-23	30	(.)	A-
31 Korea, Rep. of	29.1	48.7	30.3	35.8	907	5,143	686	5,315	-418	-3,087	BBB
32 Brunei Darussalam	..	..	..	..	1	4	..	..	..	..	..
33 Bahamas	..	..	..	..	9	235	..	..	..	..	..
34 Czech Republic	45.2	60.0	42.6	61.4	533[f]	2,540	0	966	669	-188	A-
35 Argentina	10.4	10.4	4.6	12.9	1,803	5,697	-843	9,087	-1,196	3,662	BB
36 Kuwait	44.9	45.1	58.1	46.7	7	-10	..	..	..	..	A
37 Antigua and Barbuda	89.0	74.8	87.0	82.9	15	20	..	..	..	..	..
38 Chile	34.6	27.5	31.4	28.9	927	4,792	313	789	1,194	3,825	A-
39 Uruguay	26.2	21.9	20.1	22.5	16	164	-16	336	-176	-5	BBB-
40 Slovakia	26.5	63.7	35.5	74.8	91[f]	466	0	-570	278	1,488	BB+
41 Bahrain	122.0	115.4[d]	99.7	79.3[d]	58	10	..	..	..	..	..
42 Qatar	..	..	..	..	10	70	..	..	..	..	BBB
43 Hungary	31.1	49.8	28.5	52.4	675	1,935	1,071	947	-1,379	1,800	BBB+
44 Poland	27.6	25.7[d]	20.7	30.0[d]	183	5,129	0	2,171	-18	1,117	BBB
45 United Arab Emirates	65.4	..	40.4	..	52	100	..	..	..	..	..
46 Estonia	..	79.8	..	89.4	..	581	..	70	..	63	BBB+
Medium human development											
47 Saint Kitts and Nevis	52.7	51.4	84.3	77.2	..	25	0	0	(.)	-2	..
48 Costa Rica	34.6	49.0	41.4	50.8	145	552	-42	184	-99	57	BB
49 Croatia	..	40.0	..	49.0	..	873	..	295	..	499	BBB-
50 Trinidad and Tobago	43.7	41.3	27.2	56.4	117	800	-52	0	-126	31	BBB-

... TO HAVE ACCESS TO THE RESOURCES NEEDED FOR A DECENT STANDARD OF LIVING ...

15 Resource flows

HDI rank	Exports of goods and services (as % of GDP)		Imports of goods and services (as % of GDP)		Net foreign direct investment flows (US$ millions) Annual average		Net portfolio investment flows (US$ millions) [a]		Net bank and trade-related lending (US$ millions) [b]		Sovereign long-term debt rating [c]
	1990	1998	1990	1998	1987-92	1998	1990	1998	1990	1998	1999
51 Dominica	54.5	55.4	80.5	60.3	..	20	0	0	(.)	0	..
52 Lithuania	52.1	47.2	60.6	59.1	..	926	..	0	..	57	BBB-
53 Seychelles	62.5	70.2	66.7	87.4	19	55	0	0	-6	5	..
54 Grenada	42.4	37.9	62.8	61.4	..	20	0	0	(.)	0	..
55 Mexico	18.6	31.2	19.7	33.2	4,310	10,238	1,224	3,158	4,396	9,792	BB
56 Cuba	..	..	..	..	3	30	..	..	..	..	..
57 Belarus	46.3	62.0	44.1	68.0	..	144	..	0	..	-27	..
58 Belize	63.8	48.5	61.6	53.5	14	12	0	0	6	6	..
59 Panama	38.4	33.8	33.8	43.1	-113	1,186	-2	219	-4	34	BB+
60 Bulgaria	33.1	45.2	36.7	46.3	34 [f]	401	65	9	-111	88	B
61 Malaysia	76.4	114.4	74.3	92.6	2,387	3,727	-947	278	-617	3,017	BBB
62 Russian Federation	18.2	31.7	17.9	26.8	..	2,183	310	11,834	5,252	4,748	SD [g]
63 Latvia	47.7	47.7	49.0	61.0	..	274	..	4	..	5	BBB
64 Romania	16.7	25.7	26.2	34.2	61 [f]	2,063	0	42	4	-247	B-
65 Venezuela	39.4	20.0	20.2	20.1	553	3,737	345	1,472	-922	959	B
66 Fiji	63.6	66.0	66.0	64.7	43	91	0	0	-16	-9	..
67 Suriname	28.2	..	27.4	..	-119	10	..	..	..	..	B-
68 Colombia	20.0	13.9	15.8	19.6	464	2,983	-4	1,778	-151	-1,187	BB+
69 Macedonia, TFYR	..	41.0	..	56.6	..	119	..	0	..	72	..
70 Georgia	39.9	14.0	45.7	28.0	..	251	..	0	..	7	..
71 Mauritius	65.2	64.8	72.5	65.0	25	13	0	8	45	-99	..
72 Libyan Arab Jamahiriya	..	..	..	..	52	150	..	..	..	..	..
73 Kazakhstan	..	30.6	..	35.1	17	1,158	..	100	..	725	B+
74 Brazil	8.2	7.4	7.0	10.1	1,513	28,718	129	1,951	-556	20,521	B+
75 Saudi Arabia	46.2	35.9	36.1	30.7	-35	2,400	..	..	..	..	..
76 Thailand	34.1	58.9	41.7	42.4	1,656	6,969	362	1,709	1,593	-826	BBB-
77 Philippines	27.5	55.7	33.3	59.9	518	1,713	395	605	-286	269	BB+
78 Ukraine	27.6	39.8	28.7	42.8	..	743	..	1,076	..	267	..
79 Saint Vincent and the Grenadines	65.8	50.2	76.8	71.3	..	40	0	0	0	(.)	..
80 Peru	12.0	12.0	11.6	16.7	50	1,930	0	174	18	620	BB
81 Paraguay	22.8	45.0	28.3	49.4	51	195	0	0	-9	-20	B
82 Lebanon	18.0	10.6	99.9	51.1	2	230	0	1,497	6	43	BB-
83 Jamaica	52.0	49.3	56.1	62.4	85	350	0	250	-46	-33	B
84 Sri Lanka	30.2	36.0	38.1	42.4	57	345	0	71	11	61	..
85 Turkey	13.3	24.8	17.6	28.2	578	807	632	345	466	357	B
86 Oman	52.7	..	30.6	..	103	50	0	10	-400	-330	BBB-
87 Dominican Republic	33.8	30.6	43.7	39.5	127	691	0	70	-3	10	B+
88 Saint Lucia	72.6	64.9	84.2	68.2	..	40	0	0	-1	7	..
89 Maldives	36.1	..	94.4	..	5	7	0	0	1	7	..
90 Azerbaijan	..	24.5	..	58.9	..	1,085	..	0	..	58	..
91 Ecuador	32.7	27.2	27.4	34.4	150	830	0	-10	57	-238	..
92 Jordan	61.9	49.2	92.7	70.3	21	223	0	1	216	-104	BB-
93 Armenia	35.0	18.9	46.3	52.1	8 [f]	232	0	0	0	0	..
94 Albania	14.9	9.5	23.2	32.2	..	45	0	0	31	-3	..
95 Samoa (Western)	30.6	..	65.1	..	2	10	0	0	0	0	..
96 Guyana	62.7	95.8	79.9	107.5	49 [f]	44	-1	0	-16	-4	..
97 Iran, Islamic Rep. of	22.0	13.2	23.5	14.8	-129	300	0	0	-30	564	..
98 Kyrgyzstan	30.2	35.3	48.8	51.4	..	102	..	0	..	-2	..
99 China	17.5	21.6	14.3	17.3	4,652 [f]	45,460	-48	2,860	4,668	-3,936	BBB
100 Turkmenistan	..	..	..	..	..	80	..	0	..	343	..

... TO HAVE ACCESS TO THE RESOURCES NEEDED FOR A DECENT STANDARD OF LIVING ...

211

HDI rank	Exports of goods and services (as % of GDP)		Imports of goods and services (as % of GDP)		Net foreign direct investment flows (US$ millions) Annual average		Net portfolio investment flows (US$ millions)[a]		Net bank and trade-related lending (US$ millions)[b]		Sovereign long-term debt rating[c]
	1990	1998	1990	1998	1987-92	1998	1990	1998	1990	1998	1999
101 Tunisia	43.6	42.4	50.6	45.6	160	650	-60	40	-138	4	BBB-
102 Moldova, Rep. of	48.8	46.5	51.2	75.3	..	85	..	0	..	-23	
103 South Africa	24.4	25.8	18.6	24.5	-24	371	..	922	..	-689	BB+
104 El Salvador	18.6	23.1	31.2	35.7	15	200	0	0	6	230	BB+
105 Cape Verde	12.7	24.9	43.7	56.9	1	15	0	0	(.)	-1	..
106 Uzbekistan	28.8	22.2	47.8	22.5	..	85	..	0	..	392	..
107 Algeria	23.3	23.4	25.1	23.3	..	500	-16	2	-409	-1,328	..
108 Viet Nam	26.4	43.6[d]	33.4	51.7[d]	206[f]	1,900	0	0	0	-368	..
109 Indonesia	26.1	53.9	23.7	43.8	999	-356	338	109	1,804	-3,512	CCC+
110 Tajikistan	..	..	..	..	..	30	..	0	..	-21	
111 Syrian Arab Republic	27.7	29.0	27.4	40.2	67	100	0	0	-53	-4	..
112 Swaziland	76.8	101.5	76.0	94.6	62	19	0	0	-2	0	..
113 Honduras	36.4	45.8	39.8	52.1	47	99	0	-32	33	141	..
114 Bolivia	22.8	19.7	23.9	28.9	53	872	0	0	-24	-12	BB-
115 Namibia	50.4	63.1	60.2	63.3	44	96	..	..	..	..	..
116 Nicaragua	24.9	39.1	46.3	71.5	3	184	0	0	21	-13	..
117 Mongolia	21.4	49.6	42.4	55.4	..	19	..	0	..	-12	B
118 Vanuatu	46.4	..	76.6	..	16	28	0	0	0	(.)	..
119 Egypt	20.0	16.8	32.7	23.3	806	1,076	-1	494	-35	-186	BBB-
120 Guatemala	21.0	18.6	24.8	26.9	133	584	-11	-31	7	-21	..
121 Solomon Islands	46.8	..	72.8	..	10	10	0	0	-3	(.)	..
122 Botswana	55.4	35.0	50.1	33.8	47	168	0	0	-19	-4	..
123 Gabon	46.0	51.2	30.9	40.2	56	300	0	0	29	-7	..
124 Morocco	19.4	18.1	29.0	26.0	203	258	0	174	176	470	BB
125 Myanmar	2.6	0.8[d]	4.8	1.3[d]	96	40	0	0	-8	83	..
126 Iraq	..	..	..	..	2	..	..	..	..	..	..
127 Lesotho	14.1	33.5	115.2	124.7	11	30	0	0	(.)	16	..
128 India	7.1	11.0	9.8	13.8	58	2,258	252	4,462	1,458	-946	BB
129 Ghana	16.9	26.7	25.9	36.4	14	45	0	15	-20	-29	..
130 Zimbabwe	22.9	45.9	22.8	47.8	-8	444	-30	-27	127	-266	..
131 Equatorial Guinea	32.2	101.8	69.6	173.2	10	200	0	0	0	0	..
132 Sâo Tomé and Principe	18.1	29.3	83.4	86.4	..	..	0	0	(.)	0	..
133 Papua New Guinea	40.6	68.2	48.9	70.2	138	30	0	0	49	120	B+
134 Cameroon	20.2	26.5	17.3	25.0	4	94	0	0	-12	-49	..
135 Pakistan	15.5	15.8	23.4	20.2	227	497	0	0	-63	306	B-
136 Cambodia	6.1	34.1	12.8	43.6	..	140	0	0	0	-3	..
137 Comoros	14.3	16.7	37.1	41.9	3	..	0	0	0	0	..
138 Kenya	26.2	24.6	31.4	32.3	31	42	0	4	65	-72	..
139 Congo	53.7	63.1	45.8	71.9	12	15	0	0	-100	0	..
Low human development											
140 Lao People's Dem. Rep.	11.3	3.7	24.5	4.9	4	45	0	0	0	0	..
141 Madagascar	16.6	21.2	27.3	29.2	12	100	0	0	-15	-1	..
142 Bhutan	28.3	33.2	32.3	42.6	..	..	0	0	-3	-2	..
143 Sudan	..	..	..	..	-6	10	0	0	0	0	..
144 Nepal	10.5	23.2	21.1	34.4	2	9	0	0	-14	-13	..
145 Togo	33.5	33.7	45.3	40.4	9	5	0	0	(.)	0	..
146 Bangladesh	6.3	13.8	13.8	18.9	2	317	0	3	67	-23	..
147 Mauritania	41.0	41.1	54.6	54.1	4	6	0	0	-1	-2	..
148 Yemen	14.6	34.5	20.5	53.6	198	100	0	0	161	0	..
149 Djibouti	..	41.3[d]	..	57.0[d]	..	25	0	0	-1	0	..
150 Haiti	16.0	11.5	29.2	29.1	3	6	0	0	0	0	..

. . . TO HAVE ACCESS TO THE RESOURCES NEEDED FOR A DECENT STANDARD OF LIVING . . .

HDI rank	Exports of goods and services (as % of GDP)		Imports of goods and services (as % of GDP)		Net foreign direct investment flows (US$ millions)		Net portfolio investment flows (US$ millions) [a]		Net bank and trade-related lending (US$ millions) [b]		Sovereign long-term debt rating [c]
	1990	1998	1990	1998	Annual average 1987-92	1998	1990	1998	1990	1998	1999
151 Nigeria	43.4	23.5	28.8	31.7	845	1,500	0	2	-121	-25	..
152 Congo, Dem. Rep. of the	29.5	24.0 [d]	29.2	22.1 [d]	-11	..	(.)	0	-12	0	..
153 Zambia	35.9	29.4	36.6	38.4	102	222	0	0	-9	-32	..
154 Côte d'Ivoire	31.7	44.2	27.1	37.9	-1	250	-1	-17	10	-237	..
155 Senegal	25.4	33.3	30.3	38.0	18	20	0	0	-15	-16	..
156 Tanzania, U. Rep. of	12.1	18.4	35.5	25.0	3	172	0	0	4	-16	..
157 Benin	21.8	23.3	30.5	32.1	3	26	0	0	(.)	0	..
158 Uganda	7.2	10.3	19.4	19.7	..	210	0	0	16	-2	..
159 Eritrea	..	19.9	..	89.7	..	..	..	0	..	0	..
160 Angola	38.8	51.8	20.8	41.7	178	396	0	0	..	-320	..
161 Gambia	59.9	51.1	71.6	62.1	6	14	0	0	-8	0	..
162 Guinea	30.9	21.6	30.6	23.4	20	15	0	0	-19	-10	..
163 Malawi	24.8	30.5	34.9	43.8	12	70	0	24	2	-1	..
164 Rwanda	5.6	5.4	14.1	22.9	12	7	0	0	-2	0	..
165 Mali	17.1	23.6	33.7	34.4	-1	30	0	0	-1	0	..
166 Central African Republic	14.8	15.9	27.6	25.0	..	4	0	0	-1	0	..
167 Chad	13.5	19.3	29.0	31.7	6	35	0	0	-1	0	..
168 Mozambique	8.2	11.7	36.1	30.5	12	213	0	0	26	-4	..
169 Guinea-Bissau	9.9	14.9	37.0	35.1	2	8	0	0	(.)	0	..
170 Burundi	7.9	8.1	27.8	19.6	..	..	0	0	-6	1	..
171 Ethiopia	7.8	15.8	12.4	27.7	1	178	0	0	-57	2	..
172 Burkina Faso	12.7	13.8	25.6	30.0	2	14	0	0	0	0	..
173 Niger	15.0	16.3	22.0	23.4	22	..	0	0	10	-24	..
174 Sierra Leone	24.0	22.0	17.3	31.5	12	30	0	0	4	0	..
All developing countries	27.0	31.7	26.3	30.2	31,786 T	155,225 T	2,561 T	38,281 T	10,532 T	27,091 T	..
Least developed countries	16.0	20.2	23.9	28.8	763 T	2,747 T	0 T	27 T	130 T	-345 T	..
Arab States	39.2	30.4	38.4	32.8	1,700 T	5,942 T	..	..	..	..	..
East Asia	37.0	40.2	34.9	33.4	7,445 T	52,222 T	..	8,176 T	..	-7,035 T	..
East Asia (excluding China)	54.2	65.5	53.1	55.3	2,793 T	6,762 T	..	5,315 T	..	-3,099 T	..
Latin America and the Caribbean	15.4	16.6	13.3	19.6	10,433 T	65,320 T	997 T	19,375 T	2,438 T	38,361 T	..
South Asia	10.6	12.7	14.2	15.7	222 T	3,733 T	252 T	4,536 T	1,428 T	-47 T	..
South Asia (excluding India)	17.1	16.1	22.5	19.9	164 T	1,475 T	0 T	74 T	-30 T	899 T	..
South-East Asia and the Pacific	55.9	77.9	57.2	66.2	9,750 T	21,569 T	148 T	2,701 T	2,516 T	-1,230 T	..
Sub-Saharan Africa	27.3	28.4	24.7	30.7	1,575 T	5,432 T	-31 T	930 T	-90 T	-1,880 T	..
Eastern Europe and the CIS	24.8	36.6	25.2	38.0	..	21,695 T	..	16,944 T	..	11,218 T	..
OECD	17.4	21.7	17.9	20.7	143,602 T	483,951 T	..	..	..	..	..
High human development	18.8	22.7	19.1	21.7	147,626 T	496,203 T	..	..	..	..	..
Medium human development	20.7	26.4	20.9	26.1	20,977 T	136,808 T	2,840 T	36,125 T	16,260 T	30,358 T	..
Low human development	22.2	22.3	24.5	28.9	1,471 T	4,037 T	-1 T	11 T	14 T	-725 T	..
High income	18.5	22.1	18.8	21.2	142,408 T	469,710 T	..	..	..	..	..
Medium income	23.0	30.2	22.8	29.4	19,822 T	110,791 T	3,496 T	47,821 T	7,272 T	47,338 T	..
Low income	17.2	23.1	17.5	21.9	7,844 T	56,547 T	511 T	7,404 T	7,985 T	-9,029 T	..
World	19.2	23.3	19.4	22.4	170,074 T	637,048 T	..	55,224 T	..	38,309 T	..

a. Portfolio investment flows are net and include non-debt-creating portfolio equity flows (the sum of country funds, depository receipts and direct purchases of shares by foreign investors) and portfolio debt flows (bond issues purchased by foreign investors). b. Bank and trade-related lending covers commercial bank lending and other private credits. c. Ratings cover foreign currency debt and refer to information as of February 2000. d. Data refer to 1997. e. Data refer to Belgium and Luxembourg. f. Years for annual average differ slightly from those in the column heading. g. SD refers to *selective default*, assigned when Standard & Poor's believes that the obligor has selectively defaulted on a specific issue or class of obligations but will continue to meet its payment obligations on other issues or classes of obligations in a timely manner.

Source: Columns 1-4, 9 and 10: World Bank 2000b; *columns 5 and 6:* UNCTAD 1999b; *columns 7 and 8:* calculated on the basis of data on portfolio investment (bonds and equity) from World Bank 2000b; *column 11:* Standard & Poor's 2000.

16 Resource use

HDI rank	Public expenditure on education (as % of GNP)		Public expenditure on health (as % of GDP)		Military expenditure (as % of GDP)		Trade in conventional weapons (1990 prices) [a]				Total armed forces	
							Imports		Exports			Index
							US$ millions	Index (1991 = 100)	US$ millions	Share (%) [c]	Thousands	(1985 = 100)
	1990	1995-97 [b]	1990	1996-98 [b]	1990	1998	1999	1999	1999	1995-99	1998	1998
High human development												
1 Canada	6.8	6.9 [d]	6.8	6.4	2.0	1.3	33	5	168	1.0	61	73
2 Norway	7.3	7.4	6.5	6.2	2.9	2.3	170	52	..	0.1	29	78
3 United States	5.2	5.4 [d]	5.1	6.5	5.3	3.2	111	31	10,442	48.0	1,402	65
4 Australia	5.3	5.5	5.5	5.5	2.2	1.9	341	235	298	0.6	57	82
5 Iceland	5.6	5.4	6.9	7.0	..	..	..	..	..	..	..	..
6 Sweden	7.7	8.3	7.9	7.2	2.6 [e]	2.2	79	343	157	0.6	53	81
7 Belgium	5.0 [f]	3.1 [g]	6.7	6.8	2.4	1.5	37	42	28	0.5	44	48
8 Netherlands	6.0	5.1	6.1	6.1	2.6	1.8	225	110	329	2.0	57	54
9 Japan	..	3.6 [d]	4.7	5.9	1.0	1.0	1,089	74	..	(.)	243	100
10 United Kingdom	4.9	5.3	5.1	5.9	4.0	2.7	155	17	1,078	6.6	211	64
11 Finland	5.7	7.5	6.5	5.7	1.6 [e]	1.5	821	1,346	16	(.)	32	87
12 France	5.4	6.0	6.6	7.1	3.6	2.8	105	11	1,701	10.5	359	77
13 Switzerland	4.9	5.4	5.7	7.1	1.8	1.2	508	134	58	0.3	26	132
14 Germany	..	4.8	..	8.3	2.8 [h]	1.5	126	17	1,334	5.5	334	70
15 Denmark	7.1 [i]	8.1	7.0	6.7	2.1	1.6	137	120	..	(.)	32	108
16 Austria	5.4	5.4	5.3	6.0	1.0 [j]	0.8	48	1,600	37	0.1	46	83
17 Luxembourg	2.6 [f]	4.0	5.9	6.4	0.9	0.8	..	..	..	..	1	114
18 Ireland	5.6	6.0	4.9	4.9	1.3	0.8	30	273	..	..	12	84
19 Italy	..	4.9	6.3	5.3	2.1	2.0	..	..	533	1.8	298	77
20 New Zealand	6.5	7.3	5.8	5.9	1.8 [e]	1.3	337	1,021	..	(.)	10	77
21 Spain	4.4	5.0	5.4	5.6	1.8	1.4	289	318	43	0.9	194	61
22 Cyprus	3.4	4.5	..	..	5.0	4.4 [i]	242	233	..	(.)	10	100
23 Israel	6.5	7.6 [d]	5.2	7.0	12.3	8.7	1,205	98	144	1.0	175	123
24 Singapore	3.0	3.0	1.0	1.1	4.8	5.1 [e]	163	56	1	0.1	73	132
25 Greece	2.5	3.1	3.5	5.3	4.7	4.8	633	135	1	0.1	169	84
26 Hong Kong, China (SAR)	2.8	2.9	1.6	2.1	..	..	..	..	..	..	..	..
27 Malta	4.0	5.1	..	..	0.9	0.8	..	..	..	..	2	238
28 Portugal	4.2 [f]	5.8	4.2	4.7	2.7	2.2	1	0	..	..	54	73
29 Slovenia	4.8 [i]	5.7	..	6.8	..	1.5	19	..	..	..	10	..
30 Barbados	7.9	7.2	5.0	4.6	..	..	..	..	..	..	1	60
31 Korea, Rep. of	3.5	3.7	2.1	2.5	3.7	3.1	1,245	141	..	0.1	672	112
32 Brunei Darussalam	2.5	..	1.6	0.8 [d]	..	7.6	..	..	..	..	5	122
33 Bahamas	4.3	..	2.8	2.5	..	..	54	2,700	..	..	1	180
34 Czech Republic	..	5.1	4.8	6.4	..	2.1	..	..	124	0.5	59	..
35 Argentina	3.4 [i]	3.5	4.2	4.7 [d]	1.3 [e]	1.4	223	..	..	(.)	73	68
36 Kuwait	3.5	5.0	4.0	2.9	48.5	9.3 [e]	126	21	..	0.1	15	128
37 Antigua and Barbuda	..	..	2.8	0.4	..	..	..	..	..	..	(.)	200
38 Chile	2.7 [i]	3.6	2.0	2.4	2.4 [e]	1.9	177	199	3	(.)	95	94
39 Uruguay	3.1	3.3	1.2	1.9	2.4	..	13	18	..	..	26	80
40 Slovakia	5.1	5.0	5.4	5.2	..	2.0	..	..	..	0.2	46	..
41 Bahrain	5.0	4.4	..	2.6	5.1	5.0	..	..	..	..	11	393
42 Qatar	3.4	3.4 [d]	..	2.9	..	..	117	900	..	(.)	12	197
43 Hungary	6.1	4.6	..	4.1	2.5	1.3	56	181	..	0.1	43	41
44 Poland	5.4 [i]	7.5	..	4.2	2.7	2.1	1	1	51	0.3	241	75
45 United Arab Emirates	1.7	1.8	..	4.5 [d]	4.7	3.3	595	209	..	0.1	65	150
46 Estonia	..	7.2	2.1	5.1	..	1.2	..	..	..	(.)	4	..
Medium human development												
47 Saint Kitts and Nevis	..	3.8	2.7	3.1	..	..	..	..	..	..	..	..
48 Costa Rica	4.6	5.4	6.6	6.7	0.4 [e, k]	0.6 [e, k, l]	..	..	..	..	..	..
49 Croatia	6.0 [i]	5.3	9.5	8.1	..	6.2	..	..	..	..	56	..
50 Trinidad and Tobago	4.0	4.4	2.8	2.8	..	..	..	..	..	..	3	124

... TO HAVE ACCESS TO THE RESOURCES NEEDED FOR A DECENT STANDARD OF LIVING ...

HDI rank	Public expenditure on education (as % of GNP)		Public expenditure on health (as % of GDP)		Military expenditure (as % of GDP)		Trade in conventional weapons (1990 prices)[a]				Total armed forces	
							Imports		Exports			Index (1985 = 100)
							US$ millions	Index (1991 = 100)	US$ millions	Share (%)[c]	Thousands	
	1990	1995-97 [b]	1990	1996-98 [b]	1990	1998	1999	1999	1999	1995-99	1998	1998
51 Dominica	..	..	3.9	3.9	..	..	..	..	..	..	..	..
52 Lithuania	4.6	5.5	3.0	7.2	..	1.3	4	..	..	..	11	..
53 Seychelles	8.1	7.9	3.6	5.4	4.0	2.0	..	..	..	..	(.)	17
54 Grenada	5.4	4.7	3.4	2.9	..	..	..	..	..	..	..	..
55 Mexico	3.7	4.9	2.1	2.8	0.5 e	0.6	14	67	..	..	175	136
56 Cuba	6.6 m	6.7	4.9	8.2 d	..	..	..	..	..	..	60	37
57 Belarus	4.9	5.9	2.5	4.9	..	1.0	..	..	38	0.7	83	..
58 Belize	4.8	5.0	2.2	2.2	1.2	1.5 l	..	..	..	..	1	183
59 Panama	4.9	5.1	4.6	5.8	1.4	1.4 l	..	..	..	..	..	..
60 Bulgaria	5.6	3.2	4.1	3.2	4.5	2.5	6	1	89	0.1	102	68
61 Malaysia	5.5	4.9	1.5	1.3	2.6	1.7	916	2,349	..	(.)	110	100
62 Russian Federation	3.5	3.5	2.7	4.5	12.3 e, n	3.2 e	..	..	3,125	13.1	1,159	..
63 Latvia	3.8	6.3	2.7	4.0	..	0.7	4	..	..	(.)	5	..
64 Romania	2.8	3.6	2.8	2.9	3.5	2.2	35	81	19	(.)	220	116
65 Venezuela	3.1	5.2 d	2.0	1.0 d	2.0 i	1.3 j	142	55	..	..	56	114
66 Fiji	4.7 f	5.4 d, f	2.0	2.9	2.2	1.4	..	..	..	..	4	130
67 Suriname	8.3	3.5	3.5	2.0 d	..	..	12	..	..	..	2	90
68 Colombia	2.6 f	4.4 f	1.0	1.5	2.6 e	2.6	40	83	..	..	146	221
69 Macedonia, TFYR	..	5.1	..	7.8	..	2.4	95	..	..	..	20	..
70 Georgia	..	5.2 d	3.0	0.7	..	1.0 e	60	..	..	0.1	33	..
71 Mauritius	3.6	4.6	..	1.9	0.3	0.2 l	..	..	..	..	..	..
72 Libyan Arab Jamahiriya	..	..	..	..	..	..	..	..	..	(.)	65	89
73 Kazakhstan	3.2	4.4	3.2	2.1	..	1.0	259	..	155	0.2	55	..
74 Brazil	..	5.1	3.0	3.4	1.3 j	1.4	221	201	..	0.1	313	114
75 Saudi Arabia	6.0	7.5	..	6.4	12.8 e	12.8 e	1,231	104	..	(.)	163	260
76 Thailand	3.6	4.8	1.0	1.7	2.2	2.1	185	43	..	..	306	130
77 Philippines	2.9	3.4	1.5	1.7	1.4	1.4	..	..	..	..	118	103
78 Ukraine	5.0	7.3	3.0	4.1	..	3.6	..	..	429	1.8	346	..
79 Saint Vincent and the Grenadines	6.3 i	..	4.4	4.2	..	..	..	..	..	..	..	..
80 Peru	2.3	2.9	1.0	2.2	2.0	..	108	114	..	..	125	98
81 Paraguay	1.1 f	4.0 f	0.4	2.6	1.2	..	..	..	..	..	20	140
82 Lebanon	..	2.5 f	..	3.0	5.0	3.2 e	..	..	..	..	55	317
83 Jamaica	5.4	7.5	2.6	2.3	..	..	5	..	..	..	3	157
84 Sri Lanka	2.7	3.4	1.7	1.4	2.1	4.2	26	25	..	..	115	532
85 Turkey	2.1 o	2.2	2.2	2.9	3.5	4.4	1,134	146	46	(.)	639	101
86 Oman	3.5	4.5	2.0	2.1	18.3	11.6 j	..	..	..	(.)	44	149
87 Dominican Republic	..	2.3	1.6	1.6	..	..	3	..	..	..	25	110
88 Saint Lucia	..	9.8	2.1	2.5	..	..	..	..	..	..	..	..
89 Maldives	6.3	6.4	4.9	5.1	..	..	..	..	..	..	..	..
90 Azerbaijan	7.0	3.0	2.6	1.2	..	2.7	..	..	..	..	72	..
91 Ecuador	3.1	3.5	1.5	2.5	1.9	..	24	12	..	..	57	134
92 Jordan	8.9	7.9	3.6	3.7 d	9.6	9.6	44	126	..	(.)	104	148
93 Armenia	7.3	2.0	..	3.1	..	3.6	..	..	..	..	53	..
94 Albania	5.8	3.1 d	3.3	2.7	..	1.1	..	..	..	..	54	134
95 Samoa (Western)	4.2	..	3.9	4.8	..	..	..	..	..	..	..	..
96 Guyana	4.8	5.0	2.9	4.5	0.9	0.9 e, l	..	..	..	..	2	24
97 Iran, Islamic Rep. of	4.1	4.0	2.8	1.7	2.8	3.1	67	4	..	(.)	540	177
98 Kyrgyzstan	8.3	5.3	4.2	2.7	..	1.4	..	..	..	0.1	12	..
99 China	2.3	2.3	1.2	0.7	2.7 e	1.9 e	1,688	734	79	2.0	2,820	72
100 Turkmenistan	4.3	..	3.9	3.5	..	3.6	..	..	..	..	19	..

HDI rank	Public expenditure on education (as % of GNP) 1990	1995-97 [b]	Public expenditure on health (as % of GDP) 1990	1996-98 [b]	Military expenditure (as % of GDP) 1990	1998	Trade in conventional weapons (1990 prices) [a] Imports US$ millions 1999	Index (1991 = 100) 1999	Exports US$ millions 1999	Share (%) [c] 1995-99	Total armed forces Thousands 1998	Index (1985 = 100) 1998
101 Tunisia	6.2	7.7	3.0	3.0 [d]	2.7	1.8	..	..	..	..	35	100
102 Moldova, Rep. of	5.6	10.6	4.4	4.8	..	0.6	..	..	..	0.3	11	..
103 South Africa	6.5	8.0	3.1	3.2 [d]	4.0	1.6	14	70	14	0.1	82	77
104 El Salvador	2.0	2.5	1.4	2.6	2.7	0.9	..	..	..	..	25	59
105 Cape Verde	4.0 [i]	..	..	2.8 [d]	..	0.9	..	..	..	..	1	14
106 Uzbekistan	9.5	7.7	4.6	3.3	..	1.4 [e, l]	..	..	..	..	80	..
107 Algeria	5.5 [o]	5.1 [o]	3.0	3.3 [d]	1.5 [e]	3.9	..	..	..	..	122	72
108 Viet Nam	2.1	3.0	0.9	0.4	8.7	..	154	..	..	..	484	47
109 Indonesia	1.0 [f]	1.4 [p]	0.6	0.6	1.6	1.0	213	2,663	66	0.1	299	108
110 Tajikistan	9.7	2.2	4.3	6.6	..	1.2 [j, l]	..	..	..	..	9	..
111 Syrian Arab Republic	4.3	3.1 [o]	..	..	6.9	6.3 [e]	20	5	..	(.)	320	80
112 Swaziland	5.5	5.7	1.9	2.5	1.6	..	..	..	..	..	..	..
113 Honduras	4.1 [i]	3.6	2.9	2.7	2.2	0.8 [i]	..	..	..	..	8	50
114 Bolivia	..	4.9	0.9	1.1	2.3	1.8	..	..	..	..	34	121
115 Namibia	7.5	9.1	3.8	3.8	..	2.6	..	..	..	..	9	..
116 Nicaragua	3.4 [o]	3.9 [o]	1.0	4.4	2.1 [j]	1.2	..	..	..	(.)	17	27
117 Mongolia	12.9	5.7	6.0	4.3 [d]	5.7	2.2 [e]	..	..	..	..	10	30
118 Vanuatu	4.4	4.8	2.6	2.8 [d]	..	..	..	..	..	..	..	..
119 Egypt	3.8	4.8	1.8	1.8	4.0	2.9	748	106	..	(.)	450	101
120 Guatemala	1.4 [f]	1.7 [f]	0.9	1.5	1.5	0.7 [j]	..	..	..	..	31	99
121 Solomon Islands	3.8 [i]	..	5.0	4.2	..	..	..	..	..	..	..	..
122 Botswana	6.9	8.6	1.3	2.7	3.9	3.5	34	1,133	..	..	9	213
123 Gabon	..	2.9 [o]	..	0.6	..	0.3	..	..	..	..	5	196
124 Morocco	5.5 [f]	5.3 [f]	0.9	1.3	4.1	..	..	..	..	..	196	132
125 Myanmar	..	1.2 [d, f]	1.0	0.2	3.4	3.0	27	16	..	..	350	188
126 Iraq	..	..	..	..	..	..	..	..	..	..	429	83
127 Lesotho	3.7	8.4	2.6	3.7 [d]	4.1	3.2	..	..	..	..	2	100
128 India	3.9	3.2	0.2	0.6	2.9	2.1	566	43	..	(.)	1,175	93
129 Ghana	3.3	4.2	1.4	1.6	0.4	0.8	..	..	..	..	7	46
130 Zimbabwe	8.0	7.1 [d]	..	3.1	4.5	2.6	..	..	..	..	39	95
131 Equatorial Guinea	..	1.7 [d]	5.8	..	..	..	..	..	..	..	1	59
132 Sao Tome and Principe	..	..	..	6.1 [d]	..	..	..	..	..	..	..	..
133 Papua New Guinea	..	..	3.1	2.6	2.1	1.0	..	..	..	..	4	134
134 Cameroon	3.4	..	0.9	1.0	1.7 [e]	..	..	..	..	..	13	179
135 Pakistan	2.7	2.7	0.8	0.8 [d]	5.7	4.2	839	183	..	(.)	587	122
136 Cambodia	..	2.9	..	0.6	..	2.7	2	..	..	(.)	139	397
137 Comoros	..	..	..	3.1	..	..	..	..	..	..	..	..
138 Kenya	7.1	6.5	1.7	2.2 [d]	3.3	2.3 [e]	..	..	..	..	24	177
139 Congo	6.0	6.1	1.5	1.8	..	..	..	..	..	..	10	115
Low human development												
140 Lao People's Dem. Rep.	..	2.1	0.0	1.2	..	2.4 [l]	..	..	..	..	29	54
141 Madagascar	2.2	1.9	..	1.1	1.2	1.4	..	..	..	..	21	100
142 Bhutan	..	4.1	2.1	3.2	..	..	..	..	..	..	6	200
143 Sudan	..	1.4	..	..	3.5 [e]	1.0 [l]	10	26	..	..	95	167
144 Nepal	2.0	3.2	0.8	1.3	0.8	0.9	..	..	..	..	50	200
145 Togo	5.6	4.5	1.3	1.1	3.1	..	..	..	..	..	7	194
146 Bangladesh	1.5 [f]	2.2 [f]	0.8	1.6	1.4	1.6	130	277	..	..	121	133
147 Mauritania	..	5.1 [f]	..	1.8 [d]	3.8	2.3 [l]	..	..	..	..	16	185
148 Yemen	..	7.0	1.2	2.1	8.4	6.5	53	68	..	..	66	103
149 Djibouti	..	..	..	..	..	4.4	..	..	..	..	10	320
150 Haiti	1.5	..	1.2	1.3	..	..	..	..	..	..	..	..

16 Resource use

	Public expenditure on education (as % of GNP)		Public expenditure on health (as % of GDP)		Military expenditure (as % of GDP)		Trade in conventional weapons (1990 prices) [a]				Total armed forces	
							Imports		Exports			Index (1985 = 100)
							US$ millions	Index (1991 = 100)	US$ millions	Share (%) [c]	Thousands	
HDI rank	1990	1995-97 [b]	1990	1996-98 [b]	1990	1998	1999	1999	1999	1995-99	1998	1998
151 Nigeria	1.0	0.7	1.0	0.2	0.7	0.7	..	..	..	..	77	82
152 Congo, Dem. Rep. of the	..	..	..	1.2	..	..	..	..	..	..	50	104
153 Zambia	2.6	2.2	2.6	2.3	3.7	1.8	..	..	..	..	22	133
154 Côte d'Ivoire	..	5.0	..	1.4 [d]	1.5	0.9 [l]	..	..	..	..	8	64
155 Senegal	4.1	3.7	2.8	2.6	2.0	1.4	..	..	..	..	11	109
156 Tanzania, U. Rep. of	3.4	..	1.8	1.3	..	1.4 [e]	..	..	..	..	34	84
157 Benin	..	3.2	0.5	1.6	1.8	..	..	..	..	..	5	107
158 Uganda	1.5 [f]	2.6	..	1.8	2.5	2.2	..	..	..	..	40	200
159 Eritrea	..	1.8	..	2.9	..	13.5 [l]	..	..	..	..	47	..
160 Angola	4.9 [f]	..	1.4	..	5.8	14.9	..	..	..	..	114	230
161 Gambia	4.1	4.9	..	1.4	1.1	1.1	..	..	..	..	1	160
162 Guinea	2.1 [i]	1.9	1.2	1.2	..	..	..	..	..	..	10	98
163 Malawi	3.4	5.4	..	2.8	1.3	0.8 [l]	..	..	..	..	5	94
164 Rwanda	..	..	1.9	2.1	3.7	4.3	..	..	..	..	47	904
165 Mali	..	2.2	1.6	2.0	2.1	1.9	..	..	..	..	7	151
166 Central African Republic	2.2 [f]	..	..	1.9	..	..	..	..	..	..	3	117
167 Chad	1.7 [i]	1.7 [d]	..	2.4	..	1.4	..	..	..	..	25	208
168 Mozambique	4.1	..	3.6	2.1	10.1	4.2 [j]	..	..	..	..	6	39
169 Guinea-Bissau	..	..	1.1	1.1 [d]	..	..	..	..	..	..	7	85
170 Burundi	3.4	4.0	0.8	0.6	3.4	5.8 [l]	..	..	..	..	40	769
171 Ethiopia	3.4	4.0	1.0	1.6	10.4	3.8	13	..	..	..	120	55
172 Burkina Faso	2.7	3.6	1.2	1.2	3.0	1.5	..	..	..	..	6	145
173 Niger	3.2 [o]	2.3 [o]	..	1.3	1.9	..	..	..	..	..	5	241
174 Sierra Leone	..	..	..	1.7	0.7	0.8 [l]	..	..	..	..	5	161
All developing countries	3.5	3.8	1.9	2.2	..	..	..	..	..	..	13,159 T	95
Least developed countries	..	..	..	1.6	..	..	..	..	..	..	1,512 T	141
Arab States	4.8	5.4	..	..	7.3	..	..	..	..	..	2,256 T	104
East Asia	2.8	2.9	1.6	1.5	3.2	2.3	..	..	..	..	3,502 T	77
East Asia (excluding China)	3.3	3.5	2.0	2.4	3.7	3.1	..	..	..	..	682 T	108
Latin America and the Caribbean	3.4	4.5	2.7	3.1	..	..	..	..	..	..	1,297 T	98
South Asia	3.7	3.2	0.7	0.9	3.1	2.4	..	..	..	..	2,594 T	119
South Asia (excluding India)	3.4	3.2	1.6	1.4	3.4	3.2	..	..	..	..	1,419 T	153
South-East Asia and the Pacific	..	3.3	1.0	1.2	..	..	..	..	..	..	1,920 T	91
Sub-Saharan Africa	4.9	6.1	..	2.4	..	..	..	..	..	..	942 T	106
Eastern Europe and the CIS	..	4.9	3.2	4.5	..	2.5	..	..	..	..	2,804 T	..
OECD	5.2	5.0	5.2	6.2	..	2.2	..	..	..	..	5,549 T	78
High human development	5.2	5.0	5.2	6.2	..	..	..	..	..	..	5,357 T	77
Medium human development	3.7	4.1	2.1	2.3	..	..	..	..	..	..	13,388 T	71
Low human development	..	2.5	..	1.3	..	..	..	..	..	..	1,116 T	116
High income	5.3	5.0	5.3	6.4	..	2.2	..	..	..	..	4,087 T	74
Medium income	4.1	4.6	2.6	3.2	..	..	..	..	..	..	8,506 T	67
Low income	..	2.5	0.9	0.8	..	..	..	..	..	..	7,267 T	85
World	4.9	4.8	4.7	5.6	..	..	..	..	..	..	19,860 T	74

a. Figures are trend indicator values, which are only an indicator of the volume of international arms transfers and not of the actual financial values of such transfers. b. Data refer to the most recent year available during the period specified in the column heading. c. Calculated using the 1995-99 totals for all countries and non-state actors with exports of major conventional weapons as defined by SIPRI 2000. d. Data refer to an earlier year than that specified in the column heading. e. Data refer to estimates by SIPRI 2000. f. Data refer to expenditures by the ministry of education only. g. Data refer to the Flemish community only. h. Data refer to the Federal Republic of Germany before reunification. i. Data refer to 1991. j. Data refer to estimates deemed uncertain by SIPRI 2000. k. Data refer to expenditure on border guards and air and maritime surveillance. l. Data refer to 1997. m. Data refer to expenditure on education as percentage of global social product. n. Data refer to the former Soviet Union. o. Not including expenditure on tertiary education. p. Data refer to the central government only.

Source: Columns 1 and 2: UNESCO 1999c; *columns 3 and 4:* World Bank 2000b; *columns 5-7 and 9:* SIPRI 2000; *columns 8 and 10:* calculated on the basis of weapons transfer data from SIPRI 2000; *column 11:* IISS 1999; *column 12:* calculated on the basis of armed forces data from IISS 1999.

17 Aid flows from DAC member countries

HDI rank	Net official development assistance (ODA) disbursed			ODA as % of central government budget	ODA per capita of donor country (1997 US$)		Multi-lateral ODA as % of GNP [b]	Share of ODA through NGOs (%) [c]	Aid by NGOs as % of GNP		ODA to least developed countries (as % of total)	
	Total (US$ millions) [a] 1998	As % of GNP 1987/88	As % of GNP 1998	1997/98	1987/88	1997/98	1997/98	1997/98	1987/88	1997/98	1987/88	1998
1 Canada	1,691	0.48	0.29	0.7	93	64	0.11	7.7	0.05	0.03	25	20
2 Norway	1,321	1.11	0.91	2.0	270	309	0.26	..	0.07	0.08	35	37
3 United States	8,786	0.21	0.10	0.3	52	29	0.03	..	0.05	0.03	14	15
4 Australia	960	0.41	0.27	0.8	68	59	0.07	(.)	0.02	0.04	13	16
6 Sweden	1,573	0.87	0.72	1.2	207	189	0.24	6.6	0.07	0.02	34	28
7 Belgium	883	0.44	0.35	0.7	88	81	0.14	0.3	0.01	0.02	44	28
8 Netherlands	3,042	0.98	0.80	1.8	182	192	0.23	9.6	0.08	0.07	29	26
9 Japan	10,640	0.31	0.28	0.9	81	82	0.06	3.0	(.)	0.01	20	15
10 United Kingdom	3,864	0.30	0.27	0.7	56	61	0.12	2.6	0.03	0.03	27	26
11 Finland	396	0.55	0.32	0.6	114	76	0.15	0.7	0.03	0.01	38	26
12 France	5,742	0.59	0.40	0.9	120	103	0.11	0.2	0.01	(.)	24	17
13 Switzerland	898	0.31	0.32	0.8	112	127	0.11	3.7	0.05	0.04	33	29
14 Germany	5,581	0.39	0.26	0.6	78	70	0.10	..	0.06	0.04	25	21
15 Denmark	1,704	0.88	0.99	1.8	222	316	0.39	0.4	0.02	0.02	34	33
16 Austria	456	0.21	0.22	0.5	44	61	0.09	0.5	0.02	0.02	16	19
17 Luxembourg	112	0.19	0.65	..	55	242	0.18	0.8	(.)	0.03	..	26
18 Ireland	199	0.20	0.30	0.8	19	53	0.11	0.9	0.09	0.08	32	46
19 Italy	2,278	0.37	0.20	0.3	63	31	0.10	1.0	(.)	(.)	44	36
20 New Zealand	130	0.27	0.27	0.7	39	41	0.07	3.4	0.02	0.03	17	21
21 Spain	1,376	0.08	0.24	0.6	8	33	0.09	(.)	(.)	0.02	10	9
28 Portugal	259	0.16	0.24	0.6	10	26	0.08	0.9	(.)	0.01	..	55
DAC [d]	51,888 T	0.33	0.24	0.6	72	62	0.07	2.0	0.03	0.02	24	21

Note: DAC refers to the Development Assistance Committee of the Organisation for Economic Co-operation and Development (OECD). This table does not include Greece, which joined DAC in December 1999.

a. Some non-DAC countries and areas also provide ODA. According to OECD, Development Assistance Committee 2000, net ODA disbursed in 1998 by the Czech Republic, Estonia, Greece, the Republic of Korea, Kuwait, Poland, Saudi Arabia, Taiwan (Province of China), Turkey and the United Arab Emirates totalled $990 million. b. Data for European countries include disbursements through the European Community. c. Data refer to disbursements made by DAC member countries through non-governmental organizations. d. Aggregates are as calculated in OECD, Development Assistance Committee 2000.
Source: Columns 1-12: OECD, Development Assistance Committee 2000.

... TO HAVE ACCESS TO THE RESOURCES NEEDED FOR A DECENT STANDARD OF LIVING ...

18 Aid and debt by recipient country

	Official development assistance (ODA) received (net disbursements)[a]						External debt				Total debt service (as % of exports of goods and services)	
	Total (US$ millions)		As % of GNP		Per capita (US$)		Total (US$ millions)		As % of GNP			
HDI rank	1992	1998	1992	1998	1992	1998	1985	1998	1985	1998	1985	1998
High human development												
22 Cyprus	26.4	31.6 [b]	0.4	0.4 [b]	36.7	41.9 [b]	..	..	..	..	..	..
23 Israel	2,065.8	1,065.9 [b]	3.0	1.1 [b]	411.0	178.5 [b]	..	..	..	..	..	..
24 Singapore	19.9	1.6 [b]	(.)	(.) [b]	7.2	0.5 [b]	..	..	..	..	..	..
26 Hong Kong, China (SAR)	-39.0	6.8 [b]	(.)	..	-6.8	1.0 [b]	..	..	..	..	..	..
27 Malta	4.8	21.9	0.2	0.6	13.2	57.9	..	..	..	..	..	..
29 Slovenia	..	39.6	..	0.2	..	20.0	..	..	..	..	..	..
30 Barbados	0.4	15.6	(.)	0.7	1.4	58.9	457	608	38.4	..	6.3	6.2
31 Korea, Rep. of	12.2	108.7	(.)	(.)	-0.1	-1.1	47,133	139,097	51.6	44.0	27.8	12.9
32 Brunei Darussalam	5.4	0.3 [b]	0.1	(.) [b]	20.0	1.0 [b]	..	..	..	..	..	..
33 Bahamas	1.9	22.6 [b]	0.1	..	7.1	77.0 [b]	..	..	..	..	..	..
34 Czech Republic	130.0 [b]	447.1 [b]	0.5 [b]	0.9 [b]	12.6 [b]	43.5 [b]	3,459	25,301	12.5	45.5	..	15.2
35 Argentina	264.2	76.7	0.1	(.)	7.9	2.1	50,998	144,050	60.9	49.5	60.1	58.2
36 Kuwait	2.0	5.9 [b]	(.)	(.) [b]	1.1	3.1 [b]	..	..	..	..	..	..
37 Antigua and Barbuda	4.8	9.9	1.2	1.7	73.1	147.6	..	..	..	..	..	..
38 Chile	133.3	104.5	0.3	0.2	9.8	7.1	20,384	36,302	141.7	47.6	48.4	22.3
39 Uruguay	69.3	24.1	0.6	0.1	22.1	7.3	3,919	7,600	89.7	37.3	42.6	23.5
40 Slovakia	63.6 [b]	154.5 [b]	0.6 [b]	0.8 [b]	12.0 [b]	28.7 [b]	1,108	9,893	8.2	49.0	..	15.9
41 Bahrain	65.3	41.0	1.7	0.9	126.0	64.0	..	..	..	..	..	..
42 Qatar	1.5	1.3 [b]	(.)	..	2.9	1.7 [b]	..	..	..	..	..	..
43 Hungary	222.9 [b]	208.8 [b]	0.6 [b]	0.5 [b]	21.7 [b]	20.6 [b]	13,957	28,580	70.6	62.2	39.3	27.3
44 Poland	1,438.0 [b]	901.6 [b]	1.7 [b]	0.6 [b]	37.6 [b]	23.3 [b]	33,307	47,708	48.7	30.4	15.5	9.7
45 United Arab Emirates	-9.7	4.0 [b]	(.)	(.) [b]	-5.5	1.5 [b]	..	..	..	..	..	..
46 Estonia	104.4 [b]	90.0 [b]	2.7 [b]	1.7 [b]	67.0 [b]	62.3 [b]	..	782	..	15.3	..	2.1
Medium human development												
47 Saint Kitts and Nevis	7.7	6.6	4.5	2.6	182.4	160.7	13	115	16.7	43.2	1.8	7.2
48 Costa Rica	138.2	27.3	2.1	0.3	43.8	7.8	4,400	3,971	121.0	39.0	41.5	7.6
49 Croatia	..	39.0	..	0.2	..	8.5	..	8,297	..	38.4	..	8.9
50 Trinidad and Tobago	7.7	13.7	0.2	0.2	6.1	10.4	1,448	2,193	20.6	35.7	10.2	10.2
51 Dominica	12.1	19.5	6.6	8.8	170.3	263.6	54	109	55.8	46.5	7.6	6.7
52 Lithuania	93.8 [b]	127.6 [b]	1.7 [b]	1.2 [b]	25.3 [b]	34.5 [b]	..	1,950	..	18.6	..	3.3
53 Seychelles	19.2	23.2	4.5	4.5	270.7	294.9	97	187	59.6	36.3	7.9	5.7
54 Grenada	12.1	6.1	5.5	2.0	132.5	63.6	52	183	42.4	55.9	10.7	5.0
55 Mexico	315.4	14.8	7.7	37.5	3.6	0.2	96,862	159,959	55.2	42.0	43.7	20.8
56 Cuba	24.8	79.7	..	..	2.3	7.2	..	..	..	..	..	..
57 Belarus	273.1 [b]	28.3 [b]	0.9 [b]	0.1 [b]	26.8 [b]	2.8 [b]	..	1,120	..	5.0	..	2.0
58 Belize	24.6	15.0	5.3	2.4	123.8	63.8	118	338	59.4	51.9	11.6	12.9
59 Panama	155.1	21.7	2.7	0.2	62.3	7.9	4,758	6,689	91.4	78.0	7.3	7.6
60 Bulgaria	147.7 [b]	232.3 [b]	1.4 [b]	2.3 [b]	16.6 [b]	28.2 [b]	3,852	9,907	22.0	83.0	10.2	22.1
61 Malaysia	203.9	202.0	0.4	0.3	11.0	9.1	20,269	44,773	69.9	65.3	30.4	8.7
62 Russian Federation	1,935.0 [b]	1,017.2 [b]	0.4 [b]	0.3 [b]	13.1 [b]	6.9 [b]	28,296	183,601	..	69.4	..	12.1
63 Latvia	80.3 [b]	96.8 [b]	1.2 [b]	1.6 [b]	30.6 [b]	39.7 [b]	..	756	..	11.7	..	2.5
64 Romania	257.9 [b]	355.9 [b]	1.0 [b]	1.1 [b]	11.4 [b]	15.8 [b]	7,008	9,513	..	25.3	18.7	23.5
65 Venezuela	34.1	36.6	0.1	(.)	1.7	1.6	35,334	37,003	58.4	39.6	25.0	27.4
66 Fiji	62.8	36.5	4.0	2.4	83.6	44.1	444	193	40.5	12.6	11.7	3.6
67 Suriname	79.8	58.8	19.5	8.6	195.2	142.4	..	..	..	..	..	..
68 Colombia	233.3	165.6	0.5	0.2	6.7	4.1	14,245	33,263	42.5	33.1	41.9	30.7
69 Macedonia, TFYR	..	92.0	..	3.5	..	45.8	..	2,392	..	96.7	..	13.0
70 Georgia	5.3	162.4	0.2	3.2	1.0	29.9	..	1,674	..	31.9	..	7.6
71 Mauritius	45.5	39.6	1.5	1.0	42.1	34.2	629	2,482	61.1	59.6	24.3	11.3

. . . TO HAVE ACCESS TO THE RESOURCES NEEDED FOR A DECENT STANDARD OF LIVING . . .

219

HDI rank	Official development assistance (ODA) received (net disbursements) [a] Total (US$ millions) 1992	1998	As % of GNP 1992	1998	Per capita (US$) 1992	1998	External debt Total (US$ millions) 1985	1998	As % of GNP 1985	1998	Total debt service (as % of exports of goods and services) 1985	1998
72 Libyan Arab Jamahiriya	5.6	7.1	..	..	1.1	1.3	..	..	..	..	..	..
73 Kazakhstan	9.5	207.1	(.)	1.0	0.6	13.2	..	5,714	..	26.4	..	13.0
74 Brazil	-253.9	329.1	-0.1	(.)	-1.7	2.0	103,602	232,004	49.1	30.6	39.1	74.1
75 Saudi Arabia	49.4	25.4	(.)	(.)	3.0	1.2	..	..	..	..	..	..
76 Thailand	770.2	690.4	0.7	0.6	13.5	11.3	17,546	86,172	45.9	76.4	31.9	19.2
77 Philippines	1,715.7	606.6	3.2	0.9	27.1	8.1	26,637	47,817	89.1	70.1	31.6	11.8
78 Ukraine	557.6 [b]	380.4 [b]	0.5 [b]	0.9 [b]	10.8 [b]	7.6 [b]	..	12,718	..	29.8	..	11.4
79 Saint Vincent and the Grenadines	14.4	20.5	6.4	7.5	131.9	180.8	25	420	22.3	138.9	3.8	13.7
80 Peru	407.3	501.5	1.4	0.8	18.2	20.2	12,884	32,397	73.0	52.9	27.7	28.3
81 Paraguay	96.5	76.0	1.5	0.9	21.2	14.6	1,817	2,304	58.0	26.6	19.7	5.3
82 Lebanon	123.5	236.0	2.1	1.4	33.0	56.1	870	6,725	..	40.7	..	18.7
83 Jamaica	118.6	18.5	4.1	0.3	48.5	7.2	4,103	3,995	225.6	63.1	37.6	12.8
84 Sri Lanka	639.3	489.9	6.6	3.2	36.2	26.1	3,540	8,526	59.5	54.9	16.5	6.6
85 Turkey	268.6	13.9	0.2	(.)	4.6	0.2	26,013	102,074	38.4	50.0	35.0	21.2
86 Oman	35.4	26.6	0.4	0.2	18.6	11.5	2,329	3,629	26.3	..	5.4	..
87 Dominican Republic	63.9	120.4	0.7	0.8	8.7	14.6	3,502	4,451	74.1	29.8	19.0	4.2
88 Saint Lucia	26.7	6.1	6.0	1.1	190.8	38.1	23	184	12.4	31.9	1.2	4.2
89 Maldives	36.4	25.0	20.8	7.7	158.3	95.3	83	180	116.3	58.1	11.3	3.1
90 Azerbaijan	5.6	88.7	0.1	2.2	0.8	11.2	..	693	..	17.7	..	2.3
91 Ecuador	242.0	176.1	2.0	0.9	22.6	14.5	8,703	15,140	58.9	82.5	33.0	28.8
92 Jordan	425.1	408.2	8.9	5.9	107.6	89.5	4,022	8,484	78.7	146.9	17.2	16.4
93 Armenia	22.5	138.5	0.9	7.6	6.1	36.4	..	800	..	42.0	..	8.9
94 Albania	389.7	242.2	49.4	8.9	116.4	72.1	..	821	..	26.4	..	4.5
95 Samoa (Western)	49.2	36.4	32.6	20.6	303.5	206.4	76	180	88.8	102.1	15.1	3.9
96 Guyana	90.0	93.0	34.2	14.1	111.0	108.5	1,496	1,653	388.8	248.6	27.7	19.5
97 Iran, Islamic Rep. of	106.2	163.9	0.1	0.1	1.7	2.7	6,057	14,391	3.4	12.7	4.1	20.2
98 Kyrgyzstan	3.5	216.1	0.1	13.1	0.8	46.0	..	1,148	..	69.4	..	9.4
99 China	3,045.7	2,358.9	0.7	0.3	2.6	1.9	16,696	154,599	5.5	16.4	8.3	8.6
100 Turkmenistan	5.4	16.6	0.1	0.6	1.4	3.5	..	2,266	..	87.7	..	42.0
101 Tunisia	390.1	148.3	2.6	0.7	46.1	15.8	4,884	11,078	60.6	58.0	25.0	15.1
102 Moldova, Rep. of	9.7 [b]	33.3	0.3 [b]	1.9	2.2 [b]	7.8	..	1,035	..	62.5	..	18.5
103 South Africa	..	512.3	..	0.5	..	12.4	..	24,711	..	18.9	..	12.2
104 El Salvador	403.3	179.8	6.8	1.5	74.6	29.7	1,851	3,633	50.2	30.8	24.0	10.4
105 Cape Verde	119.0	129.8	35.6	28.9	329.6	314.9	97	244	..	49.8	9.5	9.9
106 Uzbekistan	1.4	144.3	(.)	1.0	0.1	6.0	..	3,162	..	15.6	..	13.2
107 Algeria	405.9	388.8	0.9	0.8	15.6	13.0	18,260	30,665	32.4	67.5	35.6	42.0
108 Viet Nam	572.6	1,162.9	5.8	4.7	8.3	15.0	61	22,359	..	82.3	..	8.9
109 Indonesia	2,075.8	1,257.7	1.6	1.3	11.3	6.2	36,715	150,875	44.4	176.5	28.8	33.0
110 Tajikistan	11.7	105.1	0.4	4.9	2.1	17.2	..	1,070	..	49.4	..	13.7
111 Syrian Arab Republic	197.4	155.8	1.6	1.0	14.9	10.2	10,843	22,435	66.5	137.9	12.3	6.4
112 Swaziland	53.0	30.4	5.1	2.3	62.3	30.8	243	251	60.8	18.7	9.9	2.1
113 Honduras	353.2	318.2	11.6	7.1	68.2	51.7	2,730	5,002	78.5	96.9	24.7	18.7
114 Bolivia	670.6	628.1	13.3	7.6	97.0	79.0	4,805	6,077	167.2	72.8	49.5	30.2
115 Namibia	142.4	180.1	5.1	5.7	100.2	108.4	..	..	..	..	..	..
116 Nicaragua	656.2	562.2	48.6	30.2	165.6	117.0	5,758	5,968	229.0	335.9	18.4	25.5
117 Mongolia	122.7	203.5	11.8	19.6	54.1	78.8	..	739	..	74.7	..	6.3
118 Vanuatu	40.0	40.6	22.9	18.2	254.7	223.4	16	63	13.0	28.3	1.4	0.9
119 Egypt	3,602.5	1,914.9	10.2	2.4	65.1	31.2	36,102	31,964	115.0	37.3	25.8	9.5
120 Guatemala	195.3	232.6	1.9	1.2	20.1	21.5	2,677	4,565	28.0	24.3	28.1	9.8

18 Aid and debt by recipient country

HDI rank	Official development assistance (ODA) received (net disbursements) [a] Total (US$ millions) 1992	1998	As % of GNP 1992	1998	Per capita (US$) 1992	1998	External debt Total (US$ millions) 1985	1998	As % of GNP 1985	1998	Total debt service (as % of exports of goods and services) 1985	1998
121 Solomon Islands	44.8	42.6	19.1	14.4	130.9	102.7	66	152	42.6	51.6	4.5	3.3
122 Botswana	111.9	106.4	3.0	1.9	82.4	68.1	351	548	33.1	11.8	5.4	2.7
123 Gabon	68.7	44.5	1.4	0.9	69.4	37.7	1,206	4,425	39.0	90.7	11.6	12.0
124 Morocco	946.3	528.3	3.5	1.5	37.3	19.0	15,779	20,687	129.2	60.3	34.6	23.0
125 Myanmar	115.0	58.7	0.3	..	2.6	1.3	3,098	5,680	..	..	52.5	5.3
126 Iraq	139.6	115.5	..	..	7.4	5.2	..	..	..	..	..	..
127 Lesotho	143.4	66.2	11.8	6.2	75.8	32.1	175	692	36.7	64.7	6.8	8.4
128 India	2,430.2	1,594.6	0.9	0.4	2.8	1.6	40,951	98,232	17.7	23.0	22.7	20.6
129 Ghana	612.3	700.9	9.3	9.3	38.4	38.0	2,256	6,884	51.0	91.8	23.6	28.4
130 Zimbabwe	791.7	280.0	16.7	5.1	76.0	24.0	2,415	4,716	43.9	79.8	29.0	38.2
131 Equatorial Guinea	61.8	24.9	41.8	3.9	167.1	57.8	132	306	175.7	75.7	..	1.4
132 São Tomé and Principe	56.5	28.3	148.6	72.9	470.4	199.6	63	246	..	684.0	29.1	31.9
133 Papua New Guinea	439.8	361.1	11.3	10.3	109.5	78.5	2,112	2,692	90.4	76.9	32.5	8.6
134 Cameroon	715.4	423.6	6.8	5.1	58.7	29.6	3,174	9,829	40.2	119.4	23.4	22.3
135 Pakistan	1,012.9	1,049.8	2.1	1.7	8.5	8.0	13,465	32,229	43.9	52.8	24.9	23.6
136 Cambodia	205.6	337.1	10.3	11.7	21.9	31.5	7	2,210	..	77.7	..	1.5
137 Comoros	48.1	35.3	18.2	18.0	105.0	66.5	134	203	118.4	103.3	8.9	13.4
138 Kenya	885.6	473.9	11.7	4.5	35.9	16.2	4,181	7,010	70.8	61.5	38.7	18.8
139 Congo	113.5	64.6	4.4	3.9	47.9	23.2	3,050	5,119	150.7	306.9	34.4	3.3
Low human development												
140 Lao People's Dem. Rep.	164.1	281.4	13.9	21.8	36.8	56.6	619	2,437	26.1	199.1	9.2	6.3
141 Madagascar	362.7	494.2	12.7	13.4	29.3	33.9	2,529	4,394	92.7	119.5	41.7	14.7
142 Bhutan	55.0	55.7	22.3	15.9	86.5	73.3	9	120	5.6	32.1	0.0	6.3
143 Sudan	540.9	209.1	9.2	2.3	20.9	7.4	8,955	16,843	75.1	182.7	12.8	9.8
144 Nepal	433.0	404.3	12.2	8.8	21.8	17.7	590	2,646	22.2	54.2	6.8	7.0
145 Togo	222.6	128.4	13.4	8.6	59.2	28.8	935	1,448	128.9	97.4	27.3	5.7
146 Bangladesh	1,820.3	1,251.1	5.3	2.8	16.1	10.0	6,870	16,376	32.1	37.1	22.4	9.1
147 Mauritania	200.1	171.1	17.8	18.3	95.0	67.7	1,454	2,589	198.7	272.5	25.3	27.7
148 Yemen	253.9	310.2	6.9	7.9	20.3	18.8	3,339	4,138	..	104.8	..	4.2
149 Djibouti	112.5	81.0	24.1	16.3	208.4	123.9	144	288	..	..	..	..
150 Haiti	101.8	407.1	5.4	13.0	15.1	53.3	717	1,048	36.1	27.1	10.2	8.2
151 Nigeria	258.6	204.0	1.0	0.5	2.5	1.7	18,643	30,315	68.1	78.8	32.7	11.2
152 Congo, Dem. Rep. of the	269.1	125.6	3.3	2.0	6.7	2.6	6,171	12,929	93.0	208.2	24.8	1.2
153 Zambia	1,035.3	348.7	36.2	11.0	119.7	36.1	4,499	6,865	226.5	217.4	15.9	17.7
154 Côte d'Ivoire	756.6	798.3	8.8	7.8	58.9	55.1	9,659	14,852	153.4	145.4	34.8	26.1
155 Senegal	670.3	502.1	11.4	10.6	87.0	55.6	2,566	3,861	104.7	83.1	20.8	23.2
156 Tanzania, U. Rep. of	1,338.4	997.8	28.6	12.9	49.3	31.1	9,107	7,603	..	94.3	40.0	20.8
157 Benin	269.3	210.4	12.9	9.2	54.6	35.3	854	1,647	83.3	72.2	12.9	10.6
158 Uganda	725.0	470.8	26.3	7.1	41.2	22.5	1,232	3,935	35.5	58.2	38.0	23.6
159 Eritrea	..	158.2	..	20.6	..	40.8	..	149	..	19.4	..	1.5
160 Angola	346.1	335.2	9.9	9.7	34.9	27.9	2,993	12,173	47.6	297.1	6.4	34.4
161 Gambia	110.6	37.8	30.5	9.1	110.9	31.1	245	477	113.7	116.7	10.3	9.7
162 Guinea	448.4	359.2	15.9	10.3	73.3	50.7	1,466	3,546	..	102.0	..	19.5
163 Malawi	572.4	433.7	31.5	27.2	57.0	41.2	1,021	2,444	94.6	137.5	39.8	14.7
164 Rwanda	351.4	349.9	21.6	16.9	47.8	43.2	366	1,226	21.4	60.8	10.4	16.9
165 Mali	431.8	349.3	15.3	13.2	48.2	33.0	1,456	3,201	113.1	120.4	17.3	12.6
166 Central African Republic	176.3	119.9	13.5	11.6	57.3	34.5	344	921	40.1	88.8	14.2	20.9
167 Chad	239.1	167.4	18.4	9.9	40.8	22.8	217	1,091	20.9	65.5	17.5	10.6
168 Mozambique	1,462.9	1,039.3	140.1	27.9	98.9	61.3	2,871	8,208	65.9	223.0	34.5	18.0
169 Guinea-Bissau	104.2	95.7	46.7	50.5	103.6	82.4	318	964	199.6	503.7	51.9	25.6
170 Burundi	310.5	76.5	28.9	8.1	53.1	11.6	455	1,119	40.2	128.3	20.4	40.0

	Official development assistance (ODA) received (net disbursements)[a]						External debt				Total debt service (as % of exports of goods and services)	
	Total (US$ millions)		As % of GNP		Per capita (US$)		Total (US$ millions)		As % of GNP			
HDI rank	1992	1998	1992	1998	1992	1998	1985	1998	1985	1998	1985	1998
171 Ethiopia	1,177.4	647.5	12.1	10.0	23.4	10.6	5,206	10,352	78.0	160.4	28.4	11.3
172 Burkina Faso	433.8	397.5	14.9	15.6	45.7	37.0	511	1,399	35.9	54.5	10.1	10.7
173 Niger	365.1	291.4	15.8	15.0	44.2	28.7	1,195	1,659	85.5	82.1	33.7	18.4
174 Sierra Leone	133.4	106.3	22.2	16.9	30.6	21.9	709	1,243	60.4	197.7	14.7	18.2
All developing countries	45,205 T	34,449 T	1.9	3.2	11.1	7.5	857,562 T	2,051,435 T	41.3	42.8	28.3	20.1
Least developed countries	15,487 T	11,737 T	9.9	8.4	30.8	20.2	71,341 T	145,635 T	66.9	99.5	20.3	13.1
Arab States	7,287 T	4,607 T	1.9	0.9	32.8	18.1	..	..	..	..	..	..
East Asia	3,142 T	2,678 T	0.4	0.2	2.6	1.9	..	294,435 T	..	24.8	..	10.5
East Asia (excluding China)	96 T	319 T	(.)	0.1	1.6	2.9	..	139,836 T	..	44.1	..	12.9
Latin America and the Caribbean	4,705 T	4,388 T	2.5	7.3	10.4	8.8	387,738 T	751,223 T	58.0	39.2	36.8	33.7
South Asia	6,533 T	5,034 T	1.4	0.8	5.4	3.8	71,564 T	172,698 T	15.5	26.2	14.5	18.9
South Asia (excluding India)	4,103 T	3,440 T	2.0	1.4	12.3	9.5	30,613 T	74,466 T	13.3	32.0	9.4	16.7
South-East Asia and the Pacific	6,485 T	5,116 T	1.4	1.1	14.1	10.0	107,665 T	365,603 T	..	102.3	30.2	17.3
Sub-Saharan Africa	16,759 T	12,580 T	11.1	4.4	36.4	21.4	95,225 T	208,464 T	76.9	67.9	26.7	15.1
Eastern Europe and the CIS	5,768 T	5,565 T	0.6	0.7	14.8	14.0	..	360,899 T	..	48.8	..	13.5
OECD	..	..	..	..	..	..	..	..	..	..	..	..
High human development	..	..	..	..	..	..	..	..	..	..	..	..
Medium human development	32,204 T	25,302 T	1.7	3.4	8.6	6.2	675,564 T	1,787,907 T	..	41.3	26.2	18.9
Low human development	16,253 T	12,416 T	10.7	6.7	28.6	18.6	98,262 T	184,506 T	73.2	98.4	27.2	15.4
High income	..	..	..	..	..	..	..	..	..	..	..	..
Medium income	20,766 T	15,948 T	1.4	3.7	15.8	10.9	715,433 T	1,708,360 T	..	44.1	29.4	20.2
Low income	30,200 T	23,952 T	2.7	1.4	9.6	6.9	233,115 T	703,974 T	27.1	42.5	21.8	15.1
World	53,044 T	41,102 T	1.7	2.9	11.8	8.3	..	2,412,334 T	..	43.6	..	18.9

a. A negative value indicates that the repayment of ODA loans exceeds the amount of ODA received. b. Data refer to net official aid.

Source: Columns 1-6: OECD, Development Assistance Committee 2000; *columns 7-12:* World Bank 2000b.

... TO HAVE ACCESS TO THE RESOURCES NEEDED FOR A DECENT STANDARD OF LIVING ...

HDI rank	Total population (millions)			Annual population growth rate (%)		Urban population (as % of total)			Dependency ratio (%)		Population aged 65 and above (as % of total)		Total fertility rate		Contraceptive prevalence rate (%)
	1975	1998	2015	1975-1998	1998-2015	1975	1998	2015	1998	2015	1998	2015	1970-1975	1995-2000	1990-99 [a]
High human development															
1 Canada	23.2	30.6	35.3	1.2	0.9	75.6	76.9	79.8	47.0	48.7	12.5	16.2	2.0	1.6	73 [b]
2 Norway	4.0	4.4	4.7	0.4	0.4	68.2	73.8	78.0	54.4	54.8	15.7	18.0	2.2	1.9	76 [b]
3 United States	220.2	274.0	307.7	1.0	0.7	73.7	76.8	81.0	52.4	49.8	12.5	14.7	2.0	2.0	74 [b]
4 Australia	13.9	18.5	21.5	1.3	0.9	85.9	84.7	86.0	49.6	50.3	12.1	15.2	2.5	1.8	76 [b]
5 Iceland	0.2	0.3	0.3	1.0	0.7	86.6	92.0	93.8	54.2	51.4	11.4	13.7	2.8	2.1	..
6 Sweden	8.2	8.9	9.1	0.3	0.1	82.7	83.2	85.2	56.2	57.5	17.4	21.8	1.9	1.6	78 [b]
7 Belgium	9.8	10.1	10.1	0.2	0.0	94.9	97.2	98.0	51.1	51.6	16.4	19.1	1.9	1.6	79
8 Netherlands	13.7	15.7	15.9	0.6	0.1	88.4	89.2	90.9	46.8	49.2	13.6	18.5	2.0	1.5	80
9 Japan	111.5	126.3	126.1	0.5	0.0	75.7	78.5	82.0	45.4	64.3	16.1	24.6	2.1	1.4	59
10 United Kingdom	56.2	58.6	59.6	0.2	0.1	88.7	89.4	90.8	54.0	54.1	16.0	18.7	2.0	1.7	82
11 Finland	4.7	5.2	5.3	0.4	0.1	58.3	64.3	70.9	49.5	56.9	14.6	20.1	1.6	1.7	80 [b]
12 France	52.7	58.7	61.1	0.5	0.2	73.0	75.2	79.4	53.0	55.5	15.6	18.4	2.3	1.7	75
13 Switzerland	6.3	7.3	7.6	0.6	0.3	55.7	61.9	68.3	47.4	49.6	14.5	18.7	1.8	1.5	71 [b]
14 Germany	78.7	82.1	81.6	0.2	0.0	81.2	87.1	89.9	46.6	49.7	15.9	20.3	1.6	1.3	75
15 Denmark	5.1	5.3	5.3	0.2	0.0	81.8	85.5	87.8	49.0	54.4	15.2	19.2	2.0	1.7	78 [b]
16 Austria	7.6	8.1	8.3	0.3	0.1	65.2	64.5	68.5	47.1	46.8	14.7	17.8	2.0	1.4	71 [b]
17 Luxembourg	0.4	0.4	0.5	0.7	0.5	73.7	90.4	94.0	47.3	50.4	14.1	17.0	2.0	1.7	..
18 Ireland	3.2	3.7	4.2	0.6	0.7	53.6	58.1	63.9	50.1	52.5	11.4	13.6	3.8	1.9	..
19 Italy	55.4	57.4	54.4	0.1	-0.3	65.6	66.8	70.7	47.1	53.0	17.6	22.6	2.3	1.2	78 [b]
20 New Zealand	3.1	3.8	4.4	0.9	0.8	82.8	86.5	89.4	52.8	51.8	11.6	14.1	2.8	2.0	70 [b]
21 Spain	35.6	39.6	38.5	0.5	-0.2	69.6	77.1	81.3	46.1	48.1	16.5	19.7	2.9	1.2	59 [b]
22 Cyprus	0.6	0.8	0.9	1.0	0.7	43.4	55.7	64.6	55.1	51.9	11.4	14.9	2.5	2.0	..
23 Israel	3.5	6.0	7.6	2.4	1.4	86.6	91.0	92.6	61.3	52.4	9.7	11.3	3.8	2.7	..
24 Singapore	2.3	3.5	4.0	1.9	0.8	100.0	100.0	100.0	41.0	41.3	6.8	12.4	2.6	1.7	74 [b]
25 Greece	9.0	10.6	10.4	0.7	-0.1	55.3	59.7	65.1	48.6	52.4	17.1	21.4	2.3	1.3	..
26 Hong Kong, China (SAR)	4.4	6.7	7.7	1.8	0.8	89.7	95.4	96.7	39.6	38.4	10.2	13.7	2.9	1.3	..
27 Malta	0.3	0.4	0.4	1.0	0.5	80.4	90.1	92.6	47.8	54.2	11.4	16.5	2.1	1.9	..
28 Portugal	9.1	9.9	9.7	0.4	-0.1	27.7	37.0	46.6	47.3	48.3	15.4	18.2	2.7	1.4	66 [b]
29 Slovenia	1.7	2.0	1.9	0.6	-0.2	42.4	52.0	58.8	43.2	44.7	13.2	17.6	2.2	1.3	..
30 Barbados	0.2	0.3	0.3	0.4	0.4	38.6	48.9	58.4	49.1	39.6	11.0	11.3	2.7	1.5	55 [b]
31 Korea, Rep. of	35.3	46.1	51.1	1.2	0.6	48.0	84.5	92.2	39.6	41.4	6.2	10.6	4.3	1.7	79
32 Brunei Darussalam	0.2	0.3	0.4	3.0	1.6	62.0	71.1	78.7	57.0	42.5	3.0	6.6	5.4	2.8	..
33 Bahamas	0.2	0.3	0.4	2.0	1.4	73.4	87.8	91.5	55.8	48.5	5.1	7.7	3.4	2.6	62 [b]
34 Czech Republic	10.0	10.3	9.9	0.1	-0.2	57.8	65.9	70.7	44.5	46.0	13.4	18.4	2.2	1.2	69
35 Argentina	26.0	36.1	43.5	1.4	1.1	80.7	88.9	91.9	60.6	54.5	9.6	10.7	3.1	2.6	74 [b]
36 Kuwait	1.0	1.8	2.6	2.6	2.2	83.8	97.4	98.2	61.4	44.4	1.9	5.6	6.9	2.9	35 [b]
37 Antigua and Barbuda	0.1	0.1	0.1	0.5	0.5	34.2	36.3	43.3	..	..	..	..	..	..	53 [b]
38 Chile	10.3	14.8	17.9	1.6	1.1	78.4	84.3	86.9	56.0	50.0	6.9	9.7	3.6	2.4	43 [b]
39 Uruguay	2.8	3.3	3.7	0.7	0.7	83.1	90.9	93.2	60.2	56.3	12.7	13.4	3.0	2.4	84
40 Slovakia	4.7	5.4	5.5	0.6	0.1	46.3	60.2	68.0	47.1	42.1	11.2	13.5	2.5	1.4	74
41 Bahrain	0.3	0.6	0.8	3.5	1.5	79.2	91.6	95.0	50.0	36.6	2.8	6.2	5.9	2.9	62
42 Qatar	0.2	0.6	0.7	5.4	1.4	82.9	92.1	94.2	39.8	49.5	1.8	9.1	6.8	3.7	32 [b]
43 Hungary	10.5	10.1	9.4	-0.2	-0.4	52.8	66.0	73.2	46.8	45.5	14.5	17.2	2.1	1.4	73 [b]
44 Poland	34.0	38.7	39.3	0.6	0.1	55.4	64.8	71.4	47.8	44.5	11.6	14.3	2.2	1.5	75 [b]
45 United Arab Emirates	0.5	2.4	3.0	6.9	1.5	65.4	85.2	88.8	45.6	48.1	2.2	9.3	6.4	3.4	28
46 Estonia	1.4	1.4	1.2	0.0	-0.9	67.6	73.8	78.7	47.5	43.7	13.4	16.4	2.1	1.3	70
Medium human development															
47 Saint Kitts and Nevis	(.)	(.)	(.)	-0.7	-0.5	35.0	34.0	39.3	..	..	..	..	..	..	41 [b]
48 Costa Rica	2.0	3.8	5.2	3.0	1.8	41.3	50.8	60.3	61.8	52.0	4.9	7.1	4.3	2.8	75
49 Croatia	4.3	4.5	4.3	0.2	-0.2	45.1	56.9	64.4	46.6	50.2	14.0	17.6	2.0	1.6	..
50 Trinidad and Tobago	1.0	1.3	1.4	1.0	0.6	63.0	73.2	79.3	50.8	41.4	6.5	9.5	3.4	1.7	53 [b]

19 Demographic trends

HDI rank	Total population (millions)			Annual population growth rate (%)		Urban population (as % of total)			Dependency ratio (%)		Population aged 65 and above (as % of total)		Total fertility rate		Contraceptive prevalence rate (%)
	1975	1998	2015	1975-1998	1998-2015	1975	1998	2015	1998	2015	1998	2015	1970-1975	1995-2000	1990-99 [a]
51 Dominica	0.1	0.1	0.1	-0.1	0.1	55.3	70.3	76.0	..	..	..	..	..	..	50 [b]
52 Lithuania	3.3	3.7	3.5	0.5	-0.3	55.7	73.6	80.1	49.7	45.0	12.9	15.8	2.3	1.4	..
53 Seychelles	0.1	0.1	0.1	1.1	1.0	33.3	56.9	67.3	..	..	..	..	..	..	..
54 Grenada	0.1	0.1	0.1	0.1	0.4	32.6	37.0	47.2	..	..	..	..	..	..	54
55 Mexico	59.1	95.8	119.2	2.1	1.3	62.8	74.0	77.9	62.8	49.4	4.5	6.8	6.5	2.8	69
56 Cuba	9.3	11.1	11.6	0.8	0.3	64.2	77.1	82.7	45.2	44.0	9.3	14.1	3.5	1.6	82
57 Belarus	9.4	10.3	9.8	0.4	-0.3	50.3	73.2	80.4	49.6	44.0	13.2	14.2	2.2	1.4	50
58 Belize	0.1	0.2	0.3	2.4	1.9	50.2	46.4	51.0	81.5	51.0	4.3	4.4	6.3	3.7	47
59 Panama	1.7	2.8	3.5	2.1	1.3	49.0	56.9	64.9	60.2	48.6	5.4	7.8	4.9	2.6	58 [b]
60 Bulgaria	8.7	8.3	7.5	-0.2	-0.6	57.5	69.4	75.4	48.2	46.3	15.4	18.4	2.2	1.2	76 [b]
61 Malaysia	12.3	21.4	27.5	2.5	1.5	37.7	55.8	66.2	63.5	46.6	4.0	6.4	5.2	3.2	48 [b]
62 Russian Federation	134.2	147.4	142.9	0.4	-0.2	66.4	77.0	82.0	46.3	42.6	12.3	13.7	2.0	1.3	..
63 Latvia	2.5	2.4	2.1	-0.1	-0.9	65.4	73.7	78.9	49.0	45.8	13.8	16.8	2.0	1.3	..
64 Romania	21.2	22.5	21.1	0.2	-0.4	46.2	57.3	65.4	46.1	40.8	12.7	15.4	2.6	1.2	57
65 Venezuela	12.7	23.2	30.9	2.7	1.7	75.8	86.8	90.4	64.6	51.7	4.3	6.5	4.9	3.0	49 [b]
66 Fiji	0.6	0.8	1.0	1.4	1.3	36.7	41.6	50.5	58.6	49.4	4.3	7.3	4.2	2.7	32 [b]
67 Suriname	0.4	0.4	0.5	0.6	0.9	44.8	51.0	60.8	59.6	42.3	5.3	5.9	5.3	2.2	..
68 Colombia	25.4	40.8	53.2	2.1	1.6	60.7	74.1	80.0	61.4	50.1	4.6	6.4	5.0	2.8	72
69 Macedonia, TFYR	1.7	2.0	2.2	0.8	0.5	50.6	61.1	68.5	49.6	50.0	9.6	12.6	3.0	2.1	..
70 Georgia	4.9	5.1	5.1	0.1	0.0	49.5	59.7	67.7	53.8	50.1	12.2	13.8	2.6	1.9	..
71 Mauritius	0.9	1.1	1.3	1.1	0.8	43.4	40.9	48.6	47.6	42.0	6.1	8.5	3.2	1.9	75
72 Libyan Arab Jamahiriya	2.4	5.3	7.6	3.5	2.1	60.9	86.8	90.3	72.9	55.7	3.0	4.8	7.6	3.8	..
73 Kazakhstan	14.1	16.3	16.9	0.6	0.2	52.2	60.8	68.4	55.1	46.8	6.9	8.4	3.5	2.3	59
74 Brazil	108.2	165.9	200.7	1.9	1.1	61.2	80.2	86.5	53.7	46.0	4.9	7.2	4.7	2.3	77
75 Saudi Arabia	7.3	20.2	32.6	4.6	2.9	58.4	84.7	89.7	77.9	69.1	2.8	4.4	7.3	5.8	..
76 Thailand	41.4	60.3	68.9	1.7	0.8	15.1	20.9	29.3	46.5	41.2	5.5	8.5	5.0	1.7	74
77 Philippines	^3.0	72.9	96.7	2.3	1.7	35.6	56.9	67.8	69.2	51.4	3.5	5.0	5.5	3.6	47
78 Ukraine	49.0	50.9	47.9	0.2	-0.4	58.3	71.6	78.0	48.7	45.4	14.0	16.2	2.0	1.4	..
79 Saint Vincent and the Grenadines	0.1	0.1	0.1	0.8	0.6	20.6	52.2	68.0	..	..	..	..	..	..	58 [b]
80 Peru	15.2	24.8	31.9	2.2	1.5	61.5	72.0	77.9	64.1	49.7	4.6	6.5	6.0	3.0	64
81 Paraguay	2.7	5.2	7.8	3.0	2.4	39.0	54.6	65.0	78.3	62.1	3.5	4.3	5.7	4.2	59
82 Lebanon	2.8	3.2	3.9	0.6	1.3	67.0	88.9	92.6	64.3	43.5	5.7	5.9	4.9	2.7	63
83 Jamaica	2.0	2.5	2.9	1.0	0.9	44.1	55.1	63.5	63.8	47.1	7.1	7.5	5.0	2.5	66
84 Sri Lanka	13.6	18.5	21.9	1.3	1.0	22.0	22.9	32.0	51.0	47.5	6.4	9.3	4.0	2.1	66
85 Turkey	40.0	64.5	80.3	2.1	1.3	41.6	73.1	84.5	53.2	45.5	5.6	7.2	5.0	2.5	64
86 Oman	0.9	2.4	4.1	4.4	3.2	19.6	81.2	92.8	90.1	81.7	2.5	3.7	7.2	5.9	40
87 Dominican Republic	5.0	8.2	10.3	2.1	1.3	45.3	63.9	72.8	61.9	49.0	4.3	6.6	5.6	2.8	64
88 Saint Lucia	0.1	0.2	0.2	1.4	1.3	38.6	37.4	43.6	..	..	..	..	..	..	47 [b]
89 Maldives	0.1	0.3	0.4	3.0	2.6	18.0	27.7	36.3	90.7	68.0	3.5	3.3	7.0	5.4	17
90 Azerbaijan	5.7	7.7	8.8	1.3	0.8	51.5	56.6	64.0	58.0	41.3	6.5	7.7	4.3	2.0	..
91 Ecuador	6.9	12.2	15.9	2.5	1.6	42.4	61.1	70.6	65.0	50.0	4.6	6.2	6.0	3.1	57
92 Jordan	2.6	6.3	9.9	3.9	2.7	55.3	73.1	79.8	82.4	67.0	2.9	3.4	7.8	4.9	53
93 Armenia	2.8	3.5	3.8	1.0	0.4	63.0	69.4	75.0	52.5	42.4	8.1	9.6	3.0	1.7	60
94 Albania	2.4	3.1	3.5	1.1	0.7	32.8	38.3	47.6	56.6	45.3	5.8	8.2	4.7	2.5	..
95 Samoa (Western)	0.2	0.2	0.2	0.6	1.8	21.0	21.3	26.7	76.1	57.6	4.4	4.8	6.9	4.2	21
96 Guyana	0.7	0.8	1.0	0.6	0.7	30.0	37.0	48.0	54.1	41.3	4.1	5.7	4.9	2.3	..
97 Iran, Islamic Rep. of	33.3	65.8	83.1	3.0	1.4	45.8	60.6	68.8	75.3	46.1	4.2	4.8	6.5	2.8	73
98 Kyrgyzstan	3.3	4.6	5.5	1.5	1.0	37.9	39.5	47.9	71.9	48.8	5.9	5.8	4.7	3.2	60
99 China	927.8	1,255.7	1,417.7	1.3	0.7	17.3	32.7	45.9	47.5	40.6	6.5	9.3	4.9	1.8	83
100 Turkmenistan	2.5	4.3	5.6	2.4	1.5	47.6	45.2	52.4	75.0	48.8	4.2	4.4	6.2	3.6	..

19 Demographic trends

HDI rank	Total population (millions)			Annual population growth rate (%)		Urban population (as % of total)			Dependency ratio (%)		Population aged 65 and above (as % of total)		Total fertility rate		Contraceptive prevalence rate (%)
	1975	1998	2015	1975-1998	1998-2015	1975	1998	2015	1998	2015	1998	2015	1970-1975	1995-2000	1990-99 [a]
101 Tunisia	5.7	9.3	11.6	2.2	1.3	49.9	64.1	73.5	60.0	45.4	5.7	6.1	6.2	2.6	60
102 Moldova, Rep. of	3.8	4.4	4.5	0.6	0.1	35.8	53.8	63.9	52.1	43.1	9.6	10.8	2.6	1.8	74
103 South Africa	24.7	39.4	43.4	2.0	0.6	48.0	49.9	56.3	63.9	53.6	3.5	4.0	4.8	3.3	50 [b]
104 El Salvador	4.1	6.0	8.0	1.7	1.7	40.4	45.9	53.6	69.6	55.3	4.8	6.1	6.1	3.2	60
105 Cape Verde	0.3	0.4	0.6	1.7	2.1	21.4	59.3	73.5	81.2	54.0	4.6	3.2	7.0	3.6	53
106 Uzbekistan	14.0	23.6	29.9	2.3	1.4	39.1	41.8	50.1	75.6	50.8	4.5	4.6	6.0	3.4	56
107 Algeria	16.0	30.1	41.2	2.8	1.9	40.3	57.9	67.5	70.3	51.2	3.7	4.4	7.4	3.8	57
108 Viet Nam	48.0	77.6	96.6	2.1	1.3	18.8	19.5	24.3	66.4	43.0	5.2	5.3	5.8	2.6	75
109 Indonesia	135.7	206.3	250.4	1.8	1.1	19.4	38.3	52.4	56.4	44.9	4.5	6.3	5.1	2.6	57
110 Tajikistan	3.4	6.0	7.8	2.5	1.5	35.5	32.5	40.1	84.5	56.5	4.4	4.3	6.8	4.2	..
111 Syrian Arab Republic	7.4	15.3	22.6	3.2	2.3	45.1	53.5	62.1	83.6	58.0	3.0	3.4	7.7	4.0	36
112 Swaziland	0.5	1.0	1.5	3.0	2.6	14.0	33.9	47.2	85.3	68.9	2.6	3.5	6.5	4.7	21 [b]
113 Honduras	3.0	6.1	9.0	3.1	2.3	32.1	45.7	56.1	84.8	60.2	3.3	4.3	7.1	4.3	50
114 Bolivia	4.8	8.0	11.2	2.3	2.0	41.5	63.2	73.7	78.5	62.7	3.9	4.9	6.5	4.4	48
115 Namibia	0.9	1.7	2.0	2.7	1.2	20.6	38.9	53.2	83.9	74.5	3.8	3.1	6.0	4.9	29
116 Nicaragua	2.5	4.8	7.3	2.9	2.5	50.3	63.7	71.3	87.6	64.3	3.1	3.8	6.8	4.4	60
117 Mongolia	1.4	2.6	3.3	2.5	1.5	48.7	62.4	70.5	67.5	43.5	3.9	4.5	7.3	2.6	..
118 Vanuatu	0.1	0.2	0.3	2.5	2.3	15.7	19.5	27.0	84.2	63.0	3.4	4.1	6.5	4.3	15
119 Egypt	38.8	66.0	85.2	2.3	1.5	43.5	45.3	53.5	68.5	47.3	4.0	5.2	5.5	3.4	55
120 Guatemala	6.0	10.8	16.4	2.6	2.5	36.7	39.7	48.3	91.2	69.9	3.5	3.8	6.5	4.9	31
121 Solomon Islands	0.2	0.4	0.7	3.5	2.8	9.1	18.6	28.6	86.6	68.9	2.9	3.8	7.2	4.9	25
122 Botswana	0.8	1.6	2.0	3.2	1.3	12.0	68.8	88.7	82.6	64.7	2.5	2.4	6.6	4.4	48
123 Gabon	0.6	1.2	1.7	3.0	2.1	29.2	53.2	66.2	83.5	77.9	5.9	5.4	4.3	5.4	..
124 Morocco	17.3	27.4	34.8	2.0	1.4	37.7	54.0	64.3	60.7	46.2	4.3	5.3	6.9	3.1	59
125 Myanmar	30.4	44.5	53.5	1.7	1.1	23.9	26.9	36.7	51.2	42.7	4.6	6.0	5.8	2.4	33
126 Iraq	11.0	21.8	34.1	3.0	2.7	61.4	75.9	81.6	81.9	69.0	3.1	4.0	7.1	5.3	18 [b]
127 Lesotho	1.2	2.1	2.9	2.4	2.0	10.8	26.4	38.9	79.1	72.7	4.1	4.5	5.7	4.8	23
128 India	620.7	982.2	1,211.7	2.0	1.2	21.3	27.7	35.9	64.1	47.3	4.8	6.4	5.4	3.1	41
129 Ghana	9.8	19.2	29.8	2.9	2.6	30.1	37.3	47.8	88.7	73.3	3.1	3.7	6.6	5.2	22
130 Zimbabwe	6.1	11.4	13.6	2.7	1.0	19.6	33.9	45.9	82.1	56.3	2.8	2.4	7.2	3.8	66
131 Equatorial Guinea	0.2	0.4	0.6	2.9	2.4	27.1	45.9	61.4	89.7	77.2	4.0	3.7	5.7	5.6	..
132 São Tomé and Principe	0.1	0.1	0.2	2.4	1.8	26.9	45.2	56.2	..	..	..	..	..	..	10 [b]
133 Papua New Guinea	2.7	4.6	6.5	2.3	1.8	11.9	16.8	23.7	72.5	61.2	3.0	3.7	6.1	4.6	26
134 Cameroon	7.5	14.3	21.5	2.8	2.4	26.9	47.3	58.9	90.0	79.8	3.6	3.5	6.3	5.3	19
135 Pakistan	74.7	148.2	222.6	3.0	2.4	26.4	35.9	46.7	83.4	64.0	3.1	3.8	7.0	5.0	17
136 Cambodia	7.1	10.7	14.4	1.8	1.8	10.3	22.2	32.9	81.8	58.8	3.1	4.0	5.5	4.6	13
137 Comoros	0.3	0.7	1.0	3.2	2.5	21.2	32.1	42.6	84.4	66.5	2.6	3.2	7.1	4.8	21
138 Kenya	13.7	29.0	37.6	3.3	1.5	12.9	31.3	44.5	89.7	62.1	3.0	2.5	8.1	4.5	39
139 Congo	1.4	2.8	4.4	2.9	2.7	34.8	61.0	70.1	97.9	84.9	3.2	2.8	6.3	6.1	..
Low human development															
140 Lao People's Dem. Rep.	3.0	5.2	7.8	2.4	2.5	11.4	22.3	32.7	90.7	75.1	3.2	3.8	6.2	5.8	19
141 Madagascar	7.8	15.1	23.4	2.9	2.6	16.1	28.3	39.3	89.9	71.2	2.9	3.1	6.6	5.4	19
142 Bhutan	1.2	2.0	3.1	2.3	2.6	3.5	6.7	11.6	87.6	75.1	4.0	4.4	5.9	5.5	19
143 Sudan	16.0	28.3	39.8	2.5	2.0	18.9	34.2	48.7	77.3	64.7	3.1	4.2	6.7	4.6	8
144 Nepal	12.8	22.8	32.7	2.6	2.1	5.0	11.2	18.1	82.9	63.2	3.6	4.1	6.3	4.5	30
145 Togo	2.3	4.4	6.7	2.9	2.6	16.3	32.2	42.5	96.7	81.5	3.1	3.0	6.6	6.1	24
146 Bangladesh	76.6	124.8	161.5	2.1	1.5	9.3	20.0	30.8	67.0	50.0	3.2	4.3	7.0	3.1	49
147 Mauritania	1.4	2.5	3.9	2.7	2.6	20.3	55.3	68.6	88.8	75.0	3.2	3.4	6.5	5.5	4
148 Yemen	7.0	16.9	29.6	3.9	3.4	16.4	36.2	49.2	101.5	85.7	2.4	2.3	7.6	7.6	21
149 Djibouti	0.2	0.6	0.9	4.9	2.0	68.5	82.9	86.3	80.6	68.8	3.2	4.3	6.7	5.3	..
150 Haiti	4.9	8.0	10.4	2.1	1.6	21.7	33.6	44.8	83.2	63.5	3.6	3.9	5.8	4.4	18

HDI rank	Total population (millions) 1975	1998	2015	Annual population growth rate (%) 1975-1998	1998-2015	Urban population (as % of total) 1975	1998	2015	Dependency ratio (%) 1998	2015	Population aged 65 and above (as % of total) 1998	2015	Total fertility rate 1970-1975	1995-2000	Contraceptive prevalence rate (%) 1990-99 [a]
151 Nigeria	57.0	106.4	153.3	2.8	2.2	23.4	42.2	55.4	87.7	74.2	3.0	3.4	6.9	5.2	6
152 Congo, Dem. Rep. of the	23.3	49.1	80.3	3.3	2.9	29.5	29.6	39.3	103.1	89.2	2.8	2.8	6.3	6.4	8
153 Zambia	4.8	8.8	12.8	2.6	2.2	34.8	43.9	51.5	99.7	78.5	2.2	1.8	6.9	5.6	26
154 Côte d'Ivoire	6.8	14.3	20.0	3.3	2.0	32.1	45.3	55.7	88.5	71.0	2.9	3.1	7.4	5.1	15
155 Senegal	4.8	9.0	13.7	2.8	2.5	34.2	45.7	56.5	90.4	75.5	2.5	2.7	7.0	5.6	13
156 Tanzania, U. Rep. of	15.9	32.1	47.2	3.1	2.3	10.1	26.4	38.3	93.6	78.8	2.6	2.7	6.8	5.5	18
157 Benin	3.0	5.8	8.9	2.8	2.6	21.9	40.7	53.0	98.3	78.8	2.9	2.8	7.1	5.8	37
158 Uganda	11.2	20.6	34.5	2.7	3.1	8.3	13.5	20.7	108.3	94.7	2.2	1.7	6.9	7.1	15
159 Eritrea	2.1	3.6	5.5	2.4	2.6	12.2	18.0	26.2	89.2	75.5	2.8	3.4	6.5	5.7	8
160 Angola	6.1	12.1	19.7	3.0	2.9	17.8	32.9	44.1	102.2	88.0	2.9	2.9	6.6	6.8	8
161 Gambia	0.5	1.2	1.8	3.6	2.3	17.0	31.1	42.5	77.3	69.2	3.0	3.9	6.5	5.2	12
162 Guinea	4.1	7.3	10.5	2.5	2.1	16.3	31.3	42.9	90.3	73.8	2.7	3.0	7.0	5.5	29
163 Malawi	5.2	10.3	15.8	3.0	2.5	7.7	14.6	22.7	99.6	86.1	2.7	2.5	7.4	6.8	22
164 Rwanda	4.4	6.6	10.5	1.8	2.8	4.0	5.9	8.9	93.6	77.1	2.4	2.4	8.3	6.2	21
165 Mali	6.2	10.7	16.7	2.4	2.6	16.2	28.7	40.1	101.3	86.6	3.7	3.8	7.1	6.6	7
166 Central African Republic	2.1	3.5	4.8	2.3	1.9	33.7	40.3	49.7	87.7	74.3	3.9	3.4	5.7	4.9	15
167 Chad	4.0	7.3	11.2	2.6	2.6	15.6	23.1	30.9	97.0	83.1	3.4	3.1	6.6	6.1	4
168 Mozambique	10.5	18.9	25.2	2.6	1.7	8.6	37.8	51.5	92.8	84.5	3.3	2.6	6.5	6.3	10
169 Guinea-Bissau	0.6	1.2	1.6	2.7	2.0	16.0	22.9	31.7	87.9	81.4	4.1	3.9	5.4	5.8	1 [b]
170 Burundi	3.7	6.5	9.5	2.5	2.3	3.2	8.4	14.5	97.2	75.2	2.7	2.3	6.8	6.3	9 [b]
171 Ethiopia	32.2	59.6	90.9	2.7	2.5	9.5	16.7	25.8	95.8	86.6	2.9	2.7	6.8	6.3	4
172 Burkina Faso	6.1	11.3	18.1	2.7	2.8	6.3	17.4	27.4	100.4	88.1	2.6	2.4	7.8	6.6	12
173 Niger	4.8	10.1	16.7	3.3	3.0	10.6	19.6	29.1	103.3	87.5	2.5	2.6	8.1	6.8	8
174 Sierra Leone	2.9	4.6	6.7	1.9	2.3	21.4	35.3	46.7	88.8	80.3	2.9	3.0	6.5	6.1	4 [b]
All developing countries	2,928.0 T	4,575.4 T	5,750.8 T	2.0	1.4	26.1	39.0	49.1	61.7	50.7	4.9	6.4	5.4	3.0	..
Least developed countries	327.2 T	581.6 T	843.6 T	2.5	2.2	14.2	24.3	34.6	83.8	70.8	3.1	3.4	6.7	4.9	..
Arab States	137.4 T	258.4 T	365.1 T	2.8	2.1	42.1	56.2	65.4	73.0	57.4	3.6	4.5	6.6	4.1	..
East Asia	968.9 T	1,311.0 T	1,479.8 T	1.3	0.7	18.8	34.9	47.8	47.2	40.6	6.6	9.3	4.8	1.8	..
East Asia (excluding China)	41.1 T	55.3 T	62.0 T	1.3	0.7	52.5	84.8	91.6	40.7	41.1	6.6	10.6	4.2	1.7	..
Latin America and the Caribbean	317.9 T	498.2 T	624.9 T	2.0	1.3	61.2	74.6	79.9	60.5	50.2	5.2	7.1	5.1	2.7	..
South Asia	833.1 T	1,364.5 T	1,737.0 T	2.2	1.4	21.4	29.1	38.0	66.9	49.7	4.5	5.8	5.7	3.3	..
South Asia (excluding India)	212.4 T	382.3 T	525.3 T	2.6	1.9	21.6	32.7	42.7	74.6	55.8	3.5	4.4	6.7	3.8	..
South-East Asia and the Pacific	327.1 T	508.9 T	629.0 T	1.9	1.3	22.2	35.5	46.5	58.9	45.8	4.5	6.1	5.3	2.7	..
Sub-Saharan Africa	303.1 T	569.0 T	834.0 T	2.8	2.3	20.8	32.7	42.6	91.0	77.6	3.0	3.0	6.7	5.5	..
Eastern Europe and the CIS	353.8 T	398.6 T	399.9 T	0.5	0.0	57.5	67.0	72.5	50.2	44.7	11.5	13.0	2.4	1.6	..
OECD	920.7 T	1,105.0 T	1,190.6 T	0.8	0.4	70.5	76.9	81.3	50.3	50.9	12.8	16.0	2.5	1.8	..
High human development	882.4 T	1,031.3 T	1,093.7 T	0.7	0.3	72.8	78.1	82.2	49.4	51.4	13.7	17.2	2.3	1.7	..
Medium human development	2,779.4 T	4,137.2 T	4,990.7 T	1.7	1.1	29.6	41.7	51.5	57.8	46.6	5.7	7.3	4.9	2.6	..
Low human development	355.6 T	651.3 T	955.8 T	2.7	2.3	15.5	27.8	38.5	87.4	73.6	3.0	3.2	6.8	5.2	..
High income	746.6 T	864.1 T	911.1 T	0.6	0.3	75.0	78.2	81.9	49.6	52.4	14.5	18.2	2.1	1.7	..
Medium income	1,001.9 T	1,455.8 T	1,740.2 T	1.6	1.1	52.7	65.9	72.9	58.0	48.6	6.6	7.9	4.2	2.5	..
Low income	2,268.9 T	3,499.9 T	4,389.0 T	1.9	1.3	19.0	30.8	41.6	62.0	51.0	5.0	6.4	5.5	3.0	..
World	4,017.4 T	5,819.8 T	7,040.2 T	1.6	1.1	37.8	46.6	54.5	59.0	50.6	6.8	8.3	4.5	2.7	..

a. Data refer to the most recent year available during the period specified in the column heading. b. Data refer to a year or period other than that specified in the column heading, differ from the standard definition or refer to only part of the country.

Source: Columns 1-3, 13 and 14: UN 1998c; *columns 4, 5 and 9-12:* calculated on the basis of population data from UN 1998c; *columns 6-8:* UN 1996b; *column 15:* UNICEF 1999c.

... WHILE PRESERVING IT FOR FUTURE GENERATIONS ...

HDI rank	Electricity consumption [a] Total (millions of kilowatt-hours) 1997	Index (1980 = 100) 1997	Per capita (kilowatt-hours) 1980	1997	Traditional fuel consumption (as % of total energy use) 1980	1996	Commercial energy use (oil equivalent) Total (1,000 metric tons) 1980	1997	Per capita (kilograms) 1980	1997	GDP output per kilogram (US$) [b] 1980	1997	Net energy imports (as % of commercial energy use) [c] 1980	1997
High human development														
1 Canada	531,051	152	14,243	17,549	0.4	0.5	193,000	237,983	7,848	7,930	2.1	2.5	-7	-52
2 Norway	115,369	139	20,327	26,214	0.4	10.1	18,819	24,226	4,600	5,501	5.1	6.6	-196	-778
3 United States	3,610,149	152	10,334	13,284	1.3	3.6	1,811,650	2,162,190	7,973	8,076	2.7	3.6	14	22
4 Australia	183,069	190	6,599	9,986	3.8	3.7	70,372	101,626	4,790	5,484	3.3	3.8	-22	-96
5 Iceland	5,586	177	13,838	20,387	..	..	1,469	2,330	6,443	8,566	3.5	3.3	43	36
6 Sweden	147,150	179	11,655	16,616	7.7	16.2	40,984	51,934	4,932	5,869	4.5	4.6	61	36
7 Belgium	82,209	163	5,125	8,118	0.2	0.3	46,100	57,125	4,682	5,611	4.6	5.0	83	77
8 Netherlands	99,270	154	4,560	6,358	(.)	0.1	65,000	74,910	4,594	4,800	4.5	5.7	-11	13
9 Japan	1,040,108	180	4,944	8,252	0.1	0.4	346,491	514,898	2,967	4,084	9.3	10.6	88	79
10 United Kingdom	361,529	127	5,020	6,152	(.)	0.9	201,299	227,977	3,574	3,863	4.0	5.1	2	-18
11 Finland	76,828	192	8,351	14,944	4.3	5.1	25,413	33,075	5,317	6,435	3.7	4.2	73	54
12 France	450,072	181	4,615	7,693	1.3	1.0	190,111	247,534	3,528	4,224	6.1	6.4	75	48
13 Switzerland	56,048	151	5,855	7,697	0.9	1.6	20,861	26,218	3,301	3,699	12.1	11.9	66	58
14 Germany	544,063	..	..	6,630	0.3	0.3	360,441	347,272	4,603	4,231	..	7.2	48	60
15 Denmark	41,128	159	5,054	7,825	0.4	2.3	19,734	21,107	3,852	3,994	6.7	9.1	95	4
16 Austria	56,082	149	4,988	6,925	1.2	3.1	23,450	27,761	3,105	3,439	7.2	8.7	67	71
17 Luxembourg	6,466	197	10,330	15,506	(.)	..	3,643	3,394	9,984	8,052	2.4	5.5	99	99
18 Ireland	20,675	196	3,106	5,652	(.)	0.2	8,485	12,491	2,495	3,412	4.0	6.3	78	77
19 Italy	289,607	153	3,357	5,045	0.8	0.8	138,629	163,315	2,456	2,839	6.0	6.8	86	82
20 New Zealand	36,219	165	7,061	9,630	0.2	(.)	9,251	16,679	2,972	4,435	4.7	3.8	41	15
21 Spain	187,128	173	2,872	4,724	0.4	0.7	68,583	107,328	1,834	2,729	5.7	5.5	77	71
22 Cyprus	2,711	262	1,692	3,553	(.)	(.)	945	2,074	1,547	2,777	4.1	4.4	99	99
23 Israel	34,010	275	3,187	5,804	(.)	(.)	8,609	17,591	2,220	3,014	5.1	5.2	98	97
24 Singapore	26,188	382	2,836	7,642	0.4	(.)	6,062	26,878	2,656	8,661	4.4	3.6	..	100
25 Greece	51,111	220	2,413	4,836	3.0	1.2	15,960	25,556	1,655	2,435	5.8	4.8	77	62
26 Hong Kong, China (SAR)	36,260	294	2,449	5,569	0.9	0.7	5,518	14,121	1,095	2,172	10.3	10.8	99	100
27 Malta	1,515	287	1,627	3,976	..	..	402	943	1,104	2,515	4.2	7.2	..	..
28 Portugal	37,086	217	1,750	3,760	1.2	0.9	10,291	20,400	1,054	2,051	6.8	5.5	86	89
29 Slovenia	11,470	..	..	5,749	..	0.9	4,313	6,380	2,269	3,213	..	3.2	62	55
30 Barbados	678	204	1,333	2,539	25.0	6.7	..	..	..	..	..	..	..	..
31 Korea, Rep. of	248,653	621	1,051	5,437	4.0	0.7	41,238	176,351	1,082	3,834	3.5	3.1	77	86
32 Brunei Darussalam	1,705	364	2,430	5,536	0.8	1.0	2,297	2,107	11,902	6,840	2.5	2.7	-855	-735
33 Bahamas	1,414	166	4,062	4,859	(.)	..	..	..	..	..	..	..	..	..
34 Czech Republic	63,410	..	..	6,156	0.6	0.4	47,029	40,576	4,596	3,938	..	1.3	9	22
35 Argentina	78,190	..	..	2,192	5.9	3.5	41,868	61,710	1,490	1,730	5.2	4.8	7	-30
36 Kuwait	27,224	289	6,849	15,718	(.)	(.)	9,564	16,165	6,956	8,936	2.4	..	-884	-618
37 Antigua and Barbuda	99	165	984	1,500	(.)	(.)	..	..	..	..	..	..	..	..
38 Chile	33,292	283	1,054	2,276	12.3	12.7	9,525	23,012	854	1,574	2.8	3.0	41	65
39 Uruguay	7,003	207	1,163	2,145	11.1	26.0	2,636	2,883	905	883	5.5	6.6	71	62
40 Slovakia	28,877	..	..	5,375	..	0.6	20,810	17,216	4,175	3,198	..	1.1	84	73
41 Bahrain	5,041	304	4,784	8,647	(.)	(.)	3,324	8,487	9,952	13,689	1.2	0.7	-54	12
42 Qatar	6,868	283	10,616	12,070	(.)	(.)	4,796	13,575	20,943	18,835	..	..	-481	-224
43 Hungary	37,545	120	2,920	3,697	2.0	1.5	28,870	25,311	2,696	2,492	1.6	1.9	49	50
44 Poland	140,576	116	3,419	3,633	0.4	0.4	124,806	105,155	3,508	2,721	0.8	1.4	2	4
45 United Arab Emirates	20,571	327	6,204	8,917	..	..	8,576	30,874	8,222	11,967	4.6	1.6	-995	-397
46 Estonia	8,244	..	..	5,697	..	2.8	6,275	5,556	4,240	3,811	0.9	1.0	-11	32
Medium human development														
47 Saint Kitts and Nevis	90	..	..	2,308	50.0	50.0	..	..	..	..	..	..	..	..
48 Costa Rica	5,714	259	964	1,525	26.3	12.6	1,527	2,663	669	769	3.7	3.5	50	57
49 Croatia	13,633	..	..	3,040	..	3.4	..	7,650	..	1,687	..	2.8	..	48
50 Trinidad and Tobago	4,844	236	1,900	3,793	1.4	0.8	3,873	8,196	3,579	6,414	1.3	0.7	-239	-66

	Electricity consumption [a]				Traditional fuel consumption (as % of total energy use)		Commercial energy use (oil equivalent)						Net energy imports (as % of commercial energy use) [c]	
	Total (millions of kilowatt-hours)	Index (1980 = 100)	Per capita (kilowatt-hours)				Total (1,000 metric tons)		Per capita (kilograms)		GDP output per kilogram (US$) [b]			
HDI rank	1997	1997	1980	1997	1980	1996	1980	1997	1980	1997	1980	1997	1980	1997
51 Dominica	38	345	149	535	..	..	..	..	..	..	..	..	..	..
52 Lithuania	12,105	..	..	3,267	..	5.9	11,701	8,806	3,428	2,376	..	0.9	95	55
53 Seychelles	148	296	794	1,973	..	..	..	..	..	..	..	..	..	..
54 Grenada	108	432	281	1,161	..	(.)	..	..	..	..	..	..	..	..
55 Mexico	172,212	255	999	1,827	5.0	5.6	98,898	141,520	1,464	1,501	2.8	2.9	-51	-58
56 Cuba	14,087	141	1,029	1,273	27.9	26.0	14,570	14,273	1,501	1,291	..	..	73	49
57 Belarus	33,677	..	..	3,254	..	0.8	2,385	25,142	247	2,449	..	0.8	-8	87
58 Belize	192	356	370	857	50.0	40.0	..	..	..	..	..	..	..	..
59 Panama	4,436	245	930	1,630	26.6	18.6	1,865	2,328	956	856	2.8	3.6	72	65
60 Bulgaria	39,253	101	4,371	4,677	0.5	1.2	28,673	20,616	3,236	2,480	0.4	0.5	73	52
61 Malaysia	58,638	576	740	2,795	15.7	6.0	11,128	48,473	809	2,237	2.9	2.1	-50	-53
62 Russian Federation	814,400	..	..	5,516	..	1.1	763,707	591,982	5,494	4,019	0.7	0.6	2	-57
63 Latvia	6,323	..	..	2,569	..	24.1	566	4,460	222	1,806	12.6	1.2	54	63
64 Romania	57,369	84	3,061	2,544	1.3	4.7	64,694	44,135	2,914	1,957	0.6	0.7	19	30
65 Venezuela	75,145	209	2,379	3,299	0.9	0.8	35,361	57,530	2,343	2,526	1.7	1.4	-277	-255
66 Fiji	545	176	489	693	45.0	50.0	..	..	..	..	..	..	..	..
67 Suriname	1,626	103	4,442	3,947	2.4	(.)	..	..	..	..	..	..	..	..
68 Colombia	46,577	226	778	1,163	15.9	22.9	19,127	30,481	672	761	2.8	3.2	5	-122
69 Macedonia, TFYR	6,719	..	..	3,381	..	5.2	..	..	..	..	..	..	..	..
70 Georgia	7,363	..	..	1,438	..	1.4	4,474	2,295	882	423	2.7	1.6	66	70
71 Mauritius	1,278	274	482	1,128	59.1	32.4	..	..	..	..	..	..	..	..
72 Libyan Arab Jamahiriya	18,300	379	1,588	3,512	2.3	0.9	7,173	15,090	2,357	2,909	..	..	-1,248	-423
73 Kazakhstan	58,700	..	..	3,585	..	0.1	76,799	38,418	5,163	2,439	..	0.5	0	-69
74 Brazil	348,456	250	1,145	2,129	35.5	29.2	108,999	172,030	896	1,051	4.7	4.3	43	30
75 Saudi Arabia	106,979	566	1,969	5,492	(.)	(.)	35,357	98,449	3,773	4,906	3.1	1.3	-1,408	-395
76 Thailand	98,194	619	340	1,644	40.3	30.0	22,740	79,963	487	1,319	2.3	2.2	51	42
77 Philippines	39,816	221	373	557	37.0	31.7	21,212	38,251	439	520	2.7	2.2	50	57
78 Ukraine	177,848	..	..	3,483	..	0.4	97,893	150,059	1,956	2,960	..	0.3	-12	46
79 Saint Vincent and the Grenadines	80	296	276	714	..	..	..	..	..	..	..	..	..	..
80 Peru	17,953	179	579	737	15.2	27.2	11,700	15,127	675	621	4.1	4.3	-25	19
81 Paraguay	4,946	680	233	972	62.0	47.5	2,094	4,191	672	824	2.8	2.2	23	-66
82 Lebanon	7,342	260	1,056	2,336	2.4	2.8	2,483	5,244	827	1,265	..	2.3	93	96
83 Jamaica	6,255	352	834	2,486	5.0	6.3	2,378	3,963	1,115	1,552	1.3	1.0	91	85
84 Sri Lanka	5,145	308	113	282	53.5	48.0	4,493	7,159	305	386	1.5	2.0	29	39
85 Turkey	107,412	436	554	1,694	20.5	3.4	31,314	71,273	704	1,140	2.8	2.7	45	61
86 Oman	9,662	1010	847	4,192	..	..	996	6,775	905	3,003	3.9	..	-1,415	-662
87 Dominican Republic	7,335	221	582	906	27.5	15.1	3,464	5,453	608	673	2.2	2.5	62	74
88 Saint Lucia	115	198	504	777	..	..	..	..	..	..	..	..	..	..
89 Maldives	66	1650	25	251	..	..	..	..	..	..	..	..	..	..
90 Azerbaijan	17,806	..	..	2,330	..	(.)	15,001	11,987	2,433	1,529	..	0.3	1	-17
91 Ecuador	9,560	284	423	801	26.7	14.3	5,191	8,513	652	713	2.4	2.2	-126	-168
92 Jordan	6,273	586	366	1,024	(.)	(.)	1,714	4,795	786	1,081	2.2	1.4	100	96
93 Armenia	6,022	..	..	1,696	..	(.)	1,070	1,804	346	476	..	1.8	-18	70
94 Albania	5,881	183	1,204	1,878	13.1	9.3	3,049	1,048	1,142	317	0.8	2.3	-12	13
95 Samoa (Western)	65	167	252	378	50.0	33.3	..	..	..	..	..	..	..	..
96 Guyana	404	98	545	479	24.1	33.3	..	..	..	..	..	..	..	..
97 Iran, Islamic Rep. of	97,744	437	570	1,512	0.4	0.9	38,918	108,289	995	1,777	1.1	0.7	-116	-108
98 Kyrgyzstan	10,900	..	..	2,360	..	(.)	1,717	2,793	473	603	..	1.4	-28	50
99 China	1,127,356	375	307	922	8.4	5.6	598,628	1,113,050	610	907	0.3	0.8	-2	1
100 Turkmenistan	6,750	..	..	1,595	..	..	7,948	12,181	2,778	2,615	..	0.2	-1	-54

20 Energy use

	Electricity consumption [a]				Traditional fuel consumption (as % of total energy use)		Commercial energy use (oil equivalent)						Net energy imports (as % of commercial energy use) [c]	
	Total (millions of kilowatt-hours)	Index (1980 = 100)	Per capita (kilowatt-hours)				Total (1,000 metric tons)		Per capita (kilograms)		GDP output per kilogram (US$) [b]			
HDI rank	1997	1997	1980	1997	1980	1996	1980	1997	1980	1997	1980	1997	1980	1997
101 Tunisia	8,397	300	434	912	16.1	12.7	3,900	6,805	611	738	2.7	3.0	-79	2
102 Moldova, Rep. of	7,226	..	..	1,651	..	0.5	..	4,436	..	1,029	..	0.7	106	98
103 South Africa	187,740	188	3,025	4,185	4.9	..	65,417	107,220	2,372	2,636	1.9	1.5	-12	-33
104 El Salvador	3,568	231	339	604	52.9	36.5	2,537	4,095	553	691	2.9	2.5	25	35
105 Cape Verde	41	256	55	103	..	..	..	..	..	..	..	..	..	..
106 Uzbekistan	46,984	..	..	2,024	..	(.)	4,821	42,553	302	1,798	..	0.5	4	-15
107 Algeria	21,489	301	381	731	1.9	1.5	12,410	26,497	665	904	2.5	1.6	-440	-374
108 Viet Nam	19,253	457	78	252	49.1	40.5	19,347	39,306	360	521	..	0.6	7	-11
109 Indonesia	84,096	591	94	413	51.5	28.7	59,561	138,779	402	693	1.3	1.6	-116	-60
110 Tajikistan	14,103	..	..	2,380	..	..	1,650	3,384	416	562	..	0.6	-20	63
111 Syrian Arab Republic	18,259	484	433	1,222	(.)	(.)	5,348	14,642	614	983	1.7	1.2	-78	-124
112 Swaziland	..	..	..	..	..	..	..	..	..	..	..	..	..	..
113 Honduras	3,252	352	259	544	55.3	50.0	1,878	3,182	526	532	1.4	1.4	30	37
114 Bolivia	3,380	216	292	435	19.3	13.4	2,287	4,254	427	548	2.4	1.7	-85	-40
115 Namibia	..	..	..	..	..	..	..	..	..	..	..	..	..	..
116 Nicaragua	2,069	195	380	442	49.2	43.4	1,558	2,573	533	551	1.3	0.8	42	41
117 Mongolia	3,096	166	1,119	1,220	14.4	3.8	..	..	..	..	..	..	..	..
118 Vanuatu	30	150	171	169	(.)	(.)	..	..	..	..	..	..	..	..
119 Egypt	54,924	290	433	848	4.7	3.5	15,970	39,581	391	656	1.9	1.7	-114	-47
120 Guatemala	4,044	242	242	384	54.6	58.6	3,754	5,633	550	536	2.9	2.8	33	21
121 Solomon Islands	32	152	93	79	66.7	50.0	..	..	..	..	..	..	..	..
122 Botswana	..	..	..	..	35.7	..	..	..	..	..	..	..	..	..
123 Gabon	1,257	237	767	1,106	30.8	32.6	1,493	1,635	2,161	1,419	2.4	3.3	-532	-1,110
124 Morocco	14,192	288	254	528	5.2	4.8	4,778	9,275	247	340	4.5	3.9	82	88
125 Myanmar	4,211	283	44	96	69.3	63.9	9,430	13,009	279	296	..	..	-1	6
126 Iraq	29,950	262	878	1,414	0.3	0.1	12,030	27,091	925	1,240	..	..	-1,036	-129
127 Lesotho	..	..	..	..	..	..	..	..	..	..	..	..	..	..
128 India	465,867	391	173	482	31.5	21.2	242,024	461,032	352	479	0.7	0.9	8	12
129 Ghana	6,426	132	451	344	43.7	78.1	4,071	6,896	379	383	1.0	1.0	19	15
130 Zimbabwe	10,930	150	1,020	975	27.6	23.4	6,488	9,926	926	866	0.7	0.8	12	18
131 Equatorial Guinea	20	111	83	48	80.0	66.7	..	..	..	..	..	..	..	..
132 São Tomé and Principe	15	167	96	109	..	..	..	..	..	..	..	..	..	..
133 Papua New Guinea	1,795	143	406	399	65.4	62.5	..	..	..	..	..	..	..	..
134 Cameroon	2,758	190	168	198	51.7	68.8	3,687	5,756	426	413	1.7	1.5	-58	-95
135 Pakistan	59,119	395	176	410	24.4	17.3	25,479	56,818	308	442	1.0	1.1	18	26
136 Cambodia	208	208	15	20	100.0	89.3	..	..	..	..	..	..	..	..
137 Comoros	17	170	26	27	..	..	..	..	..	..	..	..	..	..
138 Kenya	4,367	242	109	154	76.8	78.9	9,791	14,138	589	494	0.6	0.7	19	18
139 Congo	559	343	98	206	77.8	52.1	845	1,242	506	459	1.5	1.8	-370	-990
Low human development														
140 Lao People's Dem. Rep.	495	228	68	98	72.3	86.5	..	..	..	..	..	..	..	..
141 Madagascar	684	157	48	24	78.4	85.6	..	..	..	..	..	..	..	..
142 Bhutan	415	1886	17	213	100.0	76.5	..	..	..	..	..	..	..	..
143 Sudan	1,340	153	47	48	86.9	76.5	8,406	11,480	450	414	0.5	0.7	16	14
144 Nepal	1,262	507	17	57	94.2	90.9	4,663	7,160	322	321	0.5	0.7	3	8
145 Togo	414	215	74	97	35.7	71.0	..	..	..	..	..	..	..	..
146 Bangladesh	12,820	483	30	105	81.3	43.3	14,900	24,327	172	197	1.3	1.7	11	10
147 Mauritania	153	165	60	62	(.)	(.)	..	..	..	..	..	..	..	..
148 Yemen	2,482	..	..	152	..	2.0	1,424	3,355	167	208	..	1.2	96	-469
149 Djibouti	187	160	416	303	..	..	..	..	..	..	..	..	..	..
150 Haiti	633	201	59	81	80.7	80.5	2,099	1,779	392	237	1.5	1.5	11	27

HDI rank	Electricity consumption [a] Total (millions of kilowatt-hours) 1997	Index (1980 = 100) 1997	Per capita (kilowatt-hours) 1980	Per capita (kilowatt-hours) 1997	Traditional fuel consumption (as % of total energy use) 1980	Traditional fuel consumption (as % of total energy use) 1996	Commercial energy use (oil equivalent) Total (1,000 metric tons) 1980	Total (1,000 metric tons) 1997	Per capita (kilograms) 1980	Per capita (kilograms) 1997	GDP output per kilogram (US$) [b] 1980	GDP output per kilogram (US$) [b] 1997	Net energy imports (as % of commercial energy use) [c] 1980	Net energy imports (as % of commercial energy use) [c] 1997
151 Nigeria	14,830	209	98	143	66.8	69.0	52,846	88,652	743	753	0.4	0.3	-181	-115
152 Congo, Dem. Rep. of the	4,431	102	161	90	73.9	90.8	8,706	14,539	322	311	1.0	0.4	(.)	1
153 Zambia	6,315	98	1,125	736	37.4	73.1	4,551	5,987	793	634	0.7	0.6	8	7
154 Côte d'Ivoire	2,760	158	214	196	52.8	55.3	3,662	5,597	447	394	2.3	2.0	34	12
155 Senegal	1,184	186	115	135	50.8	56.3	1,921	2,770	347	315	1.6	1.8	46	40
156 Tanzania, U. Rep. of	1,744	228	41	56	92.0	91.4	10,280	14,258	553	455	..	0.4	8	5
157 Benin	272	223	35	48	85.4	87.5	1,363	2,182	393	377	0.9	1.0	11	13
158 Uganda	678	186	28	34	93.6	90.6	..	..	..	..	..	..	..	..
159 Eritrea	..	..	..	..	..	..	..	..	..	..	..	..	..	..
160 Angola	1,895	126	214	162	64.9	69.3	4,538	6,848	647	587	1.1	0.9	-149	-505
161 Gambia	77	171	70	65	72.7	78.6	..	..	..	..	..	..	..	..
162 Guinea	542	143	85	74	71.4	72.4	..	..	..	..	..	..	..	..
163 Malawi	876	214	66	87	90.6	89.7	..	..	..	..	..	..	..	..
164 Rwanda	175	105	32	29	89.8	88.3	..	..	..	..	..	..	..	..
165 Mali	391	372	15	37	86.7	88.6	..	..	..	..	..	..	..	..
166 Central African Republic	104	153	29	30	88.9	91.4	..	..	..	..	..	..	..	..
167 Chad	90	191	10	13	95.9	97.6	..	..	..	..	..	..	..	..
168 Mozambique	1,174	27	364	64	43.7	91.4	8,079	7,664	668	461	0.2	0.4	8	9
169 Guinea-Bissau	53	379	18	47	80.0	57.1	..	..	..	..	..	..	..	..
170 Burundi	152	362	10	24	97.0	92.4	..	..	..	..	..	..	..	..
171 Ethiopia	1,332	193	18	22	89.6	93.0	11,157	17,131	296	287	..	0.4	5	5
172 Burkina Faso	294	260	16	27	91.3	87.4	..	..	..	..	..	..	..	..
173 Niger	373	171	39	38	79.5	80.0	..	..	..	..	..	..	..	..
174 Sierra Leone	242	120	62	55	90.0	84.2	..	..	..	..	..	..	..	..
All developing countries	3,977,263 T	329	366	884	..	..	..	..	..	..	..	..	..	..
Least developed countries	46,800 T	162	76	82	..	..	..	..	..	..	..	..	..	..
Arab States	359,480 T	363	650	1,424	..	..	138,249 T	338,180 T	882	1,314	2.6	1.5	-716	-271
East Asia	1,415,365 T	398	346	1,105	..	..	645,384 T	1,303,522 T	630	1,017	0.6	1.2	4	14
East Asia (excluding China)	288,009 T	531	1,211	5,257	..	..	46,756 T	190,472 T	1,083	3,627	4.3	3.7	79	87
Latin America and the Caribbean	857,795 T	240	990	1,749	..	..	377,189 T	575,389 T	1,063	1,180	..	..	-24	-37
South Asia	642,438 T	399	173	479	..	..	330,477 T	664,785 T	357	508	0.8	0.9	-5	-6
South Asia (excluding India)	176,571 T	421	172	472	..	..	88,453 T	203,753 T	370	583	1.1	1.0	-42	-47
South-East Asia and the Pacific	335,271 T	458	201	669	..	..	..	..	..	..	..	..	..	..
Sub-Saharan Africa	256,791 T	174	381	423	..	..	..	..	..	..	..	..	..	..
Eastern Europe and the CIS	1,633,184 T	..	..	4,095	..	..	1,317,672 T	1,173,943 T	3,630	2,963	..	0.7	7	-17
OECD	8,797,811 T	163	5,762	8,008	..	..	4,062,191 T	5,067,515 T	4,248	4,643	3.9	4.9	29	25
High human development	8,849,547 T	162	6,330	8,623	..	..	4,067,499 T	5,104,294 T	4,468	5,003	4.0	5.0	25	22
Medium human development	4,763,559 T	303	415	1,167	..	..	2,684,855 T	4,036,213 T	892	1,003	..	..	-35	-30
Low human development	60,869 T	166	86	96	..	..	..	..	..	..	..	..	..	..
High income	8,197,939 T	159	6,933	9,531	..	..	3,741,118 T	4,638,037 T	4,876	5,428	4.1	5.2	25	20
Medium income	3,558,916 T	245	1,096	2,464	..	..	2,001,642 T	2,600,178 T	1,849	1,830	..	..	-40	-39
Low income	1,917,120 T	363	208	563	..	..	..	..	..	..	..	..	..	..
World	13,673,975 T	188	1,562	2,383	..	..	6,890,949 T	9,354,236 T	1,623	1,684	..	..	..	..

a. Data refer to apparent consumption. b. Estimated real GDP (at 1995 prices) divided by kilograms of oil equivalent of commercial energy use. c. A negative value indicates that the country is a net exporter.
Source: Columns 1, 3 and 4: UN 2000c; *column 2:* calculated on the basis of electricity consumption data from UN 2000c; *columns 5 and 6:* World Bank 2000b, data from UN Statistics Division; *columns 7-14:* World Bank 2000b.

. . . WHILE PRESERVING IT FOR FUTURE GENERATIONS . . .

21 Environmental profile

HDI rank	Annual internal renewable water resources (cubic metres per capita) a 2000	Annual fresh water withdrawals — As % of water resources 1987-97 b	Annual fresh water withdrawals — Per capita (cubic metres) 1987-97 b	Average annual rate of deforestation (%) c 1980-90	Average annual rate of deforestation (%) c 1990-95	Printing and writing paper consumed (kilograms per capita) 1997	Carbon dioxide emissions — Total (millions of metric tons) 1996	Carbon dioxide emissions — Share of world total (%) 1996	Carbon dioxide emissions — Per capita (metric tons) 1996	Sulphur dioxide emissions per capita (kilograms) 1995-97
High human development										
1 Canada	87,971	1.6	1,623	..	-0.1	95.2	410.0	1.7	13.8	89.8
2 Norway	85,560	0.5	488	..	-0.3	90.0	67.1	0.3	15.4	6.8
3 United States	8,838	18.2	1,677	..	-0.3	145.9	5,309.7	22.2	19.7	63.8
4 Australia	18,638	4.3	839	..	0.0	88.7	307.1	1.3	17.0	..
5 Iceland	605,049	0.1	611	..	0.0	41.3	2.2	(.)	8.1	83.3
6 Sweden	19,977	1.5	310	..	0.0	77.9	54.2	0.2	6.2	7.8
7 Belgium	1,181	75.3	917	..	0.0	122.7 d	106.2	0.4	10.5	21.4 e
8 Netherlands	697	71.0	522	..	0.0	93.5	155.4	0.6	10.0	7.9
9 Japan	3,394	21.3	735	..	0.1	117.9	1,169.6	4.9	9.3	..
10 United Kingdom	2,465	6.4	160	..	-0.5	112.3	557.9	2.3	9.5	28.3
11 Finland	20,673	2.3	477	..	0.1	249.9	59.3	0.2	11.6	19.6 e
12 France	3,047	22.6	700	..	-1.1	72.0	362.4	1.5	6.2	..
13 Switzerland	5,416	6.5	363	..	0.0	119.7	44.3	0.2	6.1	3.6
14 Germany	1,301	43.2	583	..	0.0	94.2	862.6	3.6	10.5	17.9
15 Denmark	1,134	14.8	170	..	0.0	121.8	56.7	0.2	10.8	20.6
16 Austria	6,699	4.0	278	..	0.0	72.5	59.4	0.2	7.3	7.0
17 Luxembourg	2,090	6.3	140	..	..	..	8.3	(.)	20.2	20.0
18 Ireland	13,136	2.4	326	..	-2.6	79.6	35.0	0.1	9.8	44.6 e
19 Italy	2,804	35.8	1,005	..	-0.1	67.8	403.9	1.7	7.1	23.0
20 New Zealand	84,673	0.6	545	..	-0.6	52.8	29.8	0.1	8.3	..
21 Spain	2,821	31.8	897	..	0.0	55.1	232.9	1.0	5.9	48.7
22 Cyprus	1,006	29.7	321	..	0.0	28.0	5.4	(.)	7.1	58.8
23 Israel	121	227.9	292	..	0.0	49.5	52.4	0.2	9.3	..
24 Singapore	..	..	..	0.0	0.0	110.6	65.9	0.3	19.5	..
25 Greece	5,073	13.0	688	..	-2.3	42.0	80.7	0.3	7.7	51.2 e
26 Hong Kong, China (SAR)	..	..	..	..	..	150.3	23.1	0.1	3.7	..
27 Malta	129	359.4	149	..	0.0	35.4	1.8	(.)	4.8	..
28 Portugal	3,747	19.7	739	..	-0.9	42.6	48.0	0.2	4.9	37.7
29 Slovenia	9,317	..	..	..	0.0	22.1	13.1	0.1	6.8	60.0
30 Barbados	303	98.8	305	..	0.0	18.4	0.8	(.)	3.2	..
31 Korea, Rep. of	1,384	36.5	531	-2.0	0.2	56.5	408.7	1.7	9.0	..
32 Brunei Darussalam	25,908	1.1	319	..	0.6	1.9	5.1	(.)	16.9	..
33 Bahamas	..	..	..	..	2.6	10.3	1.7	(.)	6.0	..
34 Czech Republic	1,464	16.8	244	..	0.0	36.2	126.9	0.5	12.4	68.1
35 Argentina	9,721	7.9	822	0.6	0.3	15.9	130.1	0.5	3.7	..
36 Kuwait	10	2,690.0	307	-33.8	0.0	14.3	42.7	0.2	25.3	..
37 Antigua and Barbuda	770	9.6	78	..	..	3.6	0.3	(.)	4.9	..
38 Chile	61,007	2.3	1,634	0.1	0.4	13.8	48.9	0.2	3.4	..
39 Uruguay	17,680	7.1	1,352	-0.2	0.0	11.1	5.7	(.)	1.8	..
40 Slovakia	2,413	10.8	263	..	-0.1	40.9	39.7	0.2	7.4	37.4 e
41 Bahrain	7	5,980.8	474	..	0.0	17.0	10.6	(.)	18.6	..
42 Qatar	85	558.8	530	..	0.0	4.6	29.2	0.1	52.3	..
43 Hungary	598	104.3	612	..	-0.5	27.0	59.6	0.2	6.0	64.4
44 Poland	1,419	21.9	313	..	-0.1	20.5	357.4	1.5	9.3	56.4
45 United Arab Emirates	61	1,405.3	954	-46.6	0.0	18.7	82.0	0.3	36.3	..
46 Estonia	9,105	1.2	106	..	-1.0	38.3	16.4	0.1	11.2	..
Medium human development										
47 Saint Kitts and Nevis	..	..	..	..	..	4.1	0.1	(.)	2.5	..
48 Costa Rica	27,936	5.1	1,540	2.8	3.1	8.4	4.7	(.)	1.4	..
49 Croatia	8,429	..	..	..	0.0	12.4	17.6	0.1	3.9	17.8
50 Trinidad and Tobago	..	..	..	1.6	1.6	19.3	22.3	0.1	17.2	..

HDI rank	Annual internal renewable water resources (cubic metres per capita) [a] 2000	Annual fresh water withdrawals — As % of water resources 1987-97 [b]	Annual fresh water withdrawals — Per capita (cubic metres) 1987-97 [b]	Average annual rate of deforestation (%) [c] 1980-90	Average annual rate of deforestation (%) [c] 1990-95	Printing and writing paper consumed (kilograms per capita) 1997	Carbon dioxide emissions — Total (millions of metric tons) 1996	Carbon dioxide emissions — Share of world total (%) 1996	Carbon dioxide emissions — Per capita (metric tons) 1996	Sulphur dioxide emissions per capita (kilograms) 1995-97
51 Dominica	0	..	240	..	..	15.5	0.1	(.)	1.1	..
52 Lithuania	4,240	1.6	68	..	-0.6	6.4	13.9	0.1	3.7	20.8
53 Seychelles	..	..	..	..	..	3.4	0.2	(.)	2.3	..
54 Grenada	0	0.0	0	..	..	0.8	0.2	(.)	1.8	..
55 Mexico	4,136	19.0	812	-0.4	0.9	11.6	348.7	1.5	3.7	
56 Cuba	3,393	13.7	475	0.2	1.2	2.8	31.2	0.1	2.8	
57 Belarus	3,634	7.3	266	..	-1.0	0.6	61.8	0.3	6.0	20.0
58 Belize	66,470	0.6	469	0.3	0.3	0.9	0.4	(.)	1.6	..
59 Panama	51,616	1.1	685	1.9	2.2	6.3	6.7	(.)	2.5	..
60 Bulgaria	2,188	..	..	..	0.0	7.8	55.4	0.2	6.5	162.5
61 Malaysia	26,074	2.2	633	2.1	2.4	27.6	119.3	0.5	5.8	..
62 Russian Federation	29,358	1.8	520	..	0.0	5.2	1,582.1	6.6	10.7	16.6 [f]
63 Latvia	7,104	1.7	111	..	-0.9	17.6	9.3	(.)	3.7	23.6
64 Romania	1,657	..	..	..	0.0	4.8	119.5	0.5	5.3	40.5
65 Venezuela	35,003	0.5	382	1.1	1.1	8.6	144.7	0.6	6.5	..
66 Fiji	..	..	..	-0.2	0.4	4.4	0.8	(.)	1.0	..
67 Suriname	479,467	0.2	1,220	0.1	0.1	2.2	2.1	(.)	4.9	..
68 Colombia	50,400	0.4	228	0.6	0.5	7.4	65.4	0.3	1.8	..
69 Macedonia, TFYR	2,965	..	..	..	0.0	7.0	12.7	0.1	5.9	8.5 [g]
70 Georgia	11,702	6.0	635	..	0.0	0.6	3.0	(.)	0.6	
71 Mauritius	1,908	16.3	410	-1.2	0.0	4.3	1.7	(.)	1.5	..
72 Libyan Arab Jamahiriya	143	486.3	783	-3.2	0.0	0.3	40.6	0.2	7.3	..
73 Kazakhstan	4,649	44.6	2,019	..	-1.9	1.2	174.1	0.7	10.4	..
74 Brazil	31,849	1.0	359	0.6	0.5	13.4	273.8	1.1	1.7	..
75 Saudi Arabia	111	708.3	1,002	0.7	0.8	6.2	268.3	1.1	14.2	..
76 Thailand	3,420	15.8	596	3.1	2.6	13.5	205.7	0.9	3.5	..
77 Philippines	6,305	11.6	811	3.3	3.5	5.0	64.7	0.3	0.9	..
78 Ukraine	1,052	48.9	501	..	-0.1	3.7	397.9	1.7	7.7	22.2
79 Saint Vincent and the Grenadines	..	..	91	..	..	0.2	0.1	(.)	1.1	..
80 Peru	68,039	1.1	849	0.3	0.3	4.1	26.2	0.1	1.1	..
81 Paraguay	17,102	0.5	112	2.5	2.6	4.6	3.7	(.)	0.7	..
82 Lebanon	1,463	26.9	444	0.7	8.1	18.3	14.2	0.1	4.6	..
83 Jamaica	3,640	9.6	371	7.1	7.5	7.3	10.1	(.)	4.0	..
84 Sri Lanka	2,656	19.5	573	1.0	1.1	2.8	7.1	(.)	0.4	..
85 Turkey	2,943	18.1	560	..	0.0	7.0	178.6	0.7	2.9	
86 Oman	388	121.8	646	..	0.0	2.1	15.2	0.1	6.6	..
87 Dominican Republic	2,472	39.7	1,085	-1.8	1.6	6.3	12.9	0.1	1.6	..
88 Saint Lucia	..	..	88	..	..	7.2	0.2	(.)	1.3	..
89 Maldives	105	11.2	17	..	..	3.8	0.3	(.)	1.1	..
90 Azerbaijan	1,049	203.7	2,186	..	0.0	0.4	30.1	0.1	4.0	..
91 Ecuador	34,952	3.8	1,423	1.7	1.6	3.1	24.5	0.1	2.1	..
92 Jordan	102	144.7	187	-0.3	2.5	5.9	13.8	0.1	2.5	..
93 Armenia	2,577	32.2	817	..	-2.7	0.4	3.7	(.)	1.0	0.1
94 Albania	8,646	5.2	441	..	0.0	6.2	1.9	(.)	0.6	..
95 Samoa (Western)	..	..	..	..	1.1	0.6	0.1	(.)	0.8	..
96 Guyana	279,799	0.6	1,811	..	0.0	1.4	1.0	(.)	1.1	..
97 Iran, Islamic Rep. of	1,898	54.5	1,165	1.8	1.8	3.9	267.1	1.1	3.8	..
98 Kyrgyzstan	9,884	21.7	2,219	..	0.0	0.7	6.1	(.)	1.4	..
99 China	2,201	18.7	439	-0.6	0.1	7.8	3,369.0	14.1	2.8	..
100 Turkmenistan	305	1,748.5	5,947	..	0.0	0.1	34.3	0.1	8.3	..

. . . WHILE PRESERVING IT FOR FUTURE GENERATIONS . . .

HDI rank	Annual internal renewable water resources (cubic metres per capita) [a] 2000	Annual fresh water withdrawals		Average annual rate of deforestation (%) [c]		Printing and writing paper consumed (kilograms per capita) 1997	Carbon dioxide emissions			Sulphur dioxide emissions per capita (kilograms) 1995-97
		As % of water resources 1987-97 [b]	Per capita (cubic metres) 1987-97 [b]	1980-90	1990-95		Total (millions of metric tons) 1996	Share of world total (%) 1996	Per capita (metric tons) 1996	
101 Tunisia	367	80.4	312	-0.9	0.5	6.1	16.2	0.1	1.8	..
102 Moldova, Rep. of	228	296.3	677	..	0.0	1.6	12.1	0.1	2.7	3.9
103 South Africa	1,110	29.7	391	0.1	0.2	24.9	293.2	1.2	6.9	..
104 El Salvador	2,820	4.1	137	2.3	3.3	7.2	4.1	(.)	0.7	..
105 Cape Verde	701	8.7	76	..	-21.6	0.7	0.1	(.)	0.3	..
106 Uzbekistan	672	355.3	2,626	..	-2.6	0.1	95.1	0.4	4.1	..
107 Algeria	442	32.4	180	1.2	1.2	3.2	94.5	0.4	3.3	..
108 Viet Nam	4,591	14.8	815	0.9	1.4	1.2	37.7	0.2	10.8	..
109 Indonesia	13,380	2.6	407	0.8	1.0	7.1	245.5	1.0	1.2	..
110 Tajikistan	10,714	17.9	2,095	..	0.0	..	5.9	(.)	1.0	..
111 Syrian Arab Republic	434	205.9	1,069	2.5	2.2	3.0	44.4	0.2	3.1	..
112 Swaziland	2,619	25.0	1,178	0.0	0.0	..	0.3	(.)	0.4	..
113 Honduras	14,818	1.6	293	2.1	2.3	7.4	4.0	(.)	0.7	..
114 Bolivia	37,941	0.4	210	0.8	1.2	1.2	10.1	(.)	1.3	..
115 Namibia	3,592	4.0	185	0.3	0.3	..	..	..	..	..
116 Nicaragua	37,484	0.7	267	1.4	2.5	1.0	2.9	(.)	0.7	..
117 Mongolia	13,073	1.2	182	0.0	0.0	0.3	8.9	(.)	3.5	..
118 Vanuatu	..	..	..	..	0.8	0.3	0.1	(.)	0.4	..
119 Egypt	34	2,395.7	920	-1.8	0.0	3.2	98.0	0.4	1.5	..
120 Guatemala	11,805	0.9	126	1.7	2.0	4.2	6.8	(.)	0.6	..
121 Solomon Islands	..	..	..	0.2	0.2	0.0	0.2	(.)	0.4	..
122 Botswana	1,788	3.8	81	0.5	0.5	..	2.1	(.)	1.4	..
123 Gabon	133,755	0.0	70	0.6	0.5	0.4	3.7	(.)	3.3	..
124 Morocco	1,058	36.8	454	0.3	0.3	2.3	27.9	0.1	1.0	..
125 Myanmar	19,306	0.4	102	1.2	1.4	0.6	7.3	(.)	0.2	..
126 Iraq	1,523	121.6	2,368	0.0	0.0	0.3	91.5	0.4	4.4	..
127 Lesotho	2,430	1.0	31	-14.6	0.0	0.0	..	..	..	..
128 India	1,244	39.7	588	-1.1	0.0	2.2	999.0	4.2	1.1	..
129 Ghana	1,499	1.0	35	1.3	1.3	0.6	4.1	(.)	0.2	..
130 Zimbabwe	1,208	8.7	136	0.7	0.6	1.9	18.4	0.1	1.6	..
131 Equatorial Guinea	66,275	0.0	30	0.4	0.5	0.0	0.1	(.)	0.4	..
132 São Tomé and Principe	14,853	..	..	..	0.0	0.2	0.1	(.)	0.6	..
133 Papua New Guinea	166,645	0.0	28	-0.1	0.4	0.8	2.4	(.)	0.6	..
134 Cameroon	17,766	0.1	38	0.6	0.6	0.8	3.5	(.)	0.3	..
135 Pakistan	542	183.6	1,269	3.1	2.9	1.4	94.5	0.4	0.7	..
136 Cambodia	10,795	0.4	66	2.4	1.6	0.1	0.5	(.)	(.)	..
137 Comoros	1,469	..	..	..	5.8	0.7	0.1	(.)	0.1	..
138 Kenya	672	10.1	87	0.4	0.3	1.8	6.8	(.)	0.3	..
139 Congo	75,387	0.0	20	0.2	0.2	0.3	5.0	(.)	1.9	..
Low human development										
140 Lao People's Dem. Rep.	35,049	0.5	260	..	1.2	0.1	0.3	(.)	0.1	..
141 Madagascar	21,140	5.8	1,694	0.9	0.8	0.3	1.2	(.)	0.1	..
142 Bhutan	44,728	0.0	13	0.6	0.3	0.0	0.3	(.)	0.2	..
143 Sudan	1,187	50.9	669	1.0	0.8	0.1	3.5	(.)	0.1	..
144 Nepal	8,282	14.6	1,397	0.9	1.1	0.1	1.6	(.)	0.1	..
145 Togo	2,484	0.8	28	1.6	1.4	0.2	0.8	(.)	0.2	..
146 Bangladesh	813	13.9	134	1.8	0.9	1.1	23.0	0.1	0.2	..
147 Mauritania	150	4,075.0	8,046	0.0	0.0	0.2	3.0	(.)	1.3	..
148 Yemen	226	71.5	253	0.0	0.0	0.6	17.0	0.1	1.1	..
149 Djibouti	471	2.5	19	..	0.0	0.5	0.4	(.)	0.6	..
150 Haiti	1,473	8.1	139	4.3	3.5	0.5	1.1	(.)	0.2	..

HDI rank	Annual internal renewable water resources (cubic metres per capita) [a] 2000	Annual fresh water withdrawals		Average annual rate of deforestation (%) [c]		Printing and writing paper consumed (kilograms per capita) 1997	Carbon dioxide emissions			Sulphur dioxide emissions per capita (kilograms) 1995-97
		As % of water resources 1987-97 [b]	Per capita (cubic metres) 1987-97 [b]	1980-90	1990-95		Total (millions of metric tons) 1996	Share of world total (%) 1996	Per capita (metric tons) 1996	
151 Nigeria	1,982	1.8	46	1.6	0.9	0.6	83.5	0.3	0.7	..
152 Congo, Dem. Rep. of the	18,101	0.0	8	0.7	..	0.1	2.3	(.)	(.)	..
153 Zambia	8,747	2.1	214	0.9	0.8	0.4	2.4	(.)	0.3	..
154 Côte d'Ivoire	5,187	0.9	66	7.7	0.6	0.5	13.1	0.1	0.9	..
155 Senegal	2,785	5.7	205	0.6	0.7	0.2	3.1	(.)	0.4	..
156 Tanzania, U. Rep. of	2,387	1.5	40	1.1	1.0	0.5	2.4	(.)	0.1	..
157 Benin	1,690	1.4	28	1.4	1.2	0.3	0.7	(.)	0.1	..
158 Uganda	1,791	0.5	20	0.9	0.9	0.3	1.0	(.)	(.)	..
159 Eritrea	727	..	..	..	0.0	0.0	0.1	(.)	11.2	..
160 Angola	14,288	0.3	57	0.6	1.0	0.1	5.1	(.)	0.4	..
161 Gambia	2,298	1.0	33	1.1	0.9	0.2	0.2	(.)	0.2	..
162 Guinea	30,416	0.3	141	1.1	1.1	0.1	1.1	(.)	0.2	..
163 Malawi	1,606	5.4	98	1.2	1.6	0.1	0.7	(.)	0.1	..
164 Rwanda	815	12.2	134	-1.7	0.2	0.1	0.5	(.)	0.1	..
165 Mali	5,341	2.3	164	0.8	1.0	0.2	0.5	(.)	(.)	..
166 Central African Republic	39,001	0.0	26	0.4	0.4	0.0	0.2	(.)	0.1	..
167 Chad	1,961	1.3	33	0.7	0.8	0.0	0.1	(.)	(.)	..
168 Mozambique	5,081	0.6	40	0.7	0.7	0.0	1.0	(.)	0.1	..
169 Guinea-Bissau	13,189	0.1	17	-0.8	0.4	0.1	0.2	(.)	0.2	..
170 Burundi	538	2.8	20	-2.2	0.4	0.0	0.2	(.)	(.)	..
171 Ethiopia	1,758	2.0	50	..	0.5	0.2	3.4	(.)	(.)	..
172 Burkina Faso	1,466	2.1	39	0.7	0.7	0.1	1.0	(.)	0.1	..
173 Niger	326	14.3	65	0.0	0.0	0.0	1.1	(.)	0.1	..
174 Sierra Leone	32,960	0.2	98	2.8	3.0	0.8	0.4	(.)	0.1	..
All developing countries	6,235	..	..	..	..	6.1	8,716.5 T	36.4	2.1	..
Least developed countries	6,976	..	..	..	..	0.4	85.7 T	0.4	0.2	..
Arab States	522	..	..	..	..	3.1	910.0 T	3.8	3.7	..
East Asia	2,194	..	..	..	..	10.2	3,809.7 T	15.9	3.0	..
East Asia (excluding China)	2,013	..	..	..	..	65.1	440.7 T	1.8	8.2	..
Latin America and the Caribbean	27,328	..	..	..	..	10.4	1,195.6 T	5.0	2.5	..
South Asia	1,361	..	..	..	..	2.1	1,392.9 T	5.8	1.0	..
South Asia (excluding India)	1,660	..	..	..	..	1.7	393.9 T	1.6	1.0	..
South-East Asia and the Pacific	12,478	..	..	..	..	7.4	755.6 T	3.2	3.1	..
Sub-Saharan Africa	6,202	..	..	..	..	2.2	468.7 T	2.0	0.9	..
Eastern Europe and the CIS	12,470	..	..	..	..	7.9	3,249.6 T	13.6	8.2	..
OECD	7,928	..	..	..	..	89.0	11,902.6 T	49.7	10.9	46.1
High human development	9,374	..	..	..	..	96.6	11,950.2 T	49.9	11.7	..
Medium human development	6,890	..	..	..	..	5.8	10,316.3 T	43.1	2.8	..
Low human development	5,162	..	..	..	..	0.4	176.5 T	0.7	0.3	..
High income	9,458	..	..	..	..	109.3	10,745.1 T	44.9	12.6	..
Medium income	14,360	..	..	..	..	10.3	6,622.1 T	27.7	4.6	..
Low income	3,578	..	..	..	..	4.1	5,075.8 T	21.2	1.8	..
World	7,122	..	..	..	..	21.4	22,443.0 T	93.8 [h]	4.1	..

a. These annual averages disguise large seasonal, interannual and long-term variations. b. Data refer to the most recent year available during the period specified in the column heading. c. A positive number indicates a loss of forest area, a negative number a gain. d. Data for Belgium include data for Luxembourg. e. Preliminary data. f. Includes mobile sources. g. Figure refers to Skopje only. h. The world total is less than 100% because of the omission of data for countries not reported on and because the global total used in this calculation includes other emissions not included in national totals, such as emissions from bunker fuels and oxidation of non-fuel hydrocarbon products.

Source: Columns 1-3: WRI 2000b; columns 4 and 5: WRI 1999; column 6: UNESCO 1999c; columns 7-9: CDIAC 1999; column 10: EMEP 1999.

. . . WHILE PRESERVING IT FOR FUTURE GENERATIONS . . .

HDI rank	Major protected areas (as % of national territory)[a] 1999	Nuclear waste generated (metric tons of heavy metal)[b] 1998	Hazardous waste generated (1,000 metric tons)[c] 1991-97[d]	Municipal waste generated (kilograms per person) 1997[e]	Population served By municipal waste services (%) 1992-97[d]	Population served By public sanitation services (%) 1993-97[d]	Waste recycling (as % of apparent consumption) Paper and cardboard 1992-97[d]	Glass 1992-97[d]
High human development								
1 Canada	9.1	1,510	5,896	490	99	91	33	17
2 Norway	6.5	..	683	630	98	80	44	76
3 United States	13.1	2,700 [f]	172,732	720	100	..	41	26
4 Australia	7.0	..	426	..	..	..	..	42
5 Iceland	9.5	..	5	560	99	90	..	75
6 Sweden	8.1	232 [f]	..	360	100	93	62	76
7 Belgium	2.8	141	776	480	100	75	16	75
8 Netherlands	5.7	12	511	560	100	98	62	82
9 Japan	6.8	1,061	..	400	100	55	54	56
10 United Kingdom	20.4	785 [f]	2,077	480	100	96	40	26
11 Finland	5.5	72	559	410	100	77	57	62
12 France	13.5	1,165	..	480	100	79	41	52
13 Switzerland	25.7	64	888	600	99	94	63	91
14 Germany	26.9	430	10,780	460	100	92	70	79
15 Denmark	32.0 [g]	..	254	560	100	87	50	70
16 Austria	29.2	..	606	510	100	76	69	88
17 Luxembourg	14.4	..	139	460	100	88	..	..
18 Ireland	0.9	..	248	560	..	68	12	38
19 Italy	7.3	..	2,708	460	..	..	31	34
20 New Zealand	23.4	..	479	..	..	..	66	36
21 Spain	8.4	97 [f]	3,394	390	..	..	42	37
25 Greece	3.6	..	280	370	85	68	29	26
28 Portugal	6.6	..	1,365	380	98	56	40	44
29 Slovenia	5.9	..	..	..	..	..	..	..
31 Korea, Rep. of	6.9	370	1,912	400	98	..	57	68
34 Czech Republic	15.8	45	1,265	310	85	74	33	..
40 Slovakia	22.1	..	1,500	340	96	53	34	40
43 Hungary	7.0	53	2,588	500	85	45	49	..
44 Poland	9.1	..	4,007	320	..	54	13	..
46 Estonia	11.1	..	..	..	..	..	..	..
Medium human development								
49 Croatia	7.4	..	..	..	..	..	..	..
52 Lithuania	9.9	..	..	..	..	..	..	..
55 Mexico	3.4	43	12,700	300	77	65	2	4
57 Belarus	6.3	..	..	..	..	..	..	..
60 Bulgaria	4.5	..	..	..	..	..	..	..
62 Russian Federation	3.1	..	89,390	340	73	..	..	..
63 Latvia	12.5	..	..	..	..	..	..	..
64 Romania	4.6	..	..	..	..	..	..	..
69 Macedonia, TFYR	7.1	..	..	..	..	..	..	..
70 Georgia	2.8	..	..	..	..	..	..	..
73 Kazakhstan	2.7	..	..	..	..	..	..	..
78 Ukraine	1.6	..	..	..	..	..	..	..
85 Turkey	1.3	..	..	330	72	63	36	20
90 Azerbaijan	5.5	..	..	..	..	..	..	..
93 Armenia	7.6	..	..	..	..	..	..	..
94 Albania	2.9	..	..	..	..	..	..	..
98 Kyrgyzstan	3.5	..	..	..	..	..	..	..
100 Turkmenistan	4.1	..	..	..	..	..	..	..
102 Moldova, Rep. of	1.4	..	..	..	..	..	..	..
106 Uzbekistan	1.8	..	..	..	..	..	..	..
110 Tajikistan	4.1	..	..	..	..	..	..	..

HDI rank	Major protected areas (as % of national territory)[a] 1999	Nuclear waste generated (metric tons of heavy metal)[b] 1998	Hazardous waste generated (1,000 metric tons)[c] 1991-97[d]	Municipal waste generated (kilograms per person) 1997[e]	Population served		Waste recycling (as % of apparent consumption)	
					By municipal waste services (%) 1992-97[d]	By public sanitation services (%) 1993-97[d]	Paper and cardboard 1992-97[d]	Glass 1992-97[d]
All developing countries	..	..	..	..	..	..	..	..
Eastern Europe and the CIS	3.3	..	..	..	..	..	..	..
OECD	9.6	..	..	440 [h]	..	..	..	..
World	..	..	..	..	..	..	..	..

Note: This table includes OECD member countries, Eastern Europe and the CIS only as adequate data on the indicators it presents are limited to these countries.

a. National classifications may differ. Protected areas may include overlaps between different designations, leading to unexpectedly high percentages. Data include only areas greater than 10 square kilometres except for islands. World Conservation Union (IUCN) management categories I-V, except where otherwise noted. b. Refers to spent fuel, one part of nuclear waste. c. Refers to waste, generated mainly by industrial activities, that may lead to toxic contamination of soil, water and air if not properly managed. d. Data refer to the most recent year available during the period specified in the column heading. e. Data refer to 1997 or the latest available year. f. Provisional data. g. Total for Denmark does not include protected areas in Greenland. Greenland has two protected areas occupying a combined area of 98,250,000 hectares. h. Aggregate as calculated in OECD 1999c.

Source: Column 1: WRI 2000a; *columns 2-8:* OECD 1999c.

... WHILE PRESERVING IT FOR FUTURE GENERATIONS ...

HDI rank	Daily per capita supply of calories[a]		Daily per capita supply of protein[a]		Daily per capita supply of fat[a]		Food production index (1989-91 = 100)	Food imports (as % of merchandise imports)	Food aid in cereals (thousands of metric tons)	Food consumption (as % of total household consumption)[c]
			Total (grams)	Change (%)	Total (grams)	Change (%)				
	1970	1997	1997	1970-97	1997	1970-97	1998	1997-98[b]	1998	1997

High human development

1 Canada	2,963	3,119	98	3.2	126	8.4	121	6	..	9
2 Norway	3,022	3,357	104	18.5	136	3.0	101	7	..	13
3 United States	2,965	3,699	112	18.4	143	22.8	121	5	..	8
4 Australia	3,251	3,224	107	-0.7	132	11.4	131	5	..	14
5 Iceland	3,016	3,117	113	-8.9	121	2.8	91	10	..	13
6 Sweden	2,877	3,194	100	14.4	134	14.8	100	7	..	10
7 Belgium	3,125	3,619	102	10.8	160	24.5	..	10	..	15
8 Netherlands	3,024	3,284	106	22.7	141	6.4	97	11	..	11
9 Japan	2,704	2,932	96	17.9	83	52.3	93	16	..	11
10 United Kingdom	3,282	3,276	95	2.0	141	-0.5	98	9	..	11
11 Finland	3,121	3,100	101	13.4	127	2.8	85	7	..	11
12 France	3,300	3,518	113	8.3	164	29.7	106	10	..	12
13 Switzerland	3,480	3,223	88	-2.9	144	-3.6	97	6	..	12
14 Germany	3,166	3,382	96	8.3	144	12.8	93	9	..	11
15 Denmark	3,157	3,407	108	38.7	132	-5.8	103	12	..	10
16 Austria	3,227	3,536	103	15.4	161	29.8	106	6	..	13
17 Luxembourg	..	..	..	..	..	..	..	..	..	10
18 Ireland	3,445	3,565	111	4.6	133	6.5	107	7	..	14
19 Italy	3,422	3,507	109	11.7	147	31.9	101	11	..	14
20 New Zealand	2,941	3,395	108	12.9	137	17.7	127	9	..	12
21 Spain	2,733	3,310	107	28.1	145	62.7	109	12	..	17
22 Cyprus	3,061	3,429	109	27.4	147	40.0	108	20	..	..
23 Israel	3,014	3,278	105	7.9	113	14.8	107	7	..	..
24 Singapore	..	..	..	..	..	..	29	4	..	14
25 Greece	3,137	3,649	115	14.7	153	42.1	98	14	..	28
26 Hong Kong, China (SAR)	2,912	3,206	100	18.7	135	44.3	19	5	..	10
27 Malta	3,147	3,398	110	16.6	107	6.4	125	11	..	..
28 Portugal	2,930	3,667	113	38.0	132	70.9	93	13	..	20
29 Slovenia	..	3,101	103	..	102	..	97	7	..	13
30 Barbados	2,854	3,176	92	20.2	109	35.5	88	17	..	..
31 Korea, Rep. of	2,786	3,155	86	21.1	80	229.5	121	6	..	21
32 Brunei Darussalam	2,366	2,857	83	52.7	83	96.7	167	14 [d]	..	..
33 Bahamas	2,600	2,443	78	-0.3	81	-3.4	148	16	..	..
34 Czech Republic	..	3,244	96	..	111	..	82	6	..	15
35 Argentina	3,347	3,093	95	-10.4	110	-2.7	134	5	..	..
36 Kuwait	2,607	3,096	97	29.0	95	38.1	153	16	..	..
37 Antigua and Barbuda	2,554	2,365	81	27.2	93	12.1	99	..	..	33
38 Chile	2,637	2,796	77	10.9	82	34.6	132	7	..	..
39 Uruguay	3,045	2,816	84	-10.7	104	-11.8	132	11	..	..
40 Slovakia	..	2,984	81	..	105	..	74 [d]	6	..	17
41 Bahrain	..	..	..	..	..	..	92	12 [d]	..	..
42 Qatar	..	..	..	..	..	..	179	15 [d]	..	..
43 Hungary	3,331	3,313	85	-8.0	137	18.8	77	4	..	14
44 Poland	3,445	3,366	99	-3.8	112	7.0	92	8	..	20
45 United Arab Emirates	3,229	3,390	104	17.3	109	36.5	257	10 [d]	..	..
46 Estonia	..	2,849	95	..	91	..	45	16	..	..

Medium human development

47 Saint Kitts and Nevis	1,989	2,771	75	69.2	95	56.7	114	19	..	30
48 Costa Rica	2,370	2,649	68	17.6	80	50.9	129	8	..	..
49 Croatia	..	2,445	63	..	69	..	60	10	(.)	17
50 Trinidad and Tobago	2,486	2,661	59	-7.1	71	13.4	87	11	..	20

HDI rank	Daily per capita supply of calories [a]		Daily per capita supply of protein [a]		Daily per capita supply of fat [a]		Food production index (1989-91 = 100) 1998	Food imports (as % of merchandise imports) 1997-98 [b]	Food aid in cereals (thousands of metric tons) 1998	Food consumption (as % of total household consumption) [c] 1997
	1970	1997	Total (grams) 1997	Change (%) 1970-97	Total (grams) 1997	Change (%) 1970-97				
51 Dominica	2,051	3,059	86	72.1	78	65.4	90	26	..	32
52 Lithuania	..	3,261	98	..	83	..	66	11	..	..
53 Seychelles	1,930	2,487	79	52.5	72	112.7	143	20 [d]	..	..
54 Grenada	2,251	2,768	67	15.6	93	41.5	109	23	..	26
55 Mexico	2,706	3,097	83	18.1	88	49.4	126	6	..	..
56 Cuba	2,640	2,480	52	-23.9	49	-27.7	61	..	11	..
57 Belarus	..	3,225	94	..	96	..	67	11	..	16
58 Belize	2,266	2,907	65	14.0	76	21.7	161	20	..	28
59 Panama	2,257	2,430	65	14.0	68	39.4	96	12	..	..
60 Bulgaria	3,465	2,686	80	-15.5	90	8.4	69	9	12	15
61 Malaysia	2,560	2,977	75	48.3	87	59.4	123	6	..	..
62 Russian Federation	..	2,904	90	..	81	..	59	17	1,332	18
63 Latvia	..	2,864	79	..	87	..	46	13	..	..
64 Romania	2,882	3,253	100	18.1	82	14.3	95	8	..	24
65 Venezuela	2,352	2,321	59	0.3	66	22.5	115	12	..	..
66 Fiji	2,423	2,865	74	39.5	106	71.8	107	16 [d]	..	30
67 Suriname	2,225	2,665	65	16.2	55	22.6	89	15	..	..
68 Colombia	1,938	2,597	63	40.5	65	65.5	111	12	1	..
69 Macedonia, TFYR	..	2,664	69	..	75	..	97	16 [d]	..	..
70 Georgia	..	2,614	69	..	39	..	81	..	94	..
71 Mauritius	2,355	2,917	72	43.2	87	72.0	109	16	..	24
72 Libyan Arab Jamahiriya	2,453	3,289	78	31.4	106	44.1	130	23	..	..
73 Kazakhstan	..	3,085	97	..	66	..	49	11	..	..
74 Brazil	2,409	2,974	76	26.5	84	81.9	128	10	..	..
75 Saudi Arabia	1,895	2,783	78	61.4	79	155.1	80	18 [d]	..	..
76 Thailand	2,123	2,360	54	7.6	47	59.7	113	5	..	23
77 Philippines	1,753	2,366	56	30.5	47	41.8	125	9	3	33
78 Ukraine	..	2,795	78	..	72	..	47	..	3	21
79 Saint Vincent and the Grenadines	2,331	2,472	65	22.9	69	16.3	77	25	..	24
80 Peru	2,198	2,302	60	9.5	50	52.8	144	16	133	..
81 Paraguay	2,589	2,566	77	4.8	79	32.6	124	20	..	..
82 Lebanon	2,336	3,277	85	43.1	108	69.5	146	..	..	..
83 Jamaica	2,538	2,553	63	-6.1	77	23.8	117	17	..	26
84 Sri Lanka	2,266	2,302	52	11.6	46	-6.1	114	..	26	38
85 Turkey	3,053	3,525	98	7.2	101	38.7	115	5	..	23
86 Oman	..	..	..	..	..	..	111	17	..	..
87 Dominican Republic	2,003	2,288	50	14.7	74	52.9	104	..	14	..
88 Saint Lucia	2,008	2,734	80	58.2	72	26.1	75	26	..	39
89 Maldives	1,607	2,485	88	69.6	47	29.9	115	..	..	..
90 Azerbaijan	..	2,236	66	..	38	..	59	..	12	..
91 Ecuador	2,188	2,679	59	13.2	98	94.1	134	12	13	..
92 Jordan	2,418	3,014	75	15.9	86	52.0	153	..	100	..
93 Armenia	..	2,371	65	..	54	..	75	31	11	..
94 Albania	2,424	2,961	99	41.4	79	50.7	..	27	26	..
95 Samoa (Western)	..	..	..	..	..	..	94	..	..	..
96 Guyana	2,281	2,530	69	20.0	54	10.8	176	7 [d]	35	..
97 Iran, Islamic Rep. of	2,051	2,836	75	37.9	63	48.0	160	..	1	23
98 Kyrgyzstan	..	2,447	82	..	47	..	103	21 [d]	1	..
99 China	2,018	2,897	78	62.4	71	213.5	157	5	..	..
100 Turkmenistan	..	2,306	65	..	64	..	118	9	..	..

HDI rank	Daily per capita supply of calories [a]		Daily per capita supply of protein [a]		Daily per capita supply of fat [a]		Food production index (1989-91 = 100)	Food imports (as % of merchandise imports) [b]	Food aid in cereals (thousands of metric tons)	Food consumption (as % of total household consumption) [c]
			Total (grams)	Change (%)	Total (grams)	Change (%)				
	1970	1997	1997	1970-97	1997	1970-97	1998	1997-98	1998	1997
101 Tunisia	2,255	3,283	88	55.0	93	45.6	122	10	..	35
102 Moldova, Rep. of	..	2,567	69	..	48	..	48	8	..	28
103 South Africa	2,831	2,990	77	2.9	77	12.8	97	5	..	..
104 El Salvador	1,830	2,562	64	37.4	55	43.5	119	16	8	..
105 Cape Verde	1,628	3,015	70	79.1	80	157.9	132	..	65	..
106 Uzbekistan	..	2,433	70	..	70	..	114	..	..	..
107 Algeria	1,829	2,853	79	66.2	70	93.3	130	32	20	..
108 Viet Nam	2,146	2,484	57	13.4	36	72.2	147	..	51	40
109 Indonesia	1,842	2,886	67	72.7	57	114.0	119	11	727	45
110 Tajikistan	..	2,001	53	..	34	..	61	..	38	..
111 Syrian Arab Republic	2,319	3,351	86	35.6	95	64.9	164	21	16	..
112 Swaziland	2,347	2,483	60	-9.4	42	-0.4	96	..	..	27
113 Honduras	2,155	2,403	58	2.9	62	54.0	117	16	47	..
114 Bolivia	1,998	2,174	57	13.7	57	31.6	136	8	144	..
115 Namibia	2,162	2,183	60	-7.7	38	-12.6	124	..	1	..
116 Nicaragua	2,338	2,186	49	-31.4	47	6.7	125	18	110	..
117 Mongolia	2,133	1,917	71	-13.5	72	-17.7	90	14 [d]	45	..
118 Vanuatu	2,513	2,700	60	-9.7	93	4.6	118	20 [d]	..	..
119 Egypt	2,356	3,287	89	39.1	58	21.1	141	21	13	44
120 Guatemala	2,097	2,339	61	7.1	46	18.7	128	12	31	..
121 Solomon Islands	2,249	2,122	51	-9.1	41	-6.1	121	16 [d]	..	..
122 Botswana	2,103	2,183	70	-6.5	60	38.0	91	..	..	25
123 Gabon	2,183	2,556	73	18.7	55	44.4	111	19 [d]	..	37
124 Morocco	2,468	3,078	82	26.9	61	38.5	110	17	4	45
125 Myanmar	2,020	2,862	72	38.5	47	44.8	138	..	2	..
126 Iraq	2,261	2,619	56	-8.3	77	82.0	99	..	17	..
127 Lesotho	1,986	2,243	64	6.5	33	46.7	100	..	4	..
128 India	2,082	2,496	59	12.9	45	46.5	120	6	327	..
129 Ghana	2,242	2,611	49	-0.4	32	-20.5	144	..	27	..
130 Zimbabwe	2,225	2,145	52	-14.6	53	6.8	93	7	82	28
131 Equatorial Guinea	..	..	..	..	..	..	97	..	1	..
132 São Tomé and Principe	2,119	2,138	44	-5.2	76	15.8	188	..	3	..
133 Papua New Guinea	1,899	2,224	48	23.8	42	58.3	112	..	11	..
134 Cameroon	2,301	2,111	48	-20.6	44	-2.5	119	14 [d]	10	38
135 Pakistan	2,202	2,476	61	10.6	65	91.6	142	21	..	40
136 Cambodia	2,109	2,048	47	-1.5	33	55.6	133	..	31	..
137 Comoros	1,860	1,858	43	26.5	42	7.6	114	..	3.6	..
138 Kenya	2,187	1,976	52	-19.0	47	40.2	105	14	71	38
139 Congo	2,030	2,143	43	22.6	50	14.5	112	21 [d]	2	36
Low human development										
140 Lao People's Dem. Rep.	2,093	2,108	52	-0.7	26	22.8	135	..	12	..
141 Madagascar	2,424	2,021	46	-24.2	32	-4.8	109	15	26	..
142 Bhutan	..	..	..	..	..	..	107	21 [d]	4	..
143 Sudan	2,170	2,395	75	23.1	75	9.9	156	..	233	..
144 Nepal	1,959	2,366	61	17.8	32	18.1	118	12	46	37
145 Togo	2,293	2,469	59	19.8	50	43.8	131	..	3	..
146 Bangladesh	2,197	2,085	45	-4.5	22	41.0	112	15	1,557	41
147 Mauritania	1,910	2,622	74	-1.7	64	21.8	103	..	11	..
148 Yemen	1,768	2,051	54	9.5	36	27.9	129	29 [d]	158	..
149 Djibouti	1,846	2,084	44	2.9	61	65.1	86	..	8	..
150 Haiti	1,944	1,869	41	-8.3	40	49.1	95	..	127	..

23 Food security and nutrition

HDI rank	Daily per capita supply of calories [a]		Daily per capita supply of protein [a]		Daily per capita supply of fat [a]		Food production index (1989-91 = 100)	Food imports (as % of merchandise imports)	Food aid in cereals (thousands of metric tons)	Food consumption (as % of total household consumption) [c]
			Total (grams)	Change (%)	Total (grams)	Change (%)				
	1970	1997	1997	1970-97	1997	1970-97	1998	1997-98 [b]	1998	1997
151 Nigeria	2,392	2,735	62	11.1	71	23.9	149	..	..	48
152 Congo, Dem. Rep. of the	2,178	1,755	28	-25.3	28	-19.2	95	..	10	..
153 Zambia	2,173	1,970	52	-19.2	30	-27.1	94	10 [d]	33	47
154 Côte d'Ivoire	2,460	2,610	50	-6.0	55	29.6	127	17 [d]	4	35
155 Senegal	2,577	2,418	61	-8.6	86	22.8	99	..	12	52
156 Tanzania, U. Rep. of	1,770	1,995	49	14.4	31	13.2	103	17	36	..
157 Benin	1,958	2,487	59	25.8	44	-1.7	148	..	11	45
158 Uganda	2,319	2,085	45	-19.9	28	-19.5	113	..	57	..
159 Eritrea	..	1,622	51	..	20	..	142	..	101	..
160 Angola	2,103	1,903	40	-9.8	37	9.9	143	..	113	..
161 Gambia	2,114	2,350	50	-7.0	62	20.4	92	..	6	..
162 Guinea	2,217	2,231	48	-0.4	50	-11.7	143	..	22	32
163 Malawi	2,359	2,043	54	-25.0	30	-28.6	116	..	41	45
164 Rwanda	2,224	2,056	46	-18.6	22	80.3	82	..	144	..
165 Mali	2,195	2,029	61	-4.7	42	-16.9	116	..	12	48
166 Central African Republic	2,387	2,016	44	22.7	64	14.8	129	12 [d]	10	..
167 Chad	2,108	2,032	59	-8.2	60	22.1	157	24 [d]	7	..
168 Mozambique	1,896	1,832	35	-0.2	32	13.0	140	22 [d]	112	..
169 Guinea-Bissau	2,002	2,430	49	19.1	61	5.9	118	..	21	..
170 Burundi	2,104	1,685	51	-30.8	11	-26.7	92	..	1	..
171 Ethiopia	..	1,858	54	..	23	..	121	14 [d]	589	..
172 Burkina Faso	1,765	2,121	62	13.7	47	54.1	136	..	57	..
173 Niger	1,992	2,097	61	11.3	39	29.8	127	..	55	..
174 Sierra Leone	2,449	2,035	44	-11.3	58	-13.6	101	..	72	48
All developing countries	2,145	2,663	67	27.5	59	79.6	..	..	..	..
Least developed countries	2,108	2,099	51	1.4	34	10.0	..	..	3,803 T	..
Arab States	2,225	2,930	79	32.1	70	44.7	..	16.8	..	..
East Asia	2,050	2,906	78	59.7	71	209.8	..	5.5	..	..
East Asia (excluding China)	2,777	3,103	87	19.5	86	155.0	..	5.8	..	..
Latin America and the Caribbean	2,474	2,798	73	13.1	79	43.2	..	8.7	..	..
South Asia	2,103	2,467	59	12.7	45	50.7	..	..	1,960 T	..
South Asia (excluding India)	2,166	2,394	58	12.5	47	62.6	..	..	1,633 T	..
South-East Asia and the Pacific	1,966	2,656	62	40.0	51	77.7	..	..	..	..
Sub-Saharan Africa	2,271	2,237	53	-4.1	46	2.8	..	..	1,833 T	..
Eastern Europe and the CIS	..	2,907	86	..	81	..	..	10.7	..	..
OECD	3,033	3,380	101	12.4	125	22.8	..	8.4	..	..
High human development	3,055	3,371	103	12.0	129	21.8	..	8.3	..	..
Medium human development	2,125	2,743	70	34.7	63	95.0	..	9.4	..	..
Low human development	2,181	2,166	51	0.1	40	10.5	..	..	3,710 T	..
High income	3,041	3,412	105	14.3	134	22.4	..	8.4	..	..
Medium income	2,507	2,889	78	17.6	76	39.5	..	9.0	..	..
Low income	2,062	2,596	65	30.7	55	96.2	..	..	5,302 T	..
World	2,358	2,791	74	19.7	72	42.2	..	8.5	..	..

a. Amount available for human consumption. Per capita supply represents the average supply available for the population as a whole and does not necessarily indicate what is actually consumed by individuals. b. Data refer to the most recent year available during the period specified in the column heading. c. Data refer to the percentage share of all food purchased for household consumption, converted in PPP terms. d. Data refer to a year or period other than that specified in the column heading.

Source: Columns 1-3 and 5: FAO 1999; columns 4 and 6: calculated on the basis of data on protein and fat supply from FAO 1999; column 7: World Bank 2000b, data from FAO; column 8: World Bank 2000b; column 9: FAO 2000; column 10: World Bank 1999b.

HDI rank	Unemployed people (thousands) 1998	Unemployment rate [a] Total (% of labour force) 1998	Index (1994 = 100) 1998	Incidence of long-term unemployment [b] (as % of total unemployment) Female 1998	Male 1998	Part-time employment (as % of total employment) Female 1998	Male 1998	Involuntary part-time employment (as % of total part-time employment) Female 1997	Male 1997	Public expenditure on unemployment compensation (as % of GDP) 1997-98 [c]
High human development										
1 Canada	1,303	8.3	80	8.3	11.5	28.6	10.5	29.8	34.9	0.46
2 Norway	75	3.3	60	8.6	10.0	35.9	8.1	15.2	17.2	..
3 United States	6,204	4.5	74	7.1	8.8	19.1	8.2	8.0	7.4	..
4 Australia	756	8.0	82	29.3	36.5	40.7	14.4	8.5	17.0	0.25
5 Iceland	4	2.7 d	50 d	18.1	13.6	38.6	9.8	..	..	2.29
6 Sweden	278	8.2	87	30.1	36.3	22.0	5.6	31.3	34.7	..
7 Belgium	505	8.8	88	64.7	60.3	32.2	4.9	..	..	1.17
8 Netherlands	287	4.0	56	45.2	51.4	54.8	12.4	4.6	8.2	..
9 Japan	2,814	4.1	141	12.4	25.3	39.0	12.9	4.0 e	18.9 e	0.72
10 United Kingdom	1,812	6.3	66	24.6	38.4	41.2	8.2	9.5	23.8	..
11 Finland	285	11.4	68	23.1	31.7	13.0	6.8	40.2	32.8	2.29
12 France	3,051	11.7	95	44.9	43.2	25.0	5.8	38.8	52.9	1.86
13 Switzerland	143	4.2 f	111 f	31.9	37.9	45.8	7.2	5.8	8.4	..
14 Germany	4,279	9.4	112	52.6	51.9	32.4	4.6	12.6	17.8	0.42
15 Denmark	183	5.1	62	30.7	25.8	25.4	9.9	13.9	13.1	1.07
16 Austria	237	4.7	124	30.7	27.5	22.8	2.7	..	..	0.43
17 Luxembourg	6	2.8	88	27.2	30.0	29.6	2.6	..	..	..
18 Ireland	125	7.8	55	46.9 f	63.3 f	..	..	..	..	1.64
19 Italy	2,801	12.2	107	67.0	66.4	22.7	5.5	..	..	0.50
20 New Zealand	139	7.5	93	15.3	22.6	37.6	10.6	..	..	..
21 Spain	3,060	18.8	78	59.1	48.0	16.6	2.9	..	..	..
25 Greece	432	9.6 f	108 f	62.2 f	45.8 f	15.9	5.3	36.0	50.2	1.47
28 Portugal	234	4.9	70	45.5	43.6	15.8	5.2	24.1	16.1	..
29 Slovenia	127 g	14.6 g	103 g	..	..	..	..	..	..	..
31 Korea, Rep of	1,462	7.1 d	284 d	0.8	1.9	9.3	5.2	..	..	..
34 Czech Republic	336	6.5	171	31.5	30.9	5.4	1.7	3.7	1.8	1.50
40 Slovakia	427 g	15.6 g	105 g	..	..	..	..	..	..	..
43 Hungary	313	8.0	73	49.2	50.2	5.0	1.9	..	..	0.68
44 Poland	1,809	10.6	74	41.8	32.5	16.6	8.0	..	..	..
46 Estonia	35 g	5.1 g	100 g	..	..	..	..	..	..	2.35
Medium human development										
49 Croatia	303 g	18.6 g	108 g	..	..	..	..	..	..	..
52 Lithuania	123 g	6.9 g	153 g	..	..	..	..	..	..	1.77
55 Mexico	603	3.0 d	68 d	0.4	1.2	28.3	8.2	..	..	..
57 Belarus	106 g	2.3 g	110 g	..	..	..	..	..	..	1.91
60 Bulgaria	465 g	12.2 g	95 g	..	..	..	..	..	..	3.14
62 Russian Federation	9728 g	13.3 g	177 g	..	..	..	..	..	..	..
63 Latvia	111 g	9.2 g	142 g	..	..	..	..	..	..	..
64 Romania	1025 g	10.3 g	94 g	..	..	..	..	..	..	..
69 Macedonia, TFYR	265 g	41.4 g	138 g	..	..	..	..	..	..	..
70 Georgia	99 g	4.2 g	111 g	..	..	..	..	..	..	1.16
73 Kazakhstan	252 g	3.7 g	370 g	..	..	..	..	..	..	0.02
78 Ukraine	1003 g	4.3 g	1,433 g	..	..	..	..	..	..	..
85 Turkey	1,429	6.6 d	80 d	46.1	37.5	13.3	3.4	..	..	..
90 Azerbaijan	42 g	1.4 g	156 g	..	..	..	..	..	..	2.06
93 Armenia	134 g	8.9 g	148 g	..	..	..	..	..	..	0.49
94 Albania	235 g	17.6 g	98 g	..	..	..	..	..	..	1.02
98 Kyrgyzstan	56 g	3.1 g	388 g	..	..	..	..	..	..	0.24
100 Turkmenistan	..	..	..	..	..	..	..	..	..	..
102 Moldova, Rep. of	32 g	1.9 g	190 g	..	..	..	..	..	..	..
106 Uzbekistan	33 g	0.4 g	133 g	..	..	..	..	..	..	..
110 Tajikistan	54 g	2.9 g	161 g	..	..	..	..	..	..	..

HDI rank	Unemployed people (thousands) 1998	Unemployment rate [a] Total (% of labour force) 1998	Index (1994 = 100) 1998	Incidence of long-term unemployment [b] (as % of total unemployment) Female 1998	Male 1998	Part-time employment (as % of total employment) Female 1998	Male 1998	Involuntary part-time employment (as % of total part-time employment) Female 1997	Male 1997	Public expenditure on unemployment compensation (as % of GDP) 1997-98 [c]
All developing countries	..	..	..	..	..	..	..	..	..	..
Eastern Europe and the CIS	..	..	..	..	..	..	..	..	..	..
OECD	34,965 [h]T	7.0 [i]	86 [i]	34.2 [j]	31.7 [j]	24.0 [i]	7.0 [j]	..	..	..
World	..	..	..	..	..	..	..	..	..	..

Note: This table includes OECD countries, Eastern Europe and the CIS only.

a. Except where otherwise indicated, the unemployment rates for OECD are standardized to ensure comparability over time and across countries. b. Data refer to unemployment lasting 12 months or longer. c. Data refer to the most recent year available during the period specified in the column heading. d. Data do not refer to a standardized rate. e. Data refer to 1996. f. Data refer to 1997. g. Data are estimates by the United Nations Economic Commission for Europe (UNECE), based on national statistics. They refer to registered unemployment, which is likely to bias unemployment figures downward. h. Aggregate as calculated in OECD 1999a. i. Aggregate as calculated in OECD 1999b; it refers to countries with standardized unemployment rates. j. Aggregate as calculated in OECD 1999b.

Source: Columns 1 and 2: OECD 1999a; and UNECE 2000; *column 3:* calculated on the basis of data on unemployment rates from OECD 1999b; and UNECE 2000; *columns 4-10:* OECD 1999b.

HDI rank	Lower or single house		Upper house or senate		Voter turnout at latest elections (%) [a]	Political parties represented	
	Date of latest elections or appointments	Members elected (E) or appointed (A)	Date of latest elections or appointments	Members elected (E) or appointed (A)		In lower or single house	In upper house or senate
High human development							
1 Canada	06 1997	E	–	A	69	5 [b]	2 [b]
2 Norway	09 1997	E	–	–	78	7 [b]	–
3 United States	11 1998	E	11 1998	E	36	2 [b]	2
4 Australia	10 1998	E	10 1998	E	95	3 [b]	5 [b]
5 Iceland	05 1999	E	–	–	84	5	–
6 Sweden	09 1998	E	–	–	81	7	–
7 Belgium	06 1999	E	06 1999	E + A	91	11	10
8 Netherlands	05 1998	E	05 1999	E	73	9	8 [b]
9 Japan	10 1996	E	07 1998	E	59	7 [b]	9 [b]
10 United Kingdom	05 1997	E	–	A	72	10 [b]	3 [b]
11 Finland	03 1999	E	–	–	65	7 [b]	–
12 France	05 1997	E	09 1998	E	71	9	8 [b]
13 Switzerland	10 1999	E	10 1999	E	43	8 [b]	4
14 Germany	09 1998	E	01 2000	A	82	5	..
15 Denmark	03 1998	E	–	–	86	10	–
16 Austria	10 1999	E	11 1994 [c]	E	80	5 [b]	3
17 Luxembourg	06 1999	E	–	–	86	6	–
18 Ireland	06 1997	E	08 1997	E + A	66	7 [b]	5 [b]
19 Italy	04 1996	E	04 1996	E + A	83	4 [b]	6 [b]
20 New Zealand	11 1999	E	–	–	90	7	–
21 Spain	03 1996	E	03 1996	E	77	8 [b]	4 [b]
22 Cyprus	05 1996	E	–	–	93	5	–
23 Israel	05 1999	E	–	–	79	15 [b]	–
24 Singapore	01 1997	E + A	–	–	41	3	–
25 Greece	09 1996	E	–	–	76	5	–
26 Hong Kong, China (SAR)	..	..	–	–	..	..	–
27 Malta	09 1998	E	–	–	95	2	–
28 Portugal	10 1999	E	–	–	62	5	–
29 Slovenia	11 1996	E	–	–	74	8	–
30 Barbados	01 1999	E	01 1999	A	63	2	..
31 Korea, Rep. of	04 1996	E	–	–	64	4 [b]	–
32 Brunei Darussalam [d]	–	–	–	–	–	–	–
33 Bahamas	03 1997	E	03 1997	A	68 [e]	2	2
34 Czech Republic	06 1998	E	11 1998	E	74	5	4
35 Argentina	10 1999	E	10 1998	E	81	4 [b]	..
36 Kuwait	07 1999	E	–	–	80	0	–
37 Antigua and Barbuda	03 1999	E	03 1999	A	64	3 [b]	..
38 Chile	12 1997	E	12 1997	E + A	86	7 [b]	6 [b]
39 Uruguay	10 1999	E	10 1999	E	92	3 [b]	3 [b]
40 Slovakia	09 1998	E	–	–	84	6	–
41 Bahrain	12 1973 [f]	E	–	–	–	–	–
42 Qatar [d]	–	–	–	–	–	–	–
43 Hungary	05 1998	E	–	–	56	6 [b]	–
44 Poland	09 1997	E	09 1997	E	48	6	6
45 United Arab Emirates	12 1997	A	–	–	–	–	–
46 Estonia	03 1999	E	–	–	57	7	–
Medium human development							
47 Saint Kitts and Nevis	07 1995	E + A	–	–	68 [e]	4	–
48 Costa Rica	02 1998	E	–	–	70	7	–
49 Croatia	01 2000	E	04 1997	E + A	..	13 [b]	6
50 Trinidad and Tobago	11 1995	E	11 1995	A	63	3	2 [b]

HDI rank	Lower or single house		Upper house or senate		Voter turnout at latest elections (%) [a]	Political parties represented	
	Date of latest elections or appointments	Members elected (E) or appointed (A)	Date of latest elections or appointments	Members elected (E) or appointed (A)		In lower or single house	In upper house or senate
51 Dominica	01 2000	E + A	–	–	75 [e]	3	–
52 Lithuania	10 1996	E	–	–	53	6 [b]	–
53 Seychelles	03 1998	E	–	–	87	3	–
54 Grenada	01 1999	E	01 1999	A	57	1	..
55 Mexico	07 1997	E	07 1997	E	57	5 [b]	5 [b]
56 Cuba	01 1998	E	–	–	98	1	–
57 Belarus	11 1996 [g]	E	02 1997	E + A	..	..	..
58 Belize	08 1998	E	08 1998	A	90	2	2 [b]
59 Panama	05 1999	E	–	–	76	9	–
60 Bulgaria	04 1997	E	–	–	68	5	–
61 Malaysia	11 1999	E	03 1998	E + A	..	4 [b]	..
62 Russian Federation	12 1999	E	–	A	62	7 [b]	–
63 Latvia	10 1998	E	–	–	72	6	–
64 Romania	11 1996	E	11 1996	E	76	7	6
65 Venezuela	11 1998	E	–	–	..	8 [b]	–
66 Fiji	05 1999	E	06 1999	A	75 [e]	5 [b]	..
67 Suriname	05 1996	E	–	–	67 [e]	5	–
68 Colombia	03 1998	E	03 1998	E	45	2 [b]	2 [b]
69 Macedonia, TFYR	10 1998	E	–	–	73	7 [b]	–
70 Georgia	10 1999	E	–	–	68	3	–
71 Mauritius	12 1995	E + A	–	–	80	5	–
72 Libyan Arab Jamahiriya	03 1997	E	–	–	..	1	–
73 Kazakhstan	10 1999	E	09 1999	E + A	63	5 [b]	..
74 Brazil	10 1998	E	10 1998	E	..	12 [b]	9
75 Saudi Arabia [d]	–	–	–	–	–	–	–
76 Thailand	11 1996	E	03 1996	A	62	11	..
77 Philippines	05 1998	E	05 1998	E	79	5 [b]	2 [b]
78 Ukraine	03 1998	E	–	–	70	9 [b]	–
79 Saint Vincent and the Grenadines	06 1998	E + A	–	–	..	2	–
80 Peru	04 1995	E	–	–	63 [e]	13	–
81 Paraguay	05 1998	E	05 1998	E	80	2	2 [b]
82 Lebanon	08 1996	E	–	–	44	10 [b]	–
83 Jamaica	12 1997	E	12 1997	A	65	2	..
84 Sri Lanka	08 1994	E + A	–	–	76	7 [b]	–
85 Turkey	04 1999	E	–	–	87	5 [b]	–
86 Oman [d]	–	–	–	–	–	–	–
87 Dominican Republic	05 1998	E	05 1998	E	66	3	3
88 Saint Lucia	05 1997	E	05 1997	A	66	2	2 [b]
89 Maldives	11 1999	E + A	–	–	74	–	–
90 Azerbaijan	11 1995	E	–	–	86	9 [b]	–
91 Ecuador	05 1998	E	–	–	..	8 [b]	–
92 Jordan	11 1997	E	11 1997	A	47	..	..
93 Armenia	05 1999	E	–	–	52	6 [b]	–
94 Albania	06 1997	E	–	–	73	6 [b]	–
95 Samoa (Western)	04 1996	E	–	–	86	2 [b]	–
96 Guyana	12 1997	E	–	–	98	5 [b]	–
97 Iran, Islamic Rep. of	02 2000	E	–	–	83	2 [b]	–
98 Kyrgyzstan	02 2000	E	02 2000	E	61 [h]	..	6
99 China	11 1997	E	–	–	..	1	–
100 Turkmenistan	12 1999	E	–	–	99	1	–

HDI rank	Lower or single house		Upper house or senate		Voter turnout at latest elections (%) [a]	Political parties represented	
	Date of latest elections or appointments	Members elected (E) or appointed (A)	Date of latest elections or appointments	Members elected (E) or appointed (A)		In lower or single house	In upper house or senate
101 Tunisia	10 1999	E	–	–	92	6	–
102 Moldova, Rep. of	03 1998	E	–	–	72	4	–
103 South Africa	06 1999	E	06 1999	E	89	9 [b]	7
104 El Salvador	03 1997	E	–	–	89	9	–
105 Cape Verde	12 1995	E	–	–	77	3	–
106 Uzbekistan	12 1999	E	–	–	93	5 [b]	–
107 Algeria	06 1997	E	12 1997	E + A	66	10 [b]	4
108 Viet Nam	07 1997	E	–	–	100	1 [b]	–
109 Indonesia	06 1999	E + A	–	–	93	8 [b]	–
110 Tajikistan	02 2000	E	– [i]	–	..	..	–
111 Syrian Arab Republic	11 1998	E	–	–	82	1 [b]	–
112 Swaziland	10 1998	E + A	09 1993	E + A	..	–	–
113 Honduras	11 1997	E	–	–	73 [e]	5	–
114 Bolivia	06 1997	E	06 1997	E	70	7	5
115 Namibia	11-12 1999	E	11-12 1998	E	63	5	..
116 Nicaragua	10 1996	E	–	–	77	4 [b]	–
117 Mongolia	06 1996	E	–	–	88	4 [b]	–
118 Vanuatu	03 1998	E	–	–	75	3 [b]	–
119 Egypt	11 1995	E + A	–	–	48	6 [b]	–
120 Guatemala	11 1999	E	–	–	54	4	–
121 Solomon Islands	08 1997	E	–	–	64 [e]	2	–
122 Botswana	10 1999	E	–	–	77	3	–
123 Gabon	12 1996	E	01-02 1997	E	..	7 [b]	6 [b]
124 Morocco	11 1997	E	12 1997	E	58	15	13
125 Myanmar	04 1990 [j]	E	–	–	–	–	–
126 Iraq	03 1996	E	–	–	94	4 [b]	–
127 Lesotho	05 1998	E	05 1998	A	74	2	..
128 India	09-10 1999	E + A	03 1998	E + A	60	38 [b]	8 [b]
129 Ghana	12 1996	E	–	–	65	4	–
130 Zimbabwe	04 1995	E + A	–	–	57	2	–
131 Equatorial Guinea	03 1999	E	–	–	95	3	–
132 São Tomé and Principe	11 1998	E	–	–	65	3	–
133 Papua New Guinea	06 1997	E	–	–	81 [e]	9 [b]	–
134 Cameroon	05 1997	E	–	–	76	4 [b]	–
135 Pakistan	02 1997 [k]	E	03 1997 [k]	E	35	4 [b]	9 [b]
136 Cambodia	07 1998	E	03 1999	A	..	3	3
137 Comoros	12 1996 [k]	E	..	..	20	2 [b]	..
138 Kenya	12 1997	E + A	–	–	65	10	–
139 Congo	01 1998 [l]	A	–	–	–	–	–
Low human development							
140 Lao People's Dem. Rep.	12 1997	E	–	–	99	1 [b]	–
141 Madagascar	05 1998	E	–	–	..	9 [b]	–
142 Bhutan	1998	E + A	–	–	..	–	–
143 Sudan	03 1996 [k]	E	..	..	55	–	..
144 Nepal	05 1999	E	06 1999	E + A	66	3 [b]	4
145 Togo	03 1999	E	–	–	..	1 [b]	–
146 Bangladesh	06 1996	E	–	–	74	4 [b]	–
147 Mauritania	10 1996	E	04 1998	E	39 [e]	3 [b]	3
148 Yemen	04 1997	E	–	–	61	5 [b]	–
149 Djibouti	12 1997	E	–	–	57	1	–
150 Haiti	06 1995	E	04 1997	E	31	6 [b]	..

HDI rank	Lower or single house		Upper house or senate		Voter turnout at latest elections (%) [a]	Political parties represented	
	Date of latest elections or appointments	Members elected (E) or appointed (A)	Date of latest elections or appointments	Members elected (E) or appointed (A)		In lower or single house	In upper house or senate
151 Nigeria	02 1999	E	02 1999	E	41	3	3
152 Congo, Dem. Rep. of the	10 1993 [m]	E	..	..	..	..	..
153 Zambia	11 1996	E + A	–	–	40	4 [b]	–
154 Côte d'Ivoire	11 1995 [k]	E	..	..	71 [e]	2	..
155 Senegal	05 1998	E	01 1999	E + A	39	6	3
156 Tanzania, U. Rep. of	10 1995	E	–	–	77 [e]	5	–
157 Benin	03 1999	E	–	–	70	9 [b]	–
158 Uganda	06 1996	E	–	–	59 [e]	..	–
159 Eritrea	02 1994	E	–	–	..	..	–
160 Angola	09 1992	E	–	–	91	12	–
161 Gambia	01 1997	E + A	–	–	69	4 [b]	–
162 Guinea	06 1995	E	–	–	62	5 [b]	–
163 Malawi	06 1999	E	–	–	92	3 [b]	–
164 Rwanda	11 1994 [l]	A	–	–	–	8	–
165 Mali	07-08 1997	E	–	–	22	8	–
166 Central African Republic	11 1998	E	–	–	..	3 [b]	–
167 Chad	01 1997	E	–	–	49	10	–
168 Mozambique	12 1999	E	–	–	80	2	–
169 Guinea-Bissau	11 1999	E	–	–	80	8	–
170 Burundi	06 1993	E + A	–	–	91	2	–
171 Ethiopia	05 1995	E	05 1995	E	85 [e]	1 [b]	..
172 Burkina Faso	05 1997	E	12 1995	E + A	45	4	..
173 Niger	11 1999	E	–	–	..	5	–
174 Sierra Leone	02 1996	E	–	–	50	6	–

Note: Information is as of 1 March 2000.

a. For lower or single house. b. There are also independent and other parties not sufficiently represented to constitute a parliamentary group. c. Data valid as of 1997. d. The country has never had a parliament. e. Average turnout in the 1990s. No official data available. The figures are from International IDEA 1997. f. The first legislature of Bahrain was dissolved by decree of the emir on 26 August 1975. g. Following a referendum held on 24 November 1996, the Supreme Council elected in November-December 1995 was replaced by a bicameral National Assembly comprising some of the members of the former Supreme Council. h. Data refer to the turnout at the previous election. i. Amendments to the 1994 constitution established an upper house, the National Assembly. Elections held on 23 March 2000. j. The parliament elected in 1990 has never been convened nor authorized to sit, and many of its members were detained or forced into exile. k. Parliament has been dissolved or suspended for an indefinite period. l. Transitional appointed unicameral parliament created by decree. m. Transitional unicameral parliament dissolved following change of regime in May 1997.

Source: Columns 1-4, 6 and 7: IPU 2000a; *column 5:* IPU 2000a; and International IDEA 1997.

26 Crime

HDI rank	People incarcerated (per 100,000) 1994	Juvenile convictions (as % of total convictions) 1994	Total recorded crimes (per 100,000 people)[a] 1994	Total recorded drug offences (per 100,000 people)[b] 1994	Recorded rapes (per 100,000 women aged 15 and above) 1994	Recorded homicides		Largest city
						In country (per 100,000 people) 1994	In largest city (per 100,000 people) 1994	

<!-- High human development -->

High human development								
1 Canada	117.9	41.0	9,982	207.2	267.3	2.0	2.8	Toronto
2 Norway	..	..	..	..	..	..	..	..
3 United States	553.9	..	5,367	..	96.8	9.0	21.3	New York City
4 Australia	94.5	..	..	..	199.1	4.9	..	..
5 Iceland	..	..	..	..	..	..	..	..
6 Sweden	70.4	19.3	12,671	350.6	49.9	12.0	20.9	Stockholm
7 Belgium	74.1	..	5,733	148.4	21.1	3.4	..	..
8 Netherlands	56.8	7.3	..	..	..	..	..	..
9 Japan	37.0	0.4	1,493	18.5	3.0	1.4	1.5	Tokyo
10 United Kingdom	..	..	..	..	..	..	..	..
11 Finland	62.4	10.5	7,641	116.3	18.1	10.5	14.6	Helsinki
12 France	..	..	6,787	93.3	27.1	..	..	..
13 Switzerland	..	11.2	5,115	573.9	9.2	..	11.4	Zurich
14 Germany	..	12.0	..	..	..	..	..	..
15 Denmark	67.4	..	10,508	300.9	21.8	5.1	8.7	Copenhagen
16 Austria	91.5	4.9	6,283	149.0	16.3	3.5	5.3	Vienna
17 Luxembourg	109.2	..	5,254	..	..	..	..	..
18 Ireland	..	..	..	..	..	..	..	..
19 Italy	89.6	1.8	3,800	66.9	3.4	5.3	4.1	Rome
20 New Zealand	..	..	..	..	..	..	..	..
21 Spain	..	..	1,770	..	7.2	..	..	..
22 Cyprus	25.1	5.0	590	18.4	2.5	1.6	1.3	Nicosia
23 Israel	188.5	6.8	1,408	163.6	28.4	7.2	..	..
24 Singapore	254.9	..	1,734	62.9	6.4	1.7	..	..
25 Greece	16.4	5.8	2,909	24.3	5.8	2.9	3.1	Athens
26 Hong Kong, China (SAR)	199.1	5.6	1,449	76.2	4.2	1.6	1.6	Hong Kong
27 Malta	56.0	..	2,114	67.6	6.8	3.0	..	..
28 Portugal	102.1	15.0	..	..	..	..	..	..
29 Slovenia	52.3	14.0	2,247	21.0	28.6	5.7	6.3	Ljubljana
30 Barbados	..	..	..	..	..	..	..	..
31 Korea, Rep. of	137.8	6.0	2,945	3.9	36.2	10.2	8.4	Seoul
32 Brunei Darussalam	312.9	..	..	..	..	..	..	..
33 Bahamas	..	..	7,759	272.6	220.5	82.8	..	..
34 Czech Republic	181.5	9.7	..	..	..	..	..	..
35 Argentina	..	..	..	..	..	..	..	..
36 Kuwait	2.0	..	1,171	130.2	1.8	58.0	..	
37 Antigua and Barbuda	..	..	..	..	..	..	..	..
38 Chile	155.9	0.6	8,784	62.9	19.1	4.5	3.1	Santiago
39 Uruguay	101.9	..	2,342	45.3	..	..	..	..
40 Slovakia	138.6	12.2	2,582	1.6	10.0	3.8	6.2	Bratislava
41 Bahrain	..	..	..	..	..	..	..	..
42 Qatar	..	2.3	851	3.1	13.1	2.2	..	..
43 Hungary	123.7	9.7	3,795	2.5	18.8	4.6	5.2	Budapest
44 Poland	..	..	..	..	..	..	..	..
45 United Arab Emirates	..	..	..	..	..	..	..	..
46 Estonia	293.6	16.1	2,384	2.2	463.6	25.7	26.2	Tallinn

Medium human development								
47 Saint Kitts and Nevis	..	..	..		..	..	..	..
48 Costa Rica	119.0	..	1,487	13.8	26.4	9.7	8.4	San Jose
49 Croatia	49.9	6.5	1,422	19.0	4.9	8.1	14.6	Zagreb
50 Trinidad and Tobago	..	..	..		..	..	..	..

HDI rank	People incarcerated (per 100,000) 1994	Juvenile convictions (as % of total convictions) 1994	Total recorded crimes (per 100,000 people)[a] 1994	Total recorded drug offences (per 100,000 people)[b] 1994	Recorded rapes (per 100,000 women aged 15 and above) 1994	Recorded homicides In country (per 100,000 people) 1994	Recorded homicides In largest city (per 100,000 people) 1994	Largest city
51 Dominica	..	..	..	..	..	..	..	..
52 Lithuania	278.3	17.5	1,576	9.0	10.5	15.0	..	..
53 Seychelles	..	..	..	..	..	..	..	..
54 Grenada	..	..	..	..	..	..	..	..
55 Mexico	92.8	..	..	..	..	..	..	..
56 Cuba	..	..	..	..	..	..	..	..
57 Belarus	477.8	11.4	1,161	13.9	15.3	9.9	6.3	Minsk
58 Belize	..	..	..	..	..	..	..	..
59 Panama	215.2	..	..	115.3	34.1	12.5	..	..
60 Bulgaria	99.1	7.1	2,361	..	25.3	11.2	10.5	Sofia
61 Malaysia	122.8	0.7	390	53.1	15.5	..	..	..
62 Russian Federation	580.2	12.1	1,779	50.5	22.1	23.2	..	..
63 Latvia	359.7	10.5	1,608	10.9	11.5	16.2	17.9	Riga
64 Romania	..	..	1,042	1.2	15.1	7.6	..	..
65 Venezuela	..	..	..	..	..	..	..	..
66 Fiji	..	..	..	..	..	..	..	..
67 Suriname	..	..	..	..	..	..	..	..
68 Colombia	85.2	..	614	40.0	15.2	78.6	71.4	Bogota
69 Macedonia, TFYR	62.8	22.9	1,094	5.4	5.1	3.7	4.1	Skopje
70 Georgia	140.9	..	323	20.4	2.3	14.4	..	..
71 Mauritius	96.0	..	3607	177.0	8.5	3.4	4.8	Port Louis
72 Libyan Arab Jamahiriya	..	..	..	..	..	..	..	..
73 Kazakhstan	..	2.5	1,185	56.3	30.8	15.6	21.9	Alma-Ata
74 Brazil	..	..	..	..	..	..	..	..
75 Saudi Arabia	..	..	..	..	..	..	..	..
76 Thailand	..	..	..	..	..	..	..	..
77 Philippines	25.8	..	139	..	12.2	9.5	..	..
78 Ukraine	..	..	1,102	54.7	7.6	9.6	..	..
79 Saint Vincent and the Grenadines	..	..	7,202	..	..	14.4	..	..
80 Peru	84.0	..	..	..	..	..	..	..
81 Paraguay	..	..	..	..	..	..	..	..
82 Lebanon	..	..	..	..	..	..	..	..
83 Jamaica	..	..	2,114	236.2	127.8	29.8	62.4	Kingston and Saint Andrew
84 Sri Lanka	..	..	..	..	..	..	..	..
85 Turkey	74.4	4.6	360	3.8	2.5	2.9	4.0	Istanbul
86 Oman	..	..	..	..	..	..	..	..
87 Dominican Republic	..	..	..	..	..	..	..	..
88 Saint Lucia	..	..	..	..	..	..	..	..
89 Maldives	..	..	..	..	..	..	..	..
90 Azerbaijan	..	5.2	248	29.9	2.9	8.9	14.2	Baku
91 Ecuador	..	..	521	143.6	26.4	18.5	28.8	Guayaquil
92 Jordan	..	..	707	..	2.4	5.7	..	..
93 Armenia	..	..	..	..	..	..	..	..
94 Albania	..	..	..	..	..	..	..	..
95 Samoa (Western)	140.9	..	741	70.7	18.9	6.1	3.0	Apia
96 Guyana	174.5	..	..	..	..	..	..	..
97 Iran, Islamic Rep. of	..	..	..	..	..	..	..	..
98 Kyrgyzstan	299.7	..	895	55.4	27.0	12.3	..	..
99 China	..	..	..	..	..	..	..	..
100 Turkmenistan	..	..	..	..	..	..	..	..

HDI rank	People incarcerated (per 100,000) 1994	Juvenile convictions (as % of total convictions) 1994	Total recorded crimes (per 100,000 people) [a] 1994	Total recorded drug offences (per 100,000 people) [b] 1994	Recorded rapes (per 100,000 women aged 15 and above) 1994	Recorded homicides In country (per 100,000 people) 1994	Recorded homicides In largest city (per 100,000 people) 1994	Largest city
101 Tunisia	..	..	..		..	..	..	..
102 Moldova, Rep. of	215.1	11.2	858	6.6	15.6	9.5	..	..
103 South Africa	..	10.3	..	..	..	..	..	..
104 El Salvador	109.0	..	..	..	..	..	..	..
105 Cape Verde	..	..	..	..	..	..	..	..
106 Uzbekistan	..	..	..	..	..	..	..	..
107 Algeria	..	..	..	..	..	..	..	..
108 Viet Nam	..	..	..	..	..	..	..	..
109 Indonesia	22.6	50.6	80	0.4	2.6	..	..	..
110 Tajikistan	..	..	..	..	..	..	..	..
111 Syrian Arab Republic	..	..	16	19.4	2.7	1.3	..	..
112 Swaziland	..	..	..	..	..	..	..	..
113 Honduras	..	..	..	..	..	..	..	..
114 Bolivia	..	..	789	1.6	102.8	23.3	31.7	La Paz
115 Namibia	..	..	..	..	..	..	..	..
116 Nicaragua	74.3	..	1,072	22.4	109.7	25.6	18.7	Managua
117 Mongolia	..	..	..	..	..	..	..	..
118 Vanuatu	..	..	..	..	..	..	..	..
119 Egypt	..	22.9	36	152.2	(.)	1.5	0.7	Cairo
120 Guatemala	..	..	..	..	..	..	..	..
121 Solomon Islands	..	..	..	..	..	..	..	..
122 Botswana	..	..	..	..	..	..	..	..
123 Gabon	..	..	..	..	..	..	..	..
124 Morocco	..	..	855	55.7	11.2	1.8	..	..
125 Myanmar	..	88.4	..	..	..	..	..	..
126 Iraq	..	..	..	..	..	..	..	..
127 Lesotho	..	..	..	..	..	..	..	..
128 India	..	..	600	2.2	4.6	7.9	4.1	Mumbai
129 Ghana	..	..	..	..	..	..	..	..
130 Zimbabwe	..	..	6,220	94.1	101.2	16.0	..	..
131 Equatorial Guinea	..	..	..	..	..	..	..	..
132 São Tomé and Principe	79.2	..	1,005	..	..	..	..	..
133 Papua New Guinea	..	..	..	..	..	..	..	..
134 Cameroon	..	..	..	..	..	..	..	..
135 Pakistan	..	..	..	..	..	..	..	..
136 Cambodia	..	..	..	..	..	..	..	..
137 Comoros	..	..	..	..	..	..	..	..
138 Kenya	..	..	..	..	..	..	..	..
139 Congo	..	..	..	..	..	..	..	..
Low human development								
140 Lao People's Dem. Rep.	..	..	..	..	..	..	..	..
141 Madagascar	151.4	..	75	2.2	1.3	0.4	1.8	Antananarivo
142 Bhutan	..	..	..	..	..	..	..	..
143 Sudan	24.1	..	1,830	6.0	8.1	3.5	..	..
144 Nepal	..	..	..	..	..	..	..	..
145 Togo	..	..	..	..	..	..	..	..
146 Bangladesh	..	..	..	..	..	..	..	..
147 Mauritania	..	..	..	..	..	..	..	..
148 Yemen	..	..	..	..	..	..	..	..
149 Djibouti	..	..	..	..	..	..	..	..
150 Haiti	..	..	..	..	..	..	..	..

HDI rank	People incarcerated (per 100,000) 1994	Juvenile convictions (as % of total convictions) 1994	Total recorded crimes (per 100,000 people)[a] 1994	Total recorded drug offences (per 100,000 people)[b] 1994	Recorded rapes (per 100,000 women aged 15 and above) 1994	Recorded homicides		Largest city
						In country (per 100,000 people) 1994	In largest city (per 100,000 people) 1994	
151 Nigeria	..	..	..	..	..	..	..	..
152 Congo, Dem. Rep. of the	..	..	..	..	..	..	..	..
153 Zambia	294.1	..	779	3.7	15.7	15.8	20.2	Lusaka
154 Côte d'Ivoire	..	..	..	..	..	..	..	..
155 Senegal	..	..	..	..	..	..	..	..
156 Tanzania, U. Rep. of	..	..	..	..	..	..	..	..
157 Benin	..	..	..	..	..	..	..	..
158 Uganda	54.4	..	..	..	..	..	..	..
159 Eritrea	..	..	..	..	..	..	..	..
160 Angola	..	..	..	..	..	..	..	..
161 Gambia	..	..	..	..	..	..	..	..
162 Guinea	..	..	..	..	..	..	..	..
163 Malawi	..	..	..	..	..	..	..	..
164 Rwanda	..	..	..	..	..	..	..	..
165 Mali	..	..	..	..	..	..	..	..
166 Central African Republic	..	..	..	..	..	..	..	..
167 Chad	..	..	..	..	..	..	..	..
168 Mozambique	..	..	..	..	..	..	..	..
169 Guinea-Bissau	..	..	..	..	..	..	..	..
170 Burundi	..	..	..	..	..	..	..	..
171 Ethiopia	..	..	..	..	..	..	..	..
172 Burkina Faso	..	..	..	..	..	..	..	..
173 Niger	..	..	..	..	..	..	..	..
174 Sierra Leone	..	..	..	..	..	..	..	..

Note: These crime data are reported to the United Nations by each country, and so depend heavily on the national law enforcement and reporting system.

a. Total of all recorded crimes. b. Total of all recorded drug crimes, including possession and trafficking.

Source: Columns 1-4 and 6: calculated on the basis of data from UN 2000d; *column 5:* calculated on the basis of data from UN 2000d; and UN 1998c; *column 7:* calculated on the basis of data from UN 2000d; and UN 1995b; *column 8:* UN 2000d.

27 Personal distress	Injuries and deaths from road accidents (per 100,000 people) 1997	Suicides (per 100,000 people) Male 1993-98 c	Suicides (per 100,000 people) Female 1993-98 c	Divorces (as % of marriages) d 1996	Births to mothers under 20 (%) 1993-98 c	People killed by disasters a Total killed 1980-99	By single worst disaster 1980-99	Internally displaced people (thousands) 1998 e	Refugees b By country of asylum (thousands) 1998	By country of origin (thousands) 1998 f
High human development										
1 Canada	741	21.5	5.4	45	6.3	1,411	329	..	135.7	..
2 Norway	276	19.1	6.2	43	2.8	634	160	..	45.3	..
3 United States	1,266	19.3	4.4	49	12.8	11,539	1,265	..	524.1	..
4 Australia	..	19.0	5.1	..	4.9	647	75	..	61.8	..
5 Iceland	552	16.4	3.8	39	5.2	38	20	..	0.3	..
6 Sweden	246	20.0	8.5	64	2.0	300	200	..	178.8	..
7 Belgium	700	26.7 g	11.0 g	56	2.9	345	193	..	36.1	..
8 Netherlands	82	13.1	6.5	41	1.3	143	48	..	131.8	..
9 Japan	..	24.3	11.5	..	1.4	9,005	5,502	..	1.9	..
10 United Kingdom	559	11.0	3.2	53	7.3	1,805	329	..	116.1	..
11 Finland	183	38.7	10.7	56	2.4	930	912	..	12.3	..
12 France	304	30.4	10.8	43	1.8	1,553	178	..	140.2	..
13 Switzerland	384	30.9	12.2	40	1.3	223	105	..	81.9	..
14 Germany	621	22.1	8.1	41	2.6	575 h	101 h	..	949.2	..
15 Denmark	192	24.3	9.8	35	..	389	158	..	70.0	..
16 Austria	651	30.0	10.0	38	4.0	180	38	..	80.3	..
17 Luxembourg	374	29.0	9.8	39	2.0	0	0	..	0.7	..
18 Ireland	371	17.9	4.6	..	5.5	438	329	..	0.6	..
19 Italy	483	12.7	4.0	12	2.3	4,197	2,614	..	68.3	..
20 New Zealand	..	23.6	5.8	..	7.6	45	10	..	4.1	..
21 Spain	330	12.5	3.7	17	3.1	1,916	340	..	6.0	0.2
22 Cyprus	603	..	..	13	3.6	56	52	265	0.1	..
23 Israel	810	8.2	2.6	26	3.4	179	73	..	..	..
24 Singapore	..	14.3	8.0	..	1.8	27	24	..	(.)	..
25 Greece	330	5.7	1.2	18	4.3	1,804	1,000	..	5.9	..
26 Hong Kong, China (SAR)	..	15.9	9.1	..	2.0	509	130	..	1.0	..
27 Malta	203	5.9	2.1	..	4.8	12	12	..	0.6	..
28 Portugal	694	10.3	3.1	21	6.8	502	144	..	0.3	0.2
29 Slovenia	453	48.0	13.9	26	4.3	0 i	0 i	..	3.5	3.3
30 Barbados	..	9.5	3.7	..	14.1 g	0	0	..	..	..
31 Korea, Rep. of	..	14.5	6.7	..	0.8	3,942	458	..	..	..
32 Brunei Darussalam	..	..	..	..	6.3	..	..	..	..	..
33 Bahamas	..	2.2	0.0	..	13.8	105	100	..	0.1	..
34 Czech Republic	371	24.0	6.8	61	7.7	48 i	29 i	..	1.8	0.4
35 Argentina	..	10.6	2.9	..	15.7	762	79	..	10.9	..
36 Kuwait	..	1.8	1.9	..	4.0	2	2	..	4.2	..
37 Antigua and Barbuda	..	0.0	0.0	..	15.8	7	2	..	..	..
38 Chile	..	10.2	1.4	..	15.7	1,221	180	..	0.3	7.4
39 Uruguay	..	16.6 g	4.2 g	..	16.5	109	74	..	0.2	..
40 Slovakia	249	..	..	34	..	67 i	54 i	..	0.4	..
41 Bahrain	..	..	..	..	..	10	10	..	..	..
42 Qatar	..	..	..	..	3.4	..	..	..	..	..
43 Hungary	257	49.2	15.6	46	10.2	63	40	..	5.4	2.1
44 Poland	234	24.1	4.6	19	7.6	1,160	500	..	0.9	5.5
45 United Arab Emirates	..	..	..	..	..	209	112	..	0.5	..
46 Estonia	146	64.3	14.1	102	12.9	909 i	909 i	..	..	0.4
Medium human development										
47 Saint Kitts and Nevis	..	0.0	0.0	..	..	6	5	..	..	..
48 Costa Rica	..	8.0	1.8	..	18.9	263	69	..	23.0	..
49 Croatia	378	34.2	11.3	15	5.1	45 i	35 i	72	29.0	334.6
50 Trinidad and Tobago	..	17.4	5.0	..	13.7	13	6	..	..	..

27 Personal distress

HDI rank	Injuries and deaths from road accidents (per 100,000 people) 1997	Suicides (per 100,000 people) Male 1993-98[c]	Female 1993-98[c]	Divorces (as % of marriages)[d] 1996	Births to mothers under 20 (%) 1993-98[c]	People killed by disasters [a] Total killed 1980-99	By single worst disaster 1980-99	Internally displaced people (thousands) 1998[e]	Refugees [b] By country of asylum (thousands) 1998	By country of origin (thousands) 1998[f]
51 Dominica	..	..	..	..	25.7 g	14	11	..	..	..
52 Lithuania	187	73.7	13.7	55	11.0	16	10	..	(.)	0.4
53 Seychelles	..	..	..	..	16.2	5	5	..	..	..
54 Grenada	..	..	..	..	..	0	0	..	..	..
55 Mexico	..	5.4	1.0	..	15.6	16,456	8,776	..	28.3	..
56 Cuba	..	25.6	14.9	..	13.8	978	359	..	1.1	2.0
57 Belarus	86	48.7	9.6	68	14.1	74 i	54 i	..	0.1	..
58 Belize	..	12.0	0.9	..	17.6	22	22	..	3.4	..
59 Panama	..	..	..	..	18.4	260	57	..	1.2	..
60 Bulgaria	94	25.3	9.7	28	20.4	124	50	..	0.2	1.9
61 Malaysia	..	..	..	..	3.0	1,300	200	..	50.6	..
62 Russian Federation	139	72.9	13.7	65	..	5,264 i	1,989 i	172	128.6	5.2
63 Latvia	211	59.5	11.8	63	9.3	..	..	..	..	0.9
64 Romania	46	21.1	4.3	24	16.0	719	161	..	1.0	4.2
65 Venezuela	..	8.3	1.9	..	19.9	31,487	30,000	..	0.2	..
66 Fiji	..	..	..	..	11.2 g	173	28	..	..	..
67 Suriname	..	16.6 g	7.2 g	..	17.2	169	169	..	..	..
68 Colombia	..	5.5	1.5	..	22.7 g	28,369	21,800	..	0.2	1.9
69 Macedonia, TFYR	170	..	..	5	10.1	196 i	115 i	..	1.7	11.3
70 Georgia	49	5.4 g	2.0 g	12	19.7	461 i	270 i	277	(.)	34.5
71 Mauritius	..	20.6	6.4	..	10.6	166	159	..	..	0.1
72 Libyan Arab Jamahiriya	..	..	..	..	3.0	310	157	..	10.6	..
73 Kazakhstan	95	51.9	9.5	39	12.0	218 i	118 i	..	8.3	19.7
74 Brazil	..	5.6 g	1.6 g	..	18.8	7,345	934	..	2.3	..
75 Saudi Arabia	..	..	..	..	..	2,822	1,426	..	5.5	..
76 Thailand	..	5.6	2.4	..	11.6	4,482	458	..	138.3	20.5
77 Philippines	..	2.5	1.7	..	..	31,540	4,884	..	0.3	45.1
78 Ukraine	94	38.2 g	9.2 g	63	..	581 i	204 i	..	6.1	2.8
79 Saint Vincent and the Grenadines	..	..	..	..	21.5	3	3	..	..	..
80 Peru	..	..	..	..	13.3 g	16,267	8,000	..	0.4	2.6
81 Paraguay	..	3.4	1.2	..	4.5	132	76	..	(.)	..
82 Lebanon	..	..	..	..	..	90	45	..	3.7	5.4
83 Jamaica	..	..	..	..	23.7	367	187	..	(.)	..
84 Sri Lanka	..	44.7	16.6	..	8.3	1,422	325	603	(.)	87.3
85 Turkey	176	..	..	6	12.0	22,810	17,127	..	2.5	32.7
86 Oman	..	..	..	..	..	26	26	..	..	..
87 Dominican Republic	..	0.0	0.0	..	7.8	943	288	..	0.6	..
88 Saint Lucia	..	..	..	..	..	54	45	..	..	..
89 Maldives	..	..	..	..	10.0	10	10	..	..	..
90 Azerbaijan	38	1.5	0.3	15	9.5	498 i	293 i	576	221.6	328.5
91 Ecuador	..	6.4	3.2	..	16.4	8,075	4,000	..	0.3	..
92 Jordan	..	..	..	..	..	33	15	..	0.8	..
93 Armenia	48	3.6 g	1.0 g	18	18.1	106 i	35 i	..	310.0	190.2
94 Albania	19	2.9	1.7	7	2.9 g	187	68	..	22.3	1.5
95 Samoa (Western)	..	..	..	..	..	21	13	..	..	..
96 Guyana	..	14.6	6.5	..	..	0	0	..	..	..
97 Iran, Islamic Rep. of	..	0.3 g	0.1 g	..	..	46,170	36,000	..	1,931.3	52.2
98 Kyrgyzstan	96	17.6	3.8	25	11.3	236 i	111 i	..	14.6	7.4
99 China	..	14.3	17.9	..	..	60,549	3,656	..	292.3	99.4
100 Turkmenistan	..	8.1	3.4	18	3.2 g	40 i	40 i	..	14.6	1.5

27 Personal distress

HDI rank	Injuries and deaths from road accidents (per 100,000 people) 1997	Suicides (per 100,000 people) Male 1993-98 c	Suicides (per 100,000 people) Female 1993-98 c	Divorces (as % of marriages) d 1996	Births to mothers under 20 (%) 1993-98 c	People killed by disasters a Total killed 1980-99	People killed by disasters a By single worst disaster 1980-99	Internally displaced people (thousands) 1998 e	Refugees b By country of asylum (thousands) 1998	Refugees b By country of origin (thousands) 1998 f
101 Tunisia	..	..	..	..	..	462	117	..	0.5	0.3
102 Moldova, Rep. of	104	30.9	6.2	52	19.8	47 i	47 i	1	..	2.2
103 South Africa	..	..	..	..	..	3,323	400	..	8.4	..
104 El Salvador	..	15.6 g	7.7 g	..	22.4	3,221	1,000	..	(.)	9.6
105 Cape Verde	..	..	..	..	14.7 g	159	77	..	..	..
106 Uzbekistan	58	9.3	3.2	12	9.8	148 i	95 i	..	1.1	51.3
107 Algeria	..	..	..	..	5.4 g	3,434	2,590	..	165.2	0.7
108 Viet Nam	..	..	..	..	..	14,758	3,500	..	15.0	315.7
109 Indonesia	..	..	..	..	..	16,596	2,190	..	0.1	8.5
110 Tajikistan	37	5.1 g	2.3 g	13	..	2,077 i	1,346 i	..	3.6	56.1
111 Syrian Arab Republic	..	..	..	..	..	99	37	..	20.9	3.6
112 Swaziland	..	..	..	..	..	663	500	..	0.6	..
113 Honduras	..	..	..	..	..	6,776	5,657	..	(.)	0.1
114 Bolivia	..	..	..	..	..	1,231	329	..	0.4	..
115 Namibia	..	..	..	..	..	120	100	..	3.5	1.9
116 Nicaragua	..	4.7	2.2	..	19.3 g	3,188	2,447	..	0.5	18.9
117 Mongolia	..	..	..	..	7.5	312	41	..	..	..
118 Vanuatu	..	..	..	..	..	108	48	..	..	..
119 Egypt	..	..	..	..	2.4	4,087	600	..	6.3	0.1
120 Guatemala	..	..	..	..	..	2,012	620	..	0.8	27.6
121 Solomon Islands	..	..	..	..	..	138	101	..	0.2	..
122 Botswana	..	..	..	..	..	211	183	..	2.1	..
123 Gabon	..	..	..	..	..	142	72	..	1.1	..
124 Morocco	..	..	..	..	9.2	918	243	..	0.3	0.1
125 Myanmar	..	..	..	..	..	2,558	730	..	..	129.6
126 Iraq	..	..	..	..	..	869	700	..	104.1	590.8
127 Lesotho	..	..	..	..	..	40	22	..	..	..
128 India	..	11.4	8.0	..	..	110,131	9,843	..	185.5	0.1
129 Ghana	..	..	..	..	..	3,169	1,270	..	14.6	12.4
130 Zimbabwe	..	10.6 g	5.2 g	..	14.5	2,221	1,311	..	0.8	..
131 Equatorial Guinea	..	..	..	..	..	15	15	..	..	0.2
132 São Tomé and Principe	..	..	..	..	..	181	150	..	..	..
133 Papua New Guinea	..	..	..	..	..	3,423	2,182	..	8.2	0.2
134 Cameroon	..	..	..	..	..	4,890	1,734	..	47.7	1.6
135 Pakistan	..	..	..	..	9.0	10,742	1,229	..	1,202.5	0.4
136 Cambodia	..	..	..	..	..	922	506	..	(.)	73.1
137 Comoros	..	..	..	..	..	318	127	..	..	..
138 Kenya	..	..	..	..	..	4,905	1,000	..	238.2	4.8
139 Congo	..	..	..	..	..	690	220	..	26.4	16.8
Low human development										
140 Lao People's Dem. Rep.	..	..	..	..	..	908	500	..	..	13.5
141 Madagascar	..	..	..	..	..	1,702	304	..	..	..
142 Bhutan	..	..	..	..	..	39	22	..	..	105.7
143 Sudan	..	..	..	..	..	157,579	150,000	..	391.5	374.2
144 Nepal	..	..	..	..	..	10,398	1,300	..	126.1	..
145 Togo	..	..	..	..	..	948	600	..	11.8	2.7
146 Bangladesh	..	..	..	..	11.4 g	186,935	138,866	..	22.3	1.2
147 Mauritania	..	..	..	..	..	2,521	2,243	..	23.1	67.6
148 Yemen	..	..	..	..	..	4,298 i	2,800 i	..	61.4	1.4
149 Djibouti	..	..	..	..	..	261	145	..	23.6	3.0
150 Haiti	..	..	..	..	..	4,812	1,800	..	..	2.4

HDI rank	Injuries and deaths from road accidents (per 100,000 people) 1997	Suicides (per 100,000 people) Male 1993-98 [c]	Female 1993-98 [c]	Divorces (as % of marriages) [d] 1996	Births to mothers under 20 (%) 1993-98 [c]	People killed by disasters [a] Total killed 1980-99	By single worst disaster 1980-99	Internally displaced people (thousands) 1998 [e]	Refugees [b] By country of asylum (thousands) 1998	By country of origin (thousands) 1998 [f]
151 Nigeria	..	..	..	..	..	30,028	10,391	..	7.9	1.1
152 Congo, Dem. Rep. of the	..	..	..	..	..	3,663	500	..	240.3	152.4
153 Zambia	..	..	..	..	..	3,162	1,231	..	168.6	..
154 Côte d'Ivoire	..	..	..	..	..	298	49	..	119.9	..
155 Senegal	..	..	..	..	..	1,189	472	..	60.8	9.5
156 Tanzania, U. Rep. of	..	..	..	..	..	5,441	1,871	..	543.9	..
157 Benin	..	..	..	..	..	655	228	..	2.9	..
158 Uganda	..	..	..	..	..	1,248	197	..	204.5	9.0
159 Eritrea	..	..	..	..	..	130	72	..	2.5	345.4
160 Angola	..	..	..	..	..	4,162	2,168	..	10.6	315.9
161 Gambia	..	..	..	..	..	292	120	..	10.3	..
162 Guinea	..	..	..	..	..	1,121	356	..	413.7	0.3
163 Malawi	..	..	..	..	14.9 [g]	1,273	700	..	0.4	..
164 Rwanda	..	..	..	..	..	483	237	625	33.4	73.4
165 Mali	..	..	..	..	15.6 [g]	7,128	3,615	..	11.6	3.6
166 Central African Republic	..	..	..	..	..	94	56	..	43.0	0.2
167 Chad	..	..	..	..	..	4,918	3,000	..	8.8	59.3
168 Mozambique	..	..	..	..	..	113,974	100,000	..	0.1	..
169 Guinea-Bissau	..	..	..	..	..	1,455	781	196	6.6	8.9
170 Burundi	..	..	..	..	..	398	220	..	25.1	500.0
171 Ethiopia	..	..	..	..	..	311,602	300,000	..	262.0	53.2
172 Burkina Faso	..	..	..	..	..	9,496	4,071	..	0.6	..
173 Niger	..	..	..	..	..	6,137	3,022	..	3.7	..
174 Sierra Leone	..	..	..	..	..	1,427	352	670	9.9	411.0
All developing countries	..	..	..	..	..	1,377,318 T	-	..	7,419.0 T	..
Least developed countries	..	..	..	..	..	853,130 T	-	..	2,662.5 T	..
Arab States	..	..	..	..	..	175,509 T	-	..	799.2 T	..
East Asia	..	..	..	..	..	65,312 T	-	..	293.3 T	..
East Asia (excluding China)	..	..	..	..	..	4,763 T	-	..	1.0 T	..
Latin America and the Caribbean	..	..	..	..	..	134,667 T	-	.	74.2 T	..
South Asia	..	..	..	..	..	365,847 T	-	..	3,467.7 T	.
South Asia (excluding India)	..	..	..	..	..	255,716 T	-	..	3,282.2 T	..
South-East Asia and the Pacific	..	..	..	..	..	76,954 T	-	..	212.7 T	..
Sub-Saharan Africa	..	..	..	..	..	536,163 T	-	..	2,569.4 T	..
Eastern Europe and the CIS	137	..	..	..	..	13,284 T	-	..	774.9 T	..
OECD	703	..	..	..	..	83,098 T	-	..	2,690.6 T	..
High human development	..	..	..	..	..	48,016 T	-	..	2,681.7 T	..
Medium human development	..	..	..	..	..	501,221 T	-	..	5,313.8 T	..
Low human development	..	..	..	..	..	880,175 T	-	..	2,850.9 T	..
High income	788	..	..	..	..	39,718 T	-	..	..	..
Medium income	..	..	..	..	..	263,692 T	-	..	2,769.1 T	..
Low income	..	..	..	..	..	1,126,002 T	-	..	5,415.4 T	..
World	..	..	..	..	..	1,429,412 T	-	..	10,846.3 T	..

a. Data refer to natural and technological disasters. b. Data refer to the end of 1998. They do not include Palestinian refugees. c. Data refer to the most recent year available during the period specified in the column heading. d. Data refer to divorces and marriages in 1996. e. Includes only those to whom the United Nations High Commissioner for Refugees (UNHCR) extends assistance in pursuance to a special request by a competent organ of the United Nations. f. The origin of refugees is not available or reported for many countries. The numbers for many nationalities are therefore underestimated. g. Data refer to a year or period other than that specified in the column heading. h. Data prior to 1990 refer to combined data for the Federal Republic of Germany and the Democratic Republic of Germany. i. Data refer to a period shorter than that indicated in the heading. j. Data prior to 1991 refer to combined data for the Arab Republic of Yemen and the People's Democratic Republic of Yemen.

Source: Column 1: calculated on the basis of data on injuries and deaths from road accidents and population from UNECE 1999a; columns 2 and 3: WHO 1999b; column 4: UNECE 1999b; column 5: UN 2000a; columns 6 and 7: calculated on the basis of data on people killed by disasters from OFDA and CRED 2000; columns 8 and 9: UNHCR 1999c; column 10: UNHCR 1999a.

. . . ENSURING HUMAN SECURITY . . .

28 Gender and education

HDI rank	Female adult literacy Rate (% age 15 and above) 1998	Index (1985=100) 1998	As % of male rate 1998	Female primary age group enrolment (adjusted) Ratio (% of primary school age girls) 1997	Index (1985=100) 1997	As % of male ratio 1997	Female secondary age group enrolment (adjusted) Ratio (% of secondary school age girls) 1997	Index (1985=100) 1997	As % of male ratio 1997	Female tertiary students Per 100,000 women 1994-97 [b]	Index (1985=100) 1994-97 [b]	As % of males 1994-97 [b]	Female tertiary science enrolment (as % of female tertiary students) [a] 1994-97 [b]
High human development													
1 Canada	..	..	..	99.9	100	100	94.4	103	98	6,280	92	112	..
2 Norway	..	..	..	99.9	103	100	98.0	112	101	4,722	201	126	28.9
3 United States	..	..	..	99.9	106	100	96.2	100	100	5,847	112	121	..
4 Australia	..	..	..	99.9	100	100	96.0	108	100	5,736	255	102	28.2
5 Iceland	..	..	..	99.9	100	100	88.1	115	101	3,427	157	142	27.4
6 Sweden	..	..	..	99.9	100	100	99.9	117	100	3,445	158	124	31.0
7 Belgium	..	..	..	99.9	100	100	99.9	100	100	3,473	155	96	..
8 Netherlands	..	..	..	99.9	100	100	99.9	100	100	2,878	127	91	18.7
9 Japan	..	..	..	99.9	100	100	99.9	104	100	2,706	203	76	13.0
10 United Kingdom	..	..	..	99.9	100	100	93.2	103	103	3,289	203	103	25.3
11 Finland	..	..	..	99.9	100	100	96.2	103	102	4,551	184	106	23.8
12 France	..	..	..	99.9	100	100	98.6	99	100	3,798	167	116	30.9
13 Switzerland	..	..	..	99.9	100	100	80.3	106	92	1,543	146	59	15.8
14 Germany	..	..	..	99.9	100	100	94.9	112	99	2,323	..	80	22.9
15 Denmark	..	..	..	99.9	100	100	95.4	112	101	3,571	162	114	29.3
16 Austria	..	..	..	99.9	100	100	97.1	108	99	2,855	144	91	25.6
17 Luxembourg	..	..	..	..	..	..	..	..	..	..	..	..	..
18 Ireland	..	..	..	99.9	100	100	99.9	103	100	3,797	221	105	33.9
19 Italy	97.9	102	99	99.9	100	100	96.0	136	102	3,462	185	111	34.5
20 New Zealand	..	..	..	99.9	100	100	94.0	107	102	5,093	190	130	33.0
21 Spain	96.5	103	98	99.9	100	100	93.0	104	102	4,405	188	108	32.9
22 Cyprus	94.7	107	96	..	..	..	..	..	..	1,471	317	125	27.4
23 Israel	93.7	105	96	..	..	..	..	..	..	3,522	137	108	..
24 Singapore	87.6	112	91	90.5	93	98	74.8	112	98	2,255	202	81	..
25 Greece	95.5	106	97	99.9	100	100	93.1	114	104	3,256	185	89	..
26 Hong Kong, China (SAR)	89.1	111	93	93.2	95	104	71.5	97	107	1,437 [c]	..	79 [c]	..
27 Malta	92.0	107	101	99.9	103	100	83.3	101	96	2,254	820	107	20.8
28 Portugal	89.0	111	94	99.9	100	100	91.0	151	103	3,532	326	121	37.3
29 Slovenia	99.6	100	100	..	..	..	..	..	..	2,885	179	119	30.3
30 Barbados	..	..	..	94.5	95	95	83.1	105	94	2,920	..	138	46.2
31 Korea, Rep. of	95.9	105	97	99.9	100	100	99.9	116	100	4,629	217	61	17.1
32 Brunei Darussalam	86.7	119	92	88.5	113	101	83.9	100	105	636	196	156	36.1
33 Bahamas	96.5	102	102	99.9	101	113	95.9	103	130	..	..	..	..
34 Czech Republic	..	..	..	99.9	100	100	99.9	108	100	1,896	224	89	24.8
35 Argentina	96.6	102	100	99.9	103	100	79.8	107	108	..	..	..	..
36 Kuwait	78.5	117	94	64.0	75	96	63.2	74	100	2,214	129	169	42.7
37 Antigua and Barbuda	..	..	..	..	..	..	..	..	..	..	..	..	..
38 Chile	95.2	103	100	89.2	98	97	87.2	115	105	2,372	169	84	29.1
39 Uruguay	98.0	102	101	94.8	107	101	88.7	110	112	..	..	..	..
40 Slovakia	..	..	..	..	..	..	..	..	..	1,860	..	96	32.9
41 Bahrain	81.2	122	90	98.8	99	101	90.8	93	108	1,975 [c]	135 [c]	187 [c]	..
42 Qatar	81.7	114	102	84.5	88	103	72.0	90	97	3,278	116	531	..
43 Hungary	99.1	101	100	96.7	99	99	98.2	134	103	1,942	200	104	27.6
44 Poland	99.7	100	100	99.3	100	100	88.5	113	105	2,055	155	123	..
45 United Arab Emirates	77.1	118	105	81.3	103	98	79.9	153	105	1,722	200	608	42.3
46 Estonia	..	..	..	99.9	100	100	87.4	87	103	2,990	169	102	26.2
Medium human development													
47 Saint Kitts and Nevis	..	..	..	..	..	..	..	..	..	..	..	..	..
48 Costa Rica	95.4	103	100	92.5	110	102	56.9	109	104	2,541	..	82	..
49 Croatia	96.9	104	98	99.9	100	100	73.0	88	102	1,879	..	97	26.8
50 Trinidad and Tobago	91.5	105	96	99.9	103	100	72.2	97	102	659	153	72	38.2

28 Gender and education

HDI rank	Female adult literacy			Female primary age group enrolment (adjusted)			Female secondary age group enrolment (adjusted)			Female tertiary students			Female tertiary science enrolment (as % of female tertiary students) [a]
	Rate (% age 15 and above) 1998	Index (1985 = 100) 1998	As % of male rate 1998	Ratio (% of primary school age girls) 1997	Index (1985 = 100) 1997	As % of male ratio 1997	Ratio (% of secondary school age girls) 1997	Index (1985 = 100) 1997	As % of male ratio 1997	Per 100,000 women 1994-97 [b]	Index (1985 = 100) 1994-97 [b]	As % of males 1994-97 [b]	1994-97 [b]
51 Dominica	..	..	..	..	..	..	..	..	..	..	..	..	..
52 Lithuania	99.4	101	100	..	..	..	..	..	..	2,530	78	130	37.9
53 Seychelles	..	..	..	..	..	..	..	..	..	..	..	..	..
54 Grenada	..	..	..	..	..	..	..	..	..	..	..	..	..
55 Mexico	88.7	108	96	99.9	100	100	64.0	104	94	1,645	136	90	28.4
56 Cuba	96.3	103	100	99.9	107	100	72.6	96	108	1,223	48	152	29.8
57 Belarus	99.4	101	100	..	..	..	..	..	..	3,313	..	110	..
58 Belize	92.5	109	99	99.9	112	100	62.6	105	97	..	..	..	..
59 Panama	91.5	105	99	90.2	100	101	71.7	111	101	3,224	108	149	35.9
60 Bulgaria	97.6	103	99	99.2	102	103	75.4	78	95	3,729	271	151	45.7
61 Malaysia	82.0	119	90	99.9	100	100	68.5	129	115	646 [c]	121 [c]	91 [c]	..
62 Russian Federation	99.3	101	100	99.9	107	100	90.7	91	107	3,157	78	111	34.3
63 Latvia	99.8	100	100	99.9	100	100	80.5	87	100	2,474	129	125	36.4
64 Romania	96.9	103	98	99.9	115	100	76.3	80	101	1,893	304	109	33.6
65 Venezuela	91.4	107	99	83.6	96	103	54.2	181	124	..	..	..	..
66 Fiji	89.9	109	95	99.9	103	100	84.4	130	100	..	..	..	..
67 Suriname	..	..	..	99.9	106	100	..	..	..	..	..	..	..
68 Colombia	91.2	106	100	89.4	132	100	78.2	126	105	1,682	141	105	33.5
69 Macedonia, TFYR	..	..	..	..	..	..	..	..	..	1,696	..	120	35.9
70 Georgia	..	..	..	88.6	99	99	75.3	75	99	3,116	..	98	39.6
71 Mauritius	80.3	112	92	96.6	97	100	69.9	141	106	568	684	101	..
72 Libyan Arab Jamahiriya	65.4	159	73	99.9	106	100	99.9	122	100	1,542 [c]	..	92 [c]	..
73 Kazakhstan	..	..	..	..	..	..	..	..	..	3,090	..	118	39.2
74 Brazil	84.5	110	100	94.3	121	94	67.0	136	103	1,172	..	116	34.0
75 Saudi Arabia	64.4	155	78	58.0	137	93	52.9	127	82	1,529	190	109	43.8
76 Thailand	93.2	108	96	89.2	101	103	46.9	191	97	2,138 [c]	..	111 [c]	..
77 Philippines	94.6	105	100	99.9	102	100	78.5	118	102	3,383	..	133	..
78 Ukraine	99.4	100	100	..	..	..	..	..	..	2,963 [c]	..	111 [c]	..
79 Saint Vincent and the Grenadines	..	..	..	..	..	..	..	..	..	..	..	..	..
80 Peru	84.3	112	90	93.3	98	99	81.1	106	94	..	..	..	..
81 Paraguay	91.5	107	97	97.0	107	101	60.1	164	97	976	..	106	47.0
82 Lebanon	79.1	116	86	74.9	99	97	..	..	..	2,604	..	92	36.9
83 Jamaica	89.9	108	110	95.7	97	100	72.1	111	107	647	156	72	50.3
84 Sri Lanka	88.3	107	94	99.9	100	100	79.3	112	109	388	128	69	31.4
85 Turkey	75.0	123	81	98.1	101	98	48.5	134	72	1,636	263	55	28.7
86 Oman	57.5	217	74	66.7	105	97	65.1	319	96	662	1,226	91	32.5
87 Dominican Republic	82.8	109	100	93.6	94	105	82.1	141	109	2,600	..	140	..
88 Saint Lucia	..	..	..	..	..	..	..	..	..	..	..	..	..
89 Maldives	96.0	104	100	..	..	..	..	..	..	..	..	..	..
90 Azerbaijan	..	..	..	..	..	..	..	..	..	1,468	59	94	..
91 Ecuador	88.7	108	96	99.9	104	100	51.3	79	101	..	..	..	..
92 Jordan	82.6	130	88	..	..	..	..	..	..	..	..	..	35.5
93 Armenia	97.3	103	98	..	..	..	..	..	..	1,088	..	121	36.7
94 Albania	76.2	124	84	..	..	..	..	..	..	1,260	181	137	44.7
95 Samoa (Western)	78.2	109	96	96.8	98	101	..	..	..	..	..	..	..
96 Guyana	97.8	103	99	93.0	93	100	76.4	104	104	1,073	386	100	27.4
97 Iran, Islamic Rep. of	67.4	143	82	89.2	120	98	75.8	168	88	1,311	533	60	21.2
98 Kyrgyzstan	..	..	..	99.3	99	100	78.7	79	102	1,117	..	106	..
99 China	74.6	123	82	99.9	114	100	65.1	145	88	327	164	54	..
100 Turkmenistan	..	..	..	..	..	..	..	..	..	..	..	..	..

... AND ACHIEVING EQUALITY FOR ALL WOMEN AND MEN

HDI rank	Female adult literacy			Female primary age group enrolment (adjusted)			Female secondary age group enrolment (adjusted)			Female tertiary students			Female tertiary science enrolment (as % of female tertiary students)[a]
	Rate (% age 15 and above) 1998	Index (1985 = 100) 1998	As % of male rate 1998	Ratio (% of primary school age girls) 1997	Index (1985 = 100) 1997	As % of male ratio 1997	Ratio (% of secondary school age girls) 1997	Index (1985 = 100) 1997	As % of male ratio 1997	Per 100,000 women 1994-97[b]	Index (1985 = 100) 1994-97[b]	As % of males 1994-97[b]	1994-97[b]
101 Tunisia	57.9	148	73	99.9	114	100	72.4	167	95	1,208	295	82	32.4
102 Moldova, Rep. of	97.9	104	98	..	..	..	..	..	..	2,253	..	111	36.8
103 South Africa	83.9	108	98	99.9	123	100	96.9	140	104	1,590	..	90	29.4
104 El Salvador	75.0	115	93	89.1	128	100	36.7	114	102	1,908	150	97	28.7
105 Cape Verde	64.6	137	77	99.9	107	100	35.5	125	94	..	..	..	..
106 Uzbekistan	83.4	115	90	..	..	..	..	..	..	..	..	..	..
107 Algeria	54.3	168	71	92.6	117	93	64.0	151	88	1,002	197	68	36.3
108 Viet Nam	90.6	107	95	99.9	114	100	54.2	119	97	..	..	..	..
109 Indonesia	80.5	121	88	98.6	103	99	53.4	115	91	812	..	53	23.8
110 Tajikistan	98.6	103	99	..	..	..	..	..	..	1,211	70	47	12.6
111 Syrian Arab Republic	58.1	142	67	90.6	98	92	39.4	79	87	1,298	106	72	31.0
112 Swaziland	77.3	120	97	95.3	118	102	78.8	128	93	627	..	99	12.3
113 Honduras	73.5	115	100	88.6	95	103	37.9	77	111	871	131	79	25.9
114 Bolivia	77.8	121	85	94.9	115	95	37.1	89	86	..	..	..	..
115 Namibia	79.7	118	97	94.0	98	106	83.9	113	108	890	..	154	35.2
116 Nicaragua	69.3	109	105	80.2	106	104	52.6	102	108	1,264	132	110	34.7
117 Mongolia	51.0	150	71	87.5	88	106	63.7	69	132	2,747	104	216	53.6
118 Vanuatu	..	..	..	69.2	96	95	38.8	111	84	..	..	..	..
119 Egypt	41.8	143	64	90.6	122	91	70.1	158	88	1,467	141	64	29.4
120 Guatemala	59.7	122	80	70.2	115	91	31.7	122	83	..	..	..	..
121 Solomon Islands	..	..	..	..	..	..	..	..	..	..	..	..	..
122 Botswana	78.2	120	107	82.6	87	106	91.3	195	106	545	349	87	23.9
123 Gabon	..	..	..	..	..	..	..	..	..	..	..	..	.
124 Morocco	34.0	171	56	67.2	137	78	31.9	103	74	971	179	70	28.4
125 Myanmar	79.5	113	90	98.5	131	99	53.0	149	96	717	140	156	60.6
126 Iraq	43.2	159	68	69.6	80	88	33.8	74	66	..	..	..	..
127 Lesotho	92.9	107	131	74.3	90	118	80.3	93	122	250	208	115	31.3
128 India	43.5	139	65	71.0	111	86	48.0	133	68	479	133	61	30.4
129 Ghana	59.9	155	76	41.8	107	93	..	..	..	53 c	96 c	27 c	..
130 Zimbabwe	82.9	120	90	92.2	92	98	56.3	111	91	386	..	41	14.0
131 Equatorial Guinea	71.5	137	78	79.9	80	102	64.8	92	90	41 c	..	14 c	..
132 São Tomé and Principe	..	..	..	..	..	..	..	..	..	..	..	..	..
133 Papua New Guinea	55.1	126	78	72.5	121	85	..	..	..	209	294	50	..
134 Cameroon	67.1	151	84	59.1	86	92	34.7	90	77	..	..	..	..
135 Pakistan	28.9	168	50	..	..	..	..	..	..	220 c	153 c	59 c	..
136 Cambodia	19.9	193	35	99.9	100	100	30.9	109	66	32	..	23	11.0
137 Comoros	51.6	121	79	45.4	85	83	32.2	100	82	33	..	40	..
138 Kenya	73.5	141	84	66.6	86	105	57.4	102	89	79 c	139 c	39 c	..
139 Congo	71.5	149	83	75.8	77	94	74.3	74	79	192 c	114 c	22 c	..
Low human development													
140 Lao People's Dem. Rep.	30.2	207	49	69.2	104	90	52.9	113	72	158	148	44	..
141 Madagascar	57.8	130	80	59.4	82	102	..	..	..	168	58	80	29.9
142 Bhutan	..	..	..	12.3	119	88	..	..	..	..	..	..	..
143 Sudan	43.4	174	64	..	..	..	..	..	..	253 c	196 c	87 c	..
144 Nepal	21.7	216	38	62.5	167	67	39.7	187	58	274 c	..	32 c	..
145 Togo	38.4	161	53	70.2	144	74	40.0	167	52	108	230	21	6.6
146 Bangladesh	28.6	143	56	69.6	149	87	15.6	125	58	129 c	71 c	20 c	..
147 Mauritania	31.0	131	60	59.8	212	91	..	..	..	126	..	21	..
148 Yemen	22.7	266	35	..	..	..	..	..	..	105	..	14	16.7
149 Djibouti	51.4	159	69	27.4	104	75	15.6	103	66	23	..	77	.
150 Haiti	45.6	142	91	19.9	39	105	33.2	75	95	..	..	..	..

HDI rank	Female adult literacy			Female primary age group enrolment (adjusted)			Female secondary age group enrolment (adjusted)			Female tertiary students			Female tertiary science enrolment (as % of female tertiary students) [a]
	Rate (% age 15 and above) 1998	Index (1985 = 100) 1998	As % of male rate 1998	Ratio (% of primary school age girls) 1997	Index (1985 = 100) 1997	As % of male ratio 1997	Ratio (% of secondary school age girls) 1997	Index (1985 = 100) 1997	As % of male ratio 1997	Per 100,000 women 1994-97 [b]	Index (1985 = 100) 1994-97 [b]	As % of males 1994-97 [b]	1994-97 [b]
151 Nigeria	52.5	177	75	..	..	..	..	..	..	..	..	..	..
152 Congo, Dem. Rep. of the	47.1	174	66	47.8	91	70	28.6	99	63	..	..	..	..
153 Zambia	69.1	131	82	71.7	84	98	34.9	104	71	135	233	39	..
154 Côte d'Ivoire	35.7	202	68	50.3	114	76	23.6	84	53	263	306	31	..
155 Senegal	25.8	173	57	53.6	136	82	15.5	120	65	140 c	157 c	32 c	..
156 Tanzania, U. Rep. of	64.3	150	77	48.0	85	102	..	..	..	22	367	24	9.1
157 Benin	22.6	174	42	50.4	140	59	18.3	104	48	96	137	23	12.6
158 Uganda	54.2	146	71	..	..	..	..	..	..	118	369	49	16.7
159 Eritrea	38.2	169	58	27.9	..	91	34.3	..	83	24	..	15	..
160 Angola	..	..	..	34.1	70	97	28.0	73	82	..	..	..	..
161 Gambia	27.5	181	66	58.2	119	79	25.1	244	60	106	..	55	..
162 Guinea	..	..	..	33.2	189	58	6.9	73	31	24	47	12	6.5
163 Malawi	44.1	139	60	99.7	244	102	53.9	211	59	34	179	42	..
164 Rwanda	56.8	157	79	78.6	134	101	..	..	..	..	..	..	..
165 Mali	31.1	239	68	31.2	217	69	12.9	222	56	52	236	24	..
166 Central African Republic	31.7	206	55	37.8	80	69	12.7	68	50	35 c	167 c	16 c	..
167 Chad	30.6	227	63	35.2	185	58	9.6	135	37	13	217	14	5.6
168 Mozambique	27.0	186	46	34.3	73	76	17.1	74	62	19	380	31	20.0
169 Guinea-Bissau	17.3	197	30	38.8	111	59	16.4	162	51	..	..	..	..
170 Burundi	37.5	171	68	32.9	93	86	14.1	155	70	38 c	136 c	34 c	..
171 Ethiopia	30.5	198	72	27.0	110	62	17.5	109	55	30	125	25	12.1
172 Burkina Faso	12.6	214	39	25.2	148	64	9.4	196	58	38	158	29	7.7
173 Niger	7.4	194	33	18.5	108	61	6.5	163	53	..	..	..	..
174 Sierra Leone	..	..	..	38.8	88	79	..	..	..	..	..	..	..
All developing countries	64.5	122	80	82.7	108	94	54.8	128	83	..	..	..	..
Least developed countries	41.0	145	67	54.7	116	83	24.6	119	66	..	..	..	..
Arab States	47.3	155	66	82.1	113	91	56.8	130	85	..	..	..	..
East Asia	75.5	122	83	99.8	113	100	66.4	143	88	..	..	..	..
East Asia (excluding China)	95.1	106	96	98.2	99	101	94.5	111	102	..	..	..	..
Latin America and the Caribbean	86.7	108	98	92.4	108	98	65.8	116	102	..	..	..	..
South Asia	42.3	140	64	72.1	116	86	..	..	..	..	..	..	..
South Asia (excluding India)	38.8	142	63	..	134	..	..	..	..	..	..	..	..
South-East Asia and the Pacific	85.0	113	92	97.5	106	99	56.9	126	95	..	..	..	..
Sub-Saharan Africa	51.6	146	76	51.8	101	85	35.8	111	..	..	..	..	..
Eastern Europe and the CIS	.. d	..	..	..	..	..	..	..	..	..	..	..	..
OECD	.. d	..	..	99.7	101	100	87.8	106	98	..	..	..	..
High human development	.. d	..	..	99.3	101	100	94.7	106	101	..	..	..	..
Medium human development	69.7	118	83	88.4	109	95	59.8	129	86	..	..	..	..
Low human development	38.9	166	65	50.3	117	80	21.1	116	..	..	..	..	..
High income	.. d	..	..	99.6	102	100	95.8	105	100	..	..	..	..
Medium income	84.8	106	94	93.1	107	97	70.0	117	97	..	..	..	..
Low income	59.6	127	76	79.4	109	92	50.1	..	..	..	..	..	..
World	.. d	..	..	85.1	119	95	60.8	119	87	..	..	..	..

a. Data refer to enrolment in natural and applied sciences. b. Data refer to the most recent year available during the period specified in the column heading. c. Data refer to a year or period other than that specified in the column heading. d. Aggregate is missing or differs from that in table 2, as only literacy data from UNESCO are presented in this table.

Source: Column 1: UNESCO 2000a; *columns 2 and 3:* calculated on the basis of adult literacy data for men and women from UNESCO 2000a; *columns 4 and 7:* UNESCO 1999a; *columns 5, 6, 8 and 9:* calculated on the basis of male and female age group enrolment data from UNESCO 1999a; *column 10:* UNESCO 2000b; *columns 11 and 12:* calculated on the basis of data on male and female tertiary students from UNESCO 2000b; *column 13:* UNESCO 1999b.

...AND ACHIEVING EQUALITY FOR ALL WOMEN AND MEN

	Female economic activity rate (age 15 and above)			Unemployment rate (%) [a]				Female unpaid family workers (as % of total) [b]
				Total (age 15-64)		Youth (age 15-24)		
HDI rank	Rate (%) 1998	Index (1985 = 100) 1998	As % of male rate 1998	Female 1998	Male 1998	Female 1998	Male 1998	1997-98 [c]
High human development								
1 Canada	59.6	110.0	80.6	8.2	8.6	13.7	16.6	71
2 Norway	58.5	113.4	83.1	3.2	3.3	9.4	9.5	71
3 United States	58.2	109.9	79.9	4.7	4.5	9.8	11.1	63
4 Australia	55.3	113.3	74.9	7.3	8.4	13.2	15.7	60
5 Iceland	67.9	103.4	85.4	3.3	2.3	5.6	6.4	50
6 Sweden	62.9	108.4	88.8	8.0	8.8	16.1	17.5	67
7 Belgium	39.7	112.1	64.5	11.7	7.6	23.0	18.3	..
8 Netherlands	45.1	119.3	65.2	5.5	3.5	8.7	7.8	84
9 Japan	51.0	105.5	66.4	4.2	4.3	7.3	8.2	82
10 United Kingdom	52.4	109.6	73.2	5.3	6.9	10.5	13.8	72
11 Finland	57.5	100.8	85.7	12.1	10.9	24.5	20.0	40
12 France	47.8	106.5	75.2	13.9	10.3	30.0	21.9	..
13 Switzerland	51.4	111.7	65.2	4.3	3.2	7.0	4.7	..
14 Germany	48.4	105.4	68.7	8.7	8.5	8.2	10.4	77
15 Denmark	61.9	103.8	83.6	6.4	3.9	7.7	6.7	..
16 Austria	44.4	103.8	64.3	5.6	5.4	7.6	7.4	69
17 Luxembourg	37.6	108.8	56.6	4.2	1.9	7.1	5.8	..
18 Ireland	35.9	115.8	50.5	7.5	8.2	11.1	11.9	59
19 Italy	38.2	110.9	57.3	16.4	9.5	37.2	28.1	..
20 New Zealand	56.5	121.4	77.2	7.4	7.7	13.5	15.6	70
21 Spain	36.9	118.6	54.9	26.7	13.7	43.4	27.1	60
22 Cyprus	49.2	109.8	61.6	..	..	..	..	..
23 Israel	47.7	118.6	66.0	..	..	..	..	73
24 Singapore	50.4	105.2	63.9	..	..	..	..	77
25 Greece	37.2	118.4	56.8	17.8	8.1	42.4	23.1	73
26 Hong Kong, China (SAR)	49.0	102.7	62.8	..	..	..	..	..
27 Malta	25.2	118.3	35.4	..	..	..	..	..
28 Portugal	50.6	105.7	70.0	6.0	4.0	10.9	8.3	59
29 Slovenia	53.9	96.3	79.6	..	..	..	..	58
30 Barbados	58.6	107.9	76.6	..	..	..	..	..
31 Korea, Rep. of	52.6	109.4	68.6	5.8	7.9	12.8	20.8	90
32 Brunei Darussalam	48.5	129.0	59.9	..	..	..	..	..
33 Bahamas	68.1	112.9	84.2	..	..	..	..	..
34 Czech Republic	62.3	102.0	84.4	8.2	5.0	14.6	10.6	70
35 Argentina	34.3	118.2	44.4	..	..	..	..	..
36 Kuwait	40.2	127.7	51.4	..	..	..	..	..
37 Antigua and Barbuda	..	..	..	..	..	..	..	..
38 Chile	36.6	124.2	47.1	..	..	..	..	..
39 Uruguay	47.4	123.4	65.0	..	..	..	..	..
40 Slovakia	62.9	102.9	84.5	..	..	..	..	44
41 Bahrain	31.8	133.3	37.0	..	..	..	..	..
42 Qatar	35.5	138.0	39.4	..	..	..	..	..
43 Hungary	48.4	98.7	71.5	6.9	8.1	11.6	14.8	65
44 Poland	57.2	97.7	79.3	12.6	9.5	25.2	21.5	59
45 United Arab Emirates	31.8	128.3	36.3	..	..	..	..	..
46 Estonia	61.7	95.8	82.2	..	..	..	..	62
Medium human development								
47 Saint Kitts and Nevis	..	..	..	..	..	..	..	..
48 Costa Rica	36.3	125.2	44.6	..	..	..	..	38
49 Croatia	48.4	103.1	71.6	..	..	..	..	74
50 Trinidad and Tobago	43.2	113.5	57.0	..	..	..	..	77

HDI rank	Female economic activity rate (age 15 and above)			Unemployment rate (%) [a]				Female unpaid family workers (as % of total) [b]
	Rate (%) 1998	Index (1985 = 100) 1998	As % of male rate 1998	Total (age 15-64)		Youth (age 15-24)		
				Female 1998	Male 1998	Female 1998	Male 1998	1997-98 [c]
51 Dominica	..	..	..	..	..	..	..	..
52 Lithuania	58.0	94.7	79.3	..	..	..	..	56
53 Seychelles	..	..	..	..	..	..	..	..
54 Grenada	..	..	..	..	..	..	..	..
55 Mexico	38.4	118.6	46.1	3.6	2.6	6.4	4.7	47
56 Cuba	48.5	123.4	63.3	..	..	..	..	..
57 Belarus	59.0	96.1	81.3	..	..	..	..	..
58 Belize	26.3	118.4	30.7	..	..	..	..	..
59 Panama	42.6	114.9	53.9	..	..	..	..	25
60 Bulgaria	57.4	96.2	86.7	..	..	..	..	..
61 Malaysia	47.5	110.3	59.7	..	..	..	..	..
62 Russian Federation	59.0	96.3	80.8	..	..	..	..	..
63 Latvia	61.2	95.7	81.4	..	..	..	..	54
64 Romania	51.0	91.7	76.1	..	..	..	..	71
65 Venezuela	42.1	121.2	51.9	..	..	..	..	..
66 Fiji	34.6	151.6	42.4	..	..	..	..	..
67 Suriname	35.3	127.6	47.1	..	..	..	..	..
68 Colombia	47.3	132.7	59.1	..	..	..	..	74
69 Macedonia, TFYR	50.1	108.5	70.7	..	..	..	..	..
70 Georgia	55.7	95.0	76.9	..	..	..	..	..
71 Mauritius	37.4	121.0	47.1	..	..	..	..	54
72 Libyan Arab Jamahiriya	24.3	113.7	31.7	..	..	..	..	..
73 Kazakhstan	60.5	98.3	80.2	..	..	..	..	..
74 Brazil	44.0	110.6	52.3	..	..	..	..	..
75 Saudi Arabia	20.1	160.6	24.9	..	..	..	..	..
76 Thailand	73.1	97.4	84.6	..	..	..	..	66
77 Philippines	49.2	106.6	60.2	..	..	..	..	..
78 Ukraine	55.3	94.4	79.0	..	..	..	..	63
79 Saint Vincent and the Grenadines	..	..	..	..	..	..	..	..
80 Peru	33.5	122.2	42.2	..	..	..	..	66
81 Paraguay	36.3	109.6	42.3	..	..	..	..	..
82 Lebanon	28.7	130.5	37.5	..	..	..	..	..
83 Jamaica	69.1	103.1	85.2	..	..	..	..	95
84 Sri Lanka	41.9	117.0	54.4	..	..	..	..	56
85 Turkey	48.7	109.4	59.4	6.7	6.6	12.7	14.5	..
86 Oman	18.0	169.8	23.3	..	..	..	..	..
87 Dominican Republic	39.3	122.2	45.8	..	..	..	..	92
88 Saint Lucia	..	..	..	..	..	..	..	..
89 Maldives	65.9	104.2	78.5	..	..	..	..	..
90 Azerbaijan	54.0	96.4	73.5	..	..	..	..	..
91 Ecuador	31.8	126.3	37.7	..	..	..	..	63
92 Jordan	24.9	154.8	32.4	..	..	..	..	..
93 Armenia	62.1	99.8	85.9	..	..	..	..	..
94 Albania	59.5	104.5	72.5	..	..	..	..	..
95 Samoa (Western)	..	..	..	..	..	..	..	..
96 Guyana	41.0	124.9	48.4	..	..	..	..	..
97 Iran, Islamic Rep. of	27.6	133.0	35.2	..	..	..	..	..
98 Kyrgyzstan	60.4	101.0	82.7	..	..	..	..	..
99 China	73.2	101.8	86.2	..	..	..	..	..
100 Turkmenistan	61.7	100.4	80.1	..	..	..	..	..

. . . AND ACHIEVING EQUALITY FOR ALL WOMEN AND MEN

	Female economic activity rate (age 15 and above)			Unemployment rate (%) [a]				Female unpaid family workers (as % of total) [b]
				Total (age 15-64)		Youth (age 15-24)		
	Rate (%)	Index (1985 = 100)	As % of male rate	Female	Male	Female	Male	
HDI rank	1998	1998	1998	1998	1998	1998	1998	1997-98 [c]
101 Tunisia	36.4	110.5	45.9	..	..	..	..	..
102 Moldova, Rep. of	60.1	94.5	82.8	..	..	..	..	..
103 South Africa	46.2	103.5	58.7	..	..	..	..	..
104 El Salvador	44.5	129.4	52.6	..	..	..	..	33
105 Cape Verde	45.3	113.8	51.7	..	..	..	..	
106 Uzbekistan	61.8	101.2	83.6	..	..	..	..	
107 Algeria	27.6	147.4	36.3	..	..	..	..	
108 Viet Nam	73.8	100.6	89.5	..	..	..	..	
109 Indonesia	54.5	114.2	66.2	..	..	..	..	
110 Tajikistan	56.5	100.1	77.3	..	..	..	..	
111 Syrian Arab Republic	27.7	119.4	35.5	..	..	..	..	
112 Swaziland	41.9	105.0	51.9	..	..	..	..	..
113 Honduras	39.2	119.9	45.7	..	..	..	..	32
114 Bolivia	47.5	111.8	57.0	..	..	..	..	67
115 Namibia	53.9	100.8	67.1	..	..	..	..	..
116 Nicaragua	46.2	123.0	54.2	..	..	..	..	..
117 Mongolia	73.1	101.1	87.0	..	..	..	..	..
118 Vanuatu	..	..	..	..	..	..	..	..
119 Egypt	34.0	116.5	43.2	..	..	..	..	..
120 Guatemala	34.6	125.4	39.6	..	..	..	..	..
121 Solomon Islands	80.9	96.0	91.4	..	..	..	..	..
122 Botswana	64.7	95.0	77.6	..	..	..	..	44
123 Gabon	62.8	97.9	75.2	..	..	..	..	..
124 Morocco	40.9	108.2	51.5	..	..	..	..	..
125 Myanmar	65.9	98.4	74.7	..	..	..	..	..
126 Iraq	17.8	118.7	23.9	..	..	..	..	
127 Lesotho	47.1	100.2	55.8	..	..	..	..	
128 India	41.8	98.0	49.3	..	..	..	..	
129 Ghana	80.8	98.5	98.4	..	..	..	..	
130 Zimbabwe	66.6	99.6	78.0	..	..	..	..	
131 Equatorial Guinea	45.3	98.2	50.9	..	..	..	..	
132 São Tomé and Principe	..	..	..	..	..	..	..	
133 Papua New Guinea	67.0	98.0	77.5	..	..	..	..	
134 Cameroon	49.0	102.9	57.3	..	..	..	..	
135 Pakistan	34.4	123.3	40.5	..	..	..	..	36
136 Cambodia	81.7	99.4	95.7	..	..	..	..	
137 Comoros	62.5	96.7	72.8	..	..	..	..	
138 Kenya	74.5	99.6	84.0	..	..	..	..	
139 Congo	58.5	100.8	70.6	..	..	..	..	
Low human development								
140 Lao People's Dem. Rep.	74.6	100.0	84.0	..	..	..	..	
141 Madagascar	69.1	98.3	77.9	..	..	..	..	
142 Bhutan	57.9	100.1	64.5	..	..	..	..	
143 Sudan	34.0	110.8	39.8	..	..	..	..	
144 Nepal	56.8	100.4	66.4	..	..	..	..	
145 Togo	53.4	100.2	61.6	..	..	..	..	
146 Bangladesh	65.8	99.0	76.2	..	..	..	..	74
147 Mauritania	63.4	94.7	73.6	..	..	..	..	
148 Yemen	29.9	107.2	36.2	..	..	..	..	
149 Djibouti	..	..	..	..	..	..	..	
150 Haiti	56.8	95.2	69.5	..	..	..	..	

HDI rank	Female economic activity rate (age 15 and above)			Unemployment rate (%) [a]				Female unpaid family workers (as % of total) [b]
	Rate (%) 1998	Index (1985 = 100) 1998	As % of male rate 1998	Total (age 15-64)		Youth (age 15-24)		
				Female 1998	Male 1998	Female 1998	Male 1998	1997-98 [c]
151 Nigeria	48.0	99.9	55.7	..	..	..	..	..
152 Congo, Dem. Rep. of the	61.1	97.2	72.4	..	..	..	..	..
153 Zambia	65.4	97.9	76.2	..	..	..	..	..
154 Côte d'Ivoire	43.8	100.3	50.3	..	..	..	..	..
155 Senegal	61.3	100.3	71.8	..	..	..	..	..
156 Tanzania, U. Rep. of	82.1	97.8	92.9	..	..	..	..	..
157 Benin	74.1	97.9	89.8	..	..	..	..	..
158 Uganda	80.1	98.4	88.1	..	..	..	..	..
159 Eritrea	74.8	98.5	86.7	..	..	..	..	..
160 Angola	73.1	97.8	81.7	..	..	..	..	..
161 Gambia	69.7	100.6	77.7	..	..	..	..	..
162 Guinea	77.6	97.5	89.4	..	..	..	..	..
163 Malawi	78.3	97.7	90.3	..	..	..	..	..
164 Rwanda	83.2	98.9	89.0	..	..	..	..	..
165 Mali	71.9	98.2	80.5	..	..	..	..	..
166 Central African Republic	68.2	94.4	78.6	..	..	..	..	..
167 Chad	67.0	101.7	76.2	..	..	..	..	..
168 Mozambique	83.0	97.7	91.8	..	..	..	..	..
169 Guinea-Bissau	56.8	100.2	62.7	..	..	..	..	..
170 Burundi	82.6	99.4	88.7	..	..	..	..	..
171 Ethiopia	57.5	98.4	67.3	..	..	..	..	..
172 Burkina Faso	76.3	96.4	90.6	..	..	..	..	..
173 Niger	69.5	98.1	75.0	..	..	..	..	..
174 Sierra Leone	44.2	103.5	52.9	..	..	..	..	..
All developing countries	55.6	102.3	66.1	..	..	..	..	..
Least developed countries	64.9	98.7	74.9	..	..	..	..	..
Arab States	30.8	111.7	38.9	..	..	..	..	..
East Asia	72.3	102.0	85.4	..	..	..	..	..
East Asia (excluding China)	53.0	108.5	68.7	..	..	..	..	..
Latin America and the Caribbean	41.4	116.4	50.3	..	..	..	..	..
South Asia	42.8	100.6	50.6	..	..	..	..	..
South Asia (excluding India)	45.5	107.9	54.3	..	..	..	..	..
South-East Asia and the Pacific	60.6	105.3	72.7	..	..	..	..	..
Sub-Saharan Africa	62.0	99.1	72.1	..	..	..	..	..
Eastern Europe and the CIS	57.6	96.8	80.0	..	..	..	..	..
OECD	50.8	108.3	69.3	7.4 [d]	6.3 [d]	13.1 [d]	12.5 [d]	..
High human development	51.1	108.4	70.7	..	..	..	..	..
Medium human development	55.4	101.6	66.8	..	..	..	..	..
Low human development	61.1	98.8	70.6	..	..	..	..	..
High income	51.5	109.0	71.6	..	..	..	..	..
Medium income	47.0	102.6	59.8	..	..	..	..	..
Low income	59.8	100.7	70.4	..	..	..	..	..
World	55.0	103.1	67.8	..	..	..	..	..

a. Data refer to the number of unemployed divided by the labour force. Age ranges vary slightly among countries. b. Data refer to contributing family workers—usually people who work without pay in an economic enterprise operated by a related person living in the same household. Age ranges vary slightly among countries. c. Data refer to the most recent year available during the period specified in the column heading. d. Aggregate as calculated in OECD 1999b.

Source: Columns 1-3: calculated on the basis of data on economic activity rates for men and women from ILO 1996; columns 4-7: OECD 1999b; column 8: ILO 1999c.

... AND ACHIEVING EQUALITY FOR ALL WOMEN AND MEN

		Burden of work			Time allocation (%)					
		Work time (minutes per day)		Females as % of males	Total work time		Market activities		Non-market activities	
	Year	Females	Males		Market activities	Non-market activities	Females	Males	Females	Males
Selected developing countries										
Urban areas in:										
Colombia	1983	399	356	112	49	51	24	77	76	23
Indonesia	1992	398	366	109	60	40	35	86	65	14
Kenya	1986	590	572	103	46	54	41	79	59	21
Nepal	1978	579	554	105	58	42	25	67	75	33
Venezuela	1983	440	416	106	59	41	30	87	70	13
Average		481	453	106	54	46	31	79	69	21
Rural areas in:										
Bangladesh	1990	545	496	110	52	48	35	70	65	30
Guatemala	1977	678	579	117	59	41	37	84	63	16
Kenya	1988	676	500	135	56	44	42	76	58	24
Nepal	1978	641	547	117	56	44	46	67	54	33
Highlands	1978	692	586	118	59	41	52	66	48	34
Mountains	1978	649	534	122	56	44	48	65	52	35
Rural hills	1978	583	520	112	52	48	37	70	63	30
Philippines	1975-77	546	452	121	73	27	29	84	71	16
Average		617	515	120	59	41	38	76	62	24
National										
Korea, Rep. of	1990	488	480	102	45	55	34	56	66	44
Average for selected developing countries		544	483	113	54	46	34	76	66	24
Selected OECD countries [a]										
Australia	1992	443	443	100	44	56	28	61	72	39
Austria	1992	438	393	111	49	51	31	71	69	29
Canada	1992	429	430	100	52	48	39	65	61	35
Denmark	1987	449	458	98	68	32	58	79	42	21
Finland	1987/88	430	410	105	51	49	39	64	61	36
France	1985/86	429	388	111	45	55	30	62	70	38
Germany	1991/92	440	441	100	44	56	30	61	70	39
Israel	1991/92	375	377	99	51	49	29	74	71	26
Italy	1988/89	470	367	128	45	55	22	77	78	23
Netherlands	1987	377	345	109	35	65	19	52	81	48
Norway	1990/91	445	412	108	50	50	38	64	62	36
United Kingdom	1985	413	411	100	51	49	37	68	63	32
United States	1985	453	428	106	50	50	37	63	63	37
Average for selected OECD countries [a]		430	408	105	49	51	34	66	66	34

Note: Market activities refer to market-oriented production activities as defined by the 1993 revised UN System of National Accounts.

a. Israel, although not an OECD country, is included in this study.

Source: Goldschmidt-Clermont and Pagnossin Aligisakis 1995; and Harvey 1995.

HDI rank	Year women received right [a]		Year first woman elected (E) or appointed (A) to parliament	Women in government [b]		
	To vote	To stand for election		At all levels (%) 1998	At ministerial level (%) 1998	At sub-ministerial level (%) 1998
High human development						
1 Canada	1917, 1950	1920, 1960	1921 E	..	..	..
2 Norway	1907, 1913	1907, 1913	1911 A	22.2	20.0	22.9
3 United States	1920, 1960	1788 [c]	1917 E	33.0	26.3	33.4
4 Australia	1902, 1962	1902, 1962	1943 E	16.5	14.3	17.1
5 Iceland	1915	1915	1922 E	6.8	7.7	6.6
6 Sweden	1861, 1921	1907, 1921	1921 E	31.7	43.5	24.3
7 Belgium	1919, 1948	1921, 1948	1921 A	5.3	3.3	6.3
8 Netherlands	1919	1917	1918 E	13.9	27.8	9.8
9 Japan	1945, 1947	1945, 1947	1946 E	2.2	0.0	2.8
10 United Kingdom	1918, 1928	1918, 1928	1918 E	20.0	23.8	19.4
11 Finland	1906	1906	1907 E	16.2	28.6	13.1
12 France	1944	1944	1945 E	12.4	11.8	12.4
13 Switzerland	1971	1971	1971 E	9.4	16.7	8.3
14 Germany	1918	1918	1919 E	5.2	8.3	4.7
15 Denmark	1915	1915	1918 E	16.8	40.9	11.9
16 Austria	1918	1918	1919 E	6.5	20.0	4.3
17 Luxembourg	1919	1919	1919 E	17.7	25.0	15.2
18 Ireland	1918, 1928	1918, 1928	1918 E	10.9	21.1	8.2
19 Italy	1945	1945	1946 E	9.3	13.0	8.3
20 New Zealand	1893	1919	1933 E	27.3	8.3	30.7
21 Spain	1931	1931	1931 E	8.0	17.6	5.6
22 Cyprus	1960	1960	1963 E	2.7	0.0	4.3
23 Israel	1948	1948	1949 E	7.8	0.0	10.0
24 Singapore	1947	1947	1963 E	6.7	0.0	8.3
25 Greece	1927, 1952	1927, 1952	1952 E	6.1	4.5	6.7
26 Hong Kong, China (SAR)	–	–	–	–	–	–
27 Malta	1947	1947	1966 E	6.5	0.0	7.9
28 Portugal	1931, 1976	1931, 1976	1934 E	11.1	10.0	11.4
29 Slovenia	1945	1945	1992 E [d]	15.8	0.0	18.8
30 Barbados	1950	1950	1966 A	21.6	27.3	20.0
31 Korea, Rep. of	1948	1948	1948 E	..	..	..
32 Brunei Darussalam	– [e]	– [e]	– [e]	4.7	0.0	6.1
33 Bahamas	1961, 1964	1961, 1964	1977 A	35.6	16.7	43.9
34 Czech Republic	1920	1920	1992 E [d]	14.1	16.7	13.5
35 Argentina	1947	1947	1951 E	9.1	8.3	9.2
36 Kuwait	– [e]	– [e]	– [e]	5.0	0.0	6.7
37 Antigua and Barbuda	1951	1951	1984 A	28.9	0.0	40.7
38 Chile	1931, 1949	1931, 1949	1951 E	9.8	13.7	8.5
39 Uruguay	1932	1932	1942 E	12.0	6.7	14.3
40 Slovakia	1920	1920	1992 E [d]	22.4	19.0	23.0
41 Bahrain	1973 [f]	1973 [f]	– [f]	0.8	0.0	1.0
42 Qatar	– [e]	– [e]	– [e]	0.0	0.0	0.0
43 Hungary	1953	1958	1945 E	10.9	5.3	12.1
44 Poland	1918	1918	1919 E	11.1	17.2	9.1
45 United Arab Emirates	– [e]	– [e]	– [e]	0.0	0.0	0.0
46 Estonia	1918	1918	1919 E	16.4	11.8	17.1
Medium human development						
47 Saint Kitts and Nevis	1951	1951	1984 E	9.4	0.0	15.0
48 Costa Rica	1949	1949	1953 E	19.0	15.0	20.9
49 Croatia	1945	1945	1992 E [d]	18.9	12.0	19.9
50 Trinidad and Tobago	1946	1946	1962 E + A	16.9	13.6	18.6

HDI rank	Year women received right[a]		Year first woman elected (E) or appointed (A) to parliament	Women in government[b]		
	To vote	To stand for election		At all levels (%) 1998	At ministerial level (%) 1998	At sub-ministerial level (%) 1998
51 Dominica	1951	1951	1980 E	31.0	20.0	33.3
52 Lithuania	1921	1921	1920 A	10.1	5.6	10.8
53 Seychelles	1948	1948	1976 E + A	20.3	33.3	17.5
54 Grenada	1951	1951	1976 E + A	29.7	13.3	40.9
55 Mexico	1947	1953	1952 A	6.6	5.0	6.8
56 Cuba	1934	1934	1940 E	8.9	5.1	10.7
57 Belarus	1919	1919	1990 E[d]	8.0	2.8	9.5
58 Belize	1954	1954	1984 E + A	12.2	0.0	16.7
59 Panama	1941, 1946	1941, 1946	1946 E	5.3	5.9	4.8
60 Bulgaria	1944	1944	1945 E	12.2	15.0	9.5
61 Malaysia	1957	1957	1959 E	13.7	15.6	12.9
62 Russian Federation	1918	1918	1993 E[d]	4.7	7.5	4.3
63 Latvia	1918	1918	–	25.2	6.7	27.3
64 Romania	1929, 1946	1929, 1946	1946 E	9.3	7.7	9.8
65 Venezuela	1946	1946	1948 E	8.2	3.2	13.3
66 Fiji	1963	1963	1970 A	14.5	9.5	16.4
67 Suriname	1948	1948	1975 E	12.3	5.3	15.8
68 Colombia	1954	1954	1954 A	26.1	17.6	28.0
69 Macedonia, TFYR	1946	1946	1990 E[d]	20.0	8.7	23.9
70 Georgia	1918, 1921	1918, 1921	1992 E[d]	5.3	3.8	5.9
71 Mauritius	1956	1956	1976 E	..	..	..
72 Libyan Arab Jamahiriya	1964	1964	–	5.6	6.7	0.0
73 Kazakhstan	1924, 1993	1924, 1993	1990 E[d]	2.3	5.0	1.5
74 Brazil	1934	1934	1933 E	11.9	4.2	13.0
75 Saudi Arabia	– [e]	– [e]	– [e]	0.0	0.0	0.0
76 Thailand	1932	1932	1948 A	6.3	4.0	6.8
77 Philippines	1937	1937	1941 E	17.0	9.5	18.8
78 Ukraine	1919	1919	1990 E[d]	3.0	5.4	2.4
79 Saint Vincent and the Grenadines	1951	1951	1979 E	12.5	10.0	14.3
80 Peru	1955	1955	1956 E	19.3	10.5	21.9
81 Paraguay	1961	1961	1963 E	6.6	7.1	6.4
82 Lebanon	1952	1952	1991 A	0.0	0.0	0.0
83 Jamaica	1944	1944	1944 E	18.2	11.1	21.6
84 Sri Lanka	1931	1931	1947 E	6.7	13.3	4.8
85 Turkey	1930	1934	1935 A	13.3	5.0	19.0
86 Oman	– [e]	– [e]	– [e]	3.8	0.0	4.4
87 Dominican Republic	1942	1942	1942 E	14.3	10.0	15.8
88 Saint Lucia	1924	1924	1979 A	8.0	10.0	6.7
89 Maldives	1932	1932	1979 E	10.5	5.6	12.1
90 Azerbaijan	1921	1921	1990 E[d]	6.0	10.0	4.7
91 Ecuador	1929, 1967	1929, 1967	1956 E	8.9	20.0	5.7
92 Jordan	1974	1974	1989 A	1.1	1.6	0.0
93 Armenia	1921	1921	1990 E[d]	3.5	0.0	4.9
94 Albania	1920	1920	1945 E	11.1	10.5	12.5
95 Samoa (Western)	1990	1990	1976 A	10.5	7.1	11.6
96 Guyana	1953	1945	1968 E	19.6	15.0	23.1
97 Iran, Islamic Rep. of	1963	1963	1963 E + A	0.4	0.0	0.5
98 Kyrgyzstan	1918	1918	1990 E[d]	3.4	4.3	2.8
99 China	1949	1949	1954 E	3.7	2.6	4.0
100 Turkmenistan	1927	1927	1990 E[d]	2.5	4.0	0.0

	Year women received right [a]		Year first woman elected (E) or appointed (A) to parliament	Women in government [b]		
HDI rank	To vote	To stand for election		At all levels (%) 1998	At ministerial level (%) 1998	At sub-ministerial level (%) 1998
101 Tunisia	1957, 1959	1957, 1959	1959 E	7.7	3.2	10.0
102 Moldova, Rep. of	1978, 1993	1978, 1993	1990 E	10.8	0.0	15.3
103 South Africa	1930, 1994	1930, 1994	1933 E	15.6	14.8	15.9
104 El Salvador	1939	1961	1961 E	23.5	6.3	28.8
105 Cape Verde	1975	1975	1975 E	26.1	13.3	50.0
106 Uzbekistan	1938	1938	1990 E [d]	5.3	3.3	12.5
107 Algeria	1962	1962	1962 A	5.5	0.0	9.8
108 Viet Nam	1946	1946	1976 E	3.0	0.0	4.7
109 Indonesia	1945	1945	1950 A	1.6	3.4	1.3
110 Tajikistan	1924	1924	1990 E [d]	6.2	6.5	6.1
111 Syrian Arab Republic	1949, 1953	1953	1973 E	3.3	7.5	0.0
112 Swaziland	1968	1968	1972 E + A	11.9	5.9	16.0
113 Honduras	1955	1955	1957 [†]	15.5	11.1	17.5
114 Bolivia	1938, 1952	1938, 1952	1966 E	8.3	5.9	10.5
115 Namibia	1989	1989	1989 E	15.1	8.3	16.5
116 Nicaragua	1955	1955	1972 E	10.8	5.0	13.0
117 Mongolia	1924	1924	1951 E	2.4	0.0	3.4
118 Vanuatu	1975, 1980	1975, 1980	1987 E	5.5	0.0	7.3
119 Egypt	1956	1956	1957 E	4.9	6.3	4.2
120 Guatemala	1946	1946	1956 E	9.8	0.0	15.4
121 Solomon Islands	1974	1974	1993 E	6.7	5.6	8.3
122 Botswana	1965	1965	1979 E	19.0	14.3	20.4
123 Gabon	1956	1956	1961 E	6.5	3.4	9.1
124 Morocco	1963	1963	1993 E	5.8	0.0	8.0
125 Myanmar	1935	1946	1947 E	0.0	0.0	0.0
126 Iraq	1980	1980	1980 E	0.0	0.0	0.0
127 Lesotho	1965	1965	1965 A	13.3	6.3	14.9
128 India	1950	1950	1952 E	4.9	7.9	4.2
129 Ghana	1954	1954	1960 A [†]	8.9	9.4	8.7
130 Zimbabwe	1957	1978	1980 E + A	8.5	12.0	5.9
131 Equatorial Guinea	1963	1963	1968 E	4.0	3.7	4.3
132 São Tomé and Príncipe	1975	1975	1975 E	15.0	0.0	37.5
133 Papua New Guinea	1964	1963	1977 E	4.5	0.0	7.9
134 Cameroon	1946	1946	1960 E	6.4	6.3	6.4
135 Pakistan	1947	1947	1973 E	3.0	7.1	1.4
136 Cambodia	1955	1955	1958 E	6.8	8.3	6.0
137 Comoros	1956	1956	1993 E	4.0	6.7	0.0
138 Kenya	1919, 1963	1919, 1963	1969 E + A	6.9	0.0	8.8
139 Congo	1963	1963	1963 E	5.4	6.1	0.0
Low human development						
140 Lao People's Dem. Rep.	1958	1958	1958 E	0.0	0.0	0.0
141 Madagascar	1959	1959	1965 E	14.3	18.8	8.3
142 Bhutan	1953	1953	1975 E	5.3	0.0	8.3
143 Sudan	1964	1964	1964 E	0.0	0.0	0.0
144 Nepal	1951	1951	1952 A	1.3	3.1	0.0
145 Togo	1945	1945	1961 E	7.4	9.1	0.0
146 Bangladesh	1972	1972	1973 E	1.1	5.3	0.0
147 Mauritania	1961	1961	1975 E	5.7	4.3	6.1
148 Yemen	1967 [g]	1967 [g]	1990 E [†]	0.0	0.0	0.0
149 Djibouti	1946	1986	– [h]	2.5	0.0	2.9
150 Haiti	1950	1950	1961 E	10.0	0.0	16.0

. . . AND ACHIEVING EQUALITY FOR ALL WOMEN AND MEN

31 Women's political participation

HDI rank	Year women received right [a]		Year first woman elected (E) or appointed (A) to parliament	Women in government [b]		
	To vote	To stand for election		At all levels (%) 1998	At ministerial level (%) 1998	At sub-ministerial level (%) 1998
151 Nigeria	1958	1958	..	4.8	6.5	4.1
152 Congo, Dem. Rep. of the	1967	1970	1970 E	3.7	4.0	0.0
153 Zambia	1962	1962	1964 E + A	9.9	3.3	12.1
154 Côte d'Ivoire	1952	1952	1965 E	3.1	3.1	3.1
155 Senegal	1945	1945	1963 E	8.0	3.3	15.0
156 Tanzania, U. Rep. of	1959	1959	..	11.8	12.9	11.1
157 Benin	1956	1956	1979 E	9.5	13.0	5.3
158 Uganda	1962	1962	1962 A	11.2	13.2	9.8
159 Eritrea	1955	1955	1994 E	5.7	5.3	5.9
160 Angola	1975	1975	1980 E	11.1	13.8	10.2
161 Gambia	1960	1960	1982 E	18.9	28.6	16.7
162 Guinea	1958	1958	1963 E	13.6	8.3	20.0
163 Malawi	1961	1961	1964 E	3.8	4.2	3.7
164 Rwanda	1961	1961	1965 †	14.5	5.0	20.0
165 Mali	1956	1956	1964 E	16.1	20.8	0.0
166 Central African Republic	1986	1986	1987 E	5.4	4.0	6.5
167 Chad	1958	1958	1962 E	3.9	0.0	6.5
168 Mozambique	1975	1975	1977 E	13.7	0.0	15.8
169 Guinea-Bissau	1977	1977	1972 A	16.4	17.6	15.8
170 Burundi	1961	1961	1982 E	5.0	7.7	0.0
171 Ethiopia	1955	1955	1957 E	13.7	5.0	16.0
172 Burkina Faso	1958	1958	1978 E	10.0	10.0	9.9
173 Niger	1948	1948	1989 E	8.3	9.5	7.8
174 Sierra Leone	1961	1961	..	10.0	9.1	10.5

† No information or confirmation available.

a. Refers to year in which right to vote or stand for election on a universal and equal basis was recognized. Where two years are shown, the first refers to the first partial recognition of the right to vote or stand for election. b. Ministerial level includes ministers, secretaries of state and heads of central banks and cabinet agencies. Subministerial level includes deputy and vice ministers (or their equivalent); permanent secretaries (or their equivalent); deputy permanent secretaries, directors and advisers (or their equivalent). c. No information available on the year all women received the right to stand for election. However, the constitution does not mention gender with regard to this right. d. Refers to year women were elected to current parliamentary system. e. Women's right to vote and to stand for election has not been recognized. Brunei Darussalam, Oman, Qatar and Saudi Arabia have never had parliaments. f. According to the constitution in force (1973), all citizens are equal before the law; however, women were not able to exercise electoral rights in the only legislative elections held in Bahrain, in 1973. The first legislature of Bahrain was dissolved by decree of the emir on 26 August 1975. g. Refers to the former People's Democratic Republic of Yemen. h. The country has not yet elected or appointed a woman to the national parliament.

Source: Columns 1-3: IPU 1995 and 2000b; columns 4-6: UN 2000b.

	Total population (thousands) 1998	Life expectancy at birth (years) 1995-2000	Infant mortality rate (per 1,000 live births) 1998	Under-five mortality rate (per 1,000 live births) 1998	Total fertility rate 1995-2000	Adult literacy rate (% age 15 and above) 1998	GNP [a] Total (US$ millions) 1998	GNP [a] Per capita (US$) 1998	Daily per capita supply of calories 1997	Population without access to safe water (%) 1990-98 [b]	Refugees by country of origin (thousands) 1998
Afghanistan	21,354	45.5	165	257	6.9	35	..	.. [c]	1,745	94	2,633.9
Andorra	72 [d]	..	5	6	..	..	..	.. [e]	..	..	..
Bosnia and Herzegovina	3,675	73.3	16	19	1.4	..	..	.. [f]	2,265	..	471.6
Kiribati	81 [d]	60.0 [b, d]	54	74	4.5 [b, d]	93 [d, g]	101	1,170	2,851	..	..
Korea, Dem. People's Rep. of	23,348	72.2	23	30	2.1	..	..	.. [c]	1,837	0	..
Liberia	2,666	47.3	157	235	6.3	51	..	.. [c]	2,044	54	100.2
Liechtenstein	32 [d]	..	10	11	..	..	..	.. [e]	..	..	..
Marshall Islands	60 [d]	..	63	92	..	91 [d, g]	96	1,540	..	18	..
Micronesia, Fed. States of	114 [d]	67.0 [b, d]	20	24	4.0 [b, d]	81 [d, g]	204	1,800	..	78	..
Monaco	33 [d]	..	5	5	..	..	..	.. [e]	..	..	..
Nauru	11 [d]	..	25	30	..	..	..	..	..	..	..
Palau	19 [d]	..	28	34	..	98 [d, g]	..	.. [h]	..	12	..
San Marino	26 [d]	..	6	6	..	..	..	..	..	..	..
Somalia	9,237	47.0	125	211	7.3	24 [d, g]	..	.. [c]	1,566	69	480.8
Tonga	98 [d]	71.0 [b, d]	19	23	3.6 [b, d]	99 [d, g]	173	1,750	..	5	..
Yugoslavia	10,635	72.8	18	21	1.8	98 [d, g]	..	.. [f]	3,031	24	100.2

Note: The table presents data for countries not included in the main indicator tables.

a. Data refer to GNP calculated using the World Bank Atlas method, in current US dollars. For further details see World Bank 2000b. b. Data refer to the most recent year available during the period specified in the column heading. c. Estimated to be low income ($760 or less) by the World Bank. d. UNICEF 1999c. e. Estimated to be high income ($9,361 or more) by the World Bank. f. Estimated to be lower middle income ($761-3,030) by the World Bank. g. Data refer to a year or period other than that specified in the column heading, differ from the standard definition or refer to only part of the country. h. Estimated to be upper middle income ($3,031-9,360) by the World Bank.

Source: Columns 1, 2 and 5: unless otherwise noted, UN 1998c; *columns 3, 4 and 10:* UNICEF 1999c; *column 6:* unless otherwise noted, UNESCO 2000a; *columns 7 and 8:* unless otherwise noted, World Bank 2000b; *column 9:* FAO 1999; *column 11:* UNHCR 1999a.

Technical note. Computing the indices

The human development index

The HDI is based on three indicators: longevity, as measured by life expectancy at birth; educational attainment, as measured by a combination of the adult literacy rate (two-thirds weight) and the combined gross primary, secondary and tertiary enrolment ratio (one-third weight); and standard of living, as measured by GDP per capita (PPP US$).

Fixed minimum and maximum values
To construct the index, fixed minimum and maximum values have been established for each of these indicators:
- Life expectancy at birth: 25 years and 85 years.
- Adult literacy rate (age 15 and above): 0% and 100%.
- Combined gross enrolment ratio: 0% and 100%.
- GDP per capita (PPP US$): $100 and $40,000 (PPP US$).

For any component of the HDI individual indices can be computed according to the general formula:

$$\text{Index} = \frac{\text{Actual value} - \text{minimum value}}{\text{Maximum value} - \text{minimum value}}$$

If, for example, the life expectancy at birth in a country is 65 years, the index of life expectancy for this country would be:

$$\text{Life expectancy index} = \frac{65 - 25}{85 - 25} = \frac{40}{60} = 0.667$$

Treatment of income
Constructing the income index is a little more complex. Income enters into the HDI as a surrogate for all the dimensions of human development not reflected in a long and healthy life and in knowledge—in a nutshell, it is a proxy for a decent standard of living. The basic approach in the treatment of income has been driven by the fact that achieving a respectable level of human development does not require unlimited income. To reflect this, income is discounted in calculating the HDI according to the following formula:

$$W(y) = \frac{\log y - \log y_{min}}{\log y_{max} - \log y_{min}}$$

Illustration of the HDI methodology
The construction of the HDI is illustrated with two examples—Ireland and Viet Nam, an industrialized and a developing country.

Country	Life expectancy (years)	Adult literacy rate (% age 15 and above)	Combined gross enrolment ratio (%)	GDP per capita (PPP US$)
Ireland	76.6	99.0	91.4	21,482
Viet Nam	67.8	92.9	62.9	1,689

Life expectancy index

$$\text{Ireland} = \frac{76.6 - 25}{85 - 25} = \frac{51.6}{60} = 0.860$$

$$\text{Viet Nam} = \frac{67.8 - 25}{85 - 25} = \frac{42.8}{60} = 0.713$$

Adult literacy index

$$\text{Ireland} = \frac{99.0 - 0}{100 - 0} = \frac{99.0}{100} = 0.990$$

$$\text{Viet Nam} = \frac{92.9 - 0}{100 - 0} = \frac{92.9}{100} = 0.929$$

Combined gross enrolment index

$$\text{Ireland} = \frac{91.4 - 0}{100 - 0} = 0.914$$

$$\text{Viet Nam} = \frac{62.9 - 0}{100 - 0} = 0.629$$

Educational attainment index
Ireland = [2(0.990) + 1(0.914)]/3 = 0.965
Viet Nam = [2(0.929) + 1(0.629)]/3 = 0.829

Adjusted GDP per capita (PPP US$) index

$$\text{Ireland} = \frac{\log (21,482) - \log (100)}{\log (40,000) - \log (100)} = 0.896$$

$$\text{Viet Nam} = \frac{\log (1,689) - \log (100)}{\log (40,000) - \log (100)} = 0.472$$

Human development index
The HDI is a simple average of the life expectancy index, educational attainment index and adjusted GDP per capita (PPP US$) index, and so is derived by dividing the sum of these three indices by 3.

Country	Life expectancy index	Educational attainment index	Adjusted GDP (PPP US$) index	Sum of the three indices	HDI
Ireland	0.860	0.965	0.896	2.721	0.907
Viet Nam	0.713	0.829	0.472	2.014	0.671

The gender-related development index and the gender empowerment measure

For comparisons among countries the GDI and the GEM are limited to data available in international data sets. For this year's Report we have endeavoured to use the most recent, reliable and internally consistent data. Collecting more extensive and more reliable gender-disaggregated data is a challenge that the international community should squarely face. We continue to publish results on the GDI and the GEM—based on the best available estimates—in the expectation that it will help increase the demand for such data.

The construction of the GDI and the GEM requires that their income variable, in conformity with the income variable in the HDI, be per capita male GDP (PPP US$) and per capita female GDP (PPP US$). In the *Human Development Reports* before 1999 the GDI and GEM variable did not reflect per capita female and male GDP (PPP US$) and was subject to double discounting. This inconsistency, brought out clearly in Bardhan and Klasen (1999), was rectified in *Human Development Report 1999*.

The gender-related development index

The GDI uses the same variables as the HDI. The difference is that the GDI adjusts the average achievement of each country in life expectancy, educational attainment and income in accordance with the disparity in achievement between women and men. (For a detailed explanation of the GDI methodology see technical note 1 in *Human Development Report 1995*.) For this gender-sensitive adjustment we use a weighting formula that expresses a moderate aversion to inequality, setting the weighting parameter, ϵ, equal to 2. This is the harmonic mean of the male and female values.

The GDI also adjusts the maximum and minimum values for life expectancy, to account for the fact that women tend to live longer than men. For women the maximum value is 87.5 years and the minimum value 27.5 years; for men the corresponding values are 82.5 and 22.5 years.

Calculating the index for income is fairly complex. Values of per capita GDP (PPP US$) for women and men are calculated from the female share (s_f) and male share (s_m) of earned income. These shares, in turn, are estimated from the ratio of the female wage (w_f) to the male wage (w_m) and the percentage shares of women (ea_f) and men (ea_m) in the economically active population. When data on the wage ratio are not available, a value of 75% is used. The estimates of female and male per capita income (PPP US$) are treated in the same way as income is treated in the HDI and then used to compute the equally distributed income index.

$$\text{Female share of the wage bill} = \frac{(w_f/w_m) \times ea_f}{[(w_f/w_m) \times ea_f] + ea_m}$$

Assuming that the female share of earned income is exactly equal to the female share of the wage bill,

$$s_f = \frac{(w_f/w_m) \times ea_f}{[(w_f/w_m) \times ea_f] + ea_m}$$

If it is now assumed that the total GDP (PPP US$) of a country ($Y$) is also divided between women and men according to s_f, the total GDP (PPP US$) going to women is given by ($s_f \times Y$) and the total GDP (PPP US$) to men by [$Y - (s_f \times Y)$].

Per capita GDP (PPP US$) of women is $y_f = s_f \times Y/N_f$, where N_f is the total female population.
Per capita GDP (PPP US$) of men is $y_m = [Y - (s_f \times Y)]/N_m$, where N_m is the total male population.

Treating income the same way as in the construction of the HDI, the adjusted income for women, $W(y_f)$, is given by:

$$W(y_f) = \frac{\log y_f - \log y_{\min}}{\log y_{\max} - \log y_{\min}}$$

The adjusted income for men, $W(y_m)$, is given by:

$$W(y_m) = \frac{\log y_m - \log y_{\min}}{\log y_{\max} - \log y_{\min}}$$

The equally distributed income index is given by:

{[female population share $\times$ (adjusted female per capita PPP US$ GDP)$^{-1}$] + [male population share $\times$ (adjusted male per capita PPP US$ GDP)$^{-1}$]}$^{-1}$

The indices for life expectancy, educational attainment and income are added together with equal weight to derive the final GDI value.

Illustration of the GDI methodology

We choose Ecuador to illustrate the steps for calculating the gender-related development index. The parameter of inequality aversion, ϵ, equals 2.

Population (millions)
Total   12.175
Females   6.060
Males   6.115

Percentage share of population
Females   49.8
Males   50.2

STEP ONE
Computing the equally distributed life expectancy index

Life expectancy at birth (years)
Females   72.7
Males   67.5

Life expectancy index
Females $(72.7 - 27.5)/60 = 0.753$
Males $(67.5 - 22.5)/60 = 0.750$

Equally distributed life expectancy index
{[female population share $\times$ (female life expectancy index)$^{-1}$] + [male population share $\times$ (male life expectancy index)$^{-1}$]}$^{-1}$
$[0.498(0.753)^{-1} + 0.502(0.750)^{-1}]^{-1} = 0.752$

STEP TWO
Computing the equally distributed educational attainment index

Adult literacy rate (percent, age 15 and above)
Females   88.7
Males   92.5

Adult literacy index
Females $(88.7 - 0)/100 = 0.887$
Males $(92.5 - 0)/100 = 0.925$

Combined gross enrolment ratio (percent)
Females   72.0
Males   75.3

Combined gross enrolment index
Females $(72.0 - 0)/100 = 0.720$
Males $(75.3 - 0)/100 = 0.753$

Educational attainment index
2/3(adult literacy index) + 1/3(combined gross enrolment index)
Females   2/3(0.887) + 1/3(0.720) = 0.832
Males   2/3(0.925) + 1/3(0.753) = 0.868

Equally distributed educational attainment index
{[female population share × (educational attainment index)$^{-1}$] + [male population share × (educational attainment index)$^{-1}$]}$^{-1}$
$[0.498(0.832)^{-1} + 0.502(0.868)^{-1}]^{-1} = 0.849$

STEP THREE
Computing the equally distributed income index

Percentage share of the economically active population
Females (ea_f)   27.5
Males (ea_m)   72.5

Ratio of female non-agricultural wage
to male non-agricultural wage (w_f/w_m): 0.637

GDP per capita: $3,003 (PPP US$)

Total GDP (PPP US$): $3,003 × 12.175 million = $36,566 million (PPP US$)

$$s_f = \frac{0.637 \times 0.275}{(0.637 \times 0.275) + 0.725}$$

$$= \frac{0.175}{0.175 + 0.725}$$

$$= 0.194$$

Female total GDP (PPP US$) = 0.194 × $36,566 million (PPP US$)
                           = $7,106 million (PPP US$)
Male total GDP (PPP US$) = $36,566 million (PPP US$) − $7,106 million (PPP US$)
                         = $29,460 million (PPP US$)

Per capita female GDP (PPP US$) = $7,106 million/6.060 million = $1,173 (PPP US$)
Per capita male GDP (PPP US$) = $29,460 million/6.115 million = $4,818 (PPP US$)

$W(y_f) = [\log (1,173) - \log (100)]/[\log (40,000) - \log (100)]$
       $= (3.069 - 2.000)/(4.602 - 2.000)$
       $= 1.069/2.602$
       $= 0.411$

$W(y_m) = [\log (4,818) - \log (100)]/[\log (40,000) - \log (100)]$
        $= (3.683 - 2.000)/(4.602 - 2.000)$
        $= 1.683/2.602$
        $= 0.647$

Equally distributed income index
({female population share × $[W(y_f)]^{-1}$} + {male population share × $[W(y_m)]^{-1}$})$^{-1}$
$[0.498 \times (0.411)^{-1} + 0.502 \times (0.647)^{-1}]^{-1}$
$= [0.498 \times 2.433 + 0.502 \times 1.546]^{-1}$
$= [1.988]^{-1}$
$= 0.503$

STEP FOUR
Computing the GDI
1/3(0.752 + 0.849 + 0.503) = 0.701

The gender empowerment measure
The GEM uses variables constructed explicitly to measure the relative empow-

erment of women and men in political and economic spheres of activity.

The first two variables are chosen to reflect economic participation and decision-making power: women's and men's percentage shares of administrative and managerial positions and their percentage shares of professional and technical jobs. These are broad, loosely defined occupational categories. Because the relevant population for each is different, we calculate a separate index for each and then add the two together. The third variable, women's and men's percentage shares of parliamentary seats, is chosen to reflect political participation and decision-making power.

For all three of these variables we use the methodology of population-weighted $(1 - \epsilon)$ averaging to derive an "equally distributed equivalent percentage" (EDEP) for both sexes taken together. Each variable is indexed by dividing the EDEP by 50%.

An income variable is used to reflect power over economic resources. It is calculated in the same way as for the GDI except that unadjusted rather than adjusted GDP per capita is used.

The three indices—for economic participation and decision-making, political participation and decision-making, and power over economic resources—are added together to derive the final GEM value.

Illustration of the GEM methodology
We choose Lithuania to illustrate the steps in calculating the GEM. The parameter of inequality aversion, ϵ, equals 2.

Population (millions)
Total   3.694
Females   1.949
Males   1.745

Percentage share of population
Females   52.77
Males   47.23

STEP ONE
Calculating indices for parliamentary representation and administrative and managerial, and professional and technical, positions

Percentage share of parliamentary representation
Females   17.52
Males   82.48

Percentage share of administrative and managerial positions
Females   35.67
Males   64.33

Percentage share of professional and technical positions
Females   69.74
Males   30.26

Calculating the EDEP for parliamentary representation
$[0.528(17.52)^{-1} + 0.472(82.48)^{-1}]^{-1} = 27.9$
Calculating the EDEP for administrative and managerial positions
$[0.528(35.7)^{-1} + 0.472(64.3)^{-1}]^{-1} = 45.2$
Calculating the EDEP for professional and technical positions
$[0.528(69.7)^{-1} + 0.472(30.3)^{-1}]^{-1} = 43.2$
Indexing parliamentary representation
27.9/50 = 0.558
Indexing administrative and managerial positions
45.2/50 = 0.903
Indexing professional and technical positions
43.2/50 = 0.863
Combining the indices for administrative and managerial, and professional and technical, positions
(0.903 + 0.863)/2 = 0.883

STEP TWO
Calculating the index for female and male income

Percentage share of the economically active population
Females (ea_f)   47.9
Males (ea_m)   52.1

Ratio of female non-agricultural wage to male non-agricultural wage (w_f/w_m): 0.764

Per capita GDP (PPP US$): $6,436 (PPP US$)

Total GDP (PPP US$): $6,436 × 3.694 million = $23,772 million (PPP US$)

$$s_f = \frac{0.764 \times 0.479}{(0.764 \times 0.479) + 0.521}$$

$$= \frac{0.366}{0.366 + 0.521}$$

$$= 0.413$$

Female total GDP (PPP US$) = 0.413 × $23,772 million (PPP US$)
= $9,818 million (PPP US$)
Male total GDP (PPP US$) = $23,772 million (PPP US$) − $9,818 million (PPP US$)
= $13,954 million (PPP US$)
Per capita female GDP (PPP US$) = $9,818 million/1.949 million = $5,037 (PPP US$)
Per capita male GDP (PPP US$) = $13,954 million/1.745 million = $7,998 (PPP US$)

$$\text{Index of female per capita GDP} = \frac{5,037 - 100}{40,000 - 100}$$

$$= \frac{4,937}{39,900}$$

$$= 0.124$$

$$\text{Index of male per capita GDP} = \frac{7,998 - 100}{40,000 - 100}$$

$$= \frac{7,898}{39,900}$$

$$= 0.198$$

Calculating the equally distributed income index
$[0.528(0.124)^{-1} + 0.472(0.198)^{-1}]^{-1} = 0.150$

STEP THREE
Computing the GEM
1/3(0.558 + 0.883 + 0.150)
= 1/3(1.591)
= 0.531

The human poverty index

Computing the human poverty index for developing countries
The human poverty index for developing countries (HPI-1) concentrates on deprivations in three essential dimensions of human life already reflected in the HDI—longevity, knowledge and a decent standard of living. The first deprivation relates to survival—vulnerability to death at a relatively early age. The second relates to knowledge—being excluded from the world of reading and communication. The third relates to a decent living standard in terms of overall economic provisioning.

In constructing the HPI-1, the deprivation in longevity is represented by the percentage of people not expected to survive to age 40 (P_1), and the deprivation in knowledge by the percentage of adults who are illiterate (P_2). The deprivation in living standard is represented by a composite (P_3) of three variables—the percentage of people without access to safe water (P_{31}), the percentage of people without access to health services (P_{32}) and the percentage of moderately and severely underweight children under five (P_{33}).

The composite variable P_3 is constructed by taking a simple average of the three variables P_{31}, P_{32} and P_{33}. Thus

$$P_3 = \frac{(P_{31} + P_{32} + P_{33})}{3}$$

Following technical note 1 in *Human Development Report 1997*, the formula for the HPI-1 is given by:

$$\text{HPI-1} = [1/3(P_1^3 + P_2^3 + P_3^3)]^{1/3}$$

As an example, we compute the HPI-1 for Zambia.

Country	P_1 (%)	P_2 (%)	P_{31} (%)	P_{32} (%)	P_{33} (%)
Zambia	46.2	23.7	62.0	25.0	24.0

STEP ONE
Calculating P_3

$$x = \frac{62 + 25 + 24}{3} = 37.0$$

STEP TWO
Constructing the HPI-1

$$\begin{aligned}\text{HPI-1} &= [1/3(46.2^3 + 23.7^3 + 37.0^3)]^{1/3}\\ &= [1/3(98,611.2 + 13,312 + 50,653)]^{1/3}\\ &= [1/3(162,576.2)]^{1/3}\\ &= 54,192.067^{1/3}\\ &= 37.9\end{aligned}$$

Computing the human poverty index for industrialized countries
The human poverty index for industrialized countries (HPI-2) concentrates on deprivations in four dimensions of human life, quite similar to those reflected in the HDI—longevity, knowledge, a decent standard of living and social inclusion. (The HPI-2 is used for all OECD countries except the Czech Republic, Hungary, the Republic of Korea, Mexico, Poland and Turkey.) The first deprivation relates to survival—vulnerability to death at a relatively early age. The second relates to knowledge—being deprived of the world of reading and communication. The third relates to a decent standard of living in terms of overall economic provisioning. And the fourth relates to non-participation or exclusion.

In constructing the HPI-2, the deprivation in longevity is represented by the percentage of people not expected to survive to age 60 (P_1), and the deprivation in knowledge by the percentage of people who are functionally illiterate as defined by the OECD (P_2). The deprivation in standard of living is represented by the percentage of people living below the income poverty line, set at 50% of the median disposable household income (P_3). And the fourth deprivation, in non-participation or exclusion, is measured by the rate of long-term (12 months or more) unemployment (P_4) of the labour force.

Following technical note 1 in *Human Development Report 1998*, the formula for the HPI-2 is given by:

$$\text{HPI-2} = [1/4(P_1^3 + P_2^3 + P_3^3 + P_4^3)]^{1/3}$$

As an example, we compute the HPI-2 for Australia.

Country	P_1 (%)	P_2 (%)	P_3 (%)	P_4 (%)
Australia	8.8	17.0	2.7	11.9

Constructing the HPI-2

$$\text{HPI-2} = [1/4(8.8^3 + 17.0^3 + 2.7^3 + 11.9^3)]^{1/3}$$
$$= [1/4(681.5 + 4{,}913.0 + 19.68 + 1{,}685.2)]^{1/3}$$
$$= [1/4(7{,}299.38)]^{1/3}$$
$$= 1{,}824.85^{1/3}$$
$$= 12.2$$

Note

Calculations based on the data given in the technical note may yield results that differ from those shown because of rounding.

Primary statistical references

CDIAC (Carbon Dioxide Information Analysis Center). 1999. "CO2 Emissions." [http://cdiac.esd.ornl.gov/ftp/ndp030/global96.ems]. February 1999.

Child Info. 2000. "Child Mortality: Mongolia." [http://www.childinfo.org/cmr/cmrmgl.html]. March 2000.

EMEP (Co-operative Programme for Monitoring and Evaluation of the Long-Range Transmission of Air Pollutants in Europe). 1999. "Tables of Anthropogenic Emissions in the ECE Region." [http://www.emep.int/emis_tables/tab1.html]. November 1999.

FAO (Food and Agriculture Organization of the United Nations). 1999. "Food Balance Sheets." [http://apps.fao.org/lim500/nph-rap.pl?foodBalanceSheet&Domain=FoodBalanceSheet]. October 1999.

——. 2000. "Food Aid." [http://www.fao.org]. February 2000.

Goldschmidt-Clermont, Luisella, and Elisabetta Pagnossin Aligisakis. 1995. "Measures of Unrecorded Economic Activities in Fourteen Countries." Background paper for UNDP, *Human Development Report 1995*. United Nations Development Programme, Human Development Report Office, New York.

Harvey, Andrew S. 1995. "Market and Non-Market Productive Activity in Less Developed and Developing Countries: Lessons from Time Use." Background paper for UNDP, *Human Development Report 1995*. United Nations Development Programme, Human Development Report Office, New York.

Heston, Alan, and Robert Summers. 1999. Correspondence on data on GDP per capita (PPP US$). University of Pennsylvania, Department of Economics, Philadelphia. March.

IISS (International Institute for Strategic Studies). 1999. *The Military Balance 1999–2000*. Oxford: Oxford University Press.

ILO (International Labour Organization). 1996. *Estimates and Projections of the Economically Active Population, 1950–2010*. 4th ed. Diskette. Geneva.

——. 1997d. *Yearbook of Labour Statistics 1997*. Geneva.

——. 1999c. *Yearbook of Labour Statistics 1999*. Geneva.

——. 2000. ILO database on international labour standards (ILOLEX). [http://ilolex.ilo.ch:1567/public/english/50normes/infleg/iloeng/index.htm]. April 2000.

International IDEA (Institute for Democracy and Electoral Assistance). 1997. *Voter Turnout from 1945 to 1997: A Global Report*. Stockholm.

IPU (Inter-Parliamentary Union). 1995. *Women in Parliaments 1945–1995: A World Statistical Survey*. Geneva.

——. 2000a. Correspondence on date of latest elections, political parties represented and voter turnout. March. Geneva.

——. 2000b. Correspondence on year women received the right to vote and stand for election, and the year the first woman was elected or appointed to parliament. March. Geneva.

——. 2000c. "Parline Database." [http://www.ipu.org/parline-e/parlinesearch.asp]. March 2000.

——. 2000d. "Women in Parliament." [http://www.ipu.org/wmn-e/classif.htm]. February 2000.

ITU (International Telecommunication Union). 1998. *World Telecommunication Indicators*. Database. Geneva.

LIS (Luxembourg Income Study). 2000. "Population below Income Poverty Line." [http://lissy.ceps.lu/lim.htm]. January 2000.

Milanovic, Branko. 1998. *Income, Inequality and Poverty during the Transition from Planned to Market Economy*. Washington, D.C.: World Bank.

OECD (Organisation for Economic Co-operation and Development). 1999a. *Economic Outlook*. Paris.

——. 1999b. *Employment Outlook 1999*. Paris.

——. 1999c. *Environmental Data Compendium 1999*. Paris.

OECD (Organisation for Economic Co-operation and Development), Development Assistance Committee. 2000. *Development Co-operation 1999 Report*. Paris.

OECD (Organisation for Economic Co-operation and Development) and Statistics Canada. 2000. *Literacy in the Information Age—Final Report on the IALS*. Paris.

OFDA (Office of U.S. Foreign Disaster Assistance) and CRED (Centre for Research on the Epidemiology of Disasters). 2000. "EM-DAT: The OFDA/CRED International Disaster Database." Université Catholique de Louvain, Brussels, Belgium. [http://www.md.ucl.ac.be/cred]. March 2000.

Psacharopoulos, George, and Zafiris Tzannatos, eds. 1992. *Case Studies on Women's Employment and Pay in Latin America*. Washington, D.C.: World Bank.

SIPRI (Stockholm International Peace Research Institute). 2000. *SIPRI Yearbook 2000—Armaments, Disarmament and International Security*. Oxford: Oxford University Press.

Smeeding, Timothy. 1997. "Financial Poverty in Developed Countries: The Evidence from the Luxembourg Income Study." In UNDP, *Human Development Papers 1997: Poverty and Human Development*. New York.

Standard & Poor's. 2000. "Sovereign Long-Term Debt Ratings." [http://www.standardandpoors.com/ratings/sovereigns/index.htm]. February 2000.

UN (United Nations). 1995b. *World Urbanization Prospects: The 1994 Revision. Database*. Population Division. New York.

——. 1996b. *World Urbanization Prospects: The 1996 Revision. Database*. Population Division. New York.

——. 1998b. "Principles and Recommendations for Population and Housing Censuses. (Revision 1)." Statistical Papers Series M, No. 67/Rev. 1. Statistics Division. New York.

——. 1998c. *World Population Prospects 1950–2050: The 1998 Revision. Database*. Population Division. New York.

——. 2000a. Correspondence on births to mothers under 20. Statistics Division. January. New York.

——. 2000b. Correspondence on women in government. UN Secretariat and Department for Economic and Social Affairs, Division for the Advancement of Women. March. New York.

——. 2000c. *Energy Statistics Yearbook 1997*. New York.

——. 2000d. Fifth United Nations Survey of Crime Trends and Operations of Criminal Justice Systems. United Nations Office at Vienna, Crime Prevention and Criminal Justice Division. Vienna. [http://www.uncjin.org/]. March 2000.

———. 2000e. "Multilateral Treaties Deposited with the Secretary-General." [http://untreaty.un.org]. February 2000.

UNAIDS (Joint United Nations Programme on HIV/AIDS) and WHO (World Health Organization). 2000b. *Report on the Global HIV/AIDS Epidemic.* [http://www.who.int/emc-hiv/global_report/index.html]. March 2000.

UNCTAD (United Nations Conference on Trade and Development). 1999b. *World Investment Report 1999—Foreign Direct Investment and the Challenge of Development.* Geneva.

UNECE (United Nations Economic Commission for Europe). 1999a. Correspondence on injuries and deaths from road accidents. March. Geneva.

———. 1999b. *Trends in Europe and North America 1998–99.* Geneva.

———. 2000. Correspondence on secretariat estimates of unemployment based on national statistics. March. Geneva.

UNESCO (United Nations Educational, Scientific and Cultural Organization). 1999a. Correspondence on age group enrolment ratios. February. Paris.

———. 1999b. Correspondence on female tertiary science enrolment. December. Paris.

———. 1999c. *Statistical Yearbook 1999.* Paris.

———. 2000a. Correspondence on adult literacy rates. January. Paris.

———. 2000b. Correspondence on female tertiary students. February. Paris.

———. 2000c. Correspondence on gross enrolment ratios. February. Paris.

UNHCR (United Nations High Commissioner for Refugees). 1999a. Correspondence on refugees by country of origin. December. Geneva.

———. 1999c. *Refugees and Others of Concern to UNHCR: 1998 Statistical Overview.* Geneva.

UNICEF (United Nations Children's Fund). 1996. *The State of the World's Children 1997.* New York: Oxford University Press.

———. 1998. *The State of the World's Children 1999.* New York: Oxford University Press.

———. 1999c. *The State of the World's Children 2000.* New York: Oxford University Press.

———. 2000. Correspondence on infant mortality and under-five mortality rates. February. New York.

WHO (World Health Organization). 1999b. Correspondence on suicide rates. December. Geneva.

———. 1999c. *Global Tuberculosis Control: WHO Report 1999.* Geneva.

———. 1999d. *Weekly Epidemiological Record* 74: 265–272. [http://www.who.int]. August 1999.

———. 2000a. Correspondence on cigarette consumption per adult. February. Geneva.

———. 2000b. "WHO Estimates of Health Personnel." [http://www.who.int/whosis]. March 2000.

World Bank. 1998. *World Development Indicators 1998.* Washington, D.C.

———. 1999a. Correspondence on unpublished World Bank data on GDP per capita (PPP US$) for 1997. Development Economics Data Group. February. Washington, D.C.

———. 1999b. *World Development Indicators 1999.* Washington, D.C.

———. 2000a. Correspondence on unpublished World Bank data on GDP per capita (PPP US$) for 1998. Development Economics Data Group. February. Washington, D.C.

———. 2000b. *World Development Indicators 2000.* CD-ROM. Washington, D.C.

WRI (World Resources Institute). 1999. *World Resources 1998–99.* New York: Oxford University Press.

———. 2000a. Correspondence on major protected areas. February. Washington, D.C.

———. 2000b. Correspondence on water resources. February. Washington, D.C.

PRIMARY STATISTICAL REFERENCES

Definitions of statistical terms

Following are brief explanations of selected statistical indicators presented in the Report. Detailed definitions can be found in the original sources.

Administrators and managers Defined according to the International Standard Classification of Occupations (ISCO-1968).

Agricultural production Refers to production under divisions 1–5 of the International Standard Industrial Classification (ISIC revision 2).

Aid Refers to flows that qualify as *official development assistance (ODA)* or *official aid* (see these terms).

Bank and trade-related lending Covers commercial bank lending and other private credit.

Budget deficit or surplus Central government current and capital revenue and official grants received, less total expenditure and lending minus repayments.

Carbon dioxide (CO$_2$) emissions Anthropogenic (human-originated) carbon dioxide emissions stemming from the burning of fossil fuels and the production of cement. Emissions are calculated from data on the consumption of solid, liquid and gaseous fuels and gas flaring.

Cellular mobile subscribers People subscribing to a communications service in which voice or data are transmitted by radio frequencies.

Children reaching grade 5 The percentage of children starting primary school who eventually attain grade 5 (grade 4 if the duration of primary school is four years). The estimate is based on the reconstructed cohort method, which uses data on enrolment and repeaters for two consecutive years.

Cigarette consumption per adult The sum of production and imports minus exports of cigarettes divided by the population aged 15 years and older.

Combined gross enrolment ratio See *enrolment ratio, gross.*

Commercial energy use The domestic primary commercial energy supply. It is calculated as local production plus imports and stock changes, minus exports and international marine bunkers.

Contraceptive prevalence rate The percentage of married women of child-bearing age (15–49) who are using, or whose husbands are using, any form of contraception, whether modern or traditional.

Current account balance The difference between (a) exports of goods and services as well as inflows of unrequited transfers but exclusive of foreign aid and (b) imports of goods and services as well as all unrequited transfers to the rest of the world.

Daily per capita calorie supply The calorie equivalent of the net food supply (local production plus imports minus exports) in a country, divided by the population, per day.

Deforestation The permanent clearing of forest land for all agricultural uses and for other land uses such as settlements, other infrastructure and mining. It does not include other alterations such as selective logging.

Dependency ratio The ratio of the population defined as dependent—those under 15 and over 64—to the working-age population, aged 15–64.

Disasters Includes natural and technological disasters. Natural disasters include avalanches, cold waves, cyclones, hurricanes, typhoons, drought, earthquakes, epidemics and famine (but do not include famine relating to conflict because of a lack of reliable data). Technological disasters include accidents, chemical accidents and urban fires.

Disbursement (aid) Records the actual international transfer of financial resources or of goods or services, valued at the cost to the donor.

Doctors Physicians and all graduates of any faculty or school of medicine in any medical field (including practice, teaching, administration and research).

Drug crimes Any crimes involving drugs, including the illicit brokerage, cultivation, delivery, distribution, extraction, exportation or importation, offering for sale, production, purchase, manufacture, sale, traffic, transportation or use of narcotic drugs.

Economic activity rate The proportion of the specified group supplying labour for the production of economic goods and services during a specified period.

Education index One of the three indicators on which the human development index is built. It is based on the combined primary, secondary and tertiary gross enrolment ratio and the adult literacy rate. For details on how the index is calculated, see the technical note.

Education levels Education has been categorized as primary, secondary or tertiary in accordance with the International Standard Classification of Education (ISCED). *Primary education* (ISCED level 1) provides the basic elements of education at such establishments as primary or elementary schools. *Secondary education* (ISCED levels 2 and 3) is based on at least four years of previous instruction at the first level and provides general or specialized instruction, or both, at such institutions as middle school, secondary school, high school, teacher training school at this level and vocational or technical school. *Tertiary education* (ISCED levels 5–7) refers to education at such institutions as universities, teachers colleges and higher-level professional schools—requiring as a minimum condition of admission the successful completion of education at the second level or evidence of the attainment of an equivalent level of knowledge.

Electricity consumption The production of heat and power plants less own use and distribution losses.

Enrolment ratio, age group (adjusted) The *primary school age group enrolment ratio* is the enrolments of primary school age (regardless of the education level in which the pupils are enrolled) as a percentage of the population of official primary school age. The *secondary school age group enrolment ratio* is the enrolments of secondary school age (regardless of the education level in which the pupils are enrolled) as a percentage of the population of official secondary school age. The term *adjusted* indicates that the age groups used to calculate the ratios correspond to the structure of the education system in each country.

Enrolment ratio, gross The number of students enrolled in a level of education, regardless of age, as a percentage of the population of official school age for that level. The combined gross primary, secondary and tertiary enrolment ratio refers to the number of students at all these levels as a percentage of the population of official school age for these levels.

Exports of conventional weapons Exports of weapons as defined under *transfers of conventional weapons* (see this term).

Exports of goods and services The value of all goods and non-factor services provided to the rest of the world, including merchandise freight, insurance, travel and other non-factor services.

External debt Debt owed by a country to non-residents that is repayable in foreign currency, goods or services.

Food aid in cereals The quantity of cereals provided by donor countries and international organizations, including the World Food Programme and the International Wheat Council, as reported for a crop year.

Foreign direct investment (net inflows) Capital provided by a foreign direct investor (parent enterprise) to an affiliate enterprise in the host country. It implies that the foreign direct investor exerts significant influence on the management of the enterprise resident in the other economy. The capital provided can consist of equity capital, reinvested earnings or intracompany loans.

Fresh water withdrawals Total water withdrawals, not counting evaporation losses from storage basins. Withdrawals include water from non-renewable groundwater sources, river flows from other countries and desalination plants in countries where they are a significant source.

Functional illiteracy rate The proportion of the adult population aged 16–65 scoring at level 1 on the prose literacy scale of the International Adult Literacy Survey (IALS).

GDP See *gross domestic product*.

GDP index One of the three indicators on which the human development index is built. It is based on GDP per capita (PPP US$). For details on how the index is calculated, see the technical note.

GDP per capita (PPP US$) The GDP per capita of a country converted into US dollars on the basis of the purchasing power parity (PPP) exchange rate.

GDP per unit of energy use The US dollar estimate of real GDP (at 1995 prices) per kilogram of oil equivalent of commercial energy use.

Gender empowerment measure (GEM) A composite index using variables constructed explicitly to measure the relative empowerment of women and men in political and economic spheres of activity. Three indices—for economic participation and decision-making, for political participation and decision-making and for power over economic resources—are added to derive the final GEM value.

Gender-related development index (GDI) A composite index using the same variables as the human development index. The difference is that the GDI adjusts the average achievement of each country in life expectancy, educational attainment and income in accordance with the disparity in achievement between women and men. For more details on how the index is calculated, see the technical note.

GNP See *gross national product*.

Government consumption Includes all current expenditures for purchases of goods and services by all levels of government, excluding most government enterprises.

Government expenditure Includes non-repayable current and capital expenditure. It does not include government lending or repayments to the government or government acquisition of equity for public policy purposes.

Gross domestic investment Outlays on additions to the fixed assets of the economy plus net changes in the level of inventories.

Gross domestic product (GDP) The total output of goods and services for final use produced by an economy by both residents and non-residents, regardless of the allocation to domestic and foreign claims. It does not include deductions for depreciation of physical capital or depletion and degradation of natural resources.

Gross domestic savings Calculated as the difference between GDP and total consumption.

Gross national product (GNP) Comprises GDP plus net factor income from abroad, which is the income residents receive from abroad for factor services (labour and capital), less similar payments made to non-residents who contribute to the domestic economy.

Hazardous waste Refers to the waste streams to be controlled according to the Basel Convention on the Control of Transboundary Movements of Hazardous Wastes and Their Disposal. The data do not necessarily represent all hazardous waste nor its potential toxicity.

Health services (access to) The proportion of the population that can expect treatment for common diseases and injuries, including essential drugs on the national list, within one hour's walk or travel.

Homicides Intentional deaths purposely inflicted by another person.

Human development index (HDI) A composite index based on three indicators: longevity, as measured by life expectancy at birth; educational attainment, as measured by a combination of adult literacy (two-thirds weight) and the combined gross primary, secondary and tertiary enrolment ratio (one-third weight); and standard of living, as measured by GDP per capita (PPP US$). For more details on how the index is calculated, see the technical note.

Human poverty index (HPI) The human poverty index for developing countries (HPI-1) measures deprivations in three dimensions of human life—longevity, knowledge and a decent standard of living. The HPI for industrialized countries (HPI-2) includes, in addition to these three dimensions, social exclusion. For more details on how these indices are calculated, see the technical note.

Illiteracy rate (adult) Calculated as 100 minus the *literacy rate (adult)* (see this term).

Imports of conventional weapons Imports of weapons as defined under *transfers of conventional weapons* (see this term).

Imports of goods and services The value of all goods and non-factor services purchased from the rest of the world, including merchandise freight, insurance, travel and other non-factor services.

Industrial production Comprises value added in mining, manufacturing, construction, electricity, water and gas.

Infant mortality rate The probability of dying between birth and exactly one year of age times 1,000.

Infants with low birth-weight The percentage of babies born weighing less than 2,500 grams.

Inflation A fall in the purchasing power of money reflected in a persistent increase in the general level of prices as generally measured by the retail price index.

Internal renewable water resources Refers to the average annual flow of rivers and recharge of groundwater generated from endogenous precipitation.

Internally displaced Refers to people who are displaced within their own country and to whom the United Nations High Commissioner for Refugees extends protection or assistance, or both, in pursuance to a special request by a competent organ of the United Nations.

International tourism departures The number of departures that people make from their country of usual residence to any other country for any purpose other than a remunerated activity in the country visited.

Internet host A computer system connected to the Internet—either a single terminal directly connected or a computer that allows multiple users to access network services through it.

Involuntary part-time workers Part-time workers who say they are working part time because they could not find full-time work.

Life expectancy at birth The number of years a newborn infant would live if prevailing patterns of mortality at the time of birth were to stay the same throughout the child's life.

Life expectancy index One of the three indicators on which the human development index is built. For details on how the index is calculated, see the technical note.

Literacy rate (adult) The percentage of people aged 15 and above who can, with understanding, both read and write a short, simple statement on their everyday life.

Main telephone line Refers to a telephone line connecting a subscriber to the telephone exchange equipment.

Major protected areas See *protected areas (major)*.

Maternal mortality ratio The annual number of deaths of women from pregnancy-related causes per 100,000 live births.

Military expenditure All expenditures of the defence ministry and other ministries on recruiting and training military personnel as well as on construction and purchase of military supplies and equipment. Military assistance is included in the expenditures of the donor country.

Municipal waste Waste collected by municipalities or by their order that has been generated by households, commercial activities, office buildings, schools, government buildings and small businesses.

Nuclear waste generated Refers to spent fuel, one part of the radioactive waste generated at various stages of the fuel cycle (uranium mining and milling, fuel enrichment, reactor operation, spent fuel reprocessing). Data do not represent all radioactive waste generated, and the amounts of spent fuel generated depend on the share of nuclear electricity in the energy supply and on the nuclear plant technologies adopted.

Official aid Grants or loans that meet the same standards as for *official development assistance (ODA)* (see that term) except that recipients do not qualify as recipients of ODA. Part two of the Development Assistance Committee (DAC) list of recipient countries identifies these countries.

Official development assistance (ODA) Grants or loans to qualifying developing countries or territories, identified in part one of the Development Assistance Committee (DAC) list of recipient countries, that are undertaken by the official sector with promotion of economic development and welfare as the main objective, on concessional financial terms.

Oral rehydration therapy use rate The percentage of all cases of diarrhoea in children under five years of age treated with oral rehydration salts, recommended home fluids or both.

Paper (printing and writing) consumed Newsprint and other paper used in printing or writing. This does not cover articles manufactured from printing paper, such as stationery, exercise books, registers and the like.

Part-time employment Refers to people who usually work less than 30 hours a week in their main job. Data include only people declaring usual hours.

People incarcerated The number of people in prison. *Prison* refers to all public and privately financed institutions in which people are deprived of their liberty. These institutions could include, but are not limited to, penal, correctional or psychiatric facilities.

Population Includes all residents regardless of legal status or citizenship—except for refugees not permanently settled in the country of asylum, who are generally considered part of the population of their country of origin. Data refer to midyear estimates.

Population below income poverty line Refers to the percentage of the population living below the specified poverty line:
- *$1 a day*—at 1993 international prices, adjusted for purchasing power parity.
- *$2 a day*—at 1993 international prices, adjusted for purchasing power parity.
- *$4 a day*—at 1990 international prices, adjusted for purchasing power parity.
- *$14.40 a day*—at 1985 international prices, adjusted for purchasing power parity.
- *National poverty line*—the poverty line deemed appropriate for a country by its authorities.
- *50% of median income*—50% of the median disposable household income.

Portfolio investment flows (net) Non-debt-creating portfolio equity flows (the sum of country funds, depository receipts and direct purchases of shares by foreign investors) and portfolio debt flows (bond issues purchased by foreign investors).

Primary education See *education levels*.

Printing and writing paper See *paper (printing and writing) consumed*.

Private consumption The market value of all goods and services, including durable products, purchased or received as income in kind by households and non-profit institutions.

Probability of surviving to age 40 (60) The probability of a newborn infant surviving to age 40 (60) if the prevailing patterns of age-specific mortality at the time of birth remain the same throughout the child's life.

Professional and technical workers Defined according to the International Standard Classification of Occupations (ISCO-1968).

Protected areas (major) Natural areas of at least 1,000 hectares that are totally or partially protected.

Public expenditure on education Public spending on public education plus subsidies to private education at the primary, secondary and tertiary levels. It includes expenditure at every level of administration—central, regional and local.

Public expenditure on health Recurrent and capital spending from central and local government budgets, external borrowings and grants (including donations from international agencies and non-governmental organizations) and social health insurance funds.

Purchasing power parity (PPP) At the PPP rate, one dollar has the same purchasing power over domestic GDP as the US dollar has over US GDP. PPP could also be expressed in other national currencies or in special drawing rights (SDRs). PPP rates allow a standard comparison of real price levels between countries, just as conventional price indices allow comparison of real values over time; normal exchange rates may over- or undervalue purchasing power.

Refugees People who have fled their country because of a well-founded fear of persecution for reasons of their race, religion, nationality, political opinion or membership in a particular social group, and who cannot or do not want to return.

Safe water (access to) The proportion of the population using any of the following types of water supply for drinking: piped water, public tap, borehole or pump, well (protected or covered) or protected spring.

Sanitation (access to) The proportion of the population who have, within their dwelling or compound, a toilet connected to a sewerage system, any other flush toilet, an improved pit latrine or a traditional pit latrine.

Seats in parliament held by women Refers to seats held by women in a lower or single house and an upper house or senate, where relevant.

Secondary education See *education levels*.

Services production Refers to production under divisions 50–99 of the International Standard Industrial Classification (ISIC revision 2).

Share of ODA through NGOs The percentage of *official development assistance* (see this term) distributed through non-governmental organizations.

Shares of income or consumption The distribution of income or expenditure accruing to percentile groups of households ranked by total household income or consumption.

Sovereign long-term debt rating As determined by Standard & Poor's, an assessment of a country's capacity and willingness to repay debt according to its terms. The ratings range from AAA to CC (investment grade AAA to BBB–, and speculative grade BB+ and lower).

Sulphur dioxide (SO$_2$) emissions Emissions of sulphur in the form of sulphur oxides and of nitrogen in the form of its various oxides, which together contribute to acid rain and adversely affect agriculture, forests, aquatic habitats and the weathering of building materials.

Tax revenue Compulsory, unrequited, non-repayable receipts collected by central governments for public purposes.

Tertiary education See *education levels*.

Time allocation and time use Allocation of time between market (SNA) and non-market (non-SNA) activities according to the UN System of National Accounts (SNA).

Total armed forces Strategic, land, naval, air, command, administrative and support forces. Also included are paramilitary forces such as the gendarmerie, customs service and border guard if these are trained in military tactics.

Total debt service The sum of principal repayments and interest actually paid in foreign currency, goods or services on long-term debt, interest paid on short-term debt and repayments to the International Monetary Fund. Total debt service is an important indicator of a country's relative external debt servicing burden.

Total fertility rate The average number of children that would be born alive to a woman during her lifetime if she were to bear children at each age in accord with prevailing age-specific fertility rates.

Traditional fuel consumption Estimated consumption of fuel wood, charcoal, bagasse and animal and vegetable wastes. Traditional fuel use together with commercial energy use make up total energy use.

Transfers of conventional weapons (arms trade) Refers to orders and deliveries of major conventional weapons (rather than contracts placed), such as air-

craft, armoured vehicles, artillery, guidance and radar systems, missiles and ships. Items must be transferred voluntarily by the supplier and be destined for the armed forces, paramilitary forces or intelligence agencies of another country.

Under-five mortality rate The probability of dying between birth and exactly five years of age times 1,000.

Underweight children under age five The percentage of the population under five years of age with moderate or severe underweight, defined as a weight below minus two standard deviations from the median weight.

Unemployment All people above a specified age who are not in paid employment or self-employed, but are available and have taken specific steps to seek paid employment or self-employment.

Unpaid family workers Household members involved in unremunerated subsistence and non-market activities, such as agricultural production for household consumption, and in household enterprises producing for the market for which more than one household member provides unpaid labor.

Urban population The midyear population of areas defined as urban in each country and reported to the United Nations. Because the data are based on national definitions of what constitutes a city or metropolitan area, cross-country comparisons should be made with caution.

Voter turnout The number of votes (including blank or invalid votes) as a percentage of the number of registered voters.

Waste recycling The reuse of material that diverts it from the waste stream, except for recycling within industrial plants and the reuse of material as fuel.

Classification of countries

Countries in the human development aggregates

High human development (HDI 0.800 and above)

Antigua and Barbuda
Argentina
Australia
Austria
Bahamas
Bahrain
Barbados
Belgium
Brunei Darussalam
Canada
Chile
Cyprus
Czech Republic
Denmark
Estonia
Finland
France
Germany
Greece
Hong Kong, China (SAR)
Hungary
Iceland
Ireland
Israel
Italy
Japan
Korea, Rep. of
Kuwait
Luxembourg
Malta
Netherlands
New Zealand
Norway
Poland
Portugal
Qatar
Singapore
Slovakia
Slovenia
Spain
Sweden
Switzerland
United Arab Emirates
United Kingdom
United States
Uruguay

Medium human development (HDI 0.500–0.799)

Albania
Algeria
Armenia
Azerbaijan
Belarus
Belize
Bolivia
Botswana
Brazil
Bulgaria
Cambodia
Cameroon
Cape Verde
China
Colombia
Comoros
Congo
Costa Rica
Croatia
Cuba
Dominica
Dominican Republic
Ecuador
Egypt
El Salvador
Equatorial Guinea
Fiji
Gabon
Georgia
Ghana
Grenada
Guatemala
Guyana
Honduras
India
Indonesia
Iran, Islamic Rep. of
Iraq
Jamaica
Jordan
Kazakhstan
Kenya
Kyrgyzstan
Latvia
Lebanon
Lesotho
Libyan Arab Jamahiriya

Lithuania
Macedonia, TFYR
Malaysia
Maldives
Mauritius
Mexico
Moldova, Rep. of
Mongolia
Morocco
Myanmar
Namibia
Nicaragua
Oman
Pakistan
Panama
Papua New Guinea
Paraguay
Peru
Philippines
Romania
Russian Federation
Saint Kitts and Nevis
Saint Lucia
Saint Vincent and the
  Grenadines
Samoa (Western)
São Tomé and Principe
Saudi Arabia
Seychelles
Solomon Islands
South Africa
Sri Lanka
Suriname
Swaziland
Syrian Arab Republic
Tajikistan
Thailand
Trinidad and Tobago
Tunisia
Turkey
Turkmenistan
Ukraine
Uzbekistan
Vanuatu
Venezuela
Viet Nam
Zimbabwe

Low human development (HDI below 0.500)

Angola
Bangladesh
Benin
Bhutan
Burkina Faso
Burundi
Central African Republic
Chad
Congo, Dem. Rep. of the
Côte d'Ivoire
Djibouti
Eritrea
Ethiopia
Gambia
Guinea
Guinea-Bissau
Haiti
Lao People's Dem. Rep.
Madagascar
Malawi
Mali
Mauritania
Mozambique
Nepal
Niger
Nigeria
Rwanda
Senegal
Sierra Leone
Sudan
Tanzania, U. Rep. of
Togo
Uganda
Yemen
Zambia

Countries in the income aggregates [a]

High income (GNP per capita of $9,361 or more in 1998)

Australia
Austria
Bahamas
Belgium
Brunei Darussalam
Canada
Cyprus
Denmark
Finland
France
Germany
Greece
Hong Kong, China (SAR)
Iceland
Ireland
Israel
Italy
Japan
Kuwait
Luxembourg
Malta
Netherlands
New Zealand
Norway
Portugal
Qatar
Singapore
Slovenia
Spain
Sweden
Switzerland
United Arab Emirates
United Kingdom
United States

Middle income (GNP per capita of $761–9,360 in 1998)

Albania
Algeria
Antigua and Barbuda
Argentina
Bahrain
Barbados
Belarus
Belize
Bolivia
Botswana
Brazil
Bulgaria
Cape Verde
Chile
Colombia
Costa Rica
Croatia
Cuba
Czech Republic
Djibouti
Dominica
Dominican Republic
Ecuador
Egypt
El Salvador
Equatorial Guinea
Estonia
Fiji
Gabon
Georgia
Grenada
Guatemala
Guyana
Hungary
Iran, Islamic Rep. of
Iraq
Jamaica
Jordan
Kazakhstan
Korea, Rep. of
Latvia
Lebanon
Libyan Arab Jamahiriya
Lithuania
Macedonia, TFYR
Malaysia
Maldives
Mauritius
Mexico
Morocco
Namibia
Oman
Panama
Papua New Guinea
Paraguay
Peru
Philippines
Poland
Romania
Russian Federation
Saint Kitts and Nevis
Saint Lucia
Saint Vincent and the
  Grenadines
Samoa (Western)
Saudi Arabia
Seychelles
Slovakia
South Africa
Sri Lanka
Suriname
Swaziland
Syrian Arab Republic
Thailand
Trinidad and Tobago
Tunisia
Turkey
Ukraine
Uruguay
Uzbekistan
Vanuatu
Venezuela

Low income (GNP per capita of $760 or less in 1998)

Angola
Armenia
Azerbaijan
Bangladesh
Benin
Bhutan
Burkina Faso
Burundi
Cambodia
Cameroon
Central African Republic
Chad
China
Comoros
Congo
Congo, Dem. Rep. of the
Côte d'Ivoire
Eritrea
Ethiopia
Gambia
Ghana
Guinea
Guinea-Bissau
Haiti
Honduras
India
Indonesia
Kenya
Kyrgyzstan
Lao People's Dem. Rep.
Lesotho
Madagascar
Malawi
Mali
Mauritania
Moldova, Rep. of
Mongolia
Mozambique
Myanmar
Nepal
Nicaragua
Niger
Nigeria
Pakistan
Rwanda
São Tomé and Principe
Senegal
Sierra Leone
Solomon Islands
Sudan
Tajikistan
Tanzania, U. Rep. of
Togo
Turkmenistan
Uganda
Viet Nam
Yemen
Zambia
Zimbabwe

a. Based on World Bank classifications (valid through July 2000).

All developing countries

Algeria	Iran, Islamic Rep. of	Tanzania, U. Rep. of	Tanzania, U. Rep. of
Angola	Iraq	Thailand	Togo
Antigua and Barbuda	Jamaica	Togo	Uganda
Argentina	Jordan	Trinidad and Tobago	Vanuatu
Bahamas	Kenya	Tunisia	Yemen
Bahrain	Korea, Rep. of	Turkey	Zambia
Bangladesh	Kuwait	Uganda	
Barbados	Lao People's Dem. Rep.	United Arab Emirates	
Belize	Lebanon	Uruguay	
Benin	Lesotho	Vanuatu	
Bhutan	Libyan Arab Jamahiriya	Venezuela	
Bolivia	Madagascar	Viet Nam	
Botswana	Malawi	Yemen	
Brazil	Malaysia	Zambia	
Brunei Darussalam	Maldives	Zimbabwe	
Burkina Faso	Mali		
Burundi	Mauritania		
Cambodia	Mauritius	**Least developed**	
Cameroon	Mexico	**countries**	
Cape Verde	Mongolia	Angola	
Central African Republic	Morocco	Bangladesh	
Chad	Mozambique	Benin	
Chile	Myanmar	Bhutan	
China	Namibia	Burkina Faso	
Colombia	Nepal	Burundi	
Comoros	Nicaragua	Cambodia	
Congo	Niger	Cape Verde	
Congo, Dem. Rep. of the	Nigeria	Central African Republic	
Costa Rica	Oman	Chad	
Côte d'Ivoire	Pakistan	Comoros	
Cuba	Panama	Congo, Dem. Rep. of the	
Cyprus	Papua New Guinea	Djibouti	
Djibouti	Paraguay	Equatorial Guinea	
Dominica	Peru	Eritrea	
Dominican Republic	Philippines	Ethiopia	
Ecuador	Qatar	Gambia	
Egypt	Rwanda	Guinea	
El Salvador	Saint Kitts and Nevis	Guinea-Bissau	
Equatorial Guinea	Saint Lucia	Haiti	
Eritrea	Saint Vincent and the	Lao People's Dem. Rep.	
Ethiopia	Grenadines	Lesotho	
Fiji	Samoa (Western)	Madagascar	
Gabon	São Tomé and Principe	Malawi	
Gambia	Saudi Arabia	Maldives	
Ghana	Senegal	Mali	
Grenada	Seychelles	Mauritania	
Guatemala	Sierra Leone	Mozambique	
Guinea	Singapore	Myanmar	
Guinea-Bissau	Solomon Islands	Nepal	
Guyana	South Africa	Niger	
Haiti	Sri Lanka	Rwanda	
Honduras	Sudan	Samoa (Western)	
Hong Kong, China (SAR)	Suriname	São Tomé and Principe	
India	Swaziland	Sierra Leone	
Indonesia	Syrian Arab Republic	Solomon Islands	
		Sudan	

Eastern Europe and the Commonwealth of Independent States (CIS)

Albania
Armenia
Azerbaijan
Belarus
Bulgaria
Croatia
Czech Republic
Estonia
Georgia
Hungary
Kazakhstan
Kyrgyzstan
Latvia
Lithuania
Macedonia, TFYR
Moldova, Rep. of
Poland
Romania
Russian Federation
Slovakia
Slovenia
Tajikistan
Turkmenistan
Ukraine
Uzbekistan

OECD countries

Australia
Austria
Belgium
Canada
Czech Republic
Denmark
Finland
France
Germany
Greece
Hungary
Iceland
Ireland
Italy
Japan
Korea, Rep. of
Luxembourg
Mexico
Netherlands
New Zealand
Norway
Poland
Portugal
Spain
Sweden
Switzerland
Turkey
United Kingdom
United States

Developing countries in the regional aggregates

Arab States

Algeria
Bahrain
Djibouti
Egypt
Iraq
Jordan
Kuwait
Lebanon
Libyan Arab Jamahiriya
Morocco
Oman
Qatar
Saudi Arabia
Sudan
Syrian Arab Republic
Tunisia
United Arab Emirates
Yemen

Asia and the Pacific

East Asia
China
Hong Kong, China (SAR)
Korea, Rep. of
Mongolia

South-East Asia and the Pacific
Brunei Darussalam
Cambodia
Fiji
Indonesia
Lao People's Dem. Rep.
Malaysia
Myanmar
Papua New Guinea
Philippines
Samoa (Western)
Singapore
Solomon Islands
Thailand
Vanuatu
Viet Nam

South Asia
Bangladesh
Bhutan
India
Iran, Islamic Rep. of
Maldives
Nepal
Pakistan
Sri Lanka

Latin America and the Caribbean (including Mexico)

Antigua and Barbuda
Argentina
Bahamas
Barbados
Belize
Bolivia
Brazil
Chile
Colombia
Costa Rica
Cuba
Dominica
Dominican Republic
Ecuador
El Salvador
Grenada
Guatemala
Guyana
Haiti
Honduras
Jamaica
Mexico
Nicaragua
Panama
Paraguay
Peru
Saint Kitts and Nevis
Saint Lucia
Saint Vincent and the
  Grenadines
Suriname
Trinidad and Tobago
Uruguay
Venezuela

Southern Europe

Cyprus
Turkey

Sub-Saharan Africa

Angola
Benin
Botswana
Burkina Faso
Burundi
Cameroon
Cape Verde
Central African Republic
Chad
Comoros
Congo
Congo, Dem. Rep. of the
Côte d'Ivoire
Equatorial Guinea
Eritrea
Ethiopia
Gabon
Gambia
Ghana
Guinea
Guinea-Bissau
Kenya
Lesotho
Madagascar
Malawi
Mali
Mauritania
Mauritius
Mozambique
Namibia
Niger
Nigeria
Rwanda
São Tomé and Principe
Senegal
Seychelles
Sierra Leone
South Africa
Swaziland
Tanzania, U. Rep. of
Togo
Uganda
Zambia
Zimbabwe

Countries and regions that have produced human development reports

Arab States

Algeria, *1998, 1999*
Bahrain, *1998*
Egypt, *1994, 1995, 1996, 1997–98*
Iraq, *1995*
Kuwait, *1997, 1999*
Lebanon, *1997, 1998, 1999*
Morocco, *1997, 1999*
Occupied Palestinian territory, *1997*
Somalia, *1998*
Sudan, *1998*
Syrian Arab Republic, *1999*
Tunisia, *1999*
United Arab Emirates, *1998*
Yemen, *1998*

Asia and the Pacific

Bangladesh, *1992, 1993, 1994, 1995, 1996, 1997, 1998*
Cambodia, *1997, 1998, 1999*
China, *1997, 1999*
India, Karnataka, *1999*
India, Madhya Pradesh, *1995, 1998*
Indonesia, *1997*
Iran, Islamic Rep. of, *1999*
Lao People's Dem. Rep., *1998*
Maldives, *1999*
Mongolia, *1997, 2000*
Myanmar, *1998*
Nepal, *1998, 1999*
Pakistan, *1992*
Papua New Guinea, *1999*
Philippines, *1994, 1997, 2000*
Samoa (Western), *1998*
Sri Lanka, *1998*
Thailand, *1999*
Tuvalu, *1999*
Vanuatu, *1996*

Europe and the CIS

Albania, *1995, 1996, 1997, 1998*
Armenia, *1995, 1996, 1997, 1998*
Azerbaijan, *1995, 1996, 1997, 1998, 1999*
Belarus, *1995, 1996, 1997, 1998, 1999*
Bosnia and Herzegovina, *1998, 1999*
Bulgaria, *1995, 1996, 1997, 1998, 1999*
Bulgaria, Sofia, *1997*
Croatia, *1997, 1998*
Czech Republic, *1996, 1997, 1998*
Estonia, *1995, 1996, 1997, 1998, 1999*

Georgia, *1995, 1996, 1997, 1998, 1999*
Hungary, *1995, 1996, 1998*
Kazakhstan, *1995, 1996, 1997, 1998, 1999*
Kyrgyzstan, *1995, 1996, 1997, 1998, 1999*
Latvia, *1995, 1996, 1997, 1998, 1999*
Lithuania, *1995, 1996, 1997, 1998, 1999*
Macedonia, TFYR, *1997, 1998*
Malta, *1996*
Moldova, Rep. of, *1995, 1996, 1997, 1998*
Poland, *1995, 1996, 1997, 1998, 1999*
Romania, *1995, 1996, 1997, 1998*
Russian Federation, *1995, 1996, 1997, 1998, 1999*
Saint Helena, *1999*
Slovakia, *1995, 1997, 1998*
Slovenia, *1998*
Tajikistan, *1995, 1996, 1997, 1998, 1999*
Turkey, *1995, 1996, 1997, 1998*
Turkmenistan, *1995, 1996, 1997, 1998, 1999*
Ukraine, *1995, 1996, 1997, 1998*
Uzbekistan, *1995, 1996, 1997, 1998*
Yugoslavia, *1996, 1997*

Latin America and the Caribbean

Argentina, *1995, 1996, 1997, 1998, 1999*
Argentina, Buenos Aires, *1996, 1997, 1998, 1999*
Belize, *1997, 1998*
Bolivia, *1998, 2000*
Bolivia, Cochabamba, *1995*
Bolivia, La Paz, *1995*
Bolivia, Santa Cruz, *1995*
Brazil, *1996*
Chile, *1996, 1998, 2000*
Colombia, *1998, 1999*
Costa Rica, *1995, 1996, 1997, 1998*
Cuba, *1996, 1999*
Dominican Republic, *1997, 1999*
Ecuador, *1999*
El Salvador, *1997, 1999*
Guatemala, *1998, 1999*
Guyana, *1996*
Honduras, *1998, 1999*
Nicaragua, *1997*
Paraguay, *1995, 1996*
Peru, *1997*
Uruguay, *1999*
Venezuela, *1995, 1996, 1997, 1998, 1999*

Sub-Saharan Africa

Angola, *1997, 1998, 1999*
Benin, *1997, 1998, 1999*
Botswana, *1993, 1997*
Burkina Faso, *1997, 1998*
Burundi, *1997, 1999*
Cameroon, *1992, 1993, 1996, 1998*
Cape Verde, *1997, 1998*
Central African Republic, *1996*
Chad, *1997*
Comoros, *1997*
Côte d'Ivoire, *1997*
Equatorial Guinea, *1996, 1997*
Ethiopia, *1997, 1998*
Gabon, *1998, 1999*
Gambia, *1997*
Ghana, *1997, 1999*
Guinea, *1997*
Guinea-Bissau, *1997*
Kenya, *1999*
Lesotho, *1998*
Liberia, *1997*
Madagascar, *1997, 1999*
Malawi, *1997, 1998*
Mali, *1995, 1997, 1998, 1999*
Mauritania, *1996, 1997*
Mauritius, *1998*
Mozambique, *1998*
Namibia, *1996, 1997, 1998*
Niger, *1997, 1998*
Nigeria, *1996, 1998*
São-Tomé and Principe, *1998*
Senegal, *1998*
Sierra Leone, *1996*
South Africa, *1998*
Swaziland, *1997, 1998*
Tanzania, U. Rep. of, *1997*
Togo, *1995, 1997*
Uganda, *1996, 1998*
Zambia, *1997, 1998*
Zimbabwe, *1998*

Regional reports

Africa, *1995*
Central America, *1999*
Europe and the CIS, *1995, 1996, 1999*
Pacific Islands, *1994, 1999*
South Asia, *1997, 1998, 1999*
Southern African Development Community, *1998*

Note: Reports published as of 31 March 2000.
Source: Human Development Report Office.